The
Economist

PUBLICATIONS

ONE HUNDRED YEARS OF ECONOMIC STATISTICS

A NEW EDITION OF ECONOMIC STATISTICS 1900-1983 REVISED AND EXPANDED TO 1987

The
Economist

PUBLICATIONS

ONE HUNDRED YEARS OF ECONOMIC STATISTICS

A NEW EDITION OF ECONOMIC STATISTICS 1900-1983 REVISED AND EXPANDED TO 1987

United Kingdom, United States of America, Australia, Canada, France, Germany, Italy, Japan, Sweden

Compiled and written by Thelma Liesner

Facts On File
New York • Oxford

One Hundred Years of Economic Statistics

Facts On File, Inc.
460 Park Avenue South
New York NY 10016
USA

CIP data available on request from publisher.

ISBN 0–8160–2344–1

Text design by Susie Home
Charts by Graham Douglas
Jacket design by Rufus Segar
Composition by Paston Press, Loddon, Norfolk, UK
Printed in England by Hollen Street Press Ltd., Slough

This book is printed on acid-free paper

CONTENTS

LIST OF CHARTS

GENERAL NOTES

Sources

For the UK and the USA national official statistics have been used as far as possible in compiling the tables. For the other seven countries, statistics produced by international organisations have been used extensively although national official statistics have also been employed. Sources and explanatory notes are given at the end of each set of tables. Obvious discontinuities in the series are pointed out in these notes but for further information about the data, reference should be made to the original sources.

Index numbers

Index numbers are shown with 1980 = 100 for all countries as far as possible. The original base year will vary considerably and reference should be made to the original source for details. In most cases, indices have been linked to obtain a continuous series.

Boundary changes

Changes of boundaries affect the figures for most of the countries; the problem is particularly serious for Germany. This will clearly affect the interpretation of a number of tables.

Decimal places

Many of the series are given to one decimal place, sometimes more if the figure following the decimal is zero. This is not intended to indicate a high degree of accuracy but merely to show the movement in the series. Even so, many of the pre-1939 index numbers (based on 1980 = 100) will only indicate broad changes. For readers who wish to make more precise calculations the author will provide further data insofar as they are available.

Units of measurement

Metric measurements have been used throughout. For example, where tons are shown, the measurement is metric tons.

Billion = 1,000 mn

Symbols used

. . .	no data available or data not available at time of going to press
—	nil or negligible
Heavy horizontal bar:	significant break in series
Light horizontal bar:	minor break in series
Figures in brackets:	approximate figures obtained by extrapolation or other indirect means or in some other way not wholly consistent with the rest of the data in the table. Explanations are provided in the notes to the relevant tables.

Timing

This volume was completed in January 1989. Data published subsequently have not, in general, been incorporated.

ACKNOWLEDGEMENTS

The data presented in this volume are drawn very largely from official publications, both national and international. As in the first edition, for the earlier periods I have frequently used estimates made and data collected by academic researchers, in particular M.W. Butlin and N.G. Butlin (for Australian data), D.J. Ironside (for Canada), W.H. Hoffman (Germany), Gíorgio Fua (Italy), Osten Johansson (Sweden), C.H. Feinstein (UK), J.W. Kendrick and Simon Kuznets (USA) and B.R. Mitchell (all countries).

In addition, I have made a great many visits to libraries including the British Library and the libraries of the Canadian High Commission and the Australian High Commission in London. I am grateful to the staff in all these libraries for their help and in particular to Athalie Colquhoun of the Australian High Commission Library who went out of her way to meet my requests for information. I am also indebted to Shirley Carter and Fred Hackman of the UK Central Statistical Office who gave me a great deal of help with the official statistics for the UK. I must also thank the staff of Statistics Canada in Ottawa and Lillian Rymarowicz of the Library of Congress in Washington for their valuable assistance in the early stages of the work. C.T. Taylor of the Bank of England and Adrian Cunningham of the Reserve Bank of Australia were invaluable in obtaining for me data which I would not otherwise have been able to get hold of. Much of the data which appear in this volume were also shown in the first edition and I should not forget therefore to repeat my thanks to the many people who gave assistance on that occasion.

A very special debt of gratitude is owed to Stanley Millward who carried out tirelessly and meticulously the greater part of the calculations needed for Part IV of this volume.

As before, however, my warmest thanks go to my husband not only for his help and encouragement throughout but for his patience and understanding as the book progressed to its final stages.

Thelma Liesner
January 1989

Part I

Introduction

CONTENTS

Introduction

This second edition of *Economic Statistics* has four main aims:

(a) to bring the series up to date and to incorporate changes in the base years for the constant price estimates;
(b) to take the series back to 1885 as far as possible to give a 100-year run of economic statistics;
(c) to cover a larger number of countries; and
(d) to increase the number of series.

The general purpose of the book, like that of its predecessor, is to bring together from a wide variety of sources basic economic statistics for the main industrial countries and to make these statistics as consistent as possible.

As before, the main emphasis of the book is on the UK and the USA. Part II gives basic data on the principal components of economic activity (national output and expenditure, personal income and profits, employment and earnings, trade, finance and prices). In addition, three new tables have been included covering public finance, education and money gross domestic product, that is, gross domestic product at current prices. For these two countries 170 series are presented, most of which cover the period 1885–1987.

At the time the manuscript was completed, in January 1989, the latest available data had been incorporated; readers may wish to add later statistics as these become available. As in the first edition, the form of the tables follows, for the most part, the presentation of official statistics and this should facilitate the updating of the series. Details of the sources are shown in the notes following the tables for each country.

Since the first edition of *Economic Statistics* was published, the UK has changed the base year for the constant price series to 1985 while the USA has rebased constant price estimates on 1982. All the constant price data for the UK and USA have consequently been recalculated on the new bases. Index numbers, however, continue to be shown in this edition with 1980 as the base year even though the official series in the UK and in some other countries are now based on 1985. Index numbers on a 1985 base can, of course, be converted arithmetically to 1980. Physical quantities are, in all cases, shown in metric measurement; data from countries where metric measurements are not commonly used have been converted where necessary.

In addition to the 19 tables given for the UK and 20 tables for the USA, ten tables each for France, Germany, Italy and Japan are provided in Part III. Three new countries are also included in this section – Australia, Canada and Sweden – and the same data are presented for them in so far as the information is available. (The constant price estimates for these countries are based on 1980.) With the inclusion of these three countries, the book now covers the principal industrialised countries in the world economy.

As well as tables showing basic data for each of the nine countries, 20 tables are given in Part IV, the analytical section. These tables summarise the main data and bring out some of the more interesting trends. Further analytical data, not drawn from Parts II and III, are provided in Part IV in order to give a more complete coverage of underlying trends. Rates of growth of gross domestic product for the period 1950–87 are also given in the form of growth triangles for each country. These growth triangles enable the reader to see the rate of growth between any adjacent years, or over any longer period, at a glance.

The tables and charts in this book will show the changes which have taken place in overall economic activity during the last 100 years. No attempt has been made, however, to analyse the underlying causes of the changes that have occurred; that would not be appropriate in a book of this kind. The main purpose is to provide the statistics which can then be used for economic analysis. Nevertheless, it might be helpful to highlight the main features of the statistical tables and to point out some of the shortcomings of the available data. This is done in the next twelve sections under broad category headings as follows:

(a) trends and cycles in the total economy;
(b) growth of output by sector and by commodity;
(c) capital formation;
(d) income and expenditure;
(e) prices;
(f) earnings and productivity;
(g) employment and unemployment;
(h) population;
(i) education;
(j) trade and balance of payments;
(k) finance, public and private;
(l) transport and energy.

Trends and cycles in the total economy

Data for the last 10 or 15 years of the nineteenth century show for some countries (USA, UK and Sweden) rates of growth of gross domestic product that are comparable with, or better than, the rates of growth achieved in the years following the First World War. For all countries except the USA and Sweden, however, the rate of growth of gross domestic product has been very much

Chart I.1 Gross domestic product at constant prices, 1885–1987

Index numbers, average 1960=100

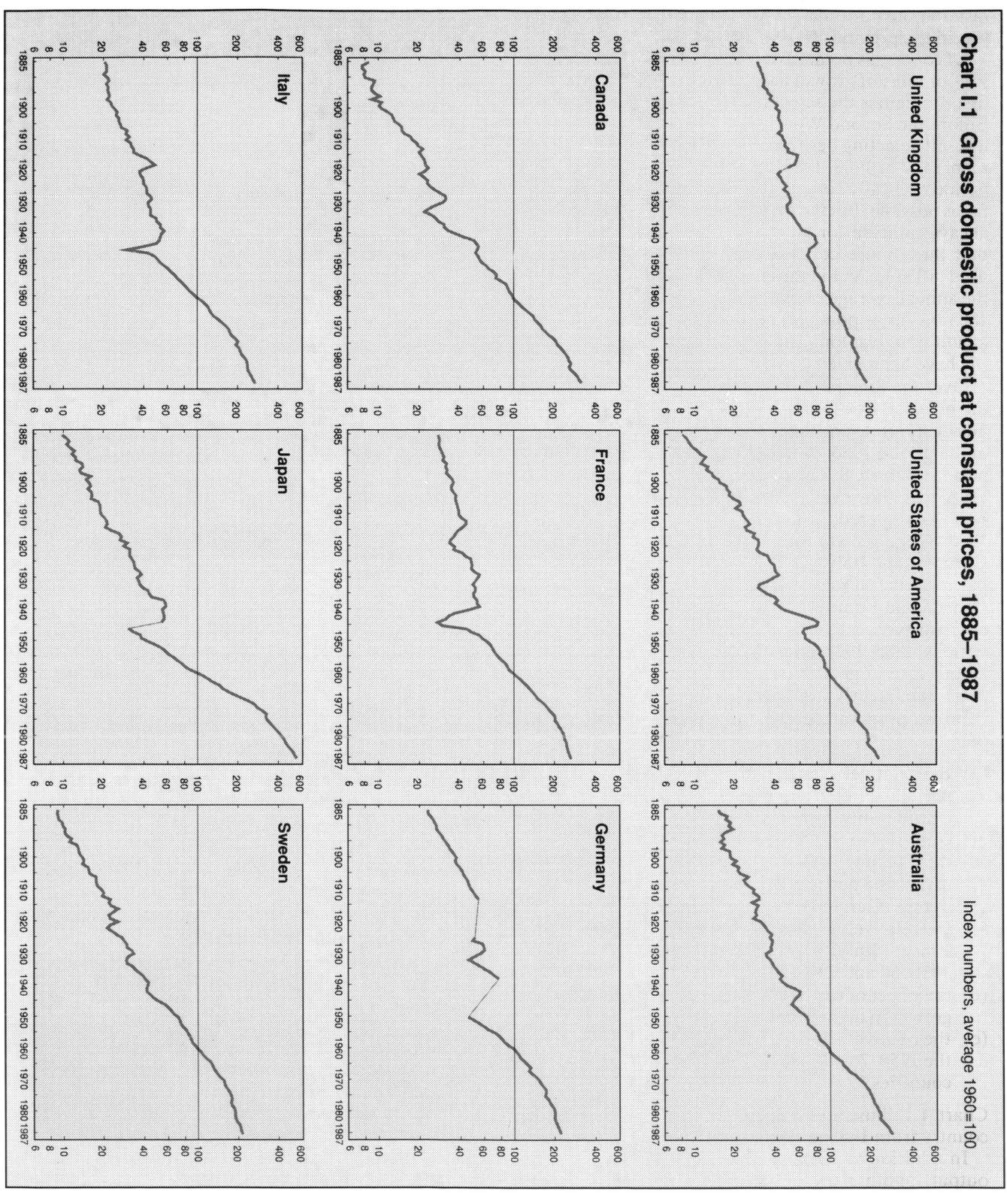

faster in the period after the Second World War than it was in the previous 60 years.

Of course, as pointed out in the first edition, comparisons of rates of growth are fraught with difficulties. The first problem is the selection of periods for comparison. Before the Second World War, the periods are more or less self-selecting because of what might be called 'natural breaks' at 1900, 1913, 1929 and 1938. In the post-war period cyclically comparable years have been chosen as far as possible, but the cycles of economic activity do not always coincide for all the countries (particularly now that three more countries are included). The periods used in Table IV.1 in the analytical section, which shows the annual average rates of growth for each country from 1885 (as far as possible), seem reasonably comparable; in addition, two long-run periods (1885–1938 and 1950–87) have been given.

Over the long periods shown in Table IV.1, seven of the nine countries (the UK, Australia, Canada, France, Germany, Italy and Japan) experienced rates of growth in the period 1950–87 in excess of those achieved in the period up to 1938. The rate of growth in Sweden and the USA was, however, remarkably similar in each long period compared, at around 3 per cent per annum. In 1950–87 the growth rate in Australia, Canada, France, Germany and Italy was well above that in the UK, with a particularly fast rate of growth in the 1960s in Australia, Canada and France. The rate of growth in Japan, however, surpassed that in all the other countries, in both periods 1885–1938 and 1950–87, showing an average annual rate of growth of nearly 3·5 per cent in the first period and nearly 7 per cent in the second period.

In the post-war period, a number of features stand out:

(a) the relatively rapid rate of growth in Japan in all periods. Even from 1973–87, the rate of growth was considerably higher in Japan than in all the other countries except Canada;

(b) the rate of growth in Germany in the period 1950–60 of nearly 8 per cent per annum which gave rise to the phrase 'German economic miracle';

(c) the relatively high annual average rates of growth in France, Italy, Australia and Canada in the periods 1950–60 and 1960–73;

(d) the effect of the oil crises on annual average rates of growth in all nine countries in the period 1973–87;

(e) the relatively slow rate of growth in the UK (even in the 1950–70 period) compared with other European countries.

Chart I.1 illustrates the pattern of growth for each country from 1885 to the present day.

In addition to looking at rates of growth by overall output, another useful measure is that of output per head, taking account of population changes. Table IV.3 does this for all nine countries in terms of national currencies (at constant prices) thus giving a broad indication for each country of the rise in the standard of living over the last 100 years.

When presenting statistics of this kind, comparisons will inevitably be made between countries. Although such comparisons can be carried out using appropriate exchange rates, it is well known that exchange rates do not necessarily reflect the costs of goods and services bought by the 'average man'. To overcome the problem, purchasing power parities have been worked out (most of the relevant work, particularly at the outset, has been done by the Organisation for Economic Cooperation and Development – OECD). These indicate the exchange rates that would have to prevail if money, changed from one country's currency into another, were to retain the same purchasing power. Table IV.4 gives gross domestic product per head (expressed in terms of US dollars at current prices and at current purchasing power parities) in each of the nine countries for the years 1970–86. From this table it can be seen that countries in North America (USA and Canada) had the highest income per head of the nine countries in 1970 and also in 1986 (the latest year for which the data were available at the time of going to press). The relative positions of the other countries have changed over the period with Japan having gained most ground. Its advance occurred notwithstanding the continuing growth in population and it clearly reflects the higher than average growth in productivity (see Table IV.2 in the analytical section).

Growth of output by sector and by commodity

For the UK and the USA, output data are shown in two forms: by broad industrial group or sector (Tables UK.3 and US.3) and with reference to actual commodities such as coal and steel (Tables UK.4 and US.4). For the other seven countries, the data are mainly for commodity output but an industrial production index is also given (Table 3 for each country).

Table UK.3 shows the breakdown of total UK output by seven main industrial groupings from 1885 to 1987 in index number form. In the case of the USA, the range of data available is much narrower. In Table US.3, output in three broad sectors is shown from 1909 and a supplementary table gives output by industrial group from 1947 in a similar form to that shown in Table UK.3.

Shifts in the contribution of each industrial group to total output can be broadly deduced by comparing the rates of growth of the different groups with those of total output. In Table I.1, the percentage change in output of

Table I.1   **Changes in output, UK and USA, selected periods, 1885–1987**

	Manufacturing		Distribution		Services		Total output	
	UK[a]	USA	UK[a]	USA	UK[a]	USA	UK[a]	USA
	% changes over the period							
1885–1900	54·6	. . .	44·8	. . .	29·0	. . .	38·3	. . .
1900–13	28.9	. . .	28·6	. . .	27·0	. . .	25·5	. . .
1920–38	57·5	. . .	25·8	. . .	13·2	. . .	35·4	. . .
1950–60	35·7	31·5	33·0	34·6	24·6	56·1	28·1	38·0
1960–70	33·9	49·7	23·1	50·0	28·1	55·6	30·3	45·2
1970–80	−3·3	31·2	7·3	36·1	23·3	47·1	16·1	31·9
1980–87	10·4	26·2	25·5	31·9	22·0	29·0	19·5	20·7

a   Including Southern Ireland before 1920.

Table I.2   **Output by sector of origin, seven countries, selected periods, 1890–1984**

	Australia			Canada			France			Germany		
	Agriculture	Mfg	Commerce	Agriculture	Mfg	Commerce	Agriculture	Mfg	Commerce	Agriculture	Mfg	Commerce
	% of total output											
1890	23	15	17				37[b]	32[b]	7[b]	33	37	8
1900	20	23	15				37[c]	34[c]	7[c]	30	40	9
1910	29	18	19				35[d]	36[d]	7[d]	25	43	9
1920	24	17	. . .	20[a]	25[a]	22[a]	. . .	. . .	. . .	. . .	. . .	. . .
1930	20	20	21	13	26	25	. . .	. . .	. . .	18	45	. . .
1940	. . .	. . .	. . .	14	33	21	22[e]	36[e]	14[e]	. . .	. . .	. . .
1950	24	29	17	13	33	22	15	38	12	11	36	13
1960	14	34	18	7	31	24	9	37	12	6	40	15
1970	6	30	18	4	25	13	6	31	13	3	42	11
1984	4	27	16	4	25	12	4	29	12	2	35	11

	Italy			Japan			Sweden		
	Agriculture	Mfg	Commerce	Agriculture	Mfg	Commerce	Agriculture	Mfg	Commerce[j]
	% of total output								
1890	51	17	17	39	8	46	33	13	22
1900	51	17[f]	16	34	11	46[i]	28	21	22
1910	42	22[f]	17	30	15	42[i]	25	26	22
1920	48	27[f]	14	27	18	40[i]	22	30	25
1930	31	25	19[h]	22	25	30[i]	13	34	21
1940	30	28	18[h]	24	33	31[i]	12	36	20
1950	29	31	9	26	25	16	12	36	11
1960	13	31	13	13	33	17	7	31	9
1970	8	35[g]	16	6	30	11	4	25	11
1984	7	35	17	3	38	14	3	25	11

a   1926.   b   1892.   c   1898.   d   Average of three-year period centred on 1909.
e   1938; figure is the percentage of net domestic product in 1938 prices.   f   Includes construction.
g   Includes mining and quarrying and public utilities.   h   Includes some services.
i   All other activities except transport and communication and construction.   j   Financial and catering services included up to 1950.

Notes Manufacturing in the years before 1950 includes other industrial activity in some instances. Commerce covers wholesale and retail trade and restaurants and hotels.
Sources *UN Year Book of National Accounts*; B. R. Mitchell, *European Historical Statistics 1750–1975*, 2nd rev. edn. Macmillan, London, 1980; B. R. Mitchell, *International Historical Statistics: Africa and Asia*, New York University Press, 1982; B.R. Mitchell, *International Historical Statistics: The Americas and Australasia*, Macmillan, London, 1983.

three of the main industrial groups and of total output is shown for seven different periods for the UK from 1885 and for four different periods from 1950 for the USA.

For the UK, the most striking feature in the period 1970 to 1987 is the shift away from the manufacturing sector and also, in the 1970s, from the distribution sector. In the USA, there appear to have been marked shifts towards the services sector in 1950–60 and again in 1970–80. For the other seven countries, the percentage contribution of different industry groups to total output has been obtained from current price data. Accordingly, Table I.2 shows the contribution of three main sectors to total output at ten-year intervals from 1890. Unfortunately, the industry groupings are not as clear cut (see notes to the table) as for the UK and USA (although the classification of different industries has also changed over the period in these two countries). Nevertheless, the decreasing importance of the agricultural sector in each of the seven countries is shown clearly in this table in contrast with the much more stable contribution to gross domestic product made by manufacturing and commerce.

The changing importance of basic materials used by the industrial sector is shown, at least to some extent, in the output figures for coal and steel. Tables UK.4 and US.4 give data on coal and steel output for the two countries as well as some information on the output of finished products such as cars and commercial vehicles. Similar information is provided for the other seven countries. One of the features which stands out from the output tables is the trend in coal and steel production in seven of the nine countries. Except in Australia and Japan, coal and steel output has shown a distinct downward trend since the late 1970s.

One of the problems in selecting items for long-run series is that many products will, because of technical developments, change quite clearly over time. For inputs such as coal and steel there are no great difficulties, but with chemicals and motor vehicles there are many ambiguities. Chemicals output has been shown in index number form for the UK and USA (but the composition of the index will have changed over the period) while motor vehicles output has been given in thousands. It hardly needs to be said that a motor vehicle made in 1986 or 1987 is not the same as a motor vehicle made in 1910. Nevertheless, the series given in the tables in Parts II and III indicate some of the changes which have taken place in the output of a number of intermediate and finished products over the last 100 years. In the analytical section, Table IV.5 shows some of the information contained in these tables in relation to total population: an indication of the growth of real income although it is a partial assessment only.

To complete the picture, some mention ought also to be made of agricultural output. The selection of commodities to represent agricultural output as a whole is even more difficult than for industrial output and the years chosen for comparison equally hazardous. Table I.3 uses corn crops for the North American and European countries and the rice crop for Japan as an indicator; data are given at ten-year intervals. One of the noticeable features of this table is the growth in output in France, Germany and, more particularly, in the UK in the period since 1950. The growth has continued into the 1980s despite the efforts of the European Commission to contain it.

Table I.3 Agricultural output, nine countries, selected periods, 1890–1987

	UK[a]	USA	Australia	Canada	France	Germany[c]	Italy	Japan	Sweden
	Index nos., 1950 = 100								
1890	120·3	53·7	12·9	16·3[b]	122·8	200·1	49·2	66·9	111·6
1900	103·4	86·6	18·4	24·8	116·9	237·8	52·1	64·4	117·3
1910	105·6	92·8	52·4	64·3	104·5	264·8	54·8	72·5	122·6
1920	92·3	99·9	52·1	73·4	94·0	145·8	49·3	98·2	105·5
1930	55·4	67·6	73·1	86·6	91·0	226·9	71·8	103·9	118·2
1940	64·4	79·9	30·1	130·0	73·9	204·8	91·8	94·6	90·7
1950	100·0	100·0	100·0	100·0	100·0	100·0	100·0	100·0	100·0
1960	188·9	140·3	121·0	139·1	150·8	146·7	86·1	133·2	153·9
1970	290·7	135·0	138·3	139·1	181·6	173·9	130·1	170·9	234·7
1980	470·3	216·1	171·3	194·7	292·7	232·2	132·2	126·3	257·9
1987	517·7	136·4	202·3	252·8	298·3	228·4	130·7	137·8	272·8

a Including Southern Ireland up to 1920.   b 1891.   c Federal Republic of Germany from 1950.

Notes For all countries except Japan, the figures refer to corn crops (wheat, rye, barley and oats for all countries except USA); the figures for Japan are for rice output.

Capital formation

A basic requirement for the growth of output is the provision of plant and machinery, buildings and infrastructure while investment in housing and other social provision such as hospitals and schools will be necessary for general development within a country. In addition, capital formation is an important component of aggregate demand.

Data on capital formation by asset and by industry are given for the UK and, as far as possible, for the USA in Tables UK.5 and US.5. Figures for capital formation in aggregate are given for the other seven countries in Tables 1 and 2 for each country (current and constant price estimates respectively).

In Table I.4, gross domestic fixed capital formation as a proportion of gross domestic (national) product is given for all nine countries at roughly ten-year intervals over the last 100 years. It can be seen from this table that of the countries for which data are available, the share of gross domestic fixed capital formation in gross domestic product was lowest in the UK in 1885. One hundred years later, the UK still has the lowest percentage of all the countries shown except for the USA. (In the case of the USA, it should be remembered that the figures refer to private investment only; they do not include capital formation by government enterprises.) In all of the other countries, the share of investment in gross domestic product has rarely fallen below 20 per cent since 1950 and in some cases, for example Japan, it has been nearer 30 per cent.

It has not been possible in this edition to provide data on the structure of investment in all nine countries but some detail is given for both the UK and the USA. For the UK, both capital formation by industry and by type of asset is given in Table UK.5 while for the USA the data are by broad sector and by type of asset (Table US.5). The information given in these tables is briefly summarised in Table I.5.

This table shows that construction (buildings and works and dwellings) was the major component of investment in both the UK and the USA in the later years of the nineteenth century and the early years of the twentieth; it still accounts for about half of total investment in both countries. Residential building has formed 20–30 per cent of total capital formation throughout the period with the exception of 1885 when it was 40 per cent in the USA.

Income and expenditure

In this section, personal income and expenditure are briefly examined. Tables UK.6 and US.6 give data on personal income and profits. Tables UK.7 and US.7 give more detailed information on consumers' expenditure. For the other seven countries, total wages and salaries (compensation of employees) and national income data are provided in Table 4 for each country while consumers' expenditure in aggregate is given in the first two tables for each country (at current and at constant prices).

If the crude figures for personal disposable income are used for comparisons, it will be seen that income rose at a much faster rate in the UK than in the USA, particularly at certain periods. This reflects, in part, different rates of inflation in the two countries. In Table I.6,

Table I.4 **Fixed capital formation as a proportion of gross domestic (national) product,[a] nine countries, selected periods, 1885–1987**

	UK	USA[b]	Australia	Canada	France	Germany	Italy	Japan	Sweden
	%								
1885	7·4	21·2[c]	17·8	12·6[d]	. . .	10·7[f]	13·9[g]	. . .	23·3[g]
1900	10·5	16·5	13·4	12·6	. . .	15·7[f]	13·6[g]	. . .	13·3[g]
1910	7·1	16·1	13·9	18·2	. . .	13·3[f]	14·9[g]	. . .	10·5[g]
1920	8·4	11·4	17·6	18·2	. . .	12·8[f]	14·7[g]	. . .	9·9[g]
1930	9·3	12·1	13·7	16·2	. . .	3·6[f]	15·1[g]	10·8[g]	15·3[g]
1940	6·9	11·2	11·7	11·9	13·2[e]	14·4[e]	15·2[g]	26·6[g]	15·1[g]
1950	13·2	16·8	22·5	20·5	17·5	19·1	19·1	25·5[g]	18·0
1960	16·4	14·6	24·6	21·9	20·6	24·3	27·7	29·5	22·2
1970	18·9	14·3	26·0	21·5	24·0	25·5	26·2	35·5	23·2
1980	18·0	16·3	25·2	23·5	23·0	22·7	24·3	31·6	20·2
1987	17·2	14·9	23·9	21·0	19·4	19·4	19·8	28·9	19·0

a Fixed capital formation and gross domestic product (gross national product for USA) at current market prices.   b Excluding government enterprises.
c 1889.   d 1890.   e 1938.   f Net investment.   g Including stocks.

Table I.5 **Capital formation in constant prices, by type of asset, UK and USA, selected periods, 1885–1987**

	Buildings & works		Dwellings		Plant & machinery	
	UK	USA[a]	UK	USA	UK	USA
	% total capital expenditure					
1885	48·3	42·4	26·5	41·6	13·9	16·0[b]
1900	40·61	60·5	26·4	22·3	18·7	17·2[b]
1910	39·3	57·4	21·6	23·5	21·5	19·1[b]
1920	40·0	43·1	17·9	20·8	21·7	36·2[b]
1930	31·6	47·1	35·0	20·4	21·8	19·9
1940	27·1[c]	29·3	37·3[c]	31·0	23·8[c]	23·9
1950	29·6	25·0	24·9	39·1	31·4	24·1
1960	33·4	30·1	23·8	35·6	29·3	25·2
1970	35·4	29·8	24·0	28·2	30·5	32·0
1980	28·6	26·4	23·1	25·3	36·7	38·2
1987	29·7	19·6	20·9	29·3	39·9	41·6

a   Excluding government expenditure on buildings and works.   b   All producers' durable goods including transport equipment.   c   1938.

Table I.6 **Real personal disposable income, UK and USA, selected periods, 1922–87**

	UK	USA
	Index nos., 1980 = 100	
1922	28·0	22·5[a]
1938	39·8	22·6[b]
1950	43·3	35·8
1960	59·0	49·3
1973	76·5	86·5
1980	100·0	100·0
1987	112·1	121·3

a   1929.   b   1939.

therefore, the growth of real personal disposable income (that is, adjusting for price changes) is set out; in times of relatively high rates of inflation this is the more meaningful measure. Not surprisingly, it can be seen from the table that the USA had a faster rate of growth of real disposable income than the UK from 1938/39 to 1987.

From the point of view of the distribution of the 'national cake', the share of wages and salaries and of rental and other property income is of interest. More reliable data are available on wages and salaries than on property income and the share of wages and salaries in national income is shown in Table I.7 for all nine countries for selected years using, for the most part, the data in Table 4 for each of the seven countries in Part III.

Table I.7 **Proportion of wages and salaries[a] in national income, nine countries, selected periods, 1900–87**

	UK	USA	Australia	Canada	France	Germany	Italy	Japan	Sweden
	% share								
1900	53.5	58·0	...	...	...	...	...	...	...
1920	67·1	67·3	...	...	...	59·9[b]	...	...	...
1938	59·4	63·3	52·1[c]	...	50·0	54·9	...	...	...
1950	62·5	59·7	49·5	55·4	44·6	50·0	41·9[d]	41·8	54·6
1960	64·0	64·2	58·2	60·2	48·8	51·2	40·0	45·5	59·5
1970	65·0	68·0	62·7	64·0	54·0	59·1	45·5	50·2	66·1
1980	68·2	69·2	64·1	64·8	63·7	64·3	52·6	62·3	73·0
1987	62·6	68·3	62·4	63·6	60·8	60·8	50·7	64·0	68·3

a   From 1950 (1960 for the UK) OECD figures of compensation of employees have been used to calculate the percentages. The figures therefore include payments in kind and pension contributions.   b   1925.   c   1939.   d   1951.

Notes National income figures for the UK and the USA are not given in the main tables; they can be obtained from **16**, **29** and **44** in UK sources and from **15** and **18** in US sources. The figures for Germany before 1950 have been taken from *Statistisches Jahrbuch*, 1974.

(The source of the data for the UK and the USA is shown at the bottom of the table.)

A number of observations can be made on this table. First, in five of the nine countries (the UK, the USA, Australia, Canada and Sweden) the share of wages and salaries in national income has been around 60 per cent or more for most of the period. Second, the share of wages and salaries in Italy has been, and remains, relatively low while in Sweden it continues to be higher than in the other countries. A third point worth mentioning is that in all countries shown, except Japan, the share of wages fell between 1980 and 1986 according to current OECD estimates.

On the expenditure side, the growth in total consumers' expenditure in real terms is shown in Table I.8 for each of the nine countries. At least two points emerge clearly from the table:

(a) the very fast rise in private consumption in Japan in the post-war period;
(b) the relatively slow rate of growth of personal consumption in the UK and in Sweden from 1960–80 not in the period 1885–1960 in Sweden).

The figures are perhaps not so surprising in view of the overall rates of growth of gross domestic product, of which private consumption is a major component, in all nine countries (see Table IV.1 in the analytical section.)

In addition to data on total consumers' expenditure, a breakdown of the total by categories is given for the UK and the USA. There are certain breaks in the series in these tables partly because the classification of particular items has changed over the period (see notes on pp. 65–118). As a further indication of changes in the standard of living, an analysis of expenditure per head on certain items in constant prices is set out in Table IV.6.

Prices

Consumer and wholesale price indices have been calculated for many years but the levels of sophistication have been variable. Price indices currently constructed are far more comprehensive than those available for the early part of the period. As the later indices have been linked to the earlier series, this should be borne in mind when the tables are consulted.

It should perhaps also be pointed out that the use of 1980 as the base year, and the fact that the indices are usually given to no more than two decimal places, will inevitably mask small changes which took place in the last 15 years of the nineteenth century and the early years of the twentieth. While it is true, therefore, that before the First World War prices (as measured) were far more stable than they have been in the post-Second World War period, there was some movement of prices although it was relatively minor. The original sources should be consulted if further accuracy is required.

Tables UK.8 and US.8 and Table 4 for each of the countries in Part III give long-run data for both wholesale and consumer prices from 1885. In this second edition, two new series (export and import prices) have been included in this table for the seven countries in Part III insofar as data were available. In Table IV.11 comparative data are set out on the rate of increase of consumer prices at certain periods. Of the many interesting features of this table, it is worth drawing attention to:

Table I.8 Total consumers' expenditure by volume, nine countries, selected periods, 1885–1987

	UK[a]	USA	Australia	Canada	France	Germany[e]	Italy	Japan	Sweden
	Index nos., 1960 = 100								
1885	. . .	11[b]	. . .	10[d]	. . .	30	27	. . .	14
1900	48	16	22	13	. . .	44	30	. . .	19
1910	52	25	32	20	. . .	54	37	. . .	25
1920	53	31	34	24	. . .	. . .	43	. . .	32
1930	61	44	39	31	. . .	62	51	45	46
1940	64	50	44	35	62[d]	73	56	40	52
1950	78	73	75	61	63	47	64	42	79
1960	100	100	100	100	100	100	100	100	100
1970	127	148	162	153	169	164	186	236	145
1980	157	199	229	248	237	227	251	382	170
1987	194	251	273	307	277	250	299	470	191

a Including Southern Ireland before 1920. b 1889. c 1890. d 1938. e Federal Republic of Germany from 1950; earlier figures refer to the pre-war boundaries.

(a) the acceleration in the rate of inflation in all countries in the period 1973–80, largely attributable to the oil price explosion;

(b) within this common experience, the vivid contrast in absolute inflation rates between Germany on the one hand and, in particular, the UK and Italy on the other;

(c) the fact that over the longer period, 1950–87, four countries (Australia, France, Sweden and the UK) experienced similar rates of increase in prices of between 6 and 7 per cent per annum.

Earnings and productivity

There is, of course, a broad relationship between prices and earnings over the long period although there is much controversy over the exact form that this relationship takes. Tables UK.12 and US.12 give data on average earnings in manufacturing (broadly defined) and similar information is presented in Table 8 for the other seven countries.

In Part IV, the average rate of rise in earnings (mainly in manufacturing) in the post-war period is given in Table IV.12. For the period 1950–86 the average annual rate of increase in earnings was around 9 per cent in the UK, Australia, Sweden and Japan and over 10 per cent in France and Italy. Countries with the lowest rate of increase over this period were Germany and the North American countries.

Two series on productivity are also given in Tables UK.12 and US.12: a series on output per person employed in the whole economy (UK) and on output per man hour in the private (business) economy in the USA together with series on output per man or output per man hour in manufacturing. In Part IV, the annual average rates of growth of productivity in the whole economy are shown for all nine countries in Table IV.2. Data from Tables 2 and 7 for the seven countries in Part III were used to construct productivity indices from which the rates of growth were calculated; the figures in Table IV.2 are therefore constrained by the availability of data in Tables 2 and 7 for each country.

What Table IV.2 shows is that over the long period (1950–86) productivity grew at around 2 per cent per annum in the UK, USA, Australia, Canada and Sweden. In France, Germany and Italy, the annual growth rate over the same period was nearer 4 per cent. Once again, however, Japan outstripped the other countries with an annual productivity growth of nearly 6 per cent over the long period and of over 8·5 per cent in the 1960s. On the other hand, the UK's rate of growth of productivity in the period 1980–86 was the highest of all the countries.

Employment and unemployment

In the section on the growth of output, the distribution of activity as measured by output data was considered (see p. 6). The same issue can also be examined from the employment side. Tables UK.11 and US.11 together with Table 7 for each of the other countries, show numbers in employment by industry group. Tables IV.7–IV.9 set out the changes that have taken place in the distribution of employment. (For the UK and the USA, the figures refer, in the main, to employees in employment but for the other seven countries they include the self-employed.)

The single most noticeable feature in these tables is the decline in employment in the agricultural sector; this is particularly remarkable in Japan and Sweden. The second common feature is the rise in employment in distribution and services in all countries and the decline in employment in manufacturing which is more marked in some countries than in others.

The level of unemployment continues to be a matter of concern in most industrialised countries despite some slight decline in the numbers without work during the 1980s. The course of unemployment over the last 100 years could therefore be of particular interest. Unfortunately, although data are available for most countries back to the 1920s, there are various problems. The method of collection and coverage of statistics on unemployment vary from country to country and the figures given in UK.12, US.12 and Table 8 for the seven other countries should not be crudely compared without referring to the notes to these tables.

For instance, the UK has recently changed the method used to calculate the percentage unemployed (as well as making various changes in the numbers to be counted as unemployed). The working population (employees in employment, unemployed, self-employed, Armed Forces and those on work-related government training programmes) is now used in the UK as the denominator as it is in the USA, Japan and some other countries. This means that the percentage figure will be lower than if the number of employees in employment is used, as was the case in the UK until 1986. Similarly, statistics are collected in different ways; in the USA, Italy and Japan data are collected by means of labour force sample surveys whereas in Germany and the UK, it is the number registering or claiming benefit at unemployment offices that is counted. Each method has advantages and disadvantages and countries have changed their coverage and definition of unemployment from time to time, particularly in the 1970s and 1980s.

Nevertheless, it is worth drawing attention to the unemployment figures of the 1930s for each country and again from 1975 onwards, compared with the 'golden era' of the 1950s and 1960s.

Population

From a crude examination of the unemployment figures, it might appear that Japan is one country (Sweden is another) which does not need to be too concerned about the level of unemployment. On the other hand, Japan's population growth over the last 100 years presents problems of a different kind. Population data are shown in Tables UK.9, US.9 and Table 5 for each of the other seven countries.

In the 100 years since 1885 the Japanese population has increased by over 200 per cent compared with 46 per cent in France, 57 per cent in the UK, 78 per cent in Sweden and 98 per cent in Italy. Japan is geographically about the same size as the UK but its population in 1986 was over twice that of the UK. Population growth in the USA, Canada and Australia was, as might be expected, a multiple of the growth in the 'older' countries. In Australia, the population grew from 2·5 mn in 1885 to over 15·5 mn in 1985; in Canada in the same period the figures were 4·5 and 25·5 mn, while in the USA population grew by 325 per cent.

Changes in population are brought about by natural increase and by migration. The last 100 years have seen a number of 'migration waves', including those from the European continent, especially Germany and Italy, to the American continent in the early years of the century and from the UK and other European countries to Australia after the two world wars.

Both the age distribution and the population of areas within a country will be affected by migratory movements. The population tables for each country show the changes in the age composition and Table IV.10 in the analytical section summarises the changes that have taken place.

The 15–64 age group currently averages around two-thirds of the total population in all nine countries and it has not varied to any great extent over the period except in Canada in 1891 and in Germany and Italy in 1986 when the 15–64 age group made up 70 per cent of the population. The proportions in the under 15 and in the 65 years and over age groups have, however, undergone quite substantial changes. The extent of the changes varies in each of the nine countries but there has been a fairly general trend in all countries for the proportion of the population in the under 15 age group to decline, more particularly from the 1970s. Correspondingly, the proportion of the population aged 65 and above has been rising in most countries over the whole period. This no doubt reflects common factors such as advances in medical care.

The geographical distribution of the population shown for the UK and the USA is a broad one and can indicate only rather general trends. In the UK, there have been changes in the definition of the South East region (see notes on p. 66) and this makes comparison over the long period rather hazardous. What is clear, however, is that the population in England and Wales grew at a somewhat faster rate than that of either Scotland or Northern Ireland between 1911 (the first year for which separate figures are available for Northern Ireland) and 1986.

In the USA over the long period the greatest growth has been in the West where population increased 15-fold between 1890 and 1985. This was the result, at least in part, of migratory factors within the USA. In the last ten years or so the rate of population growth in the South and West has continued to exceed that of the North East and North Central (now renamed Mid-West) regions where the population has been stable or growing only slowly. The only other country for which geographical data are shown is Canada because the concentration of the population of this country in the two provinces of Quebec and Ontario is really rather remarkable. Canada is a country with a land area of 9·97 mn km², but even in 1986 over 60 per cent of the population were concentrated in just over 26 per cent of the total area of the country. In 1885 roughly 75 per cent of the population lived in this area.

Education

The growth of population has been accompanied, in the nine countries considered, by the growth in education over the last 100 years. In the UK, elementary education became compulsory in 1880 although some state involvement had existed since 1833. Education systems, of a kind, were established in all of the nine countries by the last quarter of the nineteenth century including Japan, whose national education system was established in 1872. In that year, education in Japan was made compulsory for four years in the first instance. In countries with a federal constitution such as the USA and Canada, the development of compulsory education and the starting age, duration and type of institution varied from state to state and province to province. (The statistical returns also varied in their coverage and uniformity as well as their availability; the tables giving education details are therefore somewhat sparse in the early years. See Tables UK.10, US.10 and Table 6 for each of the other seven countries.) The situation in France, on the other hand, was more uniform with the central government playing an active part from an early stage.

Broadly, four phases might be distinguished in the development of education in the nine countries:

(a) the provision of elementary education with kindergartens being established at an early stage in some countries;
(b) the development of secondary education;
(c) the introduction of post-secondary education including technical and vocational training and, in recent times in some countries, remedial education;
(d) the growth in higher (university/polytechnic) education.

Within these broad categories, the statistics for each country will vary a good deal in their coverage and in the type of school or training which is subsumed under the different headings in the tables. The notes to the tables for each country indicate the coverage and, as far as possible, the changes that have taken place.

The numbers in the tables, of course, reflect a range of factors; for example, population growth, changes in the number of years of compulsory education and changing attitudes towards education. The latter point is amply illustrated by the shift in the proportion of females undertaking higher education (see Table I.9).

From this table it can be seen that the proportion of higher education students who are female has been growing steadily in all countries since the 1950s and in the USA and Sweden reached the 50 : 50 mark in 1980. The other countries have not yet got to this stage (although Australia and Canada are very close) and Japan has a lot of ground to make up. The proportion of female higher education students in Japan in 1950 was less than 10 per cent (far below the other countries) and even in 1985 it was less than 25 per cent.

Trade and balance of payments

The tables concerned with trade present data on the commodity composition of imports and exports for the UK and USA and details of trade by area for all nine countries. The figures in these tables are in current values and not volume; volume data would be much more difficult to obtain on a consistent basis back to 1885 or even 1900. For many purposes, however, current data are not inappropriate; for example, the examination of the share of different commodities in total trade or the shares of different countries in trade.

Before considering trade in detail, it would be of interest to know the extent to which the dependence of countries on trade differs and how this dependence has changed over time. The ratio of imports of goods and services to gross domestic product has been used as a proxy to measure trade dependence for all nine countries over the period 1885–1987 (as far as data permit), and the results are shown in Table I.10.

The experience of the countries included has clearly varied a good deal, but it is striking that the trade dependence of all the Western European countries has been on a rising trend in the post-war period, with especially large increases for Sweden, Germany and France. The trade dependence of the USA has also increased quite markedly since 1970. The UK has always been a major importer and exporter but it is interesting to note the decline in trade dependence since 1920. In fact, it is only in the 1980s that the ratio of imports to gross domestic product has surpassed the 1930 level. In considering the Japanese data it has to be remembered that oil forms an especially large part of total imports, so

***Table* I.9 Proportion of females in higher education, nine countries, selected periods, 1890–1985**

	UK	USA	Australia	Canada	France	Germany	Italy	Japan	Sweden
	% of total								
1890	. . .	35·7	. . .	. . .	. . .	. . .	. . .	. . .	. . .
1900	. . .	35·7	. . .	. . .	3·3	. . .	. . .	. . .	. . .
1910	. . .	39·7	11·5[b]	. . .	9·7	. . .	3·6[f]	. . .	. . .
1920	30·1[a]	47·3	. . .	16·4	14·6	7·7[e]	9·4	. . .	. . .
1930	27·3	43·7	. . .	23·7	25·7	14·8	13·2	. . .	. . .
1940	29·5	40·2	34·3[c]	23·1	33·9	. . .	20·5	. . .	27·4[g]
1950	22·9	31·6	21·6	21·3	33·9	17·1	26·3	8·4	23·7
1960	24·4	37·0	23·2	24·3	40·7	21·8	27·7	13·7	33·8
1970	29·0	41·2	29·9	35·2	31·8	30·8	37·6	18·0	38·1
1980	37·7	51·4	41·8	44·9	. . .	37·1	44·0	22·1	54·5
1985	40·4	52·5	45·2[d]	47·8	. . .	37·9	. . .	23·5	56·2

a 1923. b 1906. c 1942. d 1984. e 1921. f 1911. g 1941.

Table I.10   Trade dependence, nine countries, selected periods, 1885–1987

	UK	USA	Australia	Canada	France	Germany	Italy	Japan	Sweden
	Imports of goods and services as % of GDP in current prices								
1885	28·6	. . .	. . .	20·7[a]	. . .	. . .	13·2	. . .	24·3
1900	27·4	. . .	20·3	24·3	. . .	. . .	13·5	. . .	22·7
1910	30·6	. . .	18·7	29·4	. . .	. . .	18·8	. . .	19·8
1920	34·0	. . .	25·5	34·1	. . .	. . .	26·9	. . .	26·2
1930	23·5	4·9	11·7	28·4	. . .	. . .	14·5	18·0	16·8
1940	20·6	3·7	17·0	24·2	. . .	. . .	6·5	18·3	13·5
1950	23·6	4·3	25·6	21·0	14·0	12·7	13·2	9·2	21·5
1960	21·6	4·7	17·1	18·7	12·4	20·5	14·3	10·2	23·6
1970	21·5	6·0	14·4	20·2	15·3	19·1	17·2	9·5	24·7
1980	24·9	11·7	18·0	26·6	22·7	27·1	24·5	14·6	31·7
1987	27·3	12·2	17·7	25·7	20·7	23·7	18·9	7·8	30·4

a   1890.

Source Table 1 for each country.

that changes in the oil price have a major bearing on the ratio of imports to gross domestic product.

Details of the composition of trade by broad category in the UK and the USA are given in Tables UK.13, US.13, UK.14 and US.14. In Part IV, changes in imports and exports in each of the broad categories as a percentage of total imports and exports is shown in Tables IV.15 and IV.16. For the USA, the most noticeable change is in the percentage of petrol and petroleum products in the total value of imports. The rise began in 1974 and continued until 1980, with the proportion then gradually falling back to the 10 per cent shown for 1987. It is also worth noting that the share of consumer goods (including motor cars) rose to 40 per cent of total imports in 1987. In the UK, the change in the composition of trade that has occasioned most comment in recent years is the relatively high proportion of finished manufactures in total imports. From 5 per cent in 1920, the proportion rose to near 50 per cent in 1987.

In this context, it is of interest to ask how shares of 'world' exports of manufactures have changed over the period. In Table I.11, the UK share of exports of the eleven main industrialised countries from 1899 to 1969 is given, while in Table IV.17 figures for the shares of eight of the nine countries (Australia is excluded from the data at present) for the period 1970–87 are presented. As can be seen from Table IV.17 the countries whose share of manufactured exports has fallen since 1970 are the USA, Canada and the UK. (The UK had lost share between the beginning of the century and the 1930s, regained a good deal of it just after the Second World War and then experienced a renewed decline.) For other European countries, the share of trade in manufactures

Table I.11   UK share of exports of manufactures, 1899–1969

	Total 11 industrial countries	UK share
	$ bn	%
1899	3·1	33·2
1913	6·5	30·2
1929	11·9	22·9
1936	9·1	21·3
1948	18·6	29·3
1950	20·1	25·4
1951	28·0	21·9
1952	27·6	21·5
1953	27·2	20·9
1954	29·6	20·5
1955	33·6	19·8
1956	38·5	19·2
1957	42·5	17·9
1958	42·0	18·2
1959	45·4	17·7
1960	52·4	16·3
1961	55·3	16·2
1962	58·7	15·6
1963	65·0	15·1
1964	74·4	14·2
1965	83·0	13·8
1966	92·9	13·2
1967	99·4	12·2
1968	114·5	11·4
1969	134·1	11·2

Notes Figures from 1970–87 for the UK and seven other countries are given in Table IV.17. Eleven industrial countries comprise USA, Canada, France, Germany, Italy, Netherlands, Belgium/Luxembourg, UK, Sweden, Switzerland and Japan. East Germany included up to 1937.

Source Key Statistics of the British Economy, 1900–1970, London and Cambridge Economic Service, 1971.

has remained fairly stable over the period since 1970 while Japan has increased its share by 50 per cent.

It can be argued, of course, that shares in trade in themselves do not matter greatly as long as a country 'balances its books' externally at a reasonable level of economic activity and without resort to severe trade restrictions. In any event, the emergence of new countries as exporters of manufactures is bound to lead to a reduction in the shares of at least some of the previous incumbents.

The country of origin of imports and the destination of exports can be examined as well as the composition of trade. Tables UK.15 and US.15 and Table 10 for each of the other seven countries give figures of imports and exports by country or by area. In Part IV, some additional analysis is provided for the UK and the USA in the form of percentage shares in selected years (Tables IV.18 and IV.19).

Visible trade is only one aspect of exchange among countries. Others include trade in services such as shipping, financial services, insurance and tourism. Broad categories are shown in Tables UK.16 and US.16 together with the current account of the balance of payments. (These data are not given for the other seven countries.)

There has been much emphasis recently on the deficit on the US current account of the balance of payments in consecutive years, especially in the 1980s. Apart from the period before 1900, the US current account was nearly always in surplus until the late 1970s. The surpluses, however, as a percentage of gross domestic product were never as large as the deficits of the 1980s. The averages for the main periods (excluding the war years) are shown in Table I.12. An alternative interpretation of these figures is that they show that the rate at which the USA has recently disinvested abroad has been a good deal higher than the positive rate of investment over earlier decades.

In the case of the UK, there has similarly been much comment about the large current account surpluses during the first half of the 1980s. In fact, in historical perspective, the surplus as a percentage of gross domestic product is shown to have been rather less than the average surplus in the interwar years and a good deal lower than the average positive balance in the 30 years before the First World War.

The fluctuations in the current account as a percentage of gross domestic product over the whole period, year by year, are illustrated in Charts UK.16 and US.16.

Finance

This section has been expanded in this edition to include some information on public finance for all nine countries. The data for each country have been taken from national sources and therefore will vary a good deal in composition and coverage. This should be borne in mind when reference is made to the analytical tables and the notes to the tables for each country should be consulted. (Tables UK.18, US.18 and Table 9 for the other seven countries.)

With these reservations, the data given in the country tables have been summarised in Part IV in Tables IV.13 and IV.14. The share of taxes on income and of customs and excise duties as a proportion of total revenue is given in Table IV.13. These two sources of revenue have been selected because they are common to all countries over a long period of time. Even with these two readily identifiable sources of revenue, however, changes in composition have taken place; for example, value-added tax is included in 'taxes on business' in Italy (taxes on income in the table), whereas in the UK, value-added tax is included in customs and excise duties which explains why this is still a high proportion of total revenue in the UK. In the early years of the twentieth century and the last 15 years of the nineteenth century, customs and excise duties were the major source of revenue; income tax is, for the most part, a twentieth-century phenomenon.

On the expenditure side, interest has been centred in a number of countries on the relationship of total public expenditure to gross domestic product, as well as on the importance of different types of expenditure in the total; that is, expenditure on defence, education and social services. These relationships are set out in Table IV.14 but there is considerable variation in the composition of total expenditure as well as its component parts. The figures for total expenditure for Sweden (up to 1970) and

Table I.12   Current account of the balance of payments, UK and USA, selected periods, 1885–1987

	Average surplus or deficit		Average surplus or deficit as % of gross domestic product	
	UK	USA	UK	USA
	£ mn	$ mn	%	
1885–99	65	−6[a]	4·6	−0·04[a]
1900–13	118	113	5·9	0·40
1920–38	57	676	1·3	0·80
1950–69	54	1,940	0·23	0·35
1970–87	946	−31,419	0·55	−1·25
1980–87	2,654	−70,143	0·98	−1·94

a   1889–99.

Table I.13   Real rate of interest,[a] UK and USA, selected periods, 1950–87

	Nominal rate	'Real' rate	Nominal rate	'Real' rate
	UK		USA	
	%, average over period			
1950–60	3·06	−0·91	2·12	0·05
1960–73	5·88	0·91	4·42	1·29
1973–80	9·62	−5·18	7·47	−1·36
1980–87	11·21	5·19	9·18	4·59

a   Rate on Treasury bills.

Japan, for example, are for central government expenditure only, whereas for other countries the data cover government expenditure at all levels (on a net basis, that is, exclusive of transfers between different levels of government).

Other financial data, such as share prices and selected interest rates, money supply and exchange rates, are given for the UK and USA in Tables UK.17 and US.17. In times of rapid and continuing inflation, the concern with interest rates tends to centre on the 'real' rate of interest; that is, what the rate would be after allowance for price changes. This can be done in a very simple way by taking the average rate of interest for a selected period and deducting the average rate of growth of prices over the same period. The results of such a calculation made for the UK and the USA, using the Treasury Bill rates given in Tables UK.17 and US.17, are shown for a few periods in Table I.13.

Transport and energy

The final tables presented for the UK and the USA (Tables UK.19 and US.19) cover transport and energy consumption. The main features which these tables show are:

(a) the shift away from rail transport towards road transport for both freight and passengers;
(b) the increase in air passenger travel;
(c) the increasing importance of petroleum and natural gas relative to coal as a primary fuel input.

In the 1980s, however, there has been some recovery both in the use of railways for passengers and freight and in the importance of coal as a primary fuel input.

Part II

Statistical tables for the United Kingdom and the United States of America

UNITED KINGDOM

CONTENTS

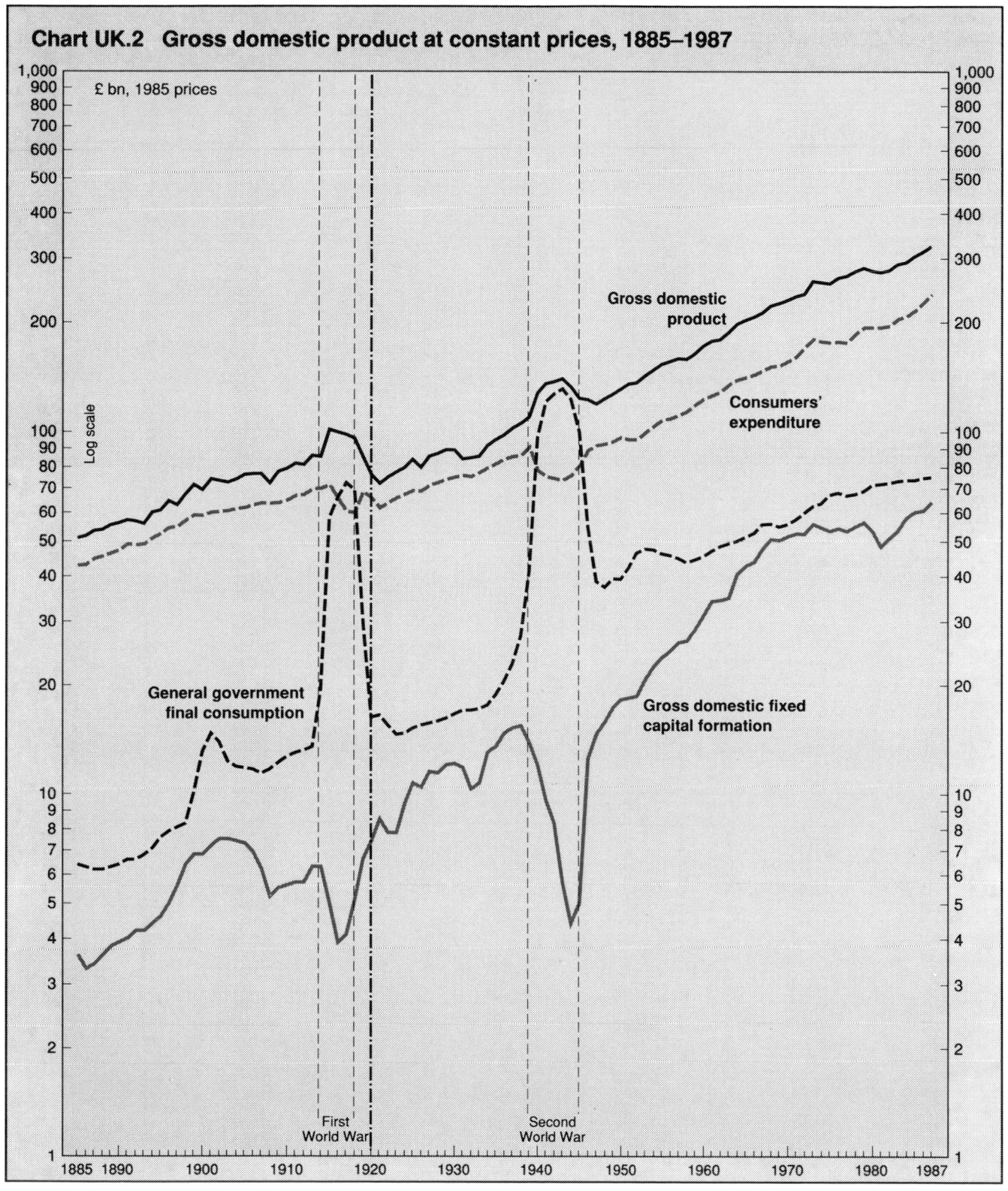

Chart UK.2 Gross domestic product at constant prices, 1885–1987

£ bn, 1985 prices

Log scale

Gross domestic product

Consumers' expenditure

General government final consumption

Gross domestic fixed capital formation

First World War

Second World War

	Consumers' expenditure	General govt final consumption	Gross domestic fixed capital formation	Value of physical change in stocks & w.i.p.	Exports of goods & services	Imports of goods & services	Gross domestic product at market prices	Less Adjustment to factor cost	Gross domestic product at factor cost
					£ mn				
1885	1,138	83	96	6	363	−370	**1,316**	87	**1,229**
1886	1,126	80	85	20	355	−350	**1,316**	87	**1,229**
1887	1,162	78	87	18	373	−362	**1,356**	88	**1,268**
1888	1,186	78	90	−2	396	−387	**1,361**	90	**1,271**
1889	1,227	80	100	22	422	−426	**1,425**	93	**1,332**
1890	1,253	85	106	15	434	−420	**1,473**	95	**1,378**
1891	1,315	87	107	8	411	−432	**1,496**	96	**1,400**
1892	1,314	87	108	11	390	−421	**1,489**	97	**1,392**
1893	1,310	89	109	−12	365	−402	**1,459**	98	**1,361**
1894	1,336	91	111	46	363	−406	**1,541**	102	**1,439**
1895	1,355	97	115	19	375	−413	**1,548**	107	**1,441**
1896	1,406	102	127	41	394	−439	**1,631**	111	**1,520**
1897	1,435	106	144	−10	392	−447	**1,620**	113	**1,507**
1898	1,500	112	172	25	395	−466	**1,738**	115	**1,623**
1899	1,561	136	192	37	431	−486	**1,871**	121	**1,750**
1900	1,637	182	205	−24	467	−535	**1,932**	128	**1,804**
1901	1,677	202	210	47	458	−540	**2,054**	136	**1,918**
1902	1,686	190	213	4	460	−537	**2,016**	146	**1,870**
1903	1,699	169	208	−17	479	−543	**1,995**	146	**1,849**
1904	1,719	163	203	2	492	−551	**2,028**	151	**1,877**
1905	1,736	163	198	27	535	−567	**2,092**	152	**1,940**
1906	1,766	163	192	5	601	−611	**2,116**	153	**1,963**
1907	1,811	163	176	−16	671	−649	**2,156**	155	**2,001**
1908	1,813	167	145	−7	597	−596	**2,119**	150	**1,969**
1909	1,831	173	154	23	615	−628	**2,168**	151	**2,017**
1910	1,877	182	158	−2	691	−683	**2,223**	164	**2,059**
1911	1,936	188	163	11	715	−685	**2,328**	167	**2,161**
1912	2,006	196	171	−13	768	−748	**2,380**	172	**2,208**
1913	2,070	203	192	31	816	−777	**2,535**	175	**2,360**
1914	2,074	324	193	4	685	−740	**2,540**	171	**2,369**
1915	2,384	1,045	171	12	750	−970	**3,392**	208	**3,184**
1916	2,581	1,332	159	−162	1,000	−1,140	**3,770**	222	**3,548**
1917	2,979	1,685	203	−50	1,085	−1,260	**4,642**	199	**4,443**
1918	3,600	1,842	286	110	940	−1,400	**5,378**	181	**5,197**
1919	4,535	935	434	−96	1,470	−1,680	**5,598**	283	**5,315**
1920	5,246	520	578	−237	2,049	−1,985	**6,171**	386	**5,785**
1921	5,020	488	482	−100	2,128	−2,036	**5,845**	370	**5,475**
1922	4,315	489	458	−100	1,666	−1,194	**5,134**	402	**4,732**
1923	3,842	435	381	−91	1,113	−1,101	**4,579**	439	**4,140**
1924	3,717	395	334	−65	1,161	−1,157	**4,385**	454	**3,931**
1925	3,777	398	374	−6	1,200	−1,324	**4,419**	430	**3,989**
1926	3,878	412	420	133	1,158	−1,357	**4,644**	429	**4,215**
1927	3,833	420	401	17	1,017	−1,292	**4,396**	449	**3,947**
1928	3,887	423	426	44	1,090	−1,257	**4,613**	479	**4,134**
1929	3,939	425	420	18	1,092	−1,235	**4,659**	493	**4,166**
1930	3,983	435	442	40	1,096	−1,269	**4,727**	476	**4,251**
1931	3,932	443	435	91	884	−1,100	**4,685**	457	**4,228**
1932	3,805	443	408	−3	632	−926	**4,359**	459	**3,900**
1933	3,683	431	347	1	578	−764	**4,276**	490	**3,786**
1934	3,696	430	357	−58	573	−739	**4,259**	486	**3,773**
1935	3,802	446	427	29	608	−799	**4,513**	507	**4,006**
1936	3,935	483	456	5	690	−848	**4,721**	522	**4,199**
1937	4,080	536	517	−6	697	−919	**4,905**	557	**4,348**
1938	4,289	617	574	60	843	−1,094	**5,289**	582	**4,707**
1939	4,392	749	592	83	757	−1,001	**5,572**	587	**4,985**
1940	4,539	1,179	540	100	700	−1,100	**5,958**	640	**5,318**
1941	4,799	2,952	520	200	600	−1,550	**7,521**	803	**6,718**
1942	5,104	4,097	480	100	600	−1,550	**8,831**	1,050	**7,781**
	5,410	4,581	450	−100	600	−1,350	**9,591**	1,151	**8,440**

Table **UK.1 (Continued)**   **Gross domestic product at current prices, 1885–1987**

	Consumers' expenditure	General govt final consumption	Gross domestic fixed capital formation	Value of physical change in stocks & w.i.p.	Exports of goods & services	Imports of goods & services	Gross domestic product at market prices	Less Adjustment to factor cost	Gross domestic product at factor cost
					£ mn				
1943	5,525	4,983	360	100	740	−1,500	**10,208**	1,218	**8,990**
1944	5,846	5,056	300	−200	970	−1,700	**10,272**	1,212	**9,060**
1945	6,391	4,190	350	−200	800	−1,700	**9,831**	1,157	**8,674**
1946	7,273	2,282	925	−126	1,430	−1,825	**9,959**	1,189	**8,770**
1947	8,028	1,735	1,199	269	1,652	−2,228	**10,655**	1,347	**9,308**
					£ bn				
1948	8·62	1·84	1·43	0·18	2·20	−2·43	**11·82**	1·44	**10·39**
1949	8·98	2·06	1·59	0·07	2·50	−2·70	**12·49**	1·46	**11·03**
1950	9·48	2·15	1·72	−0·21	3·00	−3·08	**13·06**	1·58	**11·47**
1951	10·24	2·52	1·92	0·58	3·65	−4·33	**14·57**	1·79	**12·78**
1952	10·79	3·00	2·15	0·05	3·76	−3·93	**15·81**	1·87	**13·95**
1953	11·51	3·14	2·42	0·13	3·69	−3·84	**17·05**	1·99	**15·05**
1954	12·21	3·21	2·62	0·06	3·84	−3·96	**17·98**	2·07	**15·91**
1955	13·17	3·27	2·91	0·30	4·18	−4·48	**19·35**	2·29	**17·07**
1956	13·88	3·53	3·19	0·26	4·60	−4·55	**20·91**	2·45	**18·46**
1957	14·65	3·68	3·48	0·24	4·84	−4·78	**22·11**	2·54	**19·57**
1958	15·46	3·75	3·60	0·11	4·70	−4·58	**23·05**	2·63	**20·42**
1959	16·30	4·00	3·86	0·18	4·85	−4·89	**24·29**	2·80	**21·49**
1960	17·11	4·24	4·23	0·56	5·15	−5·55	**25·74**	2·88	**22·87**
1961	18·01	4·57	4·75	0·28	5·38	−5·51	**27·48**	3·02	**24·45**
1962	19·10	4·90	4·90	−0·01	5·51	−5·61	**28·80**	3·26	**25·54**
1963	20·35	5·16	5·14	0·16	5·87	−6·03	**30·65**	3·44	**27·21**
1964	21·73	5·48	6·12	0·70	6·20	−6·82	**33·42**	3·90	**29·52**
1965	23·15	6·01	6·63	0·46	6·61	−6·97	**35·90**	4·35	**31·55**
1966	24·51	6·54	7·06	0·29	7·17	−7·26	**38·30**	4·82	**33·48**
1967	25·76	7·23	7·71	0·29	7·39	−7·85	**40·52**	5·15	**35·37**
1968	27·75	7·68	8·51	0·45	8·98	−9·38	**43·99**	5·86	**38·13**
1969	29·45	8·02	8·83	0·54	10·09	−9·93	**46·99**	6·88	**40·12**
1970	32·03	9·04	9·74	0·38	11·51	−11·11	**51·59**	7·47	**44·12**
1971	35·88	10·31	10·89	0·11	12·92	−12·16	**57·95**	7·71	**50·23**
1972	40·55	11·75	11·94	0·03	13·62	−13·74	**64·14**	8·03	**56·11**
1973	46·15	13·40	14·73	1·53	17·07	−18·95	**73·92**	8·56	**65·36**
1974	53·20	16·72	17·50	1·05	22·87	−27·16	**84·17**	8·27	**75·91**
1975	65·47	23·12	21·04	−1·35	26·86	−28·78	**106·35**	10·27	**96·09**
1976	75·98	27·04	24·50	0·90	35·10	−36·82	**126·71**	12·71	**114·00**
1977	86·89	29·47	27·04	1·82	43·31	−42·59	**145·93**	16·45	**129·48**
1978	100·22	33·41	31·06	1·80	47·48	−45·53	**168·44**	18·98	**149·46**
1979	118·65	38·89	36·93	2·16	54·90	−54·40	**197·14**	25·03	**172·11**
1980	137·90	49·02	41·56	−2·57	62·93	−57·62	**231·21**	30·76	**200·45**
1981	153·57	55·46	41·30	−2·77	67·69	−60·42	**254·83**	36·10	**218·74**
1982	168·55	60·45	44·82	−1·19	73·02	−68·04	**277·61**	40·66	**236·95**
1983	184·62	65·87	48·62	1·47	80·54	−77·90	**303·22**	43·19	**260·03**
1984	197·49	69·88	55·03	1·56	92·35	−92·99	**323·33**	45·05	**278·28**
1985	215·27	74·00	60·28	0·57	102·78	−99·17	**353·73**	49·52	**304·21**
1986	236·76	79·69	63·80	0·57	98·48	−101·58	**377·71**	56·59	**321·12**
1987	258·43	85·77	70·77	0·63	107·51	−112·03	**411·07**	62·22	**348·86**

Table UK.2   Gross domestic product at constant prices, 1885–1987

	Consumers' expenditure	General govt final consumption	Gross domestic fixed capital formation	Value of physical change in stocks & w.i.p.	Exports of goods & services	Imports of goods & services	**Gross domestic product at market prices**	*Less* Adjustment to factor cost	**Gross domestic product at factor cost**	Average estimate
				£ bn, 1985 prices						
1885	42·7	6·4	3·6	0·08	13·2	−10·1	**61·0**	10·9	**51·0**	...
1886	42·9	6·3	3·3	0·3	13·5	−10·2	**61·8**	10·9	**51·7**	...
1887	44·6	6·2	3·4	0·3	14·3	−10·8	**63·7**	11·2	**53·4**	...
1888	45·2	6·2	3·6	−0·04	15·2	−11·1	**64·2**	11·2	**53·8**	...
1889	46·1	6·3	3·8	0·3	15·9	−12·1	**66·1**	11·5	**55·4**	...
1890	47·0	6·4	3·9	0·2	15·8	−12·1	**67·0**	11·7	**56·1**	...
1891	48·9	6·6	4·0	0·1	15·1	−12·4	**68·3**	12·1	**57·2**	...
1892	48·7	6·6	4·2	0·15	14·9	−12·6	**67·9**	12·2	**56·8**	...
1893	48·9	6·8	4·2	−0·2	14·1	−12·3	**66·8**	12·1	**55·9**	...
1894	50·9	7·1	4·4	0·7	14·8	−13·3	**71·7**	12·4	**60·1**	...
1895	52·2	7·6	4·6	0·3	15·9	−14·0	**72·7**	12·7	**60·9**	...
1896	54·3	7·9	5·0	0·6	16·6	−14·8	**76·9**	13·1	**64·6**	...
1897	54·6	8·1	5·6	−0·15	16·7	−15·1	**75·3**	13·3	**63·0**	...
1898	56·9	8·3	6·4	0·4	16·7	−15·6	**80·3**	13·6	**67·4**	...
1899	58·8	10·1	6·8	0·6	17·5	−15·9	**85·1**	14·2	**71·6**	...
1900	58·7	13·1	6·8	−0·3	16·8	−16·3	**82·7**	14·3	**69·3**	...
1901	59·8	14·7	7·2	0·7	17·2	−17·0	**88·2**	14·5	**74·2**	...
1902	60·1	13·9	7·5	0·06	17·9	−17·1	**87·3**	14·5	**73·4**	...
1903	60·4	12·3	7·5	−0·2	18·6	−17·1	**86·5**	14·4	**72·7**	...
1904	61·3	11·9	7·4	0·03	19·0	−17·3	**88·1**	14·4	**74·1**	...
1905	61·6	11·8	7·3	0·4	20·6	−17·7	**90·6**	14·6	**76·3**	...
1906	62·7	11·7	6·9	0·07	22·0	−18·3	**91·0**	14·8	**76·7**	...
1907	63·5	11·4	6·2	−0·2	23·4	−18·6	**91·2**	15·0	**76·7**	...
1908	63·3	11·7	5·2	−0·1	21·7	−17·8	**89·5**	14·8	**72·3**	...
1909	63·6	12·2	5·5	0·3	22·9	−18·5	**92·1**	14·4	**77·8**	...
1910	64·6	12·7	5·6	−0·03	24·6	−19·1	**93·9**	14·6	**79·3**	...
1911	66·6	13·0	5·7	0·1	25·3	−19·6	**97·0**	15·1	**81·9**	...
1912	67·0	13·2	5·7	−0·15	26·7	−21·0	**96·4**	15·2	**81·3**	...
1913	69·4	13·5	6·3	0·4	27·5	−21·7	**101·8**	15·6	**86·1**	...
1914	69·7	19·4	6·3	0·04	22·8	−20·5	**102·3**	15·5	**85·6**	...
1915	71·3	58·1	5·0	0·1	19·0	−21·6	**119·2**	15·8	**101·5**	...
1916	65·3	66·1	3·9	−1·2	21·9	−20·0	**116·7**	14·7	**99·8**	...
1917	60·2	72·4	4·1	−0·3	15·6	−17·1	**114·4**	12·7	**98·3**	...
1918	59·7	69·1	5·1	0·6	12·2	−17·4	**111·6**	12·4	**95·9**	...
1919	68·3	30·3	6·6	−0·5	17·9	−19·6	**100·8**	14·5	**85·5**	...
1920	68·4	17·4	7·7	−0·9	19·2	−19·5	**94·8**	15·7	**79·7**	...
	65·5	16·3	7·4		20·0	−20·0	**90·8**	15·0	**76·4**	
1921	61·6	16·5	8·5	−1·1	15·9	−17·6	**85·5**	13·9	**72·1**	...
1922	63·7	15·5	7·8	−0·9	20·1	−20·3	**88·5**	13·8	**75·1**	...
1923	65·6	14·6	7·8	−0·7	22·0	−21·7	**91·3**	14·0	**77·5**	...
1924	67·2	14·7	9·4	−0·06	22·7	−23·9	**94·0**	14·5	**79·8**	...
1925	68·7	15·2	10·7	1·3	22·6	−24·5	**98·7**	14·8	**84·0**	...
1926	68·5	15·5	10·4	0·2	20·7	−25·5	**94·1**	14·5	**79·9**	...
1927	71·1	15·7	11·5	0·5	23·3	−25·9	**100·7**	15·1	**85·7**	...
1928	72·3	15·9	11·4	0·2	23·5	−25·1	**102·4**	15·3	**87·2**	...
1929	73·8	16·2	12·0	0·5	24·2	−26·3	**104·8**	15·6	**89·3**	...
1930	74·9	16·6	12·1	1·2	20·9	−26·0	**104·7**	15·6	**89·2**	...
1931	75·7	17·0	11·8	−0·04	16·8	−27·0	**99·4**	15·3	**84·3**	...
1932	75·2	17·0	10·3	0·01	16·4	−24·1	**99·6**	14·8	**84·9**	...
1933	77·1	17·2	10·7	−1·1	16·7	−24·1	**100·8**	15·2	**85·7**	...
1934	79·4	17·6	13·0	0·5	17·3	−25·2	**107·6**	15·8	**91·8**	...
1935	81·6	18·8	13·5	0·09	19·5	−26·4	**111·6**	16·4	**95·3**	...
1936	84·0	20·5	14·7	−0·09	18·9	−27·1	**115·1**	17·1	**98·2**	...
1937	85·4	22·9	15·2	0·8	19·9	−28·0	**120·0**	17·7	**102·4**	...
1938	85·4	27·4	15·4	1·2	18·6	−27·4	**123·6**	18·0	**105·6**	...
1939	90·7	41·4	13·8	1·5	17·2	−29·9	**128·4**	18·4	**110·0**	...
1940	78·3	96·7	12·0	2·3	11·8	−30·4	**146·9**	18·0	**127·9**	...
1941	75·2	121·2	9·6	0·9	10·1	−26·6	**155·8**	18·7	**135·9**	...
1942	74·4	127·1	8·3	−0·75	9·1	−22·5	**157·3**	18·6	**137·5**	...

	Consumers' expenditure	General govt final consumption	Gross domestic fixed capital formation	Value of physical change in stocks & w.i.p.	Exports of goods & services	Imports of goods & services	**Gross domestic product at market prices**	*Less* Adjustment to factor cost	**Gross domestic product at factor cost**	Average estimate
					£ bn, 1985 prices					
1943	73·5	131·4	5·7	0·9	10·1	−22·2	**160·2**	18·8	**140·1**	. . .
1944	75·7	122·9	4·4	−1·8	12·8	−24·7	**153·0**	18·8	**133·2**	. . .
1945	80·5	99·9	5·0	−1·8	10·3	−23·6	**143·5**	19·3	**123·8**	. . .
1946	88·8	54·8	12·5	1·1	17·5	−23·6	**142·7**	19·7	**122·7**	. . .
1947	91·6	38·7	14·6	2·1	17·5	−23·7	**139·2**	19·5	**119·5**	. . .
1948	92·4	37·3	15·8	1·2	21·3	−23·2	**142·7**	19·0	**123·5**	123·7
1949	93·9	39·4	17·3	0·4	23·6	−25·0	**146·8**	19·4	**127·1**	128·1
1950	96·4	39·3	18·2	−1·3	27·0	−25·2	**151·4**	19·9	**131·2**	132·2
1951	95·1	42·2	18·4	3·0	26·7	−27·0	**156·6**	20·6	**135·6**	135·8
1952	95·2	46·4	18·6	0·3	26·1	−25·0	**157·2**	20·2	**136·6**	136·2
1953	99·3	47·6	20·7	0·6	27·2	−26·9	**164·3**	21·1	**142·8**	141·5
1954	103·4	47·4	22·5	0·3	28·8	−27·9	**170·7**	22·2	**148·1**	147·4
1955	107·7	46·2	23·8	1·8	30·6	−30·7	**177·1**	23·1	**153·6**	153·1
1956	108·7	45·7	24·9	1·4	31·9	−30·8	**179·8**	22·9	**156·4**	155·0
1957	111·0	44·9	26·2	1·4	32·7	−31·6	**183·3**	23·5	**159·3**	157·6
1958	113·6	43·7	26·5	0·6	32·2	−31·9	**183·5**	24·6	**158·6**	157·1
1959	118·5	44·5	28·5	1·2	33·1	−34·0	**190·9**	26·7	**164·2**	163·6
1960	123·1	45·4	31·1	3·7	35·0	−38·0	**200·4**	28·1	**172·3**	173·2
1961	125·8	47·0	34·1	1·8	36·1	−37·8	**206·5**	28·5	**177·9**	177·6
1962	128·7	48·4	34·3	0·06	36·7	−38·6	**208·3**	28·6	**179·5**	179·9
1963	134·8	49·3	34·8	1·1	38·5	−40·2	**217·6**	29·6	**187·8**	187·4
1964	139·0	50·1	40·6	4·4	39·8	−44·4	**229·2**	31·1	**198·0**	198·1
1965	141·1	51·4	42·7	2·9	41·5	−44·8	**234·2**	31·2	**202·9**	203·8
1966	143·6	52·7	43·8	1·8	43·6	−45·9	**238·9**	31·7	**207·0**	207·6
1967	147·2	55·7	47·6	1·4	43·9	−49·0	**245·5**	32·7	**212·7**	212·1
1968	151·3	55·9	50·6	2·2	49·4	−52·8	**255·8**	33·4	**222·3**	221·4
1969	152·1	54·9	50·3	2·5	54·2	−54·5	**259·1**	33·3	**225·8**	226·8
1970	156·3	55·8	51·6	1·8	57·1	−57·1	**265·1**	34·6	**230·5**	231·4
1971	161·2	57·5	52·5	0·5	61·0	−60·2	**272·1**	35·9	**236·0**	235·0
1972	171·1	59·9	52·4	−0·13	61·7	−66·1	**278·4**	38·7	**239·4**	241·4
1973	179·9	62·5	55·8	6·9	69·0	−74·0	**301·0**	41·1	**259·6**	260·0
1974	177·2	63·7	54·5	2·9	74·1	−74·7	**298·0**	39·6	**257·7**	255·8
1975	176·3	67·2	53·4	−3·4	72·0	−69·4	**296·0**	39·4	**255·9**	253·7
1976	176·9	68·1	54·3	1·5	78·6	−72·7	**306·9**	40·9	**265·4**	260·6
1977	176·0	66·9	53·3	3·2	84·0	−73·7	**310·2**	41·1	**268·4**	267·3
1978	185·9	68·5	54·9	2·9	85·6	−76·6	**321·7**	45·2	**276·5**	275·4
1979	193·8	69·9	56·4	3·3	88·8	−84·0	**328·9**	46·6	**282·3**	282·8
1980	193·8	71·0	53·4	−3·4	89·0	−81·2	**322·5**	45·3	**277·2**	276·5
1981	193·8	71·3	48·3	−3·2	88·2	−78·9	**318·9**	44·2	**274·6**	273·4
1982	195·6	71·8	50·9	−1·3	89·0	−82·8	**322·9**	44·9	**278·0**	278·4
1983	204·3	73·3	53·5	1·3	91·1	−88·1	**335·4**	46·4	**289·0**	288·7
1984	207·9	74·0	58·1	1·1	97·1	−96·7	**341·4**	48·7	**292·7**	293·5
1985	215·3	74·0	60·3	0·6	102·8	−99·2	**353·7**	49·5	**304·2**	304·7
1986	226·8	75·4	60·8	0·6	106·6	−105·6	**364·7**	51·8	**312·9**	313·9
1987	238·5	76·0	64·2	0·6	112·5	−113·3	**378·5**	54·5	**324·0**	327·1

Table UK.3 Output by industry, index numbers, 1885–1987

	Total output	Agriculture, forestry & fishing	Production & construction	*of which:* Manufacturing	Transport & communication	Distributive trades	Services	*of which:* Public admin. & defence
				Index nos., 1980 = 100				
1885	19·6	46·7	13·2	13·0	11·2	26·8	22·4	24
1886	19·6	48·3	12·9	12·9	11·3	26·8	22·7	24
1887	20·3	45·4	14·0	14·2	12·0	28·0	23·2	25
1888	21·2	46·3	14·8	15·1	12·5	29·4	23·7	25
1889	22·2	47·3	15·8	16·2	13·3	31·4	24·0	26
1890	22·5	48·0	16·0	16·4	13·5	31·6	24·4	26
1891	22·9	49·3	16·2	16·5	13·9	32·3	24·8	27
1892	22·5	47·7	15·5	15·5	13·8	31·6	25·3	27
1893	22·3	45·7	15·2	15·4	13·7	30·7	25·6	28
1894	23·2	46·7	16·1	15·9	14·4	32·9	26·0	29
1895	23·9	46·0	16·9	17·0	15·1	34·1	26·5	29
1896	25·0	46·0	18·1	18·4	15·8	35·8	26·8	30
1897	25·4	44·7	18·6	18·5	16·1	36·4	27·3	31
1898	26·3	46·7	19·5	19·5	16·7	37·8	27·8	32
1899	26·9	45·4	20·3	20·3	17·1	38·6	28·1	32
1900	27·1	44·4	20·3	20·1	17·2	38·8	28·9	36
1901	27·5	45·1	20·3	20·0	17·5	39·4	30·2	40
1902	28·0	46·7	20·7	20·1	17·9	40·1	30·8	41
1903	27·6	42·8	20·3	19·6	18·1	39·6	30·5	38
1904	28·1	45·1	20·5	19·7	18·7	40·2	30·4	36
1905	29·2	45·8	21·7	21·4	19·3	41·8	31·1	37
1906	29·9	42·8	22·6	22·4	19·9	43·0	31·6	38
1907	30·7	46·4	23·0	23·0	20·7	44·3	32·3	39
1908	29·7	47·7	21·2	21·1	20·2	42·4	33·2	44
1909	30·2	48·7	21·3	21·3	20·8	43·2	33·7	41
1910	30·7	48·0	21·6	21·6	21·4	43·9	34·5	43
1911	31·9	47·1	23·2	23·4	22·2	45·7	35·3	44
1912	32·8	46·4	23·8	24·4	23·2	48·0	35·7	45
1913	34·0	46·4	25·3	25·9	24·2	49·9	36·7	46
1914	...	...	23·7	24·2	...	...	...	...
1920	33·2	43·1	25·1	26·3	23·7	48·2	38·3	73
1921	31·9	33·2	24·8	25·9	23·0	46·2	37·0	52
1922	28·0	33·8	20·2	20·1	20·7	40·6	34·2	57
1923	30·1	34·2	23·3	23·4	24·1	44·8	33·4	51
1924	31·1	34·7	24·7	25·1	26·4	45·5	33·3	48
1925	32·7	33·7	27·4	27·6	27·3	46·7	33·9	47
1926	33·6	36·3	28·5	28·5	27·7	48·0	34·4	48
1927	32·9	37·3	27·0	27·6	26·5	46·5	35·0	47
1928	35·7	37·4	31·1	30·5	29·2	49·6	35·9	47
1929	35·7	39·6	30·3	30·4	29·6	49·7	36·7	47
1930	36·6	39·7	31·8	31·7	30·8	50·8	36·5	48
1931	36·1	40·7	30·4	30·3	30·6	50·3	36·9	49
1932	34·8	37·1	28·4	28·2	29·1	51·0	35·8	50
1933	34·9	38·8	28·3	28·4	28·0	50·8	37·0	50
1934	36·3	41·6	30·2	30·5	28·6	52·5	37·7	50
1935	38·3	42·1	33·2	33·3	29·5	54·6	38·5	50
1936	40·0	41·0	35·7	36·3	30·4	56·4	39·4	52
1937	42·2	40·4	39·0	39·7	31·8	58·6	40·4	53
1938	43·8	40·2	41·3	42·1	33·3	59·5	41·3	56
1938	43·2	39·7	40·2	40·8	33·2	58·1	41·9	61
1946	45·4	44·0	41·2	42·7	37·9	47·5	60·8	146
1947	45·9	42·2	43·4	45·2	39·6	51·4	52·5	107
1948	48·0	45·3	47·1	49·3	42·6	53·4	50·0	94
1949	49·8	48·6	50·2	52·9	44·8	55·4	50·1	91
1950	51·6	49·2	53·2	56·9	46·3	56·9	50·8	88
1951	52·5	50·5	54·5	58·5	48·4	56·1	51·3	93
1952	52·1	51·9	52·8	55·6	49·8	55·1	52·2	96
1953	54·3	52·8	56·1	59·7	51·3	58·6	53·3	96

	Total output	Agriculture, forestry & fishing	Production & construction	*of which:* Manufacturing	Transport & communication	Distributive trades	Services	*of which:* Public admin. & defence
				Index nos., 1980 = 100				
1954	56·5	53·5	59·0	62·9	52·5	61·5	55·0	95
1955	58·4	53·1	61·9	66·8	53·8	64·3	56·5	93
1956	59·0	56·0	62·3	66·7	54·7	65·1	56·9	91
1957	60·1	57·3	63·5	68·3	54·6	66·6	58·0	89
1958	60·0	56·1	63·0	67·6	54·2	68·3	58·9	86
1959	62·7	58·2	66·2	71·5	56·5	72·1	61·3	84
1960	66·1	62·0	70·7	77·2	59·3	75·7	63·3	83
1961	67·3	62·3	71·6	77·5	60·8	77·1	64·9	84
1962	68·3	64·4	72·3	77·7	61·2	77·7	65·8	84
1963	70·5	66·9	74·3	80·4	63·2	80·8	67·9	86
1964	74·8	69·5	80·7	87·7	67·3	84·4	70·6	86
1965	76·8	71·4	83·1	90·2	68·8	86·0	72·3	87
1966	78·3	71·7	84·4	91·8	70·7	86·8	73·9	89
1967	79·6	74·1	85·4	92·3	71·5	87·5	75·4	92
1968	83·0	73·9	90·9	99·4	74·4	90·1	77·6	91
1969	84·6	73·7	93·3	103·1	77·5	90·6	78·8	90
1970	86·1	78·3	93·5	103·4	80·8	93·2	81·1	90
1971	87·4	82·4	93·1	102·4	82·9	95·2	83·2	92
1972	90·0	85·1	95·1	104·5	86·8	100·5	86·5	96
1973	95·3	87·8	102·6	114·3	93·4	105·1	90·2	98
1974	93·9	88·8	98·9	112·8	93·6	101·0	90·4	97
1975	92·1	81·9	93·6	105·1	92·5	97·5	91·4	99
1976	94·0	75·2	95·9	107·0	92·0	98·4	93·4	100
1977	96·7	85·0	99·9	109·0	94·6	97·8	94·6	99
1978	100·0	91·4	103·4	109·7	97·9	103·5	97·6	99
1979	103·0	90·0	106·9	109·5	101·9	106·5	100·4	99
1980	100·0	100·0	100·0	100·0	100·0	100·0	100·0	100
1981	98·7	102·6	96·2	94·1	100·2	98·4	100·3	100
1982	100·8	111·1	98·8	94·3	99·2	100·2	101·8	99
1983	104·2	105·2	102·9	97·0	102·2	104·6	105·0	99
1984	107·1	123·4	103·9	101·0	106·7	109·2	108·9	100
1985	110·9	117·4	108·8	103·4	109·9	114·0	112·1	99
1986	114·2	118·8	111·1	104·4	114·8	118·7	116·1	98
1987	119·5	116·8	116·0	110·4	122·7	125·5	122·0	99

25

Table UK.4   Industrial production, selected series, 1885–1987

	Coal	Crude steel	Cars & commercial vehicles	Chemicals & allied industries	Cotton cloth	Manmade fibres & mixtures	Woollen & worsted woven fabrics	Electricity
	mn tons	mn tons ingot equiv.	'000	Index nos., 1980 = 100	mn linear m		mn m²	bn kwh
1885	161·9	1·92	...	2·2	...	...	...	—
1886	160·0	2·30	...	2·4	...	...	...	—
1887	164·7	3·09	...	2·7	...	...	...	—
1888	172·7	3·36	...	3·0	...	...	...	—
1889	179·8	3·63	...	3·3	...	...	...	—
1890	184·5	3·64	...	3·3	...	...	...	—
1891	188·5	3·21	...	3·1	...	...	...	—
1892	184·7	2·97	...	3·0	...	...	...	—
1893	167·0	3·00	...	3·2	...	...	...	—
1894	191·3	3·16	...	3·6	...	...	...	—
1895	192·7	3·31	...	3·7	...	...	...	—
1896	198·5	4·20	...	4·3	...	...	...	0·1
1897	205·4	4·56	...	4·4	...	...	...	0·1
1898	205·3	4·64	...	4·5	...	...	...	0·1
1899	223·6	4·93	...	4·8	...	...	...	0·2
1900	228·8	4·98	...	4·9	...	...	...	0·2
1901	222·6	4·98	...	4·9	...	...	...	0·4
1902	230·7	4·99	...	5·1	...	...	...	0·5
1903	234·0	5·11	...	5·2	...	...	...	0·6
1904	236·1	5·11	...	5·5	...	...	...	0·8
1905	239·9	5·90	...	6·1	...	...	...	1·0
1906	255·1	6·56	...	6·7	...	...	...	1·2
1907	272·1	6·62	12	7·1	(6,483)	...	(535)	1·4
1908	265·7	5·37	11	6·3	...	...	...	1·6
1909	268·0	5·97	11	6·9	...	...	...	1·7
1910	268·6	6·47	14	7·7	...	...	...	1·9
1911	276·3	6·56	19	7·7	...	...	...	2·1
1912	264·6	6·91	23	7·9	7,361	...	604	2·4
1913	292·0	7·78	34	8·3	...	...	...	2·5
1914	270·0	7·97	...	8·0	...	...	...	3·0
1915	257·3	8·69	...	8·2	...	...	...	3·5
1916	260·5	9·13	...	8·5	...	...	...	4·1
1917	252·5	9·88	...	8·5	...	...	...	4·7
1918	231·3	9·69	...	8·6	...	...	...	4·9
1919	233·5	8·02	...	8·7	...	...	...	4·9
1920	233·2	9·22	...	9·3	...	...	...	4·3
1921	165·9	3·76	...	6·7	...	...	...	3·9
1922	253·6	5·97	73	7·9	...	...	...	4·6
1923	280·4	8·62	95	8·7	...	...	...	5·3
1924	271·4	8·33	147	9·2	5,111	37	394	6·1
1925	247·1	7·51	167	8·9	...	...	...	6·7
1926	128·3	3·66	198	8·2	...	...	...	7·1
1927	255·2	9·25	212	9·4	...	...	...	8·5
1928	241·3	8·66	212	9·8	...	...	...	9·4
1929	262·0	9·79	239	10·3	...	...	(343)	10·5
1930	247·8	7·45	237	9·8	2,907	138	288	11·0
1931	223·0	5·28	226	9·4	...	...	(272)	11·5
1932	212·0	5·34	233	10·0	...	...	(289)	12·3
1933	210·4	7·13	286	10·5	2·911	274	345	13·7
1934	214·0	8·99	342	11·4	2,849	294	352	15·6
1935	225·8	10·02	417	12·3	2,822	316	367	17·7
1936	232·1	11·97	482	12·9	...	...	(393)	20·4
1937	244·2	13·19	508	13·7	3,328	423	397	23·1
1938	230·6	10·57	445	13·0	...	...	...	24·6
1939	235·0	13·43	402	...	...	...	...	26·7
1940	227·9	13·19	134	...	...	...	...	29·0
1941	209·6	12·51	145	...	1,966	276	...	32·7
1942	208·2	12·90	161	...	1,620	258	...	36·0
1943	202·1	13·24	149	...	1,608	257	306	37·4
1944	195·9	12·33	133	...	1,507	266	251	38·8

Table UK.4 (Continued)   Industrial production, selected series, 1885–1987

	Coal	Crude steel	Cars & commercial vehicles	Chemicals & allied industries	Cotton cloth	Manmade fibres & mixtures	Woollen & worsted woven fabrics	Electricity
	mn tons	mn tons ingot equiv.	'000	Index nos., 1980 = 100	mn linear m		mn m²	bn kwh
1945	185·7	12·01	139	...	1,407	282	250	37·7
1946	193·1	12·90	366	19·5	1,487	318	289	41·7
1947	200·7	12·68	442	19·8	1,484	356	298	43·1
1948	212·9	15·12	512	21·4	1,734	455	347	47·0
1949	218·6	15·80	631	22·2	1,833	537	367	49·7
1950	219·8	16·55	784	25·2	1,941	647	376	55·6
1951	226·5	15·89	734	26·4	2,013	694	349	60·7
1952	228·2	16·37	689	25·1	1,546	550	316	62·8
1953	226·9	17·89	835	28·1	1,672	690	344	66·4
1954	227·2	18·82	1,038	31·6	1,823	714	346	73·9
1955	225·1	20·11	1,237	33·5	1,629	638	343	81·2
1956	225·6	20·99	1,004	34·9	1,474	642	332	88·3
1957	227·2	22·05	1,148	36·3	1,489	604	329	92·2
1958	219·3	19·51	1,364	36·3	1,307	550	292	99·8
1959	209·4	20·51	1,561	40·2	1,223	540	305	106·6
1960	196·7	24·70	1,811	44·5	1,183	564	307	120·5
1961	193·5	22·44	1,464	45·1	1,129	555	294	129·4
1962	200·6	20·82	1,674	46·9	957	517	274	143·6
1963	198·9	22·88	2,011	50·4	927	512	272	156·0
1964	196·7	26·19	2,332	55·5	946	558	272	164·6
1965	190·5	27·42	2,177	59·3	928	572	270	177·4
1966	177·4	24·69	2,042	62·7	837	564	253	184·1
1967	175·0	24·26	1,937	66·3	681	484	246	191·1
1968	166·7	26·26	2,225	71·9	668	507	246	204·4
1969	153·0	26·82	2,183	75·9	661	538	239	218·4
1970	144·6	27·79	2,098	80·0	627	484	215	228·2
1971	147·1	24·15	2,198	81·6	559	480	186	235·7
1972	119·5	25·29	2,329	86·2	513	470	183	242·7
1973	130·2	26·59	2,164	96·4	454	502	192	258·8
1974	109·3	22·32	1,936	101·6	409	505	175	250·5
1975	127·8	20·10	1,649	91·0	405	503	151	251·3
1976	122·2	22·27	1,705	102·8	375	493	143	254·9
1977	120·6	20·41	1,714	106·4	368	497	150	262·0
1978	121·7	20·31	1,608	107·6	380	458	144	266·8
1979	120·7	21·46	1,479	110·5	365	467	138	279·5
1980	128·2	11·28	1,314	100·0	314	350	118	266·4
1981	125·3	15·57	1,183	100·0	278	273	97	259·7
1982	121·5	13·70	1,157	100·7	261	251	100	255·4
1983	116·4	14·99	1,289	108·2	255	228	94	260·4
1984	49·5	15·12	1,134	114·3	265	239	91	266·0
1985	90·8	15·72	1,314	118·5	274	255	91	280·0
1986	104·6	14·72	1,248	121·1	275	262	93	282·3
1987	101·6	17·41	1,389	129·5	245	259	90	282·7

Table UK.5   **Gross domestic fixed capital formation by industry group and by type of asset, 1885–1987**

	Agriculture, forestry & fishing	Mfg & construction	Energy & water supply	Distribution & business services	Transport & communication	Other services	Dwellings	Other new buildings & works, etc	Vehicles, ships & aircraft	Plant & machinery
	£ mn, 1985 prices									
1885	1,523				2,008	546	1,392	2,547	606	730
1886	1,427				1,698	515	1,341	2,368	451	678
1887	1,465				1,786	472	1,431	2,368	544	678
1888	1,533				1,932	478	1,379	2,317	766	694
1889	1,598				-2,247	484	1,379	2,384	1,000	718
1890	1,622				2,352	534	1,296	2,465	1,027	751
1891	1,660				2,521	577	1,334	2,593	1,053	800
1892	1,701				2,451	664	1,450	2,588	1,022	864
1893	1,773				2,206	819	1,605	2,710	832	934
1894	1,832				2,300	831	1,644	2,751	925	958
1895	1,986				2,317	900	1,676	2,909	894	1,062
1896	2,171				2,370	943	2,005	3,006	920	1,199
1897	2,518				2,539	931	2,263	3,338	929	1,381
1898	2,837				3,076	955	2,746	3,644	1,226	1,567
1899	3,049				3,327	962	2,740	3,802	1,398	1,682
1900	3,073				3,490	1,017	2,520	3,879	1,385	1,780
1901	3,265				3,671	1,129	2,578	4,129	1,456	1,904
1902	3,406				3,782	1,272	2,707	4,420	1,425	2,002
1903	3,581				3,479	1,129	2,765	4,221	1,217	2,193
1904	3,523				3,683	1,142	2,527	4,144	1,394	2,172
1905	3,416				3,730	1,073	2,514	3,935	1,571	2,075
1906	3,145				3,771	993	2,263	3,843	1,642	1,822
1907	2,874				3,239	856	2,076	3,364	1,469	1,643
1908	2,572				2,270	838	1,850	2,853	925	1,542
1909	2,819				2,481	838	1,818	2,930	1,213	1,624
1910	2,974				2,545	831	1,650	3,016	1,354	1,646
1911	2,939				3,093	794	1,309	3,006	1,783	1,591
1912	3,073				3,053	807	1,115	3,006	1,810	1,679
1913	3,300				3,747	831	993	3,435	2,155	1,758
1914	3,615				3,327	831	844	3,277	1,783	2,169
1915	3,433				2,002	403	541	2,394	1,230	2,017
1916	2,837				1,582	199	297	1,853	1,013	1,631
1917	2,782				2,306	161	90	1,751	1,562	1,637
1918	3,605				2,562	168	52	1,955	1,938	2,117
1919	4,658				3,374	261	90	2,715	2,845	2,446
					3,239	465	528	4,007	2,722	2,519
1920	176	1,969	755	698	2,288	304	1,315	2,945	1,509	1,591
1921	150	2,137	978	576	2,063	390	2,701	2,481	1,151	2,324
1922	100	1,536	1,174	379	2,450	477	2,382	2,318	1,438	1,821
1923	100	1,368	1,341	622	2,224	607	2,169	2,700	1,271	1,988
1924	76	1,393	1,537	667	2,514	738	3,093	2,836	1,629	2,094
1925	76	1,945	1,648	530	2,675	867	3,875	3,245	1,606	2,408
1926	76	1,705	1,481	546	1,902	824	4,870	2,809	1,199	2,240
1927	76	1,705	1,705	561	2,482	932	5,333	2,836	1,582	2,554
1928	76	1,848	1,509	819	2,997	867	4,159	2,809	1,966	2,848
1929	76	1,848	1,845	773	2,611	1,084	4,729	3,327	1,893	2,658
1930	100	1,680	2,096	895	2,321	1,280	4,409	3,982	1,486	2,742
1931	76	1,393	2,236	850	1,902	1,474	4,622	3,327	1,054	3,308
1932	50	1,368	2,011	652	1,353	1,063	4,657	2,754	624	2,889
1933	50	1,368	1,928	622	903	867	6,115	2,564	527	2,533
1934	76	2,088	1,984	819	1,450	976	6,862	2,999	1,102	3,119
1935	100	2,041	2,124	925	1,935	1,040	6,542	3,300	1,414	3,224
1936	125	2,377	2,291	804	2,675	1,301	6,506	3,709	1,966	3,433
1937	150	2,952	2,011	819	2,805	1,539	6,080	4,526	1,941	3,475
1938	125	2,616	2,096	1,030	3,030	1,561	6,008	4,364	1,918	3,831
1939	...	...	...	...	...	...	3,910	4,908	1,438	3,770
1940	...	...	...	...	...	...	5,236		959	5,444
1941	...	...	...	...	...	...	3,927		1,199	4,188

	Agriculture, forestry & fishing	Mfg & construction	Energy & water supply	Distribution & business services	Transport & communi-cation	Other services	Dwellings	Other new buildings & works, etc	Vehicles, ships & aircraft	Plant & machinery
					£ mn, 1985 prices					
1942	...	...	...	...	...	...		2,946	1,438	3,561
1943	...	...	...	...	...	...		1,964	1,438	2,094
1944	...	...	...	...	...	...		1,309	1,438	1,466
1945	...	...	...	...	...	...		2,291	1,199	1,466
1946	...	...	...	...	...	...		8,509	2,158	2,722
1947	...	...	...	...	...	...	5,053	3,545	2,636	3,770
1948	1,030	3,698	1,872	864	2,675	1,084	4,693	3,818	2,636	4,607
1949	1,015	4,178	2,288	1,067	2,747	1,323	4,595	4,687	2,766	5,089
1950	970	4,766	2,483	1,159	2,570	1,579	4,498	5,356	2,551	5,673
1951	886	5,126	2,468	1,155	2,255	1,746	4,424	5,270	2,264	6,179
1952	826	4,886	2,550	1,145	2,069	1,658	5,330	5,413	2,010	5,872
1953	803	4,758	2,978	1,233	2,513	1,754	6,920	5,799	2,369	5,938
1954	856	5,105	3,370	1,497	2,627	1,801	7,142	6,421	2,544	6,600
1955	924	5,666	3,602	1,839	2,602	1,945	6,621	7,148	2,812	7,154
1956	818	6,541	3,415	1,792	3,184	2,184	6,337	7,976	3,060	7,449
1957	886	6,788	3,526	1,880	3,871	2,352	6,104	8,450	3,380	7,968
1958	1,015	6,410	3,668	2,112	3,782	2,607	5,811	8,828	3,457	7,998
1959	1,144	6,298	4,086	2,508	4,024	2,942	6,629	9,412	3,804	8,527
1960	1,190	7,495	3,899	2,910	4,299	3,109	7,367	10,375	4,260	9,093
1961	1,250	8,915	4,100	3,253	3,976	3,715	7,874	11,881	3,966	10,388
1962	1,190	8,274	4,443	3,290	3,434	4,369	8,455	12,371	3,419	10,280
1963	1,273	7,149	5,189	3,498	3,256	4,591	8,539	12,157	3,569	10,695
1964	1,280	8,088	5,935	4,075	3,846	5,453	10,532	14,137	4,208	12,021
1965	1,359	9,596	6,218	4,112	3,887	5,660	11,135	14,753	4,096	12,884
1966	1,316	9,607	7,100	3,966	3,834	5,858	11,503	14,867	3,677	13,755
1967	1,381	9,305	7,853	4,240	4,511	6,784	12,989	16,482	4,129	14,312
1968	1,537	9,990	6,590	4,875	5,415	7,502	14,021	17,360	5,124	14,622
1969	1,472	10,662	5,597	5,275	5,312	7,634	13,541	17,570	5,068	14,579
1970	1,553	11,504	5,092	5,781	5,834	8,138	12,292	18,250	5,409	15,637
1971	1,634	10,447	4,916	6,474	5,972	8,377	13,396	18,505	5,605	15,348
1972	1,785	9,228	4,418	6,882	6,292	8,606	13,777	18,086	6,337	14,766
1973	1,936	10,153	4,215	7,847	6,960	9,406	13,513	18,722	7,085	16,596
1974	1,669	11,030	5,222	7,835	6,266	8,188	12,727	17,935	6,787	17.086
1975	1,479	10,113	7,102	6,762	5,679	7,531	13,042	18,085	5,944	16,310
1976	1,469	9,568	8,154	6,989	5,188	7,589	13,457	18,149	5,750	16,894
1977	1,444	9,918	7,472	7,867	5,335	6,587	12,811	16,968	6,506	17,124
1978	1,548	10,566	7,428	8,992	5,440	6,024	12,913	16,708	7,150	18,313
1979	1,358	11.011	6,955	10,531	5,367	6,091	13,363	16,172	7,514	19,736
1980	1,213	9,368	7,110	10,520	5,065	5,950	12,379	15,334	6,296	19,660
1981	1,043	7,116	7,459	10,583	3,983	5,557	10,247	14,859	4,895	18,269
1982	1,229	6,967	7,518	11,570	3,643	6,448	10,899	16,378	5,028	18,478
1983	1,338	7,081	7,512	11,643	4,186	6,696	12,247	16,651	5,177	19,401
1984	1,242	8,363	7,072	13,694	4,859	7,299	12,571	18,135	6,107	21,262
1985	981	9,266	6,637	15,796	5,084	7,619	11,928	18,178	6,433	23,744
1986	865	8,998	6,585	15,718	4,851	7,922	12,829	18,365	5,627	24,013
1987	650	9,599	5,988	18,019	5,137	8,112	13,406	19,092	6,099	25,599

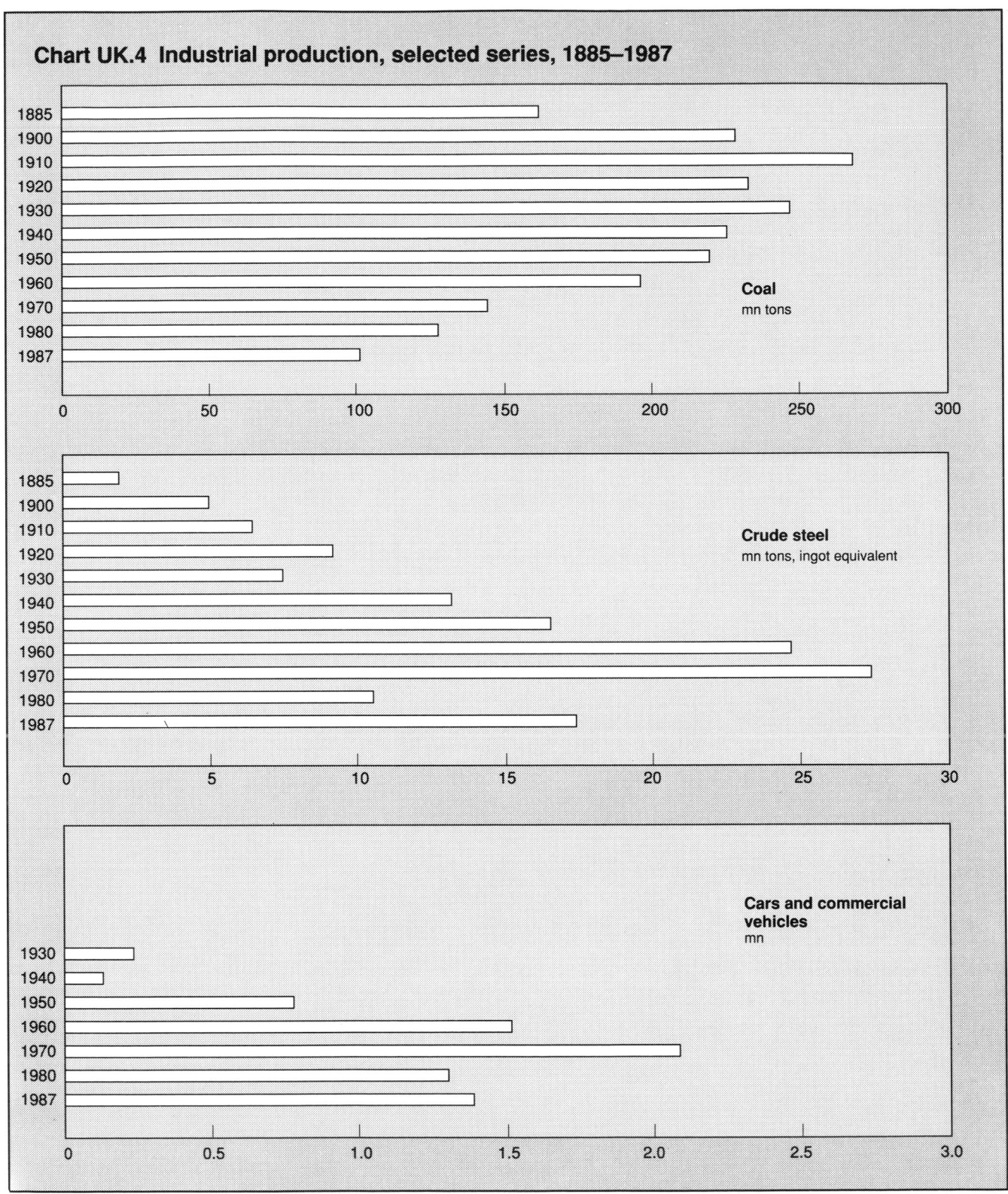

Chart UK.4 Industrial production, selected series, 1885–1987

Coal
mn tons

Crude steel
mn tons, ingot equivalent

Cars and commercial vehicles
mn

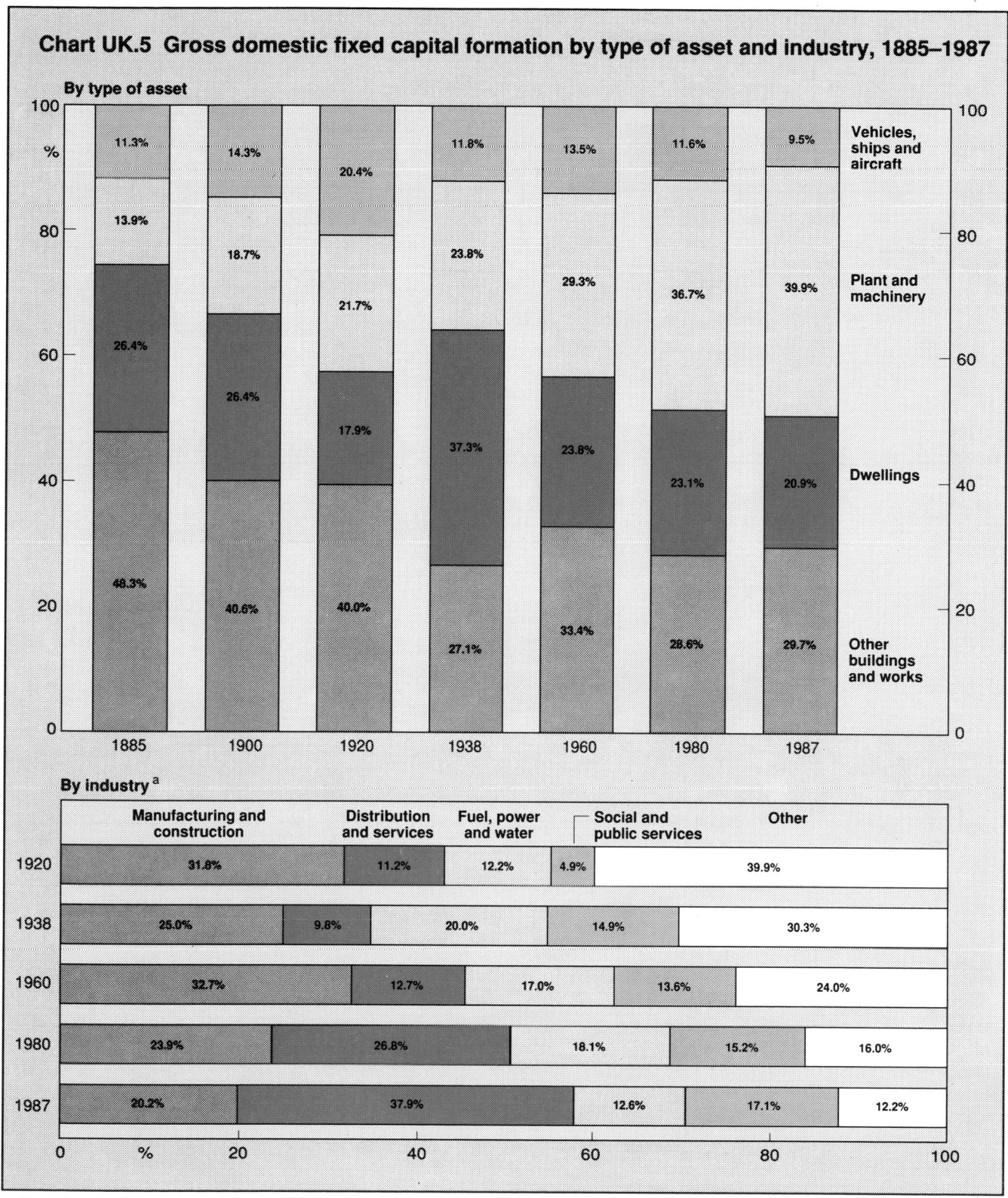

Chart UK.5 Gross domestic fixed capital formation by type of asset and industry, 1885–1987

By type of asset

	1885	1900	1920	1938	1960	1980	1987	
Vehicles, ships and aircraft	11.3%	14.3%	20.4%	11.8%	13.5%	11.6%	9.5%	
Plant and machinery	13.9%	18.7%	21.7%	23.8%	29.3%	36.7%	39.9%	
Dwellings	26.4%	26.4%	17.9%	37.3%	23.8%	23.1%	20.9%	
Other buildings and works	48.3%	40.6%	40.0%	27.1%	33.4%	28.6%	29.7%	

By industry [a]

	Manufacturing and construction	Distribution and services	Fuel, power and water	Social and public services	Other
1920	31.8%	11.2%	12.2%	4.9%	39.9%
1938	25.0%	9.8%	20.0%	14.9%	30.3%
1960	32.7%	12.7%	17.0%	13.6%	24.0%
1980	23.9%	26.8%	18.1%	15.2%	16.0%
1987	20.2%	37.9%	12.6%	17.1%	12.2%

a Excluding dwellings and transfer costs of land and buildings

Table UK.6   Personal and company income, 1885–1987

	Wages & salaries	Other income	Taxes, etc	Personal disposable income	Consumers' expenditure	Personal saving	Savings ratio	Gross trading profits of companies	Gross trading surplus of public corporations & gen. govt enterprises
					£ mn				
1885	555	...	...	...	1,138	...	...	...	...
1886	551	...	...	...	1,126	...	...	...	...
1887	579	...	...	...	1,162	...	...	...	...
1888	614	...	...	...	1,186	...	...	...	...
1889	674	...	...	...	1,227	...	...	126	...
1890	703	...	...	...	1,253	...	...	124	...
1891	703	...	...	...	1,315	...	...	116	...
1892	698	...	...	...	1,314	...	...	108	...
1893	700	...	...	...	1,310	...	...	115	...
1894	717	...	...	...	1,336	...	...	143	...
1895	731	...	...	...	1,355	...	...	152	...
1896	759	...	...	...	1,406	...	...	158	...
1897	777	...	...	...	1,435	...	...	175	...
1898	815	...	...	...	1,500	...	...	201	...
1899	848	...	...	...	1,561	...	...	227	...
1900	899	...	...	...	1,637	...	...	230	8
1901	898	...	...	...	1,677	...	...	216	8
1902	889	...	...	...	1,686	...	...	223	10
1903	897	...	...	...	1,699	...	...	208	11
1904	882	...	...	...	1,719	...	...	204	14
1905	902	...	...	...	1,736	...	...	228	13
1906	940	...	...	...	1,766	...	...	258	14
1907	996	...	...	...	1,811	...	...	271	15
1908	963	...	...	...	1,813	...	...	242	15
1909	974	...	...	...	1,831	...	...	245	17
1910	1,014	...	...	...	1,877	...	...	261	17
1911	1,051	...	...	...	1,936	...	...	272	18
1912	1,095	...	...	...	2,006	...	...	308	21
1913	1,136	...	...	...	2,070	...	...	326	20
1919	3,040	...	...	...	4,535	...	...	...	36
1920	3,470				5,246				
	3,394	1,894	331	4,957	5,020	−63	—	621	20
1921	2,767	1,823	322	4,268	4,315	−47	—	343	25
1922	2,333	1,788	320	3,801	3,842	−41	—	437	44
1923	2,338	1,772	307	3,703	3,717	−14	—	456	44
1924	2,293	1,844	313	3,824	3,777	47	1·2	477	40
1925	2,335	1,907	294	3,948	3,878	70	1.8	468	42
1926	2,245	1,948	303	3,890	3,833	57	1·5	420	40
1927	2,410	1,955	300	4,065	3,887	178	4·4	478	48
1928	2,401	2,008	313	4,096	3,939	157	3·8	474	51
1929	2,447	2,032	306	4,173	3,983	190	4·6	485	52
1930	2,385	2,041	343	4,083	3,932	151	3·7	411	54
1931	2,281	1,977	328	3,930	3,805	125	3·2	360	55
1932	2,252	1,920	345	3,827	3,683	144	3·8	321	59
1933	2,296	1,924	336	3,884	3,696	188	4·8	380	62
1934	2,398	1,922	326	3,994	3,802	192	4·8	464	67
1935	2,482	2,011	339	4,154	3,935	219	5·3	514	68
1936	2,623	2,107	358	4,372	4,080	292	6·7	627	69
1937	2,784	2,125	392	4,517	4,289	228	5·0	717	71
1938	2,863	2,180	418	4,625	4,392	233	5·0	687	72
1939	3,080	...	...	...	...	...	...	865	76
1940	3,695	...	...	...	...	...	...	1,109	77
1941	4,370	...	...	...	...	...	...	1,238	90
1942	4,860	...	...	...	...	...	...	1,377	136
1943	5,280	...	...	...	...	...	...	1,405	149
1944	5,550	...	...	...	...	...	...	1,388	134

Table UK.6 (Continued)   Personal and company income, 1885–1987

	Wages & salaries	Other income	Taxes, etc	Personal disposable income	Consumers' expenditure	Personal saving	Savings ratio	Gross trading profits of companies	Gross trading surplus of public corporations & gen. govt enterprises
					£ mn				
1945	5,680	. . .	. . .	. . .	. . .	. . .	. . .	1,350	119
1946	5,527	3,271	1,203	7,595	7,280	315	4·1	1,476	110
1947	5,935	3,477	1,229	8,183	8,036	147	1·8	1,694	159
1948	6,428	3,584	1,317	8,695	8,617	78	0·9	1,793	224
1949	6,823	3,742	1,430	9,135	8,980	155	1·7	1,843	263
1950	7,172	3,928	1,425	9,675	9,479	196	2·0	2,126	339
1951	8,008	4,041	1,594	10,455	10,238	217	2·1	2,483	381
1952	8,572	4,290	1,634	11,228	10,785	443	3·9	2,180	322
1953	9,049	4,603	1,627	12,025	11,510	515	4·3	2,313	388
1954	9,673	4,708	1,735	12,646	12,210	436	3·4	2,576	466
1955	10,566	5,038	1,901	13,703	13,172	531	3·9	2,886	431
1956	11,521	5,257	2,088	14,690	13,882	808	5·5	2,928	472
1957	12,157	5,529	2,254	15,432	14,652	780	5·1	3,075	458
1958	12,530	6,127	2,513	16,144	15,464	680	4·2	2,983	501
1959	13,114	6,649	2,622	17,141	16,296	845	4·9	3,317	572
1960	14,114	7,209	2,848	18,475	17,114	1,361	7·4	3,717	735
1961	15,229	7,840	3,256	19,813	18,008	1,805	9·1	3,625	760
1962	16,033	8,340	3,603	20,770	19,097	1,673	8·1	3,581	843
1963	16,809	9,046	3,774	22,081	20,354	1,727	7·8	4,017	948
1964	18,226	9,811	4,190	23,847	21,733	2,114	8·9	4,467	1,043
1965	19,596	10,920	4,974	25,542	23,154	2,388	9·3	4,668	1,117
1966	20,940	11,696	5,494	27,142	24,505	2,637	9·7	4,532	1,166
1967	21,735	12,549	6,021	28,263	25,761	2,502	8·9	4,580	1,259
1968	23,153	13,802	6,920	30,135	27,751	2,384	7·9	5,208	1,514
1969	24,799	14,789	7,494	32,094	29,450	2,644	8·2	5,676	1,626
1970	27,760	15,985	8,451	35,294	32,034	3,260	9·2	6,046	1,626
1971	30,394	17,777	9,342	38,829	35,879	2,950	7·6	7,082	1,724
1972	34,170	20,667	10,018	44,819	40,548	4,271	9·5	8,085	1,846
1973	39,398	23,947	11,762	51,583	46,148	5,435	10·5	10,181	2,216
1974	46,607	28,790	15,538	59,859	53,199	6,660	11·1	11,263	2,694
1975	60,333	36,113	22,028	74,418	65,474	8,944	12·0	11,603	3,221
1976	67,727	44,067	25,855	85,939	75,982	9,957	11·6	14,534	4,657
1977	74,917	49,337	27,697	96,557	86,887	9,670	10·0	19,864	5,278
1978	85,646	57,166	29,688	113,124	100,219	12,905	11·4	22,484	5,609
1979	100,444	68,583	33,306	135,721	118,652	17,069	12·6	29,429	5,774
1980	119,005	80,830	39,826	160,009	137,896	22,113	13·8	27,951	6,342
1981	127,884	93,025	44,825	176,084	153,566	22,518	12·8	27,940	8,057
1982	136,245	104,279	49,443	191,081	168,545	22,536	11·8	31,883	9,626
1983	145,469	114,227	53,741	205,955	184,619	21,336	10·4	39,810	9,968
1984	155,117	122,244	56,597	220,764	197,494	23,270	10·5	45,085	8,175
1985	168,568	130,731	61,497	237,802	215,267	22,535	9·5	53,500	7,276
1986	182,614	139,783	66,898	255,499	236,756	18,743	7·3	51,358	8,121
1987	198,191	147,854	72,739	273,306	258,431	14,875	5·4	65,596	6,446

Table UK.7 Consumers' expenditure at constant prices, selected commodities, 1900—87

	Food	Alcoholic drink & tobacco	Clothing & footwear	Energy products	Durable goods	*of which:* Cars, motor cycles, etc	Other goods	Rent, rates & water charges	Other services
					£ bn, 1985 prices				
1900	13·39	19·04	3·82	3·98	1·80	0·04	2·05	5·58	19·49
1901	13·55	18·84	3·99	3·98	1·84	0·04	2·09	5·70	20·08
1902	13·57	18·65	3·79	4·13	1·84	0·04	2·15	5·81	20·08
1903	13·85	18·15	3·64	4·07	1·79	0·04	2·18	5·91	20·08
1904	14·08	17·79	3·70	4·07	1·89	0·04	2·24	6·01	19·99
1905	14·08	17·56	3·63	3·87	1·84	0·04	2·33	6·10	20·21
1906	14·21	17·49	3·66	3·87	1·86	0·04	2·40	6·18	20·43
1907	14·13	17·60	3·64	4·16	1·96	0·04	2·47	6·29	20·65
1908	14·08	16·85	3·78	4·07	1·93	0·04	2·39	6·35	21·12
1909	14·21	15·60	3·91	4·07	1·83	0·04	2·39	6·43	21·27
1910	14·11	15·60	3·94	4·16	1·87	0·08	2·48	6·50	21·54
1911	14·63	16·21	4·22	4·30	1·92	0·08	2·56	6·58	21·74
1912	14·58	16·16	4·23	3·90	2·00	0·12	2·64	6·66	22·03
1913	14·67	16·77	4·37	4·28	2·23	0·15	2·77	6·73	22·38
1914	14·48	16·54	3·75	4·19	2·16	0·12	2·75	6·83	24·69
1915	14·67	16·24	4·06	4·42	1·99	0·04	2·85	6·87	25·83
1916	14·14	14·85	2·83	4·36	1·57	—	2·82	6·87	24·13
1917	13·19	10·89	2·63	4·22	1·49	—	2·72	6·89	23·14
1918	12·91	10·59	2·53	3·81	1·60	0·04	2·80	6·93	23·07
1919	14·65	15·38	4·12	4·16	2·20	0·23	2·90	7·02	22·33
1920	15·29	15·63	4·45	4·48	1·50	0·25	5·13	7·43	17·67
	14·56	14·88	4·28	4·28	1·46	0·25	4·92	7·08	17·03
1921	15·12	13·25	3·53	3·75	1·27	0·13	4·30	7·10	16·12
1922	16·13	11·92	3·99	4·25	1·52	0·21	4·59	7·16	16·24
1923	17·23	11·92	4·03	4·42	1·67	0·29	4·70	7·23	16·27
1924	17·27	12·42	4·09	4·74	1·77	0·40	4·76	7·29	16·76
1925	17·55	12·61	4·17	4·86	1·94	0·52	4·95	7·35	17·45
1926	17·63	12·22	4·18	4·33	2·00	0·50	4·82	7·50	17·72
1927	17·91	12·30	4·41	5·32	2·17	0·54	5·11	7·66	18·29
1928	18·26	12·14	4·44	5·26	2·26	0·54	5·24	7·83	18·85
1929	18·38	12·28	4·52	5·53	2·36	0·54	5·43	7·94	19·39
1930	18·87	12·08	4·47	5·55	2·40	0·52	5·48	8·10	20·04
1931	19·50	11·36	4·56	5·53	2·43	0·44	5·46	8·23	20·46
1932	19·52	10·31	4·37	5·44	2·63	0·48	5·41	8·33	20·87
1933	19·52	10·78	4·54	5·53	2·76	0·56	5·65	8·46	21·69
1934	19·78	11·22	4·58	5·76	3·07	0·69	5·95	8·60	22·25
1935	19·69	11·72	4·75	6·05	3·33	0·82	6·24	8·83	22·92
1936	19·95	12·25	4·90	6·37	3·47	0·92	6·43	9·06	23·66
1937	20·11	12·86	4·88	6·63	3·37	0·94	6·61	9·29	24·13
1938	20·18	13·02	4·89	6·75	3·10	0·82	6·53	9·50	24·97
1939	20·53	13·27	4·99	6·89		9·60		10·57	24·30
1940	17·65	12·64	4·20	6·34		7·69		10·71	23·56
1941	16·59	13·50	3·13	6·34		6·21		10·65	24·96
1942	17·02	13·19	3·12	5·93		5·20		10·67	25·48
1943	16·27	13·22	2·84	5·55		5·02		10·80	26·47
1944	17·14	13·52	3·18	5·58		5·06		11·05	26·71
1945	17·41	14·63	3·24	5·90		5·74		11·32	29·52
1946	21·17	14·38	3·85	6·89	1·61	0·31	6·02	12·36	27·97
1947	22·73	13·75	4·35	7·39	2·04	0·36	6·37	12·78	26·57
1948	23·22	13·19	4·81	7·07	2·18	0·31	6·54	13·14	25·81
1949	24·09	12·79	5·20	7·02	2·59	0·39	7·02	13·11	24·54
1950	25·23	12·92	5·38	7·32	2·89	0·41	7·28	13·35	24·04
1951	24·78	13·33	4·88	7·54	2·86	0·39	7·17	13·22	23·85
1952	21·81	13·40	4·80	7·47	2·78	0·54	7·23	13·32	28·33
1953	23·07	13·61	4·92	7·53	3·60	0·93	7·82	13·58	28·37
1954	23·55	13·73	5·28	7·85	4·29	1·17	8·38	13·95	29·09
1955	24·38	14·16	5·66	7·99	4·72	1·53	9·01	14·35	29·77
1956	24·78	14·41	5·88	8·30	4·17	1·22	9·21	14·61	30·05
1957	25·15	14·73	6·05	8·11	4·66	1·40	9·39	14·81	30·33

Table UK.7 (Continued)   Consumers' expenditure at constant prices, selected commodities, 1900–87

	Food	Alcoholic drink & tobacco	Clothing & footwear	Energy products	Durable goods	*of which:* Cars, motor cycles, etc	Other goods	Rent, rates & water charges	Other services
				£ bn, 1985 prices					
1958	25·45	14·84	6·07	8·66	5·41	1·83	9·94	15·09	30·00
1959	25·94	15·45	6·40	8·53	6·44	2·25	10·61	15·50	30·99
1960	26·50	16·14	6·89	9·29	6·62	2·59	11·34	15·92	31·68
1961	26·94	16·83	7·04	9·43	6·37	2·35	11·88	16·24	32·64
1962	27·21	16·57	7·01	10·35	6·68	2·67	12·23	16·79	33·76
1963	27·50	17·26	7·30	11·13	7·77	3·84	12·88	17·47	35·31
1964	27·84	17·70	7·61	11·35	8·40	4·42	13·39	17·78	36·53
1965	27·82	17·31	7·90	12·13	8·36	4·27	13·75	18·24	37·46
1966	28·13	17·93	7·90	12·67	8·22	4·26	14·18	18·67	38·09
1967	28·60	18·36	8·02	12·94	8·75	4·67	14·71	19·18	38·75
1968	28·75	18·85	8·46	13·67	9·34	4·98	15·22	19·78	39·24
1969	28·78	18·95	8·59	14·21	8·76	4·45	15·20	20·29	39·79
1970	28·90	19·67	8·96	14·50	9·48	5·08	15·38	20·79	40·96
1971	28·82	20·12	9·12	14·59	11·24	6·71	15·84	21·25	42·11
1972	28·63	21·48	9·61	15·56	13·66	8·04	17·42	21·73	44·33
1973	29·27	23·71	10·06	16·30	14·41	7·69	19·04	22·21	46·15
1974	28·86	23·96	9·94	16·24	12·62	5·87	19·46	22·63	45·37
1975	28·70	23·40	10·07	15·88	12·83	6·22	18·67	23·05	45·33
1976	28·90	23·27	10·13	16·23	13·47	6·44	18·62	23·50	44·21
1977	28·55	22·96	10·28	16·52	12·53	5·71	18·71	23·96	44·26
1978	29·35	24·31	11·24	16·91	14·34	7·11	20·00	24·40	46·73
1979	29·86	25·01	12·04	17·49	16·17	8·05	20·53	24·87	48·83
1980	29·84	24·09	11·90	17·26	15·42	7·62	20·04	25·24	51·20
1981	29·63	22·96	11·79	17·32	15·71	7·75	20·13	25·54	51·80
1982	29·53	22·00	12·23	17·41	16·50	8·01	20·57	25·94	52·08
1983	30·14	22·52	13·06	17·58	19·58	10·10	21·11	26·28	54·06
1984	29·66	22·56	13·85	17·80	19·44	9·51	22·10	26·59	55·92
1985	30·06	22·66	14·81	18·63	20·37	9·99	23·23	26·92	58·58
1986	31·05	22·51	15·90	19·36	22·02	10·77	24·76	27·27	63·98
1987	31·15	22·82	17·03	19·65	23·52	11·88	26·89	27·63	69·76

Table UK.8   Prices, 1885–1987

	Producer prices		Consumer prices					Average values		Terms of trade
	Materials & fuel purchased by mfg industry	Output of mfd products	All items	Food	Durable goods[a]	Clothing & footwear[a]	Housing[a]	Exports	Imports	
			Index nos., 1980 = 100							
1885	3·7	3·9	...	...	...	...	3·2	5·0	64·0
1886	3·5	3·8	...	...	...	...	3·1	4·7	66·0
1887	3·5	3·8	...	...	...	...	3·1	4·6	67·4
1888	3·5	3·8	...	...	...	...	3·1	4·7	66·0
1889	3·6	3·8	...	...	...	...	3·1	4·8	64·6
1890	3·6	3·8	...	...	...	...	3·3	4·8	68·7
1891	3·7	3·8	...	...	...	...	3·2	4·8	66·7
1892	3·5	3·9	...	...	...	...	3·1	4·6	67·4
1893	3·5	3·8	...	...	...	...	3·1	4·5	68·9
1894	3·3	3·6	...	...	...	...	3·0	4·2	71·4
1895	3·2	3·5	...	...	...	...	2·8	4·1	68·3
1896	3·1	3·5	...	...	...	...	2·8	4·1	68·3
1897	3·1	3·6	...	...	...	...	2·8	4·1	68·3
1898	3·3	3·8	...	...	...	...	2·8	4·1	68·3
1899	3·2	3·7	...	...	...	...	3·0	4·2	71·4
1900	3·5	3·9	3·8	4·3	4·8	3·8	3·4	4·5	75·6
1901	3·3	3·9	3·8	4·3	4·9	3·2	3·2	4·4	72·7
1902	3·3	3·9	3·8	4·3	4·9	3·9	3·1	4·3	72·1
1903	3·3	3·9	3·9	4·4	4·9	3·9	3·1	4·4	70·4
1904	3·5	3·9	3·9	4·4	5·0	4·0	3·1	4·4	70·4
1905	3·3	3·9	3·9	4·5	5·2	4·0	3·1	4·5	68·9
1906	3·5	3·9	3·9	4·5	5·3	4·0	3·2	4·7	68·1
1907	3·6	4·1	3·9	4·6	5·4	4·0	3·5	4·9	71·4
1908	3·6	4·1	4·1	4·6	5·4	4·0	3·3	4·7	70·2
1909	3·6	4·1	4·1	4·5	5·4	4·1	3·2	4·8	66·7
1910	3·8	4·1	4·1	4·7	5·4	4·1	3·3	5·1	64·7
1911	3·8	4·3	4·1	4·8	5·6	4·0	3·4	4·9	69·4
1912	4·0	4·3	4·3	5·0	5·7	4·0	3·5	5·0	70·0
1913	4·1	4·3	4·3	5·1	5·8	4·1	3·6	5·0	72·0
1914	4·1	4·3	4·5	4·9	5·5	4·1	...	...	...
1915	4·9	5·4	5·8	5·5	5·7	4·1	...	...	...
1916	6·5	6·2	7·0	6·5	7·2	4·1	...	...	...
1917	8·4	7·7	8·6	8·8	9·7	4·2	...	...	...
1918	9·3	8·7	9·4	11·2	17·4	4·3	...	...	...
1919	10·4	9·5	9·6	14·2	19·6	4·5	9·7	12·0	80·8
1920	12·5	10·8	11·3	15·6	22·4	4·8	12·7	14·3	88·8
1921	7·9	9·7	10·2	13·4	16·5	5·6	9·5	9·5	100·0
1922	6·5	7·9	7·7	11·2	13·1	5·8	7·2	7·7	93·5
1923	6·5	7·7	7·5	10·2	12·2	5·6	7·0	7·7	90·9
1924	6·8	7·7	7·5	10·2	12·3	5·5	7·0	8·1	86·4
1925	6·5	7·7	7·5	10·5	12·5	5·5	7·0	7·9	88·6
1926	6·0	7·5	7·3	9·9	12·0	5·6	6·5	7·5	86·7
1927	5·7	7·2	7·1	9·4	11·6	5·7	6·1	7·0	87·1
1928	5·7	7·2	7·0	8·7	11·8	5·7	6·1	7·2	84·7
1929	5·5	7·2	6·8	8·8	11·7	5·8	5·9	7·0	84·3
1930	4·7	6·8	6·4	8·6	11·3	5·8	5·7	6·0	95·0
1931	4·3	6·4	5·8	8·2	10·4	5·8	5·1	5·0	102·0
1932	4·1	6·2	5·6	7·4	10·0	5·8	4·8	4·6	104·3
1933	4·1	6·2	5·3	7·5	9·7	5·8	4·6	4·3	107·0
1934	4·3	6·2	5·5	7·6	9·8	5·9	4·8	4·6	104·3
1935	4·3	6·2	5·6	7·6	9·8	5·9	4·6	4·8	95·8
1936	4·6	6·4	5·8	7·7	9·9	6·0	4·8	5·0	96·0
1937	5·2	6·6	6·0	8·3	10·5	6·0	5·3	5·6	94·6
1938	4·7	6·8	6·2	8·7	10·8	6·0	5·5	5·4	101·8
1939	4·9	7·0	6·2	...	11·1	6·2	5·5	5·4	101·8
1940	6·6	7·9	7·3	...	14·4	6·3	6·3	7·5	84·0
1941	7·4	8·7	7·7	...	17·7	6·3	7·8	8·3	94·0

36

Table UK.8 (Continued)   Prices, 1885–1987

Year	Materials & fuel purchased by mfg industry	Output of mfd products	All items	Food	Durable goods[a]	Clothing & footwear[a]	Housing[a]	Exports	Imports	Terms of trade
	Producer prices		Consumer prices					Average values		
			Index nos., 1980 = 100							
1942	7·6		9·3	7·9	...	19·3	6·4	8·4	8·9	94·4
1943	7·7		9·7	7·9	...	18·7	6·5	9·7	10·4	93·3
1944	7·9		9·7	8·1	...	19·4	6·6	10·3	10·1	102·0
1945	8·1		10·1	8·3	...	19·9	6·9	9·9	10·4	95·2
1946	8·4		10·6	8·3	17·9	20·0	7·1	10·8	11·0	98·2
1947	9·2		11·2	8·8	19·3	20·4	7·5	12·2	13·7	89·1
1948	10·6 / (11)	(13)	11·8	9·4	20·6	22·6	7·6	13·1	15·1	86·7
1949	(11)	(14)	12·2	9·9	20·3	23·5	7·8	13·5	15·5	87·1
1950	14·4	14·9	12·5	10·6	21·1	23·8	8·0	14·3	17·6	92·4
1951	19·5	16·8	13·8	11·8	24·2	27·6	8·4	17·3	23·4	73·9
1952	16·9	17·7	14·9	13·7	26·0	27·5	8·8	18·6	22·8	81·6
1953	15·5	17·6	15·4	14·5	24·8	27·3	9·3	18·1	20·3	89·2
1954	15·4	17·6	15·6	14·9	24·4	27·5	9·5	17·9	20·3	88·2
1955	15·8	18·0	16·4	16·0	24·7	27·6	9·7	17·9	20·7	86·5
1956	16·4	18·8	17·2	16·6	26·5	28·2	10·1	18·8	21·3	88·3
1957	16·5	19·4	17·8	17·1	26·8	28·7	10·9	19·6	21·9	89·5
1958	15·5	19·5	18·4	17·5	26·9	28·9	12·3	19·6	20·1	97·5
1959	15·6	19·6	18·5	17·6	26·5	28·7	13·0	20·0	20·3	98·5
1960	15·6	19·9	18·6	17·5	26·4	29·1	13·3	20·3	20·5	99·0
1961	15·5	20·4	19·3	17·8	26·5	29·6	13·9	20·5	20·3	101·0
1962	15·5	20·9	20·1	18·4	26·6	30·4	14·8	20·7	20·1	103·0
1963	15·8	21·1	20·5	18·9	25·5	30·9	15·9	21·1	20·7	101·9
1964	16·5	21·7	21·2	19·4	25·8	31·2	17·1	21·6	21·3	101·4
1965	16·7	22·5	22·2	20·1	26·3	32·0	18·6	22·0	21·5	102·3
1966	17·1	23·1	23·1	20·8	26·6	32·9	19·9	22·7	21·7	104·6
1967	17·0	23·4	23·6	21·4	26·9	33·3	20·8	22·8	21·9	104·1
1968	18·5	24·3	24·7	22·2	28·3	33·8	21·8	24·7	24·3	101·6
1969	19·3	25·2	26·1	23·6	29·5	35·1	23·3	25·4	25·1	101·2
1970	20·3	27·0	27·7	25·3	31·5	37·0	25·2	27·5	26·5	103·8
1971	21·2	29·5	30·3	28·1	34·0	39·5	27·9	28·7	27·4	104·7
1972	22·1	31·0	32·5	30·5	35·1	42·3	31·3	30·1	28·1	107·1
1973	29·3	33·3	35·5	35·1	36·6	46·3	35·4	33·5	35·0	95·7
1974	43·2 / 49·0	40·9 / 42·7	41·2	41·5	42·3	54·6	42·0	42·7	51·4	83·1
1975	54·8	52·3	51·1	52·1	52·4	62·3	50·7	52·6	58·4	90·1
1976	68·4	60·9	59·6	62·5	59·4	69·0	58·4	62·5	70·9	88·2
1977	78·8	71·9	69·0	74·4	70·7	77·7	65·4	72·8	81·2	89·7
1978	81·6	79·1	74·7	79·7	81·0	84·0	73·1	78·5	83·1	94·5
1979	92·2	87·7	84·8	89·3	92·5	91·8	84·4	86·9	91·0	95·5
1980	100·0	100·0	100·0	100·0	100·0	100·0	100·0	100·0	100·0	100·0
1981	109·2	109·6	111·9	108·4	101·5	103·7	119·7	108·5	107·2	101·2
1982	117·1	118·0	121·5	117·0	106·9	107·7	135·8	115·2	113·7	101·3
1983	125·2	124·4	127·1	120·7	106·5	111·7	142·0	123·6	121·3	101·9
1984	135·5	131·6	133·4	127·4	110·4	115·3	148·0	132·3	131·6	100·5
1985	137·0	138·5	141·5	131·4	114·3	120·5	157·2	139·2	136·9	101·7
1986	126·6	144·5	146·3	135·7	118·7	123·9	169·0	125·3	129·6	96·7
1987	130·5	150·0	152·4	138·3	126·3	125·9	178·9	130·2	132·9	98·0

a Average value indices.

Table UK.9 Population, 1885–1987

	Total population	Births	Age distribution				Geographical distribution			
			0–14	15–34	35–64	65 & over	England & Wales	of which: South East	Scotland	N. Ireland
	mn	'000					mn			
1885	36·02	1,136	...	...	...	...	27·22	...	3·86	...
1886	36·31	1,146	...	...	...	...	27·52	...	3·89	...
1887	36·60	1,122	...	...	...	...	27·83	...	3·91	...
1888	36·88	1,113	...	...	...	...	28·14	...	3·94	...
1889	37·18	1,127	...	...	...	...	28·45	...	3·97	...
1890	37·49	1,097	...	...	...	...	28·76	...	4·00	...
1891	37·80	1,148	13·15		22·76	1·88	29·09	...	4·04	...
1892	38·13	1,127	...	...	...	...	29·42	...	4·08	...
1893	38·49	1,148	...	...	...	...	29·76	...	4·12	...
1894	38·86	1,119	...	...	...	...	30·10	...	4·17	...
1895	39·22	1,154	...	...	...	...	30·45	...	4·21	...
1896	39·60	1,152	...	...	...	...	30·80	...	4·25	...
1897	39·99	1,158	...	...	...	...	31·16	...	4·30	...
1898	40·38	1,159	...	...	...	...	31·52	...	4·34	...
1899	40·77	1,164	...	...	...	...	31·88	...	4·39	...
1900	41·16	1,160	13·38	14·67	11·16	1·99	32·25	...	4·44	...
1901	41·54	1,163	13·41	14·80	11·30	2·03	32·61	...	4·48	...
1902	41·89	1,175	13·49	14·87	11·49	2·08	32·95	...	4·51	...
1903	42·25	1,183	13·50	14·94	11·68	2·13	33·29	...	4·54	...
1904	42·61	1,181	13·57	15·07	11·90	2·19	33·64	...	4·56	...
1905	42·98	1,163	13·57	15·11	12·07	2·23	33·99	...	4·59	...
1906	43·36	1,171	13·62	15·19	12·27	2·30	34·34	...	4·62	...
1907	43·74	1,149	13·67	15·25	12·46	2·35	34·70	...	4·65	...
1908	44·12	1,173	13·75	15·36	12·69	2·41	35·06	...	4·68	...
1909	44·52	1,146	13·78	15·41	12·88	2·48	35·42	...	4·71	...
1910	44·92	1,123	13·85	15·48	13·06	2·52	35·79	...	4·74	...
1911	45·27	1,105	13·95	15·47	13·25	2·60	36·14	...	4·75	1·25
1912	45·44	1,097	13·89	15·44	13·49	2·63	36·33	...	4·74	1·25
1913	45·65	1,103	13·88	15·42	13·71	2·66	36·57	...	4·73	1·24
1914	46·05	1,102	13·90	15·54	14·23	2·69	36·97	...	4·75	1·24
1915	46·34	1,025	13·90	15·52	14·47	2·72	35·28	...	4·77	1·21
1916	46·51	987	13·80	15·51	13·96	2·73	34·64	...	4·80	1·21
1917	46·61	852	13·69	15·47	14·69	2·77	34·20	...	4·81	1·21
1918	46·58	849	13·46	15·41	14·87	2·81	34·02	...	4·81	1·21
1919	46·53	888	13·20	15·32	15·07	2·86	35·43	...	4·82	1·25
1920	43·72	1,127	12·34	14·37	14·40	2·63	37·25	...	4·86	1·26
1921	44·07	1,002	12·32	14·44	14·59	2·67	37·89	10·48	4·88	1·26
1922	44·37	925	12·29	14·56	14·75	2·72	38·16	10·54	4·90	1·27
1923	44·60	900	12·17	14·65	14·91	2·79	38·40	10·61	4·89	1·26
1924	44·92	865	12·08	14·84	15·11	2·83	38·75	10·70	4·86	1·26
1925	45·06	843	11·96	14·94	15·25	2·88	38·89	10·75	4·87	1·26
1926	45·23	826	11·84	14·97	15·42	2·98	39·07	10·83	4·86	1·25
1927	45·39	777	11·73	15·06	15·58	3·04	39·29	10·83	4·85	1·25
1928	45·58	783	11·57	15·14	15·72	3·12	39·48	10·89	4·85	1·25
1929	45·67	762	11·39	15·25	15·87	3·16	39·61	10·92	4·83	1·24
1930	45·87	769	11·25	15·34	16·03	3·25	39·81	10·93	4·83	1·24
1931	46·07	750	11·19	15·34	16·11	3·44	39·99	13·42	4·84	1·24
1932	46·34	730	11·17	15·36	16·29	3·52	40·20	13·64	4·88	1·25
1933	46·52	691	11·19	15·28	16·45	3·60	40·35	13·76	4·91	1·26
1934	46·67	712	11·19	15·17	16·61	3·69	40·47	13·86	4·93	1·27
1935	46·87	712	10·90	15·34	16·83	3·79	40·65	14·01	4·95	1·27
1936	47·08	720	10·69	15·44	17·07	3·88	40·84	14·19	4·97	1·28
1937	47·29	724	10·53	15·49	17·28	3·99	41·03	14·37	4·98	1·28
1938	47·49	735	10·42	15·47	17·50	4·09	41·22	14·49	4·99	1·29
1939	47·76	727	10·30	15·62	17·59	4·25	41·46	14·60	5·01	1·29
1940	48·23	702	10·23		33·64	4·35	41·86	13·26	5·06	1·30
1941	48·22	696	10·14	15·58	18·08	4·42	41·75	12·06	5·16	1·31

38

Table UK.9 (Continued)   Population, 1885–1987

	Total population	Births	Age distribution				Geographical distribution			
			0–14	15–34	35–64	65 & over	England & Wales	of which: South East	Scotland	N. Ireland
	mn	'000					mn			
1942	48·40	772	10·11	15·42	18·31	4·56	41·90	12·12	5·17	1·33
1943	48·79	811	10·17	15·33	18·57	4·72	42·26	12·12	5·19	1·34
1944	49·02	878	10·26	15·13	18·77	4·85	42·45	11·98	5·21	1·36
1945	49·18	796	10·34	14·91	18·96	4·97	42·64	12·38	5·19	1·36
1946	49·22	955	10·36	14·87	18·94	5·05	42·70	12·56	5·17	1·35
1947	49·52	1,025	10·68	14·65	19·09	5·15	43·05	12·46	5·12	1·35
1948	50·01	905	10·97	14·54	19·28	5·28	43·50	13·26	5·15	1·36
1949	50·31	855	11·16	14·39	19·46	5·35	43·79	13·58	5·16	1·37
1950	50·57	818	11·31	14·26	19·62	5·43	44·02	13·63	5·17	1·38
1951	50·29	797	11·38	13·84	19·59	5·45	43·82	13·62	5·10	1·37
1952	50·43	793	11·45	13·78	19·63	5·57	43·96	13·69	5·10	1·37
1953	50·59	804	11·53	13·86	19·59	5·63	44·11	13·71	5·10	1·38
1954	50·77	795	11·62	13·91	19·54	5·72	44·27	13·73	5·10	1·39
1955	50·95	789	11·70	13·70	19·80	5·77	44·44	13·76	5·11	1·39
1956	51·18	825	11·86	13·52	20·00	5·84	44·67	13·82	5·12	1·40
1957	51·43	851	11·96	13·40	20·16	5·94	44·91	13·89	5·13	1·40
1958	51·65	871	12·05	13·40	20·26	5·99	45·11	13·92	5·14	1·40
1959	51·96	879	12·11	13·47	20·36	6·04	45·39	13·76	5·16	1·41
1960	52·37	918	12·22	13·56	20·46	6·14	45·78	13·86	5·18	1·42
1961	52·81	944	12·36	13·71	20·53	6·21	46·20	16·07	5·18	1·43
1962	53·29	976	12·36	14·06	20·59	6·28	46·66	16·25	5·20	1·44
1963	53·63	990	12·42	14·25	20·61	6·35	46·97	16·35	5·21	1·45
1964	53·99	1,015	12·55	14·37	20·61	6·46	47·32	16·48	5·21	1·46
1965	54·35	997	12·71	14·45	20·58	6·61	47·67	16·61	5·21	1·47
1966	54·64	980	12·85	14·58	20·51	6·70	47·97	16·72	5·20	1·48
1967	54·96	962	13·02	14·65	20·44	6·85	48·27	16·82	5·20	1·49
1968	55·21	947	13·19	14·74	20·31	6·98	48·51	16·90	5·20	1·50
1969	55·46	920	13·32	14·85	20·17	7·12	48·74	16·94	5·21	1·51
1970	55·63	904	13·40	14·95	20·03	7·25	48·89	16·97	5·21	1·53
1971	55·93	902	13·47	15·12	19·94	7·41	49·15	16·99 / 17·13	5·24	1·54
1972	56·10	834	13·49	15·24	19·83	7·53	49·33	17·14	5·23	1·54
1973	56·22	780	13·45	15·39	19·72	7·66	49·46	17·13	5·23	1·53
1974	56·24	737	13·32	15·53	19·60	7·78	49·47	17·07	5·24	1·53
1975	56·23	698	13·14	15·71	19·48	7·90	49·47	17·02	5·23	1·52
1976	56·22	676	12·90	15·99	19·33	8·00	49·46	16·98	5·23	1·52
1977	56·19	657	12·61	16·24	19·24	8·10	49·44	16·95	5·23	1·52
1978	56·18	687	12·32	16·45	19·19	8·21	49·44	16·94	5·21	1·52
1979	56·24	735	12·07	16·66	19·20	8·32	49·51	16·95	5·20	1·53
1980	56·33	754	11·83	16·87	19·21	8·42	49·60	16·99	5·19	1·53
1981	56·35	731	11·60	17·03	19·25	8·47	49·63	17·01	5·18	1·54
1982	56·31	719	11·37	16·94	19·53	8·47	49·60	17·01	5·17	1·54
1983	56·35	721	11·17	16·96	19·81	8·41	49·65	17·04	5·15	1·54
1984	56·46	730	11·00	17·06	20·02	8·38	49·76	17·11	5·15	1·55
1985	56·62	751	10·90	17·16	20·00	8·56	49·92	17·19	5·14	1·56
1986	56·76	755	10·80	17·29	19·99	8·68	50·08	17·27	5·12	1·57
1987	56·93	776	10·75	17·37	20·00	8·81	50·24	17·32	5·11	1·56

Table UK.10   Education, 1885–1987

	Kindergarten	Elementary	Secondary	Post-secondary	Higher education	
					Total	*of which:* Female
		No. of pupils '000			No. of students '000	
1885	...	3,827	...	...	...	...
1886	...	3,915	...	...	...	...
1887	...	4,019	...	...	...	...
1888	...	4,111	...	...	...	...
1889	...	4,186	...	...	...	...
1890	...	4,231	...	...	...	...
1891	...	4,288	...	...	...	...
1892	...	4,409	...	...	...	...
1893	...	4,643	...	...	...	...
1894	...	4,793	...	...	...	...
1895	...	5,016	...	...	...	...
1896	...	5,094	...	...	...	...
1897	...	5,160	...	...	...	...
1898	...	5,249	...	...	...	...
1899	...	5,292	...	...	...	...
1900	...	4,817	...	...	...	...
1901	...	5,566	52	...	...	...
1902	...	5,722	...	...	...	...
1903	...	5,849	...	...	...	...
1904	...	5,940	...	...	...	...
1905	...	6,001	...	...	...	...
1906	...	5,995	...	...	...	...
1907	...	5,993	...	...	...	...
1908	...	6,060	...	...	...	...
1909	...	6,094	...	...	...	...
1910	...	6,421	76	652	...	...
1911	...	6,452	75	...	...	...
1912	...	6,473	78	857	...	...
1913	...	6,591	88	...	...	...
1914	...	...	...	...	...	...
1915	...	...	...	...	...	...
1916	...	...	...	...	...	...
1917	...	...	...	...	...	...
1918	...	...	...	...	...	...
1919	...	...	...	...	41·3	...
1920	...	6,570	299	874	45·0	...
1921	...	6,586	322	...	44·7	...
1922	...	6,492	376	...	44·9	...
1923	...	6,214	390	...	42·9	12·9
1924	...	6,180	389	...	41·8	12·9
1925	...	6,149	384	...	41·6	12·8
1926	...	6,209	393	838	42·4	12·9
1927	...	6,245	399	...	43·3	13·0
1928	...	6,217	404	...	44·3	12·9
1929	...	6,163	413	...	45·6	12·9
1930	...	6,195	422	1,032	47·6	13·0
1931	...	6,217	421	...	48·5	12·8
1932	...	6,334	399	...	50·2	12·9
1933	...	6,414	491	...	50·7	12·5
1934	...	6,256	493	...	50·6	12·2
1935	...	6,070	497	1,042	50·5	11·9
1936	...	5,917	502	...	49·7	11·4
1937	...	5,804	476	1,322	49·2	11·3
1938	...	5,712	462	...	50·0	11·6
1939	...	...	...	...	43·4	11·0
1940	...	...	...	...	37·3	11·0
1941	...	...	...	...	37·3	11·7
1942	...	...	...	...	36·8	12·5
1943	...	...	...	...	35·6	13·2
1944	...	...	...	...	37·8	14·3
1945	...	5,594	250	...	51·6	17·4

Table UK.10 (Continued)   Education, 1885–1987

	Kindergarten	Elementary	Secondary	Post-secondary	Higher education Total	of which: Female
		No. of pupils '000			No. of students '000	
1946	183	5,595	272	1,797	68·5	18·7
1947	216	5,966	282	1,943	78·5	19·4
1948	213	6,156	302	2,225	86·2	20·0
1949	205	6,313	310	2,503	88·0	20·0
1950	184	6,409	299	2,513	87·7	20·1
1951	203	6,898	336	2,556	85·8	20·1
1952	228	7,174	349	2,328	83·8	20·3
1953	200	7,338	366	2,362	82·8	20·4
1954	206	7,458 / 7,547	376 / 383	2,422	83·9	21·0
1955	211	7,688	397	2,201	87·4	22·0
1956	215	7,834	385	2,182	92·7	23·3
1957	223	7,957	407	2,202	98·5	24·3
1958	224	7,991	448	2,315	103·6	25·1
1959	218	8,018	500	2,356	107·7	25·8
1960	234	7,982	567	2,405	111·7	27·3
1961	242	8,021	566	2,756	117·6	29·8
1962	264	7,953	651	2,615	123·2	32·5
1963	(247)	7,854	751	2,997	130·8	35·0
1964	(245)	7,831	873	3,060	143·4	39·6
1965	277	7,935	880	3,248	173·7	45·9
1966	274	7,924	878	3,270	189·3	51·1
1967	296	8,373	889	3,374	205·2	56·3
1968	315	8,253	932	3,332	217·4	60·3
1969	339	8,438	974	3,278	226·1	63·8
1970	354	8,639	997	3,493	235·3	68·3
1971	384	8,830	1,016	3,579	242·6	72·3
1972	428	9,009	1,065	3,674	246·8	76·3
1973	474	9,110	1,109	3,827	251·2	80·4
1974	509	9,173	1,449	3,988	257·7	85·3
1975	532	9,201	1,490	4,219	268·7	90·6
1976	576	9,186	1,539	3,923	279·3	95·6
1977	569	9,158	1,593	3,795	288·1	100·2
1978	557	9,040	1,626	4,189	295·9	105·3
1979	573	8,864	1,654	3,943	300·5	110·5
1980	585 / 804	8,624 / 8,699	1,683 / 1,388	3,737	306·6	115·7
1981	792	8,433	1,409	3,745	308·4	118·8
1982	794	8,138	1,435	3,825	304·0	119·4
1983	823	7,841	1,430	4,036	300·6	118·9
1984	887	7,595	1,393	3,897	305·0	122·6
1985	915	7,425	1,363	4,001	310·1	125·2
1986	917	7,319	1,328	. . .	316·3	128·8
1987	900	7,141	1,350	. . .	. . .	. . .

Table UK.11   Labour market: employment, 1900–88

	Employed labour force	Agriculture, forestry & fishing	Mining & quarrying	Mfg	Construction	Gas, electricity & water	Transport & communication	Distributive trades	Services	Public administration & defence	Self-employed
						'000					
1900	18,020	...	...	...	...	...	...	...	...	...	...
1901	18,080	2,420	1,020	5,990	1,090	100	1,450	1,990	3,590	880	...
1902	18,110	...	...	...	...	...	...	...	...	...	...
1903	18,140	...	...	...	...	...	...	...	...	...	...
1904	18,050	...	...	...	...	...	...	...	...	...	...
1905	18,400	...	...	...	...	...	...	...	...	...	...
1906	18,830	...	...	...	...	...	...	...	...	...	...
1907	18,980	...	...	...	...	...	...	...	...	...	...
1908	18,340	...	...	...	...	...	...	...	...	...	...
1909	18,530	...	...	...	...	...	...	...	...	...	...
1910	19,280	...	...	...	...	...	...	...	...	...	...
1911	19,790	2,400	1,290	6,550	1,030	120	1,580	2,460	3,890	840	...
1912	19,890	...	...	...	...	...	...	...	...	...	...
1913	20,310	...	...	...	...	...	...	...	...	...	...
1914	20,250	...	...	...	...	...	...	...	...	...	...
1915	20,890	...	...	...	...	...	...	...	...	...	...
1916	21,200	...	...	...	...	...	...	...	...	...	...
1917	21,350	...	...	...	...	...	...	...	...	...	...
1918	21,490	...	...	...	...	...	...	...	...	...	...
1919	21,160	...	...	...	...	...	...	...	...	...	...
1920	21,570										
	20,297	1,741	1,325	7,208	927	185	1,641	2,352	3,521	637	...
1921	17,908	1,669	1,210	5,665	888	185	1,544	2,189	3,433	634	...
1922	17,875	1,620	1,200	5,927	808	185	1,504	2,194	3,447	598	...
1923	18,106	1,571	1,280	6,083	831	190	1,532	2,199	3,483	589	...
1924	18,378	1,582	1,295	6,187	863	194	1,555	2,211	3,552	593	...
1925	18,588	1,576	1,205	6,227	924	199	1,558	2,320	3,630	599	...
1926	18,593	1,552	1,204	6,054	950	205	1,562	2,406	3,701	610	...
1927	19,136	1,523	1.123	6,434	1,009	210	1,592	2,516	3,776	606	...
1928	19,204	1,511	1,045	6,428	1,010	216	1,600	2,591	3,852	615	...
1929	19,479	1,502	1,055	6,522	1,011	224	1,601	2,669	3,925	637	...
1930	19,115	1,460	1,034	6,066	1,035	230	1,595	2,724	3,980	664	...
1931	18,665	1,425	958	5,659	1,008	238	1,558	2,778	4,031	685	...
1932	18,753	1,413	902	5,744	930	242	1,537	2,850	4,125	687	...
1933	19,136	1,413	873	5,963	983	244	1,524	2,905	4,218	690	...
1934	19,685	1,394	883	6,235	1,079	251	1,548	2,949	4,323	698	...
1935	20,037	1,370	870	6,387	1,141	263	1,579	2,965	4,411	718	...
1936	20,670	1,335	873	6,737	1,213	272	1,620	3,023	4,511	737	...
1937	21,364	1,313	901	7,077	1,263	284	1,678	3,086	4,620	765	...
1938	21,418	1,272	904	6,970	1,266	291	1,692	3,090	4,700	801	...
1939	23,300	...	...	...	...	...	...	...	...	...	...
1940	23,100	...	...	...	...	...	...	...	...	...	...
1941	24,000	...	...	...	...	...	...	...	...	...	...
1942	24,800	...	...	...	...	...	...	...	...	...	...
1943	25,000	...	...	...	...	...	...	...	...	...	...
1944	24,700	...	...	...	...	...	...	...	...	...	...
1945	24,200	...	...	...	...	...	...	...	...	...	...
1946	23,000	...	...	...	...	...	...	...	...	...	...
1947	23,100	...	...	...	...	...	...	...	...	...	...
		1,203	881	8,294	1,475	327	1,840	2,581	4,102	1,421	
1948	23,064										
		842	879	8,128	1,334	327	1,771	2,045	3,588	1,413	...
1949	23,090	821	880	8,295	1,322	339	1,760	2,114	3,511	1,428	...
1950	23,257	806	857	8,520	1,325	360	1,769	2,130	3,573	1,402	1,802
1951	23,603	772	860	8,746	1,331	369	1,741	2,162	3,584	1,387	1,798
1952	23,590	724	877	8,669	1,324	379	1,756	2,187	3,606	1,376	1,794
1953	23,703	709	881	8,747	1,338	379	1,727	2,237	3,635	1,362	1,791
1954	24,038	702	872	8,975	1,359	379	1,714	2,314	3,706	1,368	1,789
1955	24,298	692	867	9,222	1,385	384	1,708	2,378	3,755	1,331	1,787

42

Table UK.11 (Continued)   Labour market: employment, 1900–88

	Employed labour force	Agriculture, forestry & fishing	Mining & quarrying	Mfg	Construction	Gas, electricity & water	Transport & communication	Distributive trades	Services	Public administration & defence	Self-employed
						'000					
1956	24,514	661	862	9,293	1,431	384	1,720	2,440	3,818	1,342	1,782
1957	24,543	647	873	9,285	1,412	386	1,715	2,511	3,859	1,343	1,778
1958	24,278	625	860	9,183	1,371	383	1,696	2,502	3,898	1,342	1,774
1959	23,760	630	831	9,122	1,403	381	1,674	2,558	3,989	1,347	1,770
		768	803	8,071	1,385	383	1,660	2,657	4,385	1,284	
1960	24,183	743	740	8,418	1,426	380	1,652	2,737	4,490	1,287	1,766
1961	24,457	712	707	8,535	1,482	389	1,678	2,767	4,629	1,310	1,760
1962	24,632	687	685	8,456	1,517	396	1,689	2,830	4,830	1,338	1,748
1963	24,661	691	657	8,322	1,545	406	1,670	2,863	4,947	1,385	1,735
1964	24,950	657	630	8,450	1,583	412	1,656	2,884	5,166	1,355	1,720
1965	25,204	605	597	8,561	1,621	419	1,648	2,909	5,327	1,374	1,696
1966	25,355	582	550	8,584	1,645	432	1,623	2,921	5,477	1,422	1,681
1967	24,992	542	526	8,319	1,556	434	1,617	2,795	5,530	1,471	1,762
1968	24,841	519	463	8,240	1,520	422	1,597	2,770	5,618	1,484	1,786
1969	24,857	492	421	8,353	1,459	406	1,561	2,711	5,736	1,465	1,853
1970	24,753	466	410	8,342	1,339	391	1,572	2,675	5,802	1,481	1,902
1971	24,533	432	396	8,058	1,262	377	1,568	2,610	5,910	1,509	2,021
1972	24,510	427	379	7,779	1,300	356	1,543	2,640	6,144	1,553	1,997
1973	25,076	432	363	7,830	1,380	344	1,524	2,744	6,461	1,585	2,032
1974	25,148	414	349	7,873	1,329	347	1,506	2,761	6,614	1,596	1,996
1975	25,056	397	352	7,490	1,314	353	1,518	2,763	6,861	1,657	1,993
1976	24,844	393	348	7,246	1,309	353	1,475	2,723	7,057	1,631	1,952
1977	24,865	388	350	7,292	1,270	347	1,468	2,753	7,134	1,614	1,907
1978	25,014	382	353	7,257	1,264	340	1,483	2,780	7,314	1,605	1,907
1979	25,393	368	a	7,258	1,253	722	1,473	3,063	7,299	1,721	1,906
1980	25,327	361	a	6,940	1,252	726	1,483	3,090	7,451	1,669	2,013
1981	24,346	353	a	6,220	1,139	709	1,423	2,978	7,424	1,626	2,119
1982	23,908	358	a	5,863	1,067	680	1,380	2,917	7,555	1,594	2,170
1983	23,626	350	a	5,525	1,044	648	1,345	2,891	7,659	1,606	2,221
1984	24,235	340	a	5,409	1,037	616	1,340	2,957	7,936	1,602	2,496
1985	24,618	341	a	5,365	1,022	589	1,345	3,001	8,229	1,613	2,610
1986	24,756	329	a	5,235	991	539	1,340	3,031	8,496	1,619	2,627
1987	25,306	322	a	5,145	1,009	497	1,345	3,053	8,799	1,642	2,861
1988	25,749	...	...	...	...	...	...	...	...	...	...

a   Included with gas, electricity and water under a new heading of energy and water supply in current official statistics .

43

Table UK.12 Labour market: other indicators, 1885–1987

	Output per person employed		Ave. weekly hrs of manual workers	Ave. weekly earnings of manual workers	Unemployment		Vacancies unfilled	Industrial stoppages	
	Whole economy	Mfg						Working days lost	Workers involved
	Index nos., 1980 = 100			£	'000	%	'000	'000	'000
1885	...	...	...	...	1,430	9·1	...	...	...
1886	...	...	...	...	1,590	10·0	...	...	...
1887	...	...	...	...	1,200	7·5	...	...	...
1888	...	...	...	...	790	4·9	...	...	...
1889	...	...	...	...	340	2·1	...	...	...
1890	...	...	...	...	340	2·1	...	...	...
1891	...	...	...	...	570	3·4	...	...	...
1892	...	...	...	...	1,040	6·2	...	...	...
1893	...	...	...	...	1,260	7·4	...	...	...
1894	...	...	...	...	1,170	6·8	...	...	...
1895	...	...	...	...	990	5·7	...	...	...
1896	...	...	...	...	570	3·2	...	...	...
1897	...	...	...	...	580	3·3	...	...	...
1898	...	...	...	...	500	2·8	...	...	...
1899	...	...	...	...	360	2·0	...	...	...
1900	38·1	...	(54)	1·40	450	2·4	...	3,088	185
1901	38·5	...	...	...	600	3·2	...	4,130	179
1902	39·2	...	...	...	730	3·9	...	3,438	255
1903	38·5	...	...	...	870	4·6	...	2,320	116
1904	39·4	...	...	...	1,130	5·9	...	1,464	87
1905	40·2	...	...	...	950	4·9	...	2,368	92
1906	40·2	...	...	...	690	3·5	...	3,019	218
1907	41·0	...	...	...	710	3·6	...	2,148	146
1908	41·0	...	...	...	1,520	7·7	...	10,785	293
1909	41·3	...	...	...	1,510	7·5	...	2,687	297
1910	40·3	...	(54)	...	930	4·6	...	9,867	514
1911	40·8	...	...	...	600	2·9	...	10,155	952
1912	41·8	...	...	...	670	3·3	...	40,890	1,462
1913	42·4	...	...	1·60	430	2·1	...	9,804	664
1914	...	...	...	...	660	3·2	...	9,878	447
1915	...	...	...	...	200	0·9	...	2,953	448
1916	...	...	...	...	70	0·3	...	2,446	276
1917	...	...	...	...	100	0·5	...	5,647	872
1918	...	...	...	...	140	0·6	...	5,875	1,116
1919	...	...	...	...	660	3·0	...	34,969	2,591
1920	39·8	26·6	...	...	391	1·9	...	26,568	1,932
1921	39·6	26·3	...	...	2,212	11·0	...	85,872	1,801
1922	42·6	29·3	...	...	1,909	9·6	...	19,850	552
1923	43·5	30·5	...	...	1,567	8·0	...	10,672	405
1924	45·0	33·1	46	3·00	1,404	7·1	...	8,424	613
1925	45·8	33·8	...	...	1,559	7·7	...	7,952	441
1926	44·8	33·7	...	...	1,759	8·6	...	162,233	2,734
1927	47·2	35·1	...	...	1,373	6·7	...	1,174	108
1928	47·1	35·0	...	...	1,536	7·4	...	1,388	124
1929	47·6	35·9	...	...	1,503	7·2	...	8,287	533
1930	47·8	37·0	...	...	2,379	11·1	...	4,399	307
1931	47·2	36·9	...	2·95	3,252	14·8	...	6,983	490
1932	47·2	36·6	...	...	3,400	15·3	...	6,488	379
1933	48·0	37·9	...	...	3,087	13·9	...	1,072	136
1934	49·3	39·5	...	...	2,609	11·7	...	959	134
1935	50·6	42·0	...	...	2,437	10·8	...	1,955	271
1936	51·7	43·6	...	...	2,100	9·2	...	1,829	316
1937	51·9	43·9	...	3·00	1,776	7·7	...	3,413	597
1938	51·1	43·4	46·3 / 47·7	3·45	2,164	9·2	...	1,334	274
1939	...	...	...	...	1,340	5·7	...	1,356	337
1940	...	...	...	4·45	710	3·0	...	940	299
1941	...	...	...	4·97	250	1·0	...	1,079	360

Table UK.12 (Continued)   Labour market: other indicators, 1885–1987

	Output per person employed		Ave. weekly hrs of manual workers	Ave. weekly earnings of manual workers	Unemployment		Vacancies unfilled	Industrial stoppages	
	Whole economy	Mfg						Working days lost	Workers involved
	Index nos., 1980 = 100			£	'000	%	'000	'000	'000
1942	...	...	...	5·57	110	0·4	...	1,527	456
1943	...	...	52·9	6·06	80	0·3	...	1,808	557
1944	...	...	51·2	6·22	70	0·3	...	3,714	821
1945	...	...	49·7	6·07	100	0·4	...	2,835	531
1946	50·0	...	47·6	6·04	400	1·7	629	2,158	526
1947	50·3	...	46·6	6·40	300	1·3	571	2,433	620
1948	52·7	46·8	46·7	6·90	298[a]	1·3	467	1,944	424
1949	54·5	48·9	46·8	7·13	328	1·4	383	1,807	433
1950	56·1	51·0	47·6	7·52	332	1·4	364	1,389	302
1951	56·3	51·3	47·8	8·30	264	1·1	410	1,694	379
1952	56·0	49·2	47·7	8·92	368	1·5	275	1,792	415
1953	58·0	52·3	47·9	9·46	356	1·5	275 / 192	2,184	1,370
1954	59·5	53·8	48·5	10·22	303	1·2	240	2,457	448
1955	60·9	55·8	48·9	11·15	244	1·0	281	3,781	659
1956	60·9	55·3	48·5	11·90	258	1·0	241	2,083	507
1957	62·0	56·8	48·2	12·58	327	1·3	186	8,412	1,356
1958	62·6	57·1	47·7	12·83	451	1·8	137	3,462	523
1959	65·2	60·3	48·5	13·54	480	2·0	158	5,270	645
1960	68·6	63·2	48·0	14·53	377	1·5	213	3,024	814[b]
1961	69·0	62·7	47·4	15·34	347	1·4	214	3,046	771
1962	69·6	63·5	47·0	15·86	467	1·9	150	5,798	4,420
1963	71·8	66·5	47·6	16·75	558	2·2	145	1,755	590
1964	75·2	71·6	47·7	18·11	404	1·6	222	2,277	872[b]
1965	76·5	72·6	47·0	19·59	347	1·4	267	2,925	868
1966	77·6	73·9	46·0	20·30	361	1·4	257	2,398	530[b]
1967	80·0	76·5	46·2	21·38	559	2·2	175	2,787	732
1968	83·8	82·5	46·4	23·00	586	2·3	190	4,690	2,256
1969	85·5	84·6	46·5	24·82	581	2·3	202	6,846	1,656
1970	87·3	85·1	45·7	28·05	612	2·4	188	10,980	1,793
1971	89·7	86·9	44·7	30·93	792 / 751	3·1 / 3·0	131	13,551	1,175
1972	92·1	92·0	45·0	35·82	837	3·3	147	23,909	1,726
1973	95·5	100·0	45·6	40·92	596	2·3	307	7,197	1,513
1974	93·7	98·5	45·1	48·63	600	2·3	298	14,750	1,622
1975	92·4	95·9	43·6	59·58	941	3·6	157	6,012	789
1976	94·9	100·9	44·0	66·97	1,302	5·0	122	3,284	670
1977	97·6	102·5	44·2	72·89	1,403	5·4	155	10,142	1,155
1978	100·6	103·6	44·2	83·50	1,383	5·2	210	9,405	1,003
1979	102·2	104·1	44·0	96·94	1,296	4·9	241	29,474	4,583
1980	100·0	100·0	43·0	113·06	1,665	6·2	134	11,964	842
1981	101·9	103·5	43·0	125·58	2,520	9·4	91	4,266	1,499
1982	105·7	110·4	42·9	137·06	2,917	10·9	114	5,312	2,103
1983	110·0	119·8	43·3 / 42·5	149·13 / 146·19	3,105	11·7	137	3,753	574
1984	111·7	126·4	42·8	157·50	3,160	11·7	150	27,135	1,464
1985	114·2	130·6	43·0	170·58	3,271	11·8	162	6,399	792
1986	117·0	134·6	42·7	182·25	3,289	11·8	188	1,923	721
1987	120·4	144·4	43·5	197·92	2,953	10·6	235	3,545	888

a   July figure.
b   Excludes workers becoming involved after end of year in which stoppage began.

Table UK.13 Value of imports by commodity group, 1885–1987

	Total imports	Food, beverages & tobacco	Basic materials	Fuels	Semi-manufact.	Finished manufact.	Machinery & transport equipment
				£ mn			
1885	371	160	151	...		59	...
1886	350	145	145	...		60	...
1887	362	151	150	...		61	...
1888	388	159	164	...		65	...
1889	428	174	182	...		72	...
1890	421	176	174	...		70	...
1891	435	187	176	...		72	...
1892	424	188	164	...		72	...
1893	405	179	154	...		72	...
1894	408	177	156	...		75	...
1895	417	178	156	...		82	...
1896	442	187	166	...		89	...
1897	451	193	166	...		92	...
1898	471	208	169	...		94	...
1899	485	209	177	...		99	...
1900	523	214	203	7		106	4
		220	166			127	
1901	522	224	162	6		127	4
1902	528	224	164	6		132	5
1903	543	231	168	6		136	5
1904	551	231	176	7		136	4
1905	565	231	182	7		142	6
1906	608	238	205	7		155	6
1907	646	247	235	7		154	7
1908	593	244	197	8		142	6
1909	625	254	214	7		147	6
1910	678	258	255	7		156	12
1911	680	264	248	7		160	13
1912	745	281	276	9		178	16
1913	769	290	272	12	142	49	17
1914	697	297	223	13	123	37	15
1915	852	381	273	13	143	39	19
1916	949	419	321	20	152	37	16
1917	1,064	455	354	34	136	83	18
1918	1,316	570	398	64	151	129	24
1919	1,626	706	616	40	186	74	28
1920	1,933	760	715	72	281	102	49
1921	1,086	563	260	69	139	52	30
1922	1,003	469	298	40	138	55	16
1923	1,096	506	322	37	165	61	19
1924	1,277	567	395	43	195	83	23
1925	1,321	566	418	42	206	70	28
1926	1,241	526	343	94	203	81	24
1927	1,218	535	337	52	207	83	30
1928	1,196	528	331	41	201	90	31
1929	1,221	532	337	45	206	82	37
1930	1,044	472	248	48	183	74	32
1931	861	414	172	30	161	74	26
1932	702	371	162	33	90	40	16
1933	675	338	178	31	87	37	14
1934	731	345	204	33	101	44	31
1935	756	353	208	35	109	47	21
1936	848	379	243	39	123	58	26
1937	1,028	429	308	50	164	71	34
1938	920	428	240	48	131	65	30
1939	886	397	234	48	140	60	34
1940	1,082	418	329	76	190	63	...
1941	986	420	220	97	170	71	...
1942	997	434	229	103	163	54	...
1943	1,234	512	254	156	213	84	...

Table **UK.13 (Continued)**   **Value of imports by commodity group, 1885–1987**

	Total imports	Food, beverages & tobacco	Basic materials	Fuels	Semi-manufact.	Finished manufact.	Machinery & transport equipment
				£ mn			
1944	1,309	518	272	224	174	91	...
1945	1,104	489	284	148	105	59	42
1946	1,301	636	375	89	140	33	21
1947	1,798	798	540	105	261	68	37
1948	2,064	865	643	159	287	81	55
1949	2,268	958	730	149	309	101	77
1950	2,598	1,017	914	197	350	103	71
1951	3,892	1,282	1,520	316	636	140	82
1952	3,465	1,196	1,143	339	581	187	133
1953	3,328	1,304	1,055	313	445	196	160
1954	3,359	1,314	1,026	329	512	169	119
1955	3,860	1,424	1,121	408	689	206	147
1956	3,862	1,434	1,099	414	670	234	163
1957	4,139	1,478	1,165	466	744	268	189
1958	3,834	1,489	906	439	674	303	210
1959	4,087	1,519	946	467	750	377	253
1960	4,655	1,540	1,080	480	1,005	517	347
1961	4,546	1,484	1,009	482	975	556	366
1962	4,627	1,569	924	533	955	602	395
1963	4,989	1,676	989	560	1,050	651	407
1964	5,702	1,771	1,118	585	1,323	834	545
1965	5,760	1,708	1,110	611	1,369	882	606
1966	5,951	1,712	1,061	628	1,476	990	681
1967	6,440	1,762	1,011	732	1,597	1,244	868
1968	7,900	1,900	1,206	907	2,116	1,652	1,189
1969	8,317	1,930	1,251	911	2,300	1,834	1,320
1970	9,085	2,028	1,439	949	2,468	2,099	1,520
1971	9,769	2,156	1,341	1,252	2,437	2,462	1,760
1972	11,049	2,339	1,389	1,245	2,791	3,166	2,293
1973	15,664	3,066	2,063	1,731	3,976	4,681	3,383
1974	22,917	3,712	2,692	4,640	6,023	5,624	4,002
1975	23,863	4,282	2,351	4,313	5,763	6,796	4,917
1976	31,031	4,934	3,511	5,664	7,533	8,982	6,498
1977	36,157	5,850	3,991	5,249	9,113	11,513	8,486
1978	39,441	6,064	3,783	4,798	10,280	14,039	10,211
1979	46,711	6,439	4,274	5,774	12,651	17,031	12,244
1980	48,918	6,097	4,122	6,867	13,435	17,735	12,580
1981	50,413	6,488	4,072	7,157	12,478	19,504	13,420
1982	56,624	7,198	4,010	7,399	13,962	23,137	16,489
1983	65,581	7,824	4,857	7,065	16,877	28,038	20,286
1984	78,760	8,874	5,523	10,320	19,657	33,325	23,812
1985	84,905	9,275	5,496	10,648	21,126	37,161	26,973
1986	85,568	10,033	5,066	6,278	22,556	40,254	28,808
1987	94,016	10,132	5,688	6,099	25,177	45,778	32,820

Table UK.14 Value of exports by commodity group, 1885–1987

	Total exports	Non-manufact.	Fuels	Manufact.	of which: Chemicals	Textiles	Metals & metal manufact.	Machinery & transport equipment
					£ mn			
1885	271	84		188	...	...	...	...
1886	268	82		187	...	...	...	...
1887	280	86		195	...	...	...	...
1888	299	94		205	...	...	...	...
1889	316	101		215	...	...	...	...
1890	329	105		214	...	...	...	...
1891	309	99		211	...	...	...	...
1892	292	99		193	...	...	...	...
1893	277	91		186	...	...	...	...
1894	274	91		183	...	...	...	...
1895	286	92		193	...	...	...	...
1896	296	88		208	...	...	...	...
1897	294	95		198	...	...	...	...
1898	294	97		198	...	...	...	...
1899	329	112		218	...	...	...	...
1900	354	126		229	16	111	47	31
		66	39	247				
1901	348	71	30	242	15	112	40	29
1902	349	73	28	245	17	112	43	30
1903	361	73	27	254	18	117	45	29
1904	371	76	27	263	18	129	43	41
1905	408	85	26	291	20	141	49	34
1906	461	91	32	331	21	153	61	44
1907	518	101	42	368	23	170	70	50
1908	457	90	42	320	22	143	55	60
1909	469	103	37	322	23	146	56	42
1910	534	117	38	370	25	167	65	48
1911	557	119	38	390	26	181	68	48
1912	599	132	43	414	28	185	74	54
1913	635	130	54	441	29	190	81	64
1914	526	113	42	363	25	157	63	53
1915	484	116	39	315	29	138	59	31
1916	604	113	51	420	38	192	79	32
1917	597	84	51	442	33	222	63	28
1918	532	40	52	419	31	246	51	25
1919	964	198	92	662	48	372	89	70
1920	1,558	287	124	1,133	60	557	167	71
1921	810	142	48	611	20	244	83	76
1922	824	148	80	584	22	257	78	63
1923	886	177	114	584	25	251	96	44
1924	941	205	83	637	24	280	97	45
1925	927	218	60	635	22	269	92	63
1926	779	182	26	557	23	215	86	62
1927	832	186	54	577	25	215	95	59
1928	844	184	47	593	28	212	89	65
1929	839	172	57	592	30	198	94	69
1930	658	134	53	453	30	151	68	111
1931	455	97	39	301	24	99	41	71
1932	416	86	36	280	24	103	38	57
1933	417	85	36	283	24	101	45	56
1934	447	93	37	306	25	107	51	66
1935	481	92	40	337	28	108	57	79
1936	502	100	38	352	27	113	57	84
1937	596	113	49	422	32	127	82	103
1938	532	97	47	376	29	94	66	117
1939	486	88	46	341	31	94	51	99
1940	419	65	29	318	40	100	50	72
1941	337	41	10	281	35	96	34	54

Table UK.14 (Continued) Value of exports by commodity group, 1885–1987

	Total exports	Non-manufact.	Fuels	Manufact.	*of which:* Chemicals	Textiles	Metals & metal manufact.	Machinery & transport equipment
					£ mn			
1942	276	26	7	237	26	91	23	53
1943	240	26	8	204	30	72	17	49
1944	282	39	6	232	32	74	19	68
1945	450	105	8	316	49	90	45	83
1946	965	134	15	792	81	157	132	268
1947	1,201	110	11	1,007	84	195	145	400
1948	1,628	191	53	1,325	104	294	183	574
1949	1,832	196	70	1,495	110	331	212	676
1950	2,245	295	78	1,807	136	382	260	807
1951	2,693	297	72	2,210	194	513	259	892
1952	2,711	329	134	2,161	178	365	315	967
1953	2,661	292	153	2,091	173	364	312	943
1954	2,748	299	157	2,160	202	362	304	984
1955	2,993	336	146	2,372	235	344	365	1,082
1956	3,286	367	167	2,623	245	331	448	1,235
1957	3,497	374	157	2,850	268	345	473	1,317
1958	3,391	360	136	2,796	264	293	427	1,372
1959	3,553	372	123	2,951	295	282	453	1,446
1960	3,789	393	130	3,137	319	298	466	1,541
1961	3,955	414	128	3,289	328	286	482	1,635
1962	4,062	427	151	3,362	344	280	487	1,674
1963	4,378	456	170	3,607	369	298	476	1,820
1964	4,600	476	144	3,807	414	319	511	1,844
1965	4,932	496	137	4,120	448	309	581	2,005
1966	5,275	533	139	4,413	475	296	588	2,205
1967	5,244	526	136	4,403	496	279	610	2,142
1968	6,442	639	173	5,432	603	330	746	2,623
1969	7,352	677	177	6,278	690	383	847	2,987
1970	8,073	789	207	6,821	778	409	953	3,340
1971	9,055	874	236	7,698	876	435	996	3,935
1972	9,577	990	238	8,091	954	458	1,009	4,094
1973	12,029	1,314	370	10,032	1,261	614	1,301	4,858
1974	16,191	1,664	775	13,268	2,120	757	1,704	6,156
1975	19,429	2,005	818	16,027	2,153	715	1,821	8,308
1976	25,139	2,527	1,255	20,643	3,017	948	2,306	10,190
1977	31,921	3,212	2,083	25,743	3,827	1,162	2,771	12,482
1978	35,280	3,981	2,363	27,970	4,210	1,209	2,966	13,424
1979	40,400	4,254	4,310	30,855	4,925	1,312	3,490	14,252
1980	47,054	4,739	6,414	34,804	5,301	1,336	3,953	16,291
1981	50,381	4,965	9,601	34,619	5,516	1,153	3,626	16,720
1982	55,314	5,337	11,222	37,296	6,134	1,161	3,838	18,114
1983	60,590	5,875	13,087	40,061	6,949	1,244	4,311	18,337
1984	70,373	6,741	15,290	46,668	8,236	1,433	4,577	21,535
1985	78,263	7,159	16,776	52,474	9,431	1,659	4,777	24,685
1986	72,834	7,582	8,664	54,564	9,711	1,662	4,824	25,365
1987	79,852	7,843	8,747	61,009	10,541	1,834	5,178	28,819

Table UK.15 Value of exports and imports by area, 1885–1987

	European Community		Rest of Europe		North America		Rest of World		*of which:* Japan	
	Exports to	Imports from	Exports to	Imports from	Exports to	Imports from	Exports to	Imports from	Exports to	Imports from
					£ mn					
1885	97	121	12	18	38	97	124	134	2·3	0·5
1886	90	118	12	16	45	92	121	123	2·3	0·6
1887	94	125	12	16	48	94	127	126	3·7	0·5
1888	96	134	14	18	49	89	139	146	4·1	1·0
1889	103	145	15	20	52	107	145	155	4·1	1·0
1890	106	143	14	19	53	109	154	149	4·2	1·0
1891	101	143	13	20	48	117	146	154	3·1	1·2
1892	97	142	13	17	48	123	145	141	3·3	0·8
1893	93	142	13	19	43	105	127	138	3·7	1·0
1894	92	142	13	19	37	103	131	143	3·9	1·0
1895	92	148	12	18	50	100	131	150	5	1·1
1896	96	146	13	20	38	122	148	153	6	1·2
1897	94	161	14	20	44	133	141	136	6	1·3
1898	98	163	16	20	36	147	143	139	5	1·2
1899	110	158	17	20	45	141	156	164	8	2
1900	118	178	22	22	48	163	165	158	10	2
1901	106	177	22	23	48	164	171	157	8	2
1902	103	184	20	23	56	153	169	167	5	2
1903	107	185	20	25	55	151	177	180	5	2
1904	107	168	21	39	53	145	189	196	5	2
1905	117	172	23	40	64	144	203	202	10	2
1906	137	180	26	44	70	164	227	218	13	3
1907	156	183	31	43	79	164	251	259	12	3
1908	140	172	29	42	58	153	228	224	10	2
1909	139	178	28	42	79	147	222	253	9	4
1910	155	188	32	44	86	149	259	293	10	4
1911	162	191	34	47	80	152	279	289	12	3
1912	171	209	36	45	93	165	297	322	13	4
1913	180	224	37	47	88	175	328	328	15	4
1914	140	178	32	40	85	173	267	288	9	4
1915	156	116	27	51	73	282	226	391	5	9
1916	195	118	31	53	87	356	289	433	8	13
1917	203	98	26	43	78	465	288	427	6	15
1918	206	109	26	56	42	647	256	542	7	24
1919	435	227	106	11	84	663	335	721	15	24
1920	486	287	144	135	181	666	742	840	28	30
1921	218	226	48	65	86	340	454	450	22	9
1922	248	213	50	68	105	280	416	439	25	8
1923	288	281	49	71	116	269	429	472	27	7
1924	313	331	55	75	109	312	460	557	27	8
1925	294	336	50	73	114	321	465	588	17	7
1926	216	357	37	67	104	296	418	518	14	7
1927	255	352	42	74	98	260	432	529	15	8
1928	256	350	43	68	106	250	434	524	15	9
1929	263	356	43	74	100	246	428	541	14	9
1930	221	327	44	67	71	196	317	451	8	8
1931	165	292	32	55	48	140	206	370	6	7
1932	142	183	28	42	38	129	203	344	6	7
1933	135	159	28	45	45	125	204	342	4	6
1934	135	161	34	46	44	136	228	380	4	8
1935	140	165	32	53	54	146	246	388	4	8
1936	134	174	33	61	62	172	267	437	4	10
1937	156	197	41	78	72	208	320	540	5	12
1938	139	181	38	68	53	200	296	466	2	9
1939	123	177	39	64	61	200	257	440	1	9
1940	77	...	28	...	72	364	239	579	—	6
1941	29	...	15	...	72	446	221	475	—	1
1942	25	...	14	...	50	505	187	418	—	—
1943	25	...	20	...	45	739	150	435	—	—

50

	European Community		Rest of Europe		North America		Rest of World		*of which:* Japan	
	Exports to	Imports from	Exports to	Imports from	Exports to	Imports from	Exports to	Imports from	Exports to	Imports from
					£ mn					
1944	36	...	.10	...	43	745	193	481	—	—
1945	139	...	25	...	46	527	242	455	—	—
1946	258	...	89	...	74	431	534	655	—	—
1947	249	240	126	88	107	536	705	924	—	5
1948	343	321	172	134	144	408	969	1,201	—	5
1949	367	439	169	158	145	447	1,151	1,224	1	11
1950	476	546	227	168	257	392	1,285	1,492	3	8
1951	517	774	298	345	294	641	1,584	2,132	9	17
1952	541	694	289	284	314	638	1,567	1,849	9	29
1953	607	634	336	260	334	559	1,460	1,875	18	9
1954	636	683	273	265	297	556	1,542	1,855	12	16
1955	552	776	296	322	344	764	1,801	1,988	14	24
1956	746	777	319	329	442	756	1,779	2,000	24	24
1957	775	812	319	361	483	809	1,920	2,157	29	24
1958	731	837	301	328	515	665	1,844	2,004	20	35
1959	777	881	331	353	631	689	1,814	2,164	33	43
1960	849	1,039	381	430	596	950	1,963	2,236	29	42
1961	1,047	1,080	429	433	570	846	1,909	2,187	44	40
1962	1,196	1,121	445	424	580	838	1,841	2,245	46	54
1963	1,339	1,217	501	449	583	883	1,955	2,440	53	54
1964	1,406	1,426	572	560	622	1,109	2,001	2,608	61	75
1965	1,466	1,505	598	577	728	1,131	2,141	2,566	53	78
1966	1,582	1,634	653	614	877	1,149	2,163	2,551	69	77
1967	1,582	1,868	664	692	862	1,263	2,137	2,617	88	91
1968	1,954	2,263	748	884	1,182	1,574	2,557	3,178	99	115
1969	2,340	2,260	900	962	1,223	1,636	2,888	3,359	129	105
1970	2,627	2,656	1,091	1,195	1,232	1,877	3,123	3,357	149	135
1971	2,841	3,070	1,186	1,284	1,444	1,757	3,584	3,658	158	202
1972	3,217	3,789	1,277	1,527	1,600	1,800	3,483	3,933	173	315
1973	4,271	5,646	1,554	2,202	1,935	2,386	4,269	5,430	273	446
1974	5,895	8,279	2,098	2,785	2,282	3,253	5,916	8,600	320	572
1975	6,807	9,341	2,453	2,902	2,347	3,222	7,822	8,398	310	673
1976	9,672	12,058	3,102	3,781	3,100	4,260	9,265	10,932	362	796
1977	12,604	14,825	3,946	4,412	3,784	4,960	11,587	11,960	471	1,061
1978	14,329	17,287	3,642	5,242	4,241	5,288	13,068	11,624	541	1,283
1979	18,272	21,913	4,568	6,135	4,785	6,085	12,775	12,578	606	1,488
1980	21,563	21,612	5,475	6,096	5,299	7,383	14,717	13,827	595	1,707
1981	21,996	22,728	4,978	6,371	7,107	7,372	16,300	13,942	611	2,206
1982	24,379	26,547	5,232	6,992	8,343	7,984	17,360	15,101	669	2,659
1983	27,992	31,651	5,960	8,851	9,488	9,019	17,150	16,060	799	3,355
1984	33,086	37,383	7,107	11,164	11,401	10,955	18,779	19,258	919	3,772
1985	38,160	41,445	7,410	12,075	13,310	11,697	19,383	19,688	1,011	4,115
1986	34,959	44,459	6,919	11,840	12,075	10,020	18,881	19,249	1,183	4,931
1987	39,416	49,557	7,621	12,869	12,993	10,781	19,822	20,809	1,495	5,463

Table UK.16   Balance of payments, 1885–1987

	Imports (fob)	Exports (fob)	Services		Interest, profits & dividends		Current balance	Official reserves (end year)
			Debits	Credits	Debits	Credits		
					£ mn			
1885	341	272	29	91	5	75	62	...
1886	322	270	28	85	6	80	78	...
1887	333	283	29	90	6	85	88	...
1888	357	302	30	94	6	90	91	...
1889	393	323	33	99	7	96	83	...
1890	387	334	33	100	7	101	107	...
1891	400	313	32	98	7	101	72	...
1892	390	295	31	95	7	102	63	...
1893	372	280	30	85	7	102	57	...
1894	376	277	30	86	7	100	50	...
1895	383	290	30	85	7	101	55	...
1896	407	304	32	90	7	103	50	...
1897	415	300	32	92	8	105	41	...
1898	433	302	33	93	8	109	29	...
1899	446	331	40	100	8	111	47	...
1900	485	356	50	111	8	112	34	...
1901	485	349	55	109	9	115	19	...
1902	491	350	46	110	10	119	24	...
1903	505	361	38	118	10	122	43	...
1904	512	372	39	120	11	124	52	...
1905	527	409	40	126	12	135	88	...
1906	568	462	43	139	14	148	121	...
1907	603	519	46	152	16	160	162	...
1908	550	457	46	140	17	168	150	...
1909	581	470	47	145	17	175	142	...
1910	632	536	51	155	19	189	174	...
1911	634	559	51	156	20	197	204	...
1912	694	600	54	168	22	209	203	...
1913	719	637	58	179	24	224	235	35
1914	660	540	80	145	25	215	134	...
1915	840	500	130	250	25	190	−55	...
1916	980	630	160	370	30	230	90	...
1917	1,040	620	220	465	40	235	50	...
1918	1,170	540	230	400	65	240	−275	...
1919	1,460	990	220	480	65	230	−45	88
1920	1,761 1,812	1,585 1,664	224	464	46	292	317 337	128
1921	1,022	874	172	292	44	222	193	128
1922	951	888	150	225	60	237	201	127
1923	1,011	914	146	247	64	240	183	128
1924	1,172	958	152	242	65	261	78	129
1925	1,208	943	149	215	63	295	52	147
1926	1,140	794	152	223	63	300	−18	151
1927	1,115	845	142	245	63	302	98	152
1928	1,095	858	140	234	64	304	124	153
1929	1,117	854	152	242	64	307	96	146
1930	953	670	147	214	62	277	36	148
1931	786	464	140	168	48	211	−103	121
1932	641	425	123	153	48	175	−51	206
1933	619	427	120	146	29	183	−8	372
1934	683	463	116	145	28	195	−22	415
1935	724	541	124	149	31	212	23	493
1936	784	523	135	174	34	229	−27	703
1937	950	614	144	229	37	242	−47	825
1938	849	564	152	193	37	229	−55	615
1939	800	500	200	300	90	250	−250	545
1940	1,000	400	550	200	100	260	−800	108
1941	1,100	400	450	200	130	270	−820	141
1942	800	300	550	300	170	270	−660	254
1943	800	240	700	500	190	280	−680	467

Table UK.16 (Continued) Balance of payments, 1885–1987

	Imports (fob)	Exports (fob)	Services		Interest, profits & dividends		Current balance	Official reserves (end year)
			Debits	Credits	Debits	Credits		
					£ mn			
1944	900	270	800	700	210	290	−680	601
1945	700	450	1,000	350	230	310	−870	610
1946	1,063	960	762	470	113	198	−230	664
1947	1,541	1,180	687	472	111	261	−381	512
1948	1,790	1,639	644	557	125	360	26	457
1949	2,000	1,863	697	632	132	351	−1	603
1950	2,312	2,261	764	734	162	558	307	1,178
1951	3,424	2,735	907	913	211	553	−369	834
1952	3,048	2,769	885	991	248	500	163	659
1953	2,927	2,683	908	1,004	266	495	145	899
1954	2,989	2,785	972	1,052	290	540	117	986
1955	3,386	3,073	1,095	1,104	343	517	−155	757
1956	3,324	3,377	1,230	1,221	342	571	208	799
1957	3,538	3,509	1,240	1,327	334	583	233	812
1958	3,377	3,406	1,206	1,304	389	682	360	1,096
1959	3,642	3,527	1,243	1,329	396	658	172	977
1960	4,138	3,737	1,411	1,419	438	671	228	1,154
1961	4,043	3,903	1,467	1,488	422	676	47	1,185
1962	4,103	4,003	1,505	1,523	420	754	155	1,002
1963	4,450	4,331	1,577	1,546	444	842	125	949
1964	5,111	4,568	1,708	1,658	495	889	−358	827
1965	5,173	4,913	1,798	1,762	557	992	−30	1,073
1966	5,384	5,276	1,876	1,891	577	979	128	1,107
1967	5,840	5,241	2,014	2,147	601	1,002	−281	1,123
1968	7,145	6,433	2,235	2,547	776	1,135	−264	1,009
1969	7,478	7,269	2,452	2,818	844	1,375	482	1,053
1970	8,142	8,128	2,963	3,379	898	1,494	816	1,178
1971	8,820	9,030	3,341	3,885	984	1,537	1,111	2,526
1972	10,154	9,412	3,587	4,205	2,809	3,403	198	2,405
1973	14,448	11,882	4,501	5,184	3,598	4,925	−999	2,795
1974	21,513	16,280	5,646	6,594	4,703	6,211	−3,199	2,955
1975	22,440	19,183	6,342	7,679	5,673	6,564	−1,504	2,700
1976	29,041	25,082	7,776	10,020	6,829	8,389	−941	2,485
1977	34,006	31,682	8,586	11,623	8,551	8,816	−150	10,975
1978	36,574	34,981	8,959	12,501	10,375	11,181	964	10,380
1979	43,868	40,470	10,527	14,434	16,300	17,505	−496	13,170
1980	45,794	47,147	11,830	15,779	23,886	23,690	3,122	13,275
1981	47,318	50,668	13,103	17,026	36,319	37,529	6,936	11,960
1982	53,112	55,330	14,923	17,685	42,950	44,396	4,685	12,939
1983	61,773	60,698	16,122	19,843	39,624	42,471	3,832	12,805
1984	74,843	70,263	18,145	22,086	47,266	51,699	2,022	13,219
1985	80,334	77,988	18,832	24,794	49,509	52,309	3,337	13,201
1986	81,394	72,678	20,188	25,806	42,558	47,637	−199	17,424
1987	89,584	79,422	22,446	28,084	42,566	48,089	−2,504	27,008

Table UK.17 Finance, 1885–1988

	Industrial ordinary share price index	Interest rates			Money stock (MI)	Total consumer credit outstanding	Foreign exchange rates				
		Treasury bills, ave. 3 months tender rate	Gilt-edged yields				US $	French Fr	German Mark	Italian L	Japanese ¥
			Short-dated	2½% Consols	(end of period)						
	1980 = 100	%	%	%	£ mn	£ mn	Annual average, rates to £				
1885	...	...	...	3·02	...	...	...	...	...	...	5·79
1886	...	...	...	2·97	...	...	...	...	...	...	6·29
1887	...	...	...	2·94	...	...	...	...	...	...	6·26
1888	...	...	...	2·76	...	...	...	...	...	...	6·52
1889	...	...	...	2·78	...	...	...	...	...	...	6·39
1890	...	...	...	2·85	...	...	...	...	...	...	5·80
1891	...	...	...	2·87	...	...	...	...	...	...	6·23
1892	...	...	...	2·85	...	...	...	...	...	...	6·92
1893	...	...	...	2·80	...	...	...	...	...	...	7·97
1894	...	...	...	2·72	...	...	...	...	...	...	11·64
1895	...	...	...	2·59	...	...	...	...	...	...	9·60
1896	...	...	...	2·47	...	...	...	...	...	...	9·32
1897	...	...	...	2·44	...	...	...	...	...	...	9·75
1898	...	...	...	2·48	...	...	...	...	...	...	9·87
1899	...	...	...	2·58	...	...	...	...	...	...	9·78
1900	4·5	3·996	...	2·51	...	...	4·872	25·38	20·72	...	9·91
1901	4·5	2·475	...	2·65	...	...	4·879	25·35	20·62	...	9·88
1902	4·1	2·963	3·12	2·65	...	...	4·876	25·33	20·61	...	9·81
1903	4·1	3·446	3·40	2·75	...	...	4·868	25·36	20·63	...	9·81
1904	4·1	2·904	3·40	2·83	...	...	4·872	25·33	20·61	...	9·92
1905	4·1	2·200	2·95	2·78	...	...	4·866	25·31	20·62	...	9·82
1906	4·1	3·000	3·17	2·83	...	...	4·857	25·37	20·71	...	9·85
1907	4·1	3·763	3·28	2·97	...	...	4·867	25·43	20·78	...	9·83
1908	3·7	2·246	2·91	2·90	...	...	4·868	25·32	20·66	...	9·83
1909	3·7	2·137	2·74	2·98	...	...	4·876	25·36	20·66	...	9·81
1910	4·1	3·058	2·91	3·08	...	...	4·868	25·45	20·71	...	9·86
1911	4·5	2·825	2·99	3·15	...	...	4·866	25·49	20·71	...	9·83
1912	4·5	2·004	3·04	3·28	...	...	4·870	25·50	20·75	...	9·81
1913	4·5	3·048	3·09	3·39	...	...	4·868	25·56	20·78	...	9·85
1914	...	...	...	...	...	...	4·884	...	...	...	9·90
1919	7·4	3·481	5·24	4·62	(1,501)	...	4,429	31·75	226·98	...	8·89
1920	7·4	6·212	6·23	5·32	(1,519)	...	3·661	52·47	404·59	104·6	7·62
1921	5·2	4·575	5·70	5·21	1,494	...	3·846	51·89	8,155·85	89·5	8·03
1922	6·0	2·571	4·78	4·42	1,424	...	4·427	54·60	...	93·2	9·32
1923	7·1	2·621	4·39	4·31	1,396	...	4·574	75·64	18·90	99·4	9·39
1924	7·1	3·392	4·36	4·39	1,393	...	4·417	85·24	20·28	101·3	10·52
1925	7·8	4·092	4·51	4·44	1,363	...	4·829	102·54	20·41	121·4	11·85
1926	8·2	4·512	4·35	4·55	1,365	...	4·858	152·38	20·46	125·8	10·36
1927	8·6	4·254	3·98	4·56	1,382	...	4·861	123·85	20·39	95·1	10·25
1928	10·1	4·146	4·73	4·47	1,424	...	4·886	124·10	20·39	92·6	10·49
1929	9·7	5·264	5·08	4·60	1,345	...	4·857	124·02	20·40	92·7	10·55
1930	7·8	2·484	4·31	4·48	1,388 / 1,303	Total	4·862	123·88	20·38	92·8	9·86
1931	6·3	3·593	4·54	4·39	1,189	...	4·859 / 3·694	124·06 / 94·02	20·52 / 15·73	87·0	9·25
1932	6·0	1·486	3·64	3·74	1,317	...	3·504	89·19	14·74	68·4	12·60
1933	7·1	0·591	2·09	3·39	1,346	...	4·218	84·59	13·98	63·7	16·46
1934	8·9	0·727	1·78	3·10	1,377	...	5·041	76·94	12·80	58·8	16·78
1935	9·7	0·546	2·46	2·89	1,494	...	4·903	74·27	12·18	59·3	17·07
1936	11·2	0·583	2·45	2·93	1,670	...	4·971	82·97	12·33	70·4	17·12
1937	10·4	0·563	2·90	3·28	1,698	...	4·944	124·61	12·29	94·0	17·16
1938	8·6	0·611	2·72	3·38	1,663	...	4·890	170·65	12·17	92·9	17·15
1939	8·2	1·315	3·30	3·72	1,810	...	4·460	176·65	...	85·3	17·07
1940	6·7	1·028	2·78	3·40	2,235	...	4·03	176·62	...	72·3	16·84
1941	7·1	1·006	2·47	3·13	2,719	...	4·03	...	...	...	...
1942	7·8	1·004	2·32	3·03	3,133	...	4·03	...	...	...	...
1943	9·3	1·004	2·45	3·10	3,562	...	4·03	...	...	...	...

	Industrial ordinary share price index	Interest rates			Money stock (MI) (end of period)	Total consumer credit outstanding	Foreign exchange rates				
		Treasury bills, ave. 3 months tender rate	Gilt-edged yields				US $	French Fr	German Mark	Italian L	Japanese ¥
			Short-dated	2½% Consols							
	1980 = 100	%			£ mn		Annual average, rates to £				
1944	10·4	1·004	2·37	3·14	4,069	...	4·03	...	...	...	...
1945	10·8	0·896	2·45	2·92	4,415	...	4·03	203·80	...	...	60·45
1946	11·9	0·504	2·08	2·60	4,956	...	4·03	480·00	...	...	...
1947	12·3	0·508	2·18	2·76	5,035	68	4·03	480·00	...	...	201·50
1948	11·9	0·509	2·02	3·21	5,126	105	4·03	879·73	...	...	1,088·1
1949	11·2	0·521	1·94	3·30	5,191	128	3·68	1,053·06	...	2,104	1,157·2
1950	11·5	0·516	2·03	3·54	5,283	167	2·80	980·00	...	1,749	1,010·2
1951	13·4	0·562	1·85	3·78	5,355	208	2·80	979·74	...	1,750	1,010·2
1952	11·2	2·196	2·98	4·23	4,950	241	2·79	981·48	...	1,750	1,010·2
1953	11·9	2·304	3·03	4·08	5,119	276	2·81	982·76	11·70	1,750	1,010·2
1954	15·6	1·794	2·61	3·75	5,358	384	2·81	981·64	11·73	1,750	1,006·6
1955	18·2	3·753	3·81	4·17	5,280	461	2·792	978·10	11·74	1,751	1,011·4
1956	17·1	4·945	4·67	4·73	5,300	376	2·796	982·74	11·71	1,751	1,005·1
1957	18·2	4·814	5·15	4·98	5,209	448	2·794	1,059·63	11·73	1,752	1,012·5
1958	18·6	4·563	4·75	4·98	5,191	556	2·810	1,177·51	11·72	1,745	1,010·5
1959	26·8	3·375	4·16	4·82	5,825	849	2·809	13·77	11·74	1,744	1,007·3
1960	33·9	4·887	5·60	5·42	5,707	935	2·808	13·77	11·71	1,743	1,008·2
1961	35·0	5·141	5·98	6·20	5,749	934	2·802	13·74	11·26	1,740	1,016·0
1962	32·8	4·171	5·31	5·98	5,890	887	2·808	13·76	11·224	1,743	1,007·8
1963	37·2	3·667	4·83	5·58	6,380 / 7,210	959	2·800	13·72	11·160	1,740	1,013·5
1964	39·8	4·594	5·54	6·03	7,450	1,115	2·793	13·68	11·099	1,743	1,001·1
1965	37·2	5·909	6·57	6·42	7,610	1,196	2·796	13·70	11·165	1,747	1,013·0
1966	37·6	6·122	6·77	6·80	7,600	1,104	2·793	13·72	11·168	1,744	1,012·5
1967	40·2	5·810	6·66	6·69	8,250 / 8,180	1,058	2·790	13·73	11·122	1,741	1,023·5
1968	56·8	7·031	7·59	7·39	8,640	1,089	2·394	11·85	9·555	1,492	856·3
1969	56·2	7·627	8·81	8·88	8,660	1,063	2·390	13·31	8·838	1,499	855·1
1970	49·8	6·999	7·89	9·16	9,420	1,127	2·396	13·24	8·736	1,502	857·8
1971	58·8	5·554	6·68	9·05	10,310 / 10,710	1,668	2·444	13·46	8·530	1,511	844·6
1972	74·9	5·541	7·68	9·11	12,370	2,106	2·502	12·62	7·975	1,460	752·3
1973	64·8	9·306	10·45	10·85	13,020	2,550	2·453	10·90	6·540	1,426	664·6
1974	38·1	11·357	12·51	14·95	14,460	2,386	2·340	11·25	6·049	1,522	682·7
1975	47·6	10·187	11·48	14·66	17,150	2,373	2·220	9·50	5·447	1,447	658·1
1976	57·0	11·157	12·06	14·25	19,000	2,716 / 3,670	1·805	8·61	4·552	1,497	535·4
1977	73·1	7·630	10·08	12·31	23,177	3,483	1·746	8·57	4·050	1,540	467·7
1978	82·3	8·535	11·32	11·93	26,922	4,553	1·920	8·64	3·851	1,628	402·7
1979	93·6	12·988	12·64	11·39	29,284	5,929	2·122	9·03	3·887	1,762	465·6
1980	100·0	15·127	13·84	11·88	30,436	7,138	2·328	9·82	4·227	1,992	525·6
1981	112·8	13·040	14·65	13·01	35,955	8,113	2·025	10·94	4·556	2,287	444·6
1982	130·7	11·424	12·79	11·90	40,035	9,657	1·749	11·48	4·243	2,364	435·2
1983	164·9	9·60	11·19	10·24	44,539	11,851	1·516	11·55	3·870	2,302	359·9
1984	196·2	9·30	11·29	10·16	51,559	13,984	1·336	11·63	3·791	2,339	316·8
1985	242·2	11·57	11·13	10·11	60,960	17,416	1·298	11·55	3·784	2,463	307·1
1986	300·5	10·33	10·01	9·47	74,695	19,910	1·467	10·16	3·183	2,186	246·8
1987	396·8	9·25	9·36	9·31	91,867	36,410	1·639	9·84	2·941	2,123	236·5
1988	357·0[a]	9·78	9·66[a]	9·12[a]	105,225	...	1·780	10·60	3·124	2,315	228·0

a Provisional.

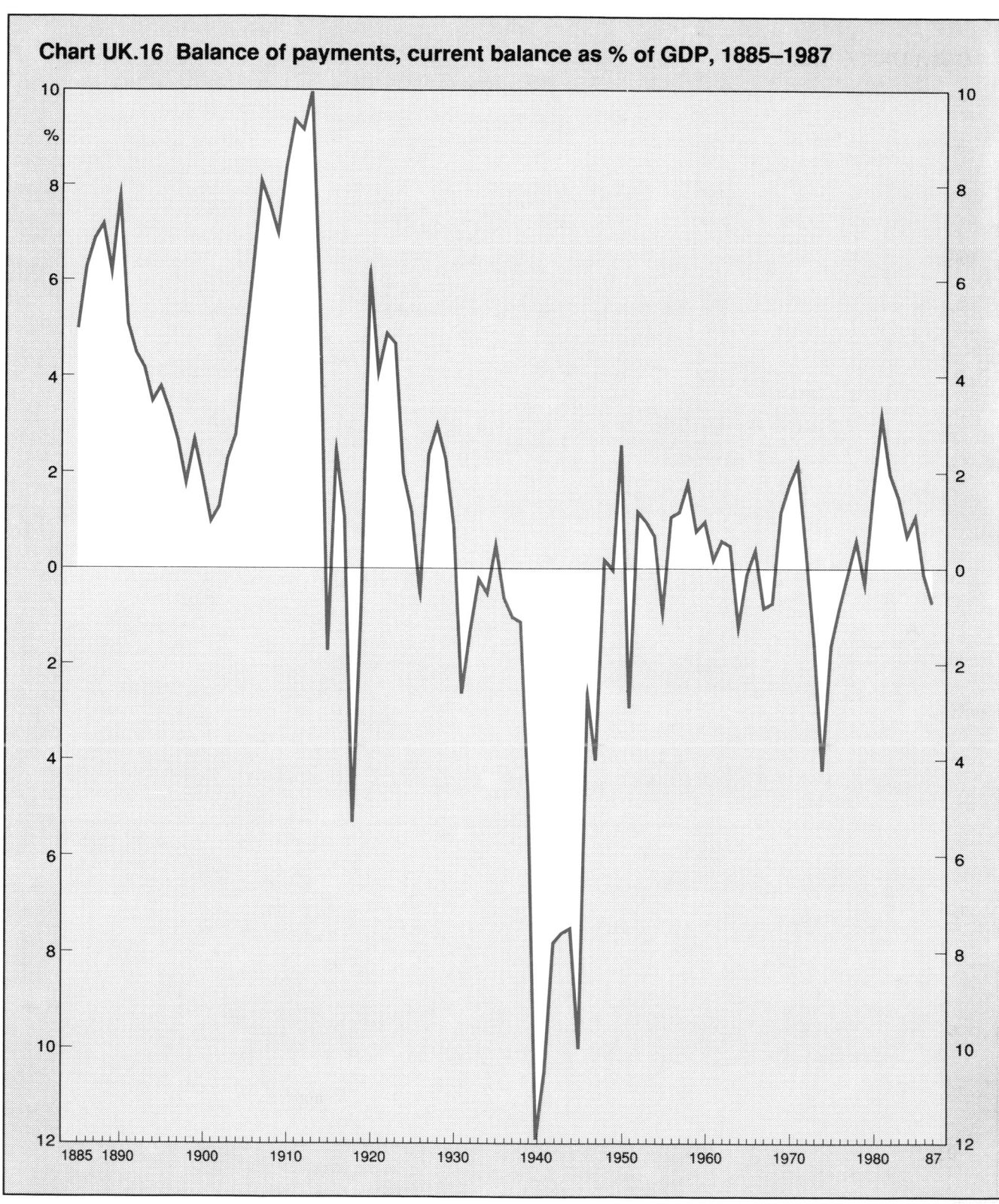

Chart UK.16 Balance of payments, current balance as % of GDP, 1885–1987

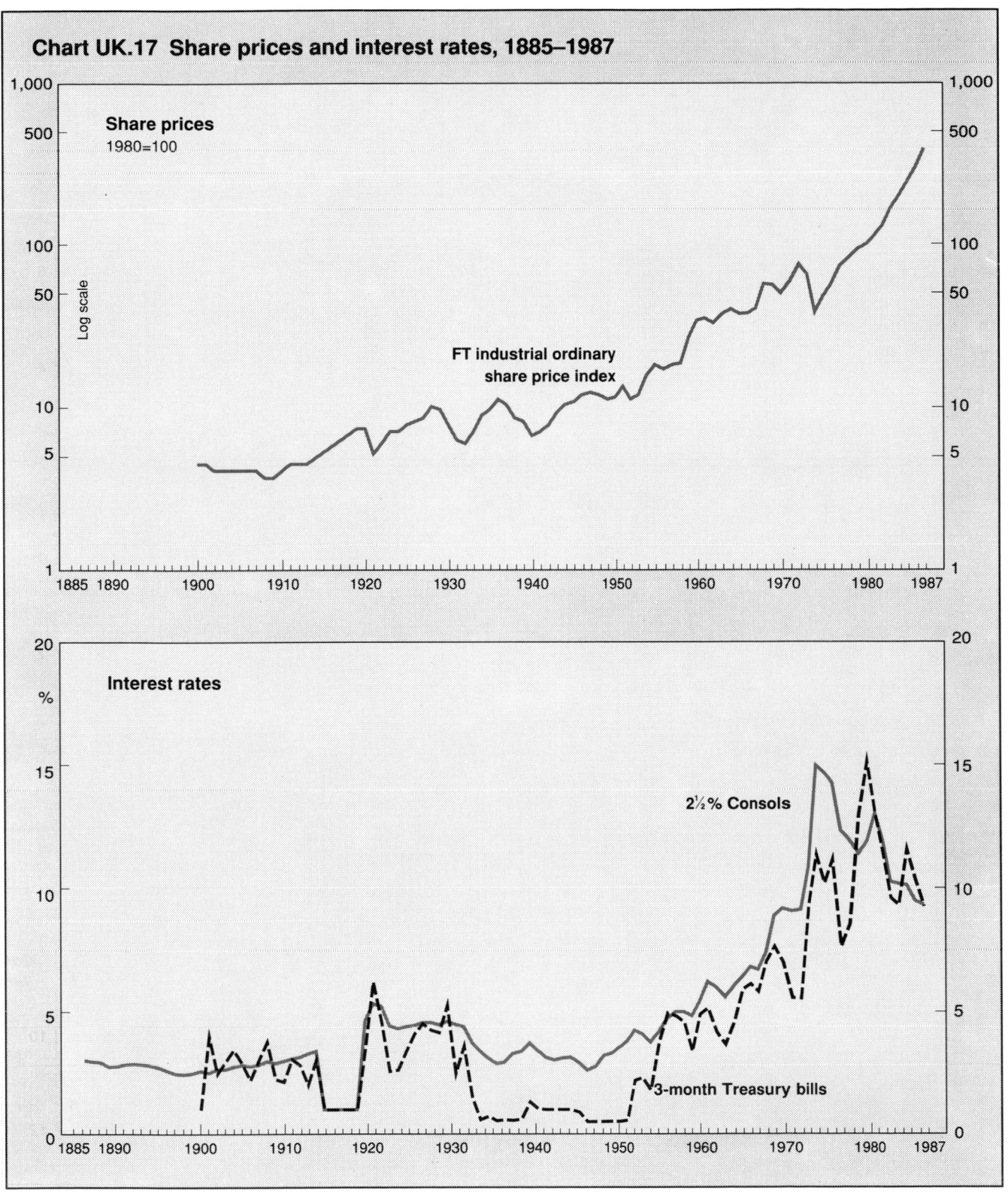

Chart UK.17 Share prices and interest rates, 1885–1987

Share prices
1980=100

Log scale

FT industrial ordinary
share price index

Interest rates

%

2½% Consols

3-month Treasury bills

Table UK.18 Public finance, 1885–1987

	Revenue					Expenditure				
	Taxes on personal income	Taxes on companies	Customs & excise	Social security contributions	Total receipts	Defence	Education	Social services	Debt interest	Total expenditure
					£ mn					
1885	15·2	...	45	...	90	...	...	...	...	...
1886	16·1	...	45	...	91	...	...	...	...	...
1887	14·3	...	46	...	90	...	...	...	...	...
1888	12·5	...	46	...	90	...	...	...	...	...
1889	12·8	...	47	...	95	...	...	...	...	...
1890	13·1	...	49	...	97	34·9	27·3		23·8	130·6
1891	13·8	...	50	...	99	...	...	...	...	...
1892	13·5	...	50	...	98	...	...	...	...	...
1893	15·2	...	50	...	98	...	...	...	...	...
1894	15·6	...	51	...	102	...	...	...	...	...
1895	16·1	...	53	...	109	43·1	39·7		22·7	156·8
1896	16·7	...	53	...	112	...	...	...	...	...
1897	17·3	...	55	...	116	...	...	...	...	...
1898	18·0	...	55	...	118	...	...	...	...	...
1899	18·8	...	61	...	130	...	...	...	...	...
1900	26·9	...	65	...	140	134·9	50·6		19·6	280·8
1901	34·8	...	68	...	153	...	...	...	...	...
1902	38·8	...	72	...	161	...	...	...	...	...
1903	30·8	...	71	...	151	...	...	...	...	...
1904	31·3	...	72	...	153	...	...	...	...	...
1905	31·4	...	71	...	154	63·1	68·3		24·4	241·7
1906	31·6	...	69	...	155	...	...	...	...	...
1907	32·4	...	68	...	157	...	...	...	...	...
1908	33·9	...	63	...	152	...	...	...	...	...
1909	13·3	...	61	...	132	...	...	...	...	...
1910	61·9	...	73	...	204	74·3	89·1		20·2	272·0
1911	44·8	...	72	...	185	...	...	...	...	...
1912	44·8	...	71	...	189	...	...	...	...	...
1913	47·2	...	73	...	198	91·3	100·8		18·7	305·4
1914	69·4	...	81	...	227	...	...	...	...	...
1915	128·3	...	121	...	337	716·6	93·4		57·7	958·1
1916	205·0	140	127	...	573	...	...	...	...	...
1917	239·5	220	110	...	707	1,123	127·8		185·2	1,515
1918	291·2	285	162	...	889	1,956	114·3		264·8	2,427
1919	359·1	290	283	...	1,340	...	...		...	...
1920	394	220	334	...	1,426	519·7	97·4	261·6	324·8	1,592
1921	399	48	324	...	1,125	270·0	106·8	283·0	307·8	1,430
1922	379	21	280	...	914	168·7	97·3	260·2	298·8	1,177
1923	330	23	268	...	837	134·9	91·4	235·4	301·7	1,025
1924	337	19	234	...	799	130·9	92·7	236·6	305·4	1,027
1925	328	14	238	...	812	133·6	97·1	242·4	304·5	1,072
1926	301	9	241	...	806	133·6	99·4	257·3	310·3	1,106
1927	312	2	251	...	843	130·0	101·9	257·4	308·3	1,106
1928	294	2	253	...	836	125·1	104·8	268·9	305·1	1,095
1929	293	2	248	...	815	123·9	108·0	276·5	304·2	1,107
1930	324	3	245	...	858	119·2	113·4	319·8	290·9	1,145
1931	364	3	256	...	851	115·4	115·7	347·1	289·7	1,174
1932	313	2	283	...	827	110·4	110·2	353·4	281·2	1,138
1933	282	2	286	...	809	112·4	107·5	343·9	228·4	1,066
1934	280	2	290	...	805	118·9	111·0	342·1	208·2	1,061
1935	289	1	304	...	845	140·8	118·3	350·2	206·7	1,117
1936	311	1	321	...	897	183·0	125·2	348·2	205·7	1,187
1937	355	3	336	...	949	254·7	131·8	352·2	209·4	1,304
1938	399	24	340	...	1,006	473·2	138·9	377·1	212·5	1,587
	371	15	372	...	904					
1939	411	28	435	...	977	...	...	...	...	...
1940	552	68	511	...	1,275	...	...	...	...	...
1941	741	234	714	...	1,857	...	...	...	...	...
1942	921	344	884	...	2,366	...	...	...	...	...

Table **UK.18 (Continued)** **Public finance, 1885–1987**

	Revenue					Expenditure				
	Taxes on personal income	Taxes on companies	Customs & excise	Social security contributions	Total receipts	Defence	Education	Social services	Debt interest	Total expenditure
					£ mn					
1943	1,184	486	1,020	...	2,926	...	...	...	...	...
1944	1,353	516	1,116	...	3,218	...	...	...	...	...
1945	1,426	474	1,209	...	3,268	...	...	...	...	...
1946	1,337	391	1,393	...	3,942	...	...	...	532	4,587
1947	1,222	286	1,621	...	4,069	...	...	...	562	4,184
1948	1,326	283	1,582	...	4,683	...	...	...	551	4,277
1949	1,495	300	1,654	...	4,972	...	...	...	548	4,450
					£ bn					
1950	1·42	0·26	1·58	0·44	5·02	0·86	0·37	1·21	0·55	4·50
1951	1·50	0·30	1·75	0·45	5·30	1·18	0·40	1·28	0·59	5·27
1952	1·67	0·38	1·76	0·48	5·59	1·57	0·44	1·42	0·65	5·87
1953	1·71	0·23	1·78	0·53	5·68	1·64	0·46	1·53	0·68	6·12
1954	1·76	0·18	1·86	0·53	5·87	1·60	0·50	1·56	0·69	6·04
1955	1·96	0·20	1·99	0·59	6·30	1·54	0·55	1·69	0·77	6·26
1956	2·02	0·19	2·09	0·64	6·58	1·63	0·64	1·82	0·80	6·73
1957	2·19	0·24	2·15	0·66	7·01	1·61	0·73	1·93	0·80	6·99
1958	2·29	0·28	2·19	0·86	7·49	1·54	0·79	2·21	0·89	7·37
1959	2·33	0·26	2·25	0·90	7·83	1·58	0·85	2·37	0·91	7·82
1960	2·29	0·26	2·37	0·91	8·10	1·63	0·92	2·49	1·02	8·34
1961	2·57	0·32	2·54	1·07	8·91	1·73	1·01	2·72	1·10	9·11
1962	2·85	0·38	2·69	1·20	9·77	1·84	1·17	2·89	1·11	9·78
1963	2·82	0·39	2·72	1·30	10·00	1·89	1·28	3·21	1·20	10·42
1964	2·94	0·41	3·04	1·44	10·87	1·99	1·42	3·43	1·26	11·22
1965	3·37	0·47	3·43	1·68	12·22	2·11	1·59	3·91	1·35	12·38
1966	4·24	0·16	3·62	1·80	13·45	2·20	1·70	4·21	1·47	13·45
1967	3·84	1·17	3·73	1·91	14·97	2·41	1·89	4·72	1·57	15·37
1968	4·37	1·29	4·24	2·16	16·91	2·44	2·10	5·29	1·79	17·10
1969	4·92	1·39	4·76	2·24	19·01	2·29	2·25	5·67	1·93	18·01
1970	5·49	1·67	5·13	2·66	21·21	2·46	2·53	6·33	2·03	20·91
1971	6·21	1·54	5·35	2·83	22·58	2·76	2·90	7·02	2·09	23·52
1972	6·35	1·44	5·67	3·34	23·98	3·06	3·41	8·24	2·28	26·44
1973	7·03	1·89	6·57	3·94	27·00	3·47	4·00	9·15	2·67	30·52
1974	9·56	2·85	7·57	5·00	33·75	4·08	4·65	11·60	3·49	39·21
1975	14·32	2·32	9·08	6·85	42·96	5·17	6·63	15·43	4·13	51·48
1976	16·71	2·15	10·65	8·42	49·98	6·21	7·32	18·93	5·29	58·52
1977	17·42	2·99	12·42	9·50	56·13	6·86	8·34	21·97	6·29	62·03
1978	18·77	3·59	13·72	10·10	62·40	7·60	9·15	25·74	7·09	72·38
1979	20·34	4·12	18·35	11·53	75·68	8·97	10·31	30·08	8·67	85·70
1980	24·31	4·84	22·56	13·94	91·71	11·44	12·75	37·07	10·87	104·20
1981	27·88	4·32	25·81	15·92	106·15	12·64	14·31	44·48	12·70	117·07
1982	30·05	5·24	28·64	18·10	117·51	14·45	15·28	50·49	13·97	128·71
1983	31·64	5·71	31·61	20·78	125·99	15·84	16·32	55·32	14·19	138·41
1984	32·98	6·88	34·99	22·31	134·48	17·16	17·08	59·08	15·76	147·21
1985	35·17	9·05	38·61	24·19	147·14	18·26	17·40	64·39	17·47	157·38
1986	37·62	11·77	42·27	26·03	153·81	19·11	19·35	69·23	17·19	161·83
1987	40·30	13·46	45·41	28·45	165·07	18·91	21·20	73·12	17·67	168·05

Table UK.19 Transport and energy, 1900–87

	Motor vehicle licences current		Railways		Airways	Energy consumption		
	Goods	Private				Coal	Petroleum (primary fuel input basis)	Natural gas
	'000		bn passenger km	bn freight net ton km	bn passenger km	mn tons coal or coal equiv.		
1900	...	...	...	...	...	165·9	1·5	...
1901	...	...	...	...	...	162·3	...	...
1902	...	...	...	...	...	167·7	...	...
1903	...	...	...	...	...	167·5	...	...
1904	4	8	...	...	...	167·4	...	...
1905	9	16	...	...	...	170·0	...	...
1906	12	23	...	...	...	175·5	...	...
1907	14	32	...	...	...	184·1	...	...
1908	18	41	...	...	...	177·7	...	...
1909	22	48	...	...	...	179·2	...	...
1910	30	53	...	...	...	181·4	2·0	...
1911	40	72	...	...	...	186·2	...	...
1912	53	88	...	...	...	180·9	...	...
1913	64	106	...	...	...	193·8	...	...
1914	82	132	...	...	...	188·3	...	...
1915	85	139	...	...	...	196·9	...	...
1916	82	142	...	...	...	205·5	...	...
1917	64	110	...	...	...	203·7	...	...
1918	41	78	...	...	...	187·8	...	...
1919	62	110	...	...	...	182·2	...	...
1920	101	187	30·9	31·4	...	186·4	...	...
1921	128	243	26·9	21·7	...	130·9	3·6	...
1922	151	315	28·5	27·5	...	166·1	4·1	...
1923	173	384	28·6	31·0	...	177·5	5·2	...
1924	203	474	29·9	31·2	...	184·5	6·0	...
1925	224	580	30·4	30·0	0·004	175·9	6·0	...
1926	257	684	27·0	23·0	0·006	123·0	7·6	...
1927	283	787	29·4	30·9	0·007	183·2	8·0	...
1928	306	885	29·9	29·0	0·010	170·4	8·1	...
1929	330	981	30·4	30·8	0·011	180·2	8·1	...
1930	348	1,056	29·4	29·1	0·010	171·1	9·1	...
1931	361	1,083	27·8	26·7	0·011	158·8	9·0	...
1932	370	1,128	26·7	24·4	0·026	156·1	9·1	...
1933	387	1,203	28·2	24·6	0·035	155·9	9·8	...
1934	413	1,308	29·8	26·5	0·047	167·5	10·4	...
1935	444	1,505	30·9	26·8	0·068	172·4	10·6	...
1936	471	1,675	32·0	28·5	0·066	182·4	11·0	...
1937	490	1,834	33·3	30·1	0·080	189·0	11·5	...
1938	506	1,984	30·6	26·6	0·086	178·5	12·6	...
1939	501	2,077	...	...	0·091	186·4	13·3	...
1940	455	1,454	...	...	0·068	197·5	11·7	...
1941	466	1,539	...	...	0·092	198·5	13·3	...
1942	466	883	...	39·0	0·164	199·7	13·1	...
1943	463	736	...	39·8	0·201	192·3	14·3	...
1944	463	773	...	40·0	0·288	189·9	20·9	...
1945	488	1,521	...	36·0	0·486	181·8	16·5	...
1946	475	1,807	47·0	33·7	0·584	189·1	13·9	...
1947	687	1,983	37·0	33·0	0·710	187·5	18·3	...
1948	788	2,003	34·2	35·4	0·892	195·3	19·0	...
1949	866	2,179	34·0	36·0	0·989	196·8	20·2	...
1950	920	2,308	32·5	36·2	1·278	204·3	22·9	...
1951	959	2,433	33·5	37·4	1·714	209·5	25·8	...
1952	990	2,565	32·9	36·6	1·999	207·4	26·9	...
1953	1,023	2,825	33·1	37·2	2·308	208·9	29·2	...
1954	1,061	3,173	33·3	36·1	2·438	215·8	32·4	...
1955	1,139	3,610	32·7	34·9	2·898	216·9	36·0	...
1956	1,206	3,981	34·0	35·1	3·383	217·4	39·1	...
1957	1,250	4,283	36·4	34·1	3·897	210·9	38·2	...

	Motor vehicle licences current		Railways		Airways	Energy consumption		
	Goods	Private				Coal	Petroleum (primary fuel input basis)	Natural gas
	'000		bn passenger km	bn freight net ton km	bn passenger km	mn tons coal or coal equiv.		
1958	1,304	4,651	35·6	30·1	4·137	201·8	49·1	0·1
1959	1,365	5,087	35·8	29·0	4·973	189·6	58·3	0·1
1960	1,439	5,657	34·7	30·5	6·371	198·6	68·1	0·1
1961	1,496	6,118	33·9	28·8	7·290	193·0	73·4	0·1
1962	1,563	6,710	31·7	26·3	7·836	194·0	80·8	0·1
1963	1,625	7,552	30·9	25·2	8·765	196·9	87·9	0·2
1964	1,677	8,441	32·0	26·2	10·339	189·6	96·1	0·4
1965	1,705	9,136	30·1	25·2	11·937	187·5	106·2	1·3
1966	1,682	9,758	29·7	23·6	13·360	176·8	114·8	1·2
1967	1,736	10,563	29·1	21·4	14·069	165·8	122·6	2·1
1968	1,682	11,087	28·7	22·7	14·095	167·3	129·4	4·8
1969	1,681	11,514	29·6	23·2	16·261	164·1	139·6	9·4
1970	1,672	11,828	30·4	24·5	17·432	156·9	150·0	17·9
1971	1,674	12,384	30·1	24·3	18·664	139·3	151·2	28·8
1972	1,937	12,770	29·1	21·0	22·169	122·4	162·2	40·9
1973	1,988[a]	13,231[a]	29·8	22·7	26·187	133·0	164·2	44·2
1974	2,041	13,708	30·9	21·6	25·397	117·9	152·5	52·9
1975	2,023	13,737	30·3	20·8	27·544	120·0	136·5	55·4
1976	2,042	14,077	28·4	20·6	31·078	122·0	134·2	58·8
1977	. . .	. . .	29·3	20·3	31·871	122·7	136·6	62·8
1978	2,011	14,148	30·0	20·0	40·442	119·9	139·3	65·1
1979	2,081	14,665	30·7	19·9	47·085	129·6	139·0	71·1
1980	2,075	15,137	30·3	17·6	50·164	120·8	121·4	71·1
1981	2,070	15,308	29·7	17·5	52·210	118·2	110·9	72·1
1982	2,096	15,691	27·2	15·9	46·404	110·7	111·1	71·7
1983	2,209	15,995	29·5	17·1	43·887	111·5	106·1	74·8
1984	2,277	16,486	29·8	12·7	48·235	79·0	135·2	76·5
1985	2,317	16,858	29·7	15·4	51·437	105·3	115·0	82·3
1986	2,388	17,396	30·8	16·5	51·401	113·5	112·6	83·6
1987	2,483	17,835	32·2	17·3	59·887	116·2	109·3	85·9

a   See notes on p. 70.

Sources

(For sources used in specific tables, see Notes.)

1 *Annual Abstract of Statistics*, Central Statistical Office, HMSO, London.

2 *Annual Statement of Trade* (now *Overseas Trade Statistics*), Department of Trade and Industry, London.

3 *Bankers' Almanac*, annual, West Sussex.

4 *Bank of England Quarterly Bulletin*, June 1970.

5 Bank of Japan, *100 Year Statistics of the Japanese Economy*, Tokyo, 1966.

6 Bowley, A.L., *Wages and Income in the UK since 1860*, Cambridge University Press, 1937.

7 *British Business*, April 15, 1983, Department of Trade and Industry, London.

8 *The British Economy, Key Statistics 1900–70*, London & Cambridge Economic Service, 1972.

9 *British Labour Statistics, Historical Abstract 1886–1968*, Department of Employment, HMSO, London, 1971.

10 *British Labour Statistics Year Book*, Department of Employment, HMSO, London, 1972–76.

11 Capie, Forrest and Webber, Alan, *A Monetary History of the United Kingdom, 1870–1982*, Vol. I, George Allen & Unwin, London, 1985.

12 *Economic Trends Annual Supplement*, 1989 edition, Central Statistical Office, HMSO, London.

13 *Economic Trends*, September 1983, Central Statistical Office, HMSO, London.

14 *Economic Trends*, September 1984, Central Statistical Office, HMSO, London.

15 *Employment Gazette*, monthly, Department of Employment, London.

16 Feinstein, C.H. *National Income, Expenditure and Output of the United Kingdom 1855–1965*, Cambridge University Press, 1972.

17 Feinstein, C.H. and Pollard, Sidney (eds), *Studies in Capital Formation in the United Kingdom, 1750–1920*, Oxford University Press, Oxford, 1988.

18 *Financial Statistics*, monthly, Central Statistical Office, HMSO, London.

19 *Financial Statistics Explanatory Handbook*, Central Statistical Office, HMSO, London.

20 Gandhi, J.K.S., PhD thesis, Cambridge University, unpublished.

21 *International Financial Statistics Year Book*, United Nations, New York, 1978.

22 Johnson, H.G. 'British Monetary Statistics', *Economica*, New series, Vol. XXVI, No. 101, London School of Economics, 1959.

23 Kendall, M.G. (ed), *Sources and Nature of the Statistics of the United Kingdom*, Vol. II, Royal Statistical Society, London, 1951.

24 Macmillan Report, *Finance and Industry* (Cmd. 3897), HMSO, London, 1930–31.

25 Mitchell, B.R., *European Historical Statistics, 1750–1975*, 2nd rev. edn., Macmillan, London, 1980.

26 *Monthly Digest of Statistics*, Central Statistical Office, HMSO, London.

27 *Monthly Digest of Statistics Supplement, Definitions and Explanatory Notes*, Central Statistical Office, HMSO, London.

28 *National Accounts Statistics, Sources and Methods*. Central Statistical Office, HMSO, London, 1968.

29 *National Income and Expenditure*, 1983 and earlier years, Central Statistical Office, HMSO, London.

30 *Overseas Trade Statistics Annual Supplement*, 1988, Department of Trade and Industry, London.

31 Peacock, Alan T. and Wiseman, Jack, *The Growth of Public Expenditure in the United Kingdom*, George Allen & Unwin (now Unwin Hyman Ltd), 1967.

32 Prest, A.R., *Consumers' Expenditure in the United Kingdom 1900–1919*, Cambridge University Press, 1954.

33 Registrar General's *Statistical Review of England and Wales*, Part II, Population, annual (now replaced by *Population Trends*, Office of Population Censuses and Surveys, London).

34 *Reserves and Liabilities* (Cmd. 8354), HMSO, London, 1951.

35 Schlote, Werner, *British Overseas Trade*, translated by W.O. Henderson and W.H. Chaloner, Blackwell, Oxford, 1952.

36 Shinjo, H., *History of the Yen: 100 Years Japanese Money Economy*, Kobe Institute, 1962.

37 Society of Motor Manufacturers & Traders, *The Motor Industry of Great Britain*, SMMT, London, 1926, 1947.

38 *Standard Industrial Classification Revised 1980*, HMSO, London.

39 *Statistical Abstract of the United Kingdom* (now *Annual Abstract of Statistics*), HMSO, London.

40 Stone, Richard and Rowe, D.A., *The Measurement of Consumers' Expenditure and Behaviour in the United Kingdom, 1920–38*, Vols. I and II, Cambridge University Press, 1953 and 1966.

41 *Trade and Industry*, February 1978, Department of Trade and Industry, London.

42 *Transport Statistics Great Britain 1977–87* and earlier issues, Department of Transport, HMSO, London.

43 *United Kingdom Balance of Payments* (the CSO 'Pink Book'), Central Statistical Office, HMSO, London.

44 *United Kingdom National Accounts* (the CSO 'Blue Book'), formerly *National Income and Expenditure*, Central Statistical Office, HMSO, London.

45 *United Nations Statistical Year Book*, New York, 1965.

Notes

Table UK.1 Gross domestic product at current prices

Sources: 16, 17, 44

Estimates published by the Central Statistical Office (CSO) have been used from 1948. Estimates published in **16** are given for the years 1920 (second line) to 1947 and for 1885–1920 (first line) for all columns except gross domestic fixed capital formation, changes in stocks and gross domestic product. For the latter period, revised estimates of gross domestic fixed capital formation and changes in stocks, published in **17**, have been included and the figures for gross domestic product have been adjusted to take account of these revisions. There was also a change in coverage of gross domestic fixed capital formation in 1948 and a consequent change in consumers' expenditure. For details see **44** and notes to Table UK.5. Southern Ireland is included in the figures up to 1920 (first line).

This table measures the 'money' national output from the expenditure side. For details of coverage of individual column headings and methodology see **28**, **29** and **44**.

Table UK.2 Gross domestic product at constant prices

Sources: 16, 17, 44

The constant price estimates published by the CSO have been used from 1948. Figures for the period 1885–1947 are based on estimates given in **16** and **17** which were roughly converted to 1985 prices. Each category of expenditure has been re-referenced to 1985 independently, however, and this means that the total for gross domestic product at constant (1985) prices may not equal the sum of the component categories; this will be the case up to 1977. For further details see **44**.

The revised estimates for gross domestic fixed capital formation and changes in stocks given in **17** have also been used in this table and the figures for gross domestic product adjusted accordingly. The change in coverage of gross domestic capital formation in 1948 also affects the figures in this table (see notes to Table UK.1).

Southern Ireland is included up to 1920 (first line).

Average estimate: all three measures of gross domestic product (based on expenditure, on income and on output) should agree. Problems of measurement, however, lead to divergences in the estimates. The average estimates are the best central estimates both of the level of national accounts and of changes over time. They are given in this table as they are used to compute rates of growth shown in later tables. For further details see **44**, p. 126.

Table UK.3 Output by industry

Sources: 16, 29, 44

The CSO estimates have been used from 1948. For 1885–1947 estimates from **16** have been linked to the official series.

From 1978, the indices have been weighted on the basis of net output in 1980. For earlier years (1948–77) successive weights based on 1948, 1954, 1958, 1963 and 1970 have been used. See **29**, 1983. The current series are classified on the basis of the Standard Industrial Classification (SIC), Revised 1980, described in **38**. The main difference between the previous classification (1968) and the 1980 classification is that some industries formerly classified under 'Mining and quarrying' and under 'Manufacturing' are now grouped into one category under the title 'Energy and water supply'. For further details see **29**, 1983.

For the period 1913–47 the data are based on 1948 classification and weights. For the period 1885–1913 the classification is broadly comparable with later years. For further details see **16**, Chapter 10. Two figures are given for 1920, the first line including and the second excluding Southern Ireland.

For details of coverage of individual column headings and methodology, see **28**, **29**, **44** and Studies in Official Statistics No. 25, *The Measurement of Changes in Production*, HMSO, London, 1976.

Table UK.4 Industrial production

Sources: 1, 8, 12, 14, 25, 37

For all series, annual figures from 1946 relate to 52 week periods.

Coal: production of deep mined and open cast coal. Includes coal consumed by the colliery and supplied to ancillary works, free coal and concessionary coal; excludes screening and washing losses. Up to 1937, includes coal produced at quarries other than open cast workings; in 1938 this output amounted to 23,352 tons.

Crude steel: steel ingots and steel for castings. From January 1974, the European Community definition of usable steel has been used; the difference is minor.

Cars and commercial vehicles: chassis delivered as such are included; armoured fighting vehicles, battery driven electric vehicles and three-wheeled vehicles are excluded. Up to 1939, estimates by the Society of Motor Manufacturers and Traders, **37**. For 1927–34 the figures are for years ended September 30.

Chemicals and allied industries: index for the output of chemical and allied industries (SIC division 2, group 25) in the index of production and construction industries. The index was rebased in 1983; for details of minor changes made to the classification see **38**.

Cotton cloth: cloth made for sale including industrial use; represents the cloth in the loom state before undergoing finishing processes. Up to 1937, estimates from Census of Production data.

Manmade fibres and mixtures: cloth made wholly from continuous filament and spun rayon, nylon and other manmade fibres and mixture cloth. Up to 1937, estimates from Census of Production data.

Woollen and worsted woven fabrics: total deliveries of all fabrics woven in the wool textile industry except blankets. Includes mixtures and manmade fibres classified as wool or worsted. Up to 1937, estimated from Census of Production data, and figures are for production not deliveries.

Electricity generated: total generated for public supply excluding railway and transport authorities. For the years 1920–48, covers authorised undertakings excluding railway and transport undertakings. Northern Ireland and Scotland partly estimated by London and Cambridge Economic Service – see **8**.

Up to 1920 (first line) figures are for sales of electricity.

Table UK.5 Gross domestic fixed capital formation

Sources: **16, 17, 29, 44** and unpublished figures from the CSO.

From 1965, industries are classified as far as possible according to the SIC, Revised 1980. For the years before 1978, totals differ from the sum of their components for the same reasons as explained in notes to Table UK.1.

Agriculture, forestry and fishing: from 1965, changes in the value of breeding livestock are included in capital formation figures.

Distribution and business services: expenditure on assets for leasing other than ships is included in this category. An analysis by user industry in current prices is given from 1975 in **29**, 1983 and **44**; see tabular summary.

Percentage of total capital expenditure on assets for leasing by user industry

	Agriculture, forestry & fishing	Mfg	Energy & construction	Transport	Other industries & services	Gen. govt
1975	2·8	54·3	4·3	14·3	11·4	12·9
1979	3·7	34·0	11·7	21·3	24·5	4·8
1983	6·6	37·8	5·5	10·2	32·9	7·0
1987	6·1	21·9	5·2	20·3	40·0	6·4

Other services: Classes 91–99 of the SIC, Revised 1980, covering public administration and defence, education, health and other public services. Previously classified as 'Social and public services' but some changes in coverage have been made in recent years; some expenditure pre-

viously included in current expenditure is now treated as capital expenditure. For further details see **44**.

Dwellings: from 1948, all expenditure on improvements, including central heating, is included; this was previously included in 'Consumers' expenditure'.

Other new buildings and works: includes the transfer costs of land and buildings and purchases less sales of land and existing buildings. Expenditure on new buildings and works for civil accommodation overseas is now included, together with expenditure on minor road improvements (both previously treated as 'Current expenditure').

Vehicles: includes railway rolling stock, buses and coaches, motor vehicles and aircraft.

Plant and machinery: includes changes in the value of breeding livestock.

For further details of each category see **44**.

For the years 1920–65, industry and asset data are based on Feinstein, **16**. There have been some revisions to the total for gross fixed capital formation since Feinstein's estimates were published, but revisions have not been made to the industry and asset data by the CSO before 1965. The differences in the totals are relatively minor. Feinstein's estimates by type of asset have been roughly adjusted to the revised totals but the industry estimates are unadjusted.

Highways and street lighting have been deducted from Feinstein's estimates of total expenditure on 'Transport and communication' and added to 'Other services' to accord with current definitions.

For the years 1885–1919, figures are based on data given in **17** and roughly converted to 1985 prices. It has not been possible in the industry classification to show manufacturing, distribution, mining and quarrying, construction, and gas, electricity and water separately. Estimates at 1900 prices are given for each of these industry groups in **17** but the estimates include Southern Ireland and no satisfactory link was possible with later figures which do not include Southern Ireland. The series was therefore linked at 1920 using estimates (excluding Southern Ireland) from **16** where the above industry groups are combined. For further details of the basis of the estimates see **16** and **17**.

Table UK.6 Personal and company income

Sources: **12, 16, 44**

Wages and salaries: include pay in cash and kind of H M Forces. For the years 1885–1920 (first line) Southern Ireland is included.

Other income: includes income from self-employment (before providing for depreciation and stock appreciation), rent, dividends and net interest including imputed rent of owner occupied dwellings; employers' contributions to national insurance and other pension funds, current transfers to charities from companies, national insurance benefits and other current grants from general government.

Taxes, etc: includes taxes on income, national insurance contributions from individuals and net transfers abroad. It does not include a new item which has recently been included in deductions from income – miscellaneous current transfers. This covers certain compulsory fees and fines such as fees for passports and driving licences. These were formerly treated as a tax on expenditure. Figures for miscellaneous current transfers from 1955 (they were nil or negligible before this date) are shown in the following table.

	£ mn		£ mn		£ mn
1955	5	1966	20	1977	136
1956	6	1967	22	1978	151
1957	7	1968	27	1979	134
1958	8	1969	33	1980	169
1959	10	1970	37	1981	177
1960	10	1971	41	1982	187
1961	12	1972	46	1983	222
1962	13	1973	55	1984	217
1963	15	1974	57	1985	229
1964	17	1975	73	1986	262
1965	18	1976	118	1987	317

For further information see **44**, p. 128.

To be consistent with the system of standardised national accounts, miscellaneous current transfers should be included in 'other income' as well as being deducted with taxes, etc, to give personal disposable income.

Personal disposable income: before providing for depreciation and stock appreciation.

Savings ratio: savings as a percentage of personal disposable income.

Gross trading profits of companies: before providing for depreciation and stock appreciation. Estimates of gross trading profits from 1969 onwards have been made by using Inland Revenue corporation tax data. For further details see **29**, 1983 p. 104.

Gross trading surpluses of public corporations and government enterprises: for details of public corporations currently included see **44**, p. 129.

For the period 1889–1945 estimates are from **16**.

Table UK.7 Consumers' expenditure

Sources: **16, 29, 44**

The classification of consumers' expenditure was changed in 1983, and most of the data have been revised by the CSO back to 1948. The figures given in this table are classified by type of commodity and include expenditure of resident and non-resident households and individuals in the UK. 'Other services' includes adjustment for international travel and for final expenditure by private non-profit-making bodies. For further details of commodity classification and treatment of private non-profit-making bodies see **44** and **13**.

For the period 1900–47, estimates from **15** have been linked to the official estimates and roughly converted to 1985 prices. The conversion to 1985 prices reflects, of course, current tax rates which probably have risen more on some commodities than on others (eg alcoholic drink and tobacco). Some differences in coverage in Feinstein's estimates should be noted.

(a) For 1900–47, 'Rent, rates and water charges' include occupiers' costs of maintenance, repairs and improvements.
(b) For 1900–19, household textiles and hardware are included in the figures for 'Durable goods' and not in 'Other goods'.

For full details see **16**.

For 1948–51, expenditure on foods includes catering expenditure; from 1952, it is included in 'Other services'.

For 1900–20 (first line), Southern Ireland is included.

Table UK.8 Prices

Sources: **7, 8, 12, 16, 25, 30**

Producer prices: the name of this index was changed from the former 'wholesale price index' in 1983 and the series was revised back to 1974. The index was rebased recently on 1985 but it has been converted arithmetically to 1980 = 100 for this table. The index was reclassified in 1983 in accordance with the Standard Industrial Classification 1980 and this affected the two indices given in the table: mineral-oil refining is no longer included with 'materials and fuels purchased by manufacturing industry' and petroleum products (rather than crude oil) are now a component of the input index (first column in the table). The indices are based on average prices for the year excluding value-added tax. The weights given to each commodity are revised from time to time to take account of the changing pattern of industry's sales and purchases. For further details see **7**.

For the period 1948–54, the index has a less comprehensive coverage; in particular, the first column excludes purchases by the food and drink industries.

For the period 1900–48, the Board of Trade index for all articles was used. The index covers goods at all stages of processing but raw materials predominate. For 1885–99, the index is based on figures given in **25**.

Consumer prices: the 'All items' index measures changes in the average level of prices of commodities and services purchased by the majority of households in the UK. From February 1975, the weights used to combine the items in the index have been revised each year on the basis of the

Family Expenditure Survey for the year ended the previous June. Weights for previous periods are as follows.

1963–74   Weights were derived from the Family Expenditure Survey for three years ended the previous June adjusted to correspond with levels of prices ruling in January of the current year.

1962–63   Weights were derived from the Family Expenditure Survey for the three years July 1958–June 1961, adjusted to correspond with the level of prices ruling in January 1962.

1956–62 (Jan)   Weights were based on expenditure in 1953/54 adjusted to correspond with the level of prices in January 1962.

Coverage of the index in the period 1900–52 was less comprehensive than for the current index. For further details see **8**.

For the years 1885–99, the all items index is based on the retail price index given in **16**.

Food: the current index is compiled in the same way as the 'All items' index and has been linked to the series in **8**. For the period 1900–14 the index is weighted on the basis of London urban working class family budgets in 1904 and covers London prices only.

Durable goods; Clothing and footwear; Housing: consumers' average value indices and not the retail price index. These are obtained by dividing the estimates of expenditure on these commodity groups for the year in question at current prices by a corresponding total revalued at 1980 prices. The coverage of the indices is therefore affected by the coverage of the expenditure series; see notes to Table UK.6.

Exports and imports average value indices: current weighted indices obtained by dividing values at current prices by values at constant prices (volume) for the year in question. For the period, 1885–99, the indices are based on estimates given in **16** which are calculated in the same way.

Terms of trade: the export average value index as a percentage of the import average value index.

Table UK.9   Population

Sources: **1, 16, 32, 33, 40** and unpublished data from the Offices of Population, Censuses and Surveys.

Total home population: persons usually resident in the UK including those temporarily absent; overseas visitors and those temporarily present excluded. The figures are on this basis from 1971; previously, overseas visitors were included and absent residents excluded.

Figures for 1885–1947 from **16** and **33**.

Up to 1919 Southern Ireland is included. The 1920 figure

for total population including Southern Ireland is 46·82 m; see **16**.

The figures for 1915–20 and 1940–50 include members of the armed forces serving overseas and merchant seamen and exclude foreign forces in the UK.

Births: for England and Wales, number of births occurring in year; for Scotland and Northern Ireland, births registered in year. Up to 1938, the figures are for births occurring in Scotland and Northern Ireland and for births registered in England and Wales. Includes Southern Ireland up to 1919; the 1920 figure for births including Southern Ireland is 1,194,000.

Geographical distribution: the South East region defined in terms of new counties after the local government reorganisation on April 1, 1974 consists of:

Bedfordshire, Berkshire, Buckinghamshire, Essex, Greater London, Hampshire, Hertfordshire, Kent, Oxfordshire, Surrey, East and West Sussex, Isle of Wight.

For 1950–64, London and the South Eastern region were combined with the South to give a close approximation to the current South East. London and the South East included:

part of Essex, part of Hertfordshire, Kent, London, administrative county of Middlesex, Surrey, East and West Sussex.

and the South included:

Berkshire, Buckinghamshire, Dorset, Oxfordshire, Isle of Wight, Southampton (renamed Hampshire in 1959).

Significant boundary changes also took place in 1931. For further details see **33** for that year. Figures for 1940–47 are for civilians only for the South East.

Table UK.10   Education

Sources: **1, 25, 39**

Figures for pupils at kindergarten, elementary and secondary schools currently cover all schools (public, grant-aided and private) in the UK. All pupils are included whether full- or part-time.

Kindergarten: children aged 2–4 years.
Elementary: children aged 5–14 years.
Secondary: pupils aged 15 and over.

The age classification is at August each year from 1980. Before 1980 it was at January each year; two figures are given for 1980.

For the period 1885–1954 (first line) figures are for Great Britain only. Up to 1938, figures refer to children within the authority of the Board of Education. Dates of returns varied and refer to a date within the year stated or to twelve months ending in that year.

The minimum school leaving age was raised to 15 years in

1947 and to 16 in 1972. Earlier data, however, are for pupils aged 5–14 years and this classification has been used throughout in this table.

Post-secondary: currently includes full-time, sandwich, part-time day and evening students at major public sector and assisted establishments of further education. Also includes students at adult education centres in England and Wales. Autumn term each year. From 1977 includes teacher training colleges in Scotland and Northern Ireland. Students at Colleges of Advanced Technology are not includes.

1910–37: figures are for England and Wales only.

Higher education: full-time students at universities in the UK excluding the Open University; academic years beginning in the year shown. Before 1948, the figures are for Great Britain only.

Table UK.11   Labour market: employment

Sources: **1, 9, 10, 15, 16**

Employed labour force: includes employees in employment, self-employed, HM forces, and those on work-related government training programmes; mid-year count. For further information see **15**, August, 1988. Current figures (from 1971) are based on Census of Employment data. For the years 1959–70, figures are consistent with Census of Employment data (see **15**, March and October 1975). For 1948–59, estimates are based on counts of national insurance cards. For 1920–47, data are taken from **16**.

Employment by sector: from 1948 (second line) figures are for employees in employment. Industries are classified according to the 1980 Standard Industrial Classification (SIC) from 1979 (second line); the 1968 SIC for 1959–79 (first line); and the 1948 SIC for 1948–59. In the 1980 classification, mining and quarrying is included with gas, electricity and water under the heading of 'Energy and water supply'; separate figures for employment in mining and quarrying are not published for the UK (although estimates for Great Britain are given in **1**).

Employees in employment series have been used for this table although in some ways it would be more useful to know the total numbers employed in each industry (that is, including the self-employed). An industrial analysis of the self-employed is published from time to time in **15**, but the employees in employment series is published annually in **1** and can be more easily kept up to date.

Figures are currently mid-year estimates; for 1949–59 (first line) they are to end-May; from 1959 (second line) and in 1948, they are to end-June.

Self-employed: an industrial analysis of the self-employed is given in **15** for Great Britain. A summary for the last few years is given in the following table.

	Mfg	Services	Agriculture
		June each year; '000	
1971	129	1,200	282
1973	133	1,138	259
1975	140	1,183	247
1977	142	1,155	254
1979	140	1,102	257
1981	146	1,273	250
1983	154	1,386	246
1985	206	1,624	249
1987	246	1,767	245

Table UK.12   Labour market: other indicators

Sources: **1, 8, 9, 10, 12, 15, 16**

Output per person employed: from 1960 the published series given in **12** and **15** have been used. The series are calculated by dividing total output by the employed labour force including the self-employed. Part-time working or hours of work are not taken into account. Similarly, output per person employed in manufacturing is obtained by dividing output in manufacturing by the number employed in manufacturing. (The current series is based on the 1980 SIC; see notes to Table UK.11 for the basis of numbers employed in earlier years.) For years before 1960, data given in Table UK.3 and Table UK.11 have been used to construct the indices. (Employees in employment figures have been adjusted to take account of the self-employed.)

Average weekly hours worked: From 1983, the series is for full-time male manual workers on adult rates in manufacturing industries. Before 1983, the figures included certain other industries (mining and quarrying, building, transport, public utilities, government industrial establishments, laundries and dry cleaning and railways). For the years 1949–80, the series was for adult (over 18 years) male full-time manual workers; railways were excluded. Throughout the series is the average of actual hours worked, including overtime, in October each year. For 1940–45, the figures are for July. From 1983, industries are classified according to the 1980 SIC; the 1968 SIC from 1969 (second line) to 1982; and the 1958 SIC for 1959–69 (first line).

Average weekly earnings: the coverage of this series is the same as for hours worked. Average earnings include bonus and overtime payments before any deductions for one week in October.

Figures up to 1937 are based on **6** and are taken from **8**. They include adult males in manufacturing, coal mining, agriculture, building, transport and public utilities.

Unemployment: the current series (from 1971) is based on records of claimants at unemployment offices. It therefore excludes unemployed people not claiming benefit but includes the severely disabled unemployed, not previously included. The figures are annual averages and include school leavers.

The collection and presentation of UK unemployment statistics have been revised a number of times in recent years. The main changes and their estimated effects are listed below.

- October 1979: fortnightly attendance at unemployment offices introduced. The effect was to add 20,000 both to the unemployment count used at the time and the claimant figures introduced later.
- November 1981: higher long-term rate of supplementary benefit introduced for men over 60 years of age who had been on supplementary benefit for one year. Over the following twelve months it was estimated that 37,000 were removed from the count.
- October 1982: registration at Job Centres became voluntary. From this date the count of the unemployed was made on the basis of claimants at unemployment benefit offices and at the same time the severely disabled were included in the count. The effect was to reduce the count by 190,000.
- March/April 1983: men over 60 no longer had to attend unemployment benefit offices. The effect was to reduce the count of the unemployed by 162,000.
- July 1985: discrepancies in the figures for Northern Ireland were corrected and this removed 5,000 from the count of the unemployed.
- March 1986: compilation of figures delayed; it now takes place three weeks rather than one week after the specified count date. At the time, this meant a once-for-all exclusion of 50,000 from the records; that is, claimants who had already ceased to be unemployed.
- September 1988: people under 18 no longer eligible for income support and are therefore no longer included in the count of the unemployed.

For further details of these changes see **15**, December 1988.

For earlier years, the figures refer to registered unemployed at local unemployment offices or careers offices on one day in each month, capable of and available for work.

The percentage figure is the number of unemployed expressed as a percentage of the total working population (employees in employment, unemployed, self-employed, HM Forces and those on work-related government training programes).

Up to 1947 the data are taken from **16**. For full details of method of calculation and coverage see **16**, Chapter 11.

Vacancies unfilled: annual averages. Vacancies notified to Job Centres (previously Employment Exchanges and Youth Employment Offices) and remaining unfilled on the day of the count. It is estimated that these vacancies represent about one-third of the total unfilled vacancies. From 1980, Community Programme vacancies and vacancies handled by Professional and Executive Recruitment are excluded but self-employed vacancies are included. The self-employed vacancies are opportunities open to the general public and reflect the trend towards contracting out work which was previously carried out by employees. Community Programme vacancies are published separately.

Industrial stoppages: working days lost and workers involved through stoppages in progress during the year.

Table UK.13   Value of imports by commodity
Sources: **2, 8, 30, 35**

In January 1988 the Standard International Trade Classification (SITC) was revised; imports are now classified in accordance with SITC (R3). The figures are on this basis from 1970; earlier figures are classified according to SITC (R2); data for the pre-war period conforms, as far as possible, with SITC (R2). Imports include goods subsequently exported and are valued cif. Up to 1947 they include silver bullion and specie. Munitions are excluded in the period 1940–45; Southern Ireland is included as part of the UK up to 1923. The data for 1885–99 are classified according to the Brussels Register of International Commodities. For further details see **35**.

Table UK.14   Value of exports by commodity
Sources: **2, 8, 30, 35**

Exports are valued fob and include re-exports. Data are classified in accordance with SITC (R3) from 1970 (see above) and in accordance with SITC (R2) before that; figures for earlier years have been adjusted as far as possible to conform with SITC (R2) except for the data for the period 1885–99 which are classified according to the Brussels Register (see above).

Southern Ireland is treated as part of the UK up to 1923.

Up to 1947, silver bullion and specie are included; munitions are excluded in the period 1940–45.

Non-manufactures include food, beverages and tobacco, crude materials, animal and vegetable oils and fats.

Table UK   Value of exports and imports by area
Sources: **2, 8, 30**

Imports are classified according to country of consignment, which is not necessarily the country of shipment, origin or manufacture. Exports are classified according to country of destination. Trade with Southern Ireland is treated as part of the UK up to 1923; the Channel Islands have been treated as part of the UK throughout.

Up to 1905 imports were classified according to country of consignment and exports according to country to which they were shipped. This makes a difference to the data for countries such as Holland and Belgium; it will therefore affect the totals for the European Community in this period.

European Community: comprises France, Belgium, Luxembourg, Netherlands, Federal Republic of Germany (pre-war the whole of Germany), Italy, Irish Republic, Denmark, Greece, Portugal and Spain.

Rest of Western Europe: comprises Iceland, Faroe Islands, Norway, Sweden, Finland, Switzerland, Austria, Andorra, Gibraltar, Vatican City, Malta, Yugoslavia and Turkey.

North America: comprises Canada, USA, Greenland, Puerto Rico, St Pierre and Miquelon.

Figures for all years have been adjusted as far as possible to accord with these areas. (The Faroe Islands, Iceland, Puerto Rico, etc., were not always separately distinguished in the early Annual Statement of Trade, but trade with these areas is relatively small and the figures in the table should not be seriously affected.)

Table UK.16 Balance of payments

Sources: **16, 43**

Imports are adjusted to a fob basis and adjustments are made to both imports and exports for coverage.

Services: includes receipts and payments for sea transport and civil aviation, financial services including insurance, banking and commodity trading, together with government payments and receipts for services and transfers.

Interest, profits and dividends: includes earnings on direct investment and on portfolio investment. For treatment of oil companies' earnings see **43**, p. 32.

Current balance: net surplus (+) or deficit (−) on both visible and invisible trade together with transfers. (Transfers are not shown separately in this table.)

Up to 1920 (first line), Southern Ireland is included in 'Imports', 'Exports' and 'Current balance'.

For the period 1885–1945 estimates published in **16** have been used for all the above series.

Official reserves: comprise gold and convertible currencies, International Monetary Fund (IMF) Special Drawing Rights (SDRs) and the UK's reserve position in the IMF. From July 1979 convertible currencies include European Currency Units (Ecus) acquired when 20 per cent of the gold and dollar holdings in the official reserves were deposited on a swap basis with the European Cooperation Monetary Fund. Gold is valued at the ruling official price of SDR35 per fine oz until the end of 1977; from 1978 it has been valued at the market price at the end of the year. Other currencies (including Ecus) are valued at closing middle market rates of exchange. For further details see **43**.

Changes in the gold valuation also took place in 1932, 1945 and 1949. For details see **8**.

For the period 1900–45 figures are taken from **8** and **34**. The Bank of England holding is included up to 1938.

Table UK.17 Finance

Sources: **3, 5, 8, 11, 14, 18, 20, 21, 22, 24, 36, 45**

Industrial ordinary share price index: from 1962, the index is the FT–Actuaries index, which is a weighted arithmetic average of the percentage price changes of the constituent shares since April 1962. The FT–Actuaries index covers 500 industrial shares excluding financial and property companies. For earlier years, the index has been linked to the series given in **8**.

Treasury bills: weighted averages of discount rates at the weekly allotments of 91 day bills. For the period 1900–27 the average is unweighted, and for the period 1900–13 the rate is for 6 months bills.

Gilt-edged yields: short-dated: gross redemption yield on representative stock of about four years' life; average of working days. Up to 1934, the series was calculated by F. W. Paish from *The Economist*'s data; average of mid-month figures.

2$\frac{1}{2}$ per cent Consols: flat-yield gross of income tax and without adjustment for accrued interest; average of working days. For the period 1900–34, the yield was on the average price for the year. In 1900 the rate of interest was $2\frac{3}{4}$ per cent but the yield has been calculated at $2\frac{1}{2}$ per cent since conversion had already been announced. Figures for 1885 to 1899 from **11**.

Money stock: the definition used here is M1, which currently comprises notes and coins in circulation with the public, plus sterling sight deposits held with UK banks by the private sector only. For further details see **19**.

From 1981, the figures have been calculated on the basis of the new monetary sector. Breaks in the series from 1963 show the effect of changes in contributors.

For the period 1952–63 (first line), the figures are end-December figures estimates published in **4**. For 1930–51 estimates made by Johnson, **22**, have been used. Figures for 1919–30 (first line) are based on the Macmillan Report, **24**.

Total consumer credit outstanding: figures are for Great Britain only. The current series has been compiled from 1976. It covers credit extended by finance houses, other specialist consumer credit grantors, clothing retailers, household goods retailers, mixed retail businesses and general mail order houses. Charges for credit and amounts outstanding on running account credit agreements are included between 1976 and 1982 (first line). For further details see **1** and **19**. Before 1976, figures refer to hire purchase and other instalment credit business. For the period 1947–55, unpublished estimates by Gandhi, **20**, have been used.

Foreign exchange rates: the current figures are averages of daily mean Telegraphic Transfer rates in London. Figures for the French franc and the German mark for

1919–38 are averages of daily quotations from *The Times* or the *Financial Times* (May–December 1922) given in **8**. For the period 1900–13 rates were calculated from **3**, also given in **8**. The Italian lira figures were calculated from data in **21** for the period 1949–54 and from **3** for the period 1926–40. The figure for 1955 is from August 22. The figures for 1939 and 1940 refer to a broken period. The Japanese yen rate for the period 1885–1940 is an average of the highest and lowest during the year taken from **5**. For 1945–48 it is based on the military exchange rate in September 1945, March 1947 and July 1948 which are quoted in **36**.

Table UK.18   Public finance

Sources: **12, 25, 29, 31, 44**

Total receipts: include trading income, rent, royalties, interest, and so on of general government. General government includes central government and local authority sectors but public corporations not included.

Up to 1938 data are for fiscal years, not calendar years.

Taxes on companies: includes corporation tax and previously, profits tax. In 1937 and 1938 national defence contributions and some land tax included.

Customs and excise: includes purchase tax when it was operative and now includes value-added tax.

Total expenditure: includes expenditure on goods and services, current and capital transfers and debt interest. From 1970, includes net lending to public corporations, private sector and overseas.

Social services: includes expenditure on health and social security benefits but excludes housing expenditure.

For the years 1890–1938, data are taken from **31** for expenditure items.

For 1885–1938, data are taken from **25** for customs and excise and total receipts. Receipts are for central government only.

Table UK.19   Transport and energy

Sources: **1, 8, 12, 14, 26, 42**

Motor vehicles licences current: the taxation system for Great Britain was changed in October 1982. As a result some 970,000 vans and light goods vehicles were regrouped under the heading of 'Private and light goods' in the published data.

Goods vehicles: include light goods vehicles, general haulage vehicles, agricultural vans and lorries and general haulage tractors.

From 1978, the data have been obtained from a full count on December 31 each year of licensing records held at the Driver and Vehicle Licensing Centre (DVLC). For the period 1974–78, figures were based on DVLC data and records held at Local Taxation offices and for 1945–74 on a sample count taken during the third quarter each year. For the period 1939–44, the figures are for licences current on August 31; for 1921–25 they are for the quarter with the greatest number of licences current; up to 1920, they are licences current at March 31 each year.

No figures are available for 1977 for Great Britain or for 1973 for Northern Ireland; the figure for 1973 in the table is for Great Britain only.

Goods vehicles exclude tractors for general haulage up to 1934.

Railways: figures are for Great Britain only. From 1963, free hauled traffic on revenue earning and on departmental trains is excluded. From 1972, freight carried by coaching trains is excluded: the figure for 1972 including this freight is 23·4 bn net ton km.

Airways: Figures include scheduled services of British Airways and private companies on both domestic and international routes. The figures refer to seat kilometres used. Charter flights are included up to 1938.

Coal: consumption by primary and secondary fuel producers plus disposals to final users and net foreign trade and stock changes in solid fuels. For the period 1923–38 colliery stock changes only are taken into account, and up to 1922 the figures are not adjusted for stock changes.

Petroleum: refinery throughput of crude oil plus net imports and stock changes minus deliveries of non-energy products. For 1900–38, estimates by A.L. King given in **8**.

Natural gas: production of natural gas excluding amount flared or reinjected but including imports and colliery methane used at collieries or sold from collieries. Non-energy supplies are included.

UNITED STATES OF AMERICA

CONTENTS

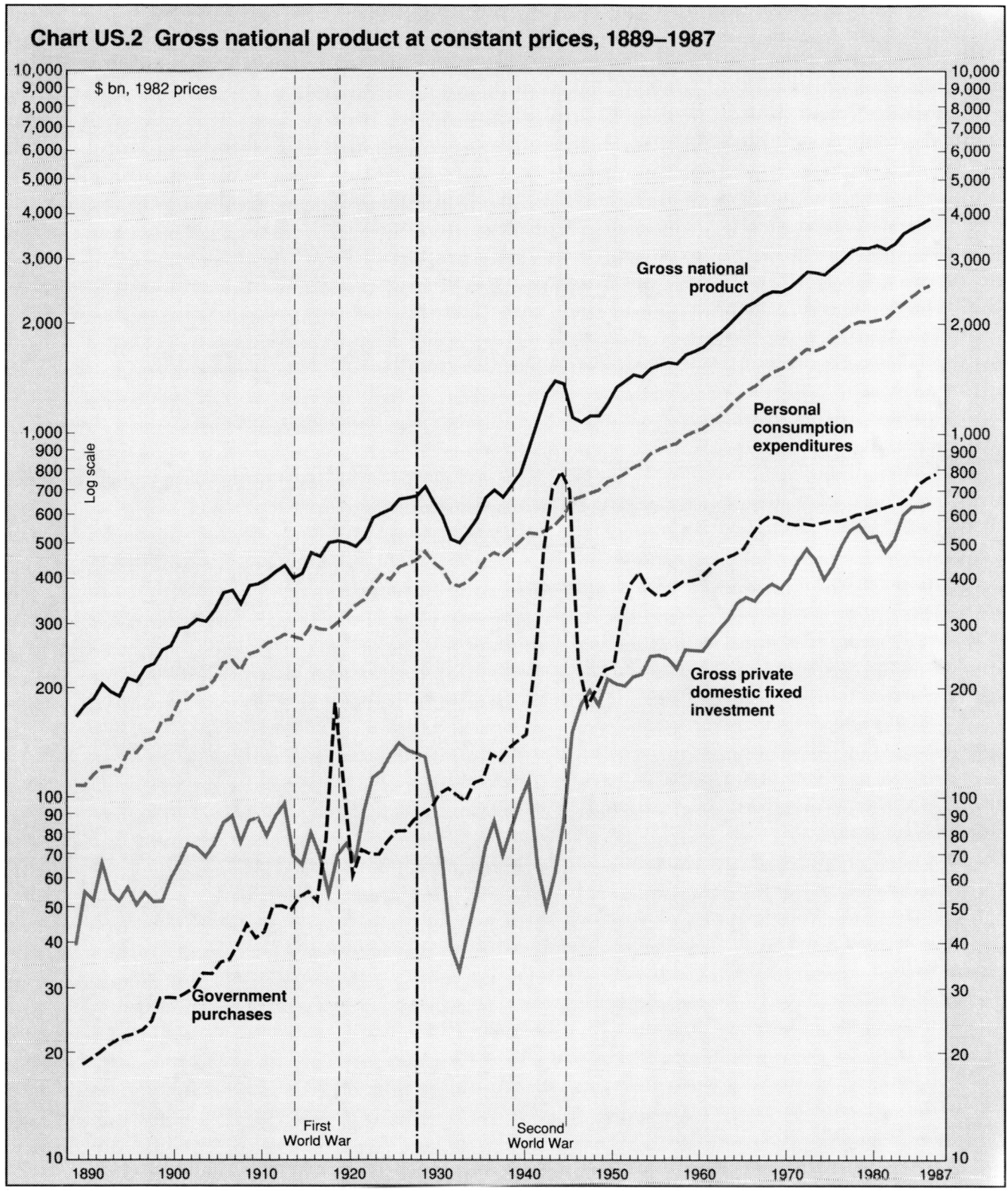

Chart US.2 Gross national product at constant prices, 1889–1987

$ bn, 1982 prices

Log scale

Gross national product

Personal consumption expenditures

Gross private domestic fixed investment

Government purchases

First World War

Second World War

Table US.1 Gross national product at current prices, 1889–1987

	Personal consumption expenditures	Government purchases	Gross private domestic fixed investment	Change in business inventories	Exports of goods and services	Imports of goods and services	Gross national product at market prices
				$ bn			
1889	9·69	0·62	2·03	0·23	−0·09		12·49
1890	9·51	0·66	2·79	0·28	−0·12		13·13
1891	10·07	0·69	2·54	0·26	−0·03		13·53
1892	10·17	0·72	3·13	0·31	−0·05		14·27
1893	10·45	0·76	2·57	0·11	−0·04		13·85
1894	9·42	0·75	2·36	0·09	—		12·62
1895	10·37	0·77	2·51	0·40	−0·13		13·93
1896	10·03	0·80	2·21	0·17	0·09		13·30
1897	10·85	0·84	2·39	0·39	0·14		14·62
1898	11·32	1·03	2·35	0·28	0·41		15·39
1899	12·80	1·10	2·58	0·61	0·27		17·36
1900	13·63	1·12	3·09	0·43	0·41		18·68
1901	15·19	1·15	3·34	0·66	0·33		20·67
1902	15·91	1·24	3·86	0·39	0·15		21·55
1903	16·97	1·41	3·82	0·43	0·23		22·86
1904	17·52	1·37	3·61	0·20	0·15		22·85
1905	18·83	1·53	4·07	0·52	0·17		25·12
1906	21·16	1·62	4·96	0·83	0·15		28·72
1907	22·55	1·89	5·39	0·45	0·12		30·40
1908	21·23	2·11	4·39	−0·26	0·24		27·70
1909	24·24	1·92	5·18	0·99	−0·16		32·17
1910	25·45	2·04	5·38	0·65	−0·16		33·36
1911	26·40	2·46	4·88	0·48	0·05		34·27
1912	28·31	2·53	5·59	0·84	0·05		37·31
1913	29·37	2·48	6·20	0·85	0·17		39·07
1914	29·44	2·68	4·41	0·02	−0·11		36·42
1915	29·84	2·81	4·33	0·17	1·60		38·74
1916	36·48	2·92	5·92	1·50	2·95		49·77
1917	44·26	5·36	6·43	0·60	3·30		59·95
1918	50·70	16·20	6·36	0·73	2·19		76·18
1919	53·26	9·46	8·31	4·05	3·82		78·91
1920	62·62	5·90	10·12	7·36	2·84		88·86
1921	58·21	6·30	7·75	0·06	1·61		73·94
1922	57·32	5·95	9·55	0·53	0·65		73·99
1923	63·77	6·19	12·69	2·99	0·48		86·12
1924	67·64	6·70	13·17	−0·94	0·99		87·56
1925	67·21	7·26	14·41	1·75	0·68		91·31
1926	72·95	7·30	15·48	1·52	0·45		97·69
1927	72·60	7·86	14·69	0·40	0·72		96·28
1928	74·89	8·18	14·46	0·38	1·01		98·16
1929	78·95	8·48	14·56	1·67	0·77		104·44
1929	77·3	8·9	14·9	1·7	7·1	−5·9	103·9
1930	69·9	9·5	11·0	−0·4	5·5	−4·5	91·1
1931	60·5	9·5	7·0	−1·1	3·7	−3·2	76·4
1932	48·6	8·4	3·6	−2·5	2·5	−2·1	58·5
1933	45·8	8·3	3·1	−1·6	2·4	−2·1	56·0
1934	51·4	10·1	4·3	−0·7	3·0	−2·4	65·6
1935	55·8	10·2	5·6	1·1	3·3	−3·2	72·8
1936	62·0	12·2	7·5	1·3	3·6	−3·5	83·1
1937	66·7	12·1	9·5	2·5	4·7	−4·3	91·3
1938	64·1	13·2	7·7	−0·9	4·4	−3·1	85·4
1939	67·0	13·6	9·1	0·4	4·6	−3·4	91·3
1940	71·0	14·2	11·2	2·2	5·4	−3·7	100·4
1941	80·8	25·0	13·8	4·5	6·1	−4·7	125·5
1942	88·6	59·9	8·5	1·8	5·0	−4·8	159·0
1943	99·5	88·9	6·9	0·6	4·6	−6·5	192·7
1944	108·2	97·1	8·7	−1·0	5·5	−7·2	211·4
1945	119·6	83·0	12·3	−1·0	7·4	−7·9	213·4
1946	143·9	29·1	25·1	6·4	15·2	−7·3	212·4
1947	161·9	26·4	35·5	−0·5	20·3	−8·3	235·2

	Personal consumption expenditures	Government purchases	Gross private domestic fixed investment	Change in business inventories	Exports of goods and services	Imports of goods and services	**Gross national product at market prices**
				$ bn			
1948	174·9	32·6	42·4	4·7	17·5	−10·6	**261·6**
1949	178·3	39·0	39·5	−3·1	16·4	−9·8	**260·4**
1950	192·1	38·8	48·3	6·8	14·5	−12·3	**288·3**
1951	208·1	60·4	50·2	10·2	19·8	15·3	**333·4**
1952	219·1	75·8	50·5	3·1	19·2	−16·0	**351·6**
1953	232·6	82·8	54·5	0·4	18·1	−16·8	**371·6**
1954	239·8	76·0	55·7	−1·6	18·8	−16·3	**372·5**
1955	257·9	75·3	64·0	5·7	21·1	−18·1	**405·9**
1956	270·6	79·7	68·0	4·6	25·2	−19·9	**428·2**
1957	285·3	87·3	69·7	1·4	28·2	−20·9	**451·0**
1958	294·6	95·4	65·1	−1·5	24·4	−21·1	**456·8**
1959	316·3	97·9	74·4	5·8	25·0	−23·5	**495·8**
1960	330·7	100·6	75·1	3·1	29·9	−24·0	**515·3**
1961	341·1	108·4	74·7	2·4	31·1	−23·9	**533·8**
1962	361·9	118·2	81·5	6·1	33·1	−26·2	**574·6**
1963	381·7	123·8	87·3	5·8	35·7	−27·5	**606·9**
1964	409·3	130·0	94·2	5·4	40·5	−29·6	**649·8**
1965	440·7	138·6	106·2	9·9	42·9	−33·2	**705·1**
1966	477·3	158·6	114·4	14·2	46·6	−39·1	**772·0**
1967	503·6	179·7	115·4	10·3	49·5	−42·1	**816·4**
1968	552·5	197·7	129·1	7·9	54·8	−49·3	**892·7**
1969	597·9	207·3	143·4	9·8	60·4	−54·7	**963·9**
1970	640·0	218·2	145·7	3·1	68·9	−60·5	**1,015·5**
1971	691·6	232·4	164·7	7·8	72·4	−66·1	**1,102·7**
1972	757·6	250·0	191·5	10·5	81·4	−78·2	**1,212·8**
1973	837·2	266·5	219·2	19·6	114·1	−97·3	**1,359·3**
1974	916·5	299·1	225·4	15·4	151·5	−135·2	**1,472·8**
1975	1,012·8	335·0	225·2	−5·6	161·3	−130·3	**1,598·4**
1976	1,129·3	356·9	261·7	16·0	177·7	−158·9	**1,782·8**
1977	1,257·2	387·3	322·8	21·3	191·6	−189·7	**1,990·5**
1978	1,403·5	425·2	388·2	28·6	227·5	−223·4	**2,249·7**
1979	1,566·8	467·8	441·9	13·0	291·2	−272·5	**2,508·2**
1980	1,732·6	530·3	445·3	−8·3	351·0	−318·9	**2,732·0**
1981	1,915·1	588·1	491·5	24·0	382·8	−348·9	**3,052·6**
1982	2,050·7	641·7	471·8	−24·5	361·9	−335·6	**3,166·0**
1983	2,234·5	675·0	509·4	−7·1	352·5	−358·7	**3,405·7**
1984	2,430·5	735·9	597·1	67·7	383·5	−442·4	**3,772·2**
1985	2,629·0	820·8	631·8	11·3	370·9	−448·9	**4,014·9**
1986	2,807·5	871·2	650·4	15·5	378·4	−482·8	**4,240·3**
1987	3,012·1	924·7	673·7	39·2	428·0	−551·1	**4,526·7**

Table US.2   Gross national product at constant prices, 1889–1987

	Personal consumption expenditures	Government purchases	Gross private domestic fixed investment	Change in business inventories	Exports of goods and services	Imports of goods and services	Gross national product at market prices
	$ bn, 1982 prices						
1889	107·5	18·8	39·6	2·5		−2·7	165·7
1890	107·2	19·5	54·9	3·1		−6·7	178·0
1891	114·9	20·3	52·1	2·8		−4·2	185·9
1892	120·4	21·2	66·0	3·7		−7·4	203·9
1893	121·0	21·9	54·8	1·3		−4·9	194·1
1894	117·4	22·5	51·9	1·2		−4·4	188·6
1895	132·1	22·8	56·5	5·1		−5·3	211·2
1896	131·7	23·4	50·6	2·3		−1·1	206·9
1897	142·1	24·7	54·6	5·2		−0·1	226·5
1898	144·5	28·6	51·6	3·6		3·2	231·5
1899	161·6	28·7	51·7	7·2		3·4	252·6
1900	163·0	28·6	59·7	4·7		3·5	259·5
1901	183·0	29·5	65·9	7·3		3·7	289·4
1902	184·6	30·5	74·2	4·1		−1·2	292·2
1903	195·6	33·4	72·6	4·5		0·5	306·6
1904	198·2	33·3	68·4	2·1		0·8	302·8
1905	209·6	35·8	74·3	5·3		0·3	325·3
1906	232·7	36·5	84·8	8·3		0·7	363·0
1907	237·1	40·4	88·7	4·3		−1·7	368·8
1908	222·1	45·4	74·9	−2·6		−1·5	338·3
1909	246·5	41·7	86·0	9·0		−3·4	379·8
1910	251·0	43·3	87·8	5·7		−3·9	383·9
1911	263·2	50·9	78·2	4·6		−0·7	396·2
1912	270·0	51·0	88·4	7·5		−2·0	414·9
1913	278·9	49·7	95·9	7·5		−0·7	431·3
1914	275·4	53·9	68·9	0·2		—	398·4
1915	270·7	55·7	65·2	1·5		17·5	410·6
1916	295·1	52·6	79·8	10·8		29·7	468·0
1917	288·7	77·5	69·3	3·1		18·5	457·1
1918	287·4	183·4	54·2	3·4		−29·9	498·5
1919	300·1	107·5	69·4	18·5		8·4	503·9
1920	314·8	61·7	74·5	27·9		19·3	498·2
1921	334·9	72·5	66·7	−0·8		13·1	486·4
1922	347·3	70·6	91·5	1·6		4·0	515·0
1923	378·8	70·5	112·9	17·9		3·0	583·1
1924	406·9	76·6	117·6	−6·4		5·7	600·4
1925	395·0	81·6	130·2	10·4		−2·1	615·1
1926	427·3	81·7	140·3	7·5		−1·7	655·1
1927	436·9	87·6	134·0	2·4		0·5	661·4
1928	446·8	91·1	131·4	−2·7		2·7	669·3
1929	471·4	94·2	128·4	10·8	42·1	−37·4	709·6
1930	439·7	103·3	98·4	−0·9	35·6	−33·3	642·8
1931	422·1	106·8	67·3	−7·1	29·3	−30·4	588·1
1932	384·9	102·2	39·0	−16·4	23·2	−23·7	509·2
1933	378·7	98·5	33·5	−10·7	22·7	−24·2	498·5
1934	390·5	110·7	42·9	−7·6	24·7	−24·6	536·7
1935	412·1	113·0	54·7	6·2	26·6	−32·5	580·2
1936	451·6	132·5	73·1	9·0	28·4	−32·5	662·2
1937	467·9	127·8	85·8	14·1	35·7	−35·9	695·3
1938	457·1	137·9	69·2	−6·0	34·1	−28·1	664·2
1939	480·5	144·1	82·1	3·9	36·2	−30·1	716·6
1940	502·6	150·2	97·4	14·4	40·0	−31·7	772·9
1941	531·1	235·6	111·1	27·8	42·0	−38·2	909·4
1942	527·6	483·7	64·7	12·0	29·1	−36·9	1,080·3
1943	539·9	708·9	49·7	0·7	25·1	−48·0	1,276·2
1944	557·1	790·8	61·6	−5·2	27·3	−51·1	1,380·6
1945	592·7	704·5	84·9	−8·4	35·2	−54·1	1,354·8
1946	655·0	236·9	150·2	27·9	69·0	−42·0	1,096·9
1947	666·6	179·8	178·9	−1·0	82·3	−39·9	1,066·7
1948	681·8	199·5	196·0	12·3	66·2	−47·1	1,108·7

Table US.2 (Continued)   Gross national product at constant prices, 1889–1987

	Personal consumption expenditures	Government purchases	Gross private domestic fixed investment	Change in business inventories	Exports of goods and services	Imports of goods and services	Gross national product at market prices
				$ bn, 1982 prices			
1949	695·4	226·0	178·4	−9·7	65·0	−46·2	1,109·0
1950	733·2	230·8	210·8	24·2	59·2	−54·6	1,203·7
1951	748·7	329·7	204·3	30·8	72·0	−57·4	1,328·2
1952	771·4	389·9	201·8	10·0	70·1	−63·3	1,380·0
1953	802·5	419·0	213·8	2·8	66·9	−69·7	1,435·3
1954	822·7	378·4	217·3	−4·8	70·0	−67·5	1,416·2
1955	873·8	361·3	243·5	16·3	76·9	−76·9	1,494·9
1956	899·8	363·7	244·9	12·9	87·9	−83·6	1,525·6
1957	919·7	381·1	240·4	3·0	94·9	−87·9	1,551·1
1958	932·9	395·3	224·8	−3·4	82·4	−92·8	1,539·2
1959	979·4	397·7	253·8	16·5	83·7	−101·9	1,629·1
1960	1,005·1	403·7	252·7	7·7	98·4	−102·4	1,665·3
1961	1,025·2	427·1	251·8	7·3	100·7	−103·3	1,708·7
1962	1,069·0	449·4	272·4	16·2	106·9	−114·4	1,799·4
1963	1,108·4	459·8	290·5	16·6	114·7	−116·6	1,873·3
1964	1,170·6	470·8	310·2	15·7	128·8	−122·8	1,973·3
1965	1,236·4	487·0	341·8	25·2	132·0	−134·7	2,087·6
1966	1,298·9	532·6	353·7	36·9	138·4	−152·1	2,208·3
1967	1,337·7	576·2	345·6	28·8	143·6	−160·5	2,271·4
1968	1,405·9	597·6	370·7	21·0	155·7	−185·3	2,365·6
1969	1,456·7	591·2	385·1	25·1	165·0	−199·9	2,423·3
1970	1,492·0	572·6	373·3	8·2	178·3	−208·3	2,416·2
1971	1,538·8	566·5	399·7	19·6	179·2	−218·9	2,484·8
1972	1,621·9	570·7	443·7	21·8	195·2	−244·6	2,608·5
1973	1,689·6	565·3	480·8	40·0	242·3	−273·8	2,744·1
1974	1,674·0	573·2	448·0	33·3	269·1	−268·4	2,729·3
1975	1,711·9	580·9	396·1	−12·8	259·7	−240·8	2,695·0
1976	1,803·9	580·3	431·4	22·1	274·4	−285·4	2,826·7
1977	1,883·8	589·1	492·2	29·1	281·6	−317·1	2,958·6
1978	1,961·0	604·1	540·2	36·8	312·6	−339·4	3,115·2
1979	2,004·4	609·1	560·2	15·0	356·8	−353·2	3,192·4
1980	2,000·4	620·5	516·2	−6·9	388·9	−332·0	3,187·1
1981	2,024·2	629·7	521·7	23·9	392·7	−343·4	3,248·8
1982	2,050·7	641·7	471·8	−24·5	361·9	−335·6	3,166·0
1983	2,146·0	649·0	510·4	−6·4	348·1	−368·1	3,279·1
1984	2,249·3	677·7	596·1	62·3	371·8	−455·8	3,501·4
1985	2,354·8	731·2	627·9	9·1	367·2	−471·4	3,618·7
1986	2,455·2	760·5	628·1	15·4	378·4	−515·9	3,721·7
1987	2,521·0	780·2	640·4	34·4	427·8	−556·7	3,847·0

Table US.3   Output by sector and industry, index numbers, 1909–87

	Business	Households & institutions	Government	Gross domestic product	Industrial production — Total industrial output	Manufacturing	Mining	Public utilities
					Index nos., 1980 = 100			
1909	13·7		8·4	13·1	...	...	...	...
1910	14·1		8·9	13·5	...	...	...	...
1911	14·5		9·2	13·9	...	...	...	...
1912	.15·2		9·6	14·6	...	...	...	...
1913	15·4		9·8	14·8	...	...	...	...
1914	14·7		10·3	14·2	...	...	...	...
1915	14·4		10·7	14·0	...	...	...	...
1916	15·6		11·0	15·1	...	...	...	...
1917	15·5		14·4	15·4	...	...	...	...
1918	16·8		29·6	18·2	...	...	...	...
1919	16·5		20·2	16·9	9·5	10·1	21·5	1·9
1920	15·6		14·8	15·6	10·0	10·4	25·0	2·1
1921	14·4		14·5	14·5	7·7	7·9	20·0	1·9
1922	16·9		14·1	16·6	9·8	10·4	21·4	2·1
1923	18·9		14·2	18·4	11·7	12·1	29·6	2·5
1924	19·1		14·8	18·6	11·0	11·4	27·0	2·6
1925	20·5		15·4	20·0	12·0	12·8	27·8	2·9
1926	21·8		15·7	21·1	12·8	13·4	30·2	3·4
1927	21·7		16·3	21·1	12·7	13·4	30·2	3·6
1928	21·9		16·6	21·3	13·3	14·1	29·9	4·0
1929	22·8	32·1	17·2	22·5	14·7	15·6	32·4	4·4
1930	20·3	31·0	18·0	20·4	12·2	12·8	28·1	4·5
1931	18·3	28·9	18·2	18·7	10·1	10·4	24·2	4·3
1932	15·6	26·3	17·8	16·2	8·0	8·0	20·2	4·0
1933	15·1	25·3	18·8	15·8	9·3	9·5	23·0	3·9
1934	16·1	27·2	21·3	17·1	10·2	10·4	24·1	4·2
1935	17·5	28·1	22·7	18·4	11·8	12·3	26·2	4·5
1936	20·1	29·6	26·3	21·1	13·9	14·7	30·1	5·1
1937	21·4	30·9	25·1	22·1	15·2	16·0	33·9	5·7
1938	20·0	29·7	27·0	21·1	10·2	12·3	29·3	5·7
1939	21·9	31·0	27·4	22·8	12·6	14·7	31·7	6·3
1940	23·7	33·4	29·0	24·6	17·0	17·3	35·2	6·9
1941	27·5	33·4	38·5	28·9	21·5	22·1	37·4	7·8
1942	31·0	34·4	60·8	34·4	24·7	25·8	38·6	8·8
1943	33·2	32·0	101·9	40·6	30·1	32·1	39·5	9·7
1944	34·8	32·0	119·9	44·0	32·2	34·7	42·3	10·3
1945	34·1	32·1	118·3	43·2	27·7	29·1	41·5	10·5
1946	32·3	33·0	56·2	34·9	23·8	24·1	40·8	10·9
1947	33·0	35·3	40·4	33·9	26·8	26·9	46·1	11·8
1948	34·5	38·4	39·8	35·2	28·0	27·9	48·5	13·2
1949	34·2	39·5	42·3	35·2	26·4	26·4	43·0	14·1
1950	37·4	41·9	43·8	38·2	30·5	30·7	48·0	16·0
1951	40·3	43·0	56·8	42·2	33·1	33·2	52·7	18·2
1952	41·5	43·1	61·8	43·8	34·4	34·5	52·2	19·8
1953	43·6	44·5	61·5	45·6	37·3	37·7	53·6	21·5
1954	43·0	45·1	60·0	45·0	35·3	35·1	52·6	23·1
1955	45·8	49·6	59·4	47·4	39·8	39·7	58·6	25·8
1956	46·7	52·3	60·0	48·4	41·6	41·3	61·7	28·4
1957	47·5	53·8	61·0	49·2	42·1	41·7	61·8	30·3
1958	47·0	56·6	61·1	48·8	39·4	38·9	56·7	31·7
1959	50·2	58·4	61·7	51·7	44·1	43·8	59·2	34·9
1960	51·0	62·8	63·6	52·8	45·0	44·6	60·4	37·3
1961	52·3	63·4	66·1	54·2	45·4	44·7	60·8	39·4
1962	55·2	65·9	68·6	57·0	49·1	48·8	62·5	42·4
1963	57·6	67·6	70·1	59·3	52·0	51·7	65·0	45·3
1964	60·9	69·5	72·5	62·5	55·6	55·3	67·6	49·2
1965	64·8	72·1	75·0	66·1	61·1	61·2	70·1	52·2
1966	68·5	74·9	80·6	70·0	66·5	66·8	73·9	56·2
1967	70·1	77·4	85·3	72·0	68·0	68·2	75·2	58·9
1968	73·1	79·8	88·3	74·9	72·3	72·6	78·4	63·8
1969	74·9	82·2	90·3	76·8	75·6	75·7	81·5	69·0
1970	74·7	81·1	90·2	76·6	73·3	72·6	84·4	73·3
1971	77·1	82·8	90·1	78·7	74·6	73·8	82·6	76·8
1972	81·5	85·0	90·0	82·5	81·4	81·1	85·1	82·1
1973	86·1	87·0	90·6	86·6	88·3	88·5	86·3	85·6
1974	85·1	87·5	92·5	86·0	88·0	88·3	86·8	84·6
1975	83·8	89·8	93·7	85·1	80·1	79·3	84·9	85·9

Table US.3 (Continued)   Output by sector and industry, index numbers, 1909–87

| | Business | Households & institutions | Government | Gross domestic product | Industrial production | | | |
					Total industrial output	Manufacturing	Mining	Public utilities
				Index nos., 1980 = 100				
1976	88·5	90·4	94·3	89·2	88·8	88·9	85·9	89·3
1977	93·1	91·3	95·5	93·3	94·0	94·4	88·9	92·1
1978	98·4	94·1	97·5	98·1	99·4	100·1	93·3	95·0
1979	100·5	96·6	98·6	100·1	103·5	104·5	94·3	97·8
1980	100·0	100·0	100·0	100·0	100·0	100·0	100·0	100·0
1981	102·1	102·4	100·8	101·9	102·7	102·5	107·2	100·5
1982	99·0	105·0	100·8	99·5	94·3	93·8	95·0	100·2
1983	103·2	107·1	101·5	103·2	100·4	101·0	87·9	102·4
1984	111·4	109·6	102·5	110·4	111·6	113·1	94·9	107·7
1985	115·3	112·9	104·1	114·0	113·7	115·8	93·0	108·1
1986	119·3	117·0	106·5	117·8	115·0	118·3	85·8	105·6
1987	123·8	120·2	108·4	122·0	119·3	123·5	86·0	107·4

Table US.3 (Supplementary)   Output by industry, index numbers, 1947–87

	Gross national product	Agriculture, forestry & fishing	Mining	Manufacturing	Construction	Transport & public utilities	Distributive trades	Services
				Index nos., 1980 = 100				
1947	33·5	73·0	49·9	34·0	47·5	34·1	31·5	25·1
1948	34·8	80·4	53·4	35·8	55·7	33·6	32·4	26·1
1949	34·8	80·1	48·5	34·0	55·3	30·9	33·2	26·6
1950	37·8	84·4	53·7	38·7	61·9	32·5	36·4	28·0
1951	41·7	82·2	59·6	43·3	68·6	35·8	36·7	29·0
1952	43·3	84·3	60·1	44·8	71·7	35·6	37·9	30·2
1953	45·0	87·0	62·2	48·1	74·2	36·4	39·1	31·4
1954	44·4	89·5	61·4	44·6	77·2	35·5	39·4	32·6
1955	46·9	90·7	67·8	49·2	82·5	38·3	43·0	34·5
1956	47·9	89·0	71·2	49·7	88·3	40·1	44·2	36·4
1957	48·7	86·5	70·9	50·0	88·1	40·9	45·0	38·2
1958	48·3	89·6	65·7	45·6	91·3	39·6	45·0	39·6
1959	51·1	86·4	69·4	50·8	99·3	42·1	48·1	41·8
1960	52·2	89·6	69·5	50·9	100·9	43·6	49·0	43·7
1961	53·6	98·4	70·5	51·0	102·2	44·3	49·5	45·5
1962	56·4	88·1	72·3	55·3	106·7	46·5	52·7	47·9
1963	58·8	88·2	75·4	59·7	109·8	49·0	54·7	50·0
1964	61·9	85·6	77·9	63·9	115·0	51·3	58·1	52·5
1965	65·5	87·5	80·7	69·5	119·9	55·0	61·9	55·2
1966	69·3	81·9	84·8	74·8	120·3	59·4	65·2	57·9
1967	71·3	86·0	88·6	74·6	118·0	60·7	67·0	60·4
1968	74·2	83·5	92·0	78·1	117·8	64·6	70·9	62·9
1969	76·0	85·7	95·1	80·7	113·6	68·3	72·3	66·4
1970	75·8	90·3	99·2	76·2	104·0	69·5	73·5	68·0
1971	77·9	92·7	97·6	77·5	100·7	71·5	77·1	70·4
1972	81·8	93·0	99·1	84·3	103·2	76·3	82·9	74·0
1973	86·1	92·3	98·4	93·4	105·4	82·8	87·3	78·1
1974	85·6	91·5	96·1	88·9	100·4	84·8	85·2	80·4
1975	84·5	95·9	92·6	82·3	92·5	84·0	86·6	81·6
1976	88·7	93·8	91·7	90·3	97·8	87·6	90·8	85·0
1977	92·8	94·0	93·1	96·9	102·2	91·5	95·8	88·9
1978	97·7	94·2	95·0	102·7	109·3	97·1	100·4	94·2
1979	100·1	99·9	95·9	104·8	107·4	100·0	102·3	98·0
1980	100·0	100·0	100·0	100·0	100·0	100·0	100·0	100·0
1981	101·9	115·5	103·1	101·6	91·2	101·0	101·4	103·3
1982	99·3	117·6	97·4	95·4	87·2	98·3	101·2	103·5
1983	102·9	97·8	92·5	101·5	91·2	102·5	105·3	107·6
1984	109·8	107·9	98·1	113·9	98·5	109·2	115·7	112·5
1985	113·5	123·1	95·9	118·2	102·4	111·1	122·0	118·1
1986	116·7	127·6	85·3	120·9	107·1	113·0	128·5	123·1
1987	120·7	126·1	86·7	126·2	108·8	119·1	131·9	129·0

Table US.4 Industrial production, selected series, 1885–1987

| | Coal | Raw steel | Passenger cars | Chemicals | Metals | | | Electricity |
| | | | | | Copper | Lead | Zinc | |
	mn tons		'000	Index nos., 1980 = 100	'000 tons			bn kwh
1885	65·1	1·7	—	...	75·2	114·5	36·9	—
1886	67·7	2·6	—	...	71·6	119·9	38·7	—
1887	80·3	3·4	—	...	82·3	142·1	45·7	—
1888	92·6	2·9	—	...	102·7	141·5	50·7	—
1889	86·8	3·4	—	...	102·9	161·8	53·4	—
1890	101·0	4·3	—	...	117·8	143·2	57·8	—
1891	107·0	3·9	—	...	128·9	179·9	73·4	—
1892	115·1	5·0	—	...	156·5	188·9	79·2	—
1893	116·5	4·1	—	...	149·4	203·5	71·5	—
1894	107·8	4·4	—	...	160·7	193·8	68·3	—
1895	122·6	6·2	—	...	172·6	213·9	81·4	—
1896	124·9	5·3	—	...	208·7	233·6	73·9	—
1897	133·9	7·2	—	...	224·1	256·0	90·7	—
1898	151·1	9·0	—	...	238·8	274·1	104·7	—
1899	175·4	10·6	—	...	257·9	270·4	117·1	—
1900	192·6	10·2	4	...	275·0	333·7	112·4	—
1901	204·8	13·4	7	...	273·1	336·6	127·7	—
1902	236·1	14·9	9	...	299·2	333·8	142·3	2·5
1903	256·5	14·4	11	...	316·6	334·7	144·4	...
1904	252·8	13·8	22	...	368·6	357·0	169·4	...
1905	285·9	19·9	24	...	403·2	352·3	184·9	...
1906	311·1	23·0	33	...	415·9	367·1	203·9	...
1907	358·1	23·0	43	...	384·3	330·9	229·5	5·9
1908	301·7	14·0	64	...	434·0	299·6	212·4	...
1909	344·5	23·8	124	...	511·0	349·4	274·3	...
1910	378·4	25·7	181	...	493·6	347·2	294·3	...
1911	368·2	23·5	199	...	505·7	387·0	300·7	...
1912	408·3	30·9	356	...	566·5	401·1	349·8	11·6
1913	434·0	30·9	462	...	560·5	438·3	375·4	...
1914	383·5	23·2	548	...	520·9	457·9	377·2	...
1915	401·5	29·2	896	...	674·9	491·8	533·5	...
1916	455·9	42·4	1,526	...	909·8	545·6	637·9	...
1917	500·6	45·2	1,746	...	859·7	570·2	647·4	25·4
1918	525·6	44·4	943	...	866·4	510·2	577·1	...
1919	422·6	34·6	1,652	...	549·9	389·7	497·9	...
1920	515·9	41·9	1,906	...	555·5	450·7	533·0	39·4
1921	377·3	20·9	1,468	...	211·5	375·6	232·8	37·2
1922	383·1	35·3	2,274	...	437·5	433·3	428·2	43·6
1923	512·2	44·4	3,625	...	670·3	496·4	554·0	51·2
1924	438·8	37·5	3,186	...	728·6	540·8	578·8	54·7
1925	471·8	45·1	3,735	...	761·2	620·9	644·8	61·5
1926	520·2	48·0	3,692	...	782·5	620·4	702·7	69·4
1927	469·7	44·7	2,937	...	748·4	603·7	651·8	75·4
1928	454·3	51·3	3,775	...	821·0	569·0	630·7	82·8
1929	485·3	56·0	4,455	...	905·0	587·9	657·3	92·2
1930	424·1	40·6	2,787	...	639·7	506·5	540·1	91·1
1931	346·6	25·8	1,948	...	479·8	367·0	372·2	87·4
1932	281·0	13·6	1,104	...	216·0	265·8	258·7	79·4
1933	302·7	23·3	1,561	...	172·9	247·4	348·6	81·7
1934	326·0	26·5	2,161	...	215·4	260·6	398·0	87·3
1935	337·8	34·6	3,274	...	350·6	300·4	469·8	95·3
1936	398·3	48·5	3,679	...	557·5	338·3	522·2	109·3
1937	404·2	51·3	3,929	...	763·9	421·8	568·3	118·9
1938	316·2	28·8	2,020	...	506·0	335·4	468·7	113·8
1939	358·2	47·9	2,889	...	660·7	375·6	529·6	127·6
1940	418·0	60·7	3,717	...	796·6	414·9	603·4	141·8
1941	466·4	75·1	3,780	...	869·2	418·6	679·6	164·8
1942	528·6	78·0	223	...	979·9	450·1	696·7	186·0
1943	535·4	80·5	—	...	989·6	411·2	675·1	217·8
1944	562·1	81·3	—	...	882·2	378·2	651·9	228·2

80

Table US.4 (Continued)   Industrial production, selected series, 1885–1987

| | Coal | Raw steel | Passenger cars | Chemicals | Metals | | | Electricity |
| | | | | | Copper | Lead | Zinc | |
	mn tons		'000	Index nos., 1980 = 100	'000 tons			bn kwh
1945	524·0	72·3	70	...	701·2	354·5	557·4	222·5
1946	484·4	60·4	2,149	...	552·2	304·4	521·5	223·2
1947	572·1	77·0	3,558	9·5	768·9	348·5	578·4	255·7
1948	543·9	80·4	3,909	10·3	757·3	354·3	571·5	282·7
1949	397·2	70·7	5,119	10·1	682·9	371·9	538·1	291·1
1950	468·4	87·8	6,666	12·7	824·9	390·8	565·5	329·1
1951	484·1	95·4	5,338	14·3	842·1	352·2	618·0	370·7
1952	423·5	84·5	4,321	15·0	839·5	354·0	604·2	399·2
1953	414·8	101·2	6,117	16·2	840·4	310·8	496·6	442·7
1954	355·4	80·1	5,559	16·5	758·0	295·2	429·6	471·7
1955	421·5	106·1	7,920	19·2	905·9	306·6	466·9	547·0
1956	454·4	104·5	5,816	20·6	1,001·7	320·1	492·0	600·7
1957	447·0	102·2	6,113	21·8	986·0	306·8	482·4	631·5
1958	372·4	77·4	4,258	22·5	888·4	242·6	373·8	645·1
1959	373·8	84·7	5,591	26·2	748·3	231·9	385·8	710·0
1960	376·9	90·1	6,675	27·2	979·9	223·8	395·0	756·0
1961	365·6	88·9	5,543	29·5	1,057·1	237·6	421·3	792·0
1962	383·0	89·1	6,933	32·7	1,114·4	215·0	458·6	852·3
1963	416·3	99·1	7,638	35·7	1,100·6	229·9	480·2	914·1
1964	441·8	115·3	7,752	39·2	1,131·1	259·5	521·5	984·0
1965	464·6	119·3	9,306	43·7	1,226·2	273·2	554·5	1,055·3
1966	484·3	121·6	8,598	47·6	1,296·6	297·0	519·5	1,144·4
1967	501·3	115·4	7,437	49·8	865·5	287·5	498·4	1,214·4
1968	494·6	119·3	8,822	56·0	1,092·8	325·9	480·3	1,329·4
1969	508·5	128·2	8,224	60·6	1,401·2	461·8	501·8	1,442·2
1970	547·0	119·3	6,550	63·1	1,560·1	519·0	484·4	1,529·6
1971	500·8	109·2	8,585	67·1	1,380·9	524·9	455·9	1,613·9
1972	539·8	120·8	8,824	75·5	1,510·3	561·5	433·9	1,749·6
1973	537·1	136·8	9,658	82·5	1,558·5	547·0	434·4	1,860·7
1974	547·0	132·1	7,331	85·5	1,448·8	602·3	453·5	1,867·1
1975	587·9	105·8	6,717	77·9	1,282·2	563·8	425·8	1,917·6
1976	616·0	116·1	8,498	87·2	1,456·6	552·9	439·5	2,037·7
1977	626·9	113·7	9,201	94·0	1,364·4	537·5	407·5	2,124·3
1978	603·3	124·3	9,165	100·4	1,352·0	528·8	274·6	2,206·3
1979	704·0	123·7	8,419	104·7	1,443·6	525·6	267·3	2,247·4
1980	747·5	101·4	6,376	100·0	1,181·0	550·7	317·5	2,286·4
1981	742·0	109·6	6,253	105·8	1,538·2	445·4	312·1	2,295
1982	756·5	67·7	5,073	97·6	1,147·0	512·6	303·0	2,241
1983	705·7	76·8	6,781	107·1	1,037·8	449·1	274·9	2,310
1984	809·2	83·9	7,773	114·3	1,102·2	323·0	253·1	2,416
1985	797·4	80·1	8,185	119·5	1,105·9	413·7	226·8	2,470
1986	803·8	74·0	7,829	124·1	1,147·3	339·8	269·6	2,489
1987	830·3	80·9	...	131·8	1,255·9	311·3	220·5	...

Table US.5 Gross domestic private investment by type of asset, 1885–1987

		Type of asset				Investment in non-residential construction by sector				
	Total private investment	Non-residential construction	Plant & machinery	Transport equipment	Non-farm, residential construction	Industrial & commercial buildings	Public utilities	Farm	Mining	Other
					$ bn, 1982 prices					
1885	41·3	17·2	6·5		16·9	. . .	. . .	. . .	. . .	. . .
1886	43·2	17·4	6·7		18·4	. . .	. . .	. . .	. . .	. . .
1887	45·0	16·3	7·2		20·3	. . .	. . .	. . .	. . .	. . .
1888	50·7	20·6	7·9		21·3	. . .	. . .	. . .	. . .	. . .
1889	54·0	24·1	8·4		21·0	. . .	. . .	. . .	. . .	. . .
1890	59·6	30·3	8·6		21·0	. . .	. . .	. . .	. . .	. . .
1891	63·3	34·0	9·0		21·0	. . .	. . .	. . .	. . .	. . .
1892	66·0	38·4	8·9		20·2	. . .	. . .	. . .	. . .	. . .
1893	66·5	38·8	9·1		20·1	. . .	. . .	. . .	. . .	. . .
1894	66·1	37·6	9·3		20·3	. . .	. . .	. . .	. . .	. . .
1895	63·5	35·3	9·1		19·9	. . .	. . .	. . .	. . .	. . .
1896	62·8	34·7	9·0		19·9	. . .	. . .	. . .	. . .	. . .
1897	62·9	33·8	9·8		19·6	. . .	. . .	. . .	. . .	. . .
1898	63·9	35·7	10·5		17·8	. . .	. . .	. . .	. . .	. . .
1899	67·5	39·5	11·1		17·3	. . .	. . .	. . .	. . .	. . .
1900	72·4	44·0	12·5		16·2	. . .	. . .	. . .	. . .	. . .
1901	77·7	47·6	14·2		15·9	. . .	. . .	. . .	. . .	. . .
1902	81·7	51·0	14·9		16·0	. . .	. . .	. . .	. . .	. . .
1903	85·3	49·9	15·7		19·2	. . .	. . .	. . .	. . .	. . .
1904	90·0	50·4	17·3		21·1	. . .	. . .	. . .	. . .	. . .
1905	93·7	50·6	18·7		22·4	. . .	. . .	. . .	. . .	. . .
1906	94·2	50·2	18·3		23·9	. . .	. . .	. . .	. . .	. . .
1907	98·3	51·9	18·8		25·6	. . .	. . .	. . .	. . .	. . .
1908	101·7	56·1	19·7		24·2	. . .	. . .	. . .	. . .	. . .
1909	99·8	56·6	18·9		23·1	. . .	. . .	. . .	. . .	. . .
1910	99·8	56·6	18·8		23·2	. . .	. . .	. . .	. . .	. . .
1911	105·0	59·6	20·6		23·2	. . .	. . .	. . .	. . .	. . .
1912	101·7	55·8	21·0		22·4	. . .	. . .	. . .	. . .	. . .
1913	96·5	49·8	20·6		22·9	. . .	. . .	. . .	. . .	. . .
1914	98·0	46·9	22·7		23·5	. . .	. . .	. . .	. . .	. . .
1915	96·1	42·5	25·0		21·6	. . .	. . .	. . .	. . .	. . .
1916	91·0	35·7	27·5		18·2	. . .	. . .	. . .	. . .	. . .
1917	93·6	34·9	30·5		16·7	. . .	. . .	. . .	. . .	. . .
1918	97·0	36·9	33·4		13·9	. . .	. . .	. . .	. . .	. . .
1919	93·6	35·8	32·3		13·2	. . .	. . .	. . .	. . .	. . .
1920	96·6	36·7	30·8		17·7	. . .	. . .	. . .	. . .	. . .
1921	106·5	40·0	30·8		25·0	. . .	. . .	. . .	. . .	. . .
1922	115·8	42·9	30·8		32·0	. . .	. . .	. . .	. . .	. . .
1923	128·3	46·0	31·6		40·7	. . .	. . .	. . .	. . .	. . .
1924	145·8	51·9	35·4		47·3	. . .	. . .	. . .	. . .	. . .
1925	156·1	56·3	37·8		50·2	. . .	. . .	. . .	. . .	. . .
1926	160·7	59·0	38·7		51·2	. . .	. . .	. . .	. . .	. . .
1927	164·1	62·0	41·3		48·0	. . .	. . .	. . .	. . .	. . .
1928	156·7	61·2	41·4		41·0	. . .	. . .	. . .	. . .	. . .
1929	139·2	54·7	24·8	13·7	33·6	20·8	17·8	1·4	5·9	8·8
1930	97·5	46·3	19·6	11·2	20·1	14·8	17·6	0·8	4·5	8·4
1931	60·2	29·7	13·5	6·3	16·8	8·0	12·4	0·4	2·5	6·5
1932	22·6	18·3	8·0	3·4	8·8	4·1	7·1	0·1	3·2	3·9
1933	22·7	14·3	7·7	3·9	6·9	4·5	4·6	0·2	2·6	2·4
1934	35·3	16·1	10·1	6·3	9·7	4·7	5·4	0·3	3·8	2·0
1935	60·9	18·1	14·2	7·9	13·6	4·7	5·9	0·7	4·6	2·1
1936	82·1	23·6	19·6	11·4	17·4	6·7	7·8	0·9	5·4	2·8
1937	99·9	29·9	22·8	13·0	18·6	9·4	9·2	1·1	7·0	3·2
1938	63·1	24·1	16·9	7·9	19·0	5·5	8·0	0·9	6·1	3·6
1939	86·0	25·2	18·6	9·6	27·1	6·0	9·1	1·1	5·7	3·5
1940	111·8	28·5	23·3	13·4	30·2	8·3	9·8	0·8	6·4	3·5
1941	138·8	33·4	28·0	15·5	31·8	11·5	10·5	1·0	6·7	3·7
1942	76·7	20·9	20·3	6·4	15·6	4·2	9·5	0·9	4·5	1·7
1943	50·4	15·6	18·2	5·7	9·1	1·5	8·4	1·1	4·1	0·4

Table US.5 (Continued)   Gross domestic private investment by type of asset, 1885–1987

	Total private investment	Type of asset				Investment in non-residential construction by sector				
		Non-residential construction	Plant & machinery	Transport equipment	Non-farm, residential construction	Industrial & commercial buildings	Public utilities	Farm	Mining	Other
					$ bn, 1982 prices					
1944	56·4	20·4	26·0	6·2	8·0	2·0	10·6	1·1	5·7	1·0
1945	76·5	27·0	37·3	10·0	9·7	6·3	11·0	1·0	6·2	1·7
1946	178·1	50·9	40·4	14·6	41·3	17·8	12·5	4·0	7·0	4·6
1947	177·9	47·5	54·0	20·6	53·2	13·5	15·8	3·8	7·8	6·6
1948	208·2	50·5	56·2	21·2	63·9	12·8	17·9	3·6	9·6	6·6
1949	168·8	49·3	45·7	20·3	59·2	10·1	18·6	3·5	9·8	7·3
1950	234·9	52·8	50·8	21·0	82·5	11·7	17·8	3·5	11·6	8·2
1951	235·2	56·5	54·4	21·3	68·6	15·1	18·1	3·3	12·2	7·8
1952	211·8	57·3	56·0	17·8	67·5	14·0	18·8	3·5	13·6	7·4
1953	216·6	62·3	58·4	19·9	70·0	16·3	20·0	3·1	14·9	8·0
1954	212·6	64·9	56·7	16·5	76·2	17·6	17·9	3·0	16·5	9·9
1955	259·8	69·4	61·6	20·7	89·1	21·6	16·8	2·9	17·8	10·3
1956	257·8	75·5	66·4	19·2	80·9	26·4	19·2	3·0	17·2	9·7
1957	243·4	75·2	65·6	21·0	75·8	25·7	19·6	2·7	16·2	11·2
1958	221·4	70·6	59·4	14·6	77·6	22·2	18·1	2·7	15·1	12·5
1959	270·3	71·9	62·8	19·8	96·5	22·7	17·0	3·6	15·5	13·1
1960	260·5	76·1	63·7	20·5	90·0	26·5	17·1	3·2	14·5	14·8
1961	259·1	77·7	62·4	19·0	89·8	28·2	16·0	3·3	14·7	15·5
1962	288·6	81·3	66·2	23·6	98·7	29·9	16·1	3·6	15·4	16·3
1963	307·1	81·6	73·5	22·6	110·2	29·0	17·3	3·5	14·5	17·3
1964	325·9	87·9	81·8	26·3	111·4	32·4	18·5	3·4	15·5	18·1
1965	367·0	101·8	93·8	33·2	110·5	42·6	20·6	3·6	15·3	19·7
1966	390·5	108·0	106·9	36·8	99·3	46·4	23·3	3·8	14·5	20·0
1967	374·4	105·4	105·1	35·8	96·6	43·2	25·0	4·3	13·8	19·1
1968	391·8	108·0	105·6	42·5	112·0	43·2	28·3	4·0	13·8	18·7
1969	410·3	112·9	112·6	44·2	111·2	46·3	28·2	4·2	14·4	19·8
1970	381·5	111·1	119·5	35·3	105·2	43·7	29·7	4·7	13·4	19·6
1971	419·3	107·3	115·9	37·3	137·0	42·1	29·4	4·6	12·3	18·9
1972	465·4	109·5	125·7	44·4	161·6	41·6	30·7	3·9	13·3	20·0
1973	520·8	117·7	148·7	53·8	158·3	46·1	32·8	5·2	14·1	19·5
1974	481·3	115·2	157·4	48·3	123·8	45·5	30·7	6·1	16·6	16·3
1975	383·3	102·8	141·1	40·1	109·5	36·4	27·2	6·5	19·5	13·2
1976	453·5	104·4	144·5	44·6	135·3	33·5	29·9	6·6	20·9	13·5
1977	521·3	108·3	163·7	55·2	161·6	35·1	28·8	6·9	24·2	13·3
1978	576·9	119·3	184·4	61·8	171·5	42·1	30·1	7·4	26·4	13·3
1979	575·2	130·6	198·6	63·8	165·2	51·0	31·1	7·1	27·3	14·1
1980	509·3	136·2	197·2	49·3	130·8	50·7	30·3	6·1	34·2	14·9
1981	545·5	148·8	202·1	47·7	121·0	54·4	29·8	4·9	44·4	15·3
1982	447·3	143·3	184·2	42·5	99·8	54·8	28·3	3·7	40·6	15·9
1983	504·0	127·2	188·9	49·1	143·7	47·0	24·8	3·1	34·5	17·8
1984	658·4	143·8	226·5	59·5	164·0	57·1	24·4	2·9	39·9	19·5
1985	637·0	149·5	247·6	61·5	167·6	68·3	25·1	2·0	35·2	18·9
1986	643·5	129·3	249·5	59·8	188·4	62·1	25·2	1·8	20·7	19·5
1987	674·8	125·5	266·4	59·1	187·8	58·5	25·7	1·6	18·8	20·9

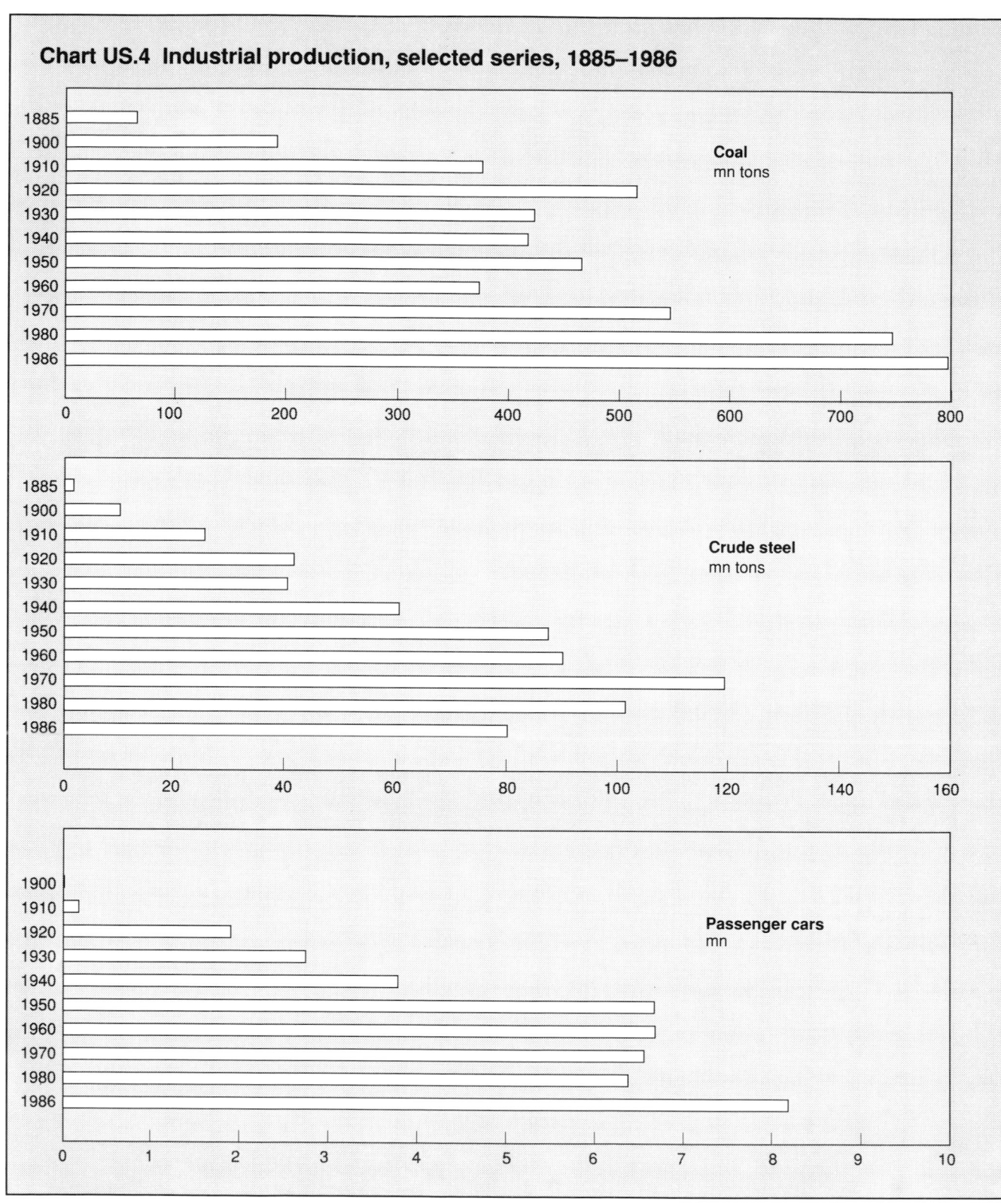

Chart US.4 Industrial production, selected series, 1885–1986

Coal
mn tons

Crude steel
mn tons

Passenger cars
mn

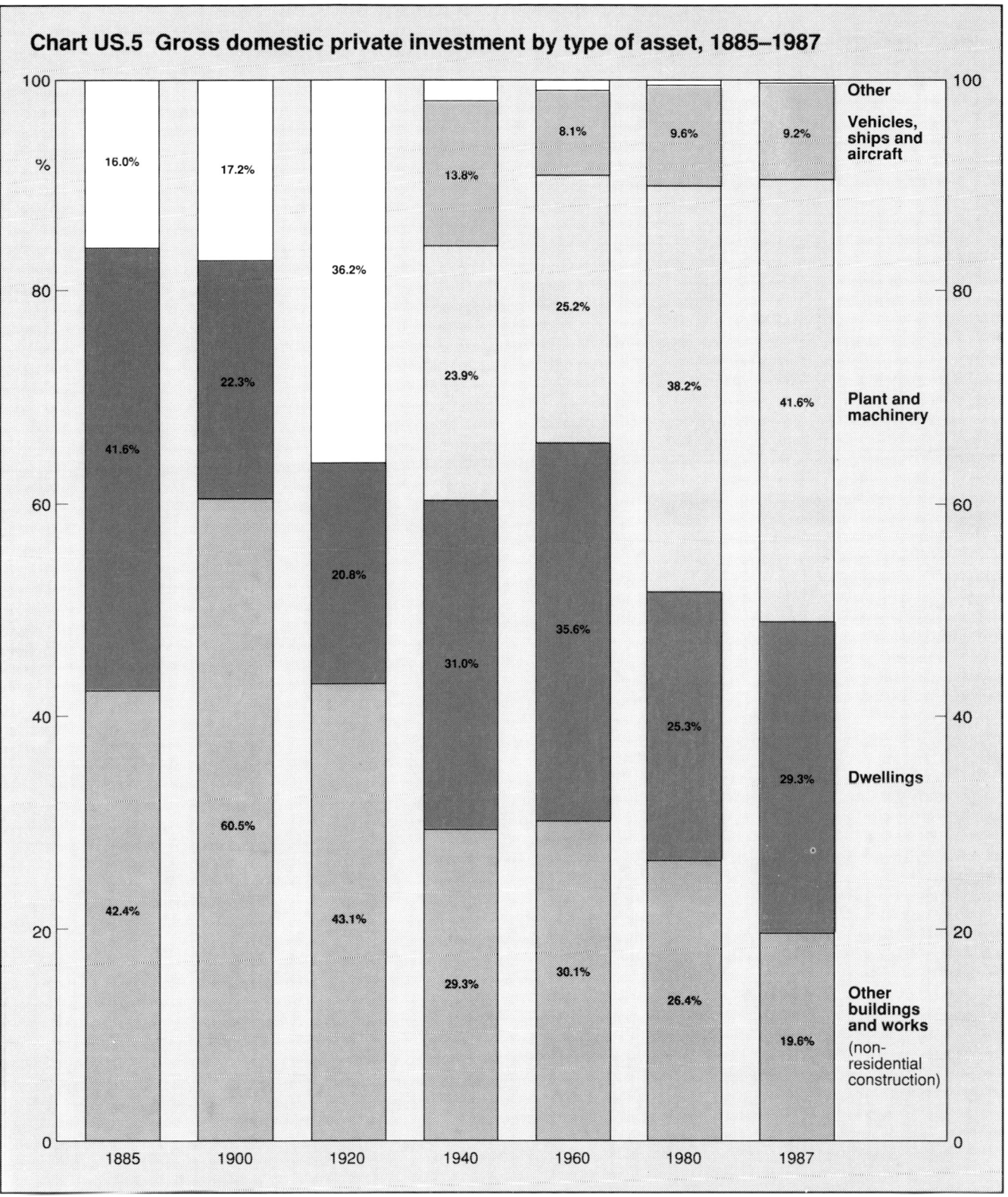

Chart US.5 Gross domestic private investment by type of asset, 1885–1987

Other

Vehicles, ships and aircraft

Plant and machinery

Dwellings

Other buildings and works (non-residential construction)

Year	Other	Vehicles, ships and aircraft	Plant and machinery	Dwellings	Other buildings and works
1885	16.0%		41.6%		42.4%
1900	17.2%		22.3%		60.5%
1920	36.2%		20.8%		43.1%
1940		13.8%	23.9%	31.0%	29.3%
1960		8.1%	25.2%	35.6%	30.1%
1980		9.6%	38.2%	25.3%	26.4%
1987		9.2%	41.6%	29.3%	19.6%

85

Table US.6   Personal and company income, 1899–1987

	Wages & salaries	Other income	Taxes, etc	Personal disposable income	Personal outlays	Personal savings	Savings ratio	Gross trading profits
				$ bn				
1899	8·9	6·6	...	...	...	...	...	...
1900	9·4	6·9	...	...	...	...	...	...
1901	10·1	7·2	...	...	...	...	...	...
1902	10·9	7·7	...	...	...	...	...	...
1903	11·7	8·0	...	...	...	...	...	...
1904	11·9	8·3	...	...	...	...	...	...
1905	13·1	8·5	...	...	...	...	...	...
1906	14·1	9·2	...	...	...	...	...	...
1907	14·7	9·8	...	...	...	...	...	...
1908	13·5	9·5	...	...	...	...	...	...
1909	15·5	11·1	...	...	...	...	...	...
1910	16·5	11·8	...	...	...	...	...	...
1911	16·7	11·5	...	...	...	...	...	...
1912	17·5	12·1	...	...	...	...	...	...
1913	19·0	12·6	...	...	...	...	...	...
1914	18·7	12·6	...	...	...	...	...	...
1915	19·5	13·2	...	...	...	...	...	...
1916	22·8	16·1	...	...	...	...	...	...
1917	27·2	19·3	...	...	...	...	...	...
1918	35·3	21·8	...	...	...	...	...	...
1919	39·6	23·4	...	...	...	...	...	...
1920	46·0	22·5	...	...	...	...	...	...
1921	37·0	19·8	...	...	...	...	...	...
1922	38·1	19·2	...	...	...	...	...	...
1923	44·6	21·1	...	...	...	...	...	...
1924	44·4	22·7	...	...	...	...	...	...
1925	46·0	24·1	...	...	...	...	...	...
1926	49·0	24·6	...	...	...	...	...	...
1927	48·9	25·1	...	...	...	...	...	...
1928	49·7	26·3	...	...	...	...	...	...
	52·1	27·5	...	...	...	...	...	...
1929	50·5	34·0	2·7	81·7	79·2	2·6	3·2	10·0
1930	46·2	29·3	2·6	73·0	71·1	1·9	2·6	3·7
1931	39·2	25·8	2·0	62·9	61·4	1·4	2·3	−0·4
1932	30·5	19·1	1·6	48·0	49·3	−1·3	−2·8	−2·3
1933	29·0	17·4	1·6	44·9	46·5	−1·6	−3·6	−1·0
1934	33·7	19·6	1·8	51·6	52·0	−0·4	−0·9	2·3
1935	36·7	23·1	2·1	57·9	56·4	1·5	2·5	3·6
1936	42·0	26·2	2·4	65·8	62·8	3·0	4·5	6·3
1937	46·1	27·8	3·5	70·5	67·5	2·9	4·2	6·9
1938	43·0	25·1	3·4	64·8	64·9	−0·1	−0·1	4·0
1939	46·0	26·7	3·0	69·7	67·9	1·8	2·6	7·2
1940	49·9	28·3	3·3	75·0	72·0	3·0	4·0	10·0
1941	62·1	33·8	4·1	91·9	81·9	10·0	10·9	17·9
1942	82·1	41·5	7·1	116·4	89·5	27·0	23·2	21·7
1943	105·6	47·0	19·6	132·9	100·2	32·7	24·6	25·3
1944	116·9	49·7	21·1	145·6	109·0	36·5	25·1	24·2
1945	117·5	54·9	23·1	149·2	120·5	28·7	19·2	19·8
1946	112·0	67·6	20·7	158·9	145·3	13·6	8·6	24·8
1947	123·1	69·2	23·5	168·8	163·6	5·2	3·1	31·8
1948	135·5	75·8	23·2	188·1	177·0	11·1	5·9	35·6
1949	134·8	73·9	20·7	187·9	180·6	7·4	3·9	29·2
1950	147·2	83·8	23·5	207·5	194·8	12·6	6·1	42·9
1951	171·5	88·4	32·3	227·6	211·0	16·6	7·3	44·5
1952	185·6	92·0	37·8	239·8	222·4	17·4	7·3	39·6
1953	199·0	95·5	39·5	255·1	236·7	18·4	7·2	41·2
1954	197·2	100·3	37·1	260·5	244·1	16·4	6·3	38·7
1955	212·1	107·3	40·6	278·8	262·8	16·0	5·8	49·2
1956	229·0	113·9	45·5	297·5	276·2	21·3	7·2	49·6
1957	239·9	122·9	49·1	313·9	291·2	22·7	7·2	48·1
1958	241·3	132·7	49·1	324·9	300·6	24·3	7·5	41·9

Table US.6 (Continued) Personal and company income, 1899–1987

	Wages & salaries	Other income	Taxes, etc	Personal disposable income	Personal outlays	Personal savings	Savings ratio	Gross trading profits
	\$ bn							
1959	259·8	138·8	54·0	344·6	322·8	21·8	6·3	52·6
1960	272·8	145·9	59·8	358·9	338·1	20·8	5·8	49·9
1961	280·5	155·0	61·9	373·8	348·9	24·9	6·6	49·8
1962	299·3	164·1	67·3	396·2	370·2	25·9	6·5	55·1
1963	314·8	173·4	72·3	415·8	391·2	24·6	5·9	59·8
1964	337·7	185·0	71·4	451·4	419·9	31·5	7·0	66·7
1965	363·7	201·6	78·5	486·8	452·5	34·3	7·0	77·4
1966	400·3	218·3	92·7	525·9	489·9	36·0	6·8	83·3
1967	428·9	236·3	103·0	562·1	516·9	45·1	8·0	80·1
1968	471·9	258·1	120·6	609·6	567·1	42·5	7·0	89·1
1969	518·3	280·9	142·5	656·7	614·5	42·2	6·4	87·2
1970	551·5	308·3	144·1	715·6	657·9	57·7	8·1	76·0
1971	583·9	340·9	148·0	776·8	710·5	66·3	8·5	87·3
1972	638·7	377·4	176·5	839·6	778·2	61·4	7·3	101·5
1973	708·7	435·7	194·6	949·8	860·8	89·0	9·4	127·2
1974	772·6	485·4	219·7	1,038·4	941·7	96·7	9·3	138·9
1975	814·6	549·1	221·0	1,142·8	1,038·2	104·6	9·2	134·8
1976	899·5	607·5	254·2	1,252·6	1,156·9	95·8	7·6	170·3
1977	993·9	674·9	289·3	1,379·3	1,288·6	90·7	6·6	200·4
1978	1,119·3	762·7	330·9	1,551·2	1,441·1	110·2	7·1	233·5
1979	1,252·1	862·9	385·7	1,729·3	1,611·3	118·1	6·8	257·2
1980	1,372·0	975·1	429·1	1,918·0	1,781·1	136·9	7·1	237·1
1981	1,510·4	1,115·2	497·8	2,127·6	1,968·1	159·4	7·5	226·5
1982	1,586·1	1,196·9	521·6	2,261·4	2,107·5	153·9	6·8	169·6
1983	1,676·2	1,282·0	530·6	2,428·1	2,297·4	130·6	5·4	207·6
1984	1,838·8	1,402·7	572·9	2,668·6	2,504·5	164·1	6·1	240·0
1985	1,974·7	1,501·1	634·8	2,841·1	2,714·1	127·1	4·5	224·3
1986	2,089·1	1,604·7	671·8	3,022·1	2,891·5	130·6	4·3	236·4
1987	2,212·7	1,702·9	734·6	3,181·1	3,060·9	120·2	3·8	276·7

Table US.7　Consumers' expenditure at constant prices, selected commodities, 1885–1987

	Food	Fuel	Clothing & footwear	Consumer durables	of which: Motor vehicles & parts	Housing	Household operation	Other services
				$ bn, 1982 prices				
1885	36·9		9·6	7·9	...		36·7	
1886	37·3		9·8	8·4	...		37·5	
1887	37·5		10·3	8·9	...		38·4	
1888	37·5		10·6	9·3	...		39·0	
1889	38·5		11·0	9·6	...		40·0	
1890	39·6		11·4	9·9	...		41·1	
1891	41·3		11·6	10·0	...		42·2	
1892	42·5		11·6	10·0	...		42·9	
1893	44·9		11·9	10·2	...		44·7	
1894	46·4		12·1	10·4	...		46·0	
1895	48·3		12·3	10·6	...		47·8	
1896	49·8		12·7	11·0	...		49·9	
1897	52·6		13·6	11·9	...		53·4	
1898	55·2		14·0	12·3	...		56·1	
1899	58·8		14·9	12·9	...		60·5	
1900	61·9		15·7	13·4	...		64·4	
1901	65·0		16·6	14·1	...		69·0	
1902	67·6		17·2	14·3	...		73·2	
1903	70·1		18·1	15·1	...		77·4	
1904	72·7		18·9	16·1	...		82·3	
1905	76·8		19·5	16·7	...		87·9	
1906	77·9		19·9	16·8	...		91·4	
1907	80·5		20·7	17·7	...		96·2	
1908	83·0		21·1	18·3	...		100·4	
1909	85·1		21·7	18·4	...		103·9	
1910	86·6		22·6	19·0	...		106·7	
1911	90·8		23·7	20·1	...		110·9	
1912	93·4		24·2	20·1	...		113·0	
1913	94·4		24·7	20·2	...		115·1	
1914	95·4		25·2	21·3	...		118·6	
1915	95·9		25·2	22·2	...		122·8	
1916	97·0		24·7	22·1	...		126·2	
1917	97·5		24·8	23·5	...		131·8	
1918	100·6		24·3	24·7	...		139·5	
1919	103·2		24·2	23·9	...		147·2	
1920	106·8		25·1	24·2	...		154·1	
1921	110·4		26·8	27·2	...		162·5	
1922	116·1		27·8	29·2	...		173·7	
1923	120·2		30·1	32·3	...		177·9	
1924	124·3		31·6	37·2	...		183·4	
1925	128·9		33·1	40·5	...		191·1	
1926	132·0		34·1	42·4	...		199·5	
1927	134·6		35·9	44·1	...		205·7	
1928	136·2		36·4	43·2	...		216·2	
1929	115·7	21·5	36·7	40·3	18·4	49·8	30·7	139·2
1930	113·7	21·0	32·9	31·9	13·6	49·3	29·8	125·7
1931	114·4	19·0	32·6	27·5	10·2	48·8	27·8	116·4
1932	107·4	18·2	29·2	21·0	6·7	47·8	25·0	104·1
1933	104·3	19·1	26·3	20·7	7·9	46·9	23·9	105·4
1934	110·1	19·8	27·9	23·4	9·7	48·6	26·2	99·9
1935	114·6	20·5	29·9	28·9	13·5	48·8	27·3	105·6
1936	129·4	22·2	32·7	35·9	17·1	49·5	29·0	112·9
1937	135·9	22·0	32·6	37·7	17·6	50·3	30·5	116·6
1938	139·2	20·4	32·9	30·4	12·0	51·0	29·0	111·3
1939	144·3	22·1	35·2	35·7	15·5	52·1	30·8	113·8
1940	150·6	23·8	36·3	40·6	18·6	53·6	32·4	116·7
1941	158·3	24·6	38·9	46·2	20·6	56·0	32·0	121·3
1942	161·8	25·3	40·3	31·3	8·4	58·1	33·4	125·7

Table US.7 (Continued) Consumers' expenditure at constant prices, selected commodities, 1885–1987

	Food	Fuel	Clothing & footwear	Consumer durables	of which: Motor vehicles & parts	Housing	Household operation	Other services
				$ bn, 1982 prices				
1943	166·3	25·7	43·0	28·1	7·7	59·8	31·2	136·2
1944	178·5	25·5	41·7	26·3	7·1	61·6	31·5	139·8
1945	193·0	27·2	43·4	28·7	7·4	62·6	32·4	145·5
1946	202·2	29·2	44·7	47·8	15·2	67·2	35·1	160·6
1947	193·9	30·8	42·5	56·5	21·8	72·8	37·6	162·2
1948	191·5	31·0	42·7	61·7	25·5	76·5	39·0	165·9
1949	193·6	27·3	43·0	67·8	32·7	80·9	40·1	164·3
1950	196·6	29·4	44·3	80·7	41·3	86·1	43·8	169·9
1951	202·5	29·3	43·7	74·7	36·3	91·9	46·2	173·0
1952	209·8	28·5	45·8	73·0	34·1	97·5	47·0	177·4
1953	217·7	27·6	46·2	80·2	39·9	102·5	48·9	182·7
1954	222·0	28·1	46·2	81·5	40·6	107·1	50·5	189·8
1955	231·3	29·9	48·6	96·9	51·5	112·1	55·5	196·0
1956	238·8	29·9	49·7	92·8	45·3	117·1	59·3	203·7
1957	243·5	29·7	49·3	92·4	45·8	122·6	61·2	208·8
1958	243·5	30·8	49·9	86·9	40·8	127·7	63·3	215·1
1959	252·1	29·4	52·3	96·9	47·4	133·6	65·7	227·4
1960	255·5	28·5	52·7	98·0	49·2	139·8	68·7	235·4
1961	259·7	26·7	53·7	93·6	44·6	145·7	70·9	244·8
1962	263·7	26·7	56·0	103·0	51·0	153·0	74·4	254·4
1963	266·5	28·0	56·9	111·8	56·4	159·4	77·0	265·9
1964	277·2	29·5	61·5	120·8	59·0	166·1	80·5	285·7
1965	290·4	31·0	64·0	134·6	67·5	174·4	83·9	300·2
1966	299·4	31·8	68·3	144·4	68·5	181·7	87·7	315·9
1967	304·0	31·8	68·8	146·2	67·4	189·3	91·9	331·1
1968	317·0	30·1	71·7	161·6	77·3	197·9	95·1	348·8
1969	324·3	28·6	73·0	167·8	80·4	207·6	99·3	364·8
1970	334·5	26·7	72·0	162·5	73·5	216·1	102·2	378·7
1971	335·9	25·9	75·3	178·3	86·4	224·5	103·6	392·1
1972	344·2	28·6	80·3	200·4	98·3	235·5	108·6	411·9
1973	340·8	30·9	86·0	220·3	106·7	246·5	112·6	427·0
1974	336·6	24·3	84·9	204·9	90·3	258·6	112·8	431·7
1975	346·4	24·2	88·1	205·6	91·1	265·7	117·5	446·6
1976	363·6	27·0	92·2	232·3	109·6	273·2	122·3	467·3
1977	377·1	26·1	97·4	253·9	121·2	279·6	128·2	490·7
1978	379·6	26·9	107·1	267·4	125·9	292·8	134·0	513·0
1979	387·5	26·2	112·1	266·5	119·4	304·1	138·3	528·8
1980	394·9	21·6	114·8	245·9	103·8	312·5	142·6	536·8
1981	392·5	19·2	122·2	250·8	106·3	318·9	142·0	548·1
1982	398·8	18·6	124·4	252·7	108·9	321·1	143·4	562·5
1983	414·0	18·6	132·6	283·1	126·8	325·4	146·2	591·1
1984	422·8	18·5	142·2	323·1	148·0	333·0	148·8	618·5
1985	435·5	19·6	147·2	355·1	164·4	341·7	151·6	659·0
1986	448·0	22·0	157·6	385·0	176·4	348·3	152·1	690·3
1987	450·4	21·1	160·5	390·9	170·4	358·3	157·0	724·2

Table US.8 Prices, 1885–1987

	Producer prices		Consumer prices				Unit value exports	Unit value imports
	All commodities	Industrial commodities	All items	Food	Apparel & upkeep	Rent		
				Index nos., 1980 = 100				
1885	11·2	...	10·9	...	...	...	12·6	8·8
1886	10·8	...	10·9	...	...	...	11·8	8·8
1887	11·2	...	10·9	...	...	...	11·8	9·1
1888	11·3	...	10·9	...	...	...	12·4	8·9
1889	10·7	...	10·9	...	...	...	11·9	9·4
1890	10·8	...	10·9	...	...	...	11·8	9·4
1891	10·7	...	10·9	...	...	...	12·2	9·2
1892	10·0	...	10·9	...	...	...	11·3	8·9
1893	10·3	...	10·9	...	...	...	11·1	9·2
1894	9·2	...	10·5	...	...	...	9·7	8·4
1895	9·4	...	10·1	...	...	...	9·9	8·0
1896	9·0	...	10·1	...	...	...	9·8	8·1
1897	9·0	...	10·1	...	...	...	9·6	7·6
1898	9·3	...	10·1	...	...	...	9·5	7·6
1899	10·0	...	10·1	...	...	...	10·0	8·2
1900	10·8	...	10·1	...	...	...	11·2	8·7
1901	10·6	...	10·1	...	...	...	11·0	8·3
1902	11·3	...	10·5	...	...	...	11·3	8·1
1903	11·4	...	10·9	...	...	...	12·0	8·4
1904	11·5	...	10·9	...	...	...	12·0	8·6
1905	11·5	...	10·9	...	...	...	11·6	9·1
1906	11·9	...	10·9	...	...	...	12·5	9·5
1907	12·5	...	11·3	...	...	...	13·3	10·0
1908	12·1	...	10·9	...	...	...	12·5	8·8
1909	13·0	...	10·9	...	...	...	13·1	8·8
1910	13·6	...	11·3	...	...	...	14·1	9·5
1911	12·5	...	11·3	...	...	...	13·0	9·6
1912	13·3	...	11·7	...	...	...	13·3	10·1
1913	13·4	13·5	12·0	11·7	16·5	25·9	13·9	10·0
1914	13·1	12·8	12·2	12·0	16·6	25·9	...	...
1915	13·3	13·1	12·3	11·8	17·0	26·0	...	...
1916	16·4	17·0	13·2	13·3	18·6	26·4	...	...
1917	22·6	22·2	15·5	17·1	22·3	26·1	...	...
1918	25·2	24·0	18·3	19·7	30·2	26·6	...	...
1919	26·6	25·0	21·0	22·0	40·1	28·8	30·5	17·8
1920	29·6	31·2	24·3	24·7	47·7	33·9	33·0	22·2
1921	18·7	20·3	21·7	18·8	36·8	38·9	21·5	12·5
1922	18·6	19·8	20·3	17·6	29·9	40·0	20·0	12·0
1923	19·3	20·2	20·7	18·1	29·9	41·0	22·8	14·1
1924	18·8	19·3	20·7	18·0	30·2	42·5	21·0	13·8
1925	19·8	19·9	21·3	19·5	29·1	42·7	21·3	15·0
1926	19·2	19·4	21·5	20·1	28·6	42·3	19·5	14·6
1927	18·4	18·2	21·1	19·4	28·0	41·6	18·3	13·6
1928	18·6	17·9	20·8	19·2	27·6	40·6	18·6	13·2
1929	18·3	17·7	20·8	19·4	27·3	39·7	18·5	12·4
1930	16·6	16·4	20·2	18·5	26·8	38·6	16·5	10·1
1931	14·0	14·5	18·5	15·2	24·4	36·5	12·7	7·9
1932	12·5	13·6	16·6	12·7	21·5	32·8	11·0	6·2
1933	12·7	13·8	15·7	12·3	20·8	28·2	11·4	6·2
1934	14·4	15·1	16·2	13·7	22·8	26·5	13·5	7·1
1935	15·4	15·1	16·6	14·7	23·0	26·4	13·7	7·2
1936	15·5	15·3	16·8	14·8	23·2	27·1	14·0	7·7
1937	16·6	16·4	17·4	15·4	24·4	28·3	14·9	8·6
1938	15·1	15·8	17·0	14·3	24·2	29·2	13·8	7·7
1939	14·8	15·8	16·8	13·9	23·9	29·2	13·5	7·8
1940	15·1	16·0	17·0	14·2	24·1	29·3	14·5	8·4
1941	16·8	17·2	17·9	15·4	25·3	29·9	15·6	9·0
1942	19·0	18·4	19·8	18·1	29·5	30·5	18·9	10·4
1943	19·8	18·7	21·0	20·2	30·8	30·5	20·8	11·3
1944	20·0	19·0	21·3	19·9	33·0	30·6	23·8	12·1

	Producer prices		Consumer prices				Unit value exports	Unit value imports
	All commodities	Industrial commodities	All items	Food	Apparel & upkeep	Rent		
					Index nos., 1980 = 100			
1945	20·3	19·3	21·8	20·4	34·7	30·7	23·7	12·4
1946	23·2	21·1	23·7	23·4	38·0	30·9	22·5	13·8
1947	28·5	25·8	27·1	28·4	44·1	31·9	26·9	17·0
1948	30·8	28·0	29·2	30·8	47·0	34·0	28·5	18·8
1949	29·3	27·4	28·9	29·6	45·2	35·5	26·5	17·9
1950	30·4	28·4	29·2	30·0	44·5	36·7	25·8	19·4
1951	33·9	31·3	31·2	33·3	48·5	38·2	29·6	24·4
1952	33·0	30·6	32·2	33·9	48·1	39·8	29·5	23·1
1953	32·5	30·9	32·4	33·4	47·7	41·9	29·2	22·2
1954	32·6	30·9	32·6	33·3	47·6	43·4	28·8	22·6
1955	32·7	31·6	32·5	32·8	47·4	44·0	29·1	22·6
1956	33·8	33·0	33·0	33·1	48·4	44·8	30·2	22·8
1957	34·7	34·0	34·1	34·1	49·2	45·7	31·1	23·2
1958	35·2	34·1	35·1	35·6	49·3	46·5	30·8	22·1
1959	35·3	34·7	35·3	35·0	49·7	47·2	30·9	21·7
1960	35·3	34·7	35·9	35·4	50·5	47·9	31·1	22·0
1961	35·2	34·5	36·3	35·8	51·0	48·5	31·7	21·7
1962	35·3	34·5	36·7	36·1	51·2	49·1	31·5	21·2
1963	35·2	34·5	37·1	36·7	51·8	49·6	31·4	21·4
1964	35·3	34·6	37·6	37·2	52·3	50·1	31·8	21·9
1965	36·0	35·1	38·3	38·0	52·8	50·6	32·8	22·2
1966	37·2	35·8	39·4	39·8	54·2	51·3	33·8	22·8
1967	37·2	36·4	40·5	40·2	56·4	52·2	34·5	23·0
1968	38·2	37·3	42·2	41·7	59·4	53·4	34·9	23·2
1969	39·6	38·6	44·5	43·8	62·9	55·2	36·1	23·9
1970	41·1	40·0	47·1	46·2	65·4	57·5	38·2	25·6
1971	42·4	41·5	49·1	47·6	67·5	60·1	39·4	26·9
1972	44·3	42·9	50·7	49·7	68·9	62·2	40·5	28·9
1973	50·1	45·8	53·9	56·9	71·5	64·9	47·4	34·1
1974	59·6	56·0	59·8	65·0	76·8	68·2	60·1	51·3
1975	65·1	62·4	65·3	70·5	80·2	71·7	67·2	55·4
1976	68·1	66·4	69·0	72·7	83·2	75·5	69·6	57·1
1977	72·3	71·0	73·5	77·3	86·9	80·1	72·4	62·0
1978	77·9	76·2	79·2	83·0	89·5	85·6	77·4	66·9
1979	87·7	86·1	88·1	92·1	93·4	91·9	88·0	79·7
1980	100·0	100·0	100·0	100·0	100·0	100·0	100·0	100·0
1981	109·2	110·7	110·4	107·9	104·8	108·7	109·2	105·5
1982	111·3	113·6	117·1	112·2	107·5	116·9	110·4	103·8
1983	112·8	114·9	120·9	114·6	110·1	123·6	111·6	99·5
1984	115·4	117·4	126·0	119·0	112·2	130·1	113·1	101·3
1985	114·8	117·8	130·0	121·7	115·5	138·1	112·2	98·8
1986	111·5	113·6	133·1	125·6	116·5	146·1	112·5	95·4
1987	114·4	116·6	137·9	130·8	121·6	152·1	114·8	102·0

Table US.9   Population, 1885–1987

	Total population	Births	Age distribution				Geographical distribution			
			0–14	15–34	35–64	65 & over	North East	Mid-West	South	West
	mn	'000	mn				mn			
1885	56·7	...	...	...	...	...	...	...	...	...
1886	57·9	...	...	...	...	...	...	...	...	...
1887	59·2	...	...	...	...	...	...	...	...	...
1888	60·5	...	...	...	...	...	...	...	...	...
1889	61·8	...	...	...	...	...	...	...	...	...
1890	63·1	...	22·2	22·6	15·2	2·4	17·41	22·41	20·03	3·13
1891	64·4	...	...	...	...	...	...	...	...	...
1892	65·7	...	...	...	...	...	...	...	...	...
1893	67·0	...	...	...	...	...	...	...	...	...
1894	68·3	...	...	...	...	...	...	...	...	...
1895	69·6	...	...	...	...	...	...	...	...	...
1896	70·9	...	...	...	...	...	...	...	...	...
1897	72·2	...	...	...	...	...	...	...	...	...
1898	73·5	...	...	...	...	...	...	...	...	...
1899	74·8	...	...	...	...	...	...	...	...	...
1900	76·1	...	26·1	27·1	19·7	3·1	21·05	26·33	24·52	4·31
1901	77·6	...	26·5	27·7	20·2	3·2	...	...	...	...
1902	79·2	...	26·9	28·3	20·8	3·3	...	...	...	...
1903	80·6	...	27·2	28·9	21·3	3·3	...	...	...	...
1904	82·2	...	27·5	29·5	21·8	3·4	...	...	...	...
1905	83·8	...	27·8	30·2	22·3	3·5	...	...	...	...
1906	85·4	...	28·2	30·8	22·9	3·6	...	...	...	...
1907	87·0	...	28·5	31·4	23·4	3·7	...	...	...	...
1908	88·7	...	28·8	32·1	24·0	3·8	...	...	...	...
1909	90·5	2,718	29·2	32·8	24·6	3·9	...	...	...	...
1910	92·4	2,777	29·6	33·5	25·3	4·0	25·87	29·89	29·39	7·08
1911	93·9	2,809	30·0	33·9	25·9	4·1	...	...	...	...
1912	95·3	2,840	30·4	34·2	26·5	4·2	...	...	...	...
1913	97·2	2,869	31·0	34·7	27·2	4·3	...	...	...	...
1914	99·1	2,966	31·6	35·2	28·0	4·4	...	...	...	...
1915	100·5	2,965	32·0	35·4	28·6	4·5	...	...	...	...
1916	102·0	2,964	32·5	35·6	29·3	4·6	...	...	...	...
1917	103·3	2,944	32·9	35·7	29·9	4·7	...	...	...	...
1918	103·2	2,948	33·3	34·5	30·5	4·8	...	...	...	...
1919	104·5	2,740	33·4	35·4	30·9	4·9	...	...	...	...
1920	106·5	2,950	33·8	36·2	31·5	4·9	29·66	34·02	33·13	9·21
1921	108·5	3,055	34·4	36·9	32·2	5·1	...	...	...	...
1922	110·1	2,882	34·8	37·3	32·7	5·2	...	...	...	...
1923	112·0	2,910	35·2	38·0	33·3	5·4	...	...	...	...
1924	114·1	2,979	35·6	38·9	34·0	5·6	...	...	...	...
1925	115·8	2,909	35·9	39·4	34·7	5·8	...	...	...	...
1926	117·4	2,839	36·1	39·9	35·4	6·0	...	...	...	...
1927	119·0	2,802	36·3	40·4	36·3	6·1	...	...	...	...
1928	120·5	2,674	36·3	40·8	37·1	6·3	...	...	...	...
1929	121·8	2,582	36·2	41·1	38·0	6·5	...	...	...	...
1930	123·1	2,318	36·0	41·5	38·8	6·7	34·43	38·59	37·86	12·32
1931	124·1	2,506	35·8	41·9	39·4	6·9	...	...	...	...
1932	124·8	2,440	35·5	42·2	40·0	7·1	...	...	...	...
1933	125·6	2,307	35·1	42·6	40·5	7·4	...	...	...	...
1934	126·4	2,396	34·7	43·0	41·1	7·6	...	...	...	...
1935	127·3	2,377	34·4	43·4	41·7	7·8	...	...	...	...
1936	128·1	2,355	33·9	43·8	42·2	8·0	...	...	...	...
1937	128·8	2,413	33·6	44·2	42·8	8·3	...	...	...	...
1938	129·8	2,496	33·3	44·6	43·4	8·5	...	...	...	...
1939	130·9	2,466	33·1	45·0	44·0	8·8	...	...	...	...
1940	132·1	2,559	32·9	45·5	44·7	9·0	35·98	40·14	41·67	14·38
1941	133·4	2,703	32·9	45·8	45·4	9·3	...	...	...	...
1942	134·9	2,989	33·1	46·0	46·1	9·6	...	...	...	...
1943	136·7	3,104	33·7	46·3	46·9	9·9	...	...	...	...
1944	138·4	2,939	34·1	46·5	47·6	10·1	...	...	...	...

Table **US.9 (Continued)**   **Population, 1885–1987**

	Total population	Births	Age distribution				Geographical distribution			
			0–14	15–34	35–64	65 & over	North East	Mid-West	South	West
	mn	'000	mn				mn			
1945	139·9	2,858	34·6	46·4	48·4	10·5	. . .	. . .	. . .	. . .
1946	141·4	3,411	35·1	46·3	49·1	10·8	. . .	. . .	. . .	. . .
1947	144·1	3,817	36·7	46·4	49·9	11·2	. . .	. . .	. . .	. . .
1948	146·6	3,637	38·0	46·4	50·7	11·5	. . .	. . .	. . .	. . .
1949	149·2	3,649	39·4	46·3	51·6	11·9	. . .	. . .	. . .	. . .
1950	152·3	3,632	40·8	46·2	52·3	12·4	39·48	44·46	47·20	20·19
1951	154·9	3,823	42·3	46·1	53·1	12·8	. . .	. . .	. . .	. . .
1952	157·6	3,913	43·9	46·0	53·9	13·2	. . .	. . .	. . .	. . .
1953	160·2	3,965	45·4	45·9	54·7	13·6	. . .	. . .	. . .	. . .
1954	163·0	4,078	47·1	45·9	55·4	14·0	. . .	. . .	. . .	. . .
1955	165·9	4,097	48·7	45·8	56·2	14·5	. . .	. . .	. . .	. . .
1956	168·9	4,218	50·3	45·9	57·1	14·9	. . .	. . .	. . .	. . .
1957	172·0	4,308	51·9	46·0	58·0	15·4	. . .	. . .	. . .	. . .
1958	174·9	4,255	53·1	46·6	58·7	15·8	. . .	. . .	. . .	. . .
1959	177·1	4,245[a]	54·4	47·0	59·5	16·2	. . .	. . .	. . .	. . .
	177·8		54·7	47·2	59·7	16·2	. . .	. . .	. . .	. . .
1960	180·7	4,258[b]	56·1	47·5	60·4	16·7	44·68	51·62	54·97	28·05
1961	183·7	4,268	57·6	47·9	61·1	17·1	. . .	. . .	. . .	. . .
1962	186·6	4,167	57·9	49·4	61·8	17·5	. . .	. . .	. . .	. . .
1963	189·2	4,098	58·5	50·6	62·4	17·8	. . .	. . .	. . .	. . .
1964	191·9	4,027	58·9	51·9	62·9	18·1	. . .	. . .	. . .	. . .
1965	194·3	3,760	59·3	53·2	63·4	18·5	. . .	. . .	. . .	. . .
1966	196·6	3,606	59·3	54·7	63·8	18·8	. . .	. . .	. . .	. . .
1967	198·7	3,521	59·1	56·4	64·2	19·1	. . .	. . .	. . .	. . .
1968	200·7	3,502	58·9	58·1	64·6	19·4	. . .	. . .	. . .	. . .
1969	202·7	3,600	58·3	59·9	64·8	19·7	. . .	. . .	. . .	. . .
1970	205·1	3,731	57·9	61·9	65·1	20·1	49·06	56·59	62·81	34·84
1971	207·7	3,556	57·7	63·9	65·5	20·6	49·49	57·03	64·11	35·57
1972	209·9	3,258	57·0	66·1	65·8	21·0	49·62	57·29	65·22	36·11
1973	211·9	3,137	56·2	68·2	66·0	21·5	49·48	57·44	66·23	36·70
1974	213·9	3,160	55·2	70·2	66·3	22·1	49·33	57·55	67·22	37·30
1975	216·0	3,144	54·4	72·3	66·6	22·7	49·33	57·65	68·12	37·95
1976	218·0	3,168	53·4	74·3	67·1	23·3	49·29	57·83	68·94	38·63
1977	220·2	3,327	53·0	76·0	67·7	23·9	49·19	58·05	69·79	39·37
1978	222·6	3,333	52·0	77·4	68·7	24·5	49·09	58·26	70·64	40·24
1979	225·1	3,494	51·4	78·9	69·6	25·1	49·00	58·41	71·55	41·14
1980	226·6	3,704	51·3	79·6	70·1	25·6	49·14	58·87	75·37	43·17
1981	229·6	3,629	51·3	81·1	71·0	26·2	49·26	59·01	77·06	44·32
1982	232·0	3,681	51·5	81·0	72·6	26·8	49·31	58·96	78·49	45·24
1983	234·3	3,639	51·7	81·2	74·0	27·4	49·51	58·94	79·73	46·12
1984	236·5	3,669	51·8	81·3	75·4	28·0	49·69	59·10	80·78	46·91
1985	238·7	3,761	51·9	81·6	76·7	28·5	49·83	59·20	81·89	47·82
1986	241·1	3,731[c]	52·0	81·8	78·1	29·2	50·02[c]	59·31[c]	82·99[c]	48·76[c]
1987	243·2	. . .	. . .	. . .	. . .	29·8	. . .	. . .	. . .	. . .

a Including Alaska.
b Including Alaska and Hawaii.
c Provisional.

Table US.10   Education, 1885–1985

| | Kindergarten | Elementary | Secondary | % of population 5–17 years | Higher education | | % of population 18–24 years |
| | | | | | Total | of which: Female | |
		No. of pupils '000			No. of students '000		
1885	...	11,398		...	...	...	...
1886	...	11,664		...	...	...	...
1887	...	11,885		...	...	...	...
1888	...	12,183		...	...	...	...
1889	...	12,392		75·2	...	...	...
1890	...	12,520	203	78·1	157	56	1·8
1891	...	12,839	212	77·3	...	...	...
1892	...	13,016	240	76·3	...	...	...
1893	...	13,229	254	76·6	...	...	...
1894	...	13,706	289	78·0	...	...	...
1895	...	13,894	350	77·6	...	...	...
1896	...	14,118	380	78·4	...	...	...
1897	...	14,414	409	78·8	...	...	...
1898	...	14,654	450	79·2	...	...	...
1899	...	14,700	476	78·2	...	...	...
1900	...	14,984	519	78·3	238	85	2·3
1901	...	15,161	542	78·3	...	...	...
1902	...	15,367	551	77·6	...	...	...
1903	...	15,417	592	71·1	...	...	...
1904	...	15,620	636	77·8	...	...	...
1905	...	15,789	680	77·9	264	...	2·3
1906	...	15,919	723	78·0	...	...	...
1907	...	16,140	751	77·8	...	...	...
1908	...	16,292	770	78·6	...	...	...
1909	...	16,665	841	79·1	...	...	...
1910	...	16,899	915	79·4	355	141	2·9
1911	...	17,050	985	79·5	354	...	2·8
1912	...	17,078	1,105	79·2	356	...	2·7
1913	...	17,474	1,135	79·8	361	...	2·8
1914	...	17,935	1,219	80·6	379	...	2·9
1915	...	18,375	1,329	81·5	404	...	3·1
1916	...	18,896	1,456	83·0	441	...	3·3
1918	...	18,920	1,934	81·8	441	...	3·6
1920	481	18,897	2,200	83·2	598	283	4·7
1922	529	19,837	2,873	85·8	681	...	5·1
1924	610	20,289	3,390	87·3	823	...	5·9
1926	673	20,311	3,757	88·8	941	...	6·6
1928	695	20,573	3,911	89·1	1,054	...	7·1
1930	723	20,556	4,399	89·5	1,101	481	7·2
1932	701	20,434	5,140	91·8	1,154	...	7·4
1934	602	20,163	5,669	92·6	1,055	...	6·6
1936	607	19,786	5,975	92·9	1,208	...	7·5
1938	607	19,141	6,227	93·7	1,351	...	8·3
1940	595	18,237	6,601	94·2	1,494	601	9·1
1942	626	17,549	6,388	93·5	1,404	...	8·4

| | Kindergarten | Elementary | Secondary | % of population 5–17 years | Higher education | | % of population 18–24 years |
| | | | | | Total | of which: Female | |
	No. of pupils '000				No. of students '000		
1944	697	17,016	5,554	89.7	1,155	. . .	6·8
1946	773	16,905	5,622	91·2	2,078	661	12·5
1948	. . .	17,302	5,653	91·1	2,403	. . .	14·7
1950	. . .	18,353	5,725	83·2	2,281	721	14·2
1951	. . .	. . .	. . .	. . .	2,102	711	. . .
1952	. . .	19,409	5,882	(87·5)	2,134	754	13·8
1953	1,474	21,072	6,290	(90·5)	2,231	808	. . .
1954	1,415	22,056	6,574	(90·9)	2,447	883	16·2
1955	1,564	22,726	6,873	(90·6)	2,653	920	. . .
1956	1,675	23,341	7,318	(90·2)	2,918	1,007	19·5
1957	1,772	23,897	7,860	(90·0)	3,037	1,052	. . .
1958	1,834	24,747	8,258	(90·6)	3,226	1,134	21·2
1959	1,923	25,679	8,485	(91·4)	3,365	1,211	. . .
1960	2,000	26,439	8,821	(91·6)	3,583	1,326	22·2
1961	2,065	26,621	9,566	(91·0)	3,861	1,452	. . .
1962	2,162	27,212	10,372	(91·2)	4,175	1,588	23·6
1963	2,177	27,738	10,883	(92·8)	4,766	1,811	. . .
1964	2,250	28,402	11,628	(94·6)	5,280	2,031	26·3
1965	2,328	28,849	11,610	(94·2)	5,921	2,291	. . .
1966	2,364	28,781	11,894	(93·1)	6,390	2,534	27·7
1967	2,432	29,210	12,250	(93·7)	6,912	2,779	25·5
1968	2,526	29,700	12,718	(95·1)	7,513	3,035	26·0
1969	2,601	29,996	13,022	(95·9)	8,005	3,258	27·3
1970	2,559	30,018	13,332	(96·7)	8,581	3,537	25·7
1971	2,483	29,782	13,816	(97·8)	8,949	3,742	26·2
1972	2,487	29,349	13,908	(97·9)	9,215	3,976	25·5
1973	2,639	28,714	14,077	(98·2)	9,602	4,231	24·0
1974	2,784	28,137	14,132	(98·3)	10,224	4,601	24·6
1975	2,945	27,542	14,304	(98·4)	11,185	5,036	26·3
1976	2,919	27,087	14,310	(98·3)	11,012	5,201	26·7
1977	2,742	26,594	14,240	(98·9)	11,286	5,497	26·1
1978	2,652	25,773	14,125	(98·7)	11,260	5,619	25·3
1979	2,675	25,256	13,714	(98·5)	11,570	5,887	25·0
1980	2,689	24,985	13,313	(98·6)	12,097	6,223	25·6
1981	2,687	24,558	12,855	(98·0)	12,372	6,397	26·2
1982	2,845	24,311	12,496	(97·2)	12,426	6,394	26·6
1983	2,860	24,137	12,355	(96·9)	12,465	6,441	26·2
1984	3,010	23,908	12,375	(96·3)	12,242	6,378	27·1
1985	3,191	23,856	12,467	(96·4)	12,247	6,429	27·8

Table US.11   Labour market: employment, 1900–87

	Number in civil work	Employed in agriculture	Mining	Mfg	Transport & public utilities	Distributive trades	Services	Govt	Self-employed
	mn					'000			
1900	27·0	11·1	637	5,468	2,282	2,502	2,048	1,094	...
1901	27·9	10·9	703	5,817	2,404	2,765	2,202	1,129	...
1902	28·8	10·8	685	6,305	2,754	2,827	2,240	1,191	...
1903	29·5	10·9	834	6,527	2,666	2,979	2,333	1,229	...
1904	29·8	11·1	801	6,199	2,743	2,992	2,371	1,277	...
1905	30·9	11·2	889	6,739	2,905	3,170	2,461	1,335	...
1906	32·6	11·5	894	7,226	3,110	3,442	2,620	1,386	...
1907	33·2	11·5	1,051	7,322	3,114	3,486	2,666	1,448	...
1908	32·1	11·2	900	6,570	3,069	3,299	2,606	1,507	...
1909	33·9	11·2	998	7,661	3,229	3,585	2,790	1,564	...
1910	34·6	11·3	1,068	7,828	3,366	3,570	2,893	1,630	...
1911	35·0	11·1	1,052	7,870	3,426	3,813	3,011	1,672	...
1912	36·2	11·1	1,083	8,322	3,552	4,073	3,107	1,717	...
1913	37·0	11·0	1,182	8,751	3,570	4,232	3,239	1,757	...
1914	36·3	10·9	1,027	8,210	3,445	4,128	3,304	1,809	...
1915	36·2	11·0	1,022	8,210	3,439	4,091	3,331	1,861	...
1916	38·0	10·8	1,168	9,629	3,579	4,476	3,534	1,916	...
1917	38·2	10·8	1,267	9,872	3,722	4,320	3,554	2,000	...
1918	38·5	10·7	1,311	10,167	3,877	4,110	3,578	2,461	...
1919	39·2	10·5	1,133	10,659	3,711	4,514	3,349	2,676	...
1920	39·2	10·4	1,239	10,658	3,998	4,467	3,512	2,603	...
1921	37·1	10·4	962	8,527	3,459	3,960	4,053	2,528	...
1922	39·6	10·6	929	9,120	3,505	4,708	4,232	2,538	...
1923	42·4	10·6	1,212	10,300	3,882	5,194	4,422	2,607	...
1924	42·0	10·6	1,101	9,671	3,807	5,047	4,509	2,720	...
1925	43·7	10·7	1,089	9,939	3,826	5,576	4,075	2,800	...
1926	44·8	10·7	1,185	10,156	3,942	5,784	4,323	2,846	...
1927	44·9	10·5	1,114	10,001	3,895	5,908	4,506	2,915	...
1928	45·1	10·5	1,050	9,947	3,828	5,874	4,671	2,995	...
1929	47·6	10·5	1,087	10,702	3,916	6,123	4,919	3,065	10,320
1930	45·5	10·3	1,009	9,562	3,685	5,797	4,821	3,148	10,311
1931	42·4	10·3	873	8,170	3,254	5,284	4,561	3,264	10,352
1932	38·9	10·2	731	6,931	2,816	4,683	4,244	3,225	10,350
1933	38·8	10·1	744	7,397	2,672	4,755	4,141	3,166	10,371
1934	40·9	9·9	883	8,501	2,750	5,281	4,349	3,299	10,493
1935	42·3	10·1	897	9,069	2,786	5,431	4,448	3,481	10,645
1936	44·4	10·0	946	9,827	2,973	5,809	4,685	3,668	10,567
1937	46·3	9·3	1,015	10,794	3,134	6,265	4,920	3,756	10,495
1938	44·2	9·7	891	9,440	2,863	6,179	4,868	3,883	10,338
1939	45·8	9·6	854	10,278	2,936	6,426	4,949	3,995	10,266
1940	47·5	9·5	925	10,985	3,038	6,750	5,150	4,202	10,150
1941	50·4	9·1	957	13,192	3,274	7,210	5,430	4,660	10,090
1942	53·8	9·3	992	15,280	3,460	7,118	5,575	5,483	9,947
1943	54·5	9·1	925	17,602	3,647	6,982	5,611	6,080	9,431
1944	54·0	9·0	892	17,328	3,829	7,058	5,606	6,043	9,273
1945	52·8	8·6	836	15,524	3,906	7,314	5,703	5,944	9,349
1946	55·2	8·3	862	14,703	4,061	8,376	6,372	5,595	9,913
1947	57·8 / 57·0	8·3 / 7·9	955	15,545	4,166	8,955	6,753	5,474	10,199
1948	58·3	7·6	994	15,582	4,189	9,272	6,981	5,650	10,211
1949	57·6	7·7	930	14,441	4,001	9,264	7,068	5,856	10,064
1950	58·9	6·2	901	15,241	4,034	9,386	7,245	6,026	9,996
1951	60·0	6·7	929	16,393	4,226	9,742	7,503	6,389	9,699
1952	60·2	6·5	898	16,632	4,248	10,004	7,734	6,609	9,637
1953	61·2	6·3	866	17,549	4,290	10,247	7,946	6,645	9,475
1954	60·1	6·2	791	16,314	4,084	10,235	8,169	6,751	9,329
1955	62·2	6·4	792	16,882	4,141	10,535	8,538	6,914	9,149
1956	63·8	6·3	822	17,243	4,244	10,858	8,886	7,278	8,981
1957	64·1	5·9	828	17,174	4,241	10,886	9,146	7,616	8,821

| | Number in civil work | Employed in agriculture | Employment by sector | | | | | | |
| | | | Mining | Mfg | Transport & public utilities | Distributive trades | Services | Govt | Self-employed |
	mn					'000			
1958	63·0	5·6	751	15,945	3,976	10,750	9,246	7,839	8,611
1959	64·6	5·6	732	16,675	4,011	11,127	9,636	8,083	8,428
1960	65·8	5·5	712	16,796	4,004	11,391	10,007	8,353	8,305
1961	65·7	5·2	672	16,326	3,903	11,337	10,308	8,594	8,177
1962	66·7	4·9	650	16,853	3,906	11,566	10,736	8,890	8,009
1963	67·7	4·7	635	16,995	3,903	11,778	11,107	9,225	7,722
1964	69·3	4·5	634	17,274	3,951	12,160	11,571	9,596	7,652
1965	71·1	4·4	632	18,062	4,036	12,716	12,013	10,074	7,526
1966	72·9	4·0	627	19,214	4,158	13,245	12,556	10,784	7,271
1967	74·4	3·8	613	19,447	4,268	13,606	13,230	11,391	7,188
1968	75·9	3·8	606	19,781	4,318	14,099	13,904	11,839	7,115
1969	77·9	3·6	619	20,167	4,442	14,705	14,681	12,195	7,199
1970	78·7	3·5	623	19,367	4,515	15,040	15,193	12,554	7,097
1971	79·4	3·4	609	18,623	4,476	15,352	15,569	12,881	7,142
1972	82·2	3·5	628	19,151	4,541	15,949	16,184	13,334	7,234
1973	85·1	3·5	642	20,154	4,656	16,607	16,903	13,732	7,316
1974	86·8	3·5	697	20,077	4,725	16,987	17,589	14,170	7,527
1975	85·8	3·4	752	18,323	4,542	17,060	18,057	14,686	7,506
1976	88·8	3·3	779	18,997	4,582	17,755	18,822	14,871	7,495
1977	92·0	3·3	813	19,682	4,713	18,516	19,770	15,127	7,758
1978	96·0	3·4	851	20,505	4,923	19,542	20,976	15,672	8,118
1979	98·8	3·3	958	21,040	5.136	20,192	22,087	15,947	8,416
1980	99·3	3·4	1,027	20,285	5,146	20,310	23,050	16,241	8,658
1981	100·4	3·4	1,139	20,170	5,165	20,547	23,917	16,031	8,753
1982	99·5	3·4	1,128	18,781	5,082	20,457	24,377	15,837	8,923
1983	100·8	3·4	952	18,434	4,954	20,881	25,162	15,869	9,213
1984	105·0	3·3	966	19,378	5,159	22,100	26,486	16,024	9,412
1985	107·2	3·2	927	19,260	5,238	23,073	27,955	16,394	9,327
1986	109·6	3·2	783	18,994	5,244	23,580	29,396	16,711	9,387
1987	112·4	3·2	742	19,112	5,377	24,059	30,727	17,063	9,681

Table US.12 Labour market: other indicators, 1885–1987

	Productivity		Average weekly hrs of mfg production workers	Average weekly earnings of mfg production workers	Unemployment		Industrial disputes	
	Gross private domestic product per man hr	Output per man hr in mfg					Workers involved	Man days idle
	Index nos., 1980 = 100			$	'000	%	'000	mn
1885	...	...	...	...	...	...	258	...
1886	...	...	...	...	...	...	610	...
1887	...	...	...	...	...	...	439	...
1888	...	...	...	...	...	...	163	...
1889	13·6	12·2	53·5	...	...	...	260	...
1890	14·3	12·6	...	...	904	4·0	373	...
1891	14·6	12·7	...	...	1,265	5·4	330	...
1892	15·5	12·8	...	...	728	3·0	239	...
1893	14·8	12·0	...	...	2,860	11·7	288	...
1894	14·9	12·6	...	...	4,612	18·4	690	...
1895	15·9	13·5	...	...	3,510	13·7	407	...
1896	15·5	12·7	...	...	3,782	14·4	249	...
1897	16·6	13·3	...	...	3,890	14·5	416	...
1898	16·8	14·7	...	...	3,351	12·4	263	...
1899	17·1	14·1	52·7	...	1,819	6·5	432	...
1900	17·4	13·7	...	...	1,420	5·0	568	...
1901	18·6	14·6	...	...	1,205	4·0	564	...
1902	17·9	15·3	...	...	1,097	3·7	692	...
1903	18·3	14·8	...	...	1,204	3·9	788	...
1904	18·3	15·5	...	...	1,691	5·4	574	...
1905	18·7	15·6	...	...	1,381	4·3	302	...
1906	20·1	15·8	...	...	574	1·7	...	...
1907	20·1	15·2	...	...	945	2·8	...	...
1908	19·1	14·2	...	...	2,780	8·0	...	...
1909	20·5	16·1	51·0	9·74	1,824	5·1	...	...
1910	20·1	15·9	...	...	2,150	5·9	...	...
1911	20·5	15·2	...	...	2,518	6·7	...	...
1912	20·9	17·5	...	...	1,759	4·6	...	...
1913	21·6	18·3	...	...	1,671	4·3	...	...
1914	20·2	18·4	49·4	10·92	3,120	7·9	...	...
1915	21·0	20·7	...	11·22	3,377	8·5	...	...
1916	22·6	20·4	...	12·63	2,043	5·1	...	...
1917	21·4	19·0	...	14·97	1,848	4·6	...	...
1918	23·2	18·9	...	19·12	536	1·4	...	...
1919	24·7	18·0	46·3	21·84	546	1·4	...	...
1920	24·5	19·1	47·4	26·02	2,132	5·2	1,420	...
1921	26·2	22·1	43·1	21·94	4,918	11·7	1,099	...
1922	25·9	25·0	44·2	21·28	2,859	6·7	1,613	...
1923	27·5	24·1	45·6	23·56	1,049	2·4	757	...
1924	28·7	25·6	43·7	23·67	2,190	5·0	655	...
1925	28·6	27·3	44·5	24·11	1,453	3·2	428	...
1926	29·4	27·8	45·0	24·38	801	1·8	330	...
1927	29·9	28·5	45·0	24·47	1,519	3·3	330	26·20
1928	29·9	29·7	44·4	24·70	1,982	4·2	314	12·60
1929	31·3	31·1	44·2	24·76	1,550	3·2	289	5·35
1930	30·1	31·3	42·1	23·00	4,340	8·7	183	3·32
1931	30·4	32·3	40·5	20·64	8,020	15·9	342	6·89
1932	29·2	30·2	38·3	16·89	12,060	23·6	324	10·50
1933	28·6	32·9	38·1	16·65	12,830	24·9	1,170	16·90
1934	31·5	34·4	34·6	18·20	11,340	21·7	1,470	19·60
1935	32·6	36·7	36·6	19·91	10,610	20·1	1,120	15·50
1936	34·2	36·9	39·2	21·56	9,030	16·9	789	13·90
1937	34·2	36·4	38·6	23·82	7,700	14·3	1,860	28·40
1938	35·2	35·9	35·6	22·07	10,390	19·0	688	9·15
1939	36·6	39·2	37·7	23·64	9,480	17·2	1,170	17·80
1940	37·6	41·1	38·1	24·96	8,120	14·6	577	6·70
1941	39·8	42·6	40·6	29·48	5,560	9·9	2,360	23·00
1942	39·9	43·4	43·1	36·68	2,660	4·7	840	4·18
1943	40·5	44·0	45·0	43·07	1,070	1·9	1,980	13·50

	Productivity		Average weekly hrs of mfg production workers	Average weekly earnings of mfg production workers	Unemployment		Industrial disputes	
	Gross private domestic product per man hr	Output per man hr in mfg					Workers involved	Man days idle
	Index nos., 1980 = 100			$	'000	%	'000	mn
1944	43·2	43·4	45·2	45·70	670	1·2	2,120	8·72
1945	45·5	42·8	43·5	44·20	1,040	1·9	3,470	38·00
1946	44·2	39·4	40·3	43·32	2,270	3·9	4,600	116·00
1947	45·2	41·7	40·4	49·13	2,311	3·9	2,170	34·60
1948	47·5	44·3	40·0	53·08	2,276	3·8	1,960	34·10
1949	48·0	46·1	39·1	53·80	3,637	5·9	3,030	50·50
1950	52·1	48·6	40·5	58·28	3,288	5·2	2,410	38·80
1951	54·2	50·2	40·6	63·34	2,055	3·2	2,220	22·90
1952	55·8	51·1	40·7	66·75	1,883	2·9	3,540	59·10
1953	57·9	52·0	40·5	70·47	1,834	2·8	2,400	28·30
1954	58·8	52·8	39·6	70·49	3,532	5·4	1,530	22·60
1955	60·5	55·5	40·7	75·30	2,852	4·3	2,650	28·20
1956	61·3	55·1	40·4	78·78	2,750	4·0	1,900	33·10
1957	62·9	56·1	39·8	81·19	2,859	4·2	1,390	16·50
1958	64·9	55·9	39·2	82·32	4,602	6·6	2,060	23·90
1959	67·0	58·6	40·3	88·26	3,740	5·3	1,880	69·00
1960	68·1	59·0	39·7	89·72	3,852	5·4	1,320	19·10
1961	70·5	60·6	39·8	92·34	4,714	6·5	1,450	16·30
1962	73·0	63·2	40·4	96·56	3,911	5·4	1,230	18·60
1963	75·9	67·7	40·5	99·23	4,070	5·5	941	16·10
1964	79·3	71·1	40·7	102·97	3,786	5·0	1,640	22·90
1965	81·6	73·3	41·2	107·53	3,366	4·4	1,550	23·30
1966	83·8	74·0	41·4	112·19	2,875	3·7	1,960	25·40
1967	86·1	74·0	40·6	114·49	2,975	3·7	2,870	42·10
1968	88·4	76·7	40·7	122·51	2,817	3·5	2,649	49·02
1969	88·4	78·0	40·6	129·51	2,832	3·4	2,481	42·87
1970	89·0	77·8	39·8	133·33	4,093	4·8	3,305	66·41
1971	91·9	82·5	39·9	142·44	5,016	5·8	3,280	47·59
1972	94·8	86·7	40·5	154·71	4,882	5·5	1,714	27·07
1973	96·6	91·4	40·7	166·46	4,365	4·8	2,251	27·95
1974	94·6	89·3	40·0	176·80	5,156	5·5	2,778	47·99
1975	96·4	91·8	39·5	190·79	7,929	8·3	1,746	31·24
1976	99·0	95·9	40·1	209·32	7,406	7·6	2,420	37·86
1977	100·7	98·3	40·3	228·90	6,991	6·9	2,040	35·82
1978	101·5	99·1	40·4	249·27	6,202	6·0	1,623	36·92
1979	100·3	99·8	40·2	269·34	6,137	5·8	1,727	34·75
1980	100·0	100·0	39·7	288·62	7,637	7·0	1,366	33·29
1981	101·4	102·2	39·8	318·00	8,273	7·5	1,081	24·73
							729	16·91
1982	101·0	104·4	38·9	330·26	10,678	9·5	656	9·06
1983	103·7	110·4	40·1	354·08	10,717	9·5	909	17·46
1984	106·3	115·0	40·7	374·03	8,539	7·4	376	8·50
1985	108·3	120·0	40·5	386·37	8,312	7·1	324	7·08
1986	110·3	124·3	40·7	396·01	8,237	6·9	529	12·14
1987	111·3	. . .	41·0	406·31	7,425	6·1	174	4·48

Table US.13   Value of imports by commodity group, 1885–1987

	Total imports	Food, feeds & beverages	Industrial supplies & materials	*of which:* Petroleum & products	Capital goods (excl. autos)	Consumer goods (non-food) (excl. autos)	Motor vehicles parts & engines
				$ mn			
1885	578	196	198	—		183	
1886	635	205	237	—		195	
1887	692	218	271	—		203	
1888	724	227	286	—		211	
1889	745	245	287	—		212	
1890	789	261	297	—		231	
1891	845	299	329	—		218	
1892	827	316	308	—		205	
1893	866	286	353	—		229	
1894	655	288	218	—		149	
1895	732	248	284	—		200	
1896	780	249	304	—		227	
1897	765	257	289	—		218	
1898	616	190	273	—		153	
1899	697	222	305	—		170	
1900	850	231	416	—		203	
1901	823	236	382	—		206	
1902	903	215	457	—		231	
1903	1,026	236	532	—		258	
1904	991	250	488	—		253	
1905	1,118	291	574	—		252	
1906	1,227	274	644	—		308	
1907	1,434	309	762	—		364	
1908	1,194	293	570	—		332	
1909	1,312	330	683	1		299	
1910	1,557	327	863	1		368	
1911	1,527	353	813	2		361	
1912	1,653	426	867	3		360	
1913	1,813	406	998	5		408	
1914	1,894	476	969	11		449	
1915	1,674	510	828	15		336	
1916	2,392	599	1,448	11		346	
1917	2,952	738	1,823	15		392	
1918	3,031	743	1,884	22		405	
1919	3,904	1,101	2,310	27		493	
1920	5,278	1,816	2,586	33		877	
1921	2,509	668	1,221	68		620	
1922	3,113	717	1,733	79		663	
1923	3,792	891	2,468	80	17	364	1
1924	3,610	942	2,245	103	14	369	1
1925	4,227	918	2,855	109	16	394	1
1926	4,431	953	2,979	126	23	433	2
1927	4,185	950	2,727	115	24	439	2
1928	4,091	951	2,618	134	27	446	3
1929	4,399	955	2,837	145	39	516	3
1930	3,061	684	1,943	146	29	347	2
1931	2,091	523	1,268	93	14	239	1
1932	1,333	404	742	61	8	142	—
1933	1,450	403	861	26	7	141	—
1934	1,655	514	933	37	11	155	—
1935	2,047	635	1,183	38	14	182	—
1936	2,423	728	1,443	41	17	215	1
1937	3,084	844	1,856	45	23	255	1
1938	1,960	566	1,150	39	16	186	2
1939	2,318	600	1,431	44	13	198	1
1940	2,625	556	1,778	70	9	166	1
1941	3,345	655	2,271	82	13	119	—
1942	2,756	575	1,868	37	27	116	—
1943	3,381	892	1,834	85	23	190	—
1944	3,929	1,178	1,961	113	21	240	—
1945	4,159	1,063	2,300	152	24	322	—

Table US.13 (Continued)   Value of imports by commodity group, 1885–1987

	Total imports	Food, feeds & beverages	Industrial supplies & materials	*of which:* Petroleum & products	Capital goods (excl. autos)	Consumer goods (non-food) (excl. autos)	Motor vehicles parts & engines
				$ mn			
1946	5,003	1,328	3,065	159	32	492	5
1947	5,829	1,673	3,626	250	55	375	6
1948	7,207	1,986	4,508	416	103	434	35
1949	6,706	2,068	4,011	478	106	404	13
1950	8,954	2,642	5,493	592	111	540	23
1951	11,068	3,087	6,952	601	170	666	38
1952	10,817	3,156	6,537	692	227	663	56
1953	10,983	3,282	6,456	762	224	757	53
1954	10,369	3,317	5,764	829	220	787	53
1955	11,562	3,108	6,843	1,026	254	991	85
1956	12,902	3,190	7,674	1,286	364	1,133	145
1957	13,412	3,306	7,595	1,548	400	1,210	339
1958	13,419	3,472	6,944	1,625	460	1,195	555
1959	15,688	3,445	8,343	1,535	591	1,632	844
1960	15,072	3,286	7,887	1,544	562	1,901	633
1961	14,759	3,331	7,714	1,643	693	1,889	383
1962	16,453	3,573	8,573	1,765	758	2,276	521
1963	17,205	3,753	8,874	1,814	823	2,389	586
1964	18,749	3,915	9,563	1,907	1,039	2,694	767
				$ bn			
1965	21·5	3·9	11·0	2·1	1·5	3·3	0·9
1966	25·6	4·5	12·2	2·1	2·1	3·9	1·9
1967	27·8	4·6	12·0	2·1	2·5	4·2	2·4
1968	33·9	5·3	14·4	2·4	2·8	5·4	4·0
1969	36·8	5·2	14·3	2·6	3·4	6·5	5·1
1970	40·9	6·1	15·1	2·9	4·0	7·4	5·7
1971	46·6	6·4	17·3	3·7	4·3	8·4	7·6
1972	56·9	7·3	20·7	4·7	5·9	11·1	9·0
1973	71·8	9·1	27·6	8·4	8·3	12·9	10·7
1974	104·5	10·6	53·6	26·6	9·8	14·4	12·4
1975	99·0	9·6	50·6	27·0	10·2	13·2	12·1
1976	124·3	11·5	63·1	34·6	12·3	17·2	16·8
1977	151·9	14·0	78·4	45·0	14·0	21·8	19·4
1978	176·5	15·4	82·3	42·3	19·7	28·9	25·0
1979	211·9	17·4	106·6	60·5	25·0	30·6	26·4
1980	247·5	18·1	127·7	79·3	31·2	34·4	27·9
1981	266·5	18·1	131·2	77·8	36·7	38·7	30·9
1982	249·5	17·1	108·2	61·3	38·3	39·7	34·1
1983	271·3	18·5	107·3	55·0	43·1	47·0	43·5
1984	334·3	21·3	120·4	57·3	61·1	61·3	56·6
1985	341·0	21·3	109·6	50·4	64·0	65·1	65·0
1986	367·7	24·3	96·6	34·4	72·1	79·2	78·1
1987	413·0	24·7	109·5	42·9	84·8	88·7	85·2

Table US.14 Value of exports by commodity group, 1885–1987

	Total exports (incl. re-exports)	Food, feeds & beverages	Industrial supplies & materials	of which: Fuels & lubricants	Capital goods (excl. autos)	Consumer goods (excl. autos)	Motor vehicles & parts
				$ mn			
1885	742	325	290	57		111	
1886	680	264	291	56		112	
1887	716	301	290	54		112	
1888	696	256	314	55		114	
1889	742	274	334	59		123	
1890	858	357	355	61		133	
1891	884	332	399	64		140	
1892	1,030	512	370	58		133	
1893	848	400	301	57		130	
1894	892	383	350	57		136	
1895	808	318	331	61		144	
1896	883	348	333	78		182	
1897	1,051	416	402	80		213	
1898	1,231	590	398	74		223	
1899	1,227	538	404	77		263	
1900	1,394	546	493	105		332	
1901	1,488	583	559	102		318	
1902	1,382	514	520	103		322	
1903	1,420	508	557	100		327	
1904	1,461	445	642	118		349	
1905	1,519	401	689	119		402	
1906	1,744	524	733	124		460	
1907	1,881	513	860	132		481	
1908	1,861	521	824	155		489	
1909	1,663	439	760	152		440	
1910	1,745	369	842	151		499	
1911	2,049	385	1,030	153		598	
1912	2,204	419	1,079	179		672	
1913	2,466	503	1,149	218		776	
1914	2,365	430	1,174	225		725	
1915	2,769	962	947	206		807	
1916	5,483	1,069	1,728	294		2,625	
1917	6,234	1,316	2,148	394		2,706	
1918	6,149	1,953	2,025	491		2,069	
1919	7,920	2,641	2,545	503		2,564	
1920	8,228	2,035	2,841	953		3,205	
1921	4,485	1,358	1,394	572		1,627	
1922	3,832	1,047	1,426	442		1,292	
1923	4,167	840	1,772	533		1,478	
1924	4,591	966	1,944	560		1,588	
1925	4,910	890	2,854	581	415	287	324
1926	4,809	835	2,784	759	445	289	328
1927	4,865	883	2,685	597	478	287	397
1928	5,128	762	2,879	627	543	308	509
1929	5,240	753	2,827	668	657	343	547
1930	3,843	542	2,111	585	547	255	284
1931	2,424	374	1,321	336	326	176	152
1932	1,611	243	996	254	131	102	78
1933	1,674	204	1,105	241	134	96	92
1934	2,133	224	1,308	285	218	127	192
1935	2,283	216	1,372	303	265	145	232
1936	2,456	203	1,424	322	342	182	246
1937	3,249	283	1,899	445	509	217	354
1938	3,094	433	1,560	446	528	202	277
1939	3,177	321	1,670	452	583	219	260
1940	4,021	246	2,045	397	954	234	259
1941	5,020	…	…	…	…	…	…
1942	8,003	…	…	…	…	…	…
1943	12,842	…	…	…	…	…	…
1944	14,162	…	…	…	…	…	…
1945	9,585	…	…	…	…	…	…

Table US.14 (Continued)   Value of exports by commodity group, 1885–1987

	Total exports (incl. re-exports)	Food, feeds & beverages	Industrial supplies & materials	*of which:* Fuels & lubricants	Capital goods (excl. autos)	Consumer goods (excl. autos)	Motor vehicles & parts
				$ mn			
1946	9,770	2,206	3,864	752	1,660	1,084	556
1947	15,359	3,178	5,997	1,275	3,199	1,333	1,153
1948	12,654	2,659	4,865	1,149	2,626	1,033	939
1949	12,053	2,335	4,877	870	2,562	923	772
1950	10,277	1,482	4,358	777	2,144	850	746
1951	15,038	2,433	6,190	1,392	2,526	1,111	1,218
1952	15,203	2,201	5,553	1,303	2,812	1,015	1,024
1953	15,775	1,838	4,826	1,041	2,929	1,086	998
1954	15,112	1,713	5,479	970	2,919	1,097	1,072
1955	15,553	2,119	6,065	1,141	3,071	1,134	1,276
1956	19,096	2,807	7,383	1,508	3,834	1,246	1,395
1957	20,859	2,781	8,669	1,839	4,487	1,336	1,349
1958	17,912	2,590	6,436	1,092	4,752	1,314	1,123
1959	17,642	2,871	6,146	868	4,617	1,371	1,187
1960	20,600	3,170	7,924	841	5,511	1,396	1,266
1961	21,037	3,418	7,705	772	5,910	1,441	1,188
1962	21,714	3,829	7,132	806	6,443	1,455	1,301
1963	23,387	4,282	7,822	953	6,604	1,558	1,468
1964	26,650	4,849	9,185	924	7,463	1,751	1,729
				$ bn			
1965	27·5	4·9	8·9	0·9	8·0	1·8	1·9
1966	30·4	5·5	9·6	1·0	8·9	2·0	2·4
1967	32·2	5·0	10·0	1·1	9·9	2·1	2·8
1968	35·3	4·8	11·0	1·0	11·1	2·3	3·5
1969	38·3	4·7	11·7	1·1	12·4	2·6	3·9
1970	44·5	5·9	13·8	1·6	14·7	2·8	3·9
1971	45·6	6·1	12·6	1·5	15·4	2·9	4·7
1972	51·7	7·5	13·9	1·6	16·9	3·6	5·5
1973	73·9	15·2	19·7	1·7	22·0	4·8	7·0
1974	101·0	18·6	29·9	3·4	30·9	6·4	8·8
1975	109·6	19·2	29·3	4·5	36·6	6·6	10·8
1976	117·5	19·8	31·6	4·2	39·1	8·0	12·2
1977	123·1	19·7	33·2	4·2	39·8	8·9	13·5
1978	144·7	25·2	37·9	3·9	46·5	10·5	15·7
1979	183·3	30·0	52·8	5·6	58·8	12·8	18·4
1980	225·1	35·7	67·8	8·0	74·2	16·6	17·5
1981	238·3	38·2	65·6	10·3	81·6	16·4	19·8
1982	214·0	31·6	61·6	12·7	73·7	14·7	17·4
1983	206·1	31·6	56·7	9·5	68·9	14·0	18·7
1984	224·1	31·6	61·2	9·3	74·1	13·8	22·5
1985	220·8	24·0	58·7	10·0	76·4	13·0	25·0
1986	225·0	23·1	58·4	8·1	79·3	14·6	24·9
1987	254·8	24·6	66·5	7·7	88·1	18·0	26·3

Table US.15 Value of exports and imports by areas, 1885–1987

	Europe		of which: UK		Germany		Rest of America		Asia		of which: Japan	
	Exports to	Imports from	Exports to	Imports from	Exports to	Imports from	Exports to	Imports from	Exports to	Imports from	Exports to	Imports from
						$ mn							
1885	599	319	398	137	62	63	104	183	21	61	3	12
1886	541	358	348	154	62	69	98	191	23	69	3	15
1887	575	391	366	165	59	81	104	211	20	72	3	17
1888	549	407	362	178	56	78	110	224	20	73	4	19
1889	579	403	383	178	68	82	125	243	19	76	5	17
1890	684	450	448	186	86	99	133	238	20	81	5	21
1891	705	459	445	195	93	97	131	282	26	79	5	19
1892	851	392	499	156	106	83	139	325	20	89	3	24
1893	662	458	421	183	84	96	152	286	17	99	3	27
1894	701	295	431	107	92	69	153	267	22	75	4	19
1895	628	384	387	159	92	81	143	246	18	84	5	24
1896	673	419	406	170	98	94	153	236	26	95	8	26
1897	813	430	483	168	125	111	159	213	39	92	13	24
1898	974	306	541	109	155	70	174	183	45	96	20	25
1899	937	354	512	118	156	84	194	199	49	112	17	27
1900	1,040	441	534	160	187	97	227	224	68	146	29	33
1901	1,137	430	631	143	192	100	241	255	53	122	19	29
1902	1,008	475	549	166	173	102	242	271	69	136	21	38
1903	1,029	547	524	190	194	120	256	297	62	159	21	44
1904	1,058	499	537	166	215	109	286	319	65	156	25	47
1905	1,021	541	523	176	194	118	318	378	135	175	52	52
1906	1,200	633	583	210	235	135	383	375	111	192	38	53
1907	1,298	747	608	246	257	162	432	424	101	224	39	69
1908	1,284	608	581	190	277	143	409	364	113	191	41	68
1909	1,147	654	515	209	235	144	387	418	83	207	27	70
1910	1,136	806	506	271	250	169	479	503	78	210	22	66
1911	1,308	768	577	261	287	163	566	488	105	231	37	79
1912	1,342	820	564	273	307	171	648	549	141	249	53	81
1913	1,479	893	597	296	332	189	763	580	140	298	58	92
1914	1,486	896	594	294	345	190	654	650	141	305	51	107
1915	1,971	614	912	256	29	91	576	734	139	272	41	99
1916	3,813	633	1,887	305	2	6	1,145	1,086	388	551	109	182
1917	4,062	551	2,009	280	—	—	1,573	1,471	469	821	186	254
1918	3,859	318	2,061	149	—	—	1,628	1,585	498	939	274	302
1919	5,188	751	2,279	309	93	11	1,738	1,844	772	1,108	366	410
1920	4,466	1,228	1,825	514	311	89	2,553	2,424	872	1,397	378	415
1921	2,364	765	942	239	372	80	1,403	1,051	533	618	238	251
1922	2,083	991	856	357	316	117	1,142	1,181	449	827	222	354
1923	2,093	1,157	882	404	317	161	1,355	1,469	511	1,020	267	347
1924	2,445	1,096	983	366	440	139	1,404	1,461	515	931	253	340
1925	2,604	1,239	1,034	413	470	164	1,541	1,499	487	1,319	230	384
1926	2,310	1,278	973	383	364	198	1,620	1,580	565	1,409	261	401
1927	2,314	1,265	840	358	482	201	1,691	1,504	560	1,268	258	402
1928	2,375	1,249	847	349	467	222	1,802	1,530	655	1,169	288	384
1929	2,341	1,334	848	330	410	255	1,934	1,621	643	1,279	259	432
1930	1,838	911	678	210	278	177	1,357	1,195	448	854	165	279
1931	1,187	641	456	135	166	127	750	824	386	574	156	206
1932	784	390	288	75	134	74	462	539	292	362	135	134
1933	850	463	312	111	140	78	455	520	292	425	143	128
1934	950	490	383	115	109	69	648	628	401	489	210	119
1935	1,029	599	433	155	92	78	706	776	378	605	203	153
1936	1,043	718	440	200	102	80	821	910	399	708	204	172
1937	1,360	843	536	203	126	92	1,158	1,113	580	967	289	204
1938	1,326	567	521	118	107	65	1,040	753	517	570	240	127
1939	1,290	617	505	149	46	52	1,131	898	562	700	232	161
1940	1,645	390	1,011	155	—	5	1,501	1,089	619	981	227	158
1941	1,847	281	1,637	136	—	3	2,047	1,657	625	1,088	60	78
1942	4,009	220	2,529	134	—	—	2,205	1,762	688	340	—	—
1943	7,633	240	4,505	105	—	—	2,418	2,458	838	235	—	—
1944	9,364	289	5,243	84	—	—	2,627	2,965	996	322	—	—

	Europe		UK		*of which:* Germany		Rest of America		Asia		*of which:* Japan	
	Exports to	Imports from	Exports to	Imports from	Exports to	Imports from	Exports to	Imports from	Exports to	Imports from	Exports to	Imports from
						\$ mn						
1945	5,515	409	2,193	90	2	1	2,564	2,874	849	407	—	—
1946	4,122	804	855	158	83	3	3,684	2,762	1,327	887	102	81
1947	5,670	817	1,103	205	128	6	6,199	3,401	2,330	1,055	415[a]	35
1948	4,279	1,121	644	290	863	32	5,307	4,100	2,130	1,346	325[a]	63
1949	4,118	925	700	228	822	46	4,861	3,995	2,256	1,240	468	82
1950	3,306	1,449	548	335	440	104	4,902	5,064	1,540	1,638	418	182
1951	5,121	2,119	1,000	466	521	233	6,607	5,826	2,410	1,983	601	205
1952	5,089	2,029	787	485	450	212	6,682	6,025	2,541	1,813	633	229
1953	5,711	2,335	826	546	363	277	6,514	6,117	2,783	1,626	686	262
1954	5,118	2,083	808	501	505	278	6,521	5,896	2,577	1,467	693	279
1955	5,126	2,453	1,006	616	607	366	6,903	6,262	2,581	1,876	683	432
1956	6,437	2,963	985	726	943	494	8,243	6,856	3,418	1,996	998	558
1957	6,844	3,147	1,164	766	1,330	607	9,001	7,048	3,961	1,985	1,319	601
1958	5,570	3,341	905	864	888	629	7,999	6,703	3,411	1,984	987	667
1959	5,559	4,607	1,097	1,137	880	920	7,692	7,071	3,284	2,603	1,079	1,029
1960	7,406	4,268	1,487	993	1,275	897	7,684	6,864	4,186	2,722	1,447	1,149
1961	7,371	4,141	1,206	898	1,343	856	7,673	6,995	4,653	2,583	1,837	1,055
1962	7,758	4,621	1,128	1,005	1,581	962	7,724	7,591	4,676	2,960	1,574	1,358
1963	8,738	4,811	1,213	1,079	1,582	1,003	7,944	7,850	5,448	3,192	1,844	1,498
1964	9,436	5,307	1,532	1,143	1,606	1,171	9,207	8,390	5,802	3,620	2,009	1,768
						\$ bn						
1965	9·4	6·3	1·6	1·4	1·7	1·3	9·9	9·2	6·0	4·5	2·1	2·4
1966	10·0	7·9	1·7	1·8	1·7	1·8	11·4	10·8	6·7	5·3	2·4	3·0
1967	10·3	8·2	2·0	1·7	1·7	2·0	11·9	11·7	7·1	5·3	2·7	3·0
1968	11·3	10·3	2·3	2·1	1·7	2·7	13·4	14·1	7·6	6·9	3·0	4·1
1969	12·6	10·3	2·3	2·1	2·1	2·6	14·7	15·5	8·3	8·3	3·5	4·9
1970	14·8	11·4	2·5	2·2	2·7	3·1	15·6	16·9	10·0	9·6	4·7	5·9
1971	14·6	12·9	2·4	2·5	2·8	3·7	16·9	18·7	9·9	11·8	4·1	7·3
1972	16·2	15·7	2·7	3·0	2·8	4·3	19·7	21·9	11·3	15·1	5·0	9·1
1973	23·2	19·8	3·6	3·7	3·8	5·3	25·0	27·3	18·4	18·2	8·3	9·7
1974	30·1	24·6	4·6	4·1	5·0	6·3	35·7	40·3	25·8	27·3	10·7	12·3
1975	32·7	21·6	4·5	3·8	5·2	5·4	38·8	38·2	28·2	27·3	9·6	11·4
1976	35·9	23·6	4·8	4·3	5·7	5·6	41·1	43·4	29·7	39·4	10·1	15·5
1977	37·3	28·8	6·0	5·1	6·0	7·2	43·8	50·7	31·4	49·3	10·5	18·6
1978	39·9	36·5	7·1	6·5	7·0	10·0	50·4	56·5	39·6	58·3	12·9	24·5
1979	54·3	41·7	10·6	8·0	8·5	11·0	61·6	68·5	48·8	66·7	17·6	26·2
1980	71·4	48·0	12·7	9·8	11·0	11·7	74·1	78·7	60·2	80·3	20·8	30·7
1981	69·7	53·4	12·4	12·8	10·3	11·4	81·7	85·4	63·8	92·0	21·8	37·6
1982	63·7	53·4	10·6	13·1	9·3	12·0	67·3	84·5	64·8	85·2	21·0	37·7
1983	58·9	55·2	10·6	12·5	8·7	12·7	64·0	93·9	63·8	91·5	21·9	41·2
1984	62·2	73·3	12·2	14·5	9·1	17·0	76·2	114·4	64·5	120·1	23·6	57·1
1985	60·0	81·7	11·3	14·9	9·1	20·2	78·3	115·9	60·7	131·9	22·6	68·8
1986	63·6	91·8	11·4	15·4	10·6	25·1	76·4	110·2	64·5	153·9	26·9	81·9
1987	71·9	97·4	14·1	17·3	11·7	27·1	93·8[b]	118·0	73·3	174·5	28·2	84·6

a Includes shipments under Army Civilian Program – \$354 mn in 1947 and \$246 mn in 1948.
b Adjusted for undocumented exports to Canada. See **18**, August 1987.

Table US.16 Balance of payments, 1885–1987

	Imports	Exports	Investment income Receipts	Investment income Payments	Net military transactions	Net travel & transport	Other services (net)	Unilateral transfers	Current balance
					$ mn				
1885	635	792	−86		—	−49	−10	−27	−15
1886	698	781	−93		—	−55	−12	−28	−105
1887	759	774	−98		—	−61	−13	−28	−185
1888	791	750	−107		—	−66	−13	−30	−257
1889	817	841	−118		—	−60	−13	−44	−211
1890	866	921	−125		—	−66	−14	−45	−195
1891	875	997	−134		—	−63	−14	−50	−139
1892	888	1,084	−143		—	−60	−13	−54	−74
1893	898	974	−139		—	−42	−14	−44	−163
1894	692	943	−113		—	−30	−9	−54	45
1895	774	855	−126		—	−71	−11	−55	−182
1896	816	1,048	−122		—	−64	−12	−49	−15
1897	803	1,136	−127		—	−63	−11	−41	91
1898	653	1,304	−133		—	−66	−9	−44	399
1899	735	1,363	−124		—	−67	−10	−48	379
1900	894	1,534	−114		—	−86	−12	−54	374
	869	1,623	38	−137	...	−148	...	−95	412
1901	912	1,585	47	−135	...	−147	...	−104	334
1902	996	1,473	57	−137	...	−139	...	−105	153
1903	1,019	1,575	67	−139	...	−144	...	−115	225
1904	1,062	1,563	70	−141	...	−151	...	−127	152
1905	1,215	1,751	76	−145	...	−169	...	−133	165
1906	1,365	1,921	86	−148	...	−198	...	−147	149
1907	1,469	2,051	87	−153	...	−220	...	−177	119
1908	1,159	1,880	89	−160	...	−223	...	−192	235
1909	1,522	1,857	100	−164	...	−245	...	−187	−161
1910	1,609	1,995	108	−172	...	−276	...	−204	−158
1911	1,576	2,228	114	−190	...	−302	...	−224	50
1912	1,866	2,532	123	−197	...	−335	...	−212	45
1913	1,829	2,600	137	−210	...	−324	...	−207	167
1914	1,815	2,230	145	−200	...	−304	...	−170	−114
1915	1,813	3,686	200	−136	...	−189	...	−150	1,598
1916	2,423	5,560	250	−118	...	−167	...	−150	2,952
1917	3,006	6,398	350	−100	...	−167	...	−205	3,270
1918	3,103	6,432	450	−100	−1,018	−203	...	−268	2,190
1919	3,995	8,891	719	−130	−757	224	−84	−1,044	3,824
1920	5,384	8,481	596	−120	−123	148	−75	−679	2,844
1921	2,572	4,586	445	−105	−65	−64	−103	−509	1,613
1922	3,184	3,929	670	−105	−42	−237	−34	−352	645
1923	3,866	4,266	840	−130	−33	−219	−16	−365	477
1924	3,684	4,741	762	−140	−36	−272	−20	−364	987
1925	4,291	5,011	912	−170	−39	−337	1	−403	684
1926	4,500	4,922	953	−200	−43	−307	1	−381	445
1927	4,240	4,982	981	−240	−38	−343	−29	−357	716
1928	4,159	5,249	1,080	−275	−44	−415	−59	−365	1,012
1929	4,463	5,347	1,139	−330	−50	−463	−32	−377	771
1930	3,104	3,929	1,040	−295	−49	−486	−3	−342	690
1931	2,120	2,494	766	−220	−48	−366	10	−319	197
1932	1,343	1,667	527	−135	−47	−278	16	−238	169
1933	1,510	1,736	437	−115	−41	−179	30	−208	150
1934	1,763	2,238	437	−135	−34	−200	58	−172	429
1935	2,462	2,404	521	−155	−41	−211	72	−182	−54
1936	2,546	2,590	569	−270	−38	−269	79	−208	−93
1937	3,181	3,451	577	−295	−41	−343	129	−235	62
1938	2,173	3,243	585	−200	−41	−209	86	−182	1,109
1939	2,409	3,347	541	−230	−46	−219	82	−178	888
1940	2,698	4,124	564	−210	−61	−27	27	−210	1,509
1941	3,416	5,343	544	−187	−162	77	211	−1,136	1,274
1942	3,499	9,187	614	−158	−953	353	969	−6,336	177
1943	4,599	15,115	509	−155	−1,763	678	1,253	−12,907	−1,869

Table US.16 (Continued)   Balance of payments, 1885–1987

	Imports	Exports	Investment income		Net military transactions	Net travel & transport	Other services (net)	Unilateral transfers	Current balance
			Receipts	Payments					
					$ mn				
1944	5,043	16,969	573	−161	−1,982	799	1,297	−14,142	−1,690
1945	5,245	12,473	589	−231	−2,434	741	148	−7,113	−1,072
1946	5,067	11,764	772	−212	−493	733	310	−2,922	4,885
1947	5,973	16,097	1,102	245	−455	946	145	−2,625	8,992
1948	7,557	13,265	1,921	−437	−799	374	175	−4,525	2,417
1949	6,874	12,213	1,831	−476	−621	230	208	−5,638	873
1950	9,081	10,203	2,068	−559	−576	−120	242	−4,017	−1,840
1951	11,176	14,243	2,633	−583	−1,270	298	254	−3,515	884
1952	10,838	13,449	2,751	−555	−2,054	83	309	−2,531	614
1953	10,975	12,412	2,736	−624	−2,423	−238	307	−2,481	−1,286
1954	10,353	12,929	2,929	−582	−2,460	−269	305	−2,280	219
1955	11,527	14,424	3,406	−676	−2,701	−297	299	−2,498	430
1956	12,803	17,556	3,837	−735	−2,788	−361	447	−2,423	2,730
1957	13,291	19,562	4,180	−796	−2,841	−189	482	−2,345	4,762
1958	12,952	16,414	3,790	−825	−3,135	−633	486	−2,361	784
1959	15,310	16,458	4,132	−1,061	−2,805	−821	573	−2,448	−1,282
1960	14,758	19,650	4,616	−1,237	−2,752	−964	638	−2,367	2,824
1961	14,357	20,108	4,999	−1,245	−2,596	−978	732	−2,662	3,822
1962	16,260	20,781	5,618	−1,324	−2,449	−1,152	911	−2,740	3,387
1963	17,048	22,272	6,157	−1,561	−2,304	−1,309	1,037	−2,831	4,414
1964	18,700	25,501	6,824	−1,784	−2,133	−1,146	1,161	−2,901	6,823
1965	21,510	26,461	7,437	−2,088	−2,122	−1,280	1,480	−2,948	5,430
1966	25,493	29,310	7,528	−2,481	−2,935	−1,331	1,496	−3,064	3,031
1967	26,866	30,666	8,020	−2,747	−3,266	−1,750	1,742	−3,255	2,583
1968	32,991	33,626	9,368	−3,378	−3,143	−1,548	1,759	−3,082	611
1969	35,807	36,414	10,912	−4,869	−3,328	−1,763	1,964	−3,125	399
1970	39,866	42,469	11,747	−5,516	−3,354	−2,038	2,329	−3,443	2,331
1971	45,579	43,319	12,707	−5,436	−2,893	−2,345	2,649	−3,856	−1,433
1972	55,797	49,381	14,764	−6,572	−3,420	−3,063	2,965	−4,052	−5,795
1973	70,499	71,410	21,808	−9,655	−2,070	−3,158	3,406	−4,103	7,140
1974	103,811	98,306	27,587	−12,084	−1,653	−3,184	4,231	−7,431[a]	1,962
1975	98,185	107,088	25,351	−12,564	−746	−2,792	4,853	−4,868	18,116
1976	124,228	114,745	29,286	−13,311	559	−2,558	5,027	−5,314	4,207
1977	151,907	120,816	32,179	−14,217	1,528	−3,565	5,679	−5,023	−14,511
1978	176,001	142,054	42,245	−21,680	621	−3,573	6,459	−5,552	−15,427
1979	212,009	184,473	64,132	−32,960	−1,778	−2,935	6,214	−6,128	−991
1980	249,749	224,269	72,506	−42,120	−2,237	−997	7,793	−7,593	1,873
1981	265,063	237,085	86,411	−52,329	1,183	144	9,278	−7,460	6,884
1982	247,642	211,198	83,549	−54,883	−274	−992	9,320	−8,956	−8,679
1983	268,900	201,820	77,251	−52,376	−243	−4,227	9,908	−9,480	−46,246
1984	332,422	219,900	85,908	−67,419	−2,099	−8,604	9,760	−12,102	−107,077
1985	388,083	215,935	88,837	−62,901	−3,431	−10,049	9,600	−15,010	−115,103
1986	368,516	223,969	90,110	−66,968	−4,372	−9,344	11,600	−15,308	−138,828
1987	409,850	249,570	103,756	−83,381	−2,368	−10,281	12,035	−13,445	−153,964

a   Includes extraordinary US government transactions with India.

Table US.17   Finance, 1885–1987

	Share prices		Interest rates				Money supply M1	Consumer credit outstanding	Ratio of consumer credit to disposable income
	Standard & Poor's index	Dow Jones average	3-month Treasury bill yield	US govt bonds yield	Federal Reserve Bank				
					High	Low			
	1980 = 100	$ per share	%	%	%		$ bn		%
								$ mn	
1885	3·9	...	...	...	...		2·86	...	...
1886	4·5	...	...	...	...		3·10	...	...
1887	4·7	...	...	...	...		3·30	...	...
1888	4·4	...	...	...	...		3·38	...	...
1889	4·5	...	...	...	...		3·55	...	...
1890	4·5	...	...	...	...		3·92	...	...
1891	4·3	...	...	...	...		4·04	...	...
1892	4·7	...	...	...	...		4·48	...	...
1893	4·0	...	...	...	...		4·20	...	...
1894	3·7	...	...	...	...		4·24	...	...
1895	3·8	...	...	...	...		4·50	...	...
1896	3·6	...	...	...	...		4·36	...	...
1897	3·8	...	...	...	...		4·58	...	...
1898	4·3	...	...	...	...		5·25	...	...
1899	5·3	...	...	...	...		6·14	...	...
1900	5·2	...	...	...	3·94		6·50	...	...
1901	6·6	...	...	...	4·24		7·46	...	...
1902	7·1	...	...	...	5·05		8·14	...	...
1903	6·1	...	...	...	4·84		8·65	...	...
1904	5·9	...	...	...	3·10		9·12	...	...
1905	7·6	...	...	...	3·82		10·20	...	...
1906	8·1	...	...	...	5·71		10·99	...	...
1907	6·6	...	...	...	6·49		11·55	...	...
1908	6·6	...	...	...	3·24		11·48	...	...
1909	8·2	...	...	...	3·26		12·73	...	...
1910	7·9	...	...	...	4·03		13·36	...	...
1911	7·8	...	...	...	3·22		14·16	...	...
1912	8·0	...	...	...	4·16		15·17	...	...
1913	7·2	...	...	...	4·64		15·75	...	...
1914	6·8	...	...	...	6·00	5·00	16·41	...	...
1915	7·0	...	...	...	5·00	4·00	12·48	...	...
1916	8·0	...	...	...	4·00	3·00	14·70	...	...
1917	7·2	...	...	...	3·50	3·00	17·08	...	...
1918	6·4	...	...	...	4·00	3·50	18·96	...	...
1919	7·4	...	...	4·73	4·75	4·00	21·79	2,642	...
1920	6·7	...	...	5·32	7·00	4·75	23·73	2,964	...
1921	5·8	...	...	5·09	7·00	4·50	21·51	2,966	...
1922	7·1	...	...	4·30	4·50	4·00	21·67	3,166	...
1923	7·2	...	...	4·36	4·50	4·00	22·93	3,652	...
1924	7·6	...	...	4·06	4·50	3·00	23·67	4,025	...
1925	9·4	...	...	3·86	3·50	3·00	25·66	4,715	...
1926	10·6	...	...	3·68	4·00	3·50	26·18	5,227	...
1927	12·9	...	...	3·34	4·00	3·50	26·10	5,344	...
1928	16·8	...	...	3·33	5·00	3·50	26·38	6,258	...
1929	21·9	125·43	...	3·60	6·00	4·50	26·64	7,116	8·6
1930	17·7	95·64	...	3·29	4·50	2·00	25·76	6,351	8·7
1931	11·5	55·47	1·40	3·34	3·50	1·50	24·14	5,315	8·3
1932	5·8	26·82	0·88	3·68	3·50	2·50	21·11	4,026	8·2
1933	7·5	36·00	0·52	3·31	3·50	2·00	19·91	3,885	8·6
1934	8·3	39·16	0·26	3·12	2·00	1·50	21·86	4,218	8·0
1935	8·9	41·97	0·14	2·79	1·50	1·50	25·88	5·190	8·9
1936	13·0	58·98	0·14	2·69	1·50	1·50	29·55	6,375	9·7
1937	13·0	58·08	0·45	2·74	1·50	1·00	30·91	6,948	9·7
1938	9·7	43·10	0·05	2·61	1·00	1·00	30·52	6,370	9·8
1939	10·2	48·01	0·02	2·41	1·00	1·00	34·15	7,222	10·3
1940	9·3	45·28	0·01	2·26	1·00	1·00	39·65	8,338	11·0
1941	8·3	41·22	0·10	2·05	1·00	1·00	46·52	9,172	10·0
1942	7·3	36·04	0·33	2·46	1·00	0·50	55·36	5,983	5·1

Table US.17 (Continued)   Finance, 1885–1987

	Share prices		Interest rates				Money supply M1	Consumer credit outstanding	Ratio of consumer credit to disposable income
	Standard & Poor's index	Dow Jones average	3-month Treasury bill yield	US govt bonds yield	Federal Reserve Bank				
					High	Low			
	1980 = 100	$ per share	%	%	%		$ bn		%
								$ mn	
1943	9·7	46·39	0·37	2·47	1·00	0·50	72·24	4,901	3·7
1944	10·5	51·39	0·38	2·48	1·00	0·50	85·34	5,111	3·5
1945	12·8	63·72	0·38	2·37	1·00	0·50	99·23	5,665	3·8
1946	14·4	71·01	0·38	2·19	1·00	0·50	106·46	8,384	5·3
1947	12·8	63·39	0·59	2·25	1·00	1·00	111·79	11,598	6·9
1948	13·1	66·32	1·04	2·44	1·50	1·00	112·31	14,447	7·7
1949	12·8	64·37	1·10	2·31	1·50	1·50	111·16	17,364	9·3
								21,471	10·4
1950	15·5	77·69	1·22	2·32	1·75	1·50	114·14	$ bn	
								25·0	12·1
1951	18·8	93·98	1·55	2·57	1·75	1·75	119·23	26·6	11·7
1952	20·6	103·71	1·77	2·68	1·75	1·75	125·22	31·8	13·3
1953	20·8	107·11	1·93	2·94	2·00	1·75	128·34	35·9	14·1
1954	25·0	124·24	0·95	2·55	2·00	1·50	130·27	37·3	14·3
1955	34·1	161·34	1·75	2·84	2·50	1·50	134·44	44·3	15·9
1956	39·3	174·54	2·66	3·08	3·00	2·50	136·02	48·2	16·2
1957	37·4	164·83	3·27	3·47	3·50	3·00	136·75	51·1	16·3
1958	38·9	169·27	1·84	3·43	3·00	1·75	138·35	51·6	15·9
1959	48·3	212·78	3·41	4·07	4·00	2·50	141·0	59·4	17·2
1960	47·1	204·57	2·93	4·01	4·00	3·00	141·8	63·9	17·2
1961	55·8	232·44	2·38	3·90	3·00	3·00	146·5	66·6	17·8
1962	52·5	221·07	2·78	3·95	3·00	3·00	149·2	72·8	18·4
1963	58·9	253·67	3·16	4·00	3·50	3·00	154·7	81·6	19·6
1964	68·5	294·23	3·55	4·15	4·00	3·50	161·9	91·3	20·2
1965	74·3	318·50	3·95	4·21	4·50	4·00	169·5	101·7	20·9
1966	71·8	308·70	4·88	4·66	4·50	4·50	173·7	108·2	20·6
1967	77·4	314·79	4·32	4·85	4·50	4·00	185·1	113·6	20·2
1968	83·1	322·19	5·34	5·25	5·50	4·50	199·4	124·9	20·5
1969	82·4	301·35	6·68	6·10	6·00	5·50	205·8	135·4	20·6
1970	70·1	243·92	6·46	6·58	6·00	5·50	216·6	141·0	19·7
1971	82·8	298·12	4·35	5·74	5·25	4·50	230·8	155·5	20·0
1972	92·0	319·36	4·07	5·63	4·50	4·50	252·0	179·3	21·4
1973	90·5	286·73	7·04	6·30	7·50	4·50	265·9	200·9	21·2
1974	69·8	237·33	7·89	6·98	8·00	7·50	277·5	210·6	20·3
1975	72·6	247·25	5·84	6·98	7·75	6·00	291·1	217·4	19·0
1976	85·9	303·91	4·99	6·78	6·00	5·25	310·4	242·0	19·3
1977	82·7	301·70	5·27	7·06	6·00	5·25	335·3	278·9	20·2
1978	80·9	283·63	7·22	7·89	9·50	6·00	363·0	325·0	21·0
1979	86·8	293·50	10·04	8·74	12·00	9·50	391·1	366·4	21·2
1980	100·0	328·20	11·43	10·81	13·00	10·00	416·6	369·1	19·2
1981	107·8	364·61	14·03	12·87	14·00	12·00	443·2	390·1	18·3
1982	100·8	345·40	10·61	12·23	12·00	8·50	481·3	409·5	18·1
1983	135·0	472·24	8·61	10·84	8·50	8·50	526·9	468·5	19·3
1984	135·1	463·10	9·52	11·99	9·00	8·00	557·5	561·5	21·0
1985	157·3	541·60	7·48	10·75	8·00	7·50	627·0	657·0	23·1
1986	199·0	702·50	5·96	8·14	7·50	5·50	730·5	723·6	23·9
1987	241·5	849·46	5·82	8·64	6·00	5·50	753·2[a]	755·6[a]	23·8[a]

a Provisional.

109

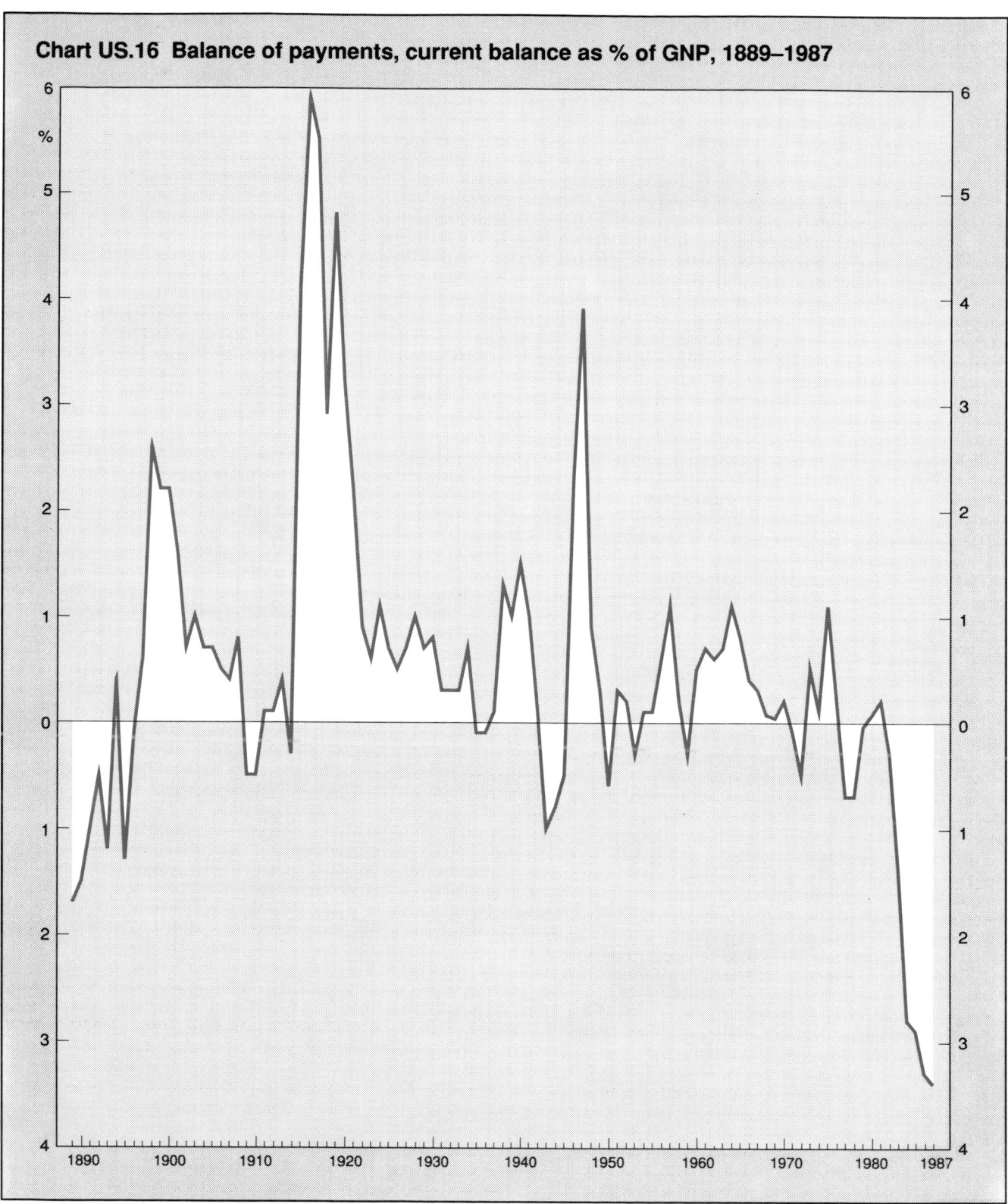

Chart US.16 Balance of payments, current balance as % of GNP, 1889–1987

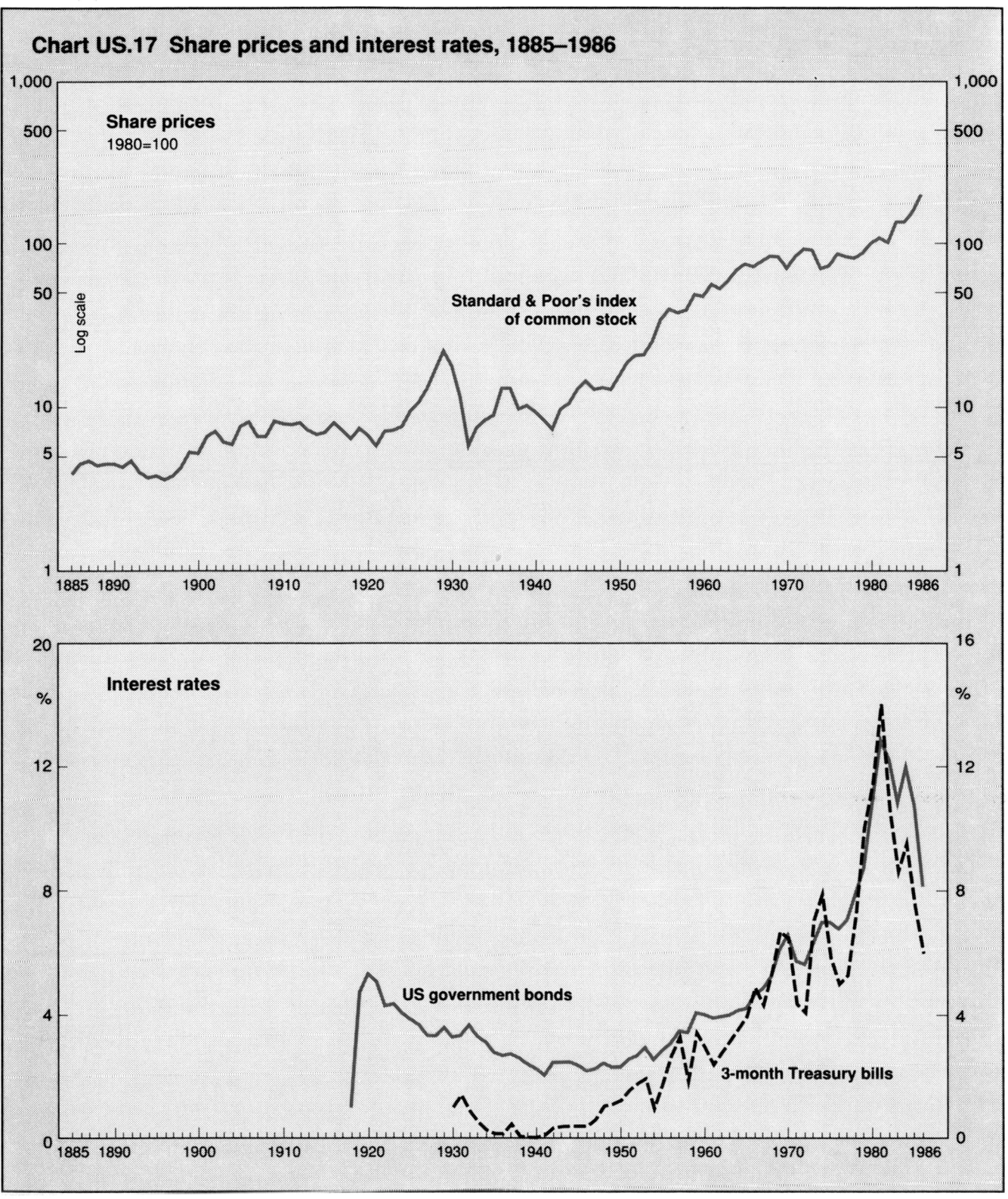

Chart US.17 Share prices and interest rates, 1885–1986

Share prices
1980=100

Log scale

**Standard & Poor's index
of common stock**

Interest rates

%

US government bonds

3-month Treasury bills

111

Table US.18   Public finance, 1885–1987

	Revenue					Expenditure				
	Taxes on personal income	Taxes on companies	Customs & excise	Sales taxes	Total receipts	Defence	Education	Social services	Debt interest	Total expenditure
					$ bn					
1885	...	...	0·29	...	0·32	0·05	...	...	...	...
1886	...	...	0·31	...	0·34	0·04	...	...	...	...
1887	...	...	0·34	...	0·37	0·05	...	...	...	...
1888	...	...	0·34	...	0·38	0·05	...	...	...	...
1889	...	...	0·35	...	0·39	0·05	...	...	...	...
1890	...	...	0·37	...	0·40	0·05	...	...	...	...
1891	...	...	0·36	...	0·39	0·06	...	...	...	...
1892	...	...	0·33	...	0·35	0·06	...	...	...	...
1893	...	...	0·36	...	0·39	0·06	...	...	...	...
1894	...	...	0·28	...	0·31	0·06	...	...	...	...
1895	...	...	0·29	...	0·32	0·06	...	...	...	...
1896	...	...	0·31	...	0·34	0·06	...	...	...	...
1897	...	...	0·32	...	0·35	0·07	...	...	...	...
1898	...	...	0·32	...	0·41	0·13	...	...	...	...
1899	...	...	0·47	...	0·52	0·27	...	...	...	...
1900	...	...	0·52	...	0·57	0·17	...	...	...	0·52
1901	...	...	0·53	...	0·59	0·18	...	...	...	0·53
1902	...	...	0·51	...	(1·69)	0·16	0·26	0·10	0·10	(1·66)
1903	...	...	0·51	...	0·56	0·17	...	...	...	0·52
1904	...	...	0·49	...	0·54	0·19	...	...	...	0·58
1905	...	...	0·49	...	0·54	0·21	...	...	...	0·57
1906	...	...	0·55	...	0·59	0·20	...	...	...	0·57
1907	...	...	0·60	...	0·67	0·19	...	...	...	0·58
1908	...	...	0·54	...	0·60	0·22	...	...	...	0·66
1909	...	...	0·55	...	0·60	0·23	...	...	...	0·69
1910	...	...	0·60	...	0·68	0·24	...	...	...	0·69
1911	...	...	0·60	...	0·70	0·24	...	...	...	0·69
1912	...	...	0·60	...	0·69	0·24	...	...	...	0·69
1913	...	...	0·63	...	(2·98)	0·25	0·58	0·17	0·17	(3·22)
1914	...	...	0·60	...	0·73	0·26	...	...	...	0·73
1915	...	...	0·54	...	0·68	0·27	...	...	...	0·75
1916	...	...	0·55	...	0·76	0·28	...	...	...	0·71
1917	...	...	0·62	...	1·10	0·60	...	...	...	1·95
1918	...	...	0·87	...	3·65	7·11	...	...	...	12·66
1919	...	...	1·05	...	5·13	13·55	...	...	...	18·45
1920	...	...	1·22	...	6·65	4·00	...	...	...	6·36
1921	...	...	1·08	...	5·57	2·58	...	...	...	5·06
1922	2·04		1·03	0·28	(9·32)	0·86	1·71	0·48	1·37	(9·30)
1923	...	...	1·27	...	3·85	0·68	...	...	...	3·14
1924	...	...	1·30	...	3·87	0·65	...	...	...	2·89
1925	...	...	1·18	...	3·64	0·59	...	...	...	2·88
1926	...	...	1·25	...	3·80	0·59	...	...	...	2·89
1927	0·95	1·35	1·10	0·46	(12·19)	0·60	2·24	0·59	1·35	(11·22)
1928	...	...	1·06	...	3·90	0·66	...	...	...	2·93
1929	1·3	1·4	1·2	0·4	11·3	0·70	...	...	0·7	10·3
1930	1·1	0·8	1·0	0·5	10·8	0·73	...	...	0·7	11·1
1931	0·6	0·5	0·9	0·6	9·5	0·73	...	...	0·9	12·4
1932	0·4	0·4	0·8	0·6	8·9	0·70	2·33	1·03	1·32	12·4
1933	0·5	0·5	1·5	0·7	9·4	...	...	...	...	10·7
1934	0·5	0·7	2·1	0·9	10·5	0·54	2·01	1·51	1·47	12·8
1935	0·7	1·0	2·1	1·2	11·4	...	...	...	...	13·4
1936	0·9	1·4	2·1	1·4	13·0	0·92	2·37	1·59	1·46	16·8
1937	1·5	1·5	2·3	1·5	15·4	...	...	...	...	15·1
1938	1·4	1·0	2·0	1·6	15·1	1·02	2·65	1·91	1·51	17·7
1939	1·1	1·4	2·1	1·7	15·4	...	...	...	...	17·6
1940	1·2	2·8	2·4	1·8	17·8	1·57	2·83	2·05	1·55	20·4
1941	1·9	7·6	3·2	2·1	25·0	...	...	...	...	28·8
1942	4·3	11·4	3·7	2·0	32·7	22·6	2·70	2·00	1·59	45·6

	Revenue					Expenditure				
	Taxes on personal income	Taxes on companies	Customs & excise	Sales taxes	Total receipts	Defence	Education	Social services	Debt interest	Total expenditure
					$ bn					
1943	16·2	14·1	4·5	2·0	49·2	...	...	...	...	93·4
1944	17·2	12·9	5·6	2·0	51·2	74·7	2·81	2·01	2·65	109·9
1945	18·9	10·7	6·6	2·3	53·4	...	...	...	...	92·9
1946	16·7	9·1	7·7	2·9	52·6	42·7	3·71	2·58	4·29	79·7
1947	19·3	11·3	7·6	3·5	57·8	...	...	...	...	43·4
1948	18·7	12·4	7·8	4·1	59·6	10·6	7·72	4·08	4·72	55·1
1949	16·1	10·2	7·9	4·3	56·6	...	...	...	...	60·0
1950	18·2	17·9	8·7	4·8	69·4	12·1	9·65	5·68	4·86	70·3
1951	26·3	22·6	9·2	5·4	85·6	...	...	...	...	79·5
1952	31·1	19·4	10·2	5·8	90·5	46·1	8·4	16·2	4·7	94·3
1953	32·3	20·3	10·8	6·3	95·0	48·9	9·4	17·1	4·8	102·0
1954	29·1	17·6	9·5	6·5	90·4	41·5	10·7	19·2	5·0	97·5
1955	31·7	22·0	10·5	7·1	101·6	38·9	12·0	20·5	5·0	98·5
1956	35·4	22·0	11·0	8·0	110·2	40·6	13·1	22·2	5·5	105·0
1957	37·6	21·4	11·6	8·6	116·7	44·5	14·3	25·5	6·0	115·8
1958	37·2	19·0	11·2	10·0	115·7	46·2	16·1	30·2	5·8	128·3
1959	40·7	23·6	12·2	11·1	130·3	46·3	16·8	31·5	6·9	131·9
1960	44·3	22·7	13·1	12·2	140·4	45·2	18·7	33·5	7·6	137·3
1961	45·5	22·8	13·2	13·0	145·9	47·8	20·6	38·1	7·2	150·1
1962	49·7	24·0	14·2	14·0	157·9	52·0	22·2	39·7	7·9	161·6
1963	52·6	26·2	14·7	15·0	169·8	51·4	24·7	41·9	8·5	169·1
1964	50·0	28·0	15·5	16·5	175·6	50·3	27·6	43·9	9·1	177·8
1965	55·5	30·9	15·5	18·2	190·2	50·9	30·7	47·8	9·4	189·6
1966	64·0	33·7	14·5	20·0	214·4	61·9	35·9	53·1	10·1	215·6
1967	70·5	32·7	15·2	21·4	230·8	73·2	40·6	62·7	10·8	245·0
1968	84·3	39·4	17·0	25·1	266·2	79·0	44·6	72·3	12·3	272·2
1969	101·3	39·7	17·9	28·6	300·1	78·7	49·4	80·9	13·5	290·2
1970	99·7	34·4	18·2	31·6	306·8	76·6	56·1	96·8	15·0	317·4
1971	98·1	37·7	19·1	35·4	327·3	73·9	62·3	114·0	15·5	346·8
1972	119·9	41·9	18·6	39·8	374·0	77·3	68·2	128·1	16·7	377·3
1973	128·4	49·3	20·0	44·1	419·6	77·3	75·2	146·9	19·3	411·7
1974	146·8	51·8	20·2	48·2	463·1	82·5	83·5	173·6	20·8	467·4
1975	143·3	50·9	22·3	51·7	480·0	89·5	95·4	214·1	24·2	544·9
1976	167·8	64·2	21·6	57·8	549·1	93·2	103·3	232·6	30·1	587·5
1977	192·9	73·0	22·9	64·0	616·6	100·7	111·0	249·6	32·6	635·7
1978	224·5	83·5	25·6	71·0	694·4	108·7	120·6	269·5	36·7	694·8
1979	263·4	88·0	26·0	77·3	779·8	121·6	132·9	299·2	41·5	768·3
1980	293·7	84·8	34·0	82·9	855·1	142·4	147·7	351·8	50·2	889·6
1981	339·6	81·1	50·3	90·7	977·2	167·2	159·6	398·3	68·5	1,006·9
1982	348·4	63·1	41·3	96·2	1,000·8	193·5	170·4	438·5	82·1	1,111·6
1983	346·4	77·2	44·9	106·6	1,061·3	214·0	181·9	466·7	96·0	1,189·9
1984	371·3	93·9	48·1	120·8	1,172·9	233·9	195·4	481·2	117·7	1,277·9
1985	411·5	96·4	46·8	131·0	1,270·8	258·8	210·9	510·9	132·8	1,402·6
1986	430·4	106·6	44·6	139·9	1,344·6	277·2	226·3	540·0	139·9	1,489·0
1987	482·9	133·8	47·2	148·7	1,469·5	...	...	...	...	...

Table US.19 Transport and energy, 1890–1987

	Vehicle registrations		Railways		Airways	Energy consumption		
	Passenger cars	Goods vehicles	bn passenger km	bn freight ton km	bn passenger km	Coal	Crude petroleum	Natural gas
	mn					quadrillion Btu		
1890	—	—	19·1	125	—	...	...	...
1891	—	—	20·7	133	—	...	...	...
1892	—	—	21·5	144	—	...	...	...
1893	—	—	22·8	153	—	...	...	...
1894	—	—	23·0	131	—	...	...	...
1895	—	—	19·6	139	—	...	...	...
1896	—	—	21·0	156	—	...	...	...
1897	—	—	19·7	156	—	...	...	...
1898	—	—	21·5	236	—	...	...	...
1899	—	—	23·5	202	—	...	...	...
1900	0·008	—	25·8	232	—	6·8	0·2	0·3
1901	0·015	—	27·9	240	—	7·5	0·25	0·3
1902	0·023	—	31·7	257	—	7·8	0·4	0·3
1903	0·033	—	33·6	283	—	9·2	0·4	0·3
1904	0·055	—	35·2	286	—	9·0	0·5	0·3
1905	0·077	0·001	38·3	304	—	10·0	0·6	0·4
1906	0·106	0·002	40·5	353	—	10·5	0·6	0·4
1907	0·140	0·003	44·6	387	—	12·2	0·8	0·4
1908	0·194	0·004	46·8	356	—	10·5	0·8	0·4
1909	0·306	0·01	46·8	358	—	11·7	0·8	0·5
1910	0·458	0·01	52·0	417	—	12·7	1·0	0·5
1911	0·619	0·02	52·0	415	—	12·4	1·0	0·5
1912	0·902	0·04	53·3	432	—	13·4	1·1	0·6
1913	1·19	0·07	55·8	494	—	14·2	1·2	0·6
1914	1·66	0·10	57·0	473	—	12·9	1·3	0·6
1915	2·33	0·2	52·3	453	—	13·3	1·4	0·7
1916	3·37	0·3	55·2 / 56·6	561 / 598	—	14·7	1·5	0·8
1917	4·73	0·4	64·5	651	—	16·2	1·8	0·9
1918	5·56	0·6	69·5	669	—	17·0	1·9	0·8
1919	6·68	0·9	75·3	600	—	13·8	2·2	0·8
1920	8·13	1·1	76·3	677	—	15·5	2·7	0·8
1921	9·21	1·3	60·7	507	—	12·3	2·7	0·7
1922	10·70	1·6	57·6	559	—	12·6	3·1	0·8
1923	13·25	1·8	61·6	680	—	15·8	4·1	1·0
1924	15·44	2·2	58·3	641	—	14·7	3·9	1·2
1925	17·5	2·6	58·2	682	—	14·7	4·3	1·2
1926	19·3	2·9	57·4	731	—	15·9	4·5	1·3
1927	20·3	3·0	54·4	706	—	15·0	4·6	1·5
1928	21·4	3·3	51·0	713	—	14·9	5·0	1·6
1929	23·1	3·6	50·2	736	—	15·4	5·5	1·9
1930	23·0	3·7	43·3	631	0·16	13·6	5·9	2·0
1931	22·4	3·7	35·2	508	0·19	11·2	5·2	1·7
1932	20·9	3·5	27·4	384	0·24	9·3	4·7	1·6
1933	20·7	3·5	26·4	410	0·32	9·6	5·0	1·6
1934	21·5	3·7	29·1	441	0·37	10·4	5·0	1·8
1935	22·6	4·0	29·8	464	0·58	10·6	5·7	2·0
1936	24·2	4·3	36·2	558	0·77	12·0	6·3	2·2
1937	25·5	4·6	39·7	594	0·76	12·6	6·8	2·5
1938	25·3	4·6	34·9	477	0·85	10·0	6·7	2·3
1939	26·2	4·8	36·5	548	1·22	11·1	7·1	2·5
1940	27·5	5·0	38·3	613	1·85	12·5	7·7	2·7
1941	29·6	5·3	47·3	782	2·49	14·2	8·6	2·9
1942	28·0	5·0	86·4	1,048	2·67	15·6	8·0	3·1
1943	26·0	4·9	140·7	1,194	3·02	17·0	8·6	3·5
1944	25·6	4·9	154·0	1,212	4·01	17·0	9·7	3·8
1945	25·8	5·2	147·7	1,118	6·13	16·0	10·1	4·0
1946	28·2	6·2	104·3	973	11·29	14·5	10·5	4·1
1947	30·8	7·0	74·0	1,076	12·74	15·8	11·4	4·5
1948	33·4	7·7	66·3	1,048	12·70	14·9	12·6	5·0
1949	36·5	8·2	56·5	865	14·21	12·6	12·1	5·3

Table US.19 (Continued)   Transport and energy, 1890–1987

	Vehicle registrations		Railways		Airways	Energy consumption		
	Passenger cars	Goods vehicles	bn passenger km	bn freight ton km	bn passenger km	Coal	Crude petroleum	Natural gas
	mn					quadrillion Btu		
1950	40·4	8·8	51·2	968	16·48	12·9	13·5	6·2
1951	42·7	9·2	55·7	1,063	21·24	13·2	14·8	7·2
1952	43·8	9·4	54·7	1,010	25·13	11·9	15·3	7·8
1953	46·4	9·8	51·0	996	29·35	11·9	16·1	8·2
1954	48·5	10·0	47·1	903	33·16	10·2	16·1	8·5
1955	52·1	10·6	45·9	1,025	39·18	11·5	17·5	9·2
1956	54·2	10·9	45·4	1,064	44·44	11·8	18·6	9·8
1957	55·9	11·2	41·7	1,017	50·30	11·2	18·6	10·4
1958	56·9	11·4	37·5	907	50·68	9·8	19·2	11·0
1959	59·5	11·9	35·6	947	58·52	9·8	19·7	12·0
1960	61·7	12·2	34·3	935	62·53	10·1	19·9	12·6
1961	63·4	12·5	32·7	925	64·09	9·8	20·2	13·1
1962	66·1	13·1	32·0	974	70·41	10·1	21·0	13·9
1963	69·1	13·7	29·8	1,022	81·03	10·5	21·6	14·6
1964	72·0	14·3	29·4	1,082	94·11	11·2	22·2	15·5
1965	75·3	15·1	28·0	1,441	110·51	11·8	23·1	16·0
1966	78·1	15·8	27·7	1,221	128·54	12·7	25·7	17·3
1967	80·4	16·5	24·6	1,189	158·89	12·2	25·2	18·1
1968	83·6	17·3	21·2	1,226	183·36	12·6	26·8	19·4
1969	86·9	18·2	19·6	1,265	201·80	12·6	28·3	20·9
1970	89·2	19·2	17·4	1,251	211·91	12·6	29·4	21·9
1971	92·7	20·3	14·3	1,220	218·28	12·0	30·5	22·5
1972	97·1	21·7	13·8	1,280	245·23	12·4	32·9	22·7
1973	102·0	23·7	15·0	1,403	260·59	13·3	34·8	22·5
1974	104·8	25·1	16·5	1,393	262·14	12·9	32·8	21·8
1975	106·7	26·2	15·9	1,233	261·95	12·9	32·8	20·0
1976	110·2	28·4	16·6	1,306	287·99	13·7	35·2	20·3
1977	112·3	29·8	16·6	1,364	310·86	14·0	37·2	19·9
1978	116·6	31·8	16·4	1,403	364·89	13·8	38·0	20·0
1979	118·5	33·4	18·0	1,494	421·56	15·1	37·1	20·7
1980	121·6	34·2	17·7	1,503	410·62	15·4	34·2	20·4
1981	123·1	35·2	7·5	1,488	400·32	15·9	32·0	19·9
1982	123·7	35·9	6·6	1,305	417·70	15·3	30·2	18·5
1983	126·2	37·7	7·0	1,352	453·42	15·9	30·0	17·3
1984	128·1	38·1	7·3	1,507	490·91	17·0	31·0	18·5
1985	131·9	39·8	8·0	1,434	541·27	17·5	30·9	17·8
1986	135·7[a]	40·9[a]	8·1	1,419	589·78	17·3	31·8	16·6
1987	...	...	...	...	650·53	...	...	...

a   Provisional.

115

Sources

(For sources used in specific tables, see Notes.)

1 *Business Statistics*, Department of Commerce, Bureau of Economic Analysis, Washington, DC, 1979, 1982.

2 *Current Population Reports*, Series P.25, No. 875 (1980), 911 and 917 (1982), 929 and 930 (1983), Bureau of the Census, Washington, DC.

3 *Digest of Education Statistics*, 1987 and other issues, Center for Education Statistics, Department of Education, Washington, DC.

4 *Economic Report of the President, 1988*, US Government Printing Office, Washington, DC.

5 *Employment and Earnings*, monthly, Bureau of Labor Statistics, Washington, DC.

6 *Employment and Earnings in the United States, 1909–78*, Bureau of Labor Statistics, Washington, DC, 1976.

7 *Federal Reserve Bulletin*, monthly, Board of Governors, Federal Reserve System, Washington, DC.

8 Friedman, M. and Schwartz, A., *Monetary Statistics of the United States*, National Bureau of Economic Research, Columbia University Press, 1970.

9 *Handbook of Methods for Surveys and Studies*, Bulletin 1910, Bureau of Labor Statistics, Washington, DC, 1976.

10 *Historical Statistics of the United States, Colonial Times to 1970*, Vols I and II, Department of Commerce, Bureau of the Census, Washington, DC, 1975.

11 Kendrick, J.W. *Productivity Trends in the United States*, National Bureau of Economic Research, Princeton University Press, 1961.

12 Kuznets, S. *Capital in the American Economy. Its Formation and Financing*. National Bureau of Economic Research, Princeton University Press, 1961.

13 Lipsey, Robert E., *Price and Quantity Trends in the Foreign Trade of the United States*, National Bureau of Economic Research, Princeton University Press, 1963.

14 Martin, Robert F. *National Income in the United States, 1799–1938*, National Industrial Conference Board Studies No. 241, New York, 1939.

15 *National Income and Product Accounts of the United States, 1929–82*, Statistical Tables, Department of Commerce, Bureau of Economic Analysis, Washington, DC, 1986.

16 *Statistical Abstract of the United States*, annual, Department of Commerce, Bureau of the Census, Washington, DC.

17 *Supplement for Producer Prices and Price Indexes*, annual, Bureau of Labor Statistics, Washington, DC.

18 *Survey of Current Business*, monthly, Department of Commerce, Bureau of Economic Analysis, Washington, DC.

Notes

Table US.1 Gross national product at current prices

Sources: **11, 15, 18**

The figures from 1929 are official Department of Commerce estimates; Alaska and Hawaii are included from 1960. Government expenditure includes gross fixed capital formation by government enterprises but excludes their current outlays.

For the years 1889–1928, data were obtained from **11**. For further details of coverage and methodology see **11** and **15**.

Table US.2 Gross domestic product at constant prices

Sources: **11, 15, 18**

The figures from 1929 are official Department of Commerce estimates. From 1960 data for Alaska and Hawaii are included.

Government expenditure includes gross fixed capital formation by government enterprises but excludes their current outlays.

The figures for 1889–1928 are based on constant price estimates in **12** adjusted to Department of Commerce concepts by Kendrick, **11**. The figures are five-year moving averages and have been linked to the official estimates to give a rough conversion to 1982 prices. Each category of expenditure has been re-referenced to 1982 prices independently. A net figure for imports and exports of goods and services has been obtained as a residual; this includes any statistical discrepancy caused by the independent re-referencing of the component categories.

For further details of coverage and methodology of current series see **15** and, for the earlier series, **11** and **12**.

Table US.3 Output by sector and industry

Sources: **1, 7, 15, 18**

The official statistics distinguish three main sectors: business, households and institutions, and government.

Business: includes the output of all corporate and non-corporate entities organised for profit, such as mutual financial institutions, private non-insured pension funds, cooperatives, non-profit organisations that primarily serve business, Federal Reserve banks, federally sponsored credit agencies and government enterprises. Owner-occupied housing and buildings and equipment used by non-profit institutions primarily serving individuals are treated as business entities.

Households and institutions: output of households consisting of families and unrelated individuals. Output is measured by compensation of the employees of the entities.

Government: includes all federal, state and local government agencies except government enterprises which are included under 'Business'.

Transactions with the rest of the world have not been shown in the table. For further details see **15**.

Industrial production: the index measures changes in the volume of output in manufacturing, mining, and the gas and electricity industries. The index is currently weighted according to value added in 1977. It is compiled by the Federal Reserve Board. For further details of coverage and methodology see **1**.

Output by industry (supplementary table): the industrial classification in this table is on an establishment basis and is in accordance with the Standard Industrial Classification (SIC) 1972. The first column is for gross national product; in the main table gross domestic product has been given. Data are in constant 1982 dollars and have been converted to index number form by the author.

Table US.4 Industrial production

Sources: **1, 7, 10, 16**

The US unit of measurement is short tons; the published figures for coal, steel and other metals have been converted to metric tons by using the factor 0·90719.

Coal: bituminous coal. From 1951 auger production is included. Based on detailed annual reports from producers.

Passenger cars: figures refer to factory sales and are for passenger cars only. Production of passenger cars was discontinued in February 1942 but some vehicles remaining in factory stocks were sold in subsequent war years. Production was resumed in July 1945 but no new cars were actually produced until 1946.

Chemicals: part of the current index of industrial production. Coverage of the index has changed over the period. For further details see **1**.

Metals: figures for copper, lead and zinc refer to the recoverable metal content of domestic mine output. Figures for lead in 1928 and 1929 exclude the output of Virginia and for 1885–1905 inclusive, figures for lead and zinc are for primary production refined from domestic and foreign ores. Figures for copper for 1885–1905 represent smelter production from domestic ores; difference in the series is slight.

Electricity: the series shown here is for utility companies publicly and privately owned. Industrial establishments generating their own electricity are excluded.

Table US.5 Gross domestic private investment

Sources: **12, 15, 18**

Official Department of Commerce estimates have been used from 1929. The series for producers' durable equipment has been roughly divided into plant and machinery and transport equipment. The total figure includes inventory changes from 1929.

Non-residential construction: includes industrial, commercial, religious and educational buildings, hospitals and institutions, public utilities, farm and mining exploration. Includes brokers' commissions.

Plant and machinery: includes residential purchases of fixed durable equipment as well as industrial and commercial.

Transport equipment: includes trucks, buses and truck trailers, automobiles, aircraft, ships and boats, and railroad equipment.

Non-farm residential construction: includes new houses, farm and non-farm, together with improvements to existing houses and brokers' commissions.

For the period 1885–1928, constant price estimates (five-year moving averages) by Kuznets, **12**, have been used as the basis of the series. They have been linked to the official series and roughly converted to 1982 prices. Each series has been linked separately; components may not therefore add to the total. The figures for the total also differ from those given in Table US.2, which have been adjusted to Department of Commerce concepts (see notes to that table).

For further details of coverage and methodology see **12** and **15**.

Table US.6 Personal and company income

Sources: **14, 15, 18**

Official estimates have been used from 1929.

Wages and salaries: include pay in cash and in kind. Retroactive wages are counted when paid rather than when earned.

Other income: employers' contributions to private pension funds on behalf of employees, group health and life insurance, proprietors' income and rent (adjusted for depreciation and stock appreciation), dividends, interest and transfer payments.
For the period 1899–1929 (first line), estimates by Martin, **14**.

Taxes: include income tax payments and personal contributions for social insurance and also non-tax payments such as passport fees, fines and penalties, donations and fees paid to schools and hospitals operated by the government.

Personal disposable income: personal income less tax and non-tax payments.

Gross trading profits: represents the profits that accrue to industry. No adjustment is made for capital gains or losses, changes in inventory values because of price changes, or receipt of domestic and foreign dividends, except those received by mutual life assurance companies.

Table US.7 Consumers' expenditure

Sources: **12, 15, 18**

Official Department of Commerce estimates have been used since 1929, classified by major commodity groups. The groups used in this table cover the following.

Food: all food and beverages including canteen purchases, military purchases and food produced and consumed on farms, and all meals purchased outside the home.

Fuel: includes gasoline and oil, fuel oil and coal but not electricity and gas.

Consumer durables: includes furniture and household equipment, ophthalmic products, durable toys, sports equipment and jewellery.

Housing: includes owner occupied housing and rented dwellings.

Household operation: includes electricity and gas, telephone, domestic services, water and other sanitary services.

Other services: transport, personal care, medical care, personal business, recreation, private education, religious and welfare activities, net foreign travel.

For the period 1885–1928 estimates for broad categories of consumers' expenditure by Kuznets, **12** in five-year moving averages, have been roughly converted to 1982 dollars. The broad groups used by Kuznets do not fully accord with Department of Commerce concepts or with the current classification; they have been included in the table to give approximate magnitudes. Kuznets's groups have been used in the table as follows.

Kuznets's group	Commodity group in Table US.7
Perishables	Food and fuel
Durables	Consumer durables including motor vehicles and parts
Semi-durables	Clothing and footwear
Services	Housing, household operation and other services

Table US.8 Prices

Sources: **10, 16, 17, 18**

Producer prices: the indices measure average changes in prices received in primary markets by producers of commodities in all stages of processing. Previously called the 'Wholesale price index'. The sample includes 2,800 commodities produced in manufacturing, agriculture, forestry and fishing, mining, gas, electricity and public utilities.

The industrial commodities index includes crude materials for further processing such as hides and skins, chemicals and allied products, and fuels. For further details of coverage and methodology see **17**.

Consumer prices: the index measures changes in the price of a 'fixed basket' of goods and services based on expenditure patterns of urban families. The weights are currently based on 1982–84 Consumer Expenditure Survey. See **16**, 1988, for further details. Before 1978, the index used in the table was based on the expenditure patterns of wage earners' and clerical workers' families – CPI (W) – covering about half the population included in the current index. The CPI (W) was based first on expenditure patterns in 1917–19; revisions were made in 1940, 1953 and 1964. For further details see **16**, 1983.

Unit value exports and imports indices: from 1922, these indices have been compiled by the US Bureau of International Commerce. They are chain indices, chained annually.

For the period 1885–1921, the indices are based on estimates made by Lipsey, **13**, also published in **10**.

Table US.9   Population

Sources: **2, 10, 16**

Total population: mid-year estimates (July 1). Includes armed forces stationed overseas. From 1959 (second line), the figures include Alaska and Hawaii.

Geographical distribution: excludes armed forces stationed abroad, and figures are as at April 1 each year. Current definition of areas is as follows, but there have been boundary changes from time to time; see **16**, 1983 and 1985, Appendix.

North-East: Maine, New Hampshire, Vermont, Massachusetts, Rhode Island, Connecticut, New York, New Jersey, Pennsylvania.

Mid-West: Ohio, Indiana, Illinois, Michigan, Wisconsin, Minnesota, Iowa, Missouri, North Dakota, South Dakota, Nebraska, Kansas. Previously (up to 1985), this area was called North Central. Now covers East North Central and West North Central grouped under Mid-West.

South: Delaware, Maryland, District of Columbia, Virginia, West Virginia, North Carolina, South Carolina, Georgia, Florida, Kentucky, Tennessee, Alabama, Mississippi, Arkansas, Louisiana, Oklahoma, Texas.

West: Montana, Idaho, Wyoming, Colorado, New Mexico, Arizona, Utah, Nevada, Washington, Oregon, California, Alaska, Hawaii.

Table US.10   Education

Sources: **3, 10, 16**

The first thee columns are for the numbers of pupils enrolled, full-time, in public day schools in the autumn (fall) term, classified by grade. Compulsory schooling usually starts at age 6 years and continues up to 16 although State laws vary.

Kindergarten: pre-grade 1 pupils.
Elementary: pupils in grades 1–8 inclusive including special education classes. Usually comprises pupils aged 6–13.
Secondary: pupils in grade 9 and above including special education classes.

For years before 1953 the data refer to the school year ending in June of the year shown.

For the period 1916–52, school data were published biennially.

Figures for per cent of population in column 4 are for population in the 5–15 age group from 1952.

Higher education: students enrolled in universities, colleges, professional schools, junior colleges, teachers' colleges, both public and private. From 1963 figures are for total enrolment including adult education, short courses and correspondence courses. Autumn (fall) term each year. Up to 1962, figures are for degree credit enrolment, that is, students working towards a bachelor's or higher degree.

Table US.11   Labour market: employment

Sources: **4, 5, 6, 16, 18**

Number in civil work: all those in civilian employment, including employees and self-employed.

Employed in agriculture: includes employees and self-employed.

Employment by sector: the estimates include all full and part time wage and salary earners who worked during or received pay for any part of the pay period which includes the twelfth of each month. Based on reports from establishments. Does not include self-employed, proprietors or domestic workers. Those on the establishment payroll at the time of the survey are included even though they may be on strike, on leave or sick. Employment in the government sector relates to civilian employment only. Data are classified in accordance with the SIC 1972.

The information provided by periodic censuses is used as a benchmark to establish the level of employment, and the sample data provide information measuring the changes between censuses. The current series is adjusted to March 1982. For further details see **5**, February 1967 and **6**.

'Services' includes finance, insurance and real estate, plus other services such as laundry and dry cleaning.

119

From 1947, the figures refer to those aged 16 and over; previously they included those aged 14 and over. From 1960, Alaska and Hawaii are included in the data.

Self-employed: active properties or partners who devote a majority of their working hours to their unincorporated businesses. The industry breakdown is summarised in the following table.

	Agriculture, etc.	Manufacturing	Construction	Other
	'000			
1980	1,682	363	1,186	5,427
1981	1,678	366	1,166	5,543
1982	1,677	358	1,131	5,757
1983	1,603	375	1,171	6,070
1984	1,586	364	1,248	6,214
1985	1,495	351	1,312	6,169
1986	1,491	375	1,381	6,140
1987	1,479	359	1,397	6,446

Table US.12   Labour market: other indicators

Sources: **4, 5, 6, 10, 16, 18**

Average weekly hours and earnings: based on reports of establishments and covering those on the payroll at the time of the survey. 'Hours' include paid hours for full- and part-time production and related workers. 'Earnings' figures include pay for overtime, holidays and vacations, and sick leave but not fringe benefits, bonuses (unless earned and paid regularly) or payments in kind. For further details see **5**, February 1967.

Productivity indices: obtained by dividing output indices by the corresponding index of manhours. The series given in the table are those for the 'Business' sector and for Manufacturing. From 1947, the series have been compiled by the Bureau of Labor Statistics. For full details see **9**, Chapters 30 and 31.

For the period 1885–1946, the series used are those published in **11**, which refer to 'real gross private domestic product'. They have been linked to the Bureau of Labor Statistics series for the 'Business' sector at 1947.

Unemployment: includes those not working during the survey week but who are available and currently looking for work. The sample consists of about 60,000 households selected to represent the total population aged 16 years and over. Households are interviewed on a rotating basis so that three-quarters of the sample is the same for any two consecutive periods. From January 1967, the lower age limit was raised from 14 to 16 years and the figures were revised back to 1947. The unemployment percentage is the number of unemployed expressed as a percentage of the total labour force (that is, including the self-employed, the unemployed and the resident Armed Forces). For further details see **5** and **6**, February 1967.

Industrial disputes: present series (from 1982) includes all known stoppages in effect during the year arising out of labour disputes involving 1,000 or more workers and continuing for at least one full day or shift. Figures cover all workers made idle for as long as one shift in establishments directly involved, even though they may not be active participants. Indirect or secondary effects are not included. Up to 1981, the figures cover all work stoppages in effect during the year involving six or more workers.

Table US.13   Value of imports by commodity

Sources: **10, 15, 18**

US imports data are classified in two ways: by broad end-use and by economic class. The first classification is used in this table from 1923. For 1885–1922 the figures are based on classification by economic class but have been broadly grouped according to end-use category given in the table. For details of the differences see **10**, p. 879. From 1946, imports include silver ore and bullion, and for 1946–59 US government imports of uranium ores and concentrates and oxides are included. For 1923–40 commodity categories (but not the total) are on an imports for consumption basis. For this reason, and because revisions to totals are not reflected in components, the columns will not always add to the total.

Table US.14   Value of exports by commodity

Sources: **10, 15, 18**

The totals for exports include re-exports. Re-exports are included in the commodity detail only from 1925. The commodity classification is the same as for Table US.13, that is by broad end-use from 1925, Figures based on classification by economic class have been included under the appropriate headings in the table but coverage will differ. For details of differences see **10**, p. 879.

From 1946, exports include silver ore and bullion.

Table US.15   Value of imports and exports by area

Sources: **10, 16, 18**

Europe: includes all East and West European countries together with Iceland and the Soviet Union.

Germany: from 1952, the data are for the Federal Republic of Germany.

Rest of America: includes Canada and all South American countries. US Virgin Island trade with foreign countries included from 1981.

Asia: includes Iran, Iraq, Jordan and Saudi Arabia together with East and South East Asia.

Revisions to the totals of imports and exports are not included in the geographical data.

Table US.16 Balance of payments

Sources: **4, 10, 16, 18**

Imports and exports: certain adjustments are made to the trade data for valuation, coverage and timing. Exports are on a f.a.s. transactions value basis in all years. Imports are on a customs valuation basis up to 1973 and f.a.s. transactions basis from 1974. For further description of adjustments, valuation and timing, see **1**.

Investment income: includes interest, dividends and earnings of unincorporated affiliates and reinvested earnings of incorporated affiliates on US direct investment abroad (net of foreign taxes); dividends and interest on foreign securities held by US residents; interest received on bank and commercial loans to foreigners; interest received by the US government on loans to foreign countries minus payments of income for investment in the USA in each of the above categories.

Other services: includes insurance, royalties and fees, miscellaneous government services.

Two figures are given for 1900. The first figure is comparable with earlier years and the second figure with later years, see **10**.

Table US.17 Finance

Sources: **1, 8, 10, 16**

Standard and Poor's index of common stock: based on the aggregate value of the common stock of 500 companies. From July 1976, the index includes 400 industrial stocks, 20 transport, 40 public utilities and 40 finance. (Before 1976 the coverage was 425 industrial, 25 transport, 50 public utilities.) The market value each year is expressed as a percentage of the average market value in the base period, 1941–43.

Dow Jones average: data published in the *Wall Street Journal*. Averages are compiled from daily closing prices of 65 representative stocks listed on the New York Stock Exchange. The composition of the stocks will change from time to time. For further details see **1**.

3-month Treasury bill yield: the rate is the open market rate in New York City.

US government bonds yield: the figures are unweighted averages of yields. For 1919–25, yields cover all outstanding, partially tax exempt, government bonds with a minimum repayment of eight years; for 1926–34, twelve-year minimum repayment period; 1935–41, 15-year minimum repayment period. From 1942, the series is for fully taxable bonds; 1942–52, minimum repayment period 15 years; 1953–87, repayment period ten years or more.

Money supply: defined as currency in circulation plus demand deposits at commercial banks and foreign demand balances at Federal Reserve banks. The figures are season-

ally adjusted averages of daily figures in December from 1959. For 1908–58 the figures are annual averages. For the period 1885–1914, data in **8** have been used. The series for this period includes time deposits, and the figures for 1885–1907 are for June.

Consumer credit outstanding: series compiled by the Board of Governors of the Federal Reserve system; figures are at end-December each year. Figures before 1940 are based largely on Department of Commerce estimates. The series is updated periodically. Includes credit extended to individuals for the purchase of capital goods that may be used in part for business purposes. The series has been revised back to 1950; two figures are therefore given for 1950. The second line is the revised figure; the first one is consistent with the earlier years.

Table US.18 Public finance

Sources: **10, 15, 18**

Total receipts: include personal tax and non-tax receipts, corporate profits, tax accruals, customs and excise duties and social insurance contributions from 1952. Figures for 1885–1928 are Federal government receipts except for 1902, 1913, 1922 and 1927 when the figures are for receipts of all levels of government including all taxes, and so on, operative in the year shown.

Total expenditure: this is a consolidated total (net of grants-in-aid to state and local governments) for all years from 1952 and for selected years before 1952. Figures for total expenditure for 1885–1928 are for Federal expenditure only except for 1902, 1913, 1922 and 1927 when a consolidated figure for all levels of government is given together with expenditure by category.

For the period 1929–31 and every alternate year from 1932 to 1952, the figure for total expenditure is that given in **15**. Where data are given for categories of expenditure, the total expenditure figure is that given in **10**.

The figures for 1900–29 are for fiscal years ending June 30 of year shown; all other data are for calendar years.

Social services: includes health and hospitals, income support, social security and welfare, and veterans' benefits and services.

Table US.19 Transport and energy

Sources: **10, 16**

Vehicle registrations: the series includes both private and publicly owned vehicles. 'Passenger cars' includes taxis, and 'Goods vehicles' covers both trucks (lorries) and buses. Based on information supplied to the US Federal Highway Administration by state vehicle registration departments. Data before 1921 are incomplete because not all states required vehicles to be registered.

Railways: passenger km: series is for revenue passenger miles of Amtrak traffic from 1981 converted to km by using the factor 1·609. Previously all three classes of railway up to 1960 and then Class I only. (Railways are classified according to size of operating revenues; in 1969 Class I railways carried over 98 per cent of the traffic.) For years up to 1916, the figures are for year-end June 30; from 1916 (second line), figures refer to calendar years.

Railways: freight ton km: see note above for coverage and timing of data. Converted to freight ton km by using the factor 1·635.

Airways: passenger km: series covers both domestic and international flights on scheduled and chartered airlines. Converted to km by using the factor 1·609.

Energy consumption: series covers primary fuel input with the exception of hydroelectricity, expressed in Btu to give a common measurement. For details of conversion factors see **10**, pp. 567 and 568.

'Crude petroleum' includes domestically produced crude oil, natural gas liquids and lease condensate plus imported crude oil and products.

Part III

**Statistical tables for
Australia, Canada, France,
Germany, Italy, Japan and Sweden**

AUSTRALIA

CONTENTS

Table A.1   Gross domestic product at current prices, 1885–1987

	Consumers' expenditure	Government current expenditure	Gross fixed capital formation	Value of physical change in stocks	Exports of goods & services	Imports of goods & services	**Gross domestic product at market prices**
				A$ mn			
1885	...	...	64	...	...	...	**360**
1886	...	...	74	...	...	...	**355**
1887	...	...	76	...	...	...	**391**
1888	...	...	81	...	...	...	**403**
1889	...	...	79	...	...	...	**443**
1890	...	...	71	...	...	...	**430**
1891	...	...	79	...	...	...	**423**
1892	...	...	46	...	...	...	**359**
1893	...	...	34	...	...	...	**321**
1894	...	...	35	...	...	...	**312**
1895	...	...	31	...	...	...	**297**
1896	...	...	41	...	...	...	**336**
1897	...	...	31	...	...	...	**323**
1898	...	...	46	...	...	...	**373**
1899	...	...	46	...	...	...	**381**
1900	...	...	46	...	...	...	**397**
1901	326	20	56	−1	103	−85	**419**
1902	324	24	72	9	97	−82	**444**
1902	335	22	75	−11	94	−77	**428**
1903	320	23	51	22	106	−74	**448**
1904	324	26	50	−3	121	−74	**444**
1905	334	28	53	12	133	−81	**479**
1906	364	32	72	17	148	−95	**538**
1907	389	32	75	−4	145	−101	**536**
1908	410	33	75	17	139	−101	**573**
1909	436	33	80	29	157	−112	**623**
1910	495	36	95	19	167	−128	**684**
1911	556	38	121	2	164	−147	**734**
1912	578	41	143	30	170	−160	**802**
1913	629	48	149	18	171	−151	**864**
1914	683	52	128	−31	142	−136	**838**
1915	757	81	121	38	166	−194	**969**
1916	774	118	119	−15	243	−217	**1,022**
1917	811	121	107	1	209	−187	**1,062**
1918	903	102	139	17	227	−243	**1,145**
1919	953	72	206	−50	300	−228	**1,253**
1920	1,027	75	243	121	268	−352	**1,382**
1921	960	73	258	24	268	−215	**1,378**
1922	1,117	90	273	39	262	−271	**1,510**
1923	1,185	85	290	32	265	−288	**1,569**
1924	1,214	88	302	72	341	−295	**1,722**
1925	1,303	88	305	−28	302	−311	**1,659**
1926	1,357	94	322	12	286	−342	**1,729**
1927	1,325	102	324	−	293	−305	**1,739**
1928	1,314	105	306	2	308	−323	**1,712**
1929	1,293	95	239	18	216	−295	**1,566**
1930	986	87	176	−13	201	−150	**1,287**
1931	913	84	119	−2	219	−123	**1,210**
1932	976	82	133	5	225	−157	**1,264**
1933	1,010	88	154	12	259	−167	**1,356**
1934	1,104	94	200	−7	244	−203	**1,432**
1935	1,211	98	220	−8	287	−234	**1,574**
1936	1,269	95	250	5	356	−258	**1,717**
1937	1,368	106	299	53	350	−319	**1,857**
1938	1,378	112	290	6	314	−281	**1,819**
1939	1,388	190	288	78	376	−340	**1,980**
1940	1,436	432	250	14	378	−365	**2,145**
1941	1,538	714	192	32	416	−395	**2,497**
1942	1,540	1,176	144	−53	428	−377	**2,858**
1943	1,470	1,072	154	−69	593	−315	**2,905**
1944	1,636	880	188	−77	528	−313	**2,842**
1945	1,798	560	288	89	557	−357	**2,935**

	Consumers' expenditure	Government current expenditure	Gross fixed capital formation	Value of physical change in stocks	Exports of goods & services	Imports of goods & services	**Gross domestic product at market prices**
				A$ mn			
1946	2,158	270	470	139	656	−572	**3,121**
1947	2,580	270	604	182	914	−803	**3,747**
1948	2,975	353	792	45	1,138	−979	**4,324**
1949	3,492	424	1,064	54	1,325	−1,260	**5,099**
				A$ bn			
1950	4·30	0·59	1·52	0·13	2·09	−1·73	**6·77**
1951	5·14	0·80	1·94	0·38	1·48	−2·44	**7·27**
1952	5·45	0·93	1·94	−0·29	1·85	−1·31	**8·24**
1953	5·99	0·87	2·13	0·11	1·79	−1·60	**9·01**
1954	6·51	0·94	2·35	0·17	1·70	−1·98	**9·60**
1955	6·99	1·04	2·57	0·23	1·73	−1·95	**10·40**
1956	7·47	1·09	2·67	−0·05	2·18	−1·74	**11·32**
1957	7·83	1·12	2·86	0·06	1·84	−1·93	**11·58**
1958	8·24	1·22	3·02	0·25	1·86	−1·96	**12·43**
1959	9·05	1·30	3·41	0·17	2·14	−2·29	**13·70**
1960	9·63	1·75	3·71	0·48	2·17	−2·59	**15·19**
1961	9·93	1·89	3·79	−0·22	2·46	−2·18	**15·57**
1962	10·65	1·99	4·12	0·25	2·48	−2·59	**16·82**
1963	11·52	2·18	4·64	0·12	3·15	−2·84	**18·68**
1964	12·47	2·49	5·40	0·56	3·04	−3·44	**20·55**
1965	13·26	2·83	5·84	0·11	3·13	−3·58	**21·60**
1966	14·34	3·22	6·14	0·36	3·47	−3·66	**23·83**
1967	15·67	3·72	6·67	0·11	3·56	−4·10	**25·47**
1968	17·06	3·90	7·50	0·68	3·88	−4·24	**28·71**
1969	18·82	4·30	8·19	0·44	4·75	−4·72	**31·79**
1970	20·82	4·90	9·11	0·45	5·07	−5·07	**35·14**
1971	23·14	5·60	10·08	0·01	5·66	−5·21	**39·36**
1972	25·97	6·35	10·93	−0·29	6·98	−5·34	**44·87**
1973	30·69	7·94	12·79	1·17	7·85	−7·83	**53·76**
1974	37·38	10·68	15·04	1·09	10·03	−10·29	**64·94**
1975	44·74	13·20	18·47	0·17	11·10	−10·83	**76·75**
1976	51·14	15·29	20·99	1·13	13·28	−13·87	**87·50**
1977	56·85	17·21	22·62	−0·45	14·07	−15·07	**95·14**
1978	64·10	18·97	25·83	1·28	16·63	−17·84	**107·76**
1979	72·36	21·27	28·52	0·79	21·72	−20·96	**121·80**
1980	82·14	24·91	34·94	0·48	22·19	−24·90	**138·69**
1981	93·58	28·46	41·17	1·56	22·89	−28·69	**155·74**
1982	105·31	32·36	40·90	−2·45	24·69	−28·53	**169·85**
1983	115·72	35·76	43·89	1·43	28·03	−30·79	**190·63**
1984	126·92	40·11	50·53	0·85	34·14	−39·01	**211·48**
1985	141·25	44·66	58·24	1·45	37·95	−45·52	**236·20**
1986	154·45	48·57	62·94	−1·54	42·20	−47·49	**260·38**
1987	169·99	52·41	69·87	−0·72	48·74	−51·72	**291·89**

Table A.2   Gross domestic product at constant prices, 1885–1987

	Consumers' expenditure	Government current expenditure	Gross fixed capital formation	Value of physical change in stocks	Exports of goods & services	Imports of goods & services	**Gross domestic product at market prices**
				A$ bn, 1980 prices			
1885	. . .	. . .	1·96	. . .	. . .	. . .	**9·04**
1886	. . .	. . .	2·37	. . .	. . .	. . .	**9·14**
1887	. . .	. . .	2·44	. . .	. . .	. . .	**10·46**
1888	. . .	. . .	2·58	. . .	. . .	. . .	**10·19**
1889	. . .	. . .	2·33	. . .	. . .	. . .	**11·05**
1890	. . .	. . .	2·10	. . .	. . .	. . .	**10·68**
1891	. . .	. . .	2·37	. . .	. . .	. . .	**11·50**
1892	. . .	. . .	1·56	. . .	. . .	. . .	**10·08**
1893	. . .	. . .	1·21	. . .	. . .	. . .	**9·53**
1894	. . .	. . .	1·32	. . .	. . .	. . .	**9·86**
1895	. . .	. . .	1·13	. . .	. . .	. . .	**9·30**
1896	. . .	. . .	1·49	. . .	. . .	. . .	**10·01**
1897	. . .	. . .	1·08	. . .	. . .	. . .	**9·45**
1898	. . .	. . .	1·57	. . .	. . .	. . .	**10·92**
1899	. . .	. . .	1·49	. . .	. . .	. . .	**10·93**
1900	. . .	. . .	1·33	. . .	. . .	. . .	**11·57**
	8·02	1·14	1·68	−0·03	2·29	−1·99	**11·08**
1901	8·39	1·33	2·28	0·23	2·06	−1·99	**12·20**
1902	8·59	1·18	2·07	−0·27	1·86	−1·90	**11·40**
1903	9·03	1·25	1·64	0·57	2·06	−1·82	**12·71**
1904	9·19	1·43	1·64	−0·08	2·30	−1·87	**12·49**
1905	9·15	1·49	1·73	0·30	2·40	−1·91	**13·06**
1906	10·38	1·65	2·10	0·43	2·55	−2·12	**14·90**
1907	9·99	1·54	2·10	−0·09	2·58	−2·25	**13·76**
1908	10·02	1·51	2·20	0·39	2·59	−2·35	**14·29**
1909	10·32	1·47	2·37	0·65	2·88	−2·57	**15·11**
1910	11·50	1·55	2·76	0·42	3·11	−2·87	**16·48**
1911	11·76	1·65	3·11	0·04	3·01	−3·25	**16·23**
1912	12·51	1·80	3·47	0·61	2·97	−3·44	**17·85**
1913	12·34	2·11	3·58	0·35	2·95	−3·15	**17·98**
1914	11·62	2·78	2·89	−0·54	2·44	−2·84	**15·84**
1915	11·50	5·29	2·26	0·64	2·33	−3·28	**17·66**
1916	9·91	7·39	1·94	−0·23	2·76	−2·92	**17·12**
1917	9·97	6·83	1·61	0·02	2·23	−2·21	**16·82**
1918	10·86	5·12	2·13	0·24	2·49	−2·53	**17·21**
1919	11·24	2·41	2·71	−0·60	2·97	−2·09	**16·26**
1920	12·14	2·06	3·03	1·49	2·65	−2·78	**18·48**
1921	12·31	2·18	3·52	0·31	3·46	−2·11	**19·46**
1922	13·82	2·70	3·85	0·48	2·86	−3·24	**20·12**
1923	15·62	2·54	4·14	0·39	2·37	−3·83	**20·90**
1924	16·23	2·53	4·25	0·86	2·70	−4·06	**22·27**
1925	16·46	2·46	4·24	−0·34	3·12	−4·05	**21·61**
1926	17·21	2·52	4·47	0·14	3·06	−4·62	**22·52**
1927	16·92	2·58	4·49	−	2·92	−4·28	**22·32**
1928	16·45	2·74	4·24	0·02	3·32	−4·58	**21·89**
1929	17·45	2·44	3·62	0·24	3·02	−4·34	**22·21**
1930	14·13	2·26	2·62	−0·19	3·71	−2·20	**20·12**
1931	14·10	2·45	1·90	−0·03	4·08	−1·83	**20·46**
1932	15·31	2·48	1·82	0·08	4·27	−2·51	**21·68**
1933	16·09	2·84	2·54	0·18	3·87	−2·73	**22·49**
1934	15·99	3·15	3·29	−0·10	4·35	−3·32	**23·00**
1935	17·52	3·28	3·60	−0·11	4·06	−3·78	**24·17**
1936	18·00	3·14	3·91	0·07	4·18	−4·01	**24·95**
1937	18·42	3·23	4·53	0·69	4·63	−4·69	**26·55**
1938	16·73	3·61	4·57	0·08	5·09	−4·18	**25·49**
1939	15·76	6·11	4·35	0·97	5·16	−4·44	**26·89**
1940	15·62	11·46	3·40	0·17	4·90	−4·03	**28·90**
1941	16·10	16·86	2·34	0·39	5·29	−3·75	**33·14**
1942	14·87	24·60	1·60	−0·61	5·06	−3·11	**36·03**
1943	14·23	21·45	1·67	−0·78	6·83	−2·44	**35·60**
1944	16·21	17·84	1·68	−0·83	5·48	−2·36	**33·54**

Table A.2 (Continued)   Gross domestic product at constant prices, 1885–1987

	Consumers' expenditure	Government current expenditure	Gross fixed capital formation	Value of physical change in stocks	Exports of goods & services	Imports of goods & services	**Gross domestic product at market prices**
				A$ bn, 1980 prices			
1945	16·72	11·56	3·07	0·90	5·13	−2·64	**32·15**
1946	19·81	5·61	4·76	1·28	4·36	−3·70	**31·18**
1947	22·11	5·42	5·59	1·50	4·35	−4·43	**33·70**
1948	24·32	5·53	6·65	0·34	4·62	−5·16	**35·37**
1949	25·99	6·02	8·13	0·37	5·00	−6·26	**38·24**
1950	26·77	6·85	10·12	0·68	4·74	−7·80	**40·44**
1951	26·62	7·85	10·84	1·85	4·31	−8·86	**41·25**
1952	26·00	8·18	9·80	−1·34	5·33	−5·11	**41·17**
1953	27·83	7·51	10·51	0·48	5·29	−6·66	**43·80**
1954	29·67	7·73	11·29	0·66	5·42	−8·10	**46·45**
1955	30·61	7·87	11·77	0·87	5·89	−7·67	**48·76**
1956	30·88	7·92	11·80	−0·15	6·64	−6·55	**49·69**
1957	31·91	7·99	12·35	0·26	5·93	−7·20	**50·77**
1958	32·93	8·66	12·92	0·94	6·79	−7·41	**54·51**
1959	35·18	8·40	14·25	0·58	7·25	−8·71	**57·45**
1960	35·83	8·73	15·02	1·75	7·62	−9·87	**59·43**
1961	36·76	9·19	15·16	−0·76	8·65	−8·41	**60·12**
1962	39·02	9·54	16·33	0·98	8·46	−9·88	**64·19**
1963	41·51	9·98	18·05	0·47	9·84	−10·96	**68·71**
1964	43·42	10·87	20·36	1·87	9·81	−13·08	**73·58**
1965	44·73	12·04	21·47	0·39	9·94	−13·41	**75·18**
1966	46·93	12·97	21·83	1·18	11·04	−13·59	**80·19**
1967	49·53	14·27	23·14	0·26	11·58	−14·95	**83·21**
1968	52·62	14·40	25·02	2·28	12·34	−15·49	**91·01**
1969	55·79	15·01	26·36	1·26	14·36	−16·71	**96·10**
1970	58·16	15·57	27·68	1·28	15·68	−16·47	**101·54**
1971	60·63	16·29	28·63	−0·03	17·18	−15·95	**107·10**
1972	63·96	16·83	28·91	−0·58	17·63	−15·98	**111·45**
1973	67·41	18·14	29·75	2·18	16·58	−20·53	**116·10**
1974	69·59	19·64	28·30	2·12	17·78	−21·05	**118·34**
1975	71·93	21·07	29·90	0·17	18·37	−19·77	**121·49**
1976	73·72	21·81	30·25	1·86	19·62	−22·04	**124·56**
1977	75·05	22·66	29·94	−0·72	20·03	−21·07	**125·75**
1978	77·66	23·43	31·65	1·76	21·74	−22·86	**131·75**
1979	79·47	23·87	31·72	1·03	23·42	−22·78	**134·28**
1980	82·14	24·91	34·94	0·48	22·19	−24·90	**138·69**
1981	85·52	25·13	37·21	1·32	22·40	−27·60	**141·21**
1982	86·83	25·85	33·31	−1·95	22·45	−25·14	**139·48**
1983	88·81	26·93	34·05	1·35	24·33	−26·46	**146·33**
1984	91·78	28·53	37·13	0·64	27·68	−30·64	**153·53**
1985	94·38	29·84	38·68	0·95	29·28	−31·10	**160·60**
1986	94·99	30·51	38·35	−0·85	31·76	−30·11	**164·97**
1987	97·67	31·33	39·97	−0·32	33·60	−32·86	**170·87**

Table A.3   Industrial production, index and selected series, 1885–1987

	Industrial production	Coal	Crude steel	Cars & commercial vehicles	Electricity
	Index nos., 1980 = 100	mn tons	mn tons	'000	bn kwh
1885	...	3·15	—	—	—
1886	...	3·12	—	—	—
1887	...	3·24	—	—	—
1888	...	3·62	—	—	—
1889	...	4·04	—	—	—
1890	...	3·52	—	—	—
1891	...	4·45	—	—	—
1892	...	4·17	—	—	—
1893	...	3·73	—	—	—
1894	...	4·21	—	—	—
1895	...	4·36	—	—	—
1896	...	4·63	—	—	—
1897	...	5·10	—	—	—
1898	...	5·50	—	—	—
1899	...	5·54	—	—	—
1900	...	6·49	—	—	—
1901	...	7·00	—	—	—
1902	...	6·97	—	—	—
1903	...	7·23	—	—	—
1904	...	6·96	—	—	—
1905	...	7·62	—	—	—
1906	...	8·73	—	—	—
1907	...	9·84	—	—	—
1908	...	10·36	—	—	—
1909	...	8·32	—	—	—
1910	...	9·89	—	—	—
1911	...	10·72	—	—	—
1912	...	11·92	—	—	—
1913	...	12·61	0·01	—	0·30
1914	...	12·64	0·02	—	...
1915	...	11·60	0·08	—	...
1916	...	9·97	0·11	—	...
1917	...	10·36	0·16	—	...
1918	...	11·01	0·19	—	...
1919	...	10·62	0·23	—	...
1920	...	13·17	0·26	—	...
1921	...	13·08	0·29	—	0·65
1922	...	12·50	0·07	—	0·80
1923	...	12·84	0·28	—	0·99
1924	...	14·11	0·37	—	1·38
1925	...	14·74	0·41	—	1·54
1926	...	14·46	0·38	—	1·73
1927	...	15·22	0·42	—	1·99
1928	...	13·65	0·41	—	2·19
1929	...	12·30	0·44	—	2·29
1930	...	11·55	0·32	—	2·44
1931	...	10·77	0·23	—	2·45
1932	...	11·38	0·23	—	2·51
1933	...	11·86	0·40	—	2·72
1934	...	12·62	0·53	—	2·91
1935	...	13·32	0·71	—	3·20
1936	...	14·65	0·83	—	3·53
1937	...	15·72	1·11	68	3·97
1938	...	15·60	1·20	83	4·35
1939	...	17·46	1·20	75	4·69
1940	...	16·26	1·33	62	5·14
1941	...	19·08	1·70	35	5·70
1942	...	20·13	1·79	32	6·26
1943	...	19·54	1·72	25	6·64
1944	...	19·01	1·61	30	6·68
1945	...	18·53	1·41	18	6·84
1946	...	19·90	1·10	11	6·91

Table **A.3 (Continued)** **Industrial production, index and selected series, 1885–1987**

	Industrial production	Coal	Crude steel	Cars & commercial vehicles	Electricity
	Index nos., 1980 = 100	mn tons	mn tons	'000	bn kwh
1947	...	21·31	1·36	33	7·53
1948	...	21·82	1·40	48	8·36
1949	...	21·03	1·23	58	9·05
1950	...	24·25	1·28	58	9·51
1951	...	25·85	1·50	81	10·50
1952	...	27·95	1·58	86	11·30
1953	...	27·10	1·86	81	12·05
1954	...	29·56	2·18	114	13·71
1955	...	29·86	2·28	127	15·20
1956	...	30·31	2·39	131	16·68
1957	38	31·15	2·85	121	18·29
1958	41	32·60	3·12	160	19·80
1959	45	33·87	3·29	170	21·20
1960	46	37·11	3·62	205	23·20
1961	46	39·72	3·86	214	24·81
1962	50	40·91	4·19	198	26·28
1963	54	42·60	4·33	279	29·28
1964	60	45·59	4·84	288	33·91
1965	63	51·06	5·21	348	36·91
1966	64	53·78	5·65	366	39·88
1967	68	56·56	6·21	369	42·93
1968	71	61·18 / 65·77	6·39	402	46·50
1969	76	69·39	6·53	422	51·18
1970	80	73·15	6·87	478	56·15
1971	83	77·92	6·80	454	57·97
1972	84	84·43	6·63	473	59·50
1973	92	85·28	7·24	452	64·80
1974	95	88·87	7·70	498	69·74
1975	88	98·7	8·06	456	73·93
1976	93	100·16	7·93	455	76·60
1977	93	104·70	7·31	448	82·52
1978	94	105·96	7·54	378	88·52
1979	100	111·25	8·14	432	93·70
1980	100	129·26	7·90	445	96·32
1981	101	120·3	7·96	356	102·46
1982	90	134·6	7·27	413	104·89
1983	94	132·4	5·30	385	109·19
1984	98	138·6	6·17	370	115·81
1985	94	155·9	5·77	409	121·63
1986	101	169·5	6·83	340	126·97
1987	...	193·2	6·12	323	...

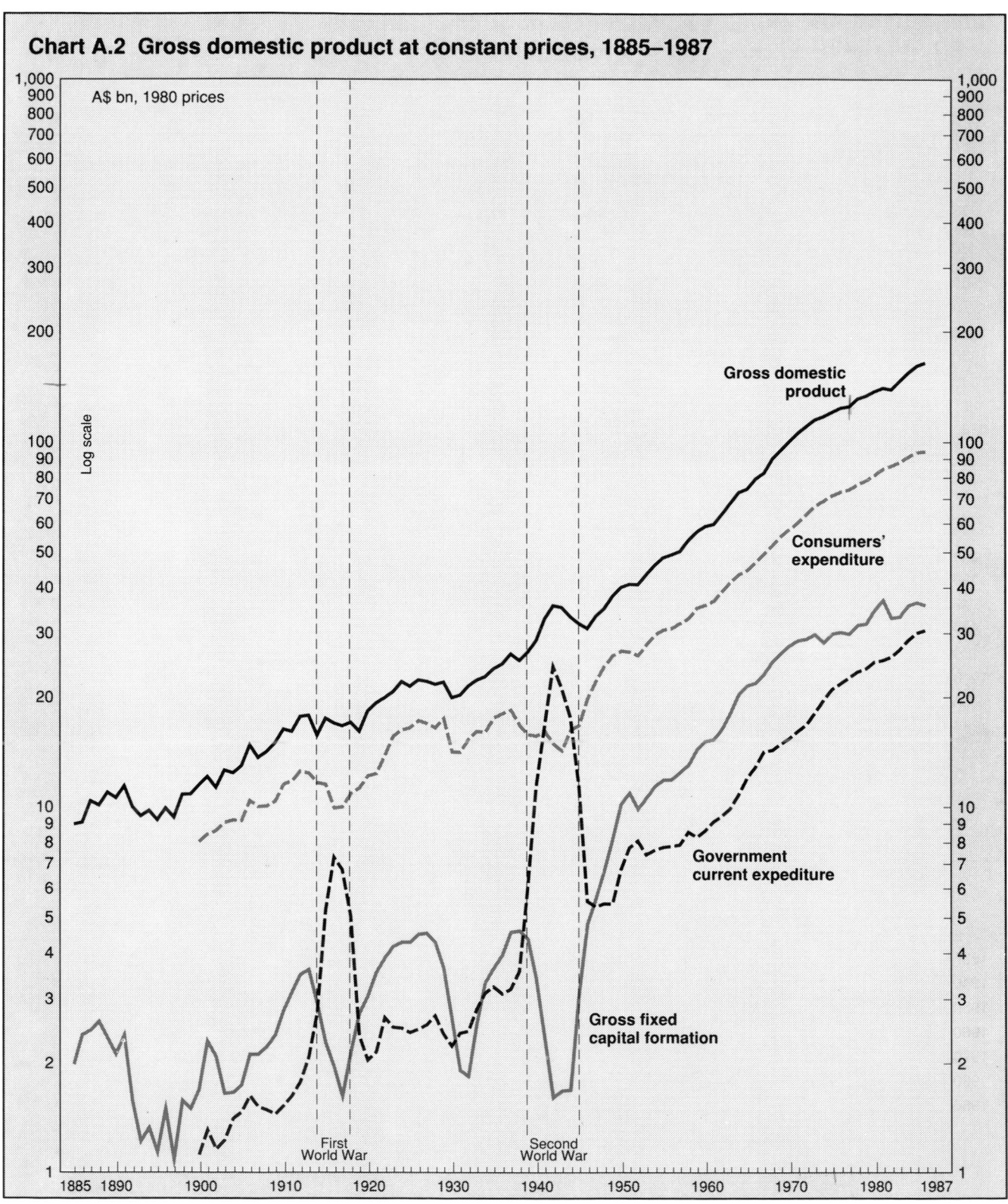

Chart A.2 Gross domestic product at constant prices, 1885–1987

A$ bn, 1980 prices

Log scale

Gross domestic product

Consumers' expenditure

Government current expediture

Gross fixed capital formation

First World War

Second World War

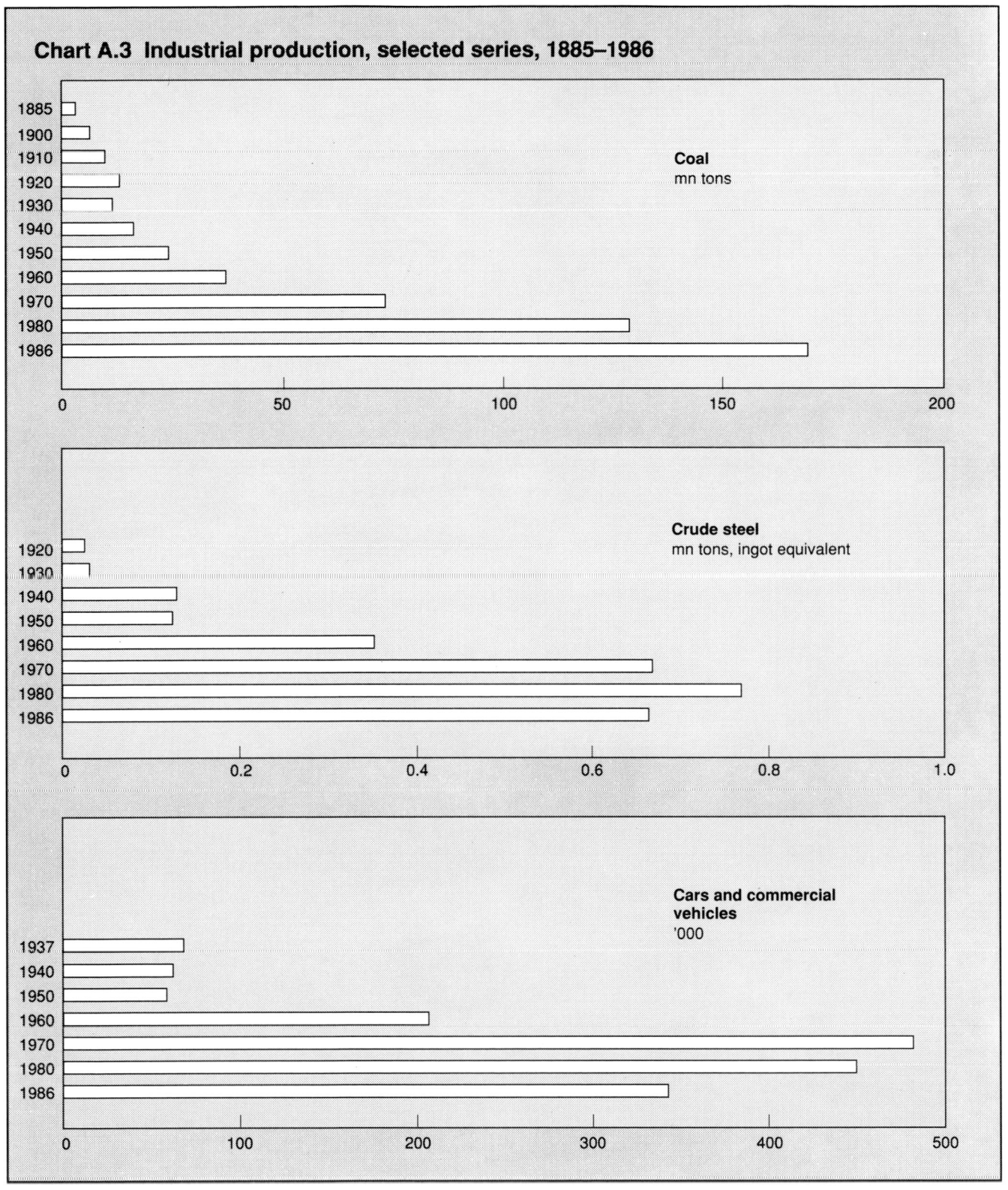

Chart A.3 Industrial production, selected series, 1885–1986

Coal
mn tons

Crude steel
mn tons, ingot equivalent

Cars and commercial
vehicles
'000

Table A.4 Prices and income, 1890–1987

	Consumer prices		Wholesale prices	Import prices	Export prices	Compensation of employees	National income
	All items	Food					
	Index nos., 1980 = 100		Index nos., 1980–81 = 100			A$ mn	
1890	6·1	...	4·7	3·3	5·4	...	...
1891	6·0	...	4·3	3·2	5·0	...	...
1892	5·9	...	4·1	3·0	4·7	...	...
1893	5·7	...	3·9	2·9	4·3	...	...
1894	5·0	...	3·4	2·8	3·8	...	...
1895	4·95	...	3·4	2·7	3·9	...	...
1896	5·0	...	4·1	2·8	4·1	...	...
1897	4·95	...	4·1	2·9	4·0	...	...
1898	4·95	...	4·1	2·9	4·3	...	...
1899	5·4	...	3·6	2·9	5·3	...	...
1900	5·1	...	4·1	3·1	4·9	...	...
1901	5·6	...	4·4	3·0	4·7	...	...
1902	5·9	...	4·7	2·9	5·1	...	...
1903	5·8	...	4·7	2·9	5·4	...	...
1904	5·5	...	4·0	3·0	5·4	...	...
1905	5·7	...	4·1	2·9	5·7	...	...
1906	5·7	...	4·3	3·1	6·0	...	...
1907	5·7	...	4·6	3·2	6·2	...	...
1908	6·0	...	5·0	3·1	5·6	...	...
1909	6·0	...	4·5	3·1	5·6	...	...
1910	6·2	...	4·5	3·2	5·8	...	...
1911	6·3	...	4·8	3·2	5·8	...	...
1912	7·0	...	5·2	3·3	6·0	...	...
1913	7·0	...	4·9	3·4	6·2	...	...
1914	7·2	5·9	6·2	3·4	6·2	...	...
1915	8·3	7·3	7·2	4·3	7·5	...	...
1916	8·4	7·7	6·9	5·4	9·2	...	...
1917	8·9	7·5	8·3	6·4	9·9	...	...
1918	9·5	7·8	8·8	7·3	9·6	...	...
1919	10·8	8·7	10·5	8·7	10·6	...	...
1920	12·2	11·0	10·3	8·9	10·6	...	...
1921	10·7	9·7	7·9	6·8	8·1	...	...
1922	10·3	8·6	8·4	6·0	9·6	...	...
1923	10·5	9·6	8·8	5·6	11·7	...	...
1924	10·4	8·9	8·4	5·6	13·2	...	...
1925	10·4	9·1	8·4	5·5	10·2	...	...
1926	10·7	9·5	8·0	5·3	9·9	...	...
1927	10·5	9·0	8·4	5·2	10·6	...	...
1928	10·5	9·1	8·0	5·1	9·7	...	...
1929	10·8	9·5	8·1	5·0	7·5	...	...
1930	10·3	8·5	7·2	5·0	5·7	...	...
1931	9·2	7·4	6·9	4·9	5·7	...	...
1932	8·8	7·2	6·5	4·6	5·5	...	...
1933	8·4	6·8	6·5	4·5	7·0	...	...
1934	8·6	7·1	6·5	4·5	5·9	...	...
1935	8·8	7·3	6·8	4·5	7·4	...	...
1936	8·9	7·4	7·2	4·7	9·0	...	...
1937	9·2	7·7	7·3	5·0	8·0	...	...
1938	9·5	8·2	7·3	4·9	6·6	...	...
1939	9·7	8·4	7·6	5·6	7·8	0·92	1·77
1940	10·1	...	8·3	6·6	8·4	1·07	1·95
1941	10·5	...	9·0	7·7	8·4	1·31	2·07
1942	11·5	9·4	9·9	8·8	9·0	1·54	2·43
1943	12·0	9·4	10·2	9·4	9·2	1·61	2·80
1944	11·8	9·1	10·3	9·7	10·2	1·58	2·86
1945	11·8	9·4	10·3	9·9	11·7	1·57	2·79
1946	12·1	9·4	10·5	11·3	16·2	1·55	2·89
1947	12·6	10·1	11·6	13·2	22·4	1·82	3·11
1948	13·9	11·5	13·1	13·8	26·3	2·17	4·04
1949	15·2	13·2	14·8	15·0	30·2	2·47	4·70
1950	16·6	15·5	17·8	18·2	51·7	3·11	6·28

Table **A.4 (Continued)** **Prices and income, 1890–1987**

	Consumer prices		Wholesale prices	Import prices	Export prices	Compensation of employees	National income
	All items	Food					
	Index nos., 1980 = 100		Index nos., 1980–81 = 100			A$ mn	
1951	19·8	20·3	21·6	20·5	37·4	3·94	6·85
1952	23·2	22·6	23·2	19·4	38·3	4·25	7·75
1953	24·3	23·4	23·2	19·0	37·4	4·53	8·42
1954	24·4	23·6	23·4	19·2	34·1	4·96	8·90
1955	25·0	24·9	24·3	19·8	31·4	5·44	9·60
1956	26·5	26·1	25·0	20·2	35·0	5·76	10·46
1957	27·1	25·6	24·7	20·5	30·5	5·98	10·53
1958	27·6	26·1	24·4	20·6	26·9	6·27	11·29
1959	28·1	27·1	25·3	20·7	29·9	6·96	12·44
1960	29·0	28·8	26·2	21·0	28·4	7·63	13·12
1961	29·9	28·3	24·4	20·9	28·7	7·89	13·35
1962	29·7	28·1	24·7	20·9	30·2	8·36	14·44
1963	29·9	28·4	25·2	21·2	34·1	9·14	16·14
1964	30·6	30·0	25·8	21·6	31·4	10·25	17·79
1965	31·8	31·5	27·0	22·1	32·0	11·09	18·57
1966	32·7	32·0	27·9	22·1	31·4	12·12	20·49
1967	33·9	33·5	28·2	21·9	29·9	13·21	21·83
1968	34·7	33·8	28·3	22·2	30·5	14·63	24·69
1969	35·8	34·6	29·0	22·9	30·8	16·45	27·28
1970	37·1	36·0	28·3	23·9	30·2	18·88	30·13
1971	39·3	37·4	29·0	25·4	31·1	21·08	33·71
1972	41·7	40·2	32·2	25·1	40·1	23·54	38·51
1973	45·6	47·8	38·1	29·2	47·8	28·90	46·50
1974	52·5	52·4	41·0	41·9	54·1	37·16	55·55
1975	60·4	57·6	44·9	47·5	58·9	42·79	65·19
1976	68·6	64·3	51·6	54·7	65·9	48·28	73·98
1977	77·0	71·3	56·2	61·8	69·2	53·07	79·70
1978	83·2	79·5	70·4	68·2	77·8	57·06	90·32
1979	90·8	90·6	91·1	89·5	94·1	63·65	100·55
1980	100·0	100·0	100·0	100·0	100·0	74·04	115·47
1981	109·7	108·6	101·6	101·7	101·1	85·45	128·64
1982	121·8	118·5	109·9	112·3	109·7	94·98	138·60
1983	134·1	127·7	113·8	116·4	112·4	100·47	155·97
1984	139·5	136·5	119·5	128·7	120·5	110·63	172·43
1985	148·8	145·1	125·4	146·3	127·0	121·57	190·96
1986	162·4	158·0	...	...	...	132·64	208·81
1987	176·2	166·8	...	...	...	145·56	233·36

135

Table A.5   Population, 1885–1986

	Total population	Males	Females	Births	Net migration	Age distribution — Under 15	Age distribution — 15–64	Age distribution — 65 & over
		mn		'000	'000		mn	
1885	2·69	1·46	1·23	95	36·7	(0·85)	(1·79)	(0·05)
1886	2·79	1·51	1·28	97	38·7	...	...	...
1887	2·88	1·56	1·32	101	33·8	...	...	...
1888	2·98	1·61	1·37	104	38·9	...	...	...
1889	3·06	1·65	1·41	105	22·6	...	...	...
1890	3·15	1·69	1·46	109	24·6	...	...	...
1891	3·24	1·74	1·50	110	26·9	1·17	1·91	0·09
1892	3·31	1·77	1·54	110	−3·1	...	...	...
1893	3·36	1·79	1·57	109	−7·4	...	...	...
1894	3·43	1·82	1·60	105	3·2	...	...	...
1895	3·49	1·86	1·64	105	2·9	...	...	...
1896	3·55	1·89	1·67	100	6·5	...	...	...
1897	3·62	1·92	1·70	101	7·0	...	...	...
1898	3·66	1·94	1·73	99	−0·5	...	...	...
1899	3·72	1·96	1·76	101	−1·7	...	...	...
1900	3·77	1·98	1·79	102	−8·8	...	...	...
1901	3·82	2·00	1·82	103	3·0	1·33	2·28	0·17
1902	3·88	2·03	1·85	103	−4·3	...	...	...
1903	3·92	2·05	1·87	98	−9·9	...	...	...
1904	3·97	2·07	1·89	104	−3·0	...	...	...
1905	4·03	2·10	1·92	105	−2·6	...	...	...
1906	4·09	2·13	1·95	108	−5·0	...	...	...
1907	4·16	2·16	2·00	110	5·2	...	...	...
1908	4·23	2·19	2·04	112	5·4	...	...	...
1909	4·32	2·24	2·08	114	21·8	...	...	...
1910	4·43	2·30	2·13	117	29·9	...	...	...
1911	4·57	2·38	2·19	122	74·4	1·41	2·84	0·21
1912	4·65	2·43	2·22	133	91·9	...	...	...
1913	4·82	2·52	2·30	136	63·2	...	...	...
1914	4·95	2·58	2·37	138	−8·2	...	...	...
1915	4·99	2·57	2·42	135	−84·4	...	...	...
1916	4·94	2·48	2·46	131	−128·7	...	...	...
1917	4·94	2·44	2·50	130	−17·8	...	...	...
1918	5·03	2·49	2·54	126	23·4	...	...	...
1919	5·19	2·61	2·58	122	166·3	...	...	...
1920	5·36	2·73	2·63	136	27·6	...	...	...
1921	5·46	2·78	2·68	136	17·5	1·73	3·46	0·25
1922	5·57	2·83	2·74	137	40·2	...	...	...
1923	5·69	2·90	2·79	135	39·7	...	...	...
1924	5·81	2·96	2·85	135	46·1	...	...	...
1925	5·94	3·03	2·91	136	39·8	...	...	...
1926	6·06	3·10	2·96	133	44·8	...	...	...
1927	6·18	3·16	3·02	134	51·6	...	...	...
1928	6·30	3·22	3·08	134	30·1	...	...	...
1929	6·39	3·26	3·13	129	11·8	...	...	...
1930	6·46	3·29	3·17	128	−8·5	...	...	...
1931	6·53	3·32	3·21	119	−10·1	...	...	...
1932	6·58	3·35	3·23	111	−3·0	...	...	...
1933	6·63	3·37	3·26	111	0·8	1·82	4·38	0·43
1934	6·68	3·39	3·29	109	3·3	...	...	...
1935	6·73	3·41	3·32	111	0·7	...	...	...
1936	6·78	3·44	3·34	116	2·6	...	...	...
1937	6·84	3·46	3·38	119	6·4	...	...	...
1938	6·90	3·49	3·41	120	10·5	...	...	...
1939	6·97	3·52	3·45	123	15·3	...	...	...
1940	7·04	3·56	3·48	126	15·1	...	...	...
1941	7·14	3·60	3·54	135	6·9	...	...	...
1942	7·18	3·61	3·57	137	7·3	...	...	...
1943	7·23	3·63	3·60	149	2·7	...	...	...
1944	7·31	3·67	3·64	153	−0·6	...	...	...

Table A.5 (Continued)   Population, 1885–1986

	Total population	Males	Females	Births	Net migration	Age distribution		
						Under 15	15–64	65 & over
	mn			'000	'000	mn		
1945	7·39	3·70	3·69	161	0·9	. . .	. . .	. . .
1946	7·47	3·74	3·73	176	−13·3	. . .	. . .	. . .
1947	7·58	3·80	3·78	182	11·2	1·90	5·07	0·61
1948	7·71	3·87	3·84	178	53·4	. . .	. . .	. . .
1949	7·91	3·97	3·94	181	147·1	2·06	5·20	0·65
1950	8·18	4·12	4·06	191	149·5	2·18	5·34	0·66
1951	8·42	4·25	4·17	193	108·9	2·29	5·45	0·68
1952	8·64	4·38	4·26	202	91·6	2·38	5·56	0·70
1953	8·82	4·47	4·35	202	41·1	2·48	5·61	0·73
1954	8·99	4·55	4·44	202	66·8	2·57	5·67	0·75
1955	9·20	4·66	4·54	208	96·2	2·67	5·76	0·77
1956	9·43	4·78	4·65	212	93·0	2·77	5·87	0·79
1957	9·64	4·88	4·76	220	77·8	2·86	5·96	0·82
1958	9·84	4·97	4·87	223	64·5	2·95	6·05	0·84
1959	10·06	5·13	5·03	227	75·8	3·03	6·17	0·86
1960	10·28	5·25	5·14	230	89·1	3·10	6·30	0·88
1961	10·51	5·37	5·27	240	58·7	3·19	6·42	0·90
1962	10·70	5·47	5·38	237	59·0	3·22	6·57	0·91
1963	10·91	5·57	5·48	236	68·1	3·26	6·72	0·93
1964	11·12	5·60	5·51	229	95·8	3·32	6·85	0·95
1965	11·34	5·71	5·62	223	101·3	3·36	7·00	0·96
1966	11·60	5·84	5·76	224	80·2	3·41	7·20	0·99
1967	11·81	5·95	5·86	229	80·8	3·46	7·35	1·00
1968	12·06	6·06	6·00	241	102·0	3·52	7·52	1·02
1069	12·30	6·20	6·10	250	118·0	3·56	7·71	1·03
1970	12·51	6·29	6·22	258	111·8	3·61	7·86	1·04
1971	12·94	6·51	6·43	276	114·4	3·71	8·14	1·09
1972	13·18	6·63	6·55	265	66·6	3·76	8·30	1·12
1973	13·38	6·72	6·66	248	61·6	3·79	8·45	1·14
1974	13·60	6·83	6·77	245	87·6	3·80	8·63	1·17
1975	13·77	6·91	6·86	233	25·0	3·80	8·78	1·20
1976	13·92	6·98	6·94	228	31·6	3·77	8·91	1·24
1977	14·07	7·06	7·02	226	52·9	3·74	9·06	1·27
1978	14·25	7·14	7·11	224	43·5	3·72	9·21	1·31
1979	14·51	7·25	7·26	223	49·0	3·72	9·42	1·37
1980	14·70	7·34	7·36	226	73·7	3·71	9·57	1·41
1981	14·92	7·45	7·48	236	98·9	3·73	9·74	1·46
1982	15·18	7·58	7·60	240	84·7	3·74	9·94	1·50
1983	15·38	7·68	7·70	243	52·5	3·75	10·10	1·53
1984	15·56	7·76	7·80	234[a]	50·8	3·73	10·26	1·57
1985	15·76	7·86	7·90	247[a]	63·4	3·72	10·43	1·61
1986	15·97	7·97	8·01	. . .	. . .	3·69	10·62	1·67

a   See notes on p. 149.

Table A.6   Education, 1891–1986

	Kindergarten	Primary	Secondary	Post-secondary	University students Total	of which: Female
		No. of pupils '000			No. of students '000	
1891		686		...	...	...
1896		703		...	...	...
1897		725		...	...	...
1898		740		...	...	...
1899		760		...	...	...
1900		777		...	...	...
1901		787		...	...	...
1902		781		...	1·9	...
1903		776		...	...	...
1904		772		...	...	...
1905		767		...	...	...
1906		762		(15·6)	2·6	0·3
1907		764		41·1	2·8	...
1098		771		...	2·9	...
1909		789		40·0	3·0	...
1910		787		42·8	3·3	...
1911		800		47·6	3·4	...
1912		827		44·4	3·8	...
1913		847		41·4	4·2	...
1914		876		40·9	4·3	...
1915		905		40·8	4·3	...
1916		929		44·8	3·8	...
1917		942		49·0	4·0	...
1918		971		52	4·6	...
1919		975		52	6·4	...
1920		994		62	7·9	...
1921		1,018		65	8·0	...
1922		1,039		68	7·8	...
1923		1,056		72	7·3	...
1924		1,091		...	7·3	...
1925		1,101		...	7·4	...
1926		1,118		...	7·8	...
1927		1,136		...	7·9	...
1928		1,158		...	8·0	...
1929		1,171		...	8·5	...
1930		1,156		...	9·5	...
1931		1,158		63	9·8	...
1932		1,155		66	9·9	...
1933	71	700	359	66	9·8	...
1934		1,144		60	10	...
1935		1,143		67	10	...
1936		1,140		74	11	...
1937		1,123		82	11	...
1938		1,184		90	12	...
1939		1,111		89	...	3·9
1940		1,156		94	...	...
1941		1,143		97	...	...
1942		1,118		88	10·8	3·7
1943		1,138		88	11·7	4·5
1944		1,153		100	13·0	...
1945	...	(895)	(253)	111	15·6	...
1946	...	(920)	(244)	134	25·6	6·2
1947	...	(950)	(237)	145	30·5	6·5
1948	...	(982)	(227)	151	32·5	6·9
1949	...	(1,031)	(233)	154	31·8	6·8
1950	...	(1,092)	(245)	162	30·6	6·6
1951	...	(1,146)	(258)	158	31·7	6·3
1952	...	(1,220)	(273)	160	29·6	5·8
1953	...	(1,278)	(294)	168	28·8	6·0

Table A.6 (Continued)   Education, 1891–1986

	Kindergarten	Primary	Secondary	Post-secondary	University students Total	of which: Female
		No. of pupils '000			No. of students '000	
1954	135	1,012	422	205	29·4	6·3
1955	144	1,071	441	213	30·8	6·8
1956	148	1,119	478	...	34·5	7·6
1957	154	1,158	517	251	36·9	8·1
1958	163	1,194	554	266	41·9	9·2
1959	164	1,202	620	285	47·2	10·7
1960	170	1,222	660	303	53·4	12·4
1961	176	1,243	690	358	57·7	13·4
1962	180	1,262	716	390	63·3	...
1963	187	1,285	724	432	69·1	17·2
1964	191	1,307	743	463	76·2	19·8
1965	196	1,339	773	491	83·3	22·0
1966	204	1,374	793	508	91·3	25·0
1967	207	1,410	814	534	95·4	26·4
1968	206	1,442	835	565	101·5	29·1
1969	203	1,474	855	617	109·7	31·8
1970	196	1,495	881	622	116·8	34·9
1971	196	1,500	907	...	123·8	39·0
1972	201	1,494	931	655	128·7	42·1
1973	204	1,481	950	629	133·1	44·9
1974	1,874		1,063[a]	411[a]	142·9	50·4
1975	220	1,481	985	872	148·3	54·3
1976	237	1,488	988	937	154·0	58·1
1977	1,875		1,120[a]	729[a]	158·4	61·5
1978	224	1,563	962	1,031	160·0	63·8
1979	198	1,579	952	1,147	160·8	65·6
1980	201	1,587	950	1,203	163·2	68·2
1981	201	1,579	969	930	166·6	71·2
1982	196	1,560	970	970	167·4	73·0
1983	195	1,516	1,041	1,058	169·4	74·8
1984	157	1,571	973	...	172·7	77·5
1985	162	1,542	1,278[b]	...	175·5	80·3
1986	168	1,520	1,290[b]	...	181·5	84·8

a   Not strictly comparable with other figures in this column as the figures for 1974 and 1977 for 'secondary' include pupils aged 16 and over. In other years, children aged 16 and over are included in post-secondary.
b   Includes all pupils over Grade 7.

Table A.7 Labour market: employment, 1910–86

	Employed labour force	Agriculture, forestry & fishing	Mining & quarrying	Manufacturing	Construction	Gas, electricity & water	Transport & communication	Distribution & services
				'000				
1910	1,754	446	98	361	143	12	131	563
1911	1,868	460	94	381	194	14	145	580
1912	1,944	462	93	393	228	15	153	600
1913	1,990	476	88	394	234	17	163	618
1914	1,952	475	78	386	184	17	167	645
1915	2,019	478	68	383	161	17	168	744
1916	2,076	466	65	383	138	17	169	838
1917	2,074	470	64	386	112	18	173	851
1918	2,042	470	61	399	126	18	169	799
1919	1,990	474	58	429	153	20	176	680
1920	2,008	488	54	434	159	20	170	683
1921	2,073	508	51	444	190	21	168	691
1922	2,154	514	52	461	218	22	178	709
1923	2,196	508	53	476	238	24	175	722
1924	2,266	524	53	486	253	25	180	745
1925	2,301	526	54	495	251	26	185	764
1926	2,363	523	53	512	265	28	196	786
1927	2,359	526	49	502	266	28	194	794
1928	2,351	531	44	503	246	28	189	810
1929	2,265	534	42	470	194	27	180	818
1930	2,100	540	47	384	140	23	167	799
1931	2,065	531	50	381	142	21	164	776
1932	2,176	548	51	416	177	21	164	799
1933	2,280	556	53	453	212	23	165	818
1934	2,382	551	57	499	251	25	165	834
1935	2,468	553	60	543	265	27	162	858
1936	2,528	552	65	574	262	27	168	880
1937	2,617	557	65	610	264	27	178	916
1938	2,645	550	64	615	252	28	187	949
1939	2,682	544	63	639	237	30	188	981
1940	2,829	537	61	704	193	27	189	1,118
1941	3,042	499	56	779	143	27	196	1,342
1942	3,222	462	50	820	131	27	204	1,528
1943	3,276	462	47	834	120	28	215	1,570
1944	3,261	479	46	812	119	29	218	1,558
1945	3,127	503	48	802	145	32	239	1,358
1946	3,063	508	53	863	215	35	252	1,137
1947	3,158	502	56	900	250	39	267	1,144
1948	3,264	500	56	933	272	39	280	1,184
1949	3,363	501	56	955	304	42	291	1,214
1950	3,503	500	60	1,001	341	42	298	1,261
1951	3,589	500	60	1,011	346	47	307	1,318
1952	3,533	504	61	963	316	47	307	1,335
1953	3,607	505	61	1,008	323	50	306	1,354
1954	3,705	501	61	1,047	351	57	308	1,380
1955	3,795	498	61	1,071	357	57	318	1,433
1956	3,819	495	61	1,073	347	60	325	1,458
1957	3,854	495	57	1,082	350	63	323	1,484
1958	3,904	486	54	1,091	362	67	322	1,522
1959	4,000	471	53	1,131	383	69	324	1,569
1960	4,092	463	52	1,156	388	71	327	1,637
1961	...	...	...	...	...	...	...	...
1962	...	...	...	...	...	...	...	...
1963	...	...	...	...	...	...	...	...
1964	4,496	463	50	1,358	387	a	345	1,892
1965	4,629	454	54	1,411	394	a	363	1,953
1966	4,824	430	58	1,329	406	a	375	2,226
1967	4,933	429	63	1,363	402	a	374	2,302
1968	5,056	440	73	1,371	422	a	387	2,363
1969	5,183	415	67	1,405	435	a	403	2,458

Table A.7 (Continued)   Labour market: employment, 1910–86

	Employed labour force	Agriculture, forestry & fishing	Mining & quarrying	Manufacturing	Construction	Gas, electricity & water	Transport & communication	Distribution & services
				'000				
1970	5,396	434	82	1,424	457	a	417	2,582
1971	5,516	413	89	1,467	471	a	412	2,664
1972	5,610	442	81	1,428	466	a	409	2,784
1973	5,783	426	70	1,481	503	a	439	2,864
1974	5,855	405	74	1,478	506	a	444	2,948
1975	5,841	398	79	1,369	511	a	455	3,030
1976	5,898	385	80	1,385	494	a	442	3,113
1977	5,995	400	80	1,383	482	a	452	3,198
1978	6,005	375	79	1,194	487	115	459	3,296
1979	6,079	399	82	1,228	469	119	473	3,309
1980	6,281	407	84	1,240	486	129	459	3,476
1981	6,394	416	99	1,236	475	125	482	3,561
1982	6,379	410	91	1,196	467	129	505	3,581
1983	6,241	412	94	1,132	388	136	505	3,573
1984	6,462	400	94	1,141	423	148	486	3,770
1985	6,646	414	102	1,109	469	138	523	3,890
1986	6,886	415	96	1,127	491	137	542	4,078

a   Included in manufacturing.

Table A.8 Labour market: other indicators, 1900–87

	Manufacturing					Industrial disputes		
	Average weekly hrs worked	Average hourly earnings	Unemployment			Stoppages	Workers involved	Working days lost
			'000	%			'000	'000
		Pence						
1900	48·93	9·0	...	3·9		...	...	...
1901	48·93	9·1	...	4·8		...	...	...
1902	48·93	9·4	...	8·5		...	...	...
1903	48·93	9·7	...	9·4		...	...	...
1904	48·93	9·8	...	8·6		...	...	...
1905	48·93	10·1	...	6·6		...	...	...
1906	48·93	10·4	...	5·2		...	...	...
1907	48·93	10·8	...	3·4		...	...	...
1908	48·93	11·3	...	3·3		...	...	...
1909	48·93	12·0	...	3·3		...	...	...
1910	48·93	12·8	...	2·9		...	...	...
1911	48·93	13·5	...	2·4		...	...	...
1912	48·93	14·0	...	5·0		...	...	...
1913	48·93	14·6	...	3·3		208	50	624
1914	48·87	14·8	...	5·9		337	71	1,090
1915	48·77	15·3	...	3·5		358	81	583
1916	48·33	16·0	...	3·3		508	171	1,679
1917	48·10	16·3	...	3·4		444	174	4,600
1918	47·88	17·3	..	3·6		298	56	581
1919	47·41	19·3	...	3·4		460	158	6,308
1920	47·07	22·6	...	5·8		554	156	1,872
1921	46·22	24·4	...	6·1		624	165	1,286
1922	46·38	24·7	...	5·0		445	116	859
1923	46·70	25·6	...	4·7		274	76	1,146
1924	46·66	25·7	...	6·3		504	152	919
1925	46·44	26·4	...	4·9		499	177	1,129
1926	45·57	27·1	...	4·2		360	113	1,310
1927	45·46	27·5	...	6·2		441	201	1,714
1928	45·27	26·9	...	6·7		287	96	777
1929	45·38	27·0	...	9·8		259	105	4,461
1930	45·44	24·5	...	16·4		183	54	1,511
1931	45·86	24	...	19·7		134	38	246
1932	45·50	22·8	...	18·9		127	33	212
1933	45·51	22	...	16·0		90	30	112
1934	45·36	22	...	14·0		155	51	370
1935	45·36	22·5	...	11·0		183	47	495
1936	45·14	23	...	8·8		235	61	497
1937	45·06	24	...	7·5		342	96	557
1938	44·89	25·3	...	8·8		376	144	1,338
1939	44·56	26·3	...	9·0		416	153	459
1940	44·15	27·0	...	4·9		350	193	1,507
1941	43·88	28·8	...	1·9		567	248	984
1942	43·74	31·0	...	1·0		602	169	378
1943	43·63	32·8	...	1·0		785	296	990
1944	43·62	32·8	...	1·2		941	276	913
1945	43·60	33·0	...	2·2		945	316	2,120
1946	43·59	33·8	7·6	2·9		869	349	1,948
1947	43·57	37·0	6·7	2·0		982	327	1,339
1948	39·96	44·5	2·6	1·5		1,141	317	1,663
1949	39·96	49	10·3	1·8		849	265	1,334
1950	39·96	54	12	0·4		1,276	432	2,063
1951	39·96	67	10	0·3		1,344	409	873
1952	39·95	79	38	1·1		1,627	516	1,164
1953	39·95	83	53	1·5		1,459	496	1,051
1954	39·95	85	22	0·6		1,490	370	902
1955	39·95	87	19	0·5		1,532	445	1,011
1956	39·95	91	32	0·8		1,306	428	1,121
1957	39·95	94	52	1·3		1,103	337	630
1958	...	95	67	1·7		987	283	440

	Manufacturing		Unemployment		Industrial disputes		
	Average weekly hrs worked	Average hourly earnings			Stoppages	Workers involved	Working days lost
			'000	%		'000	'000
		Pence					
1959	...	99	66	1·7	869	237	365
1960	...	104	47	1·2	1,145	603	725
1961	...	107	112	2·6	815	300	607
1962	...	109	93	2·1	1,183	354	509
		A$					
1963	42·8	...	81	1·9	1,250	413	582
1964	43·4	...	49	1·1	1,334	546	911
			52	1·2			
1965	...	...	54	1·2	1,346	475	816
1966	43·5	1·40	79	1·6	1,273	395	732
1967	43·7	1·48	87	1·7	1,340	483	705
1968	43·7	1·57	81	1·6	1,713	720	1,079
1969	44·1	1·66	79	1·5	2,014	1,285	1,958
1970	44·0	1·79	78	1·4	2,738	1,367	2,394
1971	43·5	2·04	93	1·7	2,404	1,327	3,069
1972	43·1	2·20	144	2·5	2,298	1,114	2,010
1973	43·6	2·58	106	1·8	2,538	803	2,635
1974	42·2	3·44	141	2·4	2,809	2,005	6,293
1975	41·3	3·82	278	4·6	2,432	1,398	3,510
1976	41·3	4·33	293	4·7	2,055	2,190	3,799
1977	41·3	4·79	359	5·7	2,090	596	1,655
1978	41·7	5·11	398	6·2	2,276	1,076	2,131
1979	42·1	5·66	378	5·8	2,042	1,863	3,964
1980	41·6	6·37	395	5·9	2,429	1,173	3,320
1981	42·7	7·13	381	5·6	2,915	1,247	4,189
1982	39·9	8·41	461	6·7	2,060	706	1,980
1983	40·8	8·88	687	9·9	1,787	470	1,641
1984	41·5	9·31	605	8·6	1,965	560	1,307
1985	42·0	9·89	598	8·1	1,845	571	1,256
1986	41·9	10·43	590	7·8	1,687	692	1,391
1987	...	...	626	8·1	1,475	605	1,316

143

Table A.9 Public finance, 1901–86

	Revenue					Expenditure			
	Taxes on personal income	Taxes on companies	Sales taxes	Customs & excise	Total receipts	Defence	Education	Social services	Total expenditure
	A$ mn								
1901	1		. . .	8·2	9·8	. . .	. . .	. . .	7·8
1902	1		. . .	17·8	22	. . .	. . .	. . .	7·8
1903	2		. . .	19·4	24	. . .	. . .	. . .	8·6
1904	2		. . .	18·2	24	. . .	. . .	. . .	8·6
1905	2		. . .	17·6	22	. . .	. . .	. . .	9·0
1906	2		. . .	18·0	24	. . .	. . .	. . .	10
1907	1		. . .	19·4	26	. . .	. . .	. . .	12
1908	1		. . .	23·2	30	. . .	. . .	. . .	13
1909	1		. . .	21·6	28	. . .	. . .	. . .	15
1910	1		. . .	23·2	32	. . .	. . .	. . .	26
1911	3		. . .	27·0	38	. . .	. . .	. . .	30
1912	4		. . .	29·2	42	. . .	. . .	. . .	34
1913	4		. . .	31·0	44	. . .	. . .	. . .	36
1914	1		. . .	30·0	44	. . .	. . .	. . .	64
1915	7		. . .	29·6	44	. . .	. . .	. . .	128
1916	15		. . .	34·6	62	. . .	. . .	. . .	162
1917	20		. . .	30·4	68	. . .	. . .	. . .	174
1918	24		. . .	26·4	74	. . .	. . .	. . .	214
1919	38		. . .	35·6	90	. . .	. . .	. . .	194
1920	39		. . .	43·2	106	. . .	. . .	. . .	186
1921	49		. . .	64	132	. . .	. . .	. . .	156
1922	53		. . .	54	128	. . .	. . .	. . .	142
1923	45		. . .	66	128	. . .	. . .	. . .	150
1924	43		. . .	72	130	. . .	. . .	. . .	150
1925	46		. . .	74	136	. . .	. . .	. . .	164
1926	48		. . .	78	140	. . .	. . .	. . .	164
1927	53		. . .	88	152	. . .	. . .	. . .	178
1928	51		. . .	84	148	. . .	. . .	. . .	170
1929	51		. . .	82	150	. . .	. . .	. . .	168
1930	53		. . .	84	154	. . .	. . .	. . .	164
1931	56		. . .	56	140	. . .	. . .	. . .	148
1932	46		. . .	58	144	. . .	. . .	. . .	142
1933	41		. . .	66	148	. . .	. . .	. . .	146
1934	48		. . .	68	148	. . .	. . .	. . .	158
1935	58		. . .	76	154	. . .	. . .	. . .	160
1936	65		. . .	82	164	. . .	. . .	. . .	168
1937	70		. . .	86	166	. . .	. . .	. . .	180
1938	78		. . .	96	178	. . .	. . .	. . .	196
1939	83		. . .	95	190	. . .	. . .	. . .	280
1940	100		. . .	108	224	. . .	. . .	. . .	510
1941	158		. . .	108	300	. . .	. . .	. . .	846
1942	229		54	114	420	. . .	. . .	. . .	1,394
1943	297		58	. . .	588	. . .	. . .	. . .	1,440
1944	379		56	. . .	684	. . .	. . .	. . .	1,286
1945	431		59	. . .	754	. . .	. . .	. . .	1,102
1946	429		67	78	782	. . .	. . .	. . .	960
1947	416		73	204	862	. . .	. . .	. . .	956
1948	466		69	232	932	. . .	. . .	. . .	1,100
1949	399	146	78	252	1,077	84	53	48	1,246 / 352
1950	392	167	85	287	1,160	109	64	56	399
1951	722	181	114	330	1,620	200	78	72	580
1952	801	302	191	428	2,058	329	101	94	797
1953	775	334	178	367	2,029	406	121	108	918
1954	788	268	191	440	2,085	339	132	109	868
1955	720	343	201	488	2,184	344	150	118	927
1956	773	373	220	512	2,346	376	173	131	1,034
1957	807	432	252	572	2,588	364	191	145	1,074

Table A.9 (Continued)   Public finance, 1901–86

	Revenue					Expenditure			
	Taxes on personal income	Taxes on companies	Sales taxes	Customs & excise	Total receipts	Defence	Education	Social services	Total expenditure
					A$ mn				
1958	870	429	276	606	2,758	337	210	157	1,112
1959	777	437	287	616	2,736	363	236	165	1,215
1960	884	456	328	672	3,030	376	264	190	1,323
1961	1,037	575	346	717	3,408	384	304	208	1,422
1962	1,074	580	298	701	3,436	396	338	225	1,543
1963	1,083	536	313	759	3,539	411	369	242	1,652
1964	1,271	601	325	814	3,950	486	414	254	1,804
1965	1,569	722	363	899	4,592	559	476	279	2,066
1966	1,729	815	370	1,023	4,754	685	519	303	2,408
1967	1,921	805	381	1,082	5,019	877	579	337	2,727
1968	2,175	856	417	1,167	5,608	1,041	656	378	3,082
1969	2,377	1,033	494	1,248	6,248	1,070	713	476	3,299
1970	2,855	1,191	569	1,353	7,160	1,011	848	542	3,665
1971	3,175	1,427	633	1,520	8,039	1,062	1,028	654	4,196
1972	3,764	1,520	681	1,682	9,811	1,127	1,222	765	4,786
1973	4,084	1,617	765	1,781	10,757	1,179	1,462	897	5,450
1974	5,485	2,013	969	2,159	13,746	1,380	1,779	1,162	6,702
1975	7,709	2,447	1,154	2,570	17,802	1,469	2,743	1,823	10,759
1976	9,213	2,618	1,408	3,375	21,504	1,618	3,407	2,625	13,318
1977	11,047	2,920	1,650	3,758	24,935	1,908	4,047	3,102	15,447
1978	12,117	3,218	1,758	3,965	27,173	2,111	4,547	3,495	17,372
1979	12,792	3,156	1,770	5,517	29,664	2,457	4,978	3,846	19,197
1980	15,033	3,555	1,865	6,868	34,584	2,640	5,613	4,268	21,542
1981	17,532	4,867	2,102	7,894	40,727	3,395	6,431	4,988	25,235
1982	21,204	5,278	2,854	8,286	47,388	3,841	7,360	5,624	28,899
1983	22,942	5,132	3,490	9,104	52,001	4,387	8,275	6,207	32,899
1984	24,692	4,953	4,165	10,482	56,917	4,537	9,077	7,257	36,459
1985	29,289	6,038	4,966	11,983	66,458	5,474	9,761	8,466	41,042
1986	32,720	6,707	5,728	12,887	73,570	6,330	10,607	9,441	45,798

Table A.10 Value of exports and imports by area/country, 1885–1987

		Exports to:					Imports from:			
			of which:					*of which:*		
	Total exports	European Community	UK	USA	Japan	Total imports	European Community	UK	USA	Japan
					A$ mn					
1885	52·6	...	...	...	...	79·8	...	...	...	...
1886	41·6	...	...	...	...	68·4	...	...	...	...
1887	48·0	...	...	...	...	59·2	...	...	...	...
1888	57·6	...	...	...	...	73·8	...	...	...	...
1889	59·2	...	...	...	...	73·2	...	...	...	...
1890	56·4	...	41·6	3·0	0·03	72·4	...	47·8	4·6	0·15
1891	78·6	...	51·0	5·6	0·03	75·4	...	53·0	5·2	0·11
1892	69·2	...	46·4	3·6	0·02	60·2	...	42·6	3·6	0·11
1893	71·6	...	47·2	1·4	0·02	47·6	...	34·6	2·4	0·07
1894	69·2	...	45·8	1·0	0·08	46·4	38·6	31·4	2·4	0·13
1895	73·0	...	47·6	2·0	0·16	59·4	38·8	33·2	2·8	0·13
1896	75·6	...	43·2	4·8	0·22	64·0	48·2	40·6	5·6	0·19
1897	81·8	...	51·6	5·4	0·22	63·0	...	42·4	6·4	0·32
1898	88·0	...	47·8	12·0	0·24	82·8	...	42·0	6·4	0·39
1899	104·0	...	53·2	5·8	0·33	68·6	...	42·4	9·0	0·46
1900	98·4	...	50·4	9·6	0·34	84·8	...	50·8	10·0	0·50
1901	99·4	...	50·4	6·8	0·25	84·8	...	50·4	11·8	0·58
1902	87·8	...	40·4	5·4	0·83	81·4	...	47·8	10·0	0·71
1903	96·6	...	40·0	5·2	0·23	75·6	...	39·8	12·8	0·66
1904	115·0	...	55·2	4·4	1·16	74·0	...	45·0	9·2	0·84
1905	113·8	...	53·4	2·2	1·16	76·6	...	40·6	10·0	0·79
1906	139·4	95·0	65·8	8·6	2·42	89·4	50·0	45·8	11·2	0·90
1907	145·6	106·8	68·0	4·8	1·41	103·6	57·6	53·6	13·6	1·12
1908	128·6	96·4	59·0	4·8	2·54	99·6	68·0	50·6	13·2	1·12
1909	130·6	98·0	61·8	5·2	3·77	102·2	66·4	51·8	11·8	1·28
1910	149·0	120·6	75·4	3·2	1·31	120·0	77·8	60·8	15·4	1·48
1911	159·0	114·2	70·6	3·0	1·67	134·0	80·0	65·4	18·0	1·71
1912	158·2	108·8	63·0	4·0	2·34	156·4	99·0	78·2	21·6	1·99
1913	157·2	120·2	69·6	5·2	2·86	159·4	103·4	82·6	21·8	1·90
1914	[75·8]	...	[34·0]	[3·4]	[1·48]	[79·6]	...	[39·8]	[11·2]	[0·97]
1915	121	84	78	9·8	—	129	69	64	22	—
1916	150	78	68	36·0	—	155	75	70	32	—
1917	196	132	116	13·6	0·01	152	72	72	32	—
1918	163	82	76	22·0	0·01	125	49	44	30	—
1919	228	130	124	18·0	0·02	204	76	70	54	—
1920	300	192	162	22·0	0·03	198	84	78	48	—
1921	264	172	136	20·0	6·2	328	169	154	72	10·4
1922	256	168	116 / 114	16·6 / 12·6	16·0 / 15·8	206	117	106	38	7·2
1923	236	136	102	19·0	18·6	264	150	136	50	7·8
1924	240	154	88	13·2	22·0	282	144	128	70	7·2
1925	324	230	138	18·0	24	314	158	138	66	8·2
1926	298	198	122	19·4	22	304	152	132	74	8·8
1927	290	182	96	16·8	20	330	162	136	82	10·4
1928	286	188	104	13·6	26	296	150	126	70	8·6
1929	290	186	106	11·0	22	288	138	114	70	9·4
1930	250 / 196	136	86	8·2	13	262 / 238	28	108	60	84
1931	182	106	68	4·6	16·2	124	56	46	22	4·8
1932	194	110	74	2·8	18·4	102	40	34	14	4·8
1933	196	110	74	2·0	18·2	130	58	48	16	7·0
1934	228	140	84	3·8	22·0	136	58	50	16	7·4
1935	208	116	86	4·2	19·2	166	72	62	22	9·2
1936	248	130	96	8·8	28·0	190	80	68	28	10·0
1937	298	172	116	17·2	15·4	206	92	78	26	8·0
1938	284	172	124	4·8	9·0	254	108	92	36	10·6
1939	246	146	106	5·2	7·6	226	98	80	30	8·2
1940	300	178	152	7·0	8·4	264	98	88	40	11·6
1941	270	124	114	48	10·6	248	...	124	44	9·0

146

Table A.10 (Continued)   Value of exports and imports by area/country, 1885–1987

		Exports to:					Imports from:			
	Total exports	*of which:* European Community	UK	USA	Japan	Total imports	*of which:* European Community	UK	USA	Japan
					A$ mn					
1942	320	88	86	96	1·8	340	. . .	142	112	1·0
1943	252	. . .	74	66	—	488	. . .	180	232	—
1944	294	. . .	80	60	—	486	. . .	142	252	—
1945	310	. . .	104	60	—	428	. . .	154	178	—
1946	394	146	108	74	3·6	356	. . .	148	104	—
			176	94	10·8			164	88	1·6
1947	618	292	180	96	11·2	416	164	150	80	1·4
1948	812	260	312	70	5·0	676	294	264	134	2·8
1949	1,086	650	460	64	15	828	454	418	84	3·4
1950	1,228	717	475	100	48	1,072	625	557	104	14
1951	1,964	1,108	641	298	124	1,482	854	714	122	32
1952	1,336	733	416	154	98	2,107	1,193	931	218	88
1953	1,702	1,099	719	116	168	1,022	511	429	170	9
1954	1,630	995	602	112	112	1,358	750	663	146	13
1955	1,520	923	571	106	118	1,682	929	757	204	36
1956	1,548	869	515	110	172	1,636	895	712	198	46
1957	1,958	1,032	555	132	278	1,434	734	593	192	26
1958	1,624	825	443	92	206	1,584	818	650	208	48
1959	1,616	807	514	124	204	1,593	790	615	218	60
1960	1,875	856	495	152	269	1,854	888	661	300	83
1961	1,938	788	463	145	323	2,175	949	681	434	131
1962	2,155	805	413	218	374	1,769	739	532	348	99
1963	2,152	746	402	266	346	2,163	908	659	460	129
1964	2,782	945	512	281	488	2,373	934	659	543	163
1965	2,651	911	516	264	441	2,905	1,121	761	692	259
1966	2,721	919	473	338	470	2,939	1,144	759	704	280
1967	3,024	832	405	359	586	3,045	1,118	724	781	296
1968	3,045	801	426	403	642	3,264	1,166	723	841	343
1969	3,374	872	425	480	832	3,469	1,189	747	883	415
1970	4,137	980	488	556	1,035	3,881	1,382	845	965	481
1971	4,376	926	494	519	1,191	4,150	1,486	887	1,042	574
1972	4,893	967	447	615	1,369	4,008	1,427	836	873	629
1973	6,214	1,321	602	759	1,932	4,121	1,363	768	860	739
1974	6,914	1,181	457	750	2,158	6,085	1,746	849	1,348	1,085
1975	8,726	1,412	475	862	2,456	8,080	2,462	1,214	1,668	1,418
1976	9,640	1,539	407	968	3,192	8,241	2,283	1,109	1,656	1,610
1977	11,652	2,013	540	1,009	3,959	10,411	2,647	1,136	2,162	2,150
1978	12,270	1,808	482	1,289	3,896	11,169	2,876	1,281	2,320	2,114
1979	14,241	2,113	572	1,790	4,107	13,752	3,601	1,492	3,226	2,426
1980	18,871	2,791	949	2,044	5,083	16,218	3,892	1,648	3,577	2,527
1981	19,177	2,455	715	2,147	5,228	18,965	3,925	1,585	4,169	3,629
1982	19,575	2,471	726	2,155	5,351	23,005	4,898	1,649	5,249	4,527
1983	22,062	3,214	1,181	2,241	5,976	21,806	4,465	1,467	4,766	4,506
1984	24,013	3,354	1,107	2,590	6,527	23,540	5,029	1,603	5,044	5,338
1985	29,708	3,859	923	3,458	7,986	29,049	6,252	1,962	6,426	6,609
1986	32,795	4,641	1,154	3,242	9,307	34,691	8,409	2,516	7,284	8,248
1987	35,783	5,635	1,375	4,195	9,088	37,022	8,804	2,706	8,118	7,737

Sources

(For sources used in specific tables, see Notes.)

1 *Australian National Accounts*, Australian Bureau of Statistics, Canberra.
2 *Australian Year Book*, Australian Bureau of Statistics, Canberra, various issues.
3 Bambrick, Susan, 'Australian Price Levels 1870–1970', *Australian Economic History Review*, March 1968.
4 Butlin, M.W., *A Preliminary Annual Data Base, 1900/01 to 1973/74*, Discussion Paper 7701, Reserve Bank of Australia, Canberra, 1977.
5 Butlin, N.G., *Australian Domestic Product, Investment and Foreign Borrowing, 1861–1938/39*, Cam-bridge University Press, 1962.
6 Butlin, N.G., *Investment in Australian Economic Growth, 1861–1900*, Cambridge University Press, 1964.
7 *Demography*, Bulletins Nos. 67 and 86, Australian Bureau of Statistics, Canberra, 1971 (now discontinued).
8 Keating, M., 'Australian Workforce and Employment, 1910/11 to 1960/61', *Australian Economic History Review*, 1967.
9 Mitchell, B.R., *International Historical Statistics: The Americas and Australasia*, Macmillan Press, 1983.
10 Norton, W.E. and Kennedy, P.J., *Australian Economic Statistics, 1949–50 to 1984–85*, Reserve Bank of Australia, Occasional Paper 8A, Canberra.
11 Organisation for Economic Cooperation and Development (OECD), *Labour Force Statistics*, annual and quarterly, Paris.
12 OECD, *National Accounts, 1950–1979*, Vol. 1, Paris, 1981.
13 OECD, *National Accounts, 1960–1987*, Vol. 1, Paris, 1989.
14 *Statistical Year Book of the League of Nations*, Geneva, various issues.
15 *Statistics of Australian Education for 1954 and earlier years*, Commonwealth Office of Education, Bulletin No. 17, 1957.
16 United Nations, *Monthly Bulletin of Statistics*, New York.
17 United Nations, *Statistical Year Book*, New York.
18 *Year Book of Labour Statistics*, International Labour Office, Geneva.

Notes

Table A.1 Gross domestic product at current prices
Sources: **4, 5, 6, 12, 13**

OECD data have been used from 1950. Figures are on the present system of national accounts from 1950. From 1900 (second line) to 1949, figures given in **4** have been used and for 1885–1900 (first line) estimates made by N.G. Butlin in **5** and **6** have been used for gross domestic fixed capital formation and gross domestic product. Statistical discrepancy is included in gross domestic product figures from 1950.

From 1900 figures are for years beginning July 1 of the year shown. For 1885–1900 (first line) they are for calendar years.

Table A.2 Gross domestic product at constant prices
Sources: **4, 5, 6, 12, 13**

OECD data have been used from 1950. See notes to Table A.1 regarding the system of national accounts used.

From 1900 (second line) to 1949 estimates in **4** have been used. Figures for the period 1900–87 are for years beginning July 1 of the year shown.

For 1885–1900 (first line), estimates given in **5** and **6** have been used for gross fixed capital formation and gross domestic product at constant (1911) prices; they have been roughly converted to 1980 prices. Figures are for calendar years.

Each category of expenditure has been re-referenced separately for the years 1885–1949 and this means that the totals for gross domestic product may not equal the sum of the components.

Table A.3 Industrial production
Sources: **9, 16**

Figures for all columns are for years ending June 30 each year except for steel and coal (see below). Data from 1975 are on a calendar year basis calculated from data in **16**.

Coal: includes lignite (brown coal) from 1920. Two figures are given for 1968; the first line is output for the year beginning July 1, 1967, to June 30, 1968. The second figure is for the year beginning July 1, 1968. Subsequently figures refer to years beginning July 1. Waste coal is excluded from 1960 onwards.

Crude steel: ingots only up to 1936. Calendar years up to 1929. From 1929 year ending June 30 or May 31 of year shown.

Cars and commercial vehicles: production and assembly of cars.

Table A.4 Prices and income

Sources: **2, 3, 5, 6, 10, 16, 17**

Consumer price index: a weighted average of retail price index numbers of six state capital cities. The index has been extended back to 1900/01 by the Australian Bureau of Statistics to give a broad indication of long-term trends in retail prices. This index has been linked to a series given in **3** at 1900/01 to give a continuous series back to 1890.

Food: a number of indices have been linked to give a continuous series back to 1914. Data are taken from **10, 16** and **17**.

Wholesale prices: series given in **3** has been used for 1890–1968/69 when it was linked to the current series for articles used in manufacturing. From 1911, figures are for year beginning July 1 of year shown.

Import prices: this index attempts to measure prices fob at the time commodities enter Australia. It is a weighted average of 50 group indices. See the Reserve Bank of Australia *Statistical Bulletin*, May 1973, for a fuller description. The Reserve Bank calculated and published the index until the 1960s when it was published officially by the Bureau of Statistics. The Reserve Bank series is linked to estimates in **3** from 1949/50. From 1911, figures are for years beginning July 1 of year shown.

Export prices: index includes gold bullion and specie. The official series is linked to estimates in **3** to give series back to 1890. From 1911, figures are for years beginning July 1 of year shown.

Compensation of employees: OECD data have been used from 1950. Figures include all payments by resident producers of wages and salaries to their employees, in kind and in cash, and of contributions, paid or imputed, to social security and pension schemes on behalf of their employees.

For the period 1939–50, estimates given in **6** have been used.

National income: OECD data have been used from 1950. National income is gross national product (gross domestic product plus net factor income from the rest of the world) minus consumption of fixed capital.

For 1939–50 estimates given in **6** have been used.

Table A.5 Population

Sources: **2, 7, 9, 11**

Total population: mid-year estimates. Tasmania and full-blooded aborigines are included from 1961. A new method of data preparation was introduced in 1961. OECD data have been used from 1964.

For the period 1885–1911 (first line), figures are for years ending December 31.

Age distribution: OECD data have been used from 1964. For 1950–63, data in **10** were used. Other figures are based on census data and estimates in **2** for various years. The age distribution data up to 1947 will not add to the total population because the age distribution figures are taken from the decennial census and there are some differences between the mid-year (or end-year) and census estimates of population.

The figures shown in brackets for 1885 are the 1881 census age distribution applied to the 1885 total population figure.

Births: exclude Northern Territory in 1900 and 1901. Figures for 1984 and 1985 are affected by late registrations in New South Wales in 1984 and the subsequent making up in 1985.

Net migration: currently refers to excess of permanent arrivals over permanent departures at December 31 of the year shown. This definition was adopted in 1971. 'Permanent' is greater than one year. There is also an adjustment for the net effect of changes in travel intention from 1976.

Table A.6 Education

Sources: **2, 9**

The figures for school pupils include those at both government and non-government schools. Schooling is compulsory for children aged 6–15 years but there are variations among the states. From 1954, it was possible to distinguish pupils at different kinds of schools.

Kindergarten: children below compulsory school age.

Elementary: children aged 6–11 years inclusive.

Secondary: children aged 12–15 years inclusive.

Post-secondary: pupils 16 years of age and over plus students undertaking technical education. Statistics of what was called technical education have been distinguished in Australian statistics back to 1905 but agricultural colleges were counted as separate units; they are not included in the data shown in this column.

Technical and further education (so-called TAFE courses) provide training for trade and technical occupations and basic training for semi-professional and professional occupations. Adult education and leisure activities are excluded from the figures here. Currently full-time, part-time and external students are included in the data.

From 1981 a new method of collection was introduced with emphasis on the individual student as the unit of account rather than on enrolment for courses. Figures now also include agricultural colleges and colleges of advanced education offering TAFE activities. Figures for 1974 exclude the Northern Territory (records lost in cyclone Tracy).

Higher education: university students enrolled for the current year on April 30. Covers full-time, part-time and external students.

Table A.7 Labour market: employment

Sources: **8, 11**

OECD data have been used from 1964. Figures refer to August each year. Coverage is for all those in the population aged 15 and over. Services excludes repair activities. From 1986 all labour force data were revised. Data for earlier years are not strictly comparable.

For 1910–60, data are taken from **8** and are annual averages for years beginning July 1 of year shown. Figures for rural, forestry and fishing have been used for the agriculture, forestry and fishing column. Distribution and services include defence forces.

Table A.8 Labour market: other indicators

Sources: **4, 9, 10, 11, 17, 18**

Average hours worked: hours worked and paid for. Figures are for October each year. Males only, including salaried employees, in manufacturing.

For the period 1900–28, figures refer to the number of hours prescribed by industrial tribunals when setting wage rates, fiscal years beginning July 1.

Average earnings: earnings per hour of adult males in manufacturing, October each year including salaried employees.

For the period 1929–64, figures are for average hourly rates for men in manufacturing, mining, construction, transport and agriculture.

For 1900–28, the index published in **4** was used to extrapolate the 1929 figure back to 1900 (year beginning July 1 of year shown).

Unemployment: data are taken from **10**. From 1964 (second line) the figures refer to total numbers seeking work as at August each year. From 1966 estimates are different in a number of ways. All series were revised to take account of the effects of under-enumeration in recent censuses and the revision to the definition of population (net immigration from overseas of less than twelve months' duration excluded). A new sample and revised questionnaire were introduced in February 1978; figures were revised in accordance with this back to 1966.

For the period 1950–64, data are taken from **10** covering persons registered with the Commonwealth Employment Service as seeking full-time work.

For 1900–49 data are taken from **4**; for 1900–19, the figures are for years beginning July 1 of year shown.

The percentage figure is currently the ratio of the unemployed to the total labour force.

Table A.9 Public finance

Sources: **1, 2, 4, 9**

Total receipts: refers to total tax revenue, not including income transferred from public trading and financial enterprises or interest and dividends received. The figure for 1901 is for the first half year; other figures are for years ending June 30 of year shown. Between 1967 and 1968 there was a change in the treatment of total revenue, see **1** and **2**.

Customs and excise: includes export taxes from 1979.

Total expenditure: combined total for all levels of government with transfer payments netted out from 1949; current expenditure only. Figures for 1885–1949 (first line) are for Commonwealth Consolidated Fund expenditures less payments to the Loan Consolidated and Reserve Trust accounts plus net loan expenditure. Figures are for year beginning July 1 of year shown.

Expenditure by function: net expenditure is used which means that any charges or any sales made are netted out.

Social services: includes health and welfare expenditures. Welfare includes expenditure on child welfare, institutions for the destitute, the old and incapacitated.

Table A.10 Value of exports and imports by area

Sources: **2, 9, 10**

From 1915 figures are for years ending June 30 of year shown.

The figure for 1914 is for six months only.

'General' trade up to 1922 (first line): imports are for countries of shipment to 1905. Imports are valued fob from 1947 (second line) and there are some slight differences in the recording of exports from that year. Bullion and specie included in total imports and exports to 1930 (first line).

European Community: comprises France, Federal Republic of Germany (the whole of Germany in the pre-Second World War period), Italy, Netherlands, Belgium, Luxembourg, Denmark, Greece, Ireland, Portugal, Spain and the UK.

CANADA

CONTENTS

Table C.1   Gross domestic product at current prices, 1890–1987

	Consumers' expenditure	Government current expenditure	Gross fixed capital formation	Value of physical change in stocks	Exports of goods & services	Imports of goods & services	**Gross domestic product at market prices**
				C$ bn			
1890	0·69	0·05	0·11	0·01	0·11	−0·17	**0·82**
1900	0·86	0·08	0·13	0·01	0·20	−0·25	**1·03**
1910	1·68	0·17	0·39	0·18	0·35	−0·63	**2·14**
1920	3·97	0·55	1·01	0·28	1·62	−1·89	**5·54**
1926	3·54	0·49	0·70	0·14	1·65	−1·52	**5·15**
1927	3·89	0·53	0·83	0·25	1·62	−1·63	**5·55**
1928	4·31	0·56	1·01	0·16	1·77	−1·81	**6·05**
1929	4·62	0·64	1·16	0·05	1·63	−1·95	**6·13**
1930	4·37	0·72	0·93	0·08	1·29	−1·63	**5·73**
1931	3·77	0·69	0·62	−0·09	0·97	−1·14	**4·70**
1932	3·19	0·58	0·32	−0·10	0·80	−0·90	**3·83**
1933	2·98	0·46	0·23	−0·09	0·83	−0·83	**3·51**
1934	3·18	0·50	0·30	0·03	1·02	−0·95	**3·98**
1935	3·34	0·54	0·37	0·04	1·14	−1·02	**4·32**
1936	3·55	0·54	0·46	−0·07	1·43	−1·18	**4·65**
1937	3·88	0·62	0·63	0·01	1·59	−1·41	**5·26**
1938	3·90	0·67	0·59	0·06	1·36	−1·26	**5·28**
1939	3·98	0·68	0·59	0·28	1·45	−1·33	**5·64**
1940	4·49	1·12	0·80	0·26	1·81	−1·63	**6·74**
1941	5·10	1·64	1·09	0·09	2·47	−1·98	**8·33**
1942	5·50	3·67	1·06	0·14	2·36	−2·31	**10·33**
1943	5·81	4·18	0·89	−0·18	3·44	−2·92	**11·09**
1944	6·27	4·98	0·90	−0·15	3·56	−3·57	**11·85**
1945	6·97	3·66	1·03	−0·31	3·60	−2·91	**11·84**
1946	8·03	1·80	1·39	0·33	3·21	−2·88	**11·85**
1947	9·09	1·54	2·09	0·40	3·64	−3·62	**13·17**
1948	10·09	1·80	2·62	0·11	4·05	−3·63	**15·12**
1949	10·92	2·13	3·03	0·05	4·02	−3·85	**16·34**
1950	12·40	1·92	3·86	0·55	4·05	−3·96	**18·83**
1951	13·76	2·80	4·42	0·87	4·93	−5·07	**21·92**
1952	15·05	3·61	5·10	0·50	5·41	−4·89	**24·79**
1953	16·06	3·81	5·73	0·60	5·21	−5·34	**26·00**
1954	16·80	3·81	5·71	−0·20	4·98	−5·05	**26·11**
1955	18·25	4·02	6·42	0·29	5·58	−5·83	**28·76**
1956	19·94	4·41	8·00	0·99	6·18	−7·04	**32·35**
1957	21·32	4·56	8·69	0·17	6·20	−7·02	**33·89**
1958	22·66	4·84	8·54	−0·30	6·11	−6·58	**35·10**
1959	24·19	4·96	8·65	0·41	6·45	−7·19	**37·23**
1960	25·55	5·26	8·84	0·41	6·73	−7·22	**39·19**
1961	25·99	6·15	8·76	0·11	7·30	−7·45	**40·62**
1962	27·72	6·55	9·26	0·67	7·94	−7·98	**44·12**
1963	29·57	6·89	9·95	0·72	8·75	−8·40	**47·37**
1964	31·73	7·50	11·67	0·59	10·07	−9·57	**51·85**
1965	34·37	8·24	13·67	1·30	10·72	−10·83	**57·15**
1966	37·57	9·61	15·92	1·28	12·56	−12·58	**63·98**
1967	40·64	11·06	16·25	0·21	14·16	−13·46	**68·61**
1968	44·30	12·65	16·49	0·74	16·17	−15·19	**74·84**
1969	48·54	14·14	18·14	1·48	17·84	−17·71	**82·42**
1970	51·26	16·39	19·01	0·24	20·08	−17·83	**88·46**
1971	55·60	18·16	21·57	0·37	21·17	−19·53	**96·55**
1972	62·26	20·05	23·88	0·78	23·74	−22·78	**107·79**
1973	71·20	22·77	28·86	1·86	29·77	−28·02	**126·42**
1974	83·20	27·35	35·78	3·59	37·81	−37·37	**150·96**
1975	96·25	33·15	41·85	1·37	38·95	−41·36	**170·11**
1976	109·99	38·15	46·71	2·33	44·25	−45·28	**196·29**
1977	121·92	43·26	50·23	1·86	51·18	−51·25	**216·09**
1978	135·59	47·20	54·58	1·05	61·15	−60·05	**239·58**

Table C.1 (Continued)   Gross domestic product at current prices, 1890—1987

	Consumers' expenditure	Government current expenditure	Gross fixed capital formation	Value of physical change in stocks	Exports of goods & services	Imports of goods & services	**Gross domestic product at market prices**
				C$ bn			
1979	151·52	52·15	63·44	4·99	75·07	−73·28	**274·09**
1980	170·41	59·10	72·29	0·34	87·58	−81·93	**307·73**
1981	193·84	68·60	86·12	1·19	96·88	−93·00	**353·45**
1982	208·10	78·44	81·33	−9·75	96·65	−82·60	**371·82**
1983	228·22	84·31	81·23	−2·90	103·44	−89·83	**402·23**
1984	248·43	88·88	84·70	4·76	126·04	−110·63	**441·31**
1985	271·48	95·46	94·22	2·98	134·98	−123·40	**475·06**
1986	293·34	100·20	101·33	2·94	137·46	−132·88	**502·25**
1987	318·43	106·19	114·38	1·95	144·21	−140·28	**544·86**

Table C.2   Gross domestic product at constant prices, 1890–1987

	Consumers' expenditure	Government current expenditure	Gross fixed capital formation	Value of physical change in stocks	Exports of goods & services	Imports of goods & services	Gross domestic product at market prices
	C$ bn, 1980 prices						
1890	6·71	0·76	1·53	0·40	0·89	−0·94	**9·85**
1900	8·91	1·15	1·66	0·44	1·66	−1·43	**13·02**
1910	13·74	2·07	4·46	4·68	2·36	−3·32	**21·93**
1920	16·71	3·26	4·76	2·88	5·05	−4·44	**27·31**
1926	17·12	4·54	5·52	1·29	8·90	−6·56	**31·61**
1927	19·12	4·75	6·82	1·71	8·94	−7·25	**34·62**
1928	20·94	4·80	8·11	1·26	10·13	−8·15	**37·78**
1929	22·24	5·40	8·97	1·00	9·54	−8·90	**37·92**
1930	21·31	5·91	7·85	0·71	8·29	−8·10	**36·30**
1931	20·27	6·25	5·83	−0·81	7·42	−6·49	**31·69**
1932	18·68	6·06	3·23	−0·99	6·87	−5·57	**28·40**
1933	18·21	5·10	2·31	−0·76	6·93	−5·29	**26·51**
1934	19·16	5·39	2·91	0·26	7·84	−5·64	**29·73**
1935	20·00	5·62	3·47	0·49	8·64	−6·05	**32·05**
1936	20·91	5·66	3·94	0·01	10·39	−6·85	**33·47**
1937	22·22	5·72	5·24	0·79	10·62	−7·57	**36·83**
1938	21·90	6·42	5·00	0·50	9·59	−7·07	**37·13**
1939	22·52	6·82	4·84	1·95	10·56	−7·55	**39·89**
1940	24·18	12·03	5·52	1·85	12·04	−8·43	**45·51**
1941	25·82	17·39	6·76	0·79	15·82	−9·76	**52·06**
1942	26·48	36·40	6·17	−0·07	14·15	−10·48	**61·71**
1943	27·26	39·84	5·00	−0·14	19·68	−12·49	**64·20**
1944	29·22	45·74	5·24	−0·23	18·99	−14·79	**66·74**
1945	32·17	31·45	6·71	−0·39	18·50	−11·77	**65·25**
1946	35·75	14·87	8·87	1·35	15·52	−10·88	**63·50**
1947	38·27	11·20	11·21	2·16	15·42	−12·22	**66·20**
1948	37·35	10·63	12·87	0·35	15·93	−11·02	**67·85**
1949	39·49	11·76	13·82	0·69	14·99	−11·32	**70·45**
1950	42·08	12·67	14·85	2·54	14·89	−12·33	**75·77**
1951	42·32	16·54	14·91	3·30	16·32	−14·30	**79·18**
1952	45·30	20·38	16·65	1·55	18·11	−14·83	**86·05**
1953	48·43	21·02	18·69	2·42	17·86	−16·21	**90·32**
1954	50·21	20·22	18·68	−0·77	17·22	−15·29	**89·33**
1955	54·55	20·65	20·41	1·32	18·52	−17·37	**97·84**
1956	58·66	21·18	24·14	3·69	19·99	−20·29	**106·24**
1957	60·85	20·81	25·86	0·80	20·15	−19·75	**108·96**
1958	63·03	21·45	25·58	−0·90	19·95	−18·26	**111·27**
1959	66·54	21·25	25·72	1·51	20·72	−20·08	**115·69**
1960	68·82	21·78	24·87	1·69	21·65	−20·04	**118·95**
1961	69·65	24·63	24·82	1·79	23·12	−20·09	**122·72**
1962	73·30	25·63	25·96	2·20	24·19	−20·56	**131·45**
1963	76·56	26·26	27·09	2·27	26·42	−21·11	**138·26**
1964	80·92	27·71	30·53	2·66	29·75	−23·88	**147·53**
1965	85·86	29·09	34·01	4·38	31·11	−26·90	**157·32**
1966	90·39	31·55	37·65	3·92	35·47	−30·60	**168·02**
1967	93·99	34·02	37·57	1·16	39·14	−32·19	**172·93**
1968	98·07	36·64	37·76	2·21	44·09	−35·36	**182·05**
1969	103·25	37·78	39·71	3·78	47·63	−39·98	**191·91**
1970	105·31	41·31	39·83	1·47	51·76	−39·29	**196·89**
1971	111·58	43·12	43·01	1·56	54·46	−42·11	**208·23**
1972	119·92	44·26	44·81	2·86	58·72	−47·92	**220·08**
1973	128·86	46·86	49·10	4·42	64·92	−54·95	**237·05**
1974	136·32	49·44	52·33	7·83	63·63	−61·04	**247·42**
1975	142·74	52·70	55·34	2·57	59·32	−59·04	**253·85**
1976	152·01	53·74	57·77	4·33	65·61	−64·14	**269·46**
1977	156·75	56·18	58·96	3·24	71·43	−65·26	**279·10**
1978	162·08	57·10	60·73	1·86	81·18	−70·09	**291·87**

***Table* C.2 (Continued)**   **Gross domestic product at constant prices, 1890–1987**

	Consumers' expenditure	Government current expenditure	Gross fixed capital formation	Value of physical change in stocks	Exports of goods & services	Imports of goods & services	**Gross domestic product at market prices**
				C$ bn, 1980 prices			
1979	166·75	57·47	65·74	7·07	85·26	−78·08	**303·24**
1980	170·41	59·10	72·29	0·34	87·58	−81·93	**307·73**
1981	174·36	60·58	80·71	1·22	91·43	−88·92	**319·08**
1982	169·77	62·02	71·84	−9·37	89·44	−75·44	**308·83**
1983	175·67	62·94	71·33	−2·59	95·17	−82·24	**318·69**
1984	183·89	63·73	72·85	4·01	112·01	−96·31	**338·98**
1985	193·76	65·44	78·86	2·87	118·73	−104·35	**354·42**
1986	201·95	66·22	82·79	3·48	123·56	−112·00	**365·53**
1987	211·44	67·28	90·74	1·57	130·89	−121·62	**380·13**

Table C.3 Industrial production, index and selected series, 1885–1987

	Industrial production	Coal	Crude steel	Cars & commercial vehicles	Crude petroleum	Natural gas	Electricity
	Index nos., 1980 = 100	mn tons	mn tons	'000	mn tons	mn m³	bn kwh
1885	. . .	1·7	—	—	0·08	—	—
1886	. . .	1·9	—	—	0·08	—	—
1887	. . .	2·2	—	—	0·09	—	—
1888	. . .	2·4	—	—	0·09	—	—
1889	. . .	2·4	—	—	0·09	—	—
1890	. . .	2·8	—	—	0·10	—	—
1891	. . .	3·2	—	—	0·10	—	—
1892	. . .	3·0	—	—	0·10	—	—
1893	. . .	3·4	—	—	0·10	—	—
1894	. . .	3·5	0·03	—	0·11	—	—
1895	. . .	3·2	0·02	—	0·10	—	—
1896	. . .	3·4	0·02	—	0·10	—	—
1897	. . .	3·4	0·02	—	0·09	—	—
1898	. . .	3·8	0·02	—	0·10	—	—
1899	. . .	4·5	0·02	—	0·11	—	—
1900	. . .	5·2	0·02	—	0·09	—	—
1901	. . .	5·9	0·03	—	0·08	—	—
1902	. . .	6·8	0·19	—	0·07	—	—
1903	. . .	7·2	0·18	—	0·06	—	—
1904	. . .	7·5	0·15	—	0·07	—	—
1905	. . .	7·9	0·41	—	0·08	—	—
1906	. . .	8·9	0·58	—	0·07	—	—
1907	. . .	9·5	0·64	—	0·10	—	—
1908	. . .	9·9	0·53	—	0·07	—	—
1909	. . .	9·5	0·68	—	0·06	—	—
1910	. . .	11·7	0·75	—	0·04	—	—
1911	. . .	10·3	0·80	—	0·04	330	—
1912	. . .	13·2	0·87	—	0·03	433	—
1913	. . .	13·6	1·06	—	0·03	580	—
1914	. . .	12·4	0·75	—	0·03	614	—
1915	. . .	11·9	0·93	—	0·03	570	—
1916	. . .	13·0	1·30	—	0·03	721	—
1917	. . .	12·7	1·58	—	0·03	776	—
1918	. . .	13·6	1·70	77	0·04	570	—
1919	5·5	12·6	0·93	76	0·03	565	5·5
1920	5·3	15·4	1·12	90	0·03	477	5·9
1921	4·6	13·7	0·68	63	0·03	399	5·6
1922	5·7	13·7	0·49	87	0·03	416	6·7
1923	6·5	15·4	0·90	125	0·02	452	8·1
1924	6·6	12·4	0·67	116	0·02	421	9·3
1925	7·2	11·9	0·76	147	0·04	479	10·1
1926	7·8	14·9	0·79	185	0·05	544	12·1
1927	8·1	15·8	0·92	167	0·06	605	14·5 / 15·4
1928	9·0	15·9	1·25	194	0·08	639	17·5
1929	9·4	15·9	1·40	239	0·14	804	19·3
1930	8·1	13·5	1·03	132	0·20	832	19·5
1931	7·1	11·1	0·68	82	0·20	733	17·6
1932	6·4	10·6	0·34	58	0·13	663	17·5
1933	6·8	10·8	0·42	60	0·14	655	18·7
1934	8·1	12·5	0·77	104	0·14	656	22·7
1935	8·8	12·6	0·96	149	0·13	705	24·9
1936	9·7	13·8	1·13	142	0·12	796	27·1
1937	11·1	14·4	1·43	187	0·31	917	30·2
1938	10·5	13·0	1·17	148	0·87	947	28·6
1939	11·3	14·2	1·41	137	1·02	996	31·0
1940	13·5	15·9	2·05	216	1·13	1,168	33·1
1941	17·0	16·5	2·46	265	1·33	1,232	36·5
1942	20·1	17·1	2·82	228	1·36	1,294	41·0
1943	21·3	16·2	2·73	178	1·30	1,254	44·0

Table **C.3 (Continued)** Industrial production, index and selected series, 1885–1987

	Industrial production	Coal	Crude steel	Cars & commercial vehicles	Crude petroleum	Natural gas	Electricity
	Index nos., 1980 = 100	mn tons	mn tons	'000	mn tons	mn m³	bn kwh
1944	21·5	15·4	2·74	158	1·30	1,276	43·6
1945	19·1	15·0	2·61	133	1·09	1,371	42·7
1946	18·1	16·2	2·11	164	1·00	1,356	44·7
1947	19·4	14·4	2·67	244	1·00	1,491	47·2
1948	20·5	16·7	2·90	248	1·66	1,659	47·3
1949	21·2	17·3	2·89	283	2·82	1,712	50·9
1950	22·7	17·4	3·07	375	3·93	1,921 / 1,870	55·4
1951	24·9	16·9	3·24	401	6·44	2,130	61·8
1952	25·9	15·9	3·36	419	8·28	2,450	66·5
1953	27·8	14·4	3·73	464	10·94	2,785	70·3
1954	27·8	13·5	2·90	345	12·98	3,330	74·5
1955	30·8	13·4	4·11	440	17·49	4,130	82·2
1956	34·1	13·5	4·81	457	23·26	4,630	88·5
1957	34·7	12·0	4·60	406	24·59	6,025	91·1
1958	34·4	10·6	3·95	355	22·38	9,320	97·5
1959	37·4	9·6	5·35	364	24·83	11,390	104·7
1960	38·2	10·0	5·27	397	25·63	14,270	114·5
1961	39·7	9·4	5·89	386	29·86	17,730	113·7
1962	43·1	9·3	6·51	508	33·02	25,270	117·5
1963	45·8	9·6	7·44	628	34·85	25,705	122·3
1964	50·0	10·3	8·28	670	37·15	34,575	144·0
1965	54·3	10·5	9·13	844	39·46	37,389	144·3
1966	58·3	10·3	9·09	870	43·25	34,119	158·1
1967	60·6	10·1	8·80	733	47·33	37,166	165·6
1968	64·5	10·0	10·16	1,145	50·43	42,301	176·4
1969	68·9	9·7	9·35	1,334	53·77	49,268	191·1
1970	69·8	15·1	11·20	1,159	60·38	56,712	204·7
1971	73·6	16·7	11·04	1,347	64·17	62,120	216·5
1972	79·2	18·8	11·86	1,430	72·89	70,129	240·2
1973	87·6	20·3	13·39	1,552	85·55	75,140	263·3
1974	90·4	21·3	13·62	1,512	80·26	73,367	280·3
1975	85·0	25·3	13·03	1,377	67·97	74,985	273·4
1976	90·2	20·8	13·33	1,642	64·52	75,680	294·0
1977	92·5	23·0	13·63	1,776	64·67	79,502	317·2
1978	95·6	25·6	14·90	1,754	64·27	76,716	335·7
1979	101·5	27·5	16·08	1,663	73·28	81,759	352·3
1980	100·0	20·2	15·89	1,375	70·40	73,861	377·5
1981	100·4	21·7	14·81	1,322	62·93	72,747	390·9
1982	90·5	22·4	11·87	1,276	62·16	74,762	387·5
1983	95·1	22·6	12·83	1,525	66·41	72,537	408·4
1984	103·4	32·1	14·70	1,842	70·68	78,659	438·0
1985	108·0	34·3	14·64	1,931	72·00	84,397	459·0
1986	108·4	30·5	14·08	1,846	72·07	78,782	468·6
1987	. . .	32·7	14·83	1.636	75·18	85.426	482·1

157

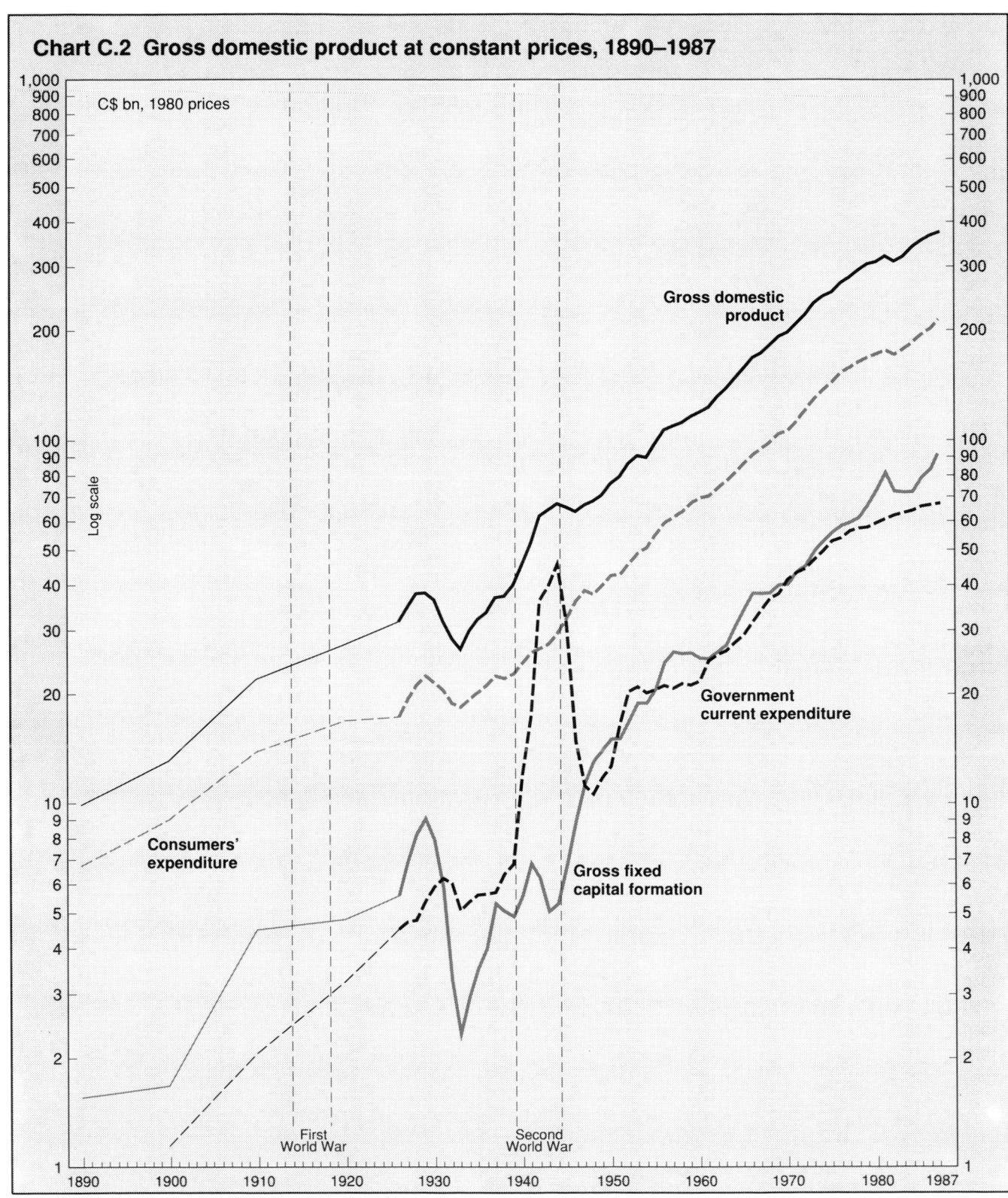

Chart C.2 Gross domestic product at constant prices, 1890–1987

C$ bn, 1980 prices

Log scale

Gross domestic product

Government current expenditure

Consumers' expenditure

Gross fixed capital formation

First World War

Second World War

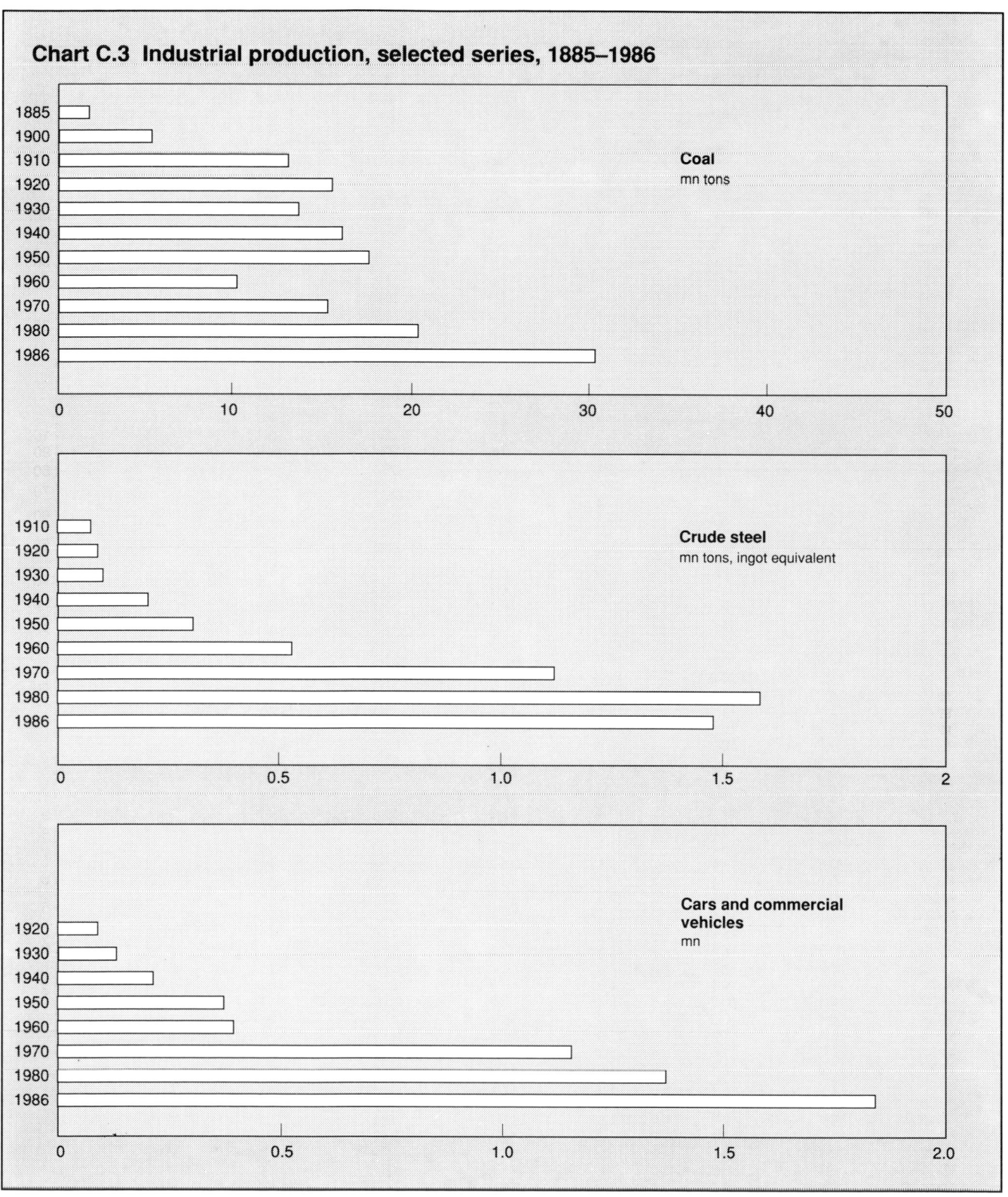

Chart C.3 Industrial production, selected series, 1885–1986

Coal
mn tons

1885	
1900	
1910	
1920	
1930	
1940	
1950	
1960	
1970	
1980	
1986	

0   10   20   30   40   50

Crude steel
mn tons, ingot equivalent

1910	
1920	
1930	
1940	
1950	
1960	
1970	
1980	
1986	

0   0.5   1.0   1.5   2

Cars and commercial vehicles
mn

1920	
1930	
1940	
1950	
1960	
1970	
1980	
1986	

0   0.5   1.0   1.5   2.0

159

Table C.4 Prices and income, 1885–1987

	Consumer prices		Producer prices					
	All items	Food	All items	Raw materials	Export prices	Import prices	Compensation of employees	National income
	Index nos., 1980 = 100				Index nos., 1971 = 100		C$ bn	
1885	...	...	8·7	...	25·2	35·8	...	...
1886	...	...	8·6	...	24·4	33·9	...	...
1887	...	...	8·7	...	24·4	32·6	...	...
1888	...	...	9·1	...	25·8	32·0	...	...
1889	...	...	9·1	...	25·7	34·1	...	...
1890	...	...	9·2	7·8	26·3	34·2	...	0·72
1891	...	...	9·2	8·0	26·4	34·8	...	...
1892	...	...	8·6	7·3	26·1	32·6	...	...
1893	...	...	8·7	7·4	25·6	32·1	...	...
1894	...	...	8·1	6·8	25·6	31·3	...	...
1895	...	...	8·0	6·8	24·5	28·5	...	...
1896	...	...	7·7	6·6	23·6	29·3	...	...
1897	...	...	7·8	6·9	23·1	28·0	...	...
1898	...	...	8·2	7·4	24·6	29·6	...	...
1899	...	...	8·3	7·3	24·2	29·9	...	...
1900	9·5	7·7	8·6	7·6	25·4	33·4	...	0·90
1901	...	...	8·7	7·9	26·0	33·7	...	...
1902	...	...	9·1	8·2	26·5	32·7	...	...
1903	...	...	9·3	8·4	27·3	33·6	...	...
1904	...	...	9·4	8·5	27·6	34·4	...	...
1905	10·7	8·4	9·7	8·6	26·7	34·3	...	...
1906	...	...	9·7	9·0	28·8	35·9	...	...
1907	...	...	10·5	9·4	30·1	38·0	...	...
1908	...	...	10·5	9·5	31·5	39·0	...	...
1909	...	...	10·7	9·9	31·4	36·2	...	...
1910	12·4	9·8	10·8	9·7	31·7	36·5	...	1·83
1911	12·6	10·1	11·1	10·0	31·4	36·9	...	...
1912	13·4	10·3	11·7	10·7	30·6	35·8	...	...
1913	13·6	10·3	11·5	10·2	31·1	36·7	...	...
1914	13·7	10·9	11·7	10·6	32·2	34·1	...	...
1915	14·0	11·1	12·6	11·6	34·6	34·1	...	...
1916	15·1	12·4	15·1	13·6	39·1	42·1	...	...
1917	17·9	16·1	20·4	17·8	55·5	52·6	...	...
1918	20·3	18·3	22·8	18·9	61·0	61·1	...	...
1919	22·3	19·6	24·0	20·4	63·9	66·1	...	...
1920	25·8	22·5	27·9	24·0	71·6	80·9	...	...
1921	22·7	17·1	19·7	16·9	51·3	59·0	...	...
1922	20·8	14·7	17·4	15·0	42·9	49·7	...	...
1923	20·8	14·8	17·5	14·4	42·6	54·2	...	...
1924	20·5	14·5	17·8	15·0	43·5	52·0	...	...
1925	20·6	15·2	18·4	15·9	47·3	51·1	...	...
1926	20·9	15·8	17·9	15·8	45·8	48·2	2·37	4·71
1927	20·6	15·5	17·5	15·7	44·1	46·0	2·51	4·96
1928	20·6	15·5	17·3	15·4	42·7	45·3	2·72	5·39
1929	20·8	15·9	17·1	15·4	42·0	44·1	2·95	5·36
1930	20·7	15·5	15·5	13·1	35·2	38·6	2·79	4·96
1931	18·7	12·2	12·9	10·2	29·2	32·6	2·42	3·91
1932	17·0	10·1	11·9	9·3	26·3	31·9	1·98	3·15
1933	16·1	10·0	12·0	9·8	26·0	30·6	1·80	2·88
1934	16·4	10·9	12·8	11·1	27·8	32·5	1·95	3·32
1935	16·5	11·1	12·9	11·6	28·3	31·9	2·09	3·65
1936	16·8	11·5	13·3	12·1	29·9	32·4	2·25	3·99
1937	17·4	12·1	14·9	14·0	34·8	35·6	2·55	4·56
1938	17·6	12·2	14·0	12·3	30·7	33·0	2·52	4·60
1939	17·4	11·8	13·6	11·7	29·4	33·0	2·63	4·93
1940	18·1	12·4	14·8	12·7	32·6	37·1	3·15	5·84
1941	19·2	13·6	16·0	14·1	33·9	40·3	3·99	7·30
1942	20·1	14·9	16·9	15·2	35·9	44·4	4·92	9·11
1943	20·4	15·3	17·6	16·2	39·8	48·9	5·72	9·85
1944	20·6	15·4	17·9	16·6	44·2	51·0	6·07	10·62

Table C.4 (Continued)   Prices and income, 1885–1987

	Consumer prices		Producer prices		Export prices	Import prices	Compensation of employees	National income
	All items	Food	All items	Raw materials				
	Index nos., 1980 = 100				Index nos., 1971 = 100		C$ bn	
1945	20·6	15·6	18·1	16·8	46·3	51·3	6·15	10·59
1946	21·4	16·5	19·1	17·3	52·1	53·6	5·83	10·73
1947	23·4	18·7	22·8	20·3	59·8	61·6	6·75	12·26
1948	26·7	22·9	27·1	24·2	65·2	70·0	7·85	14·17
1949	27·5	23·5	27·7	24·3	67·4	71·8	8·48	15·20
1950	28·3	24·1	29·6	26·3	70·7	77·2	9·15	16·53
1951	31·3	27·5	33·8	29·4	80·2	88·4	10·77	19·64
1952	32·1	27·5	31·9	27·0	79·5	77·3	12·07	22·15
1953	31·8	26·5	31·1	25·5	77·2	76·6	13·06	22·98
1954	32·0	26·4	30·6	25·3	75·1	76·7	13·45	22·89
1955	32·0	26·4	31·0	25·9	76·8	77·4	14·37	25·08
1956	32·5	26·7	32·1	26·6	79·2	79·0	16·17	27·95
1957	33·6	27·9	32·8	25·8	78·9	81·5	17·52	29·15
1958	34·5	28·8	32·9	25·3	78·7	81·6	17·98	30·27
1959	34·8	28·5	33·2	26·0	80·1	80·1	19·15	31·94
1960	35·3	28·8	33·3	25·9	80·2	80·9	20·14	33·44
1961	35·6	29·2	33·3	26·2	80·9	83·8	21·19	34·74
1962	36·0	29·7	33·7	27·6	83·6	87·6	22·79	38·02
1963	36·6	30·7	34·1	28·0	84·1	91·1	24·33	40·75
1964	37·3	31·2	34·4	27·9	85·3	92·1	26·59	44·66
1965	38·2	32·0	34·9	28·5	86·4	92·1	29·63	49·17
1966	39·6	34·0	35·9	30·0	90·0	93·2	33·58	55·10
1967	41·1	34·5	36·6	30·4	91·7	94·0	37·15	59·24
1968	42·7	35·6	37·3	30·7	95·0	95·5	40·39	64·89
1969	44·7	37·1	38·7	32·1	96·9	97·2	45·16	72·05
1970	46·1	37·9	39·7	32·7	99·3	98·1	48·95	76·48
1971	47·5	38·4	40·5	31·5	100·0	100·0	53·76	83·49
1972	49·7	41·3	42·2	33·6	103·3	102·6	60·34	94·44
1973	53·5	47·3	47·0	45·4	119·0	111·3	69·52	111·05
1974	59·3	55·0	55·9	57·8	161·5	142·9	82·87	132·86
1975	65·7	62·1	62·2	58·0	181·0	165·7	96·62	148·71
					1980 = 100			
1976	70·7	63·8	65·4	58·7	60·9	58·9	111·88	171·44
1977	76·3	69·1	70·5	64·5	64·9	66·0	124·02	186·61
1978	83·1	79·8	77·0	74·1	70·4	74·9	134·93	207·07
1979	90·7	90·4	88·1	87·3	85·3	85·8	151·74	236·39
1980	100·0	100·0	100·0	100·0	100·0	100·0	171·42	264·33
1981	112·5	111·4	110·2	119·1	106·4	111·5	197·91	301·27
1982	124·6	119·4	116·8	129·0	106·9	113·4	211·60	314·44
1983	131·8	123·8	120·9	135·8	105·5	109·4	221·80	341·32
1984	137·6	130·8	126·3	140·3	110·1	114·8	238·85	376·08
1985	143·1	134·4	129·8	139·5	111·5	118·0	257·34	404·32
1986	148·9	141·1	. . .	153·0	108·8	119·6	274·61	426·12
1987	155·5	147·5	. . .	. . .	110·0	119·0	295·66	464·92

Table C.5 Population, 1885–1986

	Total population	Males	Females	Births	Age distribution Under 15	Age distribution 15–64	Age distribution 65 & over	Geographical distribution Ontario	Geographical distribution Quebec
	mn			'000			mn		
1885	4·54	...	...	135	...	...	...	2·01	1·41
1886	4·58	...	...	141	...	...	...	2·02	1·42
1887	4·63	...	...	138	...	...	...	2·04	1·44
1888	4·68	...	...	139	...	...	...	2·06	1·45
1889	4·73	...	...	141	...	...	...	2·08	1·46
1890	4·78	...	...	138	...	...	...	2·09	1·48
1891	4·83	2·46	2·37	138	1·22	3·39	0·22	2·11	1·49
1892	4·88	...	...	133	...	...	...	2·12	1·50
1893	4·93	...	...	136	...	...	...	2·12	1·52
1894	4·98	...	...	135	...	...	...	2·13	1·53
1895	5·03	...	...	137	...	...	...	2·13	1·55
1896	5·07	...	...	148	...	...	...	2·14	1·56
1897	5·12	...	...	149	...	...	...	2·14	1·58
1898	5·18	...	...	152	...	...	...	2·15	1·59
1899	5·24	...	...	146	...	...	...	2·16	1·61
1900	5·30	...	...	146	...	...	...	2·17	1·63
1901	5·37	2·75	2·62	170	1·85	3·25	0·27	2·18	1·65
1902	5·49	...	...	175	...	...	...	2·19	1·67
1903	5·65	...	...	180	...	...	...	2·22	1·71
1904	5·83	...	...	186	...	...	...	2·25	1·75
1905	6·00	...	...	188	...	...	...	2·29	1·77
1906	6·10	...	...	188	...	...	...	2·30	1·78
1907	6·41	...	...	193	...	...	...	2·37	1·85
1908	6·63	...	...	204	...	...	...	2·41	1·90
1909	6·80	...	...	209	...	...	...	2·44	1·93
1910	6·99	...	...	216	...	...	...	2·48	1·97
1911	7·21	3·82	3·39	220	2·38	4·49	0·34	2·53	2·01
1912	7·39	...	...	236	...	...	...	2·57	2·04
1913	7·63	...	...	247	...	...	...	2·64	2·10
1914	7·88	...	...	253	...	...	...	2·71	2·15
1915	7·98	...	...	255	...	...	...	2·72	2·16
1916	8·00	...	...	247	...	...	...	2·71	2·15
1917	8·06	...	...	236	...	...	...	2·72	2·17
1918	8·15	...	...	237	...	...	...	2·74	2·19
1919	8·31	...	...	234	...	...	...	2·79	2·23
1920	8·56	...	...	254	...	...	...	2·86	2·30
1921	8·79	4·53	4·26	265	3·02	5·35	0·42	2·93	2·36
1922	8·92	4·59	4·33	260	3·05	5·44	0·43	2·98	2·41
1923	9·01	4·62	4·39	247	3·06	5·51	0·44	3·01	2·45
1924	9·14	4·68	4·46	251	3·09	5·60	0·45	3·06	2·50
1925	9·29	4·74	4·55	249	3·11	5·71	0·47	3·11	2·55
1926	9·45	4·81	4·64	240	3·15	5·81	0·49	3·16	2·60
1927	9·64	4·93	4·71	241	3·17	5·97	0·50	3·22	2·66
1928	9·84	5·05	4·79	244	3·20	6·12	0·52	3·28	2·72
1929	10·03	5·16	4·89	242	3·23	6·26	0·54	3·33	2·77
1930	10·21	5·27	4·94	250	3·26	6·39	0·56	3·39	2·83
1931	10·38	5·37	5·00	247	3·28	6·52	0·58	3·43	2·87
1932	10·51	5·44	5·07	243	3·29	6·63	0·59	3·47	2·93
1933	10·63	5·50	5·13	230	3·29	6·73	0·61	3·51	2·97
1934	10·74	5·55	5·19	228	3·28	6·83	0·63	3·54	3·02
1935	10·85	5·60	5·25	228	3·27	6·93	0·65	3·58	3·06
1936	10·95	5·64	5·31	228	3·25	7·03	0·67	3·61	3·10
1937	11·05	5·69	5·36	228	3·22	7·14	0·69	3·64	3·14
1938	11·15	5·74	5·41	237	3·20	7·24	0·71	3·67	3·18
1939	11·27	5·79	5·48	238	3·19	7·35	0·73	3·71	3·23
1940	11·38	5·84	5·54	253	3·18	7·45	0·75	3·75	3·28
1941	11·51	5·90	5·61	264	3·20	7·54	0·77	3·79	3·33
1942	11·65	5·97	5·68	282	3·22	7·64	0·79	3·88	3·39
1943	11·80	6·04	5·76	293	3·25	7·74	0·81	3·92	3·46
1944	11·95	6·11	5·83	294	3·29	7·83	0·83	3·96	3·50

162

Table C.5 (Continued) Population, 1885–1986

	Total population	Males	Females	Births	Age distribution Under 15	Age distribution 15–64	Age distribution 65 & over	Geographical distribution Ontario	Geographical distribution Quebec
	mn	mn	mn	'000	mn	mn	mn	mn	mn
1945	12·07	6 15	5·92	301	3·34	7·88	0·85	4·00	3·56
1946	12·29	6·26	6·03	344	3·42	7·99	0·88	4·09	3·63
1947	12·55	6·39	6·16	373	3·54	8·09	0·92	4·18	3·71
1948	12·82	6·53	6·30	360	3·68	8·18	0·96	4·28	3·79
1949	13·45	6·83	6·61	367	3·94	8·49	1·02	4·38	3·88
1950	13·71	6·96	6·76	372	4·07	8·59	1·05	4·47	3·97
1951	14·01	7·09	6·92	381	4·25	8·67	1·09	4·60	4·06
1952	14·46	7·33	7·13	404	4·45	8·89	1·12	4·79	4·17
1953	14·85	7·52	7·32	418	4·63	9·07	1·15	4·94	4·27
1954	15·29	7·75	7·53	436	4·83	9·28	1·18	5·12	4·39
1955	15·70	7·96	7·74	443	5·04	9·45	1·21	5·27	4·52
1956	16·08	8·15	7·93	451	5·23	9·61	1·24	5·40	4·63
1957	16·61	8·42	8·19	469	5·46	9·88	1·27	5·64	4·77
1958	17·08	8·65	8·43	470	5·69	10·09	1·30	5·82	4·90
1959	17·48	8·85	8·63	479	5·86	10·29	1·33	5·97	5·02
1960	17·87	9·04	8·83	479	6·03	10·48	1·36	6·11	5·14
1961	18·24	9·22	9·02	476	6·19	10·66	1·39	6·24	5·26
1962	18·58	9·38	9·20	470	6·31	10·85	1·42	6·35	5·37
1963	18·93	9·54	9·39	466	6·42	11·06	1·45	6·48	5·48
1964	19·29	9·71	9·58	453	6·50	11·31	1·48	6·63	5·58
1965	19·64	9·88	9·76	419	6·56	11·58	1·51	6·79	5·69
1966	20·02	10·05	9·96	388	6·59	11·88	1·54	6·96	5·78
1967	20·38	10·23	10·15	371	6·59	12·22	1·58	7·13	5·86
1968	20·70	10·39	10·31	364	6·56	12·53	1·61	7·26	5·93
1969	21·00	10·53	10·47	370	6·51	12·84	1·65	7·39	5·99
1970	21·30	10·67	10·63	372	6·45	13·15	1·70	7·55	6·01
1971	21·57	10·80	10·77	362	6·38	13·44	1·74	7·70	6·03
1972	21·80	10·90	10·90	347	6·29	13·73	1·79	7·81	6·05
1973	22·04	11·01	11·03	343	6·18	14·03	1·84	7·91	6·08
1974	22·36	11·16	11·21	351	6·09	14·39	1·89	8·05	6·12
1975	22·70	11·31	11·38	359	6·00	14·76	1·94	8·17	6·18
1976	22·99	11·45	11·54	360	5·99	15·09	2·00	8·26	6·23
1977	23·29	11·59	11·70	361	5·81	15·41	2·07	8·35	6·28
1978	23·53	11·70	11·84	359	5·71	15·70	2·13	8·44	6·30
1979	23·77	11·80	11·97	366	5·60	15·96	2·21	8·50	6·34
1980	24·04	11·93	12·11	371	5·52	16·23	2·29	8·57	6·39
1981	24·34	12·07	12·27	371	5·48	16·50	2·36	8·62	6·44
1982	24·63	12·21	12·43	373	5·47	16·73	2·43	8·72	6·48
1983	24·89	12·32	12·56	374	5·47	16·93	2·49	8·82	6·52
1984	25·12	12·43	12·69	377	5·46	17·11	2·56	8·95	6·54
1985	25·36	12·54	12·82	379	5·45	17·27	2·64	9·06	6·58
1986	25·59	12·65	12·94	378	5·44	17·42	2·73	9·18	6·63

Table C.6 Education, selected years, 1885–1986

	Kindergarten	Elementary	Secondary	Post-secondary	Higher education Total	of which: Female
		No. of pupils '000			No. of students '000	
1885		911		. . .	. . .	. . .
1890		943		. . .	. . .	. . .
1895		1,091		. . .	. . .	. . .
1900		1,055		. . .	. . .	. . .
1905		1,128		. . .	. . .	. . .
1910		1,318		. . .	. . .	. . .
1915		1,552		. . .	. . .	. . .
1920		1,834		. . .	23·2	3·8
1925		1,993		. . .	25·7	5·5
1930		2,099		. . .	32·9	7·8
1935		2,132		. . .	35·1	7·8
1940		2,075		. . .	36·4	8·4
1945		2,039		. . .	64·7	13·5
1950		2,391		. . .	68·6	14·6
1951	84	2,147	395	. . .	. . .	. . .
1955	103	2,681	507	33·3	72·7	15·2
1958	132	3,033	662	42·4	95·0	21·2
1959	138	3,155	715	46·3	101·9	23·5
1960	146	3,267	789	49·4	113·7	27·6
1961	157	3,357	895	53·4	128·6	33·0
1962	169	3,438	1,002	55·6	141·1	38·1
1963	184	3,526	1,091	62·2	158·0	44·6
1964	204	3,619	1,171	66·0	177·6	52·7
1965	268	3,680	1,250	69·4	204·2	64·3
1966	295	3,754	1,304	80·2	230·3	74·6
1967	328	3,819	1,366	99·4	253·5	83·0
1968	374	3,844	1,476	129·5	265·8	88·6
1969	405	3,841	1,576	142·7	294·1	101·1
1970	402	3,816	1,666	166·1	309·5	108·8
1971	377	3,763	1,723	173·8	323·0	116·4
1972	386	3,670	1,757	191·0	322·4	118·9
1973	389	3,531	1,799	201·5	332·1	126·4
1974	424	3,432	1,814	211·2	347·0	137·5
1975	399	3,482	1,711	221·6	370·4	151·8
1976	391	3,407	1,713	226·2	376·5	159·2
1977	380	3,321	1,706	241·7	374·2	161·0
1978	382	3,208	1,701	249·8	368·0	160·6
1979	386	3,119	1,677	252·1	371·4	164·6
1980	398	3,071	1,634	260·8	382·6	171·7
1981	392	3,070	1,560	273·4	401·9	183·1
1982	400	3,049	1,542	295·6	426·4	195·0
1983	401	3,023	1,548	316·2	450·5	208·4
1984	414	3,004	1,525	321·6	461·2	216·9
1985	422	2,989	1,514	322·6	467·3	223·4
1986	430	2,997	1,509	. . .	. . .	. . .

Table C.7   Labour market: employment, 1921–86

	Employed labour force	Agriculture, forestry & fishing	Mining & quarrying	Manufacturing	Gas, electricity & water	Construction	Transport & communication	Distribution & services
				'000				
1921	3,121	1,165	55	557	. . .	66	257	. . .
1922	3,230	1,192	55	561	. . .	71	267	. . .
1923	3,323	1,213	59	613	. . .	75	273	. . .
1924	3,344	1,206	59	585	. . .	71	279	. . .
1925	3,423	1,220	56	590	. . .	82	269	. . .
1926	3,550	1,251	55	632	. . .	98	283	. . .
1927	3,690	1,284	60	656	. . .	113	291	. . .
1928	3,796	1,305	64	698	. . .	118	309	. . .
1929	3,848	1,307	67	743	. . .	139	319	. . .
1930	3,689	1,238	66	691	. . .	148	301	. . .
1931	3,670	1,216	60	605	24	154	246	899
1932	3,470	1,237	55	528	23	118	208	885
1933	3,449	1,257	52	481	21	81	190	861
1934	3,707	1,277	58	560	20	165	193	886
1935	3,777	1,298	64	579	21	125	194	898
1936	3,895	1,319	70	592	21	132	207	914
1937	4,115	1,339	80	657	21	139	212	934
1938	4,066	1,359	79	632	23	134	204	948
1939	4,120	1,379	82	627	22	127	206	959
1940	4,184	1,344	84	712	24	126	219	973
1941	4,271	1,224	89	904	26	170	247	1,043
1942	4,434	1,139	81	1,131	25	144	262	1,077
1943	4,491	1,118	68	1,250	26	149	276	1,103
1944	4,485	1,136	60	1,263	27	110	292	1,161
1945	4,447	1,144	52	1,196	29	113	305	1,184
1946	4,738	1,297	72	1,144	34	184	308	1,204
	4,666		74	1,214	33	224	344	1,481
1947	4,832	1,239	69	1,264	38	251	373	1,599
1948	4,875	1,215	74	1,268	41	286	371	1,621
1949	4,913	1,172	84	1,303	45	317	364	1,631
1950	4,976	1,139	75	1,316	46	331	376	1,694
1951	5,097	1,084	79	1,350	51	348	398	1,788
1952	5,169	1,011	92	1,333	58	338	421	1,906
1953	5,235	967	91	1,384	58	347	423	1,965
1954	5,243	993	102	1,326	61	334	397	2,031
1955	5,364	954	109	1,373	62	368	403	2,095
1956	5,585	914	117	1,435	67	412	433	2,207
1957	5,731	870	118	1,492	73	438	438	2,297
1958	5,706	813	107	1,459	78	427	429	2,381
1959	5,870	801	88	1,494	75	442	445	2,510
1960	5,965	789	93	1,470	73	418	442	2,670
1961	6,055	778	79	1,515	77	406	432	2,762
		785	80	1,452	71	376	492	2,798
1962	6,225	757	81	1,502	75	393	513	2,903
1963	6,375	754	72	1,552	76	406	521	2,993
1964	6,609	738	87	1,650	69	410	522	3,132
1965	6,862	694	134	1,636	77	463	540	3,317
1966	7,152	646	121	1,744	77	499	543	3,523
1967	7,379	663	114	1,756	80	475	580	3,711
1968	7,537	650	117	1,754	90	470	582	3,875
1969	7,780	636	116	1,819	93	482	600	4,034
1970	7,919	604	125	1,768	89	467	609	4,257
1971	8,104	607	128	1,766	87	489	620	4,407
1972	8,344	575	122	1,823	93	494	641	4,596
1973	8,761	573	120	1,927	99	539	676	4,827
1974	9,125	579	124	1,978	96	586	695	5,067
1975	9,284	564	139	1,871	107	603	705	5,296
1976	9,477	562	145	1,921	111	635	713	5,390
1977	9,651	553	153	1,888	108	634	712	5,603
1978	9,987	574	160	1,956	119	634	740	5,802

***Table* C.7 (Continued)   Labour market: employment, 1921–86**

	Employed labour force	Agriculture, forestry & fishing	Mining & quarrying	Manufacturing	Gas, electricity & water	Construction	Transport & communication	Distribution & services
	'000							
1979	10,395	590	169	2,071	118	644	785	6,017
1980	10,708	583	196	2,111	124	624	782	6,288
1981	11,006	597	210	2,122	128	651	784	6,514
1982	10,644	558	175	1,930	122	597	763	6,500
1983	10,734	587	170	1,886	119	566	750	6,656
1984	11,000	586	182	1,968	123	572	735	6,834
1985	11,311	590	191	1,981	124	587	760	7,080
1986	11,634	590	185	2,015	121	627	777	7,319

Table C.8   Labour market: other indicators, 1890–1987

	Manufacturing		Unemployment		Industrial disputes		
	Average weekly hrs worked	Average hourly earnings			Stoppages	Workers involved	Working days lost
		C$	'000	%		'000	'000
1890	59	0·13	84	...	...	...	...
1900	56·7	0·14	74	...	...	...	...
1901	...	...	...	...	97	24·1	737·8
1902	...	...	...	...	124	12·7	203·3
1903	...	...	...	...	171	38·4	859·0
1904	...	...	...	...	103	11·4	192·9
1905	...	0·14	...	...	95	12·5	246·1
1906	...	...	...	...	149	23·4	378·3
1907	...	...	...	...	183	34·1	520·1
1908	...	...	...	...	72	26·1	703·6
1909	...	...	...	...	88	18·1	880·7
1910	53·3	0·16	84	...	94	22·2	731·3
1911	...	...	...	...	99	29·3	1,821·1
1912	...	...	...	...	179	42·9	1,135·8
1913	...	...	...	...	143	40·5	1,036·3
1914	...	...	...	...	58	9·7	490·9
1915	...	...	...	...	62	11·4	95·0
1916	...	...	...	...	118	26·5	236·8
1917	...	0·29	...	...	158	50·3	1,123·5
1918	...	0·33	...	...	228	79·7	647·9
1919	...	0·35	...	...	332	148·9	3,400·9
1920	...	0·43	65	...	310	60·3	799·5
1921	...	0·40	192	5·8	159	28·3	1,048·9
1922	...	0·37	150	4·4	89	43·8	1,528·7
1923	...	0·38	110	3·2	77	34·3	671·8
1924	...	0·39	158	4·5	64	34·3	1,295·1
1925	...	0·39	157	4·4	86	28·9	1,193·3
1926	49·6	0·40	108	3·0	75	23·8	266·6
1927	49·4	0·40	67	1·8	72	22·3	152·6
1928	49·3	0·41	65	1·7	96	17·6	224·2
1929	49·2	0·42	116	2·9	88	12·9	152·1
1930	48·1	0·41	371	9·1	67	13·8	91·8
1931	44·9	0·42	481	11·6	86	10·7	204·2
1932	42·0	0·40	741	17·6	111	23·4	255·0
1933	41·1	0·38	826	19·3	122	26·6	317·5
1934	43·5	0·41	631	14·5	189	45·8	574·5
1935	44·6	0·41	625	14·2	120	33·3	288·7
1936	45·4	0·42	571	12·8	155	34·8	277·0
1937	47·1	...	411	9·1	274	71·9	886·4
1938	47·2	0·45	522	11·4	142	20·4	148·7
1939	47·2	0·46	529	11·4	120	41·0	224·6
1940	47·9	0·49	423	9·2	166	60·6	266·3
1941	48·4	0·54	195	4·4	229	87·1	433·9
1942	48·2	0·62	135	3·0	352	113·9	450·2
1943	46·8	0·67	76	1·7	401	218·4	1,041·2
1944	56·6	0·71	63	1·4	195	75·3	490·1
1945	44·3 / 44·1	0·74	73	1·6	196	96·1	1,457·4
1946	42·7	0·81	163	3·4	225	139·5	4,516·4
1947	42·5	0·92	110	2·2	232	104·1	2,397·3
1948	42·3	1·02	114	2·3	147	42·8	885·8
1949	42·2	1·07	141	2·8	132	51·4	1,063·7
1950	42·3	1·14	186	3·6	158	192·2	1,389·0
1951	41·7	1·31	126	2·4	257	102·9	901·7
1952	41·5	1·40	155	2·9	216	120·8	2,880·0
1953	41·3	1·47	162	3·0	167	56·0	1,324·7
1954	40·7	1·51	250	4·6	156	62·3	1,475·2
1955	41·0	1·57	245	4·4	149	60·1	1,875·4

Table C.8 (Continued) Labour market: other indicators, 1890–1987

| | Manufacturing | | Unemployment | | Industrial disputes | | |
| | Average weekly hrs worked | Average hourly earnings | | | Stoppages | Workers involved | Working days lost |
		C$	'000	%		'000	'000
1956	41·0	1·66	197	3·4	221	88·7	1,246·0
1957	40·4	1·75	278	4·6	242	91·4	1,634·9
1958	40·2	1·80	432	7·0	253	112·4	2,872·3
1959	40·7	1·88	372	6·0	203	100·1	2,286·9
1960	40·4	1·93	446	7·0	268	49·4	738·7
1961	40·6	...	466	7·1	272	98·0	1,336·1
1962	40·7	...	390	5·9	290	74·3	1,417·9
1963	40·8	2·13	374	5·5	318	83·4	917·1
1964	41·0	2·21	324	4·7	327	100·5	1,580·6
1965	41·1	2·33	280	3·9	478	171·9	2,349·9
1966	40·8	2·50	251	3·4	582	411·6	5,178·2
1967	40·3	2·67	296	3·8	498	252·0	3,974·8
1968	40·3	2·88	358	4·4	559	223·6	5,082·7
1969	40·0	3·12	362	4·4	566	306·8	7,757·9
1970	39·7	3·19	476	5·6	503	261·7	6,559·6
1971	39·7	3·47	535	6·1	547	239·6	2,866·6
1972	40·0	3·73	553	6·2	556	706·5	7,753·5
1973	39·6	4·05	515	5·5	677	348·5	5,776·1
1974	38·9	4·58	514	5·3	1,173	580·9	9,221·9
1975	38·6	5·27	690	6·9	1,103	506·4	10,908·8
1976	38·7	5·89	726	7·1	921	1,570·9	11,609·9
1977	38·7	6·38	850	8·0	803	217·6	3,307·9
1978	38·8	6·84	908	8·3	1,058	401·7	7,392·8
1979	38·8	7·44	836	7·4	1,050	462·5	7,834·2
1980	38·5	8·19	865	7·4	1,028	441·0	8,975·4
1981	38·5	9·17	898	7·5	1,048	338·6	8,878·5
1982	37·7	10·25	1,314	10·9	677	444·3	5,795·4
1983	38·4	10·59	1,448	11·8	645	329·3	4,444·0
1984	38·5	11·16	1,399	11·2	717	186·8	3,871·8
1985	38·8	11·59	1,328	10·4	829	162·2	3,125·5
1986	38·7	11·95	1,236	9·5	735	483·6	7,106·4
1987	38·8	12·24	1,167	8·8	658	582·7	3,984·5

Table C.9 Public finance, 1885–1986

	Revenue					Expenditure				
	Taxes on personal income	Taxes on companies	Customs & excise	General sales tax	Total receipts	Defence	Education	Social services	Debt interest	Total expenditure
					C$ mn					
1885	...	...	25·2	...	34	4·5	...	...	...	48
1886	...	...	28·7	...	36	1·6	...	...	...	60
1887	...	...	28·2	...	36	1·9	...	...	...	40
1888	...	...	30·6	...	39	1·4	...	...	...	43
1889	...	...	31·5	...	40	1·4	...	...	...	42
1890	...	...	30·3	...	39	1·4	...	...	...	40
1891	...	...	28·4	...	37	1·4	...	...	...	39
1892	...	...	29·3	...	38	1·5	...	...	...	40
1893	...	...	27·5	...	36	1·4	...	...	...	39
1894	...	...	25·4	...	34	1·7	...	...	...	41
1895	...	...	27·7	...	37	2·2	...	...	...	41
1896	...	...	28·6	...	38	2·6	...	...	...	42
1897	...	...	29·5	...	41	1·8	...	...	...	41
1898	...	...	34·8	...	47	2·6	...	...	...	43
1899	...	...	38·1	...	51	3·6	...	...	...	49
1900	...	...	38·6	...	53	3·2	...	...	...	50
1901	...	0·6	43·1	...	58	2·8	...	...	...	56
1902	...	0·6	48·7	...	69	2·6	...	...	...	61
1903	...	0·6	53·4	...	71	3·7	...	...	...	59
1904	...	0·8	54·1	...	71	4·2	...	...	...	70
1905	...	0·9	60·1	...	80	5·7	...	...	...	77
1906	...	1·2	51·5	...	68	4·4	...	...	...	81
1907	...	1·5	73·0	...	96	6·9	...	...	...	110
1908	...	1·6	62·0	...	86	6·5	...	...	...	131
1909	...	1·8	75·0	...	102	6·1	...	...	...	114
1910	...	1·9	88·7	...	118	9·2	...	...	...	122
1911	...	2·1	104·3	...	136	9·7	...	...	...	136
1912	...	2·2	133·2	...	169	11·4	...	...	...	143
1913	...	2·6	126·1	...	163	13·5	...	...	...	185
1914	...	3·2	97·5	...	133	72·4	...	...	...	246
1915	...	3·9	122·6	...	172	172·5	...	...	...	338
1916	...	3·9	160·6	...	233	312·0	...	...	...	497
1917	...	4·1	173·6	...	261	343·8	...	...	...	574
1918	8·0	5·9	189·2	...	313	438·7	...	...	...	696
1919	13·2	12·1	227·1	...	350	346·6	...	...	...	740
1920	32·5	20·9	241·6	38	437	30·2	...	...	...	529
1921	39·8	45·7	154·8	61	395	17·5	...	...	...	476
1922	31·7	35·2	170·5	90	410	14·2	...	...	...	441
1923	25·7	35·9	182·4	98	408	13·4	...	...	...	372
1924	25·2	39·2	169·3	63	353	13·2	...	...	...	352
1925	23·9	39·4	195·4	73	383	14·1	...	...	...	356
1926	18·1	38·4	214·8	81	401	14·8	...	...	...	359
1927	23·2	41·7	234·0	71	431	17·6	...	...	...	380
1928	24·8	44·3	271·3	63	462	19·6	...	...	...	394
1929	27·2	51·8	263·7	44	453	21·8	...	...	...	405
1930	26·6	55·2	203·4	20	358	23·4	...	...	...	442
1931	24·8	49·1	171·0	42	335	17·9	...	...	...	449
1932	26·0	50·9	133·0	57	312	13·5	...	...	...	532
1933					325					458
	43	31	148	61	742	15·0	107	168	299	950
1934	...	...	160	(72)	...	(13·9)	...	...	...	...
1935	...	...	154	(78)	...	(17·2)	...	...	...	...
1936	...	...	169	(113)	...	(22·9)	...	...	...	...
1937	65	79	189	144	1,027	32·7	117	236	273	1,143
1938	...	...	170	(122)	...	(34·8)	...	...	...	...
1939	72	89	194	145	1,077	125·7	129	208	266	1,277
1940	...	...	324	(180)	...	(730·1)	...	...	...	...
1941	339	353	446	259	2,073	1,253	138	151	256	2,376
1942	...	...	...	(232)	...	(2,563)	...	...	...	...
1943	727	741	619	331	3,173	4,016	151	177	323	5,572

Table C.9 (Continued) Public finance, 1885–1986

	Revenue					Expenditure				
	Taxes on personal income	Taxes on companies	Customs & excise	General sales tax	Total receipts	Defence	Education	Social services	Debt interest	Total expenditure
					C$ mn					
1944	...	...	...	(209)	...	(4,000)	...	...	...	...
1945	715	645	554	242	3,624	2,517	186	375	489	5,683
1946	701	682	660	335	3,749	466	225	500	512	3,357
1947	696	653	739	416	3,793	195	273	579	499	3,097
1948	806	625	671	440	3,820	269	342	660	475	3,339
1949	670	707	604	481	3,790	385	392	805	472	3,782
1950	714	961	751	561	4,440	607	442	870	464	4,139
					C$ bn					
1951	1·03	1·30	0·86	0·72	5·55	1·42	0·50	0·92	0·53	5·36
1952	1·28	1·34	0·90	0·84	6·24	1·92	0·57	1·16	0·50	6·28
1953	1·33	1·30	0·93	0·88	6·45	1·82	0·63	1·22	0·52	6·48
1954	1·37	1·12	0·88	0·88	6·30	1·72	0·68	1·32	0·54	6·68
1955	1·38	1·14	0·99	0·99	6·87	1·76	0·75	1·39	0·54	7·03
1956	1·64	1·40	1·09	1·13	7·90	1·82	0·84	1·47	0·59	7·81
1957	1·74	1·51	1·05	1·12	8·22	1·71	1·04	1·69	0·64	8·54
1958	1·61	1·30	1·04	1·11	8·07	1·66	1·11	1·96	0·70	9·16
1959	1·88	1·48	1·15	1·29	9·14	1·54	1·33	2·24	0·83	9·98
1960	2·09	1·65	1·13	1·28	9·72	1·53	1·58	2·47	0·82	10·78
1961	2·25	1·57	1·16	1·49	10·28	1·65	1·82	2·77	0·88	11·76
1962	2·51	1·69	1·29	1·67	11·25	1·60	2·14	3·06	1·04	12·70
1963	2·68	1·79	1·25	1·90	12·10	1·72	2·18	3·26	1·15	13·49
1964	3·19	2·12	1·30	2·32	13·90	1·56	2·45	3·66	1·15	14·44
1965	3·64	2·28	1·43	2·73	15·39	1·57	2·62	3·96	1·26	15·91
1966	4·36	2·31	1·55	3·08	17·33	1·66	3·48	4·54	1·36	18·73
1967	5·33	2·42	1·61	3·41	19·80	1·78	4·20	5·52	1·54	21·49
1968	6·31	2·87	1·65	3·49	22·52	1·80	4·81	6·27	1·78	23·81
1969	7·98	3·70	1·71	3·97	27·82	1·82	5·55	7·40	1·85	26·8
1970	9·15	3·19	1·90	4·07	32·14	1·73	5·99	10·03	2·52	31·44
1971	10·19	3·18	2·15	4·66	35·37	1·87	6·54	11·81	2·94	36·26
1972	12·01	3·90	2·41	5·39	40·59	1·91	6·95	14·14	3·27	41·01
1973	11·81	6·72	2·71	6·60	47·01	2·12	7·30	16·61	3·79	47·71
1974	16·21	7·84	3·20	7·47	60·06	2·29	8·79	20·66	4·55	59·30
1975	19·32	7·66	3·36	7·18	66·29	2·63	10·65	25·12	5·58	71·81
1976	22·28	7·56	3·79	8·50	75·75	3·23	12·19	28·45	6·39	80·58
1977	23·42	7·94	4·08	9·39	82·52	3·65	13·85	31·73	7·64	90·85
1978	25·59	8·81	4·69	9·25	92·08	4·09	14·95	34·72	9·50	100·44
1979	30·21	9·99	5·00	10·46	105·64	4·40	16·46	38·28	11·25	112·22
1980	35·41	11·73	5·48	11·64	121·81	4·94	18·07	45·08	13·65	132·36
1981	42·56	11·80	6·04	13·23	146·12	5·84	20·83	51·77	18·46	153·52
1982	47·09	9·49	5·87	13·63	152·52	6·76	23·20	63·52	22·52	179·58
1983	49·01	10·28	6·80	15·72	164·01	...	24·98	71·22	24·36	194·23
1984	51·60	13·03	7·57	17·92	177·99	...	25·31	77·09	29·85	211·66
1985	58·36	13·57	8·52	21·11	191·11	...	28·11	81·92	32·68	225·77
1986	63·49	14·90	8·83	23·93	200·67	...	28·49	87·19	35·51	237·24

Table C.10 Value of exports and imports by country, 1885–1986

	Total exports	Exports to:			of which:	Total imports	Imports from:			of which:
		UK	USA	Rest of world	Japan		UK	USA	Rest of world	Japan
					C$ mn					
1885	87	42	40	5	...	100	42	48	10	...
1886	85	42	37	6	...	96	41	45	10	1·5
1887	90	45	38	7	...	105	45	45	15	1·6
1888	90	40	43	7	0·1	101	39	48	14	1·2
1889	87	38	44	5	...	109	42	51	16	1·2
1890	94	48	41	5	...	112	43	52	17	1·3
1891	97	49	41	7	...	112	42	54	16	1·3
1892	112	65	39	8	...	115	41	53	21	1·9
1893	114	64	44	6	...	115	43	58	14	1·5
1894	116	69	36	11	...	109	39	53	17	1·4
1895	109	62	41	6	...	101	31	55	15	1·6
1896	116	67	44	5	...	105	33	59	13	1·6
1897	134	77	49	8	0·1	107	29	62	16	1·3
1898	160	105	46	9	0·1	126	32	79	15	1·4
1899	155	99	45	11	0·1	149	37	93	19	2·0
1900	183	108	69	6	0·1	173	45	110	18	1·8
1901	195	105	72	18	0·2	178	43	110	25	1·6
1902	210	117	71	22	0·3	197	49	121	27	1·5
1903	225	131	72	22	0·3	225	59	138	28	1·4
1904	211	118	73	20	0·3	244	62	151	31	1·9
1905	201	102	77	22	0·5	252	60	163	29	1·9
1906	247	133	98	16	0·5	284	69	176	39	1·7
1907	192	...	...	...	...	250	...	...	...	...
1908	263	126	91	46	0·7	353	95	211	47	2·2
1909	260	126	85	49	0·8	289	71	180	38	2·0
1910	299	139	104	56	0·7	370	95	228	47	2·2
1911	290	132	105	53	0·6	453	110	285	58	2·4
1912	308	147	102	59	0·5	522	117	357	48	2·5
1913	377	170	140	67	1·1	671	139	441	91	3·5
1914	455	215	164	76	1·6	619	132	411	76	2·6
1915	461	187	174	100	1·0	456	90	429	...	2·8
1916	779	452	201	126	1·0	508	80	399	29	4·0
1917	1,179	742	281	156	1·3	846	122	678	46	8·1
1918	1,586	845	418	323	5·0	964	81	804	79	12
1919	1,270 / 1,288	541	455	274	12·0	921 / 940	73	750	98	14
1920	1,298	489	464	...	7·7	1,337	126	801	...	14
1921	814	313	542	...	6·4	799	214	856	...	11
1922	894	299	293	...	15·0	762	117	516	...	8
1923	1,016	379	369	...	15·0	903	141	541	...	7
1924	1,042	360	431	...	27·0	808	154	601	...	6
1925	1,252	396	417	...	22	890	151	510	...	7
1926	1,269	508	475	...	35	1,001	164	610	...	10
1927	1,235	447	466	...	30	1,078	164	687	...	11
1928	1,358	411	478	...	33	1,211	186	719	...	13
1929	1,172	430	500	...	42	1,288	194	868	...	13
1930	887	282	515	...	31	996	189	847	...	13
1931	595	210 / 174	350 / 235	...	19 / 17	619	150 / 98	584 / 352	...	9 / 6
1932	495	179	165	151	12	445	94	264	87	4·6
1933	532	211	173	148	13	397	98	217	82	3·1
1934	653	271	224	158	17	510	113	294	103	4·4
1935	735	304	273	158	15	547	117	312	118	3·6
1936	947	396	345	206	20	628	123	369	136	4·3
1937	1,009	403	372	234	26	798	147	491	160	5·9
1938	846	341	279	226	21	665	119	425	121	4·6
1939	933	324	390	219	28	736	114	497	125	4·9
1940	1,185	512	452	221	12	1,023	161	744	118	6·1
1941	1,588	661	610	317	1·6	1,274	219	1,004	51	2·4
1942	2,312	748	897	667	—	1,505	161	1,305	39	1·0

172

Table C.10 (Continued) Value of exports and imports by country, 1885–1986

		Exports to:			of which:		Imports from:			of which:
	Total exports	UK	USA	Rest of world	Japan	Total imports	UK	USA	Rest of world	Japan
						C$ mn				
1943	2,923	1,037	1,167	719	—	1,686	135	1,424	127	—
1944	3,398	1,238	1,335	825	—	1,730	111	1,447	172	—
1945	3,214	971	1,227	1,016	—	1,514	122	1,202	190	—
1946	2,299	594	884	821	1	1,841	137	1,387	317	—
1947	2,790	747	1,030	1,013	—	2,543	184	1,952	407	—
1948	3,087	683	1,499	905	8	2,618	294	1,799	525	3
1949	3,004	702	1,505	797	6	2,714	302	1,915	497	6
1950	3,143	468	2,021	654	20	3,125	401	2,090	634	12
1951	3,946	630	2,296	1,020	73	4,005	415	2,752	838	13
1952	4,337	744	2,303	1,290	102	3,916	352	2,888	676	13
1953	4,152	663	2,413	1,076	118	4,248	445	3,115	688	13
1954	3,926	651	2,309	966	96	3,967	382	2,871	714	19
1955	4,328	768	2,548	1,012	91	4,568	393	3,331	844	37
1956	4,834	811	2,803	1,220	128	5,547	476	4,031	1,040	61
1957	4,884	721	2,847	1,316	139	5,473	507	3,887	1,079	61
1958	4,899	772	2,808	1,319	105	5,050	519	3,460	1,071	70
1959	5,144	786	3,083	1,275	140	5,509	589	3,709	1,211	103
1960	5,390	915	2,932	1,543	179	5,483	589	3,687	1,207	110
1961	5,903	909	3,107	1,887	232	5,769	618	3,864	1,287	117
1962	6,357	909	3,608	1,840	215	6,258	563	4,300	1,395	125
1963	6,990	1,007	3,766	2,217	296	6,558	527	4,445	1,586	130
1964	8,303	1,200	4,271	2,832	330	7,488	574	5,164	1,750	174
1965	8,767	1,174	4,840	2,753	316	8,633	619	6,045	1,969	230
						C$ bn				
1966	10·25	1·12	6·05	3·08	0·39	10·07	0·67	7·20	2·20	0·27
1967	11·42	1·17	7·09	3·16	0·57	10·87	0·65	7·95	2·27	0·29
1968	13·79	1·23	9·29	3·27	0·61	12·36	0·70	9·05	2·61	0·36
1969	14·87	1·11	10·55	3·21	0·63	14·13	0·79	10·24	3·10	0·50
1970	16·82	1·50	10·90	4·42	0·81	13·95	0·74	9·92	3·29	0·58
1971	17·82	1·40	12·03	4·39	0·83	15·62	0·84	10·95	3·83	0·80
1972	20·15	1·39	13·97	4·79	0·96	18·67	0·95	12·88	4·84	1·07
1973	25·42	1·60	17·13	6·69	1·81	23·33	1·01	16·50	5·82	1·01
1974	32·44	1·93	21·40	9·11	2·23	31·72	1·13	21·39	9·20	1·43
1975	33·33	1·82	21·70	9·81	2·13	34·72	1·22	23·64	9·86	1·21
1976	38·48	1·90	25·90	10·68	2·40	37·49	1·15	25·80	10·54	1·52
1977	44·55	1·95	31·11	11·49	2·52	42·36	1·28	29·82	11·26	1·79
1978	53·18	2·01	37·18	13·99	3·06	50·11	1·60	35·25	13·26	2·27
1979	65·64	2·62	44·54	18·48	4·10	62·87	1·93	45·57	15·37	2·16
1980	76·16	3·25	48·17	24·74	4·37	69·27	1·97	48·61	18·69	2·80
1981	83·81	3·36	55·49	24·96	4·52	79·48	2·39	54·54	22·55	4·06
1982	84·53	2·73	57·69	24·11	4·59	67·86	1·90	47·87	18·09	3·53
1983	90·61	2·51	66·01	22·09	4·76	75·61	1·81	54·08	19·72	4·41
1984	112·38	2·54	84·93	24·91	5·67	95·46	2·31	68·17	24·98	5·71
1985	119·48	2·48	93·06	23·94	5·74	104·36	3·28	73·82	27·26	6·12
1986	120·52	2·72	93·18	24·62	5·94	112·68	3·72	77·34	31·62	7·63

Sources

(For sources used in specific tables, see Notes.)

1 *Canada Year Book,* Statistics Canada, Ottawa, various issues.
2 *Canadian Statistical Review,* monthly, Statistics Canada, Ottawa, various issues.
3 *Consolidated Government Finance,* Statistics Canada, Ottawa, various issues.
4 *Education in Canada,* Annual Statistical Review, Statistics Canada, Ottawa, various issues.
5 Firestone, O.J. *Canada's Economic Development 1867–1953,* Bowes and Bowes, London, 1958.
6 *Historical Statistics of Canada,* M.C. Urquhart and K.A.H. Buckley (eds), Macmillan Company of Canada, Toronto, 1965.
7 *Historical Statistics of Canada,* F.H. Leacy (ed.), Statistics Canada, 1983.
8 *Industry price indexes,* monthly, Statistics Canada, Ottawa.
9 Mitchell, B.R., *International Historical Statistics: The Americas and Australasia,* Macmillan Press, 1983.
10 Organisation for Economic Cooperation and Development (OECD), *Labour Force Statistics, 1966–86,* Paris, 1988 and earlier issues.
11 OECD, *National Accounts 1950–1979,* Vol. 1, Paris, 1981.
12 OECD, *National Accounts 1960–1987,* Vol. 1, Paris, 1989.
13 *Prices and Price Indexes,* monthly, Statistics Canada, Ottawa.
14 *The Labour Force,* monthly, Statistics Canada, Ottawa.
15 United Nations, *Monthly Bulletin of Statistics,* New York.
16 United Nations, *Statistical Year Book,* New York.
17 *Vital Statistics,* August 1974, Statistics Canada, Ottawa.
18 *Year Book of Labour Statistics,* International Labour Office, Geneva.

Notes

Table C.1 Gross domestic product at current prices

Sources: **5, 7, 11, 12**

OECD data have been used from 1950. Figures are on the present system of national accounts from 1950. Consumers' expenditure and government current expenditure from 1985–87 estimated by OECD Secretariat.

For the period 1926–49, data given in **7** have been used.

For 1890–1920, estimates given in **5** for selected years have been used in order to take the series back as far as possible.

Table C.2 Gross domestic product at constant prices

Sources: **5, 7, 11, 12**

OECD data have been used from 1950. See note to Table C.1 on system of national accounts. Consumers' expenditure and government current expenditure from 1985–87 estimated by OECD Secretariat.

For the period 1926–49, data given in **7** (1971 dollars) have been roughly converted to 1980 prices and linked with the OECD data at 1950.

For 1890–1920, estimates given in **5** for selected years at 1935–39 prices have been linked at 1929 and roughly converted to 1980 prices.

Each category of expenditure has been re-referenced separately for 1890–1949 and this means that the total for gross domestic product may not equal the sum of components.

Table C.3 Industrial production

Sources: **6, 7, 9, 15**

Industrial production index: includes manufacturing industries, mining and public utilities.

Coal and steel: figures published in **7** converted to metric tons. From 1976 data are taken from **15**.

Crude petroleum: from 1976 estimates given in **15**. Synthetic crude petroleum is included. For 1885–1975, data are taken from **9**.

Natural gas: from 1976 data are taken from **15**. Figures in **15** are in terajoules, converted to m^3 using the conversion factors given in **15**.

For 1885–1975, data are taken from **9**. From 1950 (second line) figures exclude shrinkage.

Electricity: in 1956 there was a change in the electricity series in that some power previously treated as sales by a utility company to an industrial customer were, after 1956, treated as energy produced by an industrial establishment and therefore not included in the data. Figures have been revised back to 1950 on this basis.

Railway industrial establishments are excluded up to 1927 (first line). From 1976, data are taken from **15**.

Table C.4 Prices and income

Sources: **1, 5, 7, 8, 11, 12, 13**

Consumer price index: represents the expenditure of all private households and families in urban centres with a population of 30,000 or more. Weights are periodically updated; those currently in use are based on the 1982 Family Expenditure Survey. For further details see **7**.

The figures for 1900 and 1905 are for December only.

Producer prices: the 'all items' index is the industry selling price index covering approximately 110 industries within manufacturing. It is linked to the general wholesale price index at 1956 although coverage of the current industry selling price index is wider. For further details see **7** and **8**.

Raw materials: currently raw materials price index published in **8**. Includes products used at the primary stage of production (approximately 70 commodities). It is linked at 1977 to an earlier index which included raw materials and partly manufactured goods; this index formed part of the general wholesale price index. For further details see **7** and **8**.

Export and import prices: the present published series is a current weighted index of imports and exports on a balance of payments basis. For 1976–81, the index was current weighted on a customs basis. Figures for 1885–1975 are base weighted indices with 1971 = 100.

Compensation of employees: OECD data have been used from 1950. Figures include all payments by resident producers of wages and salaries to their employees, in kind and in cash, and of contributions, paid or imputed, to social security and pension schemes on behalf of their employees.

For the period 1926–49, data are taken from **7**.

National income: OECD data have been used from 1950. National income is gross national product (gross domestic product plus net factor incomes from the rest of the world) minus consumption of fixed capital (depreciation).

For the period 1926–49, data are taken from **7**. Figures for net national income plus indirect taxes less subsidies have been used for this period.

For 1890–1910, estimates given in **5** have been used.

Table C.5 Population

Sources: **1, 7, 10, 17**

Total population: OECD data from 1964. Figures refer to resident population on June 1 each year. 1986 census results are not incorporated.

For the years 1885–1901, figures are for April 1 each year.

Age distribution: census figures for 1891, 1901, 1911. From 1921 they are mid-year estimates.

Births: number of live births each year.

Table C.6 Education

Sources: **1, 4, 7, 9**

Compulsory school ages vary from 6–16, 6–14, 7–14 and 7–15 depending on the province and type of area (rural or urban). Published data have distinguished between levels of education since 1951. From 1951 the figures refer to the school year beginning in the year shown. Enrolment in trade schools, private business colleges and apprentice programmes are not included in the data.

Kindergarten: pupils in pre-grade 1 classes; mainly children under 6 years. Private kindergarten and nursery schools excluded 1965–74.

Elementary: pupils in grades 1–8 (usually children aged 6–13 years).

Secondary: children in grade 9 and above (usually children in age group 14–17. A change in classification in Quebec in 1975 affected the figures for grades 1–8 and grade 9 and above (see **4**).

Before 1951, the figures are for pupils at public elementary and secondary schools; the dates of returns varied.

Post-secondary: these figures refer to community college enrolment; full-time students in the academic year beginning in the year shown.

Higher education: full-time university students, graduate and undergraduate. Academic year beginning in the year shown.

Table C.7 Labour market: employment

Sources: **7, 10**

OECD data have been used from 1970. Figures are annual averages. Total employment includes all those in civilian employment (including self-employed) and the armed forces. Distribution of economic activity is based on the 1980 industrial classification from 1984; previously the 1970 classification was used.

For the period 1961–69, figures are based on the 1960 industrial classification; for 1946–61 (first line) they are based on the 1948 industrial classification.

Figures from 1931 are at June 1 each year.

For 1921–30, figures are estimated by using employment by industry indices except for agriculture.

Table C.8 Labour market: other indicators

Sources: **5, 7, 10, 16, 18**

Average weekly hours worked: figures relate to hourly rated wage earners in manufacturing. The figure for 1983 is a ten-month average; otherwise annual averages are used. Before 1983 only wage earners in establishments with 20 or more employees are included.

For 1926–45 (first line), figures are for average hours worked by employed persons in non-agricultural activities.

For 1890–1910, estimates are taken from 5; the figures include manufacturing and certain construction and hand trades.

Average weekly earnings: earnings per hour of employees paid by the hour in manufacturing. The figure for 1983 is a ten-month average; otherwise annual averages. See note to hours worked on coverage of establishments. Figures for 1934–49 include males only in manufacturing. For 1934–45 the data refer to one week in the month of highest employment of all establishments covered by the annual census of manufactures. In 1946 and 1947 data are for the last week in November and in 1948 and 1949, the last week in October. Figures for 1917–33 are average annual earnings in manufacturing industries, male and female production workers, roughly adjusted by the author to a weekly rate.

For 1890–1910 the coverage is the same as for hours worked.

Unemployment: OECD data from 1964, annual averages. For 1946–63, data are taken from 14, annual averages.

For 1921–45, data are taken from 9 and for 1890–1920, estimates of numbers unemployed are taken from 5.

The percentage figure is currently the ratio of the unemployed to the total labour force.

Industrial disputes: numbers refer to strikes and lockouts beginning in the year shown, all industries.

The number of workers involved and days lost include industrial disputes in existence during the year.

Table C.9 Public finance

Sources: **1, 3, 7, 9**

Total receipts: total consolidated revenue from all levels of government from 1933. Figures for 1885–1932 are budgetary revenues exclusive of earmarked funds but including tax credits to the Old Age Security Fund. Up to 1905, figures are for years beginning July 1; for 1907–33, years

beginning April 1. The figure for 1906 is for nine months, July 1, 1906–March 31, 1907.

Taxes on persons and companies: from 1933 figures are on a consolidated basis; before this date they are for Federal government taxes only.

Customs and excise: excise duties include those on tobacco and alcohol.

Sales tax: data are taken from **9** for 1920–32, for 1934–36 and for alternate years from 1938–45.

Total expenditure: total consolidated expenditure for all levels of government from 1933.

For the period 1885–1932, Federal government expenditure exclusive of debt repayments.

Up to 1906 the figures are for years ending June 30; thereafter years beginning April 1. Data are taken from **9**.

Defence expenditure: the figures are for Federal government from 1885–1932, for 1934–36 and for alternate years from 1938–45.

Social services: includes health expenditure, old age security, unemployment benefit and family allowances.

Debt interest: intergovernment interest payments have not been eliminated entirely.

Data for 1984–86 are estimated.

Table C.10 Value of exports and imports by country

Sources: **1, 7, 9**

Total imports and exports: exports include re-exports. From 1946 non-commercial and special transactions are excluded. Figures refer to calendar years from 1919. For the period 1908–19 they are for fiscal years ending March 31 of the year shown; the 1907 figure is for nine months. Figures for 1885–1906 are for years ending June 30 of the year shown.

Country classification: exports are domestic exports only. Calendar years are used from 1932; years ending March 31 for 1907–31 (the second figure for 1931 is for nine months); years ending June 30 for 1885–1906.

FRANCE

CONTENTS

Table F.1 Gross domestic product at current prices, 1930–87

	Consumers' expenditure	Government current expenditure	Gross fixed capital formation	Value of physical change in stocks	Exports of goods & services	Imports of goods & services	Gross domestic product at market prices
				Fr bn			
1930	...	...	...	...	...	...	**2·67**
1931	...	...	...	...	...	...	**2·52**
1932	...	...	...	...	...	...	**2·27**
1933	...	...	...	...	...	...	**2·19**
1934	...	...	...	...	...	...	**1·96**
1935	...	...	...	...	...	...	**1·93**
1936	...	...	...	...	...	...	**2·21**
1937	...	...	...	...	...	...	**2·66**
1938	3·31	0·57	0·59		0·48	−0·49	**3·27** / **4·46**
1949	59·37	9·92	17·90		12·76	−12·79	**87·16**
1950	67·69	12·39	19·82		16·19	−15·26	**100·83**
	64·8	12·4	17·8	6·1	14·6	−14·2	**101·5**
1951	80·3	16·2	23·1	5·4	19·7	−20·3	**124·4**
1952	93·3	21·4	26·8	6·1	20·3	−21·5	**146·4**
1953	97·6	22·7	26·8	5·0	20·5	−20·0	**152·6**
1954	102·8	22·1	28·9	6·0	22·4	−20·5	**161·7**
1955	110·4	22·2	33·0	5·2	23·7	−21·7	**172·8**
1956	122·6	26·7	37·4	8·6	23·7	−26·9	**192·1**
1957	138·2	29·9	44·3	7·0	26·5	−30·0	**215·9**
1958	156·8	32·3	50·9	9·8	30·5	−31·8	**248·5**
1959	170·2	36·7	55·4	6·1	37·7	−33·6	**272·6**
1960	179·6	42·8	62·7	8·4	43·6	−37·4	**300·7**
1961	196·7	47·2	72·2	5·4	46·0	−40·0	**328·0**
1962	219·7	53·2	81·3	7·9	47·3	−43·9	**366·2**
1963	248·2	60·3	94·4	5·9	52·1	−50·6	**410·6**
1964	271·1	66·2	108·4	10·3	57·9	−58·7	**455·4**
1965	289·2	70·4	118·7	7·4	65·3	−60·9	**490·3**
1966	312·8	75·4	130·7	10·1	71·0	−69·5	**530·7**
1967	338·7	81·3	142·0	9·7	75·9	−74·3	**573·3**
1968	369·6	92·2	151·2	10·6	82·7	−82·9	**623·1**
1969	419·6	103·8	173·2	17·6	100·2	−104·0	**710·5**
1970	459·6	116·6	192·9	20·2	125·4	−121·2	**793·5**
1971	511·1	131·9	218·3	13·3	145·2	−135·6	**884·2**
1972	570·3	146·8	244·5	16·1	165·1	−154·9	**987·9**
1973	645·0	167·7	285·2	22·1	198·6	−188·7	**1,129·8**
1974	749·6	200·2	336·1	30·1	269·6	−282·7	**1,303·0**
1975	862·3	243·4	354·3	−9·7	279·8	−262·3	**1,467·9**
1976	993·5	287·8	407·2	24·5	332·9	−345·4	**1,700·5**
1977	1,117·1	329·5	439·3	29·5	392·9	−390·5	**1,917·8**
1978	1,264·0	383·7	488·4	17·4	445·5	−416·4	**2,182·6**
1979	1,442·0	436·7	555·1	32·5	526·9	−512·1	**2,481·1**
1980	1,653·3	509·3	645·8	34·3	604·4	−638·8	**2,808·3**
1981	1,907·2	595·0	700·5	−7·5	714·3	−744·8	**3,164·8**
1982	2,200·8	701·3	774·3	18·8	790·4	−859·5	**3,626·0**
1983	2,435·5	782·1	809·6	−14·1	900·7	−907·4	**4,006·5**
1984	2,651·3	854·3	840·4	−12·4	1,053·3	−1,025·0	**4,361·9**
1985	2,869·0	911·5	902·9	−19·4	1,123·9	−1,093·0	**4,695·0**
1986	3,045·5	965·3	960·1	12·1	1,074·6	−1,022·6	**5,034·9**
1987	3,220·2	1,008·1	1,024·1	30·8	1,099·8	−1,094·3	**5,288·7**

Table F.2 Gross domestic product at constant prices, 1930–87

	Consumers' expenditure	Government current expenditure	Gross fixed capital formation	Value of physical change in stocks	Exports of goods & services	Imports of goods & services	Gross domestic product at market prices
				Fr bn, 1980 prices			
1930	...	...	...	...	...	...	**647·2**
1931	...	...	...	...	...	...	**620·6**
1932	...	...	...	...	...	...	**594·1**
1933	...	...	...	...	...	...	**620·6**
1934	...	...	...	...	...	...	**620·6**
1935	...	...	...	...	...	...	**600·5**
1936	...	...	...	...	...	...	**607·4**
1937	...	...	...	...	...	...	**640·8**
1938	431·3	201·5	76·1	6·4	44·2	−71·9	**640·8**
1946	...	...	...	...	...	...	**533·6**
1947	...	...	...	...	...	...	**580·9**
1948	...	...	...	...	...	...	**667·3**
1949	416·3	171·0	134·7	13·2	54·1	−75·0	**700·2**
1950	441·1	177·8	135·9	15·4	70·2	−77·6	**755·6**
1951	473·5	191·6	143·5	12·1	81·0	−87·7	**799·5**
1952	491·9	222·6	138·3	13·2	77·0	−93·8	**826·4**
1953	513·3	227·2	139·0	10·3	78·7	−92·7	**847·2**
1954	533·0	214·0	150·7	12·5	87·3	−96·7	**882·6**
1955	565·1	207·4	170·4	10·4	91·8	−103·2	**923·8**
1956	600·2	229·3	184·9	15·8	87·5	−123·7	**978·7**
1957	641·7	236·9	202·5	12·8	92·1	−127·3	**1,037·3**
1958	649·7	226·7	214·2	15·8	98·9	−126·3	**1,067·6**
1959	666·1	240·2	221·0	9·6	112·2	−123·9	**1,101·3**
1960	696·9	244·5	237·9	25·1	134·0	−140·4	**1,180·3**
1961	738·4	256·2	263·8	16·9	140·8	−150·1	**1,245·3**
1962	790·5	268·3	286·1	21·2	143·3	−160·2	**1,328·3**
1963	845·1	277·4	311·3	15·3	153·5	−182·7	**1,399·4**
1964	892·6	288·9	343·9	28·3	163·7	−210·4	**1,490·6**
1965	928·4	298·2	367·9	18·7	182·5	−215·1	**1,561·8**
1966	973·3	306·3	394·6	27·4	194·6	−237·8	**1,643·2**
1967	1,022·9	319·3	418·4	23·7	208·7	−257·5	**1,720·3**
1968	1,063·6	337·2	441·6	26·7	228·4	−290·7	**1,793·5**
1969	1,127·8	351·1	482·0	44·2	264·3	−347·5	**1,918·9**
1970	1,175·8	365·8	504·3	45·2	306·9	−369·2	**2,028·9**
1971	1,233·9	380·2	540·9	28·2	335·3	−392·6	**2,125·9**
1972	1,294·7	393·6	573·5	27·2	375·7	−444·6	**2,220·1**
1973	1,363·7	406·9	622·1	40·1	416·1	−507·9	**2,340·9**
1974	1,380·2	411·9	630·0	56·4	452·9	−517·7	**2,413·7**
1975	1,419·5	429·9	589·4	−9·5	445·3	−467·5	**2,407·0**
1976	1,488·6	447·8	608·6	31·4	481·7	−549·0	**2,509·1**
1977	1,529·4	458·5	597·6	36·9	517·1	−549·6	**2,589·0**
1978	1,585·9	482·1	610·1	16·9	547·7	−566·0	**2,676·6**
1979	1,633·8	496·7	629·3	38·5	588·5	−623·3	**2,763·4**
1980	1,653·3	509·3	645·8	34·3	604·4	−638·8	**2,808·3**
1981	1,687·2	525·2	633·6	−5·8	626·6	−625·5	**2,841·3**
1982	1,745·5	545·0	624·9	23·8	616·1	−641·7	**2,913·7**
1983	1,761·6	556·5	602·6	−1·0	638·8	−624·5	**2,933·9**
1984	1,780·5	563·0	586·9	−0·14	683·5	−641·3	**2,972·5**
1985	1,821·7	575·9	603·3	−5·0	694·8	−669·0	**3,021·7**
1986	1,883·7	590·8	620·6	17·8	689·9	−718·1	**3,084·6**
1987	1,931·5	604·7	643·6	36·1	707·9	−772·1	**3,151·8**

Table F.3   Industrial production, index and selected indicators, 1885–1987

	Industrial production	Coal	Crude steel	Cars & commercial vehicles	Crude petroleum	Natural gas	Electricity
	Index nos., 1980 = 100	mn tons	mn tons	'000	'000 tons	mn m³	bn kwh
1885	10·9	19·5	0·55	—	—	—	—
1886	11·1	19·9	0·43	—	—	—	—
1887	11·2	21·3	0·49	—	—	—	—
1888	11·6	22·6	0·59	—	—	—	—
1889	12·2	24·3	0·63	—	—	—	—
1890	12·0	26·1	0·68	—	—	—	—
1891	12·6	26·0	0·78	—	—	—	—
1892	13·3	26·2	0·83	—	—	—	—
1893	12·9	25·7	0·79	—	—	—	—
1894	13·1	27·4	0·82	—	—	—	—
1895	12·4	28·0	0·88	—	—	—	—
1896	13·5	29·2	1·18	—	—	—	—
1897	13·9	30·8	1·33	—	—	—	—
1898	14·3	32·4	1·4	—	—	—	—
1899	14·9	32·9	1·5	—	—	—	—
1900	14·2	33·4	1·6	—	—	—	—
1901	13·4	32·3	1·4	—	—	—	0·34
1902	14·0	30·0	1·6	—	—	—	0·37
1903	14·2	34·9	1·8	—	—	—	0·43
1904	14·8	34·2	2·1	—	—	—	0·48
1905	15·2	35·9	2·3	14	—	—	0·53
1906	15·6	34·2	2·5	. . .	—	—	0·60
1907	16·6	36·8	2·8	. . .	—	—	0·67
1908	16·6	37·4	2·7	. . .	—	—	0·75
1909	17·8	37·8	3·0	. . .	—	—	0·85
1910	19·2	38·4	3·4	38	—	—	1·02
1911	19·8	39·2	3·8	. . .	—	—	1·23
1912	21·6	41·1	4·4	. . .	—	—	1·48
1913	21·6	40·8	4·7	45	—	—	1·80
1914	. . .	27·5	2·8	. . .	—	—	2·15
1915	. . .	19·5	1·1	. . .	—	—	1·90
1916	. . .	21·3	1·8	. . .	—	—	2·18
1917	. . .	28·9	2·0	. . .	—	—	2·40
1918	. . .	26·3	1·8	. . .	—	—	2·70
1919	12·3	22·4	1·3 / 2·2	. . .	47	—	2·90
1920	13·3	25·3	2·7	40	55	—	3·50 / 5·80
1921	11·9	29·0	3·1	55	56	—	6·50
1922	16·8	31·9	4·5	75	70	—	7·30
1923	19·0	38·6	5·2	110	70	—	8·17
1924	23·3	45·0	6·7	145	74	—	9·95
1925	23·1	48·1	7·5	177	65	—	11·14
1926	27·1	52·5	8·6	192	67	—	12·44
1927	23·7	52·9	8·3	191	73	—	12·58
1928	23·9	52·4	9·5	223	74	—	14·25
1929	26·3	55·0	9·7	254	75	—	15·60
1930	26·3	55·1	9·4	232	76	—	16·85
1931	22·7	51·0	7·8	201	74	—	15·67
1932	19·4	47·3	5·6	164	75	—	14·95
1933	21·2	48·0	6·6	189	79	—	16·40
1934	19·8	48·7	6·2	181	78	—	16·74
1935	19·0	47·1	6·3	165	76	—	17·47
1936	20·4	46·2	6·7	204	70	—	18·47
1937	21·6	45·4	7·9	202	70	—	20·08
1938	19·8	47·6	6·1	227	72	—	20·80
1939	. . .	50·2	8·0	. . .	70	—	22·10
1940	. . .	41·0	4·4	. . .	. . .	—	20·68
1941	. . .	43·9	4·3	55	58	—	20·28

	Industrial production	Coal	Crude steel	Cars & commercial vehicles	Crude petroleum	Natural gas	Electricity
	Index nos., 1980 = 100	mn tons	mn tons	'000	'000 tons	mn m³	bn kwh
1942	12·1	43·8	4·5	39	65	3	20·03
1943	10·7	42·4	5·1	19	68	46	21·07
1944	7·5	26·6	3·1	10	59	66	16·03
1945	9·9	35·0	1·7	35	29	85	18·37
1946	16·6	49·3	4·4	95	52	110	22·83
1947	19·6	47·3	5·7	136	50	147	25·81
1948	22·4	45·1	7·2	198	52	174	28·85
1949	24·1	53·0	9·2	286	58	228	29·93
1950	25·3	52·5	8·7	357	128	246	33·03
1951	28·3	55·0	9·8	447	291	282	38·15
1952	28·7	57·4	10·9	500	350	258	40·57
1953	28·9	54·5	10·0	498	367	233	41·46
1954	31·4	56·3	10·6	600	505	251	45·57
1955	34·0	57·4	12·6	725	878	256	49·63
1956	37·2	57·4	13·4	828	1,264	306	53·83
1957	40·3	59·1	14·1	928	1,410	439	57·43
1958	42·1	60·0	14·6	1,128	1,386	682	61·60
1959	43·5	59·8	15·2	1,283	1,618	1,645	64·51
1960	47·9	58·2	17·3	1,370	1,977	2,846	72·12
1961	50·2	55·3	17·6	1,245	2,163	4,010	76·49
1962	54·0	55·2	17·2	1,537	2,370	4,740	83·09
1963	55·2	50·2	17·6	1,737	2,522	4,861	88·25
1964	60·1	55·3	19·8	1,615	2,846	5,090	93·78
1965	61·3	54·0	19·6	1,616	2,988	5,048	101·44
1966	65·5	50·3	19·6	2,024	2,932	5,161	106·11
1967	67·1	47·6	19·7	2,010	2,832	5,563	111·64
1968	69·4	41·9	20·4	2,076	2,688	5,682	117·92
1969	77·1	40·6	22·5	2,459	2,496	6,506	131·52
1970	81·3	37·8	23·8	2,740	2,309	6,880	140·71
1971	85·6	33·0	22·8	3,010	1,861	7,149	149·00
1972	87·8	32·7	24·1	3,317	1,486	7,512	163·57
1973	93·5	28·5	25·3	3,581	1,254	7,536	174·70
1974	95·1	25·7	27·0	3,447	1,080	7,632	180·67
1975	89·4	25·6	21·5	3,287	1,028	7,356	178·51
1976	95·1	25·1	23·2	3,828	1,057	7,632	194·87
1977	95·9	24·4	22·1	3,998	1,037	8,924	202·56
1978	96·7	22·4	22·8	4,067	1,117	9,169	217·29
1979	100·0	21·1	23·4	4,184	1,197	9,037	231·06
1980	100·0	20·7	23·2	3,994	1,416	7,701	246·67
1981	99	21·5	21·3	3,426	1,676	7,386	264·54
1982	98	20·0	18·4	3,533	1,644	6,853	266·46
1983	98	19·6	17·6	3,560	1,656	7,912	288·37
1984	99	19·0	19·0	3,334	2,064	6,580	309·81
1985	99	17·1	19·0	3,244	2,652	5,781	328·57
1986	100	16·3	17·8	3,194	2,952	4,388	. . .
1987	102	13·5	17·7	3,493	3,240	5,495	. . .

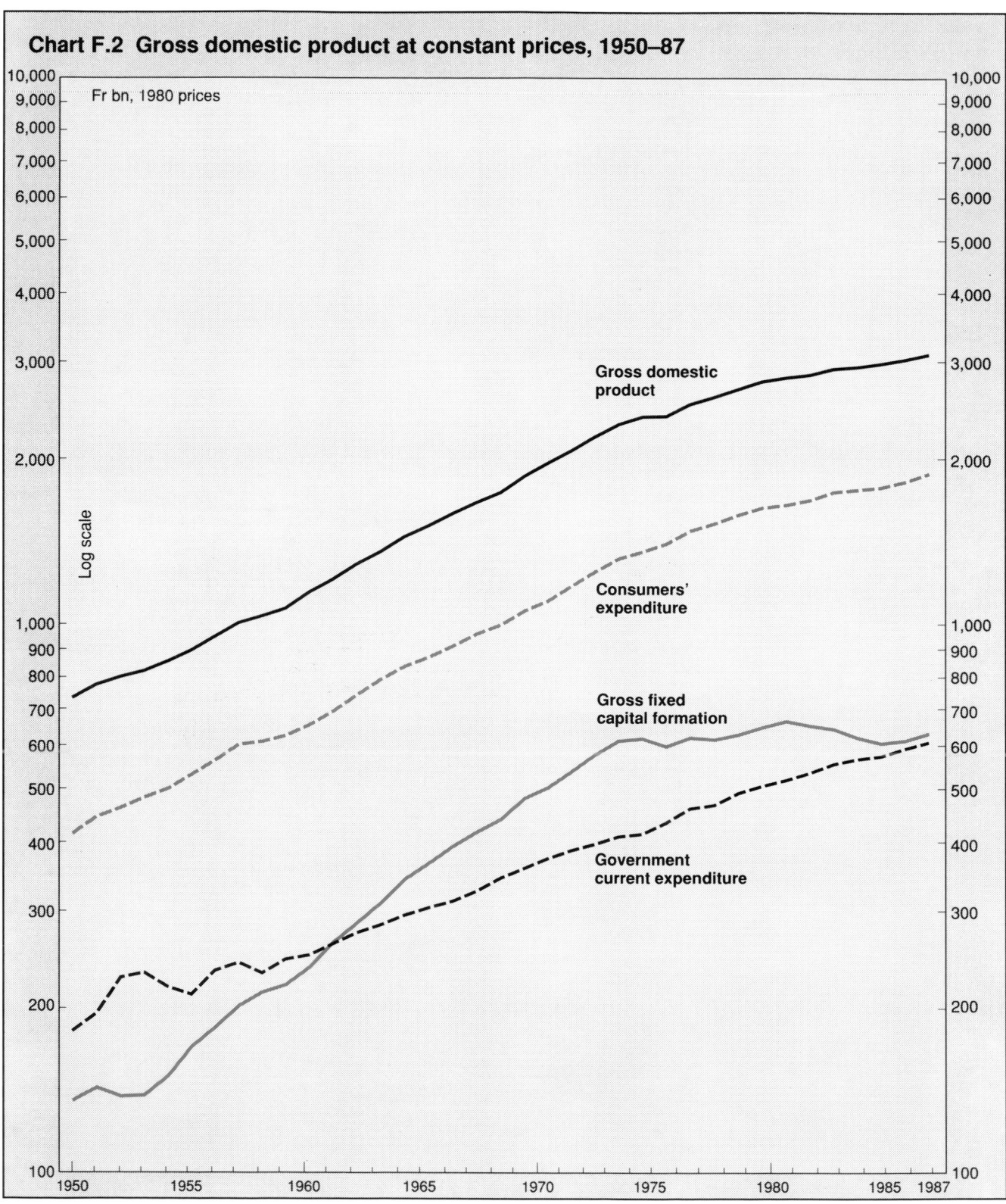

Chart F.2 Gross domestic product at constant prices, 1950–87

Fr bn, 1980 prices

Log scale

Gross domestic product

Consumers' expenditure

Gross fixed capital formation

Government current expenditure

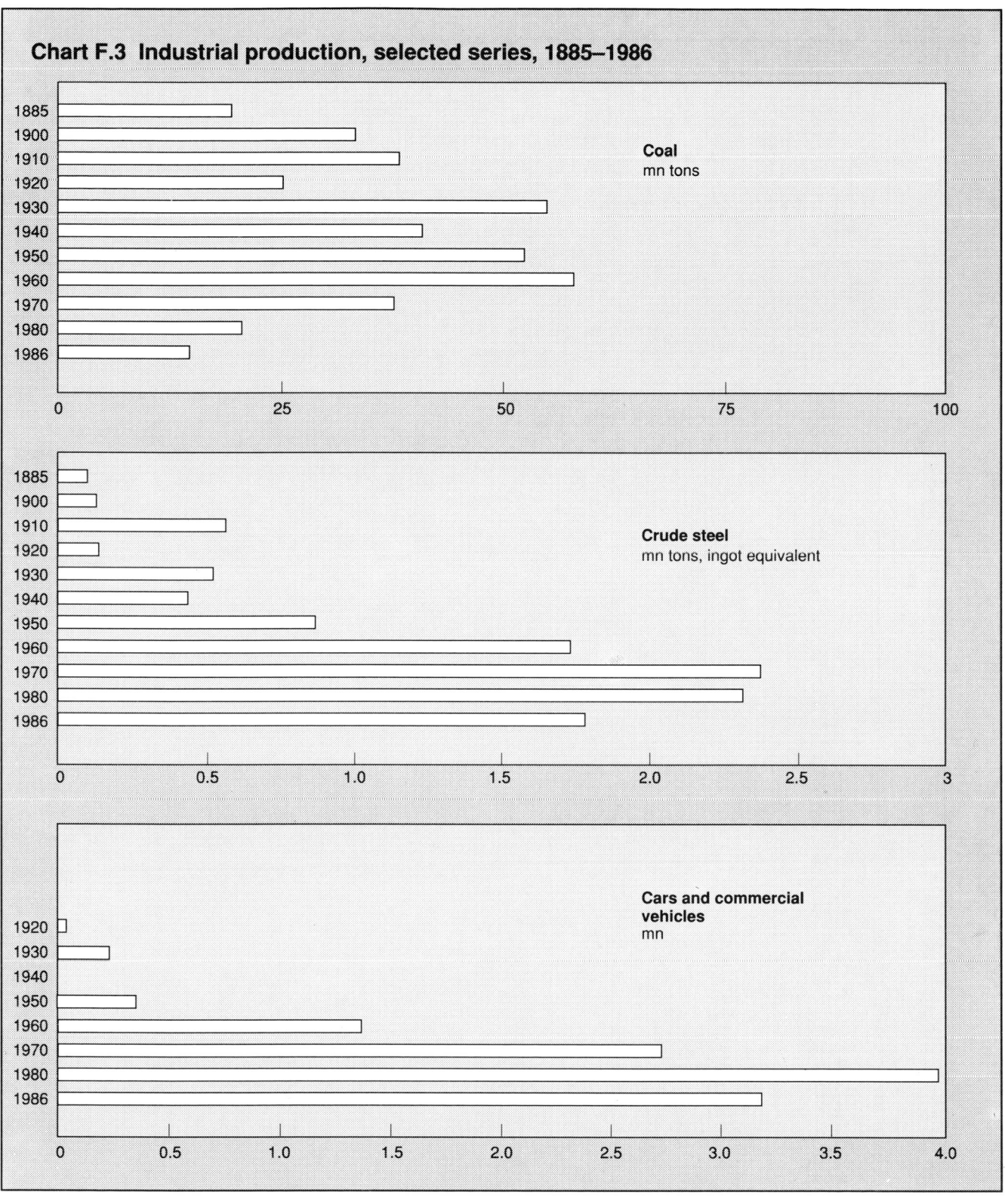

Chart F.3 Industrial production, selected series, 1885–1986

Coal
mn tons

1885	
1900	
1910	
1920	
1930	
1940	
1950	
1960	
1970	
1980	
1986	

0 · 25 · 50 · 75 · 100

Crude steel
mn tons, ingot equivalent

1885	
1900	
1910	
1920	
1930	
1940	
1950	
1960	
1970	
1980	
1986	

0 · 0.5 · 1.0 · 1.5 · 2.0 · 2.5 · 3

Cars and commercial vehicles
mn

1920	
1930	
1940	
1950	
1960	
1970	
1980	
1986	

0 · 0.5 · 1.0 · 1.5 · 2.0 · 2.5 · 3.0 · 3.5 · 4.0

183

Table F.4 Prices and income, 1885–1987

	Consumer prices		Wholesale prices		Export prices	Import prices	Compensation of employees	National income
	All items	Food	All items	Raw materials				
	Index nos., 1980 = 100						Fr bn	
1885	0·12	...	0·13	...	...	...	...	...
1886	0·12	...	0·13	...	...	...	...	...
1887	0·12	...	0·12	...	...	...	...	...
1888	0·12	...	0·13	...	...	...	...	...
1889	0·12	...	0·13	...	...	...	...	...
1890	0·12	...	0·13	...	...	...	...	...
1891	0·12	...	0·13	...	...	...	...	...
1892	0·12	...	0·13	...	...	...	...	...
1893	0·12	...	0·12	...	...	...	...	...
1894	0·12	...	0·11	...	...	...	...	...
1895	0·12	...	0·11	...	...	...	...	...
1896	0·12	...	0·11	...	...	...	...	...
1897	0·12	...	0·11	...	...	...	...	...
1898	0·12	...	0·11	...	...	...	...	...
1899	0·12	...	0·12	...	...	...	...	...
1900	0·12	...	0·13	...	...	...	...	...
1901	0·12	...	0·12	...	...	...	...	...
1902	0·12	...	0·12	...	...	...	...	...
1903	0·12	...	0·12	...	...	...	...	...
1904	0·12	...	0·12	...	...	...	...	...
1905	0·12	...	0·13	...	...	...	...	...
1906	0·12	...	0·13	...	...	...	...	...
1907	0·12	...	0·14	...	...	...	...	...
1908	0·12	...	0·13	...	...	...	...	...
1909	0·12	...	0·13	...	...	...	...	...
1910	0·12	...	0·14	...	...	...	...	...
1911	0·13	...	0·15	...	...	...	...	...
1912	0·13	...	0·15	...	...	...	...	...
1913	0·13	...	0·15	...	...	...	0·16	0·36
1914	0·13	...	0·15	...	...	...	...	...
1915	0·15	...	0·21	...	...	...	...	...
1916	0·18	...	0·28	...	...	...	...	...
1917	0·21	...	0·40	...	...	...	...	...
1918	0·27	...	0·51	...	...	...	...	...
1919	0·34	...	0·54	...	...	...	...	...
1920	0·47	...	0·77	...	...	...	0·57	...
1921	0·41	...	0·52	...	...	...	0·59	1·26
1922	0·39	...	0·49	...	...	...	0·58	1·31
1923	0·44	...	0·63	...	...	...	0·63	1·47
1924	0·50	...	0·74	...	...	...	0·74	1·70
1925	0·53	...	0·83	...	...	...	0·80	1·89
1926	0·69	...	1·06	...	...	...	0·93	2·29
1927	0·72	...	0·93	...	...	...	0·95	2·31
1928	0·72	...	0·94	0·97	...	...	1·03	2·50
1929	0·77	0·87	0·92	0·94	...	...	1·16	2·70
1930	0·78	0·87	0·80	0·79	...	...	1·22	2·67
1931	0·75	0·87	0·68	0·61	...	...	1·17	2·52
1932	0·68	0·65	0·61	0·48	...	...	1·08	2·27
1933	0·65	0·65	0·58	0·48	...	...	...	2·19
1934	0·63	0·65	0·54	0·45	...	...	...	1·96
1935	0·58	0·65	0·51	0·45	...	...	0·87	1·93
1936	0·62	0·87	0·60	0·51	...	...	0·98	2·21
1937	0·78	0·87	0·83	0·68	...	...	1·20	2·66
1938	0·88	0·87	0·95	0·85	...	...	1·8	3·6
1939	0·94	0·87	0·95	0·85	...	...	...	...
1940	1·1	1·1	1·3	1·71	...	...	...	...
1941	1·3	1·3	1·6	1·99	...	...	...	...
1942	1·6	1·5	1·9	1·99	...	...	...	...
1943	2·0	2·0	2·2	2·85	...	...	...	...
1944	2·4	2·4	2·4	4·84	...	...	...	...

Table F.4 (Continued)   Prices and income, 1885–1987

	Consumer prices		Wholesale prices		Export prices	Import prices	Compensation of employees	National income
	All items	Food	All items	Raw materials				
	Index nos., 1980 = 100						Fr bn	
1945	3·5	3·3	3·5	6·83	...	...	...	...
1946	5·4	5·7	6·0	13·9	...	...	11·3	26·0
1947	8·1	9·4	9·1	17·1	...	...	16·8	33·0
1948	12·8	14·8	15·7	21·4	...	...	28·0	54·3
1949	14·4	15·9	17·5	32·2	...	...	34·9	65·4
1950	15·8	17·4	18·9	30·2	...	...	40·3	90·4
1951	18·5	20·3	24·2	28·5	...	...	51·6	109·9
1952	20·7	22·2	25·3	27·3	...	...	62·2	129·2
1953	20·3	21·8	24·2	28·5	24·9	24·0	65·0	135·4
1954	20·3	21·2	23·7	27·9	23·5	23·8	70·6	144·1
1955	20·5	21·5	23·7	28·5	23·7	23·4	76·6	155·0
1956	21·5	21·8	24·7	29·8	24·9	24·4	86·5	172·7
1957	22·1	22·4	26·2	31·0	26·5	26·6	96·8	194·2
1958	25·4	26·4	29·2	31·7	29·2	27·9	110·9	224·1
1959	27·0	27·0	30·6	34·2	31·5	30·6	121·5 / 119·8	244·4 / 241·2
1960	28·0	27·7	31·3	35·2	32·9	31·7	133·8	274·2
1961	28·8	28·9	32·0	36·4	32·8	30·9	149·6	298·4
1962	28·8	29·2	32·9	36·4	33·0	30·7	169·1	336·7
1963	30·4	30·7	34·1	37·4	33·4	31·1	192·7	376·6
1964	31·3	32·0	34·6	39·6	34·7	31·7	215·1	419·3
1965	32·2	32·6	35·1	40·1	35·1	32·3	231·9	451·5
1966	33·1	33·5	35·9	41·6	35·9	32·6	250·1	487·8
1967	33·9	33·8	35·6	40·6	35·7	32·4	270·0	526·2
1968	35·5	35·0	36·1	39·6	35·3	31·7	301·8	572·5
1969	37·8	37·0	39·2	45·1	37·8	34·0	345·2	654·5
1970	39·8	39·4	42·8	49·6	41·9	37·5	391·4	724·5
1971	42·2	41·7	43·7	48·1	44·4	38·7	441·5	804·1
1972	44·6	45·3	46·2	49·1	44·9	39·1	493·5	894·4
1973	47·8	49·6	52·1	61·9	49·4	41·9	566·4	1,021·1
1974	54·6	55·5	64·4	82·4	61·7	61·1	678·9	1,168·8
1975	60·9	62·2	65·0	67·8	65·2	61·5	801·8	1,306·7
1976	66·9	68·5	71·7	76·6	71·2	67·9	932·9	1,510·9
1977	72·9	77·2	76·6	82·7	78·2	75·9	1,061·2	1,699·6
1978	79·7	83·5	80·1	84·0	82·2	76·6	1,203·1	1,934·3
1979	88·0	91·3	89·8	94·9	90·1	84·4	1,363·2	2,197·3
1980	100·0	100·0	100·0	100·0	100·0	100·0	1,575·8	2,475·0
1981	113·4	114·0	111	111·1	113·0	117·8	1,792·6	2,777·9
1982	126·8	128·4	123	119·0	129·0	132·6	2,054·6	3,171·4
1983	139·0	140·3	137	...	142·0	142·9	2,259·3	3,486·3
1984	149·3	151·4	155	...	158·8	157·8	2,425·8	3,786·8
1985	158·0	158·9	161	...	166·3	161·0	2,581·1	4,078·8
1986	162·2	164·4	...	...	...	...	2,696·1	4,388·9
1987	167·3	167·3	...	...	...	...	2,801·6	4,605·0

Table **F.5** Population, 1881–1986

	Total population	Males	Females	Births	Under 15	15–64	65 & over
					Age distribution		
	mn			'000	mn		
1881	37·41	18·66	18·75	937	10·00	24·38	3·03
1886	37·93	18·90	19·03	913	10·23	24·65	3·05
1891	38·13	18·93	19·20	866	10·01	24·96	3·16
1896	38·27	18·92	19·35	866	9·94	25·13	3·20
1901	38·49	18·94	19·55	857	9·89	25·34	3·25
1906	38·84	19·10	19·75	807	9·99	25·55	3·30
1911	39·23	19·25	19·94	742	9·99	25·88	3·37
1921	38·78	18·45	20·35	812	8·69	26·52	3·57
1926	40·22	19·31	20·92	768	8·92	27·51	3·74
1931	41·26	19·93	21·33	734	9·34	27·97	3·94
1936	41·19	19·80	21·39	631	10·07	27·00	4·13
1946	40·13	19·12	21·01	840	8·59	27·10	4·44
1947	40·45	19·30	21·15	867	8·72	27·20	4·52
1948	40·91	19·59	21·32	867	8·94	27·31	4·60
1949	41·31	19·81	21·50	869	9·17	27·38	4·69
1950	41·65	20·00	21·64	858	9·38	27·45	4·73
	41·84	20·11	21·72		9·50	27·58	4·76
1951	42·16	20·29	21·87	823	9·72	27·62	4·81
1952	42·46	20·45	22·01	819	9·94	27·66	4·86
1953	42·75	20·61	22·14	801	10·15	27·69	4·91
1954	43·06	20·78	22·28	807	10·36	27·73	4·96
1955	43·43	20·97	22·46	802	10·62	27·79	5·02
1956	43·84	21·19	22·66	803	10·94	27·84	5·06
1957	44·31	21·44	22·88	813	11·27	27·94	5·11
1958	44·79	21·69	23·10	809	11·55	28·07	5·17
1959	45·24	21·93	23·31	826	11·80	28·19	5·25
1960	45·68	22·16	23·52	816	12·05	28·32	5·32
1961	46·16	22·52	23·75	835	12·20	28·55	5·41
1962	47·00	22·85	24·15	829	12·32	29·14	5·54
1963	47·85	22·31	24·55	865	12·41	29·78	5·66
1964	48·41	23·62	24·79	874	12·44	30·20	5·77
1965	48·76	23·74	25·02	862	12·48	30·37	5·91
1966	49·16	23·94	25·23	860	12·51	30·62	6·04
1967	49·55	24·13	25·42	838	12·52	30·84	6·18
1968	49·92	24·32	25·60	833	12·54	31·06	6·31
1969	50·32	24·54	25·78	840	12·57	31·33	6·42
1970	50·77	24·79	25·98	848	12·61	31·63	6·54
1971	51·25	25·05	26·20	879	12·66	31·94	6·66
1972	51·70	25·29	26·41	875	12·77	32·22	6·77
1973	52·12	25·52	26·60	855	12·74	32·50	6·88
1974	52·46	25·70	26·76	799	12·70	32·77	6·99
1975	52·70	25·81	26·89	745	12·61	32·99	7·10
1976	52·91	25·89	27·02	720	12·51	33·21	7·19
1977	53·15	25·99	27·15	745	12·39	33·46	7·29
1978	53·38	26·09	27·29	737	12·28	33·70	7·40
1979	53·61	26·19	27·42	757	12·15	33·96	7·49
1980	53·88	26·31	27·57	800	12·06	34·32	7·50
1981	54·18	26·46	27·73	806	12·00	34·80	7·39
1982	54·48	26·60	27·88	797	11·95	35·28	7·26
1983	54·73	26·71	28·02	749	11·88	35·70	7·15
1984	54·95	26·80	28·15	760	11·79	36·08	7·08
1985	55·17	26·90	28·27	768	11·70	36·33	7·14
1986	55·39	27·00	28·39	778	11·60	36·48	7·32

Table F.6 Education, 1885–1985

| | Kindergarten | Elementary | Secondary | | Higher education | |
| | | | 1st cycle | 2nd cycle | Total | *of which:* Female |
	No. of pupils '000				No. of students '000	
1885	735	5,517	93·0		...	...
1886	742	5,521	94·6		...	...
1887	688	5,617	95·7		...	...
1888	707	5,623	93·0		...	...
1889	707	5,602	91·5		...	...
1890	710	5,594	90·8		...	...
1891	706	5,556	91·9		...	...
1892	709	5,554	94·0		...	...
1893	714	5,548	95·9		...	...
1894	715	5,540	95·9		...	...
1895	720	5,534	96·5		...	...
1896	729	5,532	96·2		...	...
1897	744	5,535	96·2		...	...
1898	752	5,539	95·8		...	...
1899	847	5,530	96·8		29·4	1·0
1900	754	5,526	98·7		29·9	1·0
1901	754	5,550	102		30·4	1·1
1902	706	5,553	107		31·3	1·3
1903	680	5,555	112		32·4	1·6
1904	671	5,568	117		33·6	1·9
1905	661	5,567	120		35·7	2·3
1906	652	5,585	123		38·2	2·6
1907	631	5,600	123		39·9	3·2
1908	628	5,630	124		40·8	3·6
1909	620	5,639	126		41·0	3·8
1910	621	5,655	126		41·2	4·0
1911	620	5,682	128		41·2	3·9
1912	609	5,669	131		41·1	4·1
1913	...	...	133		42·0	4·3
1914	...	...	197		11·2	2·6
1915	...	...	109		12·6	3·2
1916	...	...	118		14·1	3·8
1917	322	4,072	124		19·4	4·5
1918	241	3,893	121		29·9	5·0
1919	227	3,836	140		45·1	6·0
1920	203	3,697 / 4,452	146·2		49·9	7·3
1921	247	4,614	157·9		50·9	8·1
1922	232	4,210	159·9		50·4	8·8
1923	245	3,973	163·8		50·9	9·0
1924	263	3,828	167·6		53·1	10·4
1925	315	3,754	169·8		58·5	12·2
1926	367	3,854	165·7		61·0	13·6
1927	405	3,917	162·9		64·5	15·1
1928	394	4,099	165·5		67·0	16·0
1929	382	4,359	169·5		73·6	18·4
1930	373	4,635	182·9		78·7	20·2
1931	371	4,915	201·8		82·7	21·7
1932	388	5,111	221·4		84·7	22·6
1933	400	5,200	230·9		87·2	23·5
1934	407	5,230	234·6		82·1	22·7
1935	410	5,261	240·2		73·8	20·3
1936	403	5,332	248·4		72·1	20·3
1937	403	5,437	264·2		75·3	21·7
1938	396	5,422	277·3		79·0	24·0
1939	258	5,032	259·2		55·5	21·7
1940	288	4,913	247·2		76·5	25·9
1941	299	4,924	249·0		89·9	30·2
1942	297	4,865	...		105·9	34·6
1943	204	4,666	...		90·7	31·8

Table F.6 (Continued)   Education, 1885–1985

	Kindergarten	Elementary	Secondary		Higher education	
			1st cycle	2nd cycle	Total	*of which:* Female
	No. of pupils '000				No. of students '000	
1944	242	4,576	...	...	97·0	33·7
1945	290	4,746	...	...	123·3	40·2
1946	343	4,702	734	...	129·0	41·6
1947	387	4,635	747	...	128·8	42·7
1948	418	4,882	729	...	129·0	42·8
1949	463	4,669	746	...	136·7	46·6
1950	511 581	4,726	788	...	139·6	47·3
1951	1,226	4,197	797	...	142·1	49·1
1952	1,226	4,440	844	...	147·8	52·7
1953	1,220	4,705	871	...	151·1	53·1
1954	1,271	4,978	922	...	155·8	55·5
1955	1,272	5,295	969	...	157·5	57·1
1956	1,284	5,577	1,065	...	170·0	63·2
1957	1,308	6,313	1,129	...	180·6	66·1
1958	1,297	6,047	1,196	...	192·1	71·6
1959	1,268	5,796	1,265	...	202·1	77·2
1960	1,338	5,901	1,493	...	210·9	85·9
1961	1,399	5,681	1,608	...	232·6	96·8
1962	1,500	5,682	1,715	1,063	270·8	113·5
1963	1,598	5,668	1,560	1,480	308·2	129·8
1964	1,692	5,715	1,693	1,399	348·9	148·7
1965	1,778	5,650	1,901	1,303	393·7	179·6
1966	1,885	5,576	1,976	1,340	459	200·3[a]
1967	1,990	5,496	2,140	1,366	508	230·8[a]
1968	2,040	5,346	2,390	1,409	587	...
1969	2,116	5,218	2,619	1,462	615	...
1970	2,214	5,147	2,771	1,498	661	210·3
1971	2,298	5,042	2,916	1,555	697	...
1972	2,371	5,038	2,977	1,684	717	...
1973	2,455	5,013	2,984	1,747	784	...
1974	2,540	4,976	2,968	1,816	807	...
1975	2,591	4,964	2,989	1,880	849	...
1976	2,599	4,971	3,014	1,929	826	...
1977	2,576	5,034	2,980	1,967	844	...
1978	2,503	5,074	2,958	2,018	863	...
1979	2,412	5,077	2,964	2,042	861	...
1980	2,383	5,017	2,950	2,062	856	...
1981	2,374	4,903	2,961	2,093	882	...
1982	2,407	4,390	3,031	2,104	906	...
1983	2,461	4,557	3,115	2,107	923	...
1984	2,526	4,419	3,180	2,126	953	...
1985	2,563	4,340	3,191	2,184	967	...

a   Including some female students at non-university institutions.

Table F.7 Labour market: employment, 1930–86

	Employed labour force	Agriculture, forestry & fishing	Mining & quarrying	Manufacturing	Construction	Gas, electricity & water	Transport & communication	Distribution & services
				mn				
1930	(8·90)	...		(5·91)	...	...	...	...
1931	(8·24)	...		(5·47)	...	...	...	...
1932	(7·20)	...		(4·78)	...	...	...	...
1933	(7·07)	...		(4·69)	...	...	...	...
1934	(6·85)	...		(4·54)	...	...	...	...
1935	(6·54)	...		(4·34)	...	...	...	...
1936	(6·60)	...		(4·38)	...	...	...	...
1937	(7·00)	...	0·37	3·50	0·70	0·10	0·78	1·70
1938	(7·19)	...		(4·80)	...	...	...	...
1939	(7·28)	...		(4·93)	...	...	...	...
1940	...	...		...	...	...	...	...
1941	(6·44)	...		(4·22)	...	...	...	...
1942	(6·51)	...		(4·46)	...	...	...	...
1943	...	...		(4·23)	...	...	...	...
1944	...	...		(4·23)	...	...	...	...
1945	...	...		(4·28)	...	...	...	...
1946	(7·11)	...	0·45	3·43	0·75	0·11	0·81	1·56
1947	(7·41)	...	0·47	3·66	0·76	0·12	0·82	1·59
1948	(7·53)	...	0·47	3·77	0·78	0·12	0·81	1·60
1949	(7·60)	...	0·44	3·84	0·82	0·12	0·79	1·60
1950	(7·60)	...	0·42	3·86	0·83	0·12	0·76	1·61
1951	(7·70)	...	0·41	3·95	0·86	0·12	0·74	1·63
1952	(7·72)	...	0·41	3·93	0·90	0·12	0·72	1·64
1953	(7·65)	...	0·39	3·87	0·92	0·12	0·71	1·64
1954	(7·67)	...	0·39	3·88	0·95	0·12	0·69	1·65
1954	18·70	5·21	0·39	5·02	1·36	0·15	0·99	5·58
1955	18·72	5·04	0·38	5·04	1·43	0·15	0·99	5·69
1956	18·74	4·85	0·37	5·10	1·47	0·16	0·99	5·78
1957	18·87	4·64	0·37	5·25	1·53	0·16	1·01	5·89
1958	18·82	4·45	0·37	5·29	1·52	0·17	1·02	6·00
1959	18·67	4·34	0·36	5·21	1·53	0·17	1·03	6·04
1960	18·71	4·19	0·35	5·24	1·55	0·18	1·04	6·16
1961	18·72	4·04	0·33	5·29	1·58	0·18	1·05	6·25
1962	18·82	3·88	0·32	5·35	1·57	0·15	1·09	6·60
1963	19·13	3·74	0·31	5·49	1·66	0·15	1·13	6·81
1964	19·42	3·60	0·30	5·60	1·76	0·15	1·16	7·00
1965	19·54	3·47	0·28	5·37	1·84	0·15	1·15	7·28
1966	19·69	3·34	0·27	5·40	1·88	0·16	1·16	7·48
1967	19·76	3·22	0·26	5·37	1·90	0·16	1·17	7·69
1968	19·73	3·07	0·24	5·29	1·92	0·16	1·18	7·86
1969	20·04	2·90	0·23	5·44	1·97	0·16	1·20	8·14
1970	20·33	2·75	0·22	5·59	2·00	0·16	1·21	8·39
1971	20·44	2·61	0·21	5·68	1·98	0·16	1·21	8·59
1972	20·57	2·47	0·20	5·75	1·98	0·16	1·22	8·80
1973	20·86	2·35	0·19	5·88	2·00	0·17	1·23	9·04
1974	21·06	2·24	0·18	5·95	2·00	0·17	1·26	9·25
1975	20·86	2·16	0·18	5·80	1·91	0·17	1·26	9·39
1976	21·02	2·08	0·17	5·75	1·90	0·17	1·27	9·68
1977	21·19	2·01	0·16	5·72	1·89	0·18	1·29	9·93
1978	21·26	1·95	0·15	5·64	1·86	0·18	1·31	10·17
1979	21·31	1·91	0·14	5·56	1·84	0·19	1·32	10·35
1980	21·33	1·85	0·14	5·50	1·84	0·19	1·32	10·49
1981	21·20	1·79	0·13	5·32	1·81	0·19	1·32	10·63
1982	21·24	1·73	0·13	5·25	1·76	0·20	1·35	10·82
1983	21·17	1·68	0·13	5·14	1·68	0·21	1·37	10·97
1984	20·98	1·63	0·12	5·00	1·57	0·21	1·38	11·08
1985	20·89	1·58	0·12	4·85	1·52	0·21	1·37	11·26
1986	20·97	1·54	0·11	4·75	1·50	0·21	1·37	11·50

Table F.8 Labour market: other indicators, 1890–1987

	Manufacturing				Industrial disputes		
	Average weekly hrs worked	Average hourly wage rates	Unemployment		Stoppages	Workers involved	Working days lost
		Fr	'000	%		'000	'000
1890	...	...	...	...	313	119	1,340
1891	...	...	...	...	267	109	1,717
1892	...	...	...	...	261	49	918
1893	...	...	...	...	634	170	3,175
1894	...	...	...	...	391	55	1,062
1895	...	...	...	7·0	405	46	617
1896	...	...	...	6·7	476	50	644
1897	...	...	...	6·9	356	69	781
1898	...	...	...	7·3	368	82	1,216
1899	...	...	...	6·6	739	177	3,551
1900	...	...	...	6·8	902	223	3,761
1901	...	...	...	7·8	523	111	1,862
1902	...	...	...	9·9	512	213	4,675
1903	...	...	...	9·4	567	123	2,442
1904	...	...	...	10·2	1,026	271	3,935
1905	...	...	...	9·0	830	178	2,747
1906	...	...	...	7·6	1,309	438	9,439
1907	...	...	...	7·0	1,275	198	3,562
1908	...	...	...	8·6	1,073	99	1,752
1909	...	...	...	7·3	1,025	167	3,560
1910	...	...	...	5·8	1,502	281	4,830
1911	...	...	...	5·7	1,471	231	4,096
1912	...	...	...	5·4	1,116	268	2,318
1913	...	...	...	4·7	1,073	220	2,224
1914	...	...	...	...	672	162	2,187
1915	...	...	...	...	98	9	55
1916	...	...	...	...	314	41	236
1917	...	...	...	...	696	294	1,482
1918	...	...	...	...	499	176	980
1919	...	...	...	...	2,026	1,151	15,478
1920	...	...	13	...	1,832	1,317	23,112
1921	...	...	28	...	475	402	7,027
1922	...	...	13	...	665	290	3,935
1923	...	...	10	...	1,068	331	4,172
1924	...	...	10	...	1,083	275	3,863
1925	...	...	12	...	931	249	2,046
1926	...	...	11	...	1,660	349	4,072
1927	...	...	47	...	396	111	1,046
1928	...	...	16	...	816	204	6,377
1929	...	3·83	10	...	1,213	240	2,765
1930	48·0	4·08	13	...	1,093	582	7,209
1931	46·7	4·08	64	...	286	48	950
1932	43·7	3·99	301	...	362	72	1,244
1933	45·3	3·89	305	...	343	87	1,199
1934	44·7	3·89	368	...	385	101	2,393
1935	44·5	3·80	464	...	376	109	1,182
1936	45·7	4·42	470	...	16,907	2,423	...
1937	40·2	5·60	380	...	2,616	1,133	...
1938	38·7	6·19	402	...	1,220	324	...
1939	40·7	...	418	...	...	...	...
1940	...	...	961	...	...	...	...
1941	...	...	395	...	...	...	...
1942	...	...	124	...	...	...	...
1943	...	...	42	...	...	...	...
1944	...	...	23	...	...	...	...
1945	...	...	68	...	...	...	...
1946	...	...	57	...	528	180	386
1947	...	...	46	...	2,285	2,998	22,673
1948	44·6	66·1	78	...	1,425	6,561	13,133
1949	43·8	73·9	131	1·2	1,426	4,330	7,129

Table F.8 (Continued) Labour market: other indicators, 1890–1987

	Manufacturing		Unemployment		Industrial disputes		
	Average weekly hrs worked	Average hourly wage rates			Stoppages	Workers involved	Working days lost
		Fr	'000	%		'000	'000
1950	44·4	81·4	153	1·4	2,586	1,527	11,729
1951	44·8	104·3	120	1·2	2,514	1,754	3,495
1952	44·2	120·7	132	1·2	1,759	1,155	1,733
1953	44·1	124·2	180	1·5	1,761	1,784	9,722
1954	44·6	131·5	184 / 311	1·5 / 1·6	1,479	1,319	1,440
1955	44·9	141·6	283	1·4	2,672	1,061	3,079
1956	45·6	152·4	212	1·1	2,440	982	1,423
1957	46·1	164·4	161	0·8	2,623	2,964	4,121
1958	45·3	183·8	183	0·9	954	1,112	1,138
1959	45·0	195·1	254	1·3	1,512	940	1,938
1960	45·7	2·09	240	1·2	1,494	1,072	1,070
1961	46·0	2·25	212	1·1	1,963	2,552	2,601
1962	46·2	2·44	230	1·2	1,884	1,472	1,901
1963	46·3	2·65	273	1·4	2,382	2,646	5,991
1964	46·1	2·84	216	1·1	2,281	2,603	2,497
1965	45·6	3·00	236	1·2	1,674	1,237	980
1966	45·9	3·18	326	1·6	1,711	3,341	2,523
1967	45·4	3·37	436	2·1	1,675	2,824	4,204
1968	45·3	3·79	554	2·7	. . .	. . .	. . .
1969	45·4	4·21	484	2·3	2,480	1,444	2,224
1970	44·8	4·66	530	2·5	3,319	1,160	1,742
1971	44·5	5·18	585	2·7	4,358	3,235	4,388
1972	44·0	5·82	611	2·8	3,464	2,721	3,755
1973	43·6	6·92	593	2·7	3,731	2,246	3,915
1974	42·9	8·20	632	2·8	3,381	1,564	3,380
1975	41·7	9·66	901	4·0	3,888	1,827	3,869
1976	41·7	10·94	997	4·4	4,348	2,023	5,011
1977	41·3	12·40	1,134	4·9	3,281	1,920	2,434
1978	41·0	13·98	1,201	5·2	3,195	705	2,081
1979	40·8	15·78	1,361	5·9	3,121	967	3,172
1980	40·7	18·14	1,467	6·3	2,118	501	1,523
1981	40·3	20·72	1,750	7·4	2,405	329	1,442
1982	39·3	23·97	1,923	8·1	3,113	398	2,250
1983	38·9	26·70	1,974	8·3	2,837	456	1,321
1984	38·7	28·86	2,323	9·7	2,537	504	1,317
1985	38·6	31·56	2,442	10·2	1,901	276	727
1986	38·6	33·28	2,489	10·4	1,391	264	568
1987	38·7	34·35	2,532	10·5	1,391	223	512

Table F.9 Public finance, 1885–1986

	Revenue					Expenditure			
	Taxes on personal income	Taxes on companies	Customs & excise	Turnover & transactions taxes	Total receipts	Defence	Education	Social services	Total expenditure
					Fr mn				
1885	402		892	—	3,057	600	168	...	3,467
1886	406		899	—	2,940	582	135	...	3,204
1887	411		914	—	2,968	556	134	...	3,261
1888	415		953	—	3,108	548	134	...	3,221
1889	418		967	—	3,108	566	136	...	3,247
1890	451		967	—	3,229	580	183	...	3,288
1891	444		1,009	—	3,364	709	177	...	3,258
1892	437		1,011	—	3,370	678	169	...	3,380
1893	464		1,017	—	3,366	650	173	...	3,451
1894	468		1,021	—	3,458	648	192	...	3,480
1895	471		975	—	3,416	637	191	...	3,434
1896	475		1,003	—	3,436	646	194	...	3,445
1897	478		1,038	—	3,528	684	201	...	3,524
1898	467		1,102	—	3,620	659	199	...	3,528
1899	479		1,069	—	3,657	664	204	...	3,589
1900	484		1,083	—	3,815	673	205	...	3,747
1901	489		959	—	3,576	727	206	...	3,756
1902	489		922	—	3,582	732	209	...	3,699
1903	495		982	—	3,668	706	217	...	3,597
1904	499		1,015	—	3,739	702	224	...	3,639
1905	505		996	—	3,766	715	236	...	3,707
1906	508		1,068	—	3,837	860	251	...	3,852
1907	516		1,112	—	3,968	822	250	...	3,880
1908	524		1,113	—	3,966	835	268	...	4,021
1909	530		1,149	—	4,141	871	272	...	4,186
1910	536		1,231	—	4,274	915	279	...	4,322
1911	547		1,448	—	4,689	1,015	297	...	4,548
1912	558		1,365	—	4,857	1,088	295	...	4,743
1913	571		1,475	—	5,092	1,262	305	...	5,067
1914	552		1,184	—	4,549	6,048	321	...	10,065
1915	496		1,281	—	4,131	15,988	322	...	20,925
1916	556		1,928	—	5,259	21,610	333	...	28,113
1917	743		2,250	—	6,943	25,686	394	...	35,320
1918	399	114	2,038	—	7,621	29,095	609	...	41,897
1919	636	233	2,894	—	13,282	16,011	1,167	...	39,970
1920	847	480	3,804	1,757	22,502	6,107	1,191	...	39,644
1921	1,768	1,052	4,744	1,927	23,119	5,371	1,248	...	32,845
1922	1,597	1,034	4,774	2,314	23,888	4,747	1,436	...	45,188
1923	2,145	1,650	5,129	3,045	26,224	4,311	1,557	...	38,293
1924	2,932	2,009	5,720	4,120	30,568	4,082	1,585	...	42,511
1925	3,356	3,120	4,160	4,583	33,455	4,344	2,151	...	36,275
1926	3,470	2,527	8,412	7,517	41,902	5,063	2,429	...	41,976
1927	2,916	4,799	10,179	8,645	45,746	7,870	2,795	...	45,869
1928	3,149	4,450	11,409	9,318	48,177	6,162	3,037	...	44,248
1929	3,525	5,109	15,945	12,403	64,268	7,891	4,262	...	59,335
1930	3,397	4,699	13,180	8,744	50,794	10,149	3,786	...	55,712
					Fr bn				
1931	3·4	4·3	14·3	7·6	47·9	7·6	4·0	...	53·2
1932	3·0	3·6	10·0	5·2	36·0	5·1	3·1	...	40·7
1933	2·7	3·0	12·7	6·9	43·5	7·0	4·0	...	54·9
1934	2·7	2·9	11·5	6·4	41·1	5·9	3·1	...	49·9
1935	1·9	2·3	11·4	5·9	39·5	5·9	3·8	...	49·9
1936	2·1	2·2	11·7	6·1	38·7	7·9	4·1	...	55·8
1937	2·9	2·5	12·7	7·0	44·2	11·8	4·6	...	72·8
1938	4·4	3·7	13·9	9·8	54·6	...	...	...	82·3
1939	5·2	4·4	15·6	13·5	63·0	...	...	...	150·1
1940	4·5	4·1	13·8	18·2	72·0	...	...	...	204·0

Table F.9 (Continued)   Public finance, 1885–1986

	Revenue					Expenditure			
	Taxes on personal income	Taxes on companies	Customs & excise	Turnovers & transactions taxes	Total receipts	Defence	Education	Social services	Total expenditure
	Fr bn								
1941	9·4	4·2	9·1	20·9	80·2	...	...	...	121
1942	13·8	9·2	6·3	26·0	97·3	...	...	...	133
1943	18·3	14·3	5·4	37·5	124·3	...	...	...	160
1944	22·7	15·4	4·7	35·1	129·9	...	...	...	259
1945	37·4	13·3	13	66	222·3	...	...	...	465
1946	43·0	27·8	34	153	434·1	151·0	38·6	23·7	521
1947	97·9	83·7	62	230	670·2	203·0	64·6	27·1	690
1948	118·1	98·1	96	396	1,021	283·1	105·3	39·7	992
1949	135·7	123·9	154	625	1,442	312·8	133·5	46·3	1,205
1950	210·0	153·8	198	745	2,077	416·1	155·6	52·5	2,357
1951	237·9	216·3	256	1,008	2,515	807·4	208·3	75·6	2,914
1952	303·9	243·1	284	1,099	2,888	1,256·0	254·3	80·2	3,656
1953	395·3	285·9	307	1,091	3,103	1,289·7	268·1	86·5	3,801
1954	365·4	274·1	324	1,153	3,356	1,197·5	290·9	104·0	3,702
1955	341·0	291·0	380	1,161	3,450	1,085·0	323·7	123·2	3,945
1956	431·9	372·0	453	1,209	3,878	1,394·5	380·7	156·3	4,648
1957	503·2	393	598	1,376	4,985	1,466·6	453·1	151·6	5,640
1958	636·0	522	725	1,531	5,228	1,478·9	557·4	170·4	5,490
1959	796·3	592	777	1,754	6,014	1,632·6	658·1	189·3	5,946
1960	7·3	5·9	8·3	19·6	62·0	16·7	7·1	2·1	60·0
1961	8·7	6·4	11·3	21·6	67·8	17·8	8·5	2·5	66·5
1962	9·7	6·5	12·7	24·3	74·5	18·5	10·7	2·6	76·9
1963	11·4 / 18·2	6·7 / 6·9	14·3	28·3	85·1	18·6	12·8	3·1	90·8
1964	23·0	8·7	16·1	28·8	94·7	19·1	16·2	14·8	104·6
1965	25·1	8·2	16·7	30·2	101·8	20·0	18·5	15·7	112·5
1966	26·8	8·4	17·5	34·0	108·4	24·3	22·7	17·0	120·5
1967	28·4	9·5	18·5	36·0	117·1	25·9	25·9	18·5	133·0
1968	25·3	0·5	17·7	48·6	125·7	27·6	29·0	20·4	147·0
1969	30·5	12·7	20·1	67·3	157·2	29·4	34·0	25·2	171·4
1970	31·9	17·5	22·0	70·3	174·6	30·3	36·9	26·3	180·4
1971	32·7	17·9	23·0	81·0	187·8	32·5	41·9	32·3	196·0
1972	37·5	20·1	25·1	94·1	212·6	35·3	46·4	35·4	216·8
1973	45·2	24·1	28·5	98·1	241·8	37·6	49·9	36·7	204·3
1974	55·4	36·9	29·7	121·8	293·3	41·6	57·0	39·6	238·5
1975	62·5	29·2	30·7	135·9	316·2	48·3	68·3	49·8	269·4
1976	79·9	38·9	34·3	163·3	380·8	55·0	78·3	52·2	305·9
1977	95·4	42·5	40·6	170·0	421·1	63·0	89·6	61·1	347·8
1978	109·2	42·3	49·1	193·9	476·6	72·3	104·0	76·3	412·2
1979	122·4	48·8	62·0	227·6	552·7	82·9	120·4	93·1	478·0
1980	146·8	61·4	66·0	261·7	626·3	95·3	133·7	109·1	547·0
1981	168·7	69·9	73·8	299·1	723·9	111·5	134·9	125·9	636·3
1982	198·2	83·3	84·5	349·7	852·9	131·5	188·7	176·5	816·3
1983	220·1	78·6	91·5	385·6	925·7	141·5	208·8	199·9	903·1
1984	244·5	81·8	98·6	416·8	1,001·5	150·8	223·1	199·7	960·8
1985	254·2	87·6	120·0	452·8	1,081·1	159·5	238·6	200·9	1,018·2
1986	271·4	104·1	130·4	475·5	1,163·5	177·9	250·4	202·7	1,102·4

195

Table F.10 Value of exports and imports by country, 1885–1987

	Total exports	Exports to: Germany	Italy	UK	USA	Total imports	Imports from: Germany	Italy	UK	USA
						Fr mn				
1885	3,088	300	177	832	254	4,088	374	263	537	272
1886	3,249	298	193	858	282	4,208	335	309	526	293
1887	3,246	316	192	820	271	4,026	322	308	476	325
1888	3,247	308	119	864	256	4,107	333	181	529	248
1889	3,704	342	144	996	274	4,317	338	134	538	307
1890	3,753	342	150	1,026	329	4,437	351	122	627	317
1891	3,570	364	126	1,013	248	4,768	366	124	589	486
1892	3,461	355	133	1,027	240	4,188	337	132	530	534
1893	3,236	336	128	965	205	3,854	323	151	493	317
1894	3,078	325	98	916	186	3,850	310	122	481	327
1895	3,374	334	134	1,002	289	3,720	310	115	496	283
1896	3,401	340	115	1,033	225	3,799	308	127	511	314
1897	3,598	380	151	1,136	242	3,956	309	132	486	438
1898	3,511	394	143	1,024	210	4,472	334	138	506	623
1899	4,153	457	192	1,242	255	4,518	360	159	591	427
1900	4,109	465	156	1,230	255	4,698	427	149	675	510
1901	4,013	444	155	1,201	253	4,369	402	140	602	457
1902	4,252	487	175	1,283	248	4,394	418	154	567	425
1903	4,252	513	172	1,195	255	4,802	444	152	556	540
1904	4,451	555	190	1,217	251	4,502	429	151	524	483
1905	4,867	629	213	1,260	295	4,779	477	154	593	512
1906	5,265	640	247	1,299	402	5,627	583	182	751	588
1907	5,596	650	264	1,373	396	6,223	638	194	884	671
1908	5,051	617	242	1,183	315	5,640	608	165	794	657
1909	5,718	726	293	1,266	474	6,246	661	165	888	728
1910	6,234	804	344	1,279	456	7,174	861	189	931	614
1911	6,077	795	278	1,220	380	8,066	980	190	994	827
1912	6,713	822	302	1,365	431	8,231	999	209	1,049	890
1913	6,880	867	306	1,457	423	8,421	1,069	241	1,116	895
1914	4,869	511	215	1,165	377	6,402	614	174	857	795
1915	3,937	—	388	1,101	446	11,036	—	433	3,038	3,028
1916	6,214	—	782	1,123	622	20,640	—	717	5,969	6,163
1917	6,013	—	971	1,018	682	27,554	—	815	6,808	9,771
1918	4,723	—	780	1,083	420	22,306	—	818	6,396	7,140
						Fr bn				
1919	11·88	1·56	0·68	2·12	0·89	35·80	0·76	1·02	8·80	9·22
1920	26·89	1·50	1·25	4·24	2·26	49·91	2·67	1·28	10·32	10·87
1921	19·77	1·88	0·69	3·19	2·19	22·75	2·62	0·62	2·94	3·54
1922	21·38	1·97	0·80	3·98	2·01	24·28	1·45	0·77	3·27	3·85
1923	30·87	1·08	1·17	6·36	2·47	32·86	1·17	1·14	5·04	4·85
1924	42·37	3·96	1·48	7·90	3·15	40·16	2·05	1·48	4·77	5·59
1925	45·76	3·83	2·23	9·27	3·09	44·10	2·35	1·73	5·69	6·38
1926	59·68	4·38	2·62	10·59	3·67	59·60	4·93	2·23	6·14	7·82
1927	54·93	6·63	2·06	9·00	3·15	53·05	4·17	1·55	6·33	6·81
1928	51·38	5·62	2·13	7·94	3·03	53·44	5·00	1·53	5·31	6·18
1929	50·14	4·74	2·21	7·63	3·34	58·22	6·61	1·52	5·86	7·16
1930	42·84	4·16	1·68	6·89	2·44	52·51	7·94	1·53	5·30	6·15
1931	30·44	2·75	0·99	5·09	1·54	42·21	6·14	1·44	3·85	3·80
1932	19·71	1·70	0·60	1·98	0·96	29·81	3·61	0·63	2·46	2·90
1933	18·47	1·71	0·50	1·70	0·87	28·43	3·04	0·62	2·18	2·86
1934	17·85	1·99	0·55	1·57	0·84	23·10	2·23	0·48	1·65	2·19
1935	15·50	1·05	0·60	1·64	0·72	20·97	1·74	0·41	1·58	1·79
1936	15·49	0·67	0·14	1·96	0·88	25·41	1·77	0·22	1·80	2·53
1937	23·94	1·57	0·63	2·75	1·54	42·39	3·49	0·57	3·39	4·03
1938	30·59	1·85	0·49	3·56	1·68	46·06	3·15	0·58	3·24	5·28
1939	31·59	1·04	0·32	4·15	2·27	43·79	2·09	0·50	2·98	5·84
1940	17·51	0·65	0·26	2·14	1·21	45·77	0·10	0·82	3·68	8·49
1941	15·78	6·25	0·50	0·11	0·13	24·94	3·92	0·50	0·15	0·50
1942	29·66	17·80	0·30	0·14	—	25·95	7·52	0·42	—	0·14
1943	35·41	29·19	0·05	0·15	—	13·96	8·38	0·14	0·03	0·07

	Total exports	Exports to:				Total imports	Imports from:			
		Germany	Italy	UK	USA		Germany	Italy	UK	USA
				Fr bn						
1944	25·56	22·42	—	0·08	—	9·77	4·81	0·03	0·03	1·41
1945	11·40	0·11	—	0·32	0·59	57·03	1·67	0·10	5·06	27·18
1946	101·4	2·34	0·65	5·34	6·40	264·7	12·79	2·35	15·10	83·86
1947	223·3	5·85	2·17	15·45	5·98	397·1	15·16	2·74	12·47	120·1
1948	434·0	23·38	4·61	31·83	15·81	672·7	35·96	11·38	18·83	118·7
1949	783·9	39·29	15·83	70·11	15·74	926·3	68·44	17·09	32·82	162·7
1950	1,078	84·31	28·01	98·81	43·69	1,073	69·79	37·25	39·95	131·6
1951	1,484	69·83	35·23	133·72	88·43	1,615	101·5	47·77	56·90	181·7
1952	1,416	78·89	37·96	85·19	54·84	1,592	114·7	33·91	60·11	159·7
1953	1,406	98·54	45·45	76·03	63·52	1,458	110·0	22·53	66·61	135·0
1954	1,510	123·3	57·53	84·42	54·06	1,522	120·3	27·59	70·03	133·4
1955	1,736	176·9	66·54	125·41	72·88	1,674	154·0	36·81	75·82	160·5
1956	1,623	166·2	65·36	97·24	78·27	1,978	199·0	49·84	108·45	238·6
1957	1,889	201·8	75·48	103·12	89·86	2,267	250·1	56·47	97·43	300·5
1958	2,153	224·5	72·76	105·15	126·4	2,357	274·2	55·45	84·31	236·7
1959	27·7	3·63	1·32	1·24	2·29	25·2	3·65	0·88	0·98	2·12
1960	33·9	4·66	1·98	1·71	1·95	31·0	4·89	1·25	1·13	1·95
1961	35·7	5·41	2·41	1·81	2·06	33·0	5·63	1·51	1·48	2·06
1962	36·3	6·28	2·73	1·72	2·10	37·1	6·54	2·05	1·92	3·83
1963	39·9	6·62	3·69	1·96	2·08	43·1	7·76	2·55	2·57	4·45
1964	44·4	7·73	3·43	2·26	2·32	49·7	9·11	3·13	2·68	5·61
1965	49·6	9·58	3·62	2·29	2·94	51·0	9·44	3·59	2·58	5·37
1966	53·8	10·37	4·44	2·46	3·26	58·6	11·27	4·69	2·88	5·92
1967	56·2	9·73	5·18	2·87	3·28	61·1	12·32	5·30	2·92	6·02
1968	62·6	11·63	5·77	2·98	3·78	68·8	14·73	6·56	3·04	6·51
1969	77·0	15·88	8·06	3·16	4·22	89·1	20·04	9·02	4·00	7·59
1970	98·5	20·49	11·11	3·83	5·30	105·1	23·43	9·81	4·80	10·53
1971	113·0	24·31	12·43	5·19	6·10	117·0	26·38	11·69	5·29	9·99
1972	131·5	27·79	15·11	7·04	6·97	135·7	30·20	13·84	6·65	11·02
1973	159·7	30·92	18·75	10·10	7·50	166·1	37·66	14·99	7·69	13·76
1974	220·2	37·92	25·69	14·35	10·74	254·7	48·87	19·01	10·82	19·76
1975	223·4	36·99	20·34	14·60	8·79	231·3	43·57	20·34	10·99	17·50
1976	266·2	46·01	29·06	16·07	12·06	308·0	59·16	27·50	15·06	22·57
1977	311·6	53·34	32·66	20·24	16·05	346·2	64·07	33·16	18·06	24·05
1978	344·6	59·82	37·64	24·96	19·25	368·4	70·01	37·38	20·30	26·88
1979	414·7	71·70	47·61	32·03	20·40	457·1	82·84	46·07	25·60	34·39
1980	469·7	75·35	58·63	32·74	20·78	570·8	92·16	53·41	30·78	45·35
1981	549·5	81·36	62·35	39·06	30·31	654·2	104·61	58·60	35·92	52·31
1982	606·1	89·56	68·38	43·88	34·33	757·6	127·57	72·78	45·98	59·74
1983	694·7	108·07	74·11	52·68	43·82	799·8	135·46	79·36	56·80	61·76
1984	813·0	119·44	88·55	64·37	65·90	903·8	147·29	89·19	72·78	69·91
1985	870·8	130·51	95·32	71·55	73·35	962·7	159·06	96·80	78·99	73·25
1986	826·0	133·09	97·25	72·71	61·03	891·8	172·36	103·39	58·08	67·01
1987	858·6	142·78	103·84	75·58	62·44	945·00	186·70	110·80	66·95	67·66

Sources

(For sources used in specific tables, see Notes.)

1 *Annuaire Statistique de la France,* Institut national de la statistique et des études économiques, Paris, 1987 and earlier years.
2 *Annuaire Statistique de la France, Résumé Rétrospectif,* 1966.
3 International Labour Office, *Technical Guide,* Vol. II, Geneva, 1972, 1976, 1980.
4 League of Nations, *Year Book of Labour Statistics,* Geneva.
5 Maddison, Angus, *Phases of Capitalist Development,* Oxford University Press, 1982.
6 Mitchell, B.R., *European Historical Statistics, 1750–1975,* 2nd rev. ed., Macmillan, London, 1980.
7 Organisation for Economic Cooperation and Development (OECD), *Labour Force Statistics,* annual and quarterly, Paris.
8 OECD, *National Accounts, 1950–1979,* Vol. 1, Paris, 1981.
9 OECD, *National Accounts, 1960–1987,* Vol. 1, Paris, 1989.
10 *Statistical Year Book of the League of Nations,* Geneva.
11 Supplements to the United Nations, *Statistical Year Book* and *Monthly Digest of Statistics,* New York, 1967, 1972 and 1977.
12 United Nations, *Monthly Bulletin of Statistics,* New York.
13 United Nations, *Statistics of National Income and Expenditure,* Series H, No. 7, New York, 1955.
14 United Nations, *Statistical Year Book,* New York.
15 *Year Book of Labour Statistics,* ILO, Geneva.

Notes

Table F.1 Gross domestic product at current prices

Sources: **1, 2, 8, 9**

From 1950, OECD data have been used. For the period 1960–80, the national accounts are classified according to the present system; for 1950–59, they are on an earlier system of classification. The main differences are explained in **8**.

For 1930–50 (first line), the last column refers to gross *national* product.

For 1930–37, the figures are estimates by Colin Clark reprinted in **2**.

For 1938–50 (first line), the figures are INSEE estimates reprinted in **2**.

Exports and imports for the years 1938–50 (first line) are exports and imports of goods and services and income from the rest of the world.

Table F.2 Gross domestic product at constant prices

Sources: **1, 2, 8, 9**

From 1950, OECD data have been used. For the period 1960–80, the national accounts are classified according to the present system; for 1950–59, they are on an earlier system. See notes to Table F.1.

For the years 1938 and 1949, constant price estimates published in **2** were linked to the OECD estimates at 1950 and roughly adjusted to 1980 prices. Figures for gross domestic product for the years 1930–37 and 1946–48 were obtained by using the index of gross domestic product given in **5** and extrapolating the 1938 figure.

Table F.3 Industrial production

Sources: **1, 6, 12, 14**

Industrial production: the current index covers mining, manufacturing (except the clothing industry), public utilities (except water) and construction work including civil engineering. For further details of method, composition and linking, see notes to Table 3.03–2 and 3.08–1 in **1**, 1983, pp. 308–09.

Coal: includes coal and lignite. For 1900–18 and 1939–44 parts of Alsace Lorraine are excluded.

Crude steel: includes Alsace Lorraine from 1919 (second line).

Cars and commercial vehicles: figures to 1938 are for years ended September 30. Alsace Lorraine is excluded from 1941–44.

Natural gas: published figures are now given in terajoules. From 1977, the published figures have been converted to cubic metres using the conversion factors given in **12**.

Table F.4   Prices and income

Sources: **1, 6, 8, 9, 10, 12, 13, 14**

Consumer prices: the current series is a chain index, the weights being changed at the beginning of each calendar year. The coverage of the index has changed over the period to make it more comprehensive. For further details see **11**.

Wholesale prices: the 'All items' index is based on the series given in **1**, 1983, p. 307. For details of the way the index has been linked at successive periods see notes on p. 308 of **1**, 1983. The 'Raw materials' index is published in **14**; it includes both domestic and imported raw materials. For further details see **11**.

Import and export price indices: the current series of unit value indices published in **1** have been linked at 1975 to a previous series, *Indices des valeurs moyennes* (average value indices).

Compensation of employees: OECD data have been used from 1950; see **8** and **9**. The figures include wages and salaries in cash and kind paid to employees, contributions on behalf of employees to social security schemes and private pension funds, as well as family allowances and private health insurance paid by employers. The 1938 figure and figures for 1946–49 are from **13** converted to new francs. Figures for 1913 and 1920–37 are taken from **2**.

National income: OECD data have been used from 1950. 'National income' is defined as the sum of compensation of employees received by residents, net entrepreneurial and property income of residents, and indirect taxes minus subsidies. Figures for 1938 and 1946–49 are from **13** but have been converted to new francs. For 1913 and 1920–37, figures are taken from **2**.

Two figures have been given for 1959 for the last two columns because of the change in classification; see notes to Table F.1.

Table F.5   Population

Sources: **1, 7**

OECD data have been used from 1950 (second line); the figures are mid-year estimates of resident population including armed forces temporarily stationed abroad.

For the period 1901–50 (first line), the figures are as at January 1 each year.

Alsace Lorraine is excluded from the figures before 1919.

Births: the estimates up to 1890 are incomplete. During the First World War the number of births in departments affected by the war were estimated.

Table F.6   Education

Sources: **1, 2, 6**

Figures for schools are for pupils in both public and private schools during the school year.

Kindergarten: pupils in what is now called pre-elementary; previously called *maternelles* and *enfantines* (*enfantines* not included until 1951).

Elementary: includes pupils in basic schooling. Compulsory schooling begins at age six; the school leaving age was raised to 16 in 1959. From 1936 to 1958, compulsory schooling finished at 14 years and before 1936 at 13 years. From 1959 the figures include special schools.

Secondary: currently the figures are for students at Colleges of Secondary Education (CES) and Colleges of General Education (CEG) but coverage has altered over the period.

For 1885–1945, the figures refer to pupils at state *lycées* and colleges.

1946–61: figures include public and private secondary schools including preparatory classes for the Grande Ecole.

The system of first and second cycles was introduced in 1961 after the reform of the education system in 1959. The second cycle is what might be called post-secondary education. It includes pre-professional education and preparation for apprenticeships. It does not include preparatory classes for the Grande Ecole.

Alsace Lorraine is excluded for the years 1885–1922 and 1939–44. For 1917–20 (first line), invaded departments are excluded from the figures for elementary schools.

Higher education: students at universities only and not those at other institutions of higher education. It does not include preparatory classes for the Grande Ecole or Ecole d'ingénieurs.

Table F.7   Labour market: employment

Sources: **4, 7, 15**

OECD data have been used from 1954. The figures from 1954 (second line) are annual averages of those in civil employment and include employees, self-employed and unpaid family workers working for at least one-third of normal working time. The figures do not include the temporarily out of work or the unemployed.

The estimates are based on the French national industrial classification, which has been changed from time to time. From 1965, the estimates are more closely adjusted to the International Standard Industrial Classification and for 1965–68 have been estimated by the OECD Secretariat. For further details see **7** 1966–86.

There have been revisions to the total in employment from time to time, but the industry data have not always been revised in detail. When this has occurred, the unrevised data have been given in the industry columns together with the *revised* figures for the employed labour force. Industry figures will not therefore always add to the total (cf. 1959–61).

For 1930–54 (first line), the figures for the 'Employed labour force' are for wage and salary earners in mining, manufacturing, construction, transport, commerce, personal and public services. For the years 1930–36, fewer groups in transport and commerce are included. The figures for 1938 are for January–August. Figures available for the *total* labour force have been obtained from census data covering the economically active population, which includes employers and self-employed, employees and unemployed. For the years 1931 and 1936 (census years), the economically active population numbered just over 21·5 and 20 mn, respectively.

The industry classification also covers wage earners and salaried employees only for the period 1930–54. The figures are annual averages of the estimated number of employees in work on a specific date; no distinction is made between full- and part-time work. For the years 1930–36 and 1938–45, the figures given in the industry columns include wage earners and salaried employees in mining, manufacturing and transport. The economically active population in manufacturing in 1931 was returned as 5·9 mn and in 1936 as 5·1 mn. The figures for agriculture were 7·7 mn in 1931 and 7·2 mn in 1936. For further details see **4** and **15**.

Table F.8 Labour market: other indicators

Sources: **1, 4, 7, 15**

Manufacturing: average weekly hours worked: the current series is the average of scheduled working hours in the reporting establishments in a particular week. Thus, overtime is counted only when an entire establishment or a major section of it has extra working hours scheduled. When there is a temporary layoff, the figure of zero hours is included in the average figure. The series covers wage earners of both sexes over 18 years of age. Comprehensive revisions were made in 1954 and in 1972.

Figures for 1930–39 include mining and transport and communication. The figure for 1938 is for the period January to August.

Manufacturing: average hourly wage rates: series refers to rates of pay in force on January 1, April 1, July 1 and October 1; annual figure is an average of these four. Covers wage earners over 18 years of age of both sexes. Includes collective bonus payments but excludes overtime pay, individual bonuses or reimbursements. There was a change in the value of the franc in 1960: 1 new franc = 100 old francs. Since 1969, an average earnings figure has also been published. For further details of these series see **3**, **4** and **15**.

Unemployment: OECD data have been used from 1954. The figures refer to persons available for work seeking employment and are based on census results, annual labour force sample surveys and the Ministry of Labour series. The figures are therefore different from those published in United Nations publications. From June 1972, the figures exclude certain unemployed over the age of 60 (recipients of income maintenance benefits).

Before 1954, the figures are for job applicants still registered at the end of each month; annual figures are averages of monthly figures.

The percentage figure is currently the ratio of the unemployed to the total labour force, excluding conscripts.

Industrial disputes: exclude agriculture and public administration.

Table F.9 Public finance

Sources: **1, 2**

Total receipts: includes revenue from all sources.

Taxes on personal income: currently includes *taxe* (*impôt*) *sur le revenu* and *taxe sur le salaire* (including income from pensions and annuities). It was previously called *impôt sur personnes physiques*.

Taxes on companies: currently includes *impôt sur les sociétés*. Other taxes on companies such as stamp duties and value-added tax have not been included. For 1917–49, includes *bénéfices industriels et commerciaux*, *bénéfices agricoles* and *bénéfices professionnels et commerciaux*.

For the period 1885–1917, the first two columns are for direct taxes, mainly taxes on land in the early period.

Turnover tax: *taxe sur le chiffre d'affaires* and *taxe deluxe*. Now also includes value-added tax.

Total expenditure: covers total general expenditure. The budgets of the Comité Française de Liberation National in 1943 and the provisional government of 1944 included for those years.

Defence expenditure: for 1885–1937 the figures are for what was called 'war expenditure' but they do not include naval expenditure.

Social services: includes public health expenditure.

All figures are in new francs from 1960 (1 new franc = 100 old francs).

For 1885–1928 and from 1933 data are for the calendar year. Figures for 1931 and 1932 are for years ending March 31; 1929 is for 15 months ending March 31, 1930, and 1932 is for nine months ending December 31, 1932.

Table F.10 Value of exports and imports by country

Sources: **1, 6**

For 1885–1923, exports to and imports from the UK include trade with Cyprus, Malta, Gibraltar and Southern Ireland. For 1948–59, the Saarland is included as part of France. Alsace Lorraine became part of France from 1919. From 1948, trade with Germany refers to the Federal Republic of Germany.

The figures are in new francs from 1959 (100 old francs = 1 new franc). From 1934, statistics have been collected on the basis of countries of origin or consumption; previously they were classified according to consignment and destination. There were also changes in the method of collection or of valuation in 1923 and in 1928 and 1956.

GERMANY

CONTENTS

Table G.1   Gross domestic product at current prices, 1885–1987

	Consumers' expenditure	Government current expenditure	Gross fixed capital formation[a]	Value of physical change in stocks	Exports of goods & services	Less Imports of goods & services	Gross domestic product at market prices[b]
				Marks bn			
1885	15·0	1·3	2·0	...		0·51	18·7
1886	15·2	1·3	2·0	...		0·49	18·9
1887	15·2	1·4	2·2	...		0·43	19·3
1888	15·9	1·7	2·4	...		0·69	20·7
1889	17·0	1·7	2·9	...		0·59	22·3
1890	17·9	1·9	3·4	...		0·43	23·7
1891	18·4	1·8	2·1	...		0·33	22·6
1892	18·9	1·8	3·1	...		0·19	24·1
1893	19·1	1·9	2·9	...		0·36	24·4
1894	19·3	1·9	2·5	...		0·64	24·4
1895	20·1	2·0	2·8	...		0·34	25·3
1896	20·7	2·1	3·6	...		0·59	27·0
1897	21·7	2·2	4·2	...		0·67	28·7
1898	22·6	2·3	5·3	...		0·82	31·0
1899	23·6	2·4	5·4	...		0·37	31·8
1900	24·3	2·6	5·1	...		0·41	32·4
1901	24·6	2·7	3·9	...		0·42	31·6
1902	25·2	2·7	3·5	...		0·49	31·9
1903	26·2	2·8	5·0	...		0·44	34·4
1904	27·1	3·0	5·6	...		0·64	36·3
1905	28·3	3·2	6·1	...		1·31	38·9
1906	29·9	3·5	6·7	...		0·52	40·6
1907	31·5	3·7	7·6	...		0·16	43·0
1908	32·5	3·7	5·6	...		0·56	42·4
1909	33·9	4·0	6·0	...		0·42	44·4
1910	34·8	4·1	6·1	...		0·75	45·8
1911	35·9	4·3	7·3	...		0·64	48·1
1912	38·0	4·6	8·6	...		0·45	51·6
1913	38·2	5·1	8·2	...		0·94	52·4
1925	52·8	7·9	8·6	...		−1·99	67·3
1926	51·9	8·2	4·3	...		1·15	65·5
1927	62·0	8·8	12·2	...		−2·66	80·5
1928	64·3	9·9	11·0	...		−1·20	84·0
1929	63·9	9·9	5·8	...		−0·13	79·5
1930	58·5	9·7	2·6	...		1·10	71·9
1931	51·1	8·5	−3·2	...		2·03	58·5
1932	44·9	7·5	−2·1	...		0·42	50·8
1933	45·7	8·9	1·9	...		0·28	56·8
1934	49·5	10·9	4·7	...		−0·53	64·6
1935	50·7	13·9	7·5	...		−0·11	72·0
1936	51·9	17·7	9·0	...		0·40	78·9
1937	55·2	18·8	13·6	...		0·29	87·9
1938	58·4	25·8	14·1	...		−0·34	98·0
1950	62·9	14·2	18·7	3·6	11·1	12·5	98·1
1951	73·1	17·6	22·9	4·3	18·4	16·2	120·0
1952	81·2	20·8	26·8	5·1	21·7	18·6	137·0
1953	88·7	21·4	30·4	1·9	24·8	19·6	147·7
1954	94·6	22·3	34·1	2·6	30·1	24·6	159·1
1955	106·1	24·2	42·6	4·6	35·7	31·2	182·0
1956	118·0	25·7	47·4	3·0	42·9	35·9	200·9
1957	128·5	27·9	48·8	4·8	50·9	42·0	218·9
1958	138·4	31·3	52·4	3·6	51·9	43·1	234·4
1959	147·7	34·3	60·1	3·7	58·1	48·7	255·1
1960	161·2	38·3	69·0	7·9	66·9	58·5	284·8
1960	171·8	40·4	73·6	9·2	57·5	49·8	302·7
1961	188·3	45·8	83·5	6·7	59·8	52·4	331·7
1962	204·8	52·8	92·9	5·7	62·7	58·1	360·8
1963	216·8	59·4	97·7	2·6	68·2	62·4	382·4

Table G.1 (Continued)   Gross domestic product at current prices, 1885–1987

	Consumers' expenditure	Government current expenditure	Gross fixed capital formation[a]	Value of physical change in stocks	Exports of goods & services	Less Imports of goods & services	Gross domestic product at market prices[b]
				Marks bn			
1964	233·5	62·1	111 7	6·4	75·9	69·4	**420·2**
1965	257·6	69·6	119·9	10·7	82·9	81·6	**459·2**
1966	275·1	75·4	124·2	5·3	93·5	85·3	**488·2**
1967	282·6	80·1	114·2	−0·5	101·0	83·0	**494·3**
1968	300·7	82·7	119·4	11·1	113·9	94·6	**533·3**
1969	330·9	93·1	138·9	17·3	129·5	112·7	**596·9**
1970	368·8	106·5	172·0	14·2	143·0	129·3	**675·3**
1971	409·4	126·8	196·1	4·5	158·0	144·3	**750·6**
1972	452·1	141·1	209·2	4·8	172·6	156·0	**823·7**
1973	495·4	163·2	219·3	12·5	203·0	176·0	**917·3**
1974	533·7	190·2	212·7	5·0	262·5	219·6	**984·6**
1975	585·3	210·0	209·4	−5·4	254·7	227·1	**1,026·9**
1976	632·5	221·7	225·6	17·2	289·7	265·1	**1,121·7**
1977	683·2	235·0	242·4	9·5	306·6	278·9	**1,197·8**
1978	728·9	252·9	266·0	6·4	321·2	290·0	**1,285·3**
1979	785·0	273·3	303·4	23·5	351·1	344·0	**1,392·3**
1980	840·8	297·8	335·8	13·8	391·8	401·1	**1,478·9**
1981	887·8	318·2	335·2	−11·4	445·7	434·6	**1,540·9**
1982	918·0	326·2	326·9	−11·5	479·0	440·7	**1,597·9**
1983	964·2	336·2	343·8	−1·8	483·8	451·3	**1,674·8**
1984	1,003·6	350·2	354·6	6·6	540·2	499·4	**1,755·8**
1985	1,038·3	365·7	360·8	−0·7	593·5	527·1	**1,830·5**
1986	1,068·6	382·6	377·4	−2·1	580·5	479·9	**1,931·2**
1987	1,112·0	397·2	389·3	10·5	577·0	476·9	**2,009·1**

a   For 1885–1938 figures are for net investment.
b   For 1885–1938 figures are for net social product at market prices.

Table G.2   Gross domestic product at constant prices, 1885–1987

	Consumers' expenditure	Government current expenditure	Gross fixed capital formation	Value of physical change in stocks	Exports of goods & services	Imports of goods & services	**Gross domestic product at market prices**
				Marks bn, 1980 prices			
1885	110·1	15·6	...	...	...	...	**170·4**
1886	112·1	15·9	...	...	...	...	**171·4**
1887	113·5	16·9	...	...	...	...	**178·3**
1888	117·8	20·4	...	...	...	...	**185·8**
1889	121·0	20·7	...	...	...	...	**190·7**
1890	123·6	22·8	...	...	...	...	**196·7**
1891	126·0	21·1	...	...	...	...	**196·7**
1892	129·4	21·7	...	...	...	...	**204·6**
1893	139·3	22·9	...	...	...	...	**215·1**
1894	140·7	23·0	...	...	...	...	**220·0**
1895	148·3	23·3	...	...	...	...	**230·5**
1896	149·9	24·5	...	...	...	...	**238·9**
1897	154·5	26·0	...	...	...	...	**245·9**
1898	160·4	26·8	...	...	...	...	**256·3**
1899	164·0	28·0	...	...	...	...	**265·7**
1900	163·9	30·3	...	...	...	...	**276·7**
1901	165·9	31·2	...	...	...	...	**270·7**
1902	169·7	31·5	...	...	...	...	**276·7**
1903	176·5	32·3	...	...	...	...	**292·1**
1904	181·2	34·0	...	...	...	...	**304·0**
1905	184·5	36·9	...	...	...	...	**310·4**
1906	185·6	40·0	...	...	...	...	**319·9**
1907	194·5	41·4	...	...	...	...	**333·8**
1908	202·2	41·5	...	...	...	...	**339·7**
1909	204·2	44·1	...	...	...	...	**346·2**
1910	201·3	43·9	...	...	...	...	**359·1**
1911	208·7	44·3	...	...	...	...	**371·5**
1912	217·6	47·1	...	...	...	...	**387·4**
1913	217·3	52·8	...	...	...	...	**404·8**
1925	213·1	59·8	...	...	...	...	**380·0**
1926	210·0	63·2	...	...	...	...	**364·6**
1927	238·4	65·7	...	...	...	...	**432·6**
1928	241·9	68·9	...	...	...	...	**442·6**
1929	239·7	67·6	...	...	...	...	**447·5**
1930	229·8	66·9	...	...	...	...	**419·7**
1931	222·0	65·1	...	...	...	...	**377·5**
1932	217·0	64·7	...	...	...	...	**342·2**
1933	225·2	79·5	...	...	...	...	**376·5**
1934	239·3	100·7	...	...	...	...	**412·3**
1935	240·5	127·4	...	...	...	...	**450·0**
1936	243·9	161·6	...	...	...	...	**496·7**
1937	258·4	167·4	...	...	...	...	**527·0**
1938	268·7	231·3	...	...	...	...	**567·7**
1948[a]	68·2	37·2	...	...	...	...	**129·2**
1949	153·0	79·9	...	...	...	...	**290·8**
1950	175·0	80·5	75·0	8·4	24·8	−19·4	**338·6**
1951	188·8	88·3	78·9	8·4	33·7	−20·5	**374·1**
1952	206·0	96·9	85·8	10·6	38·0	−25·7	**407·0**
1953	228·5	97·2	100·4	4·0	44·0	−30·3	**440·8**
1954	242·3	99·7	113·0	5·7	54·5	−39·0	**474·6**
1955	267·4	104·3	136·4	9·9	63·5	−48·7	**531·7**
1956	290·9	104·9	148·3	6·5	73·1	−55·4	**569·9**
1957	309·1	109·9	148·2	10·1	84·6	−64·0	**601·9**
1958	324·6	119·0	154·3	7·6	87·4	−70·9	**623·2**
1959	343·1	129·8	172·5	8·0	97·9	−81·7	**669·4**
1960	370·6	137·5	189·9	16·9	110·7	−96·7	**728·9**
1961	392·7	145·9	202·5	10·8	114·9	−104·1	**762·7**
1962	414·2	159·7	210·5	10·2	119·7	−115·6	**798·8**

Table G.2 (Continued)   Gross domestic product at constant prices, 1885–1987

	Consumers' expenditure	Government current expenditure	Gross fixed capital formation	Value of physical change in stocks	Exports of goods & services	Imports of goods & services	Gross domestic product at market prices
				Marks bn, 1980 prices			
1963	425·8	169·4	213·5	4·3	129·2	−121·3	**820·9**
1964	448·2	172·5	237·8	9·7	140·1	−132·6	**875·7**
1965	479·0	181·0	248·9	17·1	149·3	−151·5	**923·7**
1966	493·7	186·7	251·9	9·7	164·3	−155·4	**950·9**
1967	498·9	193·5	234·5	−0·8	177·0	−153·4	**949·7**
1968	522·5	194·4	243·0	17·0	199·6	−174·0	**1,002·5**
1969	564·1	203·0	266·8	28·0	218·1	−202·7	**1,077·3**
1970	606·8	211·9	291·9	24·4	230·7	−232·9	**1,132·8**
1971	638·1	222·8	309·6	7·3	245·1	−257·3	**1,165·6**
1972	666·6	232·1	317·9	8·3	262·5	−272·7	**1,214·7**
1973	687·0	243·6	316·8	18·4	290·3	−284·5	**1,271·6**
1974	691·5	253·4	286·4	6·3	326·1	−288·6	**1,275·1**
1975	713·9	262·8	271·3	−7·5	303·9	−289·6	**1,254·8**
1976	740·3	266·8	281·0	22·8	333·4	−321·6	**1,322·7**
1977	771·8	270·4	291·0	13·2	346·4	−331·1	**1,361·8**
1978	801·4	280·8	304·7	8·3	357·5	−351·9	**1,400·9**
1979	830·4	290·3	326·7	25·1	372·9	−386·4	**1,459·0**
1980	840·8	297·8	335·8	13·8	391·8	−401·1	**1,478·9**
1981	836·4	303·3	319·7	−10·7	422·2	−389·4	**1,481·4**
1982	825·2	300·7	302·9	−9·6	436·4	−383·8	**1,471·8**
1983	839·6	301·4	312·4	−1·5	432·7	−390·8	**1,493·9**
1984	852·3	308·8	314·9	5·5	467·4	−412·9	**1,536·0**
1985	864·0	315·3	315·1	−0·9	500·1	−427·1	**1,566·5**
1986	893·4	323·2	325·4	4·5	497·3	−440·8	**1,603·0**
1987	924·7	328·3	331·3	9·9	499·5	−459·4	**1,634·3**

a   Six months only.

Table G.3   Industrial production, index and selected series, 1885–1987

	Industrial production	Coal	Crude steel	Cars & commercial vehicles	Crude petroleum	Natural gas	Electricity
	Index nos., 1980 = 100	mn tons	mn tons	'000	'000 tons	mn m³	bn kwh
1885	3·7	73·7	1·20	—	6	—	—
1886	3·7	73·7	1·31	—	10	—	—
1887	3·9	76·2	1·68	—	10	—	—
1888	4·2	82·0	1·79	—	12	—	—
1889	4·7	85·0	2·00	—	10	—	—
1890	4·8	89·3	2·14	—	15	—	—
1891	4·9	94·3	2·45	—	15	—	—
1892	5·0	92·4	2·65	—	14	—	—
1893	5·1	95·4	3·03	—	14	—	—
1894	5·4	98·8	3·62	—	17	—	—
1895	5·9	103·9	3·89	—	17	—	—
1896	6·0	112·5	4·70	—	20	—	—
1897	6·3	120·5	4·89	—	23	—	—
1898	6·7	128·0	5·28	—	26	—	—
1899	6·9	135·8	5·87	—	27	—	—
1900	7·3	149·6	6·46	—	50	—	1·0
1901	7·1	152·7	6·14	—	44	—	1·3
1902	7·2	150·5	7·47	—	50	—	1·4
1903	7·8	162·3	8·43	—	63	—	1·6
1904	8·2	169·4	8·56	—	90	—	2·2
1905	8·4	173·8	9·67	—	79	—	2·6
1906	8·8	193·5	10·70	—	81	—	2·7
1907	9·5	205·7	11·62	4·3	106	—	3·2
1908	9·4	215·2	10·73	5·0	141	—	3·9
1909	9·8	217·5	11·52	7·9	137	—	4·8
1910	10·4	222·3	13·10	10·2	140	—	5·4
1911	11·0	234·5	14·30	13·1	137	—	6·0
1912	11·7	255·8	16·36	17·9	135	—	7·4
1913	12·0	277·3	17·61	...	121	—	8·0
1914	...	245·3	13·81	...	110	—	8·8
1915	...	234·8	12·28	...	99	—	9·8
1916	...	253·4	14·87	...	93	—	11·0
1917	...	263·2	15·50	...	91	—	12·0
1918	...	258·9	14·09	...	38	—	13·0
1919	...	210·3	8·71 / 7·85	...	37	—	13·5
1920	...	219·4	9·28	...	35	—	15·0
1921	...	237·0	10·00	...	38	—	17·0
1922	...	256·3	11·71	...	42	—	17·0
1923	...	180·4	6·31	...	51	—	15·4
1924	...	243·2	9·84	...	59	—	17·3
1925	12·4	272·5	12·20	49	79	—	20·3
1926	11·1	285·3	12·34	37	95	—	21·2
1927	14·3	304·2	16·31	97	97	—	25·1
1928	14·3	317·2	14·52	123 / 138	92	—	27·9
1929	14·4	337·9	16·25	128	103	—	30·7
1930	12·6	288·7	12·54	96	174	—	29·1
1931	10·2	251·9	8·29	78	229	—	25·8
1932	8·8	227·3	5·77	51	230	—	23·5
1933	9·9	236·5	7·62	105	239	—	25·7
1934	12·2	262·2	11·92	174	318	12	30·7
1935	14·4	290·1	16·45	247	427	14	35·7 / 36·7
1936	16·4	319·7	19·21	301	445	22	42·5
1937	18·3	369·2	19·85	331	451	21	49·0
1938	20·1	381·2	22·66	338	552	18	55·3
1939	...	400·1	23·73	...	741	30	61·4
1940	...	409·4	21·54	...	1,056	...	63·0
1941	...	422·6	20·84	...	901	...	70·0

Table G.3 (Continued) Industrial production, index and selected series, 1885–1987

	Industrial production	Coal	Crude steel	Cars & commercial vehicles	Crude petroleum	Natural gas	Electricity
	Index nos., 1980 = 100	mn tons	mn tons	'000	'000 tons	mn m^3	bn kwh
1942	...	433·8	20·48	...	743	...	71 5
1943	...	443·9	20·76	...	710	...	73·9
1944	...	395·4	18·32	...	720	...	...
1945	...	59·8	...	...	543	71	...
1946	...	105·5	2·56	23	649	109	22·0
1947	...	129·8	3·06	23	577	78	27·8
1948	10·1	151·9	5·56	57	636	67	34·1
1949	14·9	177·0	9·16	159	842	54	40·7
1950	18·6	188·2	12·12	301	1,119	68	46·1
1951	22·3	203·8	13·51	370	1,367	84 / 57	53·7
1952	23·9	208·5	15·81	424	1,755	57	58·7
1953	25·5	210·7	15·42	484	2,189	58	62·9
1954	29·2	217·5	17·43	674	2,666	87	70·5
1955	32·9	222·9	21·34	902	3,147	240	78·9
1956	35·6	231·4	23·19	1,070	3,506	367	87·8
1957	37·7	231·9	24·51	1,206	3,960	357	94·7
1958	38·8	228·1	22·79	1,488	4,432	344	98·2
1959	41·5	237·2	29·44	1,711	5,103	388	106·2
1960	46·2	240·3	34·10	2,047	5,530	448	116·4 / 119·0
1961	49·4	241·7	33·46	2,139	6,204	481	127·3
1962	51·6	244·1	32·56	2,343	6,776	616 / 807	138·4
1963	53·1	250·6	31·60	2,654	7,383	1,171	150·4
1964	57·2	255·0	37·34	2,897	7,673	1,808	164·8
1965	61·3	238·7	36·82	2,963	7,884	2,639	172·3
1966	62·1	225·2	35·32	3,035	7,868	3,390	177·9
1967	60·5	209·7	36·74	2,468	7,927	4,338	184·7
1968	67·9	214·4	41·16	3,091	7,982	6,487	203·3
1969	76·0	219·8	45·32	3,711	7,876	8,912	226·1
1970	81·8	224·1	45·04	3,825	7,535	13,008	242·6
1971	83·4	220·8	40·31	3,957	7,420	15,720	259·6
1972	86·7	218·2	43·71	3,790	7,098	17,448	274·8
1973	92·4	221·7	49·52	3,920	6,638	18,984	299·0
1974	90·7	226·9	53·23	3,068	6,191	19,824	311·7
1975	84·7	220·1	40·41	3,153	5,741	18,804	301·8
1976	91·5	230·4	42·42	3,839	5,524	18,408	333·7
1977	94·1	214·3	38·99	4,104	5,401	19,143	335·3
1978	94·9	213·7	41·25	4,200	5,059	20,471	353·4
1979	100·0	223·9	46·04	4,260	4,774	20,742	372·2
1980	100·0	224·4	43·81	3,911	4,632	20,807	368·8
1981	98·3	226·2	42·16	3,902	4,464	22,159	367·1
1982	95·0	223·7	36·35	4,030	4,260	19,106	365·2
1983	95·8	214·0	36·11	4,158	4,116	20,897	372·0
1984	99	211·6	39·38	4,048	4,056	18,773	392·9
1985	105	209·2	40·50	4,460	4,104	20,314	406·7
1986	107	201·4	37·13	4,452	4,020	18,041	406·8
1987	107	191·2	36·25	4,523	3,792	19,172	...

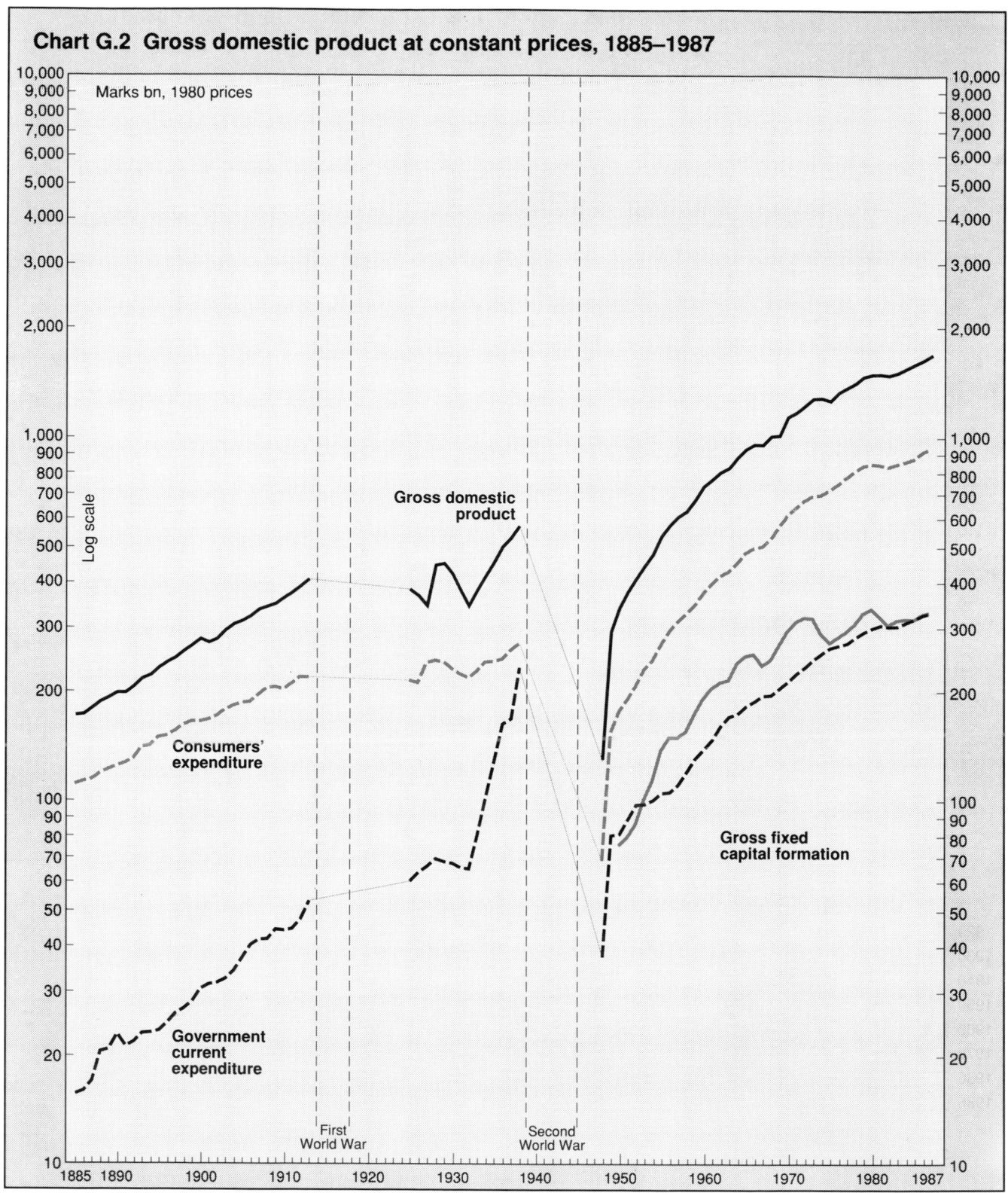

Chart G.2 Gross domestic product at constant prices, 1885–1987

Marks bn, 1980 prices

Log scale

Gross domestic product

Consumers' expenditure

Gross fixed capital formation

Government current expenditure

First World War

Second World War

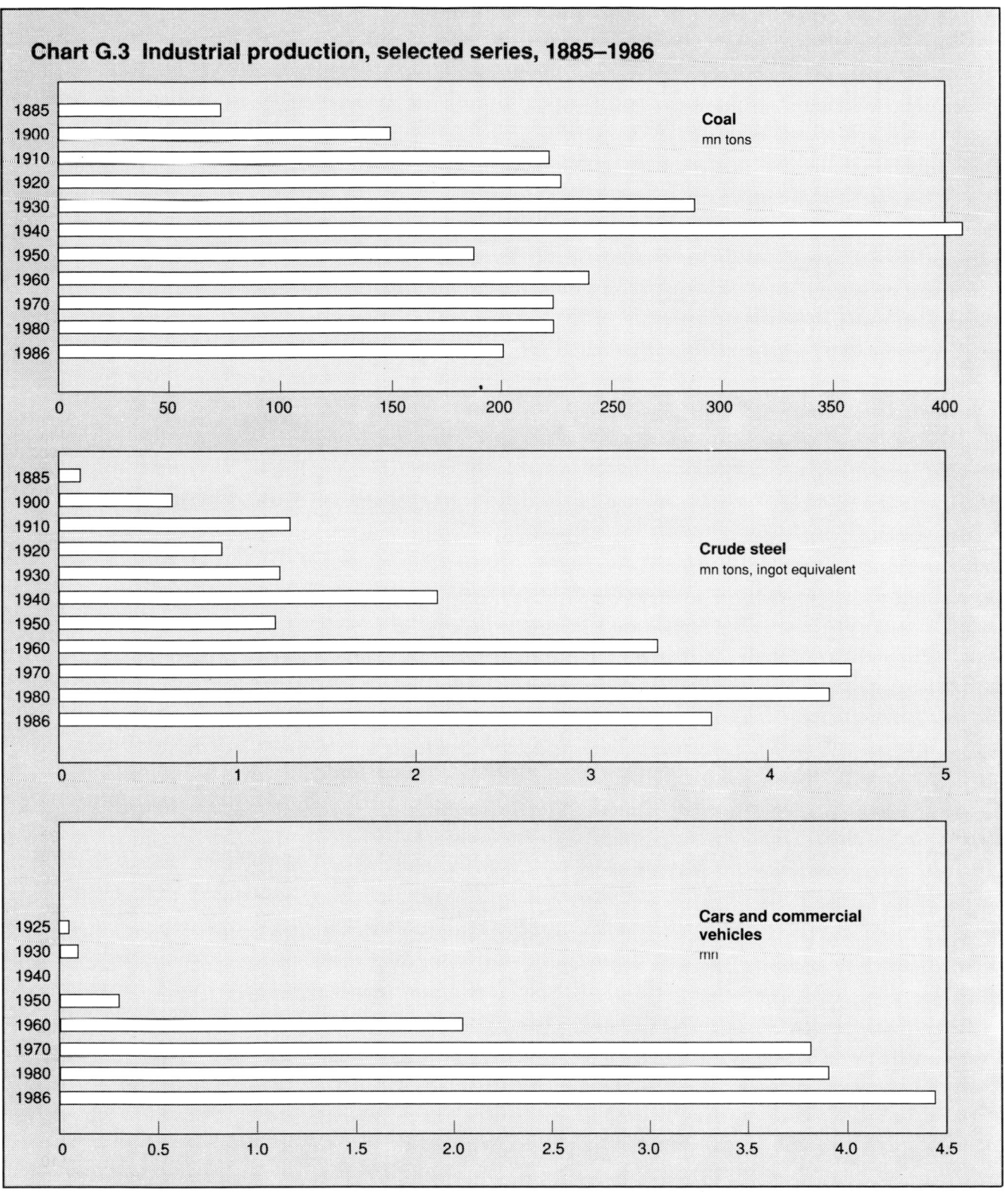

Chart G.3 Industrial production, selected series, 1885–1986

Coal
mn tons

Crude steel
mn tons, ingot equivalent

Cars and commercial vehicles
mn

Table G.4   Prices and income, 1885–1987

	Consumer prices		Producer prices		Export prices	Import prices	Compensation of employees	National income
	All items	Food	All items	Raw materials				
	Index nos., 1980 = 100[a]						Marks bn	
1885	13·8	...	17·4	...	19·1	20·8	12·12	15·93
1886	13·4	...	16·7	...	18·3	20·6	12·50	16·28
1887	13·4	...	16·9	...	18·4	20·6	12·90	17·14
1888	13·8	...	17·4	...	18·7	21·0	13·51	18·05
1889	14·4	...	19·0	...	19·3	21·7	14·20	19·16
1890	14·8	...	20·0	...	19·3	21·4	14·76	20·59
1891	15·2	...	19·9	...	18·5	21·0	15·15	20·47
1892	15·0	...	18·5	...	17·4	19·7	15·30	21·04
1893	14·8	...	17·8	...	17·2	19·2	15·45	21·14
1894	14·6	...	16·9	...	16·1	17·9	15·77	21·30
1895	14·4	...	16·7	...	16·0	17·9	16·19	21·78
1896	14·2	...	16·7	...	16·4	17·9	16·95	22·98
1897	14·6	...	17·6	...	16·3	18·5	17·71	24·73
1898	15·0	...	18·3	...	16·4	18·5	18·61	26·50
1899	15·0	...	19·2	...	17·2	19·5	19·44	27·48
1900	15·2	...	20·8	...	17·8	20·7	20·39	28·86
1901	15·4	...	19·2	...	17·0	19·6	20·59	28·24
1902	15·4	...	18·7	...	16·5	19·9	20·90	29·13
1903	15·4	...	19·0	...	16·6	20·1	21·81	30·51
1904	15·6	...	19·0	...	16·8	20·6	22·80	32·02
1905	16·2	...	19·9	...	17·0	21·5	23·85	34·31
1906	17·2	...	21·3	...	16·9	22·8	25·45	36·17
1907	17·4	...	22·4	...	17·8	23·6	26·99	38·66
1908	17·4	...	20·8	...	16·8	21·7	27·27	38·54
1909	17·8	...	21·1	...	16·6	22·6	27·96	39·51
1910	18·2	...	21·5	...	16·7	22·9	29·43	41·89
1911	18·8	...	21·8	...	16·8	23·4	31·17	44·19
1912	19·8	...	23·6	...	17·2	24·4	32·82	47·30
1913	19·8	...	23·1	...	17·4	24·3	34·11	48·81
1914	20·4	...	24·1	...	...	...	...	...
1915	25·6	...	32·3	...	...	...	...	...
1916	33·6	...	34·6	...	...	...	...	...
1917	50·0	...	40·7	...	...	...	...	...
1918	59·8	...	49·5	...	...	...	...	...
1919	82·1	...	94·9	...	...	...	...	...
1920	201·7	...	339·0	...	...	...	...	..
1921	265·5	...	436·2	...	...	...	...	
1922	b	...	b	...	...	...		...
1923	b	...	b	...	...	...		...
1924	26·6	...	28·0	...	23·3	33·5	...	...
1925	28·9	...	29·7	...	24·2	34·2	52·13	58·59
1926	28·9	...	30·0	...	23·5	31·2	52·27	57·56
1927	30·1	30·5	31·3	1937 = 100	24·1	30·2	60·77	71·99
1928	30·8	30·5	32·3	139	24·3	31·0	67·40	78·22
1929	31·3	31·1	32·6	137	23·8	31·3	70·91	80·10
1930	30·1	29·5	29·7	125	22·6	27·3	67·47	72·89
1931	27·7	25·8	26·4	107	20·1	21·7	57·06	57·83
1932	24·5	24·2	22·8	92	17·8	16·9	45·69	37·46
1933	24·0	22·9	22·2	92	16·6	15·2	45·30	45·73
1934	24·6	21·8	23·5	95	15·3	14·7	50·04	55·10
1935	25·0	22·6	24·1	95	14·3	15·5	53·40	64·05
1936	25·3	24·2	24·8	98	14·4	16·0	56·94	69·96
1937	25·4	26·6	25·1	100	15·9	18·0	61·05	79·10
1938	25·5	26·6	25·1	98	16·6	16·6	65·23	87·65
1939	25·7	...	25·4	99	...	...	...	...
1940	26·5	...	26·1	103	...	...	...	...
1941	27·1	...	26·7	104	...	...	...	...
1942	27·8	...	27·1	106	...	...	...	...
1943	28·1	...	27·7	106	...	...	...	...
1944	28·8	...	27·7	106	...	...	...	...

Table **G.4 (Continued)**   **Prices and income, 1885–1987**

	Consumer prices		Producer prices		Export prices	Import prices	Compensation of employees	National income
	All items	Food	All items	Raw materials				
	Index nos., 1980 = 100[a]						Marks bn	
1945	29·8	30·0	. . .	. . .	. . .	. . .	. . .	. . .
1946	32·5	31·9	. . .	1980 = 100	. . .	. . .	. . .	. . .
1947	34·8	33·9	. . .	. . .	. . .	. . .	. . .	. . .
1948	36·7 / 43·0	39·7	49·0	40·3	. . .	. . .	. . .	. . .
1949	42·5	46·5	47·4	40·3	. . .	. . .	. . .	. . .
1950	39·8	43·1	46·3	39·8	42·1	54·4	44·89	89·78
1951	42·9	46·9	54·5	50·2	51·8	68·5	54·43	109·88
1952	43·8	49·4	56·1	54·9	54·6	64·5	60·66	125·45
1953	43·0	48·4	54·5	52·3	51·4	56·2	66·97	135·71
1954	43·1	48·9	53·4	51·3	51·4	54·4	73·19	145·95
1955	43·8	49·5	55·0	52·8	52·5	54·5	83·47	167·35
1956	44·9	50·7	55·6	54·4	54·0	56·5	93·53	184·71
1957	45·9	51·8	56·6	55·0	55·2	55·8	102·53	200·76
1958	46·8	53·0	56·1	54·4	53·9	52·9	110·70	214·71
1959	47·3	54·1	56·1	54·4	53·5	51·6	118·36	233·43
1960	48·0	54·7	56·6	54·4	54·2	51·9	132·92 / 143·16	260·43 / 279·37
1961	49·1	55·3	57·2	54·4	54·1	50·0	161·64	304·28
1962	50·5	55·8	57·7	54·4	54·2	49·5	178·84	329·27
1963	52·1	57·6	57·7	55·0	54·2	50·5	191·86	347·11
1964	53·3	58·7	57·7	56·0	55·5	51·4	209·93	380·64
1965	55·1	61·0	59·4	57·7	56·8	52·6	232·96	414·89
1966	57·0	62·7	59·9	58·3	57·9	53·6	250·83	439·63
1967	57·8	62·7	59·4	56·0	57·9	52·4	250·35	443·18
1968	58·6	62·2	56·1	53·8	57·3	52·2	268·84	480·05
1969	59·8	63·9	57·7	55·4	59·6	53·0	302·62	539·60
1970	61·7	65·2	61·0	56·6	61·4	52·5	359·29	607·67
1971	64·8	67·8	63·4	57·1	63·5	52·7	407·77	674·27
1972	68·3	71·7	65·1	58·8	64·8	52·4	449·12	739·74
1973	72·9	77·0	69·4	65·1	68·9	59·1	509·87	824·31
1974	77·9	80·9	78·7	77·7	80·7	76·4	562·05	879·14
1975	82·6	84·8	82·3	77·9	83·8	75·1	585·93	913·46
1976	86·3	88·7	85·4	83·1	87·0	79·7	630·02	1,001·94
1977	89·3	93·3	87·7	83·8	88·5	80·9	674·70	1,066·24
1978	91·6	94·6	88·7	81·6	89·9	77·9	720·24	1,148·13
1979	95·0	95·9	93·0	88·9	94·1	87·0	776·39	1,239·96
1980	100·0	100·0	100·0	100·0	100·0	100·0	842·84	1,311·46
1981	106·3	104·8	107·7	116·0	105·8	113·6	881·20	1,356·46
1982	112·0	111·3	113·6	119·0	110·4	116·2	900·37	1,395·99
1983	115·6	114·3	113·7	117	112·3	115·8	917·57	1,468·97
1984	118·4	116·0	116·9	124	116·2	122·8	950·49	1,547·92
1985	120·9	116·9	117·5	123	119·4	124·6	987·18	1,612·51
1986	120·7	117·6	108·8	91	116·8	101·0	1,037·13	1,704·46
1987	121·0	117·0	. . .	. . .	115·5	94·4	1,077·17	1,770·18

a   For raw materials, 1937 = 100 until 1946.
b   The years of hyperinflation.

211

Table G.5 Population, 1880–1986

	Total population	Males	Females	Births	Age distribution Under 15	Age distribution 15–64	Age distribution 65 & over
	mn	mn	mn	'000	mn	mn	mn
1880	45·10	22·12	22·98	1,696	15·02	27·92	2·16
1885	46·71	...	...	1,730	...	...	...
1886	47·13	...	...	1,746	...	...	...
1887	47·63	...	...	1,757	...	...	...
1888	48·17	...	...	1,761	...	...	...
1889	48·72	...	...	1,773	...	...	...
1890	49·24	24·14	25·10	1,759	16·25	30·48	2·51
1891	49·76	...	...	1,840	...	...	...
1892	50·27	...	...	1,796	...	...	...
1893	50·76	...	...	1,866	...	...	...
1894	51·34	...	...	1,841	...	...	...
1895	52·00	...	...	1,877	...	...	...
1896	52·75	...	...	1,915	...	...	...
1897	53·57	...	...	1,927	...	...	...
1898	54·41	...	...	1,965	...	...	...
1899	55·25	...	...	1,980	...	...	...
1900	56·05	27·58	28·46	1,996	18·38	34·92	2·75
1901	56·87	...	...	2,032	...	...	...
1902	57·68	...	...	2,025	...	...	...
1903	58·63	...	...	1,953	...	...	...
1904	59·48	...	...	2,026	...	...	...
1905	60·31	...	...	1,987	...	...	...
1906	61·15	...	...	2,022	...	...	...
1907	62·01	...	...	2,000	...	...	...
1908	62·86	...	...	2,015	...	...	...
1909	63·72	...	...	1,978	...	...	...
1910	64·57	...	...	1,925	...	...	...
1911	65·36	32·26	33·10	1,871	20·98	41·11	3·27
1912	66·15	...	...	1,870	...	...	...
1913	66·98	...	...	1,839	...	...	...
1922	61·90	...	...	1,425	...	...	...
1923	62·31	...	...	1,318	...	...	...
1924	62·70	...	...	1,291	...	...	...
1925	62·41	30·20	32·21	1,311	14·79	44·00	3·62
1926	63·63	...	...	1,245	...	...	...
1927	64·02	...	...	1,179	...	...	...
1928	64·39	...	...	1,200	...	...	...
1929	64·74	...	...	1,164	...	...	...
1930	65·08	...	...	1,144	...	...	...
1931	65·42	...	...	1,048	...	...	...
1932	65·72	...	...	993	...	...	...
1933	65·22	31·69	33·53	971	15·00	45·66	4·56
1934	66·41	...	...	1,198	...	...	...
1935	66·87	...	...	1,264	...	...	...
1936	67·35	...	...	1,279	...	...	...
1937	67·83	...	...	1,277	...	...	...
1938	68·56	...	...	1,349	...	...	...
1939	69·31	33·91	35·40	1,413	14·97	48·93	5·41
1946	43·29	...	...	733	...	...	...
1947	44·68	...	...	781	...	...	...
1948	45·74	...	...	806	...	...	...
1949	46·51	...	...	833	...	...	...
1950	47·85	22·31	25·54	813	(10·43)	(32·97)	(4·45)
1951	48·37	22·58	25·79	796	...	...	...
1952	48·69	22·73	25·96	799	...	...	...
1953	49·14	22·96	26·18	796	...	...	...
1954	49·69	23·24	26·45	816	...	...	...

	Total population	Males	Females	Births	Age distribution		
					Under 15	15–64	65 & over
	mn			'000	mn		
1955	50·19	23·49	26·69	820	(9·79)	(35·38)	(5·02)
1956	53·01	24·75	28·26	856	11·04	36·55	5·42
1957	53·66	25·07	28·58	892	11·23	36·83	5·59
1958	54·29	25·38	28·91	904	11·38	37·19	5·73
1959	54·88	25·67	29·21	952	11·55	37·45	5·88
1960	55·43	25·97	29·46	969	11·82	37·60	6·01
1961	56·18	26·41	29·76	1,013	12·18	37·74	6·26
1962	56·84	26·80	30·04	1,019	12·46	37·96	6·41
1963	57·39	27·10	30·29	1,054	12·73	38·06	6·59
1964	57·97	27·41	30·56	1,065	12·99	38·18	6·81
1965	58·62	27·79	30·83	1,044	13·24	38·35	7·03
1966	59·15	28·06	31·09	1,050	13·49	38·41	7·25
1967	59·29	28·05	31·24	1,019	13·69	38·14	7·46
1968	59·50	28·13	31·37	970	13·86	37·99	7·65
1969	60·07	28·48	31·59	903	14·01	38·22	7·84
1970	60·65	28·87	31·78	811	14·06	38·60	7·99
1971	61·30	29·26	32·04	779	14·12	38·97	8·22
1972	61·67	29·47	32·20	701	14·04	39·22	8·41
1973	61·98	29·65	32·33	636	13·87	39·51	8·60
1974	62·05	29·67	32·38	626	13·62	39·65	8·78
1975	61·83	29·50	32·33	601	13·29	39·61	8·94
1976	61·53	29·32	32·21	603	12·87	39·59	9·07
1977	61·40	29·24	32·16	582	12·45	39·73	9·22
1978	61·33	29·21	32·12	576	12·01	39·95	9·37
1979	61·36	29·25	32·11	582	11·57	40·29	9·50
1980	61·57	29·42	32·15	621	11·19	40·83	9·55
1981	61·68	29·50	32·18	625	10·80	41·43	9·45
1982	61·64	29·48	32·16	621	10·39	41·97	9·27
1983	61·42	29·37	32·06	594	9·96	42·39	9·08
1984	61·18	29·24	31·93	584	9·54	42·66	8·98
1985	61·02	29·18	31·84	586	9·23	42·74	9·05
1986	61·07	29·23	31·83	626	. . .	. . .	. . .

Table G.6 Education, 1900–87

| | Kindergarten | Elementary | Secondary | | Post-secondary | Higher education | |
| | | | Gymnasien | Other | | Total | of which: Female |
	No. of pupils '000					No. of students '000	
1900	...	8,966	...	...	...	...	...
1905	...	9,779	...	...	...	...	...
1910	...	10,310	1,016		...	...	...
1921	...	8,894	800	329	2,121	107·4	8·3
1925	...	6,662	821	259	2,507	83·0	7·2
1931	...	7,590	786	230	...	131·1	19·4
1935	...	...	674	...	...	81	11
1936	...	7,892	672	235	...	62	10
1937	...	7,758	671	272	...	58	7
1939	...	7,487	734	277	...	45	8
1940	...	7,289	757	201	...	...	...
1949	...	...	...	...	...	106	19
1950	...	6,314	620	286	2,000	111	19
1951	...	5,786	643	334	2,101	112	19
1952	...	5,309	682	370	2,300	114	19
1953	...	5,141	728	396	2,391	116	20
1954	...	4,832	763	413	2,527	121	21
1955	...	4,636	775	428	2,604	127	23
1956	...	4,574	768	418	2,545	145	29
1957	...	4,775	806	416	2,410	168	33
1958	...	4,883	824	426	2,298	188	39
1959	4·3	5,138	861	485	2,114	203	44
1960	...	5,291	853	502	1,921	220	48
1961	6·6	5,343	848	527	1,896	237	53
1962	8·0	5,445	847	556	1,881	252	58
1963	9·4	5,469	859	628	1,891	265	62
1964	10·1	5,525	890	669	1,945	271	63
1965	11·1	5,607	958	721	2,001	275	63
1966	12·3	5,711	1,038	788	1,980	290	70
1967	13·7	5,755	1,194	922	2,037	295	74
1968	12·9	5,887	1,271	1,017	2,019	314	78
1969	22·4	6,077	1,349	1,131	1,907	386	117
1970	33·4	6,347	1,379	1,185	1,904	422	130
1971	50·4	6,477	1,443	1,320	1,917	598	171
1972	65·6	6,510	1,567	1,429	1,998	658	199
1973	80·2	6,500	1,687	1,529	2,045	727	231
1974	86·0	6,481	1,780	1,621	2,067	789	262
1975	88·4	6,425	1,864	1,707	2,077	836	282
1976	83·3	6,278	1,914	1,834	2,053	872	294
1977	78·7	6,019	1,972	1,913	2,128	906	314
1978	70·8	5,722	2,013	1,942	2,265	939	334
1979	62·8	5,354	2,089	1,950	2,401	970	353
1980	62·1	5,044	2,119	1,926	2,477	1,032	383
1981	60·7	4,775	2,106	1,886	2,491	1,121	422
1982	59·8	4,501	2,051	1,824	2,494	1,198	458
1983	58·7	4,247	1,959	1,741	2,513	1,267	482
1984	58·1	4,006	1,851	1,638	2,555	1,312	496
1985	60·1	3,828	1,749	1,538	2,563	1,336	506
1986	62·3	3,722	1,656	1,475	2,495	1,368	518
1987	65·9	3,668	1,602	1,421	2,413	1,411	536

Table G.7 Labour market: employment, 1929–86

	Employed labour force[a]	Agriculture, forestry & fishing	Mining & quarrying	Manufacturing	Construction	Gas, electricity & water	Transport & communication	Distribution & services
				mn				
1929	(17·60)	...		6·50		...	...	...
1930	(16·41)	...		5·66		...	...	...
1931	(14·34)	...		4·68		...	...	...
1932	(12·52)	...		3·86		...	...	...
1933	(13·02)	...		4·28		...	...	...
1934	(15·04)	...		5·41		...	...	...
1935	(15·95)	...		5·89		...	...	...
1936	(17·11)	...		6·39		...	...	...
1937	(18·39)	...		6·91		...	...	...
1938	(19·50)	...		7·35		...	...	...
1939	(20·60)	...		7·67		...	...	...
1940	(18·77)	...		7·01		...	...	...
1941	(18·77)	...		7·32		...	...	...
1942	(18·58)	...		7·08		...	...	...
1943	(19·13)	...		7·45		...	...	...
1944	(18·77)	...		7·64		...	...	...
1948	(11·88)	...		4·88		...	...	...
1949	(12·16)	...		5·15		...	...	...
	(12·59)			5·44				
1950	20·37	5·02		8·73			6·62	
1951	20·90	4·85		9·12			6·93	
1952	21·29	4·70		9·37			7·23	
1953	21·80	4·54		9·77			7·50	
1954	22·38	4·40		10·27			7·71	
1955	23·21	4·29		10·89			8·04	
1956	23·79	4·18		11·36			8·26	
	24·75	4·18		11·68			8·89	
1957	25·21	4·11		11·95			9·16	
1958	25·36	3·98		12·08			9·30	
1959	25·57	3·82		12·36			9·39	
1960	25·95	3·62		12·66			9·67	
1961	26·24	3·45	0·51	10·15	2·02	0·29	1·47	8·36
1962	26·29	3·31	0·50	10·21	2·07	0·28	1·50	8·42
1963	26·32	3·14	0·48	9·91	2·16	0·28	1·52	8·83
1964	26·30	3·00	0·47	9·92	2·17	0·27	1·55	8·92
1965	26·42	2·88	0·45	10·11	2·21	0·26	1·58	8·93
1966	26·32	2·79	0·42	10·05	2·17	0·24	1·55	9·10
1967	25·46	2·64	0·38	9·55	1·99	0·22	1·52	9·16
1968	25·49	2·52	0·35	9·64	2·03	0·20	1·49	9·26
1969	25·87	2·40	0·34	10·07	2·07	0·19	1·48	9·32
1970	26·17	2·26	0·34	10·31	2·07	0·19	1·48	9·52
1971	26·32	2·13	0·43	9·84	2·27	0·21	1·55	9·89
1972	26·21	2·02	0·42	9·65	2·25	0·20	1·58	10·09
1973	26·41	1·92	0·40	9·70	2·25	0·21	1·61	10·32
1974	26·04	1·84	0·37	9·48	2·09	0·22	1·61	10·43
1975	25·29	1·77	0·36	9·01	1·88	0·24	1·58	10·45
1976	25·06	1·68	0·36	8·81	1·88	0·22	1·54	10·57
1977	25·01	1·59	0·33	8·77	1·84	0·23	1·52	10·73
1978	25·17	1·54	0·35	8·75	1·86	0·22	1·52	10·93
1979	25·52	1·48	0·34	8·79	1·93	0·23	1·54	11·21
1980	25·80	1·44	0·34	8·84	1·95	0·24	1·55	11·44
1981	25·61	1·41	0·36	8·60	1·93	0·24	1·55	11·53
1982	25·18	1·40	0·33	8·32	1·83	0·25	1·53	11·52
1983	24·79	1·39	0·32	8·01	1·78	0·24	1·52	11·53
1984	24·84	1·38	0·32	7·93	1·78	0·24	1·51	11·69
1985	25·01	1·36	0·32	8·01	1·70	0·24	1·51	11·87
1986	25·27	1·34	0·32	8·13	1·66	0·24	1·53	12·05

a   For years 1929–50 see notes on p. 224.

Table G.8 Labour market: other indicators, 1899–1987

	Manufacturing				Industrial disputes		
	Average weekly hrs worked	Average hourly earnings	Unemployment		Stoppages	Workers involved	Working days lost
		Marks	'000	%		'000	'000
1899	...	...	...	1·2	1,311	265	3,381
1900	...	...	...	2·0	1,468	321	3,712
1901	...	...	...	6·7	1,091	149	2,427
1902	...	...	...	2·9	1,106	150	1,951
1903	...	...	...	2·7	1,444	251	4,158
1904	...	...	...	2·1	1,990	310	5,285
1905	...	...	...	1·6	2,657	966	18,984
1906	...	...	...	1·1	3,626	839	11,567
1907	...	...	...	1·6	2,512	575	9,017
1908	...	...	...	2·9	1,524	281	3,666
1909	...	...	...	2·8	1,652	291	4,152
1910	...	...	...	1·9	3,228	681	17,848
1911	...	...	...	1·9	2,798	896	11,466
1912	...	...	...	2·0	2,834	1,031	10,724
1913	...	...	...	2·9	2,464	655	11,761
1914	...	...	...	7·2	1,223	238	2,844
1915	...	...	...	3·3	141	48	46
1916	...	...	...	2·2	240	423	245
1917	...	...	...	1·0	562	1,468	1,862
1918	...	...	...	1·2	532	716	1,453
1919	...	...	...	3·7	3,719	2,761	33,083
1920	...	...	...	3·8	3,807	2,009	16,755
1921	...	...	...	2·8	4,455	2,036	25,874
1922	...	...	...	1·5	4,785	2,566	27,734
1923	...	...	...	9·6	2,046	1,917	12,344
1924	...	...	...	13·5	1,973	2,066	36,198
1925	...	...	...	6·7	1,708	1,115	2,936
1926	...	...	...	18·0	351	131	1,222
1927	...	...	...	8·8	844	686	6,144
1928	(45·36)	...	...	8·4	739	986	20,339
1929	46·02	96·8	1,899	9·3	429	268	4,251
1930	44·22	94·0	3,076	15·3	353	302	4,029
1931	42·48	86·9	4,520	23·3	463	297	1,890
1932	41·46	73·0	5,575	30·1	648	172	1,130
1933	42·96	70·7	4,804	26·3	(69)	(13)	...
1934	44·58	72·5	2,718	14·9	...	...	...
1935	44·46	73·6	2,151	11·6	...	...	...
1936	46·7	74·8	1,593	8·3	...	...	...
1937	47·6	76·4	912	4·6	...	...	...
1938	48·5	78·9	429	2·1	...	...	...
1939	48·7	81·2	119	...	...	...	...
1940	49·2	83·9	52	...	...	...	...
1948	44·6	1·05	592	4·2	...	...	...
1949	43·8	1·20	1,230	8·3	892	58	271
1950	44·4	1·28	1,580	10·2	1,344	79	380
1951	44·8	1·45	1,432	9·0	1,528	174	1,593
1952	44·2	1·56	1,379	8·4	2,529	84	443
1953	48·0	1·59	1,259	7·5	1,359	51	1,488
1954	48·7	1·63	1,221	7·0	538	116	1,587
1955	48·8	1·73	928	5·1	866	600	847
1956	47·8	1·90	761	4·0	268	52	1,580
1957	46·4	2·09	662	3·4	86	45	1,072
1958	45·5	2·23	683	3·5	1,484	202	782
1959	45·6	2·36	480	2·4	55	22	62
1960	45·6	2·62	237	1·2	28	17	38
1961	45·3	2·90	161	0·8	119	20	61
1962	44·7	3·23	142	0·7	195	79	451
1963	44·3	3·46	174	0·8	187	316	1,846
1964	43·6	3·74	157	0·7	34	6	17

216

Table **G.8 (Continued)** **Labour market: other indicators, 1899–1987**

	Manufacturing		Unemployment		Industrial disputes		
	Average weekly hrs worked	Average hourly earnings			Stoppages	Workers involved	Working days lost
		Marks	'000	%		'000	'000
1965	44·1	4·12	147	0·6	20	6	49
1966	43·7	4·42	161	0·6	205	196	27
1967	42·0	4·60	459	1·7	742	60	390
1968	43·0	4·79	323	1·2	36	25	25
1969	43·8	5·28	179	0·7	86	90	249
1970	43·8	5·96	149	0·6	. . .[a]	184	93
1971	43·0	6·66	185	0·7	. . .	536	4,484
1972	42·7	7·24	247	0·9	. . .	23	66
1973	42·8	8·03	273	1·0	. . .	185	563
1974	41·9	8·94	582	2·1	. . .	250	1,051
1975	40·4	9·69	1,074	4·0	. . .	36	69
1976	41·4	10·35	1,060	4·0	. . .	169	534
1977	41·7	11·14	1,030	3·9	. . .	34	24
1978	41·6	11·73	993	3·7	. . .	487	4,281
1979	41·8	12·36	876	3·3	. . .	77	483
1980	41·6	13·18	889	3·8	. . .	45	128
1981	41·1	13·92	1,272	5·5	. . .	253	58
1982	40·7	14·64	1,833	7·5	. . .	40	15
1983	40·5	15·14	2,258	9·1	. . .	94	41
1984	41·0	15·49	2,266	9·1	. . .	537	5,618
1985	40·7	16·20	2,304	9·3	. . .	78	34
1986	40·4	16·80	2,228	9·0	. . .	116	28
1987	40·1	17·53	2,229	8·9	. . .	155	33

a   Series discontinued.

217

Table G.9 Public finance, 1885–1987

	Revenue					Expenditure				
	Taxes on personal income	Taxes on companies	Customs & excise	Turnover taxes	Total receipts	Defence	Education	Social services	Debt interest	Total expenditure
					Marks mn					
1885	...	...	339	...	369	481	312	...	...	...
1886	...	...	353	...	388	506	318	...	...	...
1887	...	...	382	...	417	543	331	...	...	...
1888	...	...	466	...	507	822	347	...	...	...
1889	...	...	586	...	629	752	362	...	...	...
1890	...	...	625	...	661	937	376	...	...	...
1891	...	...	641	...	675	743	390	...	...	...
1892	...	...	620	...	631	766	407	...	...	...
1893	...	...	607	...	638	805	426	...	...	...
1894	...	...	642	...	691	781	444	...	...	...
1895	...	...	670	...	706	742	463	...	...	...
1896	...	...	732	...	790	733	481	...	...	...
1897	...	...	733	...	792	794	519	...	...	...
1898	...	...	782	...	847	797	561	...	...	...
1899	...	...	786	...	852	843	599	...	...	...
1900	...	...	807	...	887	1,015	641	...	...	...
1901	...	...	817	...	901	1,057	688	...	...	...
1902	...	...	818	...	909	948	710	...	...	...
1903	...	...	819	...	906	927	762	...	...	...
1904	...	...	835	...	928	1,011	794	...	...	...
1905	...	...	952	...	1,055	1,171	827	...	...	...
1906	...	...	932	...	1,075	1,306	854	...	...	...
1907	...	...	1,067	...	1,206	1,434	931	...	...	...
1908	...	...	952	...	1,121	1,250	975	...	...	...
1909	...	...	1,124	...	1,360	1,345	1,062	...	...	...
1910	...	...	1,211	...	1,499	1,295	1,144	...	...	...
1911	...	...	1,369	...	1,676	1,317	1,224	...	...	...
1912	...	...	1,345	...	1,662	1,477	1,289	...	...	...
1913	...	...	1,339	...	1,665 / 2,095	1,819	1,265	1,181	422	7,478
1914	...	...	1,337	...	2,399	...	...	...	...	...
1915	...	...	941	...	1,769	...	...	...	...	...
1916	...	...	1,027	...	2,045	...	...	...	...	...
1917	...	...	...	...	7,682	...	...	...	...	...
1918	...	...	...	...	6,830	...	...	...	...	...
1919	...	...	...	...	9,712	...	...	...	...	...
1920	...	...	11,157	4,988	53,046	...	...	...	...	...
1921	...	...	21,216	11,474	149,570	...	...	...	...	...
1922	...	...	...	...	...	...	...	...	...	...
1923	...	...	...	...	...	...	...	...	...	...
1924	2,191	314	1,550	1,918	4,650	...	...	...	...	...
1925	2,170	187	1,962	1,416	4,731	633	2,145	5,295	91	15,743
1926	2,160	382	2,460	876	5,313	685	2,249	6,658	145	17,923
1927	2,650	478	2,939	878	6,357	752	2,547	7,128	215	20,144
1928	2,939	608	2,876	1,000	6,568	811	3,008	8,728	334	23,209
1929	2,837	559	2,899	1,013	6,741	755	3,176	10,177[a]	470	24,237
1930	2,566	450	3,063	996	6,634	755	3,033	11,118[a]	579	24,509
					Marks bn					
1931	2·07	0·30	2·78	0·99	...	0·72	2·58	10·59[a]	0·62	21·36
1932	1·29	0·11	2·62	1·35	...	0·71	2·16	9·01[a]	0·60	17·68
1933	1·25	0·21	2·79	1·52	...	1·60	...	...	0·63	18·38
1934	1·67	0·32	3·09	1·87	...	1·90	...	...	0·63	21·62
1935	2·44	0·59	3·47	2·02	...	3·48	...	...	0·69	21·96
1936	3·13	1·05	3·65	2·39	...	5·35	...	...	0·81	23·65
1937	3·98	1·55	4·14	2·75	...	7·60	...	...	1·31	26·93
1938	5·26	2·42	4·65	3·36	...	15·85	...	...	...	37·16
1939	7·00	3·23	6·12	3·74	...	...	...	...	...	...
1940	...	...	...	3·93	...	...	...	...	...	...
1941	...	...	...	4·15	...	...	...	...	...	...

Table G.9 (Continued) Public finance, 1885–1987

	Revenue					Expenditure				
	Taxes on personal income	Taxes on companies	Customs & excise	Turnover taxes	Total receipts	Defence	Education	Social services	Debt interest	Total expenditure
					Marks bn					
1942	...	...	...	4·16	...	...	...	...	...	...
1943	...	...	...	4·18	...	...	...	...	...	...
1946	5·07	0·66	...	1·77	...	...	...	...	...	...
1947	5·52	0·76	...	2·30	...	...	...	...	...	...
1948	1·93	0·28	...	0·84	...	...	...	...	...	...
	3·31	0·86	...	2·20	...	...	...	...	...	...
1949	4·75	1·48	...	3·84	...	...	...	...	[0·05]	...
1950	3·89	1·45	3·66	4·77	16·10	4·7	2·1	7·6	(0·10)	28·1
1951	5·10	2·27	5·29	6·82	21·67	7·9	2·6	9·9	(0·15)	37·4
1952	7·58	2·78	5·60	8·38	27·00	7·9	3·0	10·2	(0·21)	41·5
1953	8·61	2·99	5·93	8·87	29·56	5·5	3·5	12·6	(0·21)	44·3
1954	8·46	3·07	5·98	9·59	30·79	5·9	3·9	12·7	(0·35)	47·7
1955	8·75	3·11	6·97	11·12	34·18	6·1	4·2	13·7	(1·00)	51·2
1956	10·13	3·64	7·65	12·18	38·42	7·3	4·9	15·6	(1·06)	59·9
1957	11·17	4·51	8·14	12·60	40·92	7·5	5·4	17·5	(1·13)	66·4
1958	11·41	5·19	8·52	12·96	42·88	8·7	6·0	18·4	(1·16)	71·5
1959	13·18	5·12	9·76	14·24	48·05	9·5	6·5	20·1	(1·35)	76·6
1960	16·86	6·43	11·00	15·87	56·25	8·5	5·6	15·5	(1·44)	64·6
	17·07	6·51	11·09	16·15	56·99					
1961	21·27	7·47	12·59	17·87	66·23	13·2	8·2	22·2	(1·43)	95·3
1962	24·53	7·79	13·76	19·21	73·26	17·1	9·2	23·9	(1·53)	107·2
1963	27·30	7·69	14·73	20·04	77·95	19·4	10·5	24·2	(1·94)	116·8
1964	30·19	8·02	16·30	21·93	85·49	19·0	12·3	27·8	(2·05)	128·1
1965	31·54	8·17	17·91	24·22	91·40	18·9	14·3	31·3	(2·23)	140·6
1966	35·13	7·69	18·98	25·06	97·13	19·5	15·5	32·4	(2·75)	146·7
1967	35·34	7·06	21·25	24·72	99·30	21·0	16·3	35·0	(3·63)	155·9
1968	38·35	8·55	21·85	25·69	105·58	17·5	17·5	35·9	(3·70)	159·2
1969	44·05	10·90	23·63	36·75	128·10	19·9	20·3	37·2	(4·02)	174·7
1970	51·09	8·72	24·78	38·13	136·88	19·8	24·8	40·4	(4·61)	196·3
1971	61·14	7·17	26·51	42·90	153·08	21·8	31·3	45·2	(5·05)	225·2
1972	72·91	8·50	29·98	46·98	174·55	24·8	35·7	50·3	(5·56)	251·3
1973	87·71	10·89	33·74	49·83	199·20	27·3	40·4	52·1	(6·51)	277·7
1974	98·75	10·40	33·56	51·91	212·74	30·7	47·3	62·0	(7·74)	316·5
						30·7	49·4	199·4		458·1
1975	99·19	10·05	34·40	54·08	214·50	32·4	53·8	248·3	(14·45)	526·8
1976	111·47	11·84	36·65	58·46	237·14	33·7	54·9	267·4	(17·73)	559·5
1977	126·28	16·83	38·55	62·68	264·93	34·3	57·4	284·3	(20·53)	592·6
1978	129·44	19·82	40·69	73·27	283·87	36·7	61·3	298·6	(21·73)	636·7
1979	134·62	22·91	42·33	84·21	306·82	38·6	66·3	317·8	(24·72)	688·7
1980	148·36	21·32	43·52	93·45	329·43	40·9	73·0	339·1	(29·23)	741·3
1981	149·49	20·16	45·34	97·79	336·50	44·2	76·5	367·8	(36·18)	790·9
1982	154·01	21·46	46·60	97·72	344·46	46·0	77·6	389·1	(44·66)	828·0
1983	157·16	23·68	48·90	105·87	361·91	48·5	78·1	396·8	(50·95)	848·5
1984	162·72	26·31	50·68	110·48	377·74	49·5	77·6	412·3	(53·02)	876·2
1985	176·20	31·84	51·17	109·83	397·58	50·8	80·8	425·4	...	907·0
1986	182·11	32·30	52·16	111·14	411·28	52·0	83·6	442·8	...	942·2
1987	194·87	27·30	53·11	118·80	428·35	...	...	...	...	...

a Including health expenditure.

Table **G.10**   **Value of exports and imports by country, 1885–1987**

	Total exports	Exports to:				Total imports	Imports from:			
		France	Italy	UK	USA		France	Italy	UK	USA
					Marks mn					
1885	2,854	248	85	453	155	2,923	218	76	452	122
1886	2,976	249	84	443	212	2,874	222	90	453	106
1887	3,136	219	99	491	231	3,109	213	91	461	143
1888	3,207	219	81	480	236	3,253	214	111	496	153
1889	3,167	209	102	647	395	4,015	271	149	665	317
1890	3,335	231	93	690	417	4,162	258	140	601	397
1891	3,176	237	87	679	358	4,151	251	133	565	403
1892	2,954	201	90	629	347	4,010	255	134	548	535
1893	3,092	201	84	670	354	3,962	239	149	565	427
1894	2,961	188	81	632	270	3,942	211	125	512	450
1895	3,318	202	82	676	368	4,119	223	138	536	483
1896	3,525	201	89	713	383	4,307	230	132	551	528
1897	3,635	210	88	699	397	4,681	246	146	568	652
1898	3,757	205	92	741	333	5,076	261	161	566	876
1899	4,217	216	112	801	377	5,463	298	193	673	894
1900	4,611	277	123	862	440	5,769	303	181	719	1,004
1901	4,431	249	123	907	385	5,421	272	178	553	986
1902	4,678	253	125	958	449	5,631	304	189	557	893
1903	5,015	272	131	982	469	6,003	330	196	594	935
1904	5,223	274	141	985	495	6,354	365	187	615	943
1905	5,732	293	164	1,042	542	7,129	402	211	718	992
1906	6,359	383	231	1,067	637	8,021	434	241	825	1,237
1907	6,847	449	303	1,060	653	8,745	454	285	977	1,320
1908	6,399	438	311	997	508	7,663	420	236	697	1,283
1909	6,597	455	289	1,015	606	8,519	485	288	723	1,263
1910	7,475	543	324	1,102	633	8,927	509	275	767	1,188
1911	8,106	599	348	1,140	640	9,683	524	285	809	1,343
1912	8,967	689	401	1,161	698	10,674	552	305	843	1,586
1913	10,097	790	394	1,438	713	10,751	584	318	876	1,711
1923	6,102	67	245	557	475	6,150	186	150	1,015	1,172
1924	6,674	114	240	612	491	9,132	694	372	827	1,709
1925	9,284	489	425	937	604	12,429	558	496	944	2,196
1926	10,415	670	486	1,163	744	9,984	378	388	576	1,603
1927	10,801	562	462	1,178	776	14,114	806	528	963	2,073
1928	12,055	693	547	1,180	796	13,931	741	467	894	2,026
1929	13,486	935	602	1,306	991	13,359	642	443	865	1,790
1930	12,036	1,149	484	1,219	685	10,349	519	365	639	1,307
1931	9,592	834	341	1,134	488	6,713	342	268	453	791
1932	5,741	483	223	446	281	4,653	190	181	259	592
1933	4,872	395	227	406	246	4,199	184	166	238	483
1934	4,178	282	246	383	158	4,448	177	185	206	373
1935	4,270	253	278	375	170	4,156	154	188	256	241
1936	4,778	255	241	406	172	4,228	99	209	264	232
1937	5,919	313	311	432	209	5,495	156	221	309	282
1938	5,264	229	349	374	157	5,449	159	284	309	455
1939	5,653	129	362	228	125	5,207	78	287	181	198
1940	4,868	—	724	—	11	5,012	—	508	—	16
1941	6,840	315	1,192	—	3	6,925	752	938	—	8
1942	7,560	546	1,305	—	—	8,691	1,404	1,022	—	—
1943	8,588	560	950	—	—	8,258	1,416	781	—	—
					Marks bn					
1948	1·82	0·22	0·07	0·26	0·10	3·16	0·01	0·07	0·13	1·57
1949	3·81	0·51	0·22	0·38	0·16	7·33	0·09	0·32	0·18	2·59
1950	8·36	0·61	0·49	0·36	0·43	11·37	0·69	0·51	0·49	1·74
1951	14·58	0·97	0·67	0·88	0·99	14·73	0·62	0·55	0·50	2·72
1952	16·91	1·08	0·63	0·96	1·04	16·20	0·61	0·64	0·53	2·51
1953	18·53	1·08	1·24	0·79	1·24	16·01	0·78	0·74	0·65	1·66
1954	22·04	1·19	1·34	0·86	1·23	19·34	0·97	0·84	0·85	2·23

Table G.10 (Continued)   Value of exports and imports by country, 1885–1987

	Total exports	Exports to:				Total imports	Imports from:			
		France	Italy	UK	USA		France	Italy	UK	USA
					Marks bn					
1955	25·72	1·46	1·43	1·03	1·61	24·47	1·45	1·04	0·87	3·20
1956	30·86	1·95	1·66	1·26	2·07	27·96	1·35	1·22	1·15	3·97
1957	35·97	2·25	2·00	1·41	2·49	31·70	1·55	1·55	1·14	5·63
1958	37·00	2·16	1·85	1·46	2·64	31·13	1·60	1·70	1·36	4·19
1959	41·18	2·97	2·20	1·66	3·78	35·82	2·76	2·18	1·63	4·58
1960	47·95	4·20	2·85	2·15	3·72	42·72	4·00	2·63	1·96	5·97
1961	50·98	4·78	3·39	2·12	3·45	44·36	4·62	3·04	1·97	6·10
1962	52·98	5·44	4·11	1·95	3·86	49·50	5·27	3·74	2·35	7·03
1963	58·31	6·43	5·46	2·21	4·20	52·28	5·50	3·70	2·47	7·94
1964	64·92	7·42	4·59	2·72	4·79	58·84	6·27	4·47	2·78	8·07
1965	71·65	7·79	4·50	2·80	5·74	70·45	7·84	6·56	3·14	9·20
1966	80·63	9·22	5·66	3·13	7·18	72·67	8·62	6·68	3·16	9·18
1967	87·05	10·05	6·89	3·47	7·86	70·18	8·49	6·44	2·93	8·56
1968	99·55	12·24	7·57	4·03	10·84	81·18	9·78	8·07	3·41	8·85
1969	113·56	15·12	9·26	4·59	10·63	97·97	12·70	9·49	3·91	10·25
1970	125·28	15·48	11·17	4·46	11·44	109·61	13·90	10·84	4·26	12·07
1971	136·01	16·98	11·45	5·45	13·14	120·12	15·92	12·69	4·41	12·42
1972	149·02	19·41	12·56	7·05	13·80	128·74	18·16	13·90	4·58	10·76
1973	178·40	23·13	14·98	8·40	15·09	145·42	18·96	14·04	5·16	12·22
1974	230·58	27·34	18·73	11·01	17·34	179·73	20·90	14·98	6·27	13·97
1975	221·59	25·96	16·19	10·09	13·15	184·31	22·15	17·23	6·94	14·23
1976	256·64	33·67	19·00	12·18	14·41	222·17	25·83	18·90	8·54	17·56
1977	273·61	33·64	18·73	14·61	18·20	235·18	27·31	20·73	10·45	17·02
1978	284·91	34·90	19·43	16·88	20·18	243·71	28·28	23·18	12·07	17·43
1979	314·47	39·99	24·53	21·03	20·76	292·04	33·20	25·80	17·22	20·27
1980	350·33	46·62	29·94	22·92	21·48	341·38	36·59	27·08	22·86	25·69
1981	396·90	51·91	31·31	26·16	25·98	369·18	40·12	27·56	27·50	28·39
1982	427·74	60·13	32·38	31·32	28·12	376·46	42·88	28·71	27·00	28·21
1983	432·28	55·56	32·09	35·40	32·85	390·19	44·57	31·57	27·14	27·71
1984	488·22	61·34	37·66	40·58	46·83	434·26	45·84	34·17	33·29	31·10
1985	537·16	64·00	41·79	45·97	55·53	463·81	49·28	37·15	37·16	32·34
1986	526·36	62·33	42·88	44·60	55·21	413·74	47·08	38·09	29·76	26·86
1987	527·38	63·61	46·06	46·63	49·88	409·64	47·48	39·21	29·39	25·61

Sources

(For sources used in specific tables, see Notes.)

1 Andic, Suphan and Veverka, Jindrich, 'The Growth of Government Expenditure in Germany since Unification', *Finanzarchiv* 1963/64, Tübingen.

2 Hoffman, W.H., *Das Wachstum der Deutschen Wirtschaft seit der Mitte des 19 Jahrhunderts*, Springer-Verlag, Berlin and Heidelberg, 1965.

3 International Labour Office, *Technical Guide*, Vol. II, Geneva, 1972, 1976, 1980.

4 League of Nations, *Year Book of Labour Statistics*.

5 Mitchell, B.R., *European Historical Statistics, 1750–1975*, 2nd edn, Macmillan, London, 1980.

6 Organisation for Economic Cooperation and Development (OECD), *Labour Force Statistics*, annual and quarterly, Paris.

7 OECD, *National Accounts, 1950–1979*, Vol. 1, Paris, 1981.

8 OECD, *National Accounts, 1960–1987*, Vol. 1, Paris, 1989.

9 *Statistisches Jahrbuch*, annual, W. Kohlhammer GmbH, Stuttgart and Mainz.

10 *Statistical Year Book of the League of Nations*, Geneva.

11 Supplement to the United Nations *Statistical Year Book* and *Monthly Bulletin of Statistics*, New York, 1967, 1972 and 1977.

12 United Nations, *Monthly Bulletin of Statistics*, New York.

13 United Nations, *Statistics of National Income and Expenditure*, Series H, No. 7, New York, 1955.

14 United Nations, *Statistical Year Book*, New York.

15 *Year Book of Labour Statistics*, ILO, Geneva.

Notes

Table G.1 Gross domestic product at current prices

Sources: **2, 7, 8**

From 1950, OECD data for the Federal Republic of Germany have been used. The break in the series at 1960 is due to a change in the system of national accounts; for details see **7**.

For 1885–1938, data from **2** have been used and are for the German Reich. The figures shown in the columns for imports and exports of goods and services are the net foreign balance in this period.

Table G.2 Gross domestic product at constant prices

Sources: **2, 7, 8, 13**

From 1950, OECD data for the Federal Republic of Germany have been used. There is a break in the series in 1960 when there was a change in the system of classification (see notes to Table G.1).

For 1948–49, constant price estimates published in **13** were linked to OECD data at 1950 and roughly adjusted to 1980 prices. The figure for 1948 is for six months only. For 1900–38, the figures are for the German Reich and are based on estimates made by Hoffmann, **2**, roughly adjusted to 1980 prices. The figures for gross domestic product have been obtained by using an index of output (based on Hoffman's estimates) and extrapolating the 1936 figure published in **13** grossed up to include the German Reich. Hoffmann's figures are for *net* national product and were not, therefore, used for this column. Similarly, Hoffmann's estimates for capital formation have not been used as they are net and not gross figures.

Table G.3 Industrial production

Sources: **5, 9, 10, 12, 14**

Industrial production: a combined base weighted index of output in manufacturing, mining and electricity and gas industries. The Saar is included from 1950. Figures from 1938 are for the Federal Republic of Germany; 1900–37 covers the German Reich. For further details of method of construction and weights see **11**.

Coal: includes brown and hard coal.

Cars and commercial vehicles: the figures for 1946–48 are for the British and American occupation zones only. For 1900–28 (first line), chassis production for export is excluded from the figures.

Natural gas: published figures are now given in terajoules. From 1977, the published figures have been converted to cubic metres using the conversion factors given in **12**. From 1951 (second line) to 1962 (first line), natural gas from oil wells is included.

Electricity: the Saar is included from 1960 (second line).

The following boundary changes affect the figures in this table: 1900–18 parts of Alsace Lorraine included; 1921–34 the Saar excluded; 1945–58 the Saar excluded; from 1945 Federal Republic of Germany only for most of the series.

Table G.4 Prices and income

Sources: **2, 5, 7, 8, 9, 10, 14**

Consumer prices: from 1924, the retail price index shown in **9**, 1987, which shows a comprehensive index back to 1924 has been used. This index has been linked to an earlier index to provide a series back to 1885. Commodity coverage of the earlier index would have covered food, heating and lighting, clothing and rent.

Producer prices: the official title of the 'All items' index is

'Index of producers' prices of industrial products'. It is a base weighted index, and the commodity coverage has been widened considerably in recent years. From 1968, value-added tax has been excluded from the prices making up the index. In 1924, prices for the index were based on gold following the 'great inflation' and, from 1925, a new series was spliced on to the old index. From 1948, the series is for the Federal Republic of Germany and excludes the Saar before 1960 and West Berlin before 1962.

The official title of the 'Raw materials' index is 'Price index of basic materials'. It is a base weighted index relating to basic materials purchased by goods-producing sectors (excluding agriculture and forestry). The price relatives include customs duties (imported goods) and turnover compensation tax.

The series for 1928–44 is for the German Reich based on 1937 = 100. It includes some semi-manufactured goods.

For further details of the current series see **11**.

Export and import prices: from 1954, the published series given in **9** has been used. This was linked to an earlier series based on data given in **2** to give figures back to 1885.

Compensation of employees: OECD data have been used from 1950. The figures include wages and salaries in cash and in kind paid to employees, together with contributions on behalf of employees to social security schemes and private pension funds as well as family allowances and private health insurance paid by employers. Two figures are given for 1960 because of the change in classification (see notes to Table G.1). See also **7**.

For 1900–38 Hoffmann's estimates of *arbeitseinkommen* have been given; see **2** for composition of the series. These cover the German Reich, whereas the figures from 1950 are for the Federal Republic of Germany.

National income: OECD data have been used from 1950. National income is defined as the sum of compensation of employees, net entrepreneurial and property income of residents and indirect taxes less subsidies. Two figures have been given for 1960 because of the change in classification (see notes to Table G.1). For further details, see **7**.

Estimates by Hoffmann, **2** for the German Reich have been given for the period 1900–38. They refer to Netto-sozialprodukt and may not be comparable with the figures from 1950. For further details of composition, see **2**. Hoffmann's estimates show a minus figure for income from capital in some years and for factor incomes from abroad for the years 1926–38.

Table G.5 Population

Sources: **2, 6**

OECD data have been used from 1950. From 1956, the figures are annual averages of the resident (*de jure*) population. For 1950–55, they are mid-year estimates and exclude West Berlin. The figures for 1900–49 are taken from Hoffmann, **2**, and are mid-year estimates. The figures for 1880, 1890, 1900, 1911, 1925, 1933 and 1939 are census data. Federal Republic only from 1946.

Age distribution: for the years 1890–1955 the population distribution relates to those under 14 years and 14–64 years. The years 1950 and 1955 have been estimated by the author on the basis of data in **2**.

Births: figures for 1914–16 include Alsace Lorraine. From 1922 part of Upper Silesia excluded. Heligoland not included before 1891.

Table G.6 Education

Sources: **5, 9**

The current system provides compulsory schooling from 6 to 15 years of age but at least part-time education is normally compulsory up to the age of 18.

Kindergarten: includes *Schulkindergarten* and *Vorklassen*.

Elementary: basic schooling; figures are for pupils at *Grundschulen* and *Hauptschulen*, previously known as *Volksschulen*. Data refer to pupils enrolled for the school year. Public sector schools only in the pre-war period and figures are for May of the year shown. After four years at the *Grundschulen* children attend *Hauptschulen* for a further five years to complete their compulsory education.

Secondary: the figures for pupils at *Gymnasien* are at May 15 each year. Pupils attend the *Gymnasien* for nine years after completion of four years at *Grundschulen*. Figures for 1951–56 exclude Hamburg and Bremen. 'Other secondary' includes *Realschulen* (intermediate schools) which pupils attend for six years after completing four years at the *Grundschulen* and *Sonderschulen* (special schools). In the period before 1945, figures refer mainly to intermediate or middle school pupils.

Post-secondary: includes *Berufschulen*, *Beruffachschulen* and *Fachschulen* (covering full-time vocational training and technical schools). Both public and private schools are included.

Higher education: students in universities and other institutions of higher education in the *Wintersemester*. Includes full- and part-time students from 1963.

Table G.7 Labour market: employment

Sources: **4, 6, 14, 15**

OECD data have been used from 1950. The figures are annual averages of those in civil employment and include employees, self-employed and unpaid family workers working for at least one-third of normal working time. The unemployed and temporarily stopped are not included.

From 1948, the figures are for the Federal Republic of Germany; the Saar is included from 1950 (second line) and West Berlin from 1956 (second line). The classification of industrial activity was changed in 1960. From 1972, the data are not strictly comparable with earlier years because of a change in the way in which national data were converted to the International Standard Industrial Classification.

'Distribution and services' includes wholesale and retail trades, restaurants and hotels, finance, insurance, real estate and business services, commercial, social and personal services.

For 1929–50 (first line), the figures for the 'Employed labour force' are for wage earners and salaried employees only in mining, manufacturing, construction, commerce, personal and public services and agriculture. The numbers are based on sickness insurance statistics published in 4 and from 1936 have been extrapolated by means of an index published in 14, 1948, and 15, 1954. The figures include the Saar from 1935 and Austria and Sudetenland for 1939–44. Figures available for the *total* labour force are from census data covering the economically active population which includes employers and self-employed, employees and unemployed. For the years 1933 (excluding the Saar) and 1939 (1937 territory), the economically active population numbered just over 32 mn and 34·5 mn, respectively.

The figures given for this period in the industry classifications are for wage earners and salaried employees in manufacturing. For 1939–44 they include employees in the mining and building industries. The economically active population in manufacturing was 9·97 mn in 1933 and 11·51 mn in 1939. For further details see 4.

Table G.8 Labour market: other indicators

Sources: **4, 5, 15**

Manufacturing: average weekly hours worked: the current series is of average weekly hours *paid for* in the reporting week. This comprises, in addition to hours actually worked, hours not worked but paid for, such as annual vacation, paid public holidays and paid sick leave. It covers wage earners of both sexes including foremen but excluding apprentices. Sample revised in 1973. Construction workers and public utilities employees are included for 1953–56, building workers for 1936–40 and mining in 1939 and 1940.

The figures are for the Federal Republic of Germany from 1948; the Saar is included from 1960 and West Berlin from 1964.

Manufacturing: average hourly earnings: the current series is of average hourly earnings per wage earner, both sexes, without distinction as to age, and including foremen (but not apprentices). Earnings include cash payments before deduction of taxes and social security contributions payable by workers; payment for normal working hours, overtime pay, holiday pay, sick leave, bonuses and gratuities, cost of living allowances and special premiums are included; also includes family allowances paid directly by the employer. Federal Republic of Germany from 1948; the Saar included from 1960 and West Berlin from 1964.

From 1929 to 1941 includes mining and transport. For further details see 3 and 4.

Unemployment: refers to unemployed registered at employment offices at each month-end; the annual figure is the average of months. 1948–60 data are for a specific date: June 30 for 1948–54 and September 30 for 1955–60. 1887–1928 data are for the unemployed in trade unions. From 1949 data refer to the Federal Republic of Germany. See also 3. The percentage figure is the ratio of unemployed to total employees (civilian and military).

Industrial disputes: figures for 1933 are for the first quarter. For 1949 and 1950, American and British zones only. Data from 1950 are for Federal Republic of Germany including West Berlin from 1960.

Table G.9 Public finance

Sources: **1, 2, 5, 9, 14**

Total receipts: total tax revenue (including customs and excise); excludes *Gemeinde* revenues. Includes Saar and West Berlin from 1960 (second line).

Taxes on personal income: includes *Lohnsteuer* (wages tax) and *Einkommensteuer* (income tax).

Taxes on companies: figures are for *Körperschaftsteuer*.

Turnover taxes (Umsatzsteuer): currently mainly value-added tax. Previously it was a turnover tax which was levied at each stage of production.

Excise duties: include those on tobacco, coffee, brandy, sparkling wine and fuel oil.

Total expenditure: general government expenditure including Länder. 1913 and 1925–38 expenditure data are from 1. 1885–1912 defence and education data are from 2.

Debt interest: from 1949 data are from 14 and are for fiscal years ending March 31 up to 1954. From 1975, data are for interest payments in years ending December 31. In 1983 accounting methods changed and data after this date are not strictly comparable. 1949 data in this column are from a different source from data in the other columns.

Figures for revenue are for fiscal years (April 1–March 31) for 1885–1949. From 1950, data are in calendar years.

Figures are in calendar years for expenditure in 1913, 1925–38 and from 1950; and for debt interest from 1955.

Table G.10 Value of exports and imports by country

Source: **5, 9**

Figures refer to the Federal Republic of Germany from 1948. For 1923–35 and 1945–59, the Saar is excluded. Austria became part of Germany in 1938. Trade with UK included Southern Ireland up to 1923. Alsace Lorraine is included to 1918. Figures from 1923 are post-inflation values. From 1906, figures refer to countries of origin and consumption; German free ports are not included in customs area before this date.

ITALY

CONTENTS

Table It.1 Gross domestic product at current prices, 1885–1987

	Consumers' expenditure	Government current expenditure	Gross fixed capital formation	Value of physical change in stocks	Exports of goods & services	Imports of goods & services	**Gross domestic product at market prices**
				L bn			
1885	9·10	1·00	1·58		1·22	−1·50	**11·40**
1886	9·11	0·99	1·92		1·29	−1·50	**11·81**
1887	8·81	1·04	1·52		1·31	−1·66	**11·02**
1888	8·48	1·13	1·39		1·22	−1·24	**10·98**
1889	9·58	1·16	0·56		1·28	−1·44	**11·14**
1890	9·89	1·14	1·20		1·21	−1·38	**12·06**
1891	9·93	1·11	1·55		1·20	−1·19	**12·60**
1892	9·30	1·09	0·89		1·28	−1·22	**11·34**
1893	9·18	1·11	1·19		1·30	−1·25	**11·53**
1894	9·09	1·12	0·72		1·36	−1·15	**11·14**
1895	9·59	1·09	0·71		1·39	−1·26	**11·52**
1896	9·36	1·09	0·91		1·40	−1·27	**11·49**
1897	9·36	1·07	0·55		1·45	−1·26	**11·17**
1898	10·03	1·07	1·32		1·58	−1·49	**12·51**
1899	9·99	1·08	1·20		1·82	−1·58	**12·51**
1900	10·44	1·11	1·81		1·72	−1·79	**13·29**
1901	10·21	1·12	2·26		1·77	−1·81	**13·55**
1902	10·21	1·15	1·59		1·88	−1·81	**13·02**
1903	11·19	1·16	1·86		1·93	−1·92	**14·22**
1904	10·95	1·19	1·84		2·05	−1·99	**14·04**
1905	11·32	1·22	1·89		2·24	−2·15	**14·52**
1906	12·26	1·24	2·13		2·48	−2·65	**15·46**
1907	12·98	1·25	3·67		2·52	−3·01	**17·41**
1908	13·17	1·34	2·94		2·40	−3·04	**16·81**
1909	13·83	1·45	3·75		2·57	−3·25	**18·35**
1910	14·34	1·70	2·70		2·82	−3·41	**18·15**
1911	15·21	1·92	3·64		2·91	−3·49	**20·19**
1912	16·14	2·08	3·72		3·07	−3·88	**20·13**
1913	16·38	2·11	3·99		3·25	−3·84	**21·89**
1914	16·24	3·20	2·57		2·95	−3·11	**21·85**
1915	18·12	8·85	1·36		3·22	−4·51	**27·04**
1916	26·40	16·02	0·56		3·93	−8·14	**38·77**
1917	37·08	23·43	1·59		4·11	−13·32	**52·89**
1918	49·58	30·14	2·05		4·26	−15·06	**70·97**
1919	55·24	24·99	5·55		7·10	−16·15	**76·73**
1920	83·42	18·38	14·95		13·08	−27·51	**102·32**
1921	81·82	22·14	10·58		10·22	−18·37	**106·39**
1922	85·70	17·66	15·49		11·71	−17·01	**113·55**
1923	90·70	13·02	21·00		14·07	−18·35	**120·44**
1924	90·96	12·47	24·43		17·97	−27·07	**118·76**
1925	114·15	12·40	32·68		22·80	−27·52	**154·51**
1926	124·15	13·93	30·31		22·85	−27·63	**163·61**
1927	112·11	13·56	21·82		18·95	−22·07	**144·37**
1928	106·81	12·94	29·55		17·97	−23·54	**143·73**
1929	107·31	13·19	27·71		18·12	−22·87	**143·46**
1930	99·50	13·62	19·53		14·96	−18·70	**128·91**
1931	85·50	14·74	16·45		12·73	−12·80	**116·62**
1932	82·40	14·98	16·36		8·85	−9·11	**113·48**
1933	77·39	15·44	14·40		8·37	−9·53	**106·07**
1934	77·35	15·13	15·34		7·36	−8·44	**106·74**
1935	81·17	17·78	23·25		6·66	−8·45	**120·41**
1936	83·93	24·48	21·74		6·50	−6·67	**129·98**
1937	99·47	26·52	30·29		12·08	−14·51	**153·85**
1938	121·0	26·30	28·74		11·60	−12·30	**175·34**
1939	117·3	30·50	34·93		11·01	−11·31	**182·43**
1940	144·7	37·10	32·15		11·16	−13·67	**211·44**
1941	168·0	44·95	31·16		13·29	−12·00	**245·40**
1942	218·1	62·78	26·21		14·34	−14·20	**307·23**
1943	298·9	99·31	17·95		20·69	−23·10	**413·75**
1944	623·8	143·0	8·05		18·32	−53·98	**739·19**

226

Table It.1 (Continued) Gross domestic product at current prices, 1885–1987

	Consumers' expenditure	Government current expenditure	Gross fixed capital formation	Value of physical change in stocks	Exports of goods & services	Imports of goods & services	Gross domestic product at market prices
			L bn				
1945	1,198	232·4	41·33		11·96	−148·7	1,334
1946	2,208	483·0	630·00		125·1	−269·0	3,177
1947	4,524	682·6	1,617		381·9	−1,003·3	6,203
1948	5,375	873·8	1,342		714·6	−937·7	7,368
1949	5,718	778·8	1,426		781·7	−964·1	7,741
1950	6,245	831·7	1,650		943·0	−1,023·0	8,647
1951	7,487	1,244	1,894	272	1,250	−1,415	10,732
1952	8,336	1,413	2,210	4	1,147	−1,540	11,570
1953	9,055	1,482	2,480	82	1,332	−1,636	12,795
1954	9,414	1,648	2,735	6	1,455	−1,624	13,634
1955	10,102	1,775	3,093	228	1,646	−1,812	15,032
1956	11,080	1,941	3,371	187	1,903	−2,122	16,360
1957	11,726	2,060	3,808	152	2,298	−2,479	17,565
1958	12,461	2,259	3,888	159	2,350	−2,255	18,862
1959	12,994	2,416	4,185	206	2,592	−2,364	20,029
1960	13,980	2,623	4,804	407	3,187	−3,250	21,751
	16,737	3,032	7,411	272	3,265	−3,334	26,749
1961	18,297	3,353	8,483	323	3,717	−3,708	29,747
1962	20,651	3,881	9,701	274	4,137	−4,277	33,423
1963	24,157	4,728	11,279	191	4,549	−5,322	38,283
1964	26,188	5,342	11,420	94	5,247	−5,163	41,907
1965	28,007	6,061	10,664	152	6,294	−5,299	45,095
1966	30,888	6,457	11,268	196	7,015	−6,159	48,860
1967	34,214	6,892	12,876	270	7,604	−7,040	53,820
1968	36,508	7,512	14,532	10	8,685	−7,504	58,337
1969	40,043	8,144	16,621	216	9,968	−9,078	64,403
1970	45,253	8,878	19,000	592	11,189	−10,920	72,478
1971	49,163	10,871	19,725	233	12,486	−11,800	78,965
1972	54,092	12,376	20,991	255	14,195	−13,600	86,587
1973	64,437	14,251	26,378	1,662	16,889	−18,907	103,441
1974	79,966	17,128	35,039	2,555	24,715	−29,901	127,614
1975	92,609	19,841	36,455	−193	28,562	−28,721	144,510
1976	113,133	23,706	44,403	3,112	38,658	−40,882	180,561
1977	135,606	29,709	52,616	1,910	49,996	−47,860	219,089
1978	157,257	36,130	58,685	1,615	59,605	−54,190	256,169
1979	189,912	44,976	72,026	3,595	75,406	−72,245	311,427
1980	239,344	57,013	94,780	9,694	85,063	−95,462	390,432
1981	286,510	74,156	111,568	4,660	108,748	−117,593	468,049
1982	335,433	87,386	121,730	6,461	125,535	−131,421	545,124
1983	387,459	103,568	135,014	2,985	140,586	−136,131	633,571
1984	444,444	118,034	154,926	12,521	165,771	−167,898	727,798
1985	500,496	133,249	171,706	13,497	185,022	−188,340	815,630
1986	551,842	145,120	180,260	11,417	181,961	−168,362	902,238
1987	604,870	163,866	195,086	11,389	193,132	−185,748	982,595

Table It.2   Gross domestic product at constant prices, 1885–1987

	Consumers' expenditure	Government current expenditure	Gross fixed capital formation	Value of physical change in stocks	Exports of goods & services	Less Imports of goods & services	**Gross domestic product at market prices**
				L bn			
1885	25,924	4,235	3,893	1,276	2,113	**34,130**
1886	25,214	4,214	6,103	1,413	2,189	**35,316**
1887	25,735	4,540	5,682	1,557	2,609	**35,262**
1888	25,073	4,815	5,090	1,435	1,932	**35,262**
1889	25,451	4,896	3,117	1,518	2,252	**33,645**
1890	26,586	4,784	4,262	1,334	1,998	**35,855**
1891	26,681	4,662	4,591	1,253	1,644	**36,664**
1892	26,350	4,642	2,900	1,444	1,822	**35,047**
1893	26,161	4,754	4,459	1,510	1,919	**36,179**
1894	26,208	5,181	3,209	1,662	1,843	**35,963**
1895	26,681	5,365	3,459	1,678	2,008	**36,503**
1896	27,012	5,456	3,565	1,670	1,990	**37,042**
1897	26,681	5,324	2,026	1,700	1,937	**35,532**
1898	27,107	5,293	4,801	1,769	2,181	**37,958**
1899	27,627	5,365	4,038	2,018	2,305	**38,390**
1900	28,715	5,487	5,952	1,884	2,577	**40,331**
1901	29,283	5,578	7,563	2,018	2,727	**42,380**
1902	29,803	5,548	5,446	2,177	2,779	**41,571**
1903	30,607	5,426	6,853	2,196	2,858	**43,458**
1904	30,844	5,568	6,103	2,315	2,910	**43,458**
1905	31,506	5,701	6,583	2,533	3,172	**44,698**
1906	32,405	5,772	7,096	2,671	3,749	**45,399**
1907	34,297	5,792	11,476	2,651	4,169	**50,198**
1908	35,196	6,067	9,076	2,513	4,221	**48,958**
1909	35,953	6,220	12,068	2,671	4,509	**52,193**
1910	34,960	7,054	8,583	2,830	4,536	**49,012**
1911	36,332	7,930	11,180	2,810	4,536	**53,109**
1912	37,420	8,531	11,023	2,889	4,824	**53,918**
1913	37,609	8,673	12,121	3,047	4,772	**56,075**
1914	37,845	13,234	7,833	2,790	3,880	**56,075**
1915	38,792	34,509	3,473	2,711	4,903	**62,545**
1916	39,643	57,414	947	2,394	6,083	**70,633**
1917	38,555	73,599	1,026	1,255	5,899	**74,946**
1918	40,022	77,468	1,611	1,472	5,322	**80,877**
1919	38,886	51,815	4,051	2,078	5,506	**69,554**
1920	41,583	27,078	8,721	2,750	6,948	**62,006**
1921	40,873	29,114	5,965	2,078	4,745	**62,545**
1922	42,813	22,497	9,142	2,394	4,483	**65,241**
1923	44,374	15,270	12,068	2,790	4,745	**66,319**
1924	44,090	13,743	12,733	3,423	5,296	**66,319**
1925	45,840	12,826	15,594	3,700	5,899	**69,554**
1926	46,834	13,946	13,851	3,502	5,611	**70,094**
1927	47,780	14,353	11,772	3,304	5,112	**70,201**
1928	48,726	14,455	17,757	3,403	5,899	**74,946**
1929	49,672	14,455	17,626	3,502	5,873	**76,564**
1930	48,726	14,252	12,693	3,008	5,034	**71,172**
1931	47,307	16,898	11,115	2,849	3,775	**72,250**
1932	48,726	17,509	12,825	2,157	2,936	**74,946**
1933	49,672	18,425	11,641	2,157	3,303	**74,946**
1934	48,726	18,629	12,627	1,880	2,910	**74,946**
1935	49,672	21,886	19,204	1,662	2,858	**82,495**
1936	47,780	28,910	16,574	1,524	2,071	**83,573**
1937	51,091	28,300	21,177	2,572	4,090	**88,965**
1938	57,241	26,773	18,875	2,295	3,225	**88,965**
1939	52,984	29,623	22,427	2,097	2,858	**94,357**
1940	52,984	32,168	17,034	1,741	2,858	**90,043**
1941	49,672	35,120	15,455	1,820	2,150	**88,426**
1942	46,550	46,012	11,970	1,583	2,071	**87,347**
1943	39,738	61,384	7,366	1,543	2,333	**83,034**

Table It.2 (Continued)   Gross domestic product at constant prices, 1885–1987

	Consumers' expenditure	Government current expenditure	Gross fixed capital formation	Value of physical change in stocks	Exports of goods & services	Less Imports of goods & services	Gross domestic product at market prices
				L bn			
1944	33,872	46,216	5,242		316	1,521	**65,241**
1945	29,898	29,012	4,012		99	1,888	**49,173**
1946	41,015	27,485	16,245		1,039	2,700	**71,711**
1947	48,726	20,461	24,400		1,860	5,663	**80,338**
1948	53,930	21,377	17,165		2,948	5,034	**84,651**
1949	57,241	17,814	18,349		3,225	5,139	**88,426**
1950	60,553	18,527	20,980		3,641	5,558	**94,357**
1951	62,918	21,072	22,008	1,537	4,650	6,502	**101,366**
1952	67,044	21,954	25,101	21	4,551	7,230	**105,858**
1953	71,184	22,437	28,384	437	5,585	8,239	**113,799**
1954	72,273	23,398	31,627	68	6,127	8,504	**117,948**
1955	75,351	23,807	35,531	1,254	6,838	9,325	**125,826**
1956	78,912	24,609	37,880	989	7,949	10,614	**131,707**
1957	82,160	25,030	41,300	805	9,641	11,783	**138,689**
1958	85,441	26,400	42,392	903	10,855	12,199	**145,412**
1959	89,700	27,554	46,065	1,207	12,771	13,603	**154,899**
1960	95,205	28,670	51,737	2,273	15,303	18,759	**164,706**
1961	102,325	29,924	57,720	2,632	17,560	21,336	**178,221**
1962	109,634	31,090	63,357	2,129	19,380	24,521	**189,278**
1963	119,800	32,423	68,476	1,396	20,636	30,046	**199,897**
1964	123,770	33,794	64,492	653	22,866	28,199	**205,489**
1965	127,808	35,131	59,070	1,008	27,435	28,763	**212,205**
1966	136,960	36,522	61,623	1,274	30,504	32,799	**224,905**
1967	147,073	38,123	68,855	1,720	32,690	37,222	**241,051**
1968	154,675	40,099	76,288	66	37,224	39,411	**256,827**
1969	164,877	41,221	82,202	1,314	41,600	47,014	**272,487**
1970	177,418	42,280	84,699	3,362	44,022	54,542	**286,957**
1971	182,623	44,671	81,969	1,243	47,091	55,946	**291,672**
1972	188,833	47,048	82,719	1,289	52,086	62,085	**301,013**
1973	199,923	48,185	89,112	6,772	53,815	68,450	**322,179**
1974	205,195	49,537	92,094	6,825	58,364	69,296	**335,520**
1975	201,982	51,137	80,355	−446	60,590	62,568	**323,319**
1976	208,926	52,255	82,240	5,823	68,121	71,771	**342,303**
1977	211,860	53,719	81,950	2,819	73,935	71,746	**348,800**
1978	217,633	54,954	81,868	2,145	81,443	77,573	**358,170**
1979	228,362	55,837	86,641	4,209	89,148	88,075	**375,735**
1980	239,344	57,013	94,780	9,694	85,063	95,462	**390,432**
1981	242,916	58,567	92,601	1,787	91,011	92,010	**394,872**
1982	245,370	60,237	87,285	4,021	90,397	91,483	**395,827**
1983	246,846	61,981	87,160	1,527	92,956	90,124	**399,986**
1984	253,012	63,518	91,761	5,165	99,105	99,882	**412,679**
1985	260,750	65,708	94,073	5,928	102,350	104,228	**424,581**
1986	271,791	67,740	95,368	6,933	104,474	109,475	**436,831**
1987	284,262	70,067	100,362	8,472	108,188	120,954	**450,397**

Table It.3   Industrial production, index and selected series, 1885–1987

	Industrial production	Coal	Crude steel	Cars & commercial vehicles	Crude petroleum	Natural gas	Electricity
	Index nos., 1980 = 100	mn tons	mn tons	'000	'000 tons	mn m³	bn kwh
1885	3·6	0·19	—	—	—	—	0·003
1886	3·5	0·24	0·02	—	—	—	0·003
1887	3·7	0·33	0·07	—	—	—	0·004
1888	3·6	0·37	0·12	—	—	—	0·005
1889	3·6	0·39	0·16	—	—	—	0·006
1890	3·6	0·38	0·11	—	1	—	0·008
1891	3·3	0·29	0·08	—	—	—	0·015
1892	3·3	0·30	0·06	—	—	—	0·022
1893	3·3	0·32	0·07	—	—	—	0·028
1894	3·6	0·27	0·06	—	2	—	0·033
1895	3·7	0·31	0·05	—	2	—	0·045
1896	3·6	0·28	0·07	—	2	—	0·050
1897	3·7	0·31	0·06	—	2	—	0·075
1898	3·7	0·34	0·09	—	2	1	0·10
1899	3·9	0·39	0·11	—	2	1	0·14
1900	4·3	0·5	0·12	—	2	1	0·16
1901	4·3	0·4	0·13	—	2	1	0·22
1902	4·7	0·4	0·14	—	3	2	0·30
1903	4·7	0·3	0·19	—	3	2	0·40
1904	4·9	0·3	0·20	—	4	3	0·45
1905	5·2	0·4	0·27	—	6	3	0·55
1906	5·8	0·5	0·39	—	8	6	0·70
1907	6·3	0·4	0·43	—	8	6	0·95
1908	6·5	0·5	0·54	—	7	7	1·15
1909	6·7	0·6	0·66	—	6	8	1·30
1910	6·7	0·6	0·73	—	7	9	1·50
1911	6·7	0·6	0·74	—	10	9	1·80
1912	7·2	0·7	0·92	—	8	7	2·00
1913	7·0	0·7	0·93	—	7	6	2·20
1914	6·7	0·8	0·91	—	6	6	2·58
1915	8·7	0·9	1·01	—	6	6	2·93
1916	8·7	1·3	1·27	—	7	6	3·43
1917	7·8	1·7	1·33	—	6	7	4·00
1918	7·5	2·1	0·93	—	5	7	4·30
1919	7·3	1·1	0·73	—	5	9	4·00
1920	7·3	1·6	0·77	—	5	8	4·69
1921	6·7	1·0	0·70	—	5	8	4·54
1922	7·5	0·9	0·98	—	4	7	4·73
1923	8·1	1·1	1·14	—	5	7	5·61
1924	9·0	1·0	1·36	—	5	7	6·45
1925	10·2	1·2	1·79	50	8	7	7·26
1926	10·2	1·4	1·78	64	5	6	8·39
1927	9·9	1·1	1·60	55	6	6	8·74
1928	10·8	0·8	1·96	58	6	6	9·63
1929	11·1	1·0	2·12	55	6	7	10·38
1930	10·5	0·8	1·74	47	8	9	10·67
1931	9·5	0·6	1·41	29	16	12	10·47
1932	9·5	0·7	1·40	30	27	13	10·59
1933	10·1	0·7	1·77	42	27	14	11·65
1934	9·9	0·8	1·85	45	20	15	12·60
1935	10·6	0·9	2·21	51	16	12	13·80
1936	10·6	1·6	2·03	53	16	13	13·65
1937	12·3	2·1	2·09	77	14	15	15·43
1938	12·3	2·3	2·32	71	13	17	15·54
1939	13·4·	3·1	2·28	69	12	20	18·42
1940	13·6	4·4	2·26	48	11	28	19·43
1941	12·7	4·4	2·06	39	12	42	20·76
1942	11·0	4·9	1·93	30	13	55	20·23
1943	8·5	3·3	1·73	21	11	55	18·25
1944	5·2	1·1	1·03	14	7	49	13·55

Table It.3 (Continued)   Industrial production, index and selected series, 1885–1987

	Industrial production	Coal	Crude steel	Cars & commercial vehicles	Crude petroleum	Natural gas	Electricity
	Index nos., 1980 = 100	mn tons	mn tons	'000	'000 tons	mn m^3	bn kwh
1945	3·6	1·6	0·40	10	7	42	12·65
1946	8·7	2·7	1·15	29	11	64	17·49
1947	11·2	3·3	1·69	42	10	94	20·57
1948	12·2	1·9	2·13	59	9	117	22·69
1949	13·2	2·0	2·06	86	9	249	20·78
1950	15·3	1·8	2·36	129	8	510	24·68
1951	17·4	2·1	3·06	148	18	966	29·22
1952	17·6	2·0	3·54	139	64	1,433	30·84
1953	19·4	1·9	3·50	165	85	2,280	32·62
1954	21·1	1·8	4·21	217	72	2,967	35·57
1955	23·3	1·5	5·40	270	204	3,627	38·12
1956	24·9	1·6	5·91	316	570	4,466	40·59
1957	26·6	1·5	6·79	352	1,262	4,987	42·73
1958	28·1	1·5	6·27	403	1,546	5,175	45·49
1959	30·7	1·9	6·76	501	1,695	6,118	49·35
1960	35·4	1·5	8·23	645	1,998	6,447	56·24
1961	39·3	2·2	9·12	760	1,972	6,862	60·57
1962	43·2	2·5	9·49	947	1,808	7,113	64·86
1963	46·9	1·9	10·16	1,180	1,784	7,223	71·34
1964	47·8	1·7	9·79	1,091	2,669	7,638	76·74
1965	50·2	1·4	12·68	1,176	2,207	7,758	82·97
1966	55·8	1·6	13·64	1,366	1,757	8,765	89·99
1967	60·0	2·9	15·89	1,543	1,615	9,340	96·83
1968	63·8	2·1	16·96	1,664	1,506	10,405	104·01
1969	65·7	2·2	16·43	1,596	1,479	11,927	110·45
1970	70·8	1·7	17·28	1,848	1,405	13,135	117·42
1971	70·8	1·4	17·45	1,817	1,291	13,383	124·86
1972	73·8	1·0	19·81	1,833	1,152	14,185	135·26
1973	80·8	1·3	20·99	1,951	1,047	15,320	145·52
1974	84·6	1·2	23·80	1,758	1,031	15,294	.148·91
1975	76·9	1·2	21·84	1,448	1,071	14,578	147·33
1976	86·2	1·2	23·45	1,579	1,102	15,663	163·55
1977	87·7	1·1	23·33	1,570	1,083	13,685	166·54
1978	89·2	1·9	24·28	1,644	1,478	13,681	175·04
1979	95·4	2·1	24·25	1,621	1,632	12,549	181·25
1980	100·0	1·9	26·50	1,612	1,800	12,492	185·74
1981	98	2·0	24·78	1,429	1,464	13,999	178·91
1982	95	1·3	23·99	1,452	1,728	15,317	181·82
1983	92	1·7	21·68	1,574	2,208	12,950	180·11
1984	95	1·8	23·08	1,596	2,244	13,705	179·54
1985	97	1·8	23·89	1,538	2,352	14,091	182·23
1986	99	1·5	22·74	1,822	2,508	15,961	189·58
1987	103	. . .	23·66[a]	1,913	3,900	23,672	. . .

a   1988 figure.

231

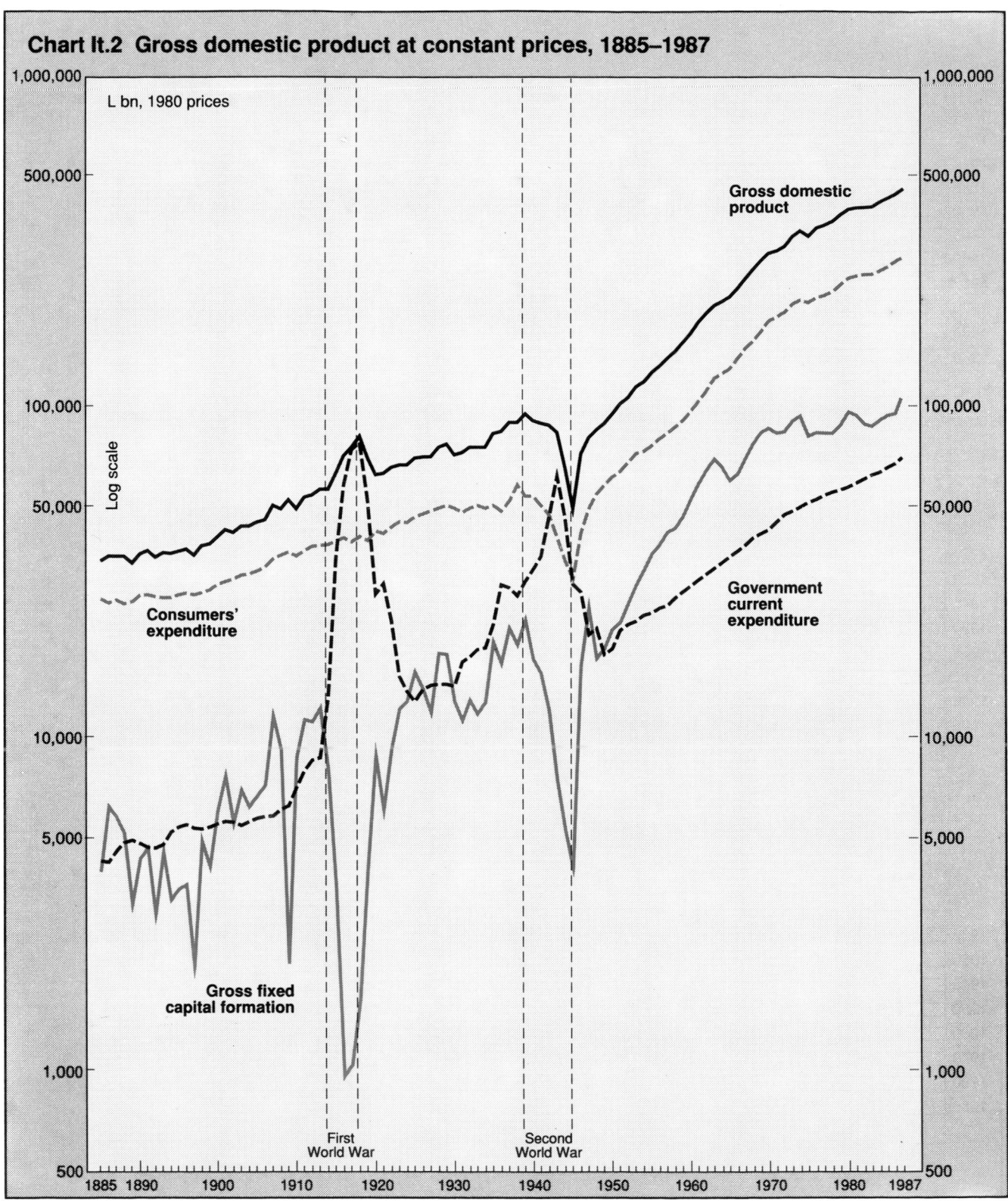

Chart It.2 Gross domestic product at constant prices, 1885–1987

L bn, 1980 prices

Log scale

Gross domestic product

Consumers' expenditure

Government current expenditure

Gross fixed capital formation

First World War

Second World War

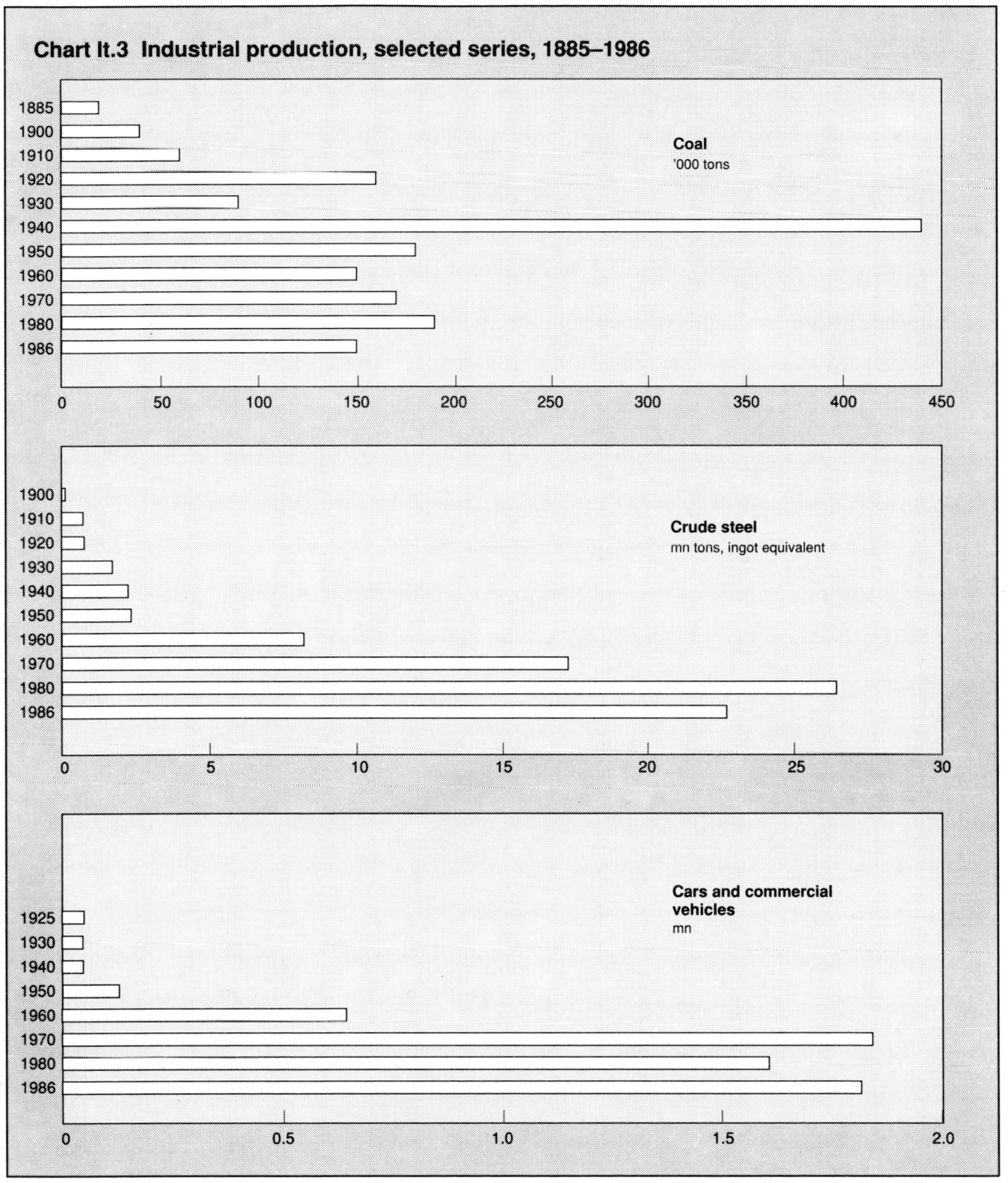

Chart It.3 Industrial production, selected series, 1885–1986

Coal
'000 tons

Crude steel
mn tons, ingot equivalent

Cars and commercial vehicles
mn

233

Table It.4 Prices and income, 1885–1987

	Consumer prices		Producer prices		Export prices	Import prices	Compensation of employees	National income
	All items	Food	All items	Producers' goods				
	Index nos., 1980 = 100							L bn
1885	0·050	...	0·070	...	...	...	...	10·17
1886	0·050	...	0·070	...	...	...	...	10·59
1887	0·047	...	0·069	...	...	...	...	9·77
1888	0·048	...	0·070	...	...	...	...	9·68
1889	0·050	...	0·071	...	...	...	...	9·85
1890	0·052	...	0·074	...	...	...	...	10·77
1891	0·050	...	0·074	...	...	...	...	11·33
1892	0·048	...	0·073	...	...	...	...	10·13
1893	0·045	...	0·072	...	...	...	...	10·28
1894	0·044	...	0·071	...	...	...	...	9·93
1895	0·046	...	0·071	...	...	...	...	10·35
1896	0·046	...	0·070	...	...	...	...	10·35
1897	0·045	...	0·070	...	...	...	...	10·09
1898	0·047	...	0·071	...	...	...	...	11·39
1899	0·048	...	0·070	...	...	...	...	11·41
1900	0·058	...	0·063	...	...	...	...	12·15
1901	0·058	...	0·063	...	...	...	...	12·50
1902	0·058	...	0·061	...	...	...	...	11·92
1903	0·060	...	0·060	...	...	...	...	13·05
1904	0·060	...	0·058	...	...	...	...	12·89
1905	0·060	...	0·060	...	...	...	...	13·52
1906	0·062	...	0·062	...	...	...	...	14·37
1907	0·064	...	0·067	...	...	...	...	16·08
1908	0·064	...	0·065	...	...	...	...	15·27
1909	0·062	...	0·066	...	...	...	...	16·59
1910	0·064	...	0·066	...	...	...	...	16·52
1911	0·065	...	0·071	...	...	...	...	18·31
1912	0·066	...	0·077	...	...	...	...	19·06
1913	0·066	...	0·075	...	...	...	...	19·29
1914	0·066	...	0·072	...	...	...	...	19·08
1915	0·072	...	0·095	...	...	...	...	21·22
1916	0·089	...	0·138	...	...	...	...	28·89
1917	0·128	...	0·205	...	...	...	...	38·10
1918	0·176	...	0·309	...	...	...	...	46·95
1919	0·179	...	0·336	...	...	...	...	57·73
1920	0·236	...	0·442	...	...	...	...	86·85
1921	0·280	...	0·405	...	...	...	...	87·70
1922	0·278	...	0·407	...	...	...	...	96·66
1923	0·277	...	0·411	...	...	...	...	105·5
1924	0·286	...	0·409	...	...	...	...	109·0
1925	0·322	...	0·458	...	...	...	...	136·9
1926	0·346	...	0·468	...	...	...	...	145·5
1927	0·316	0·224	0·393	...	...	...	...	126·9
1928	0·292	0·224	0·380	0·375	...	...	...	127·5
1929	0·298	0·228	0·362	0·355	...	...	...	127·1
1930	0·288	0·214	0·326	0·312	...	...	...	112·9
1931	0·260	0·187	0·283	0·265	...	...	...	100·2
1932	0·248	0·178	0·264	0·251	...	...	...	96·9
1933	0·237	0·167	0·239	0·218	...	...	...	89·2
1934	0·225	0·160	0·236	0·218	...	...	...	89·9
1935	0·228	0·164	0·257	0·244	...	...	...	101·2
1936	0·246	0·176	0·290	0·285	...	...	...	107·4
1937	0·270	0·178	0·337	0·335	...	...	...	127·8
1938	0·292	0·178	0·362	0·338	...	...	...	137·9
1939	0·305	0·356	0·377	0·358	...	...	...	152·6
1940	0·356	0·356	0·442	0·412	...	...	...	176·0
1941	0·411	0·356	0·493	0·476	...	...	...	207·2
1942	0·478	0·534	0·551	0·522	...	...	...	261·4
1943	0·796	0·890	0·830	...	...	...	...	351·4
1944	3·4	4·2	3·1	...	...	...	...	656·2

	Consumer prices		Producer prices		Export prices	Import prices	Compensation of employees	National income
	All items	Food	All items	Producers' goods				
	Index nos., 1980 = 100						L bn	
1945	6·7	8·0	7·4	...	...	...	...	1,184
1946	8·0	9·6	10·4	9·2	...	...	...	2,776
1947	12·9	15·4	18·7	17·2	...	...	...	5,495
1948	13·7	16·2	19·7	18·0	...	...	...	6,454
1949	13·9	16·2	18·6	18·2	...	...	...	6,963
1950	13·7	15·6	17·6	18·2	...	...	...	7,711
1951	15·0	16·6	20·1	20·2	25·5	19·5	4,075	9,714
1952	15·6	17·3	18·9	19·8	24·2	19·2	4,503	10,475
1953	16·0	17·7	18·9	19·6	24·0	17·7	4,953	11,673
1954	16·4	18·3	18·8	19·2	23·3	17·0	5,417	12,455
1955	16·8	18·9	18·9	20·0	22·6	17·2	5,941	13,766
1956	17·3	19·7	19·3	20·4	22·1	17·7	6,480	15,010
1957	17·5	19·7	19·5	20·9	22·8	18·7	7,049	16,094
1958	18·0	20·3	19·1	20·0	21·7	16·4	7,569	17,314
1959	18·0	19·9	18·6	19·8	20·0	15·3	8,104	18,404
1960	18·3	20·1	18·8	20·0	20·8	15·1	8,977 / 9,857	19,971 / 24,647
1961	18·8	20·1	18·8	20·2	20·0	14·6	10,956	27,475
1962	19·6	21·0	19·3	20·4	20·2	14·6	12,748	30,832
1963	21·1	22·9	20·3	21·3	19·5	15·2	15,510	35,156
1964	22·3	24·0	21·0	21·9	20·0	15·3	17,352	38,341
1965	23·4	25·4	21·4	21·7	20·3	15·4	18,317	41,280
1966	23·8	25·9	21·6	21·9	20·2	15·7	19,589	44,874
1967	24·9	26·3	21·4	21·9	20·2	15·8	21,668	49,547
1968	25·2	26·3	21·6	22·2	20·0	15·8	23,560	53,827
1969	25·7	27·0	22·2	23·6	20·7	16·0	25,960	59,504
1970	27·1	28·1	24·0	26·2	21·8	16·6	30,356	66,694
1971	28·5	29·2	24·6	26·5	23·4	17·4	34,735	72,452
1972	30·1	31·2	25·6	27·2	23·9	17·9	38,762	79,260
1973	33·3	34·8	30·2	33·3	27·7	22·7	47,091	94,375
1974	39·6	41·0	42·5	46·6	38·8	38·7	58,619	114,813
1975	46·3	48·3	46·1	50·1	43·1	41·0	71,220	127,572
1976	54·2	56·8	56·7	58·6	55·3	53·5	86,973	160,413
1977	64·2	67·4	66·5	68·0	65·9	62·0	106,525	194,598
1978	71·8	76·4	72·1	75·2	70·7	65·1	124,343	228,145
1979	82·4	86·5	83·3	85·4	82·8	77·6	148,929	279,298
1980	100·0	100·0	100·0	100·0	100·0	100·0	184,196	350,268
1981	117·8	116·3	116·6	117·5	123·1	129·4	224,167	414,892
1982	137·2	135·4	132·8	132·6	142·0	145·6	261,041	480,366
1983	157·3	152·0	145·7	143·2	152·5	152·6	300,156	559,239
1984	174·3	165·9	160·8	158·8	167·1	169·8	334,511	643,586
1985	190·3	180·3	172·6	169·1	180·7	182·5	374,432	722,816
1986	201·5	190·2	171·1	159·9	172·3	150·2	404,341	796,536
1987	211·0	198·3	...	...	...	...	440,509	868,957

235

Table It.5 Population, 1881–1986

	Total population	Males	Females	Births	Age distribution Under 15	15–64	65 & over
	mn			'000	mn		
1881	28·46	14·26	14·20	1,081	9·16	17·84	1·46
1901	32·48	16·16	16·32	1,058	11·16	19·35	1·97
1911	34·67	17·02	17·65	1,094	11·73	20·57	2·36
1921	37·97	18·73	19·25	1,163	11·79	23·43	2·75
1931	41·18	20·13	21·04	1,026	12·24	25·92	3·02
1936	42·92	21·07	21·85	963	13·17	26·59	3·20
1950	46·77	23·05	24·05	909	12·47	30·86	3·78
1951	47·10	23·21	24·21	861	12·43	31·12	3·86
1952	47·35	23·34	24·33	844	12·39	31·34	3·94
1953	47·61	23·48	24·48	839	12·32	31·62	4·02
1954	47·07	22·93	24·14	871	12·26	31·93	4·12
1955	47·39	23·08	24·31	869	12·19	32·23	4·22
1956	47·66	23·20	24·45	874	12·17	32·46	4·29
1957	47·93	23·31	24·62	879	12·21	32·61	4·36
1958	48·32	23·51	24·81	870	12·25	32·77	4·46
1959	48·60	23·67	24·93	901	11·42	32·93	4·24
1960	48·97	23·85	25·12	910	11·47	33·10	4·41
1961	49·16	23·87	25·28	930	11·40	33·27	4·49
1962	49·56	24·10	25·47	937	11·34	33·59	4·63
1963	49·94	24·28	25·66	960	11·45	33·76	4·72
1964	50·44	24·55	25·89	1,016	11·52	34·06	4·86
1965	50·84	24·72	26·12	990	11·72	34·12	5·00
1966	51·23	24·92	26·31	980	11·56	34·34	5·33
1967	51·66	25·18	26·49	949	11·81	34·56	5·29
1968	52·04	25·37	26·67	930	11·78	34·84	5·42
1969	52·38	25·52	26·86	932	12·16	34·79	5·42
1970	52·77	25·70	27·07	901	12·11	35·10	5·56
1971	53·12	25·89	27·23	906	12·32	35·13	5·68
1972	53·50	26·07	27·43	888	12·31	35·20	5·99
1973	53·88	26·24	27·64	875	12·28	35·51	6·09
1974	54·39	26·50	27·89	869	12·29	35·90	6·20
1975	54·76	26·68	28·08	828	12·29	36·11	6·35
1976	55·07	26·84	28·23	782	12·39	36·29	6·39
1977	55·27	26·92	28·35	741	12·34	36·45	6·49
1978	55·45	27·00	28·45	709	12·07	36·75	6·62
1979	55·60	27·07	28·53	670	11·78	37·02	6·80
1980	55·66	27·09	28·57	640	11·38	37·12	7·15
1981	55·77	27·14	28·63	623	11·21	37·35	7·22
1982	56·00	27·25	28·74	619	10·76	37·88	7·35
1983	56·23	27·36	28·87	602	10·42	38·38	7·44
1984	56·34	27·43	28·92	586	10·09	39·00	7·25
1985	56·50	27·49	29·01	575	9·92	39·29	7·29
1986	56·58	27·54	29·04	555	9·53	39·41	7·64

Table It.6 Education, 1885–1986

	Kindergarten	Elementary	Secondary	Higher education Total	of which: Female
	No. of pupils '000			No. of students '000	
1885	253	...	...	16·1	...
1886	259	...	...	17·0	...
1887	262	...	...	17·2	...
1888	268	...	...	17·6	...
1889	278	...	...	17·6	...
1890	280	...	...	18·1	...
1891	292	...	...	18·7	...
1892	303	...	...	19·8	...
1893	303	...	...	20·9	...
1894	314	...	...	22·2	...
1895	317	...	...	23·1	...
1896	...	...	...	24·3	...
1897	325	...	...	24·7	...
1898	347	...	...	24·6	...
1899	356	...	...	25·2	...
1900	...	...	...	26·0	...
1901	356	...	...	26·6	...
1902	...	...	...	25·7	...
1903	...	...	...	25·4	...
1904	...	...	...	25·1	...
1905	...	...	...	25·6	...
1906	...	...	...	26·6	...
1907	...	...	...	26·8	...
1908	...	...	...	27·3	...
1909	...	...	...	27·0	...
1910	...	...	...	26·9	...
1911	...	...	...	27·8	1·0
1912	...	...	...	27·1	1·4
1913	...	...	...	28·0	1·6
1914	...	...	...	29·6	1·9
1915	501	...	...	29·0	2·3
1916	...	...	...	32·9	2·6
1917	...	...	...	38·7	3·1
1918	...	...	...	46·1	4·0
1919	...	...	...	53·7	4·7
1920	...	...	...	53·2	5·0
1921	398	...	...	49·1	5·2
1922	...	...	...	46·6	5·5
1923	...	...	...	43·2	5·4
1924	474	...	...	43·8	5·6
1925	...	...	...	45·2	5·8
1926	608	3,635	387	42·9	5·6
1927	669	3,838	380	42·5	5·5
1928	722	4,052	386	40·4	4·8
1929	750	4,340	346	44·9	6·0
1930	746	4,595	325	46·3	6·1
1931	726	4,762	392	47·6	6·5
1932	706	4,799	454	53·7	6·7
1933	705	4,818	510	57·3	7·5
1934	720	4,841	555	62·0	8·3
1935	735	5,074	604	64·9	9·6
1936	747	5,187	685	71·5	11·6
1937	766	5,051	755	74·9	13·4
1938	751	5,095	821	77·4	15·1
1939	772	5,149	860	85·5	18·2
1940	781	5,213	919	127·1	26·0
1941	775	5,110	982	145·8	32·2
1942	...	...	...	168·3	38·7
1943	...	...	...	157·3	42·1
1944	...	...	...	170·6	46·2

238

Table It.6 (Continued)   Education, 1885–1986

	Kindergarten	Elementary	Secondary	Higher education Total	of which: Female
		No. of pupils '000		No. of students '000	
1945	870	4,868	369	189·7	47·6
1946	863	5,222	379	190·8	47·5
1947	889	5,367	368	180·1	44·4
1948	918	5,449	374	168·0	43·6
1949	900	5,442	374	146·5	39·0
1950	932	5,359	388	145·2	38·2
1951	990	5,239	416	142·7	39·6
1952	1,012	5,341	460	138·8	37·9
1953	1,043	5,437	507	137·8	38·2
1954	1,052	5,553	556	136·5	37·2
1955	1,068	5,647	594	139·0	38·3
1956	1,072	5,758	625	145·4	39·7
1957	1,080	5,788	657	154·6	42·4
1958	1,088	5,826	679	163·9	45·3
1959	1,132	5,809	706	176·2	49·1
1960	1,154	5,832	762	191·8	53·2
1961	1,195	5,960	838	206·0	59·1
1962	1,233	5,985	927	225·8	68·3
1963	1,268	6,105	1,030	240·2	77·0
1964	1,305	6,201	1,155	259·3	88·7
1965	1,335	6,315	1,259	297·8	105·7
1966	1,365	6,377	1,372	338·5	124·8
1967	1,409	6,511	1,434	370·1	141·0
1968	1,435	6,656	1,501	415·6	159·5
1969	1,560	6,814	1,569	488·4	188·2
1970	1,587	7,025	1,656	560·6	210·8
1971	1,620	7,213	1,732	631·2	237·7
1972	1,686	7,396	1,820	657·6	254·1
1973	1,735	7,500	1,916	675·2	266·4
1974	1,631	7,549	1,968	708·8	284·9
1975	1,823	7,614	2,097	736·3	291·4
1976	1,866	7,605	2,198	762·1	306·0
1977	1,894	7,587	2,270	762·8	314·9
1978	1,917	7,486	2,347	777·8	330·9
1979	1,852	7,422	2,386	767·7	334·2
1980	1,841	7,329	2,415	764·0	336·4
1981	1,805	7,189	2,444	724·5	322·8
1982	1,757	7,054	2,470	717·4	322·4
1983	1,696	6,879	2,509	745·0	342·8
1984	1,639	6,707	2,547	766·8	...
1985	1,633	6,470	2,608	763·2	...
1986	1,622	6,245	2,659	787·0	...

Table It.7 Labour market: employment, 1929–86

	Employed labour force	Agriculture, forestry & fishing	Mining & quarrying	Manufacturing	Construction	Gas, electricity & water	Transport & communication	Distribution & services
				mn				
1929	...	...	...	1·11	...	...	...	...
1930	...	...	...	...	...	...	...	...
1931	17·26	8·08		5·31[a]		...	0·79	3·08
1932	...	...		...	...		...	...
1933	...	...		...	...		...	...
1934	...	...		0·85			...	...
1935	...	...		1·00			...	...
1936	18·75	8·84	0·13	3·98	0·98	0·07	0·70	4·06
1937	...	...		1·16			...	...
1938	...	...		1·22			...	...
1939	...	...		1·26			...	...
1940	...	...		1·35			...	...
1941	...	...		1·36			...	...
1942	...	...		1·35			...	...
1947	...	...		1·73			...	...
1948	...	...		1·70			...	...
1949	...	...		1·68			...	...
1950	...	...		1·67			...	...
1951	20·14	8·06		1·68				4·39
1952	...	...		1·67			...	...
1953	...	...		1·68			...	...
1954	...	...		1·70			...	...
1954	18·57	8·00	0·14	4·15	1·24	0·13	0·66	4·25
1955	19·34	7·96	0·15	4·42	1·32	0·14	0·73	4·62
1956	19·93	7·45	0·15	4·97	1·59	0·11	0·70	4·96
1957	19·97	7·11	0·15	5·17	1·62	0·11	0·72	5·09
1958	20·00	6·97	0·14	5·18	1·65	0·11	0·73	5·22
1959	19·99	6·85	0·14	5·25	1·67	0·11	0·75	5·22
1960	20·00	6·57	0·15	5·35	1·78	0·11	0·80	5·24
1961	20·02	6·21	(0·15)	5·54	1·82	(0·13)	0·86	5·31
1962	19·86	5·82	(0·15)	5·61	1·95	(0·13)	0·91	5·29
1963	19·48	5·29	(0·15)	5·69	2·01	(0·15)	0·92	5·27
1964	19·29	4·94	(0·14)	5·56	2·10	(0·16)	1·02	5·37
1965	19·43	5·10		7·18			7·15	
1966	19·10	4·81		7·06			7·22	
1967	19·32	4·71		7·20			7·40	
1968	19·29	4·42		7·29			7·58	
1969	19·11	4·20		7·44			7·46	
1970	19·22	3·88		7·59			7·75	
1971	19·18	3·88		7·62			7·68	
1972	18·85	3·59		7·47			7·79	
1973	19·01	3·48		7·45			8·07	
1974	19·39	3·40		7·61			8·38	
1975	19·49	3·26		7·64			8·59	
1976	19·61	3·23		7·53			8·86	
1977	19·79	3·13	0·21[b]	5·44	1·97	...	1·12	7·93
1978	19·86	3·07	0·20[b]	5·39	2·00	...	1·12	8·09
1979	20·06	2·99	0·21[b]	5·37	2·00	...	1·12	8·37
1980	20·31	2·90	0·22[b]	5·44	2·04	...	1·13	8·58
1981	20·36	2·73	0·22[b]	5·33	2·09	...	1·15	8·84
1982	20·30	2·52	0·22[b]	5·23	2·08	...	1·13	9·12
1983	20·35	2·53	0·21[b]	5·08	2·06	...	1·11	9·36
1984	20·42	2·43	0·21[b]	4·88	1·96	...	1·07	9·88
1985	20·51	2·30	0·21[b]	4·77	1·92	...	1·09	10·23
1986	20·61	2·24	0·22[b]	4·72	1·88	...	1·12	10·44

a   Including mining and quarrying and construction.
b   Including gas, electricity and water.

241

Table It.8   Labour market: other indicators, 1888–1987

| | Manufacturing | | | | Industrial disputes | | |
| | Average hrs worked per month | Average hourly earnings | Unemployment | | Stoppages | Workers involved | Working days lost |
		L	'000	%		'000	'000
1888	...	...	...	...	107	30	...
1889	...	...	...	...	133	25	...
1890	...	...	...	...	152	45	...
1891	...	...	...	...	164	44	...
1892	...	...	...	...	140	34	...
1893	...	...	...	...	154	25	...
1894	...	...	...	...	217	98	...
1895	...	...	...	...	243	104	...
1896	...	...	...	...	310	47	...
1897	...	...	...	...	379	46	...
1898	...	...	...	...	424	85	...
1899	...	...	...	...	1,701	430	...
1900	...	...	...	...	1,053	350	...
1901	...	...	...	...	617	136	...
1902	...	...	...	...	847	215	...
1903	...	...	...	...	715	155	...
1904	...	...	...	...	1,649	382	...
1905	...	...	...	...	2,268	581	...
1906	...	...	...	...	1,674	324	...
1907	...	...	...	...	1,071	189	...
1908	...	...	...	...	1,109	196	...
1909	...	...	...	...	1,255	386	...
1910	...	...	...	...	1,090	241	...
1911	...	...	...	...	907	465	...
1912	...	...	...	...	905	217	...
1913	...	...	...	...	599	174	...
1914	...	...	...	...	905	217	...
1915	...	...	...	...	608	180	...
1916	...	...	...	...	577	138	...
1917	...	...	...	...	470	175	...
1918	...	...	...	...	313	159	...
1919	...	...	...	...	1,871	1,555	...
1920	...	...	...	...	2,070	2,314	...
1921	...	...	...	...	1,134	724	...
1922	...	...	...	...	575	448	...
1923	...	...	...	...	201	66	...
1924	...	...	...	...	368	187	...
1925	...	...	110	...	618	308	...
1926	...	...	114	...	...	...	...
1927	...	...	278	...	169	19	...
1928	180[a]	...	324	...	77	3	...
1929	182	2·11	301	...	83	3	...
1930	175	2·13	425	...	82	3	...
1931	171	1·99	734	...	67	4	...
1932	169	1·93	1,006	...	23	0·6	...
1933	174	1·88	1,019	...	34	0·8	...
1934	172	1·81	964	...	38	0·6	...
1935	158	1·76	...	...	43	0·6	...
1936	157	1·84	...	...	...	...	...
1937	163	2·17	874	4·6	...	...	...
1938	159	2·23	810	4·3	...	...	...
1939	157[b]	2·50	706	3·8[c]	...	...	...
	Average hrs worked per day						
1946	...	...	1,324	...	...	...	...
1947	...	...	1,620	...	...	...	...
1948	7·95	134	1,742[d]	8·9	...	...	...
1949	7·97	142	1,673	8·6	1,159	2,894	16,578

242

Table It.8 (Continued)   Labour market: other indicators, 1888–1987

	Manufacturing		Unemployment		Industrial disputes		
	Average hrs worked per month	Average hourly earnings			Stoppages	Workers involved	Working days lost
		L	'000	%		'000	'000
1950	7·97	143	1,615	8·3	1,250	3,537	7,761
1951	8·07	157	1,721	8·8	1,178	2,135	4,515
1952	8·07	165	1,850	9·5	1,558	1,472	3,531
1953	8·10	169	1,947	10·0	1,412	4,679	5,828
1954	8·12	175	1,959	10·0	1,990	2,045	5,377
1955	8·12	185	1,481	7·6	1,981	1,403	5,622
1956	8·02	198	1,847	9·4	1,904	1,678	4,137
1957	8·03	207	1,643	8·2	1,731	1,227	4,619
1958	8·02	216	1,322	6·6	1,937	1,283	4,172
1959	8·05	221	1,117	5·6	1,925	1,900	9,190
1960	8·07	232	836	4·2	2,471	2,338	5,786
1961	8·08	248	710	3·5	3,502	2,698	9,891
1962	8·00	286	611	3·0	3,652	2,910	22,717
1963	8·00	334	504	2·5	4,145	3,694	11,395
1964	7·92	371	549	2·7	3,841	3,246	13,089
1965	7·87	386	714	3·6	3,191	2,310	6,993
1966	7·88	401	759 / 1,192	3·9 / 5·7	2,387	1,888	14,474
1967	7·92	426	1,106	5·3	2,658	2,244	8,568
1968	7·92	445	1,172	5·6	3,377	4,862	9,240
1969	7·83	489	1,160	5·6	3,788	7,507	37,825
1970	7·80	606	1,111	5·3	4,162	3,722	20,887
1971	7·73	703	1,109	5·3	5,598	3,891	14,799
1972	7·78	788	1,296	6·3	4,765	4,405	19,497
1973	7·67	966	1,303	6·2	3,769[e]	6,133	23,419
1974	7·67	1,209	1,111	5·3	5,174[e]	7,824	19,467
1975	7·68	1,794	1,226	5·8	3,601	14,110	27,189
1976	7·67	2,133	1,420	6·6	2,706	11,898	25,378
1977	7·70	2,673	1,538	7·0	3,308	13,803	16,566
1978	7·72	3,244	1,560	7·1	2,479	8,774	10,177
1979	7·65	3,849	1,686	7·6	2,000	16,237	27,530
1980	7·73	4,684	1,684	7·5	2,238	13,825	16,457
1981	7·75	5,742	1,769	7·8	2,204	8,227	10,527
1982	7·70	6,693	1,923	8·4	1,747	10,483	18,563
1983	7·70	7,712	2,140	9·3	1,565	6,844	14,003
1984	7·77	8,539	2,304	9·9	1,816	7,357	8,703
1985	. . .	. . .	2,382	10·1	1,341	4,843	3,831
1986	. . .	. . .	2,610	10·9	1,469	3,607	5,644
1987	. . .	. . .	2,832	11·8	1,149	4,273	. . .

a   Average for February – December.   b   Average for first four months.   c   December figure.
d   Excluding third quarter.   e   Excluding political strikes.

Table It.9 Public finance, 1885–1986

	Revenue					Expenditure				
	Taxes on personal income	Taxes on companies	Customs	Tax on monopolies	Total receipts	Defence	Education	Social services	Debt interest	Total expenditure
					L mn					
1885	202	118	204	259	1,413	331	...	...	817	1,508
1886	207	124	191	254	1,409	337	...	...	827	1,467
1887	211	133	205	249	1,453	365	...	...	836	1,499
1888	216	142	212	246	1,500	431	...	...	856	1,606
1889	286	148	206	247	1,501	561	...	...	884	1,768
1890	231	148	231	249	1,562	429	...	...	935	1,675
1891	234	142	211	252	1,540	398	...	...	945	1,657
1892	234	145	204	254	1,528	366	...	...	949	1,613
1893	234	141	204	255	1,551	348	...	...	957	1,653
1894	234	141	188	259	1,517	354	...	...	968	1,743
1895	287	136	195	261	1,570	328	...	...	994	1,655
1896	289	135	198	261	1,633	439	...	...	988	1,727
1897	288	141	202	261	1,615	375	...	...	987	1,652
1898	286	139	209	261	1,629	366	...	...	977	1,648
1899	287	143	214	270	1,658	351	...	...	996	1,650
1900	289	141	203	270	1,671	356	...	...	1,000	1,659
1901	291	140	187	276	1,721	372	...	...	991	1,692
1902	295	140	183	285	1,744	373	...	...	1,006	1,809
1903	298	143	179	285	1,795	362	...	...	1,013	1,793
1904	298	148	176	293	1,787	362	...	...	1,021	1,776
1905	301	151	170	303	1,843	377	...	...	1,032	1,820
1906	305	164	198	312	1,946	374	...	...	1,053	2,414
1907	276	174	232	319	1,954	405	...	...	990	2,079
1908	256	180	240	340	1,946	422	...	...	973	2,179
1909	272	175	256	355	2,134	467	...	...	993	2,431
1910	284	188	249	376	2,237	499	...	...	1,026	2,448
1911	297	196	270	388	2,403	577	...	...	1,075	2,650
1912	313	207	259	407	2,475	755	...	...	1,071	2,841
1913	329	207	271	423	2,529	1,000	...	...	1,107	3,137
1914	346	205	259	440	2,524	833	155	20	1,025	3,009
1915	383	206	193	468	2,560	3,187	161	28	1,106	5,795
1916	435	232	310	607	3,734	8,222	162	17	1,273	12,543
1917	461	328	470	724	5,345	14,768	176	15	1,855	21,622
1918	492	430	535	958	7,533	21,448	227	24	2,680	26,502
1919	581	541	530	1,294	9,676	26,840	342	147	3,603	33,335
1920	709	876	513	1,706	15,207	13,734	702	160	5,915	27,827
					L bn					
1921	1·02	1·30	0·53	2·60	18·82	24·52	0·86	0·19	6·59	37·49
1922	1·63	1·04	0·62	2·82	19·70	22·50	0·99	0·24	7·34	37·21
1923	2·01	1·37	0·52	2·92	18·80	8·58	0·98	0·08	7·83	24·09
1924	2·91	1·95	0·52	3·01	20·58	8·14	1·06	0·08	7·82	24·24
1925	2·98	2·35	0·91	3·08	20·44	6·28	1·22	0·16	7·89	21·93
1926	3·56	2·74	0·66	3·26	21·04	5·52	1·43	0·16	9·27 / 4·10	22·76
1927	4·16	2·80	0·65	3·47	21·45	6·25	1·46	0·17	4·76	24·59
1928	3·88	2·30	1·46	3·48	20·07	5·37	1·39	0·15	4·68	29·65
1929	3·78	2·41	2·10	2·65	20·20	5·65	1·39	0·17	4·48	20·84
1930	3·80	2·27	1·85	2·79	19·84	5·72	1·44	0·17	4·61	20·86
1931	3·63	2·78	1·67	2·95	20·39	6·27	1·51	0·15	4·65	25·86
1932	3·50	2·85	1·94	2·89	19·32	6·12	1·61	0·16	4·81	25·24
1933	3·31	2·69	1·87	2·86	18·22	6·08	1·77	0·17	5·20	22·86
1934	3·22	2·60	1·84	2·82	18·06	5·47	1·77	0·20	7·98	28·14
1935	3·18	2·73	1·73	2·79	18·82	5·30	1·69	0·20	4·48	21·87
1936	3·16	3·14	1·41	2·83	20·37	6·15	1·71	0·21	5·15	66·92
1937	3·39	3·43	1·30	2·97	24·70	6·72	1·81	0·26	5·68	48·07
1938	3·79	4·28	1·37	3·25	27·47	8·22	2·02	0·38	6·21	40·63
1939	4·18	4·83	1·16	3·42	27·58	10·73	2·15	0·39	6·79	42·63
1940	4·48	6·01	1·26	3·74	32·35	11·89	2·74	0·47	6·77	70
1941	4·86	7·73	1·12	4·27	34·23	12·63	3·28	0·61	8·81	106

Table It.9 (Continued) Public finance, 1885–1986

	Revenue					Expenditure				
	Taxes on personal income	Taxes on companies	Customs	Tax on monopolies	Total receipts	Defence	Education	Social services	Debt interest	Total expenditure
					L bn					
1942	5·24	9·22	1·16	5·81	41·22	13·20	3·81	0·77	11·65	123
1943	6·25	9·81	1·25	7·89	50·38	15·90	4·23	0·99	15·10	160
1944	7·05	9·92	0·50	6·99	47·24	22·72	4·52	1·06	17·79	247
1945	8·03	15·43	0·13	10·02	64·64	17·27	9·67	3·52	13·92	319
1946	17·59	57·10	1·20	34·72	160·2	167	30	50	32	622
1947	35·75	196·1	3·73	62·57	382·4	171	56	62	40	1,215
1948	75·66	229·5	12·93	110·8	850·5	350	110	82	75	1,907
1949	103·6	313·0	7·18	171·3	1,137·8	333	135	102	94	1,735
1950	124·2	326·2	6·14	202·4	1,419·1	414	168	106	103	1,948
1951	154·0	401·8	57·0	220·4	1,720·1	524	195	204	105	2,213
1952	191·2	442·6	74·0	243·5	1,737·2	578	231	230	123	2,434
1953	174·2	493·5	87·8	265·8	1,804·2	652	253	283	147	2,429
1954	201·1	566·9	109·1	284·8	2,001·3	625	280	259	187	2,510
1955	233·0	609·2	117·6	305·1	2,314·5	688	324	289	197	2,759
1956	270·2	669·4	133·5	327·8	2,509·5	674	359	321	232	2,901
1957	321·0	738·1	148·7	346·8	2,808·4	738	423	300	223	3,069
1958	350·1	785·6	157·2	366·3	3,098·6	783	463	337	221	3,715
1959	399·7	837·1	150·6	389·0	3,248·4	780	517	381	247	3,621
1960	434·2	958·5	184·7	420·2	3,684·2	853	577	424	268	4,601
1961	495·3	1,080·6	201·9	445·2	3,949·1	883	710	492	271	4,682
1962	570·1	1,219·5	224·2	478·8	4,548·2	960	816	527	288	5,376
1963	672·3	1,428·7	257·0	521·4	5,251·0	1,083	1,048	630	289	6,110
1964	808·0	1,584·6	273·3	557·4	5,952.8	1,210	1,252	750	290	6,782
	512·5	767·0	112·6	285·6	3,147·2				121	3,614
1965	1,029	1,760	223	584	6,862	...	...	...	287	8,464
1966	1,120	1,935	227	627	7,453	...	...	...	316	9,517
1967	1,192	2,141	252	657	8,409	...	...	...	389	10,322
1968	1,336	2,279	199	693	9,310	...	...	...	467	11,841
1969	1,491	2,504	210	747	10,013	...	...	...	521	13,933
1970	1,532	2,776	235	793	10,996	...	...	...	598	14,314
1971	1,796	3,049	220	800	12,169	...	...	...	724	17,589
1972	2,045	3,086	233	862	13,367	...	...	...	963	19,103
1973	2,333	3,639	267	761	15,250	1,793	4,591	...	1,237	23,808
1974	4,490	6,729	334	863	19,625	2,304	5,339	...	1,732	29,558
1975	4,945	6,110	16	999	23,842	2,421	6,125	...	3,081	38,469
1976	7,220	8,423	24	1,130	35,800	...	...	...	4,701	46,985
1977	10,464	11,340	23	1,318	44,075	3,213	8,657	13,587	6,664	62,157
1978	12,135	13,341	22	1,528	55,145	3,779	10,010	15,068	9,149	83,367
1979	15,826	14,939	18	1,760	68,511	4,779	12,696	22,991	11,232	103,947
1980	23,535	21,184	28	2,038	93,430	5,823	16,239	36,643	16,293	142,757
1981	31,218	25,271	34	2,536	113,016	6,873	18,882	40,430	21,241	178,744
1982	38,665	30,007	52	3,309	149,393	8,786	21,815	42,571	32,645	208,817
1983	50,559	36,334	69	3,821	184,073	10,616	26,774	56,367	42,344	260,150
1984	56,423	42,761	72	4,261	204,720	13,183	28,955	63,761	53,738	296,933
1985	64,470	46,047	70	4,730	227,845	14,660	32,318	80,719	60,017	353,365
1986	69,880	47,642	...	5,134	255,208	15,548	35,112	103,713	72,040	406,502

Table It.10 Value of exports and imports by country, 1885–1987

	Total exports	Exports to:				Total imports	Imports from:			
		France	Germany	UK	USA		France	Germany	UK	USA
					L mn					
1885	951	367	104	71	46	1,460	288	119	314	72
1886	1,028	446	108	71	52	1,458	311	129	276	55
1887	1,002	405	115	79	66	1,605	326	166	306	64
1888	892	170	80	115	61	1,175	156	145	264	77
1889	951	165	91	113	76	1,391	167	156	314	75
1890	896	161	119	111	77	1,319	163	141	320	82
1891	877	150	131	115	74	1,127	144	134	262	74
1892	958	147	145	113	100	1,173	169	144	245	79
1893	964	148	146	104	82	1,191	159	147	252	96
1894	1,027	144	143	122	91	1,095	131	140	249	107
1895	1,038	136	170	115	102	1,187	162	144	235	124
1896	1,052	153	160	110	86	1,180	134	145	230	122
1897	1,092	116	179	114	93	1,192	161	150	223	125
1898	1,204	146	192	117	107	1,413	116	157	254	166
1899	1,431	202	236	148	118	1,507	152	194	300	168
1900	1,338	169	221	154	121	1,700	167	203	359	226
1901	1,374	175	235	151	140	1,718	179	206	279	234
1902	1,464	168	246	143	177	1,723	184	222	287	211
1903	1,483	171	226	132	166	1,813	193	236	282	212
1904	1,564	171	206	134	191	1,878	188	252	319	239
1905	1,694	182	222	130	226	2,016	205	287	348	238
1906	1,894	213	252	132	240	2,514	228	394	450	311
1907	1,938	198	301	156	236	2,881	256	527	523	393
1908	1,718	204	245	132	204	2,913	276	521	501	405
1909	1,855	199	307	168	272	3,112	329	504	491	390
1910	2,065	218	293	210	264	3,246	334	525	476	363
1911	2,190	206	301	223	247	3,389	327	550	510	415
1912	2,383	223	328	264	262	3,702	390	626	577	515
1913	2,497	231	343	261	268	3,646	283	613	592	523
1914	2,195	174	319	306	262	2,923	206	503	505	443
1915	2,512	438	204	391	283	4,704	240	230	849	1,749
1916	3,053	738	—	447	315	8,390	595	12	1,977	3,415
1917	3,276	912	—	483	244	13,990	993	18	2,165	6,192
1918	3,305	1,207	—	727	169	16,039	1,234	16	2,666	6,641
1919	6,004	1,403	85	773	630	16,623	760	88	2,444	7,350
1920	11,628	1,696	574	1,379	939	26,822	1,904	1,097	4,609	8,689
					L bn					
1921	8·04	0·97	0·81	0·80	1·08	16·91	1·07	1·29	1·68	5·71
1922	9·16	1·37	0·97	1·12	1·02	15·74	1·15	1·25	2·02	4·40
1923	10·95	1·58	0·70	1·21	1·52	17·16	1·32	1·31	2·20	4·61
1924	14·27	1·82	1·57	1·49	1·24	19·37	1·47	1·52	2·17	4·65
1925	18·17	2·02	2·03	1·85	1·90	26·20	2·36	2·25	2·73	6·20
1926	18·54	2·11	2·22	1·76	1·93	25·88	2·14	2·96	1·88	5·61
1927	15·52	1·28	2·23	1·53	1·64	20·38	1·80	2·11	1·83	3·96
1928	14·44	1·36	1·86	1·40	1·52	21·92	1·36	2·30	1·79	4·01
1929	14·77	1·30	1·78	1·46	1·72	21·30	1·30	2·74	2·04	3·56
1930	12·12	1·23	1·56	1·19	1·33	17·35	1·50	2·26	1·68	2·54
1931	10·21	1·12	1·09	1·20	1·05	11·64	0·83	1·59	1·10	1·33
1932	6·81	0·52	0·78	0·74	0·69	8·27	0·48	1·15	0·74	1·11
1933	5·99	0·46	0·73	0·69	0·53	7·43	0·41	1·14	0·73	1·12
1934	5·22	0·35	0·83	0·53	0·39	7·68	0·44	1·25	0·71	0·96
1935	5·24	0·31	0·85	0·43	0·42	7·79	0·47	1·43	0·57	0·88
1936	5·54	0·19	1·09	0·16	0·55	6·04	0·13	1·62	0·05	0·90
1937	10·44	0·44	1·50	0·64	0·78	13·94	0·49	2·59	0·56	1·54
1938	10·50	0·33	2·20	0·59	0·78	11·27	0·25	3·02	0·73	1·34
1939	10·82	0·24	1·90	0·52	0·77	10·31	0·15	3·03	0·57	0·98
1940	11·52	0·29	3·56	0·28	0·39	13·22	0·13	5·14	0·42	1·22
1941	14·51	0·22	7·11	—	—	11·47	0·21	6·89	—	0·09
1942	16·05	0·18	7·64	—	—	14·04	0·12	8·37	—	0·02

Table It.10 (Continued)   Value of exports and imports by country, 1885–1987

	Total exports	Exports to:				Total imports	Imports from:			
		France	Germany	UK	USA		France	Germany	UK	USA
						L bn				
1947	341	. . .	. . .	. . .	. . .	937	. . .	. . .	. . .	. . .
1948	576	23·1	16·6	45·5	51·3	844	7·9	17·6	27·8	317·7
1949	641	36·2	54·3	67·0	26·4	883	21·5	39·7	34·6	311·0
1950	753	65·3	73·8	85·8	47·7	926	41·8	75·9	51·1	217·9
1951	1,030	92·7	80·2	138·6	70·5	1,355	58·5	99·9	50·1	284·5
1952	867	56·7	88·0 / 86·7	71·2	87·2	1,460	58·9	136·7 / 135·5	83·4	307·5
1953	942	49·1	103·9	67·8	90·1	1,513	75·9	179·6	116·9	202·8
1954	1,024	60·4	115·2	81·0	80·2	1,524	97·5	203·7	102·6	186·5
1955	1,160	67·5	145·7	84·1	99·6	1,695	108·4	214·7	90·5	253·1
1956	1,341	95·9	180·0	86·6	125·9	1,984	100·2	247·6	107·2	325·4
1957	1,595	101·1	224·7	99·2	161·9	2,296	121·4	281·2	121·8	427·1
1958	1,611	84·6	226·9	109·2	177·5	2,010	94·7	243·3	109·9	358·0
1959	1,821	112·1	295·1	135·7	216·0	2,105	162·1	292·9	116·7	234·1
1960	2,280	172·1	375·8	156·3	239·7	2,953	248·7	418·8	151·9	418·4
1961	2,614	199·7	465·5	175·7	238·8	3,265	299·5	509·4	179·2	539·7
1962	2,918	269·1	562·0	174·8	275·6	3,797	334·3	642·1	239·9	553·3
1963	3,159	328·1	564·2	169·1	298·2	4,745	460·6	813·2	290·9	651·6
1964	3,724	406·5	707·2	207·8	316·9	4,533	446·5	738·5	248·1	615·8
1965	4,500	463·9	953·3	210·6	386·7	4,611	451·5	681·4	213·8	620·9
1966	5,024	582·6	1,007·1	238·6	465·2	5,368	542·2	857·9	251·5	656·6
1967	5,441	675·6	959·7	263·0	539·8	6,142	654·8	1,060	271·0	665·0
1968	6,366	801·2	1,189	281·2	681·3	6,429	728·2	1,148	272·8	748·4
1969	7,330	1,061	1,440	263·9	795·3	7,792	968·4	1,462	313·0	886·0
1970	8,254	1,065	1,780	313·3	846·1	9,356	1,235	1,861	352·9	967·1
1971	9,362	1,267	2,129	362·2	918·4	9,901	1,396	1,994	360·0	890·4
1972	10,849	1,536	2,487	463·0	1,062	11,265	1,772	2,286	395·5	930·8
1973	12,989	1,881	2,821	648·2	1,111	16,343	2,443	3,302	559·7	1,352
1974	19,826	2,498	3,662	1,025	1,504	26,714	3,510	4,734	808·9	2,038
1975	22,866	3,017	4,243	1,041	1,487	25,200	3,334	4,296	831·9	2,184
1976	31,167	4,684	5,884	1,495	2,010	36,731	4,975	6,231	1,284	2,983
1977	39,968	5,715	7,413	2,106	2,666	42,429	5,895	7,140	1,582	2,950
1978	47,505	6,773	9,037	2,876	3,385	47,868	6,966	8,310	1,912	3,239
1979	59,926	8,873	11,336	3,916	3,877	64,597	9,032	11,107	2,613	4,381
1980	66,719	10,094	12,211	4,064	3,555	85,564	11,858	14,180	3,784	5,291
1981	86,040	11,686	13,351	4,999	5,841	103,674	12,938	16,191	4,012	7,032
1982	99,231	15,103	15,491	6,219	6,999	116,216	14,531	18,658	4,601	7,864
1983	110,537	16,254	18,331	7,019	8,526	122,002	15,362	19,372	4,750	7,246
1984	129,027	18,078	20,782	8,716	14,045	148,162	18,436	23,666	6,384	9,111
1985	149,724	21,003	24,172	10,424	18,357	172,809	21,546	28,742	8,540	10,294
1986	145,331	22,704	26,355	10,298	15,605	148,994	21,654	30,507	7,597	8,496
1987	150,454	24,571	27,959	11,193	14,456	161,597	23,592	34,076	8,514	8,619

247

Sources

(For sources used in specific tables, see Notes.)

1 *Annuario Statistico Italiano*, Istituto Centrale di Statistica, Rome.
2 Fua, Gíorgio, (ed.), *La Sviluppo Economico in Italia*, Vol. III, Franco Angeli Libri, Milan, 1975.
3 International Labour Office, *Technical Guide*, Vol. II, Geneva, 1972, 1976, 1980.
4 League of Nations, *Yearbook of Labour Statistics*.
5 Mitchell, B.R., *European Historical Statistics, 1750–1975*, 2nd rev. edn. Macmillan, London, 1980.
6 Organisation for Economic Cooperation and Development (OECD), *Labour Force Statistics*, annual and quarterly, Paris.
7 OECD, *National Accounts, 1950–1979*, Vol. 1, Paris, 1981.
8 OECD, *National Accounts, 1960–1987*, Vol. 1, Paris, 1989.
9 *Sommario di Statistiche Storiche Italiane, 1861–1955*, Istituto Centrale di Statistica, Rome, 1958.
10 *Sommario di Statistiche Storiche dell'Italia, 1861–1975*, Istituto Centrale di Statistica, Rome, 1976.
11 *Statistical Year Book of the League of Nations*, Geneva.
12 Supplements to the United Nations *Statistical Year Book* and *Monthly Bulletin of Statistics*, New York, 1967, 1972 and 1977.
13 United Nations, *Monthly Bulletin of Statistics*, New York.
14 United Nations, *Statistical Year Book*, New York.
15 *Year Book of Labour Statistics*, International Labour Office, Geneva.

Notes

Table It.1 Gross domestic product at current prices

Sources: **2, 7, 8**

From 1951, OECD data have been used. There is a break in the series in 1960 when the system of national accounts was revised. The main differences are explained in **7**. From 1960–79 the figures have been estimated by the OECD Secretariat.

For the period 1885–1950, the figures are based on data given in **2**. For full details of method of compilation and coverage see **2**.

Table It.2 Gross domestic product at constant prices

Sources: **2, 7, 8**

From 1951, OECD data have been used. See Note to Table It.1 concerning the break in the series in 1960. From 1960–79 the figures have been estimated by the OECD Secretariat. Consumers' expenditure and government current expenditure in 1983 and 1984 also estimated by OECD Secretariat.

For the period 1885–1950, constant price data (base 1938) given in **2** have been linked to OECD data and roughly converted to 1980 prices. These estimates have been used in preference to those given in **10** because they are more detailed. Each category of expenditure has been re-referenced to 1980 prices independently and the sum of the components may not therefore add to the total for gross domestic product.

Table It.3 Industrial production

Sources: **5, 13, 14**

Industrial production index: the current base weighted index was introduced in 1973 with base weights of 1970. The index includes mining, manufacturing (except for some subgroups of miscellaneous manufactures), electricity and gas. Before the introduction of the revised index in 1973, the index for manufacturing, which forms part of the combined index, excluded printing and publishing and repair shops.

For 1929–38, the series includes building and public works; mining is excluded for 1929–32.

Coal: includes both coal and lignite.

Natural gas: published figures are now given in terajoules. From 1977, the published figures have been converted to cubic metres using the conversion factors given in **13**.

Electricity: figures are for gross production.

Table It.4   Prices and income

Sources: **1, 2, 7, 8, 10, 13, 14**

Consumer prices: the indices are weighted arithmetic averages with fixed base weight. The national index represents a weighted arithmetic average of indices relating to four major areas of the country (North West, North East, Central and Southern, and Insular). The index for 'Food' includes tobacco.

Producer prices: the current series was revised in 1976 and now includes 344 commodities. It is a base weighted index. The current series for raw materials is called a 'Producers goods' index and is part of the 'All items' index. It was linked to the earlier raw materials index in 1953.

For further details of these price series see **12**.

Export and import prices: data from **10** are linked to indices given in **1**.

Compensation of employees: OECD data have been used from 1951. The figures include wages and salaries in cash and in kind paid to employees together with contributions on behalf of employees to social security schemes and private pension funds. Two figures are given for 1960 because of the change in classification (see notes to Table It.1).

National income: OECD data have been used from 1951. National income is gross national product (gross domestic product plus net factor income from the rest of the world) minus consumption of fixed capital. Two figures are given for 1960 because of the change in classification (see notes to Table It.1).

For the period 1885–1950, the series shown is for *Reddito Nationale* given in **9** and **10**.

Table It.5   Population

Sources: **6, 9, 10**

OECD data have been used from 1950. From 1954, the figures are annual averages of the present-in-area (*de facto*) population. Permanent inmates of institutions (religious communities, old people's homes, prisons, etc) are excluded; these numbered about 605,000 in 1971.

For the period 1950–53, the estimates are for mid-year and the breakdown by sex is of the resident population (i e, includes those working abroad). The figures for 1901–36 are census figures. The figure for 1921 includes the territories acquired by Italy after the First World War.

Age distribution: figures for 1950–58 are based on resident population estimates (i e, they include Italians working abroad) and do not, therefore, add up to total population figures given in the table. Up to and including 1958, the age distribution is for under 15 years and 15–64 years; from 1959 it is under 14 years and 14–64 years.

Table It.6   Education

Sources: **1, 9, 10**

Schooling is compulsory in Italy from the age of 6 years but pre-school facilities have been available since the nineteenth century.

Kindergarten: includes pupils at *scuole del grado preparatorio*; in the early period, *scuole materne*.

Elementary: pupils at elementary schools only from 1885–1940; from 1945 the figures also include pupils at *scuole medie* (middle schools) which were established after the Second World War.

Secondary: figures are for pupils/students at *scuole secondarie superiori* which includes professional, technical and scientific training.

Higher education: students '*in corso*' in institutions of higher education (mainly universities). Data refer to the academic year.

Table It.7   Labour market: employment

Sources: **4, 6**

OECD data have been used from 1954. The figures are annual averages of those in civilian employment and include employees, self-employed and unpaid family workers working for at least one third of normal working time. The unemployed and temporarily stopped are not included. Up to 1968, permanent inmates of institutions were excluded from the figures. In 1977, definitions and classifications were revised. The figures from 1966 are on the revised basis; previous years are not strictly comparable. Figures for 1966 on the previous classification are:

Employed labour force	18·46 mn
Agriculture	4·59 mn
Industry	7·53 mn
Other activities	6·34 mn

The figures were also revised in 1956.

'Distribution and services' includes the wholesale and retail trades, restaurants and hotels, finance, insurance, real estate and business services, community, social and personal services (including, since 1969, permanent inmates of institutions).

For 1930–54 (first line), the figures are for wage earners only in manufacturing industries and are based on the Ministry of Corporations index. The annual figure is an average of the figures for the last week of each month. The 1931, 1936 and 1951 figures are from census data and refer to the economically active population (employers, self-employed, employees and unemployed).

For further details see **4**.

Table It.8   Labour market: other indicators

Sources: **4, 5, 6, 15**

Manufacturing: average hours worked per month: the current series is an average of hours actually worked per *day* including overtime in the reporting week. Covers wage earners of both sexes including apprentices. Data are based on quarterly surveys covering all establishments employing ten or more workers during the last week of each quarter. The scope of the series was revised in 1965 and in 1978.

For 1928–38, the figures are for average hours of work per month.

Manufacturing: average hourly earnings: the current series is an average of earnings of hourly paid workers including overtime and other bonus payments. Covers wage earners of both sexes including apprentices. For 1948–74 the figures exclude payments for annual vacation and public holidays. Data are based on quarterly surveys as above. The scope of the series was revised in 1965 and in 1978.

Unemployment: OECD data have been used from 1966. The current series includes all persons aged 14 years and over looking for work during the reference week including school leavers. From 1977, the definition was widened to include housewives, students, pensioners, etc, who stated that they were looking actively for work. The figures have been revised on this basis back to 1966; two figures are given for 1966. From 1955, the figures are based on labour force sample surveys, the coverage of which has varied.

For 1932–54, the figures refer to numbers unemployed on the register at the end of the month. For 1925–32, the figures are for insured workers only.

The percentage figure is currently the ratio of the unemployed to the total labour force.

For further details of all these series see **3, 15**.

Table It.9   Public finance

Sources: **1, 2, 9, 10**

Total receipts: include all central government current revenues. Loan receipts excluded.

Taxes on persons: from 1974 shown as *imposte sul reddito delle personne fisische* together with small amounts for *richezzi mobile*.

For 1885–1973, figures are for *richezzi mobile* and are given in **9** and **10**.

Taxes on companies: the figures in this column are for *imposte sugli affari* (tax on business). Up to 1973 this consisted of profits tax (*imposte sull'entrata*) and stamp duties (*registro e bollo*). From 1974 value-added tax has been included in the total; by 1986, VAT formed over 80 per cent of the total given in this column.

Taxes on monopolies: includes taxes on tobacco and salt monopolies. The salt monopoly tax was discontinued after 1972.

Figures are for the fiscal year ending June 30 of the year shown until 1964; the second figure for 1964 is for the six months July to December; from 1965, figures are for calendar years.

Total expenditure: figures are for central government expenditure as given in **1**, **9**, and **10** and are for fiscal years ending June 30 of the year shown until 1964; the second figure for 1964 is for the six months July to December. From 1965, data refer to calendar years. The figure for 1885 is for ten months.

For the years 1885–1964, data for categories of expenditure are taken from **2**.

Debt interest: figures are for debt interest and administration costs for the period 1885–1926 (first line) from estimates in **2**. From 1926 (second line) debt interest only from estimates in **10**.

Table It.10   Value of exports and imports by country

Sources: **1, 9, 10**

Changes in definition affected the trade figures in 1907 and 1930. Trade with Germany included Austria for 1937–45. From 1952 (second line) the figures for Germany refer to the Federal Republic of Germany. Trade with the UK included Southern Ireland up to 1923.

JAPAN

CONTENTS

251

Table J.1 Gross domestic product at current prices, 1930–87

	Consumers' expenditure	Government current expenditure	Gross fixed capital formation	Value of physical change in stocks	Exports of goods & services[b]	Imports of goods & services[c]	**Gross domestic product at market prices[a]**
				¥ bn			
1930	10·6	1·6		1·5	2·7	−2·5	**13·9**
1931	9·1	1·9		1·3	2·3	−2·2	**12·5**
1932	9·5	2·2		1·4	2·4	−2·5	**13·0**
1933	10·2	2·5		1·8	3·0	−3·1	**14·3**
1934	10·6	2·4		2·8	3·5	−3·7	**15·7**
1935	10·8	2·6		3·1	4·2	−4·1	**16·7**
1936	11·4	2·7		3·6	4·5	−4·4	**17·8**
1937	12·8	4·7		5·8	6·1	−6·0	**23·4**
1938	13·9	6·7		6·4	5·8	−5·9	**26·8**
1939	16·5	7·1		8·9	6·6	−6·1	**33·1**
1940	19·2	9·6		10·5	7·3	−7·2	**39·4**
1941	20·7	13·5		11·7	6·1	−7·1	**44·9**
1942	23·7	17·1		14·6	5·0	−6·1	**54·4**
1943	26·0	22·9		15·9	4·9	−5·8	**63·8**
1944	26·6	27·7		20·7	4·0	−4·3	**74·5**
1945							
1946	333·1	54·8		105·4	4·8	−24·1	**474·0**
1947	915·1	102·2		345·2	27·7	−81·5	**1,308·7**
1948	1,741·1	282·3		752·2	81·1	−190·6	**2,666·1**
1949	2,261·1	393·8		830·6	216·5	−326·8	**3,375·2**
1950	2,397·3	437·3		1,007·3	469·1	−364·3	**3,946·7**
1951	2,862·2	465·4		1,620·7	868·3	−713·5	**5,104·1**
1952	3,862	669	1,276	386	732	−710	**6,215**
1953	4,665	780	1,554	142	724	−849	**7,016**
1954	5,162	860	1,696	140	794	−854	**7,797**
1955	5,529	894	1,703	421	921	−872	**8,597**
1956	6,012	936	2,289	507	1,130	−1,168	**9,706**
1957	6,597	1,009	2,948	740	1,278	−1,499	**11,073**
1958	7,057	1,105	2,939	252	1,270	−1,105	**11,517**
1959	7,722	1,209	3,435	418	1,483	−1,334	**12,933**
1960	9,395	1,282	4,638	623	1,714	−1,641	**16,011**
1961	11,031	1,484	6,167	963	1,791	−2,100	**19,336**
1962	12,653	1,747	7,065	443	2,066	−2,031	**21,943**
1963	14,772	2,070	7,929	548	2,266	−2,471	**25,114**
1964	17,028	2,352	9,362	851	2,800	−2,852	**29,541**
1965	19,239	2,690	9,782	695	3,451	−2,991	**32,866**
1966	22,142	3,054	11,562	815	4,031	−3,434	**38,170**
1967	25,405	3,410	14,287	1,528	4,311	−4,211	**44,730**
1968	28,974	3,934	17,567	1,910	5,348	−4,757	**52,976**
1969	33,300	4,558	21,441	1,938	6,558	−5,567	**62,228**
1970	38,333	5,455	26,043	2,573	7,926	−6,985	**73,345**
1971	43,230	6,421	27,637	1,215	9,452	−7,254	**80,701**
1972	49,901	7,537	31,524	1,299	9,779	−7,645	**92,395**
1973	60,308	9,336	40,938	1,885	11,291	−11,261	**112,497**
1974	72,912	12,240	46,695	3,396	18,258	−19,257	**134,244**
1975	84,763	14,890	48,136	476	18,982	−18,919	**148,328**
1976	95,784	16,417	51,945	1,092	22,582	−21,247	**166,573**
1977	107,076	18,243	55,982	1,280	24,308	−21,267	**185,622**
1978	117,923	19,753	62,147	1,027	22,729	−19,174	**204,405**
1979	130,078	21,486	70,171	1,813	25,627	−27,629	**221,546**
1980	141,324	23,568	75,821	1,613	32,887	−35,036	**240,177**
1981	149,385	25,585	78,941	1,403	37,977	−35,927	**257,364**
1982	159,606	26,796	79,987	1,189	39,391	−37,341	**269,628**
1983	167,809	27,956	79,217	217	39,275	−34,258	**280,256**
1984	175,984	29,449	83,176	1,138	45,066	−36,866	**297,947**
1985	184,764	30,685	87,825	2,254	46,307	−35,532	**316,303**
1986	191,651	32,571	91,302	1,293	38,090	−24,791	**330,116**
1987	198,784	33,101	99,409	648	38,432	−26,644	**343,730**

a Gross national product, 1930–51.   b Exports and income from abroad, 1930–51.   c Imports and income paid abroad, 1930–51.

Table J.2 Gross domestic product at constant prices, 1930–87

	Consumers' expenditure	Government current expenditure	Gross fixed capital formation	Value of physical increase in stocks	Exports of goods & services	Less Imports of goods & services	Gross domestic product at market prices
				¥ bn, 1980 prices			
1930	16,873	5,032	1,577		. . .	. . .	**20,323**
1931	16,717	6,809	1,681		. . .	. . .	**20,925**
1932	16,717	7,401	1,577		. . .	. . .	**21,227**
1933	16,717	7,697	1,891		. . .	. . .	**22,130**
1934	17,182	7,401	3,152		. . .	. . .	**24,388**
1935	16,562	7,697	3,258		. . .	. . .	**24,990**
1936	17,027	7,697	3,572		. . .	. . .	**25,893**
1937	17,801	12,433	4,833		. . .	. . .	**31,915**
1938	17,646	16,283	5,043		. . .	. . .	**32,969**
1939	16,717	13,914	6,305		. . .	. . .	**33,271**
1940	15,015	14,506	6,199		. . .	. . .	**31,314**
1941	14,550	18,058	6,410		. . .	. . .	**31,765**
1942	13,932	19,242	6,936		. . .	. . .	**32,217**
1943	13,156	21,907	6,095		. . .	. . .	**32,217**
1944	10,835	21,611	6,830		. . .	. . .	**31,012**
1945	. . .	. . .	. . .		. . .	. . .	**. . .**
1946	10,526	3,257	4,308		. . .	. . .	**17,462**
1947	11,454	2,369	5,149		. . .	. . .	**18,968**
1948	13,002	4,144	5,253		. . .	. . .	**21,377**
1949	14,395	4,736	4,308		. . .	. . .	**21,829**
1950	15,634	5,328	3,992		. . .	. . .	**24,238**
1951	17,027	5,921	4,939		. . .	. . .	**27,399**
1952	19,968	7,105	4,378	719	1,096	1,687	**30,410**
1953	22,467	7,208	5,054	101	1,266	2,221	**32,648**
1954	23,578	7,380	5,441	327	1,387	2,473	**34,497**
1955	25,440	7,345	5,552	1,130	1,594	2,619	**37,455**
1956	27,421	7,316	6,734	989	1,948	3,455	**40,276**
1957	29,140	7,273	7,974	1,348	2,136	4,363	**43,216**
1958	31,239	7,604	8,347	577	2,136	3,207	**45,740**
1959	33,671	8,002	9,547	913	2,699	4,491	**49,911**
1960	37,039	8,361	12,481	1,147	3,007	5,573	**56,455**
1961	40,892	8,854	15,397	1,999	3,165	7,044	**63,254**
1962	43,978	9,620	17,572	980	3,708	6,964	**68,889**
1963	47,845	10,419	19,671	1,157	3,967	8,323	**74,727**
1964	53,004	10,761	22,759	1,573	4,827	9,466	**83,452**
1965	56,057	11,172	23,811	1,297	5,971	9,993	**88,309**
1966	61,679	11,808	27,155	1,291	6,986	11,212	**97,703**
1967	68,089	12,276	32,075	2,399	7,456	13,759	**108,531**
1968	73,901	13,062	38,635	3,104	9,240	15,430	**122,513**
1969	81,545	13,834	45,926	2,870	11,161	17,544	**137,799**
1970	87,588	14,819	53,673	4,910	13,114	21,556	**152,556**
1971	92,605	15,592	56,095	2,363	15,227	22,781	**159,106**
1972	101,239	16,462	61,714	2,273	15,871	25,122	**172,442**
1973	110,534	17,357	69,515	3,056	16,797	31,232	**186,023**
1974	110,226	17,892	62,914	4,619	20,779	32,657	**183,759**
1975	115,085	19,096	62,147	683	20,946	29,410	**188,537**
1976	119,107	19,990	63,805	1,349	24,494	31,179	**197,556**
1977	124,163	20,866	66,335	1,695	27,360	32,406	**208,004**
1978	130,895	21,961	72,003	922	27,091	34,247	**218,616**
1979	139,337	22,920	75,795	2,291	27,986	38,354	**229,958**
1980	141,324	23,568	75,821	1,613	32,887	35,036	**240,177**
1981	143,141	24,698	78,207	1,478	37,559	35,640	**249,447**
1982	149,043	25,178	78,837	1,336	37,927	35,799	**256,527**
1983	153,856	25,919	78,633	443	40,566	34,815	**264,613**
1984	158,066	26,638	82,493	1,569	47,718	38,611	**277,883**
1985	162,404	27,097	87,287	2,666	49,968	38,460	**290,983**
1986	167,589	28,863	92,501	1,649	47,565	40,220	**297,962**
1987	174,044	28,705	102,037	725	49,325	44,078	**310,775**

Table J.3 Industrial production, index and selected series, 1885–1987

	Industrial production	Coal	Crude steel	Cars & commercial vehicles	Crude petroleum	Natural gas	Electricity
	Index nos., 1980 = 100	mn tons	'000 tons	'000	'000 tons	mn m³	bn kwh
1885	0·12	1·3	—	—	4	—	—
1886	0·16	1·4	—	—	5	—	—
1887	0·20	1·7	—	—	4	—	—
1888	0·25	2·0	—	—	5	—	—
1889	0·27	2·4	—	—	7	—	—
1890	0·29	2·6	—	—	7	—	—
1891	0·28	3·2	—	—	7	—	—
1892	0·33	3·2	—	—	9	—	—
1893	0·35	3·3	—	—	14	—	—
1894	0·46	4·3	—	—	23	—	—
1895	0·52	4·8	—	—	19	—	—
1896	0·60	5·0	—	—	26	—	—
1897	0·62	5·2	—	—	29	—	—
1898	0·71	6·7	—	—	35	—	—
1899	0·81	6·7	—	—	72	—	—
1900	0·89	7·4	—	—	116	—	—
1901	0·92	8·9	1	—	149	—	—
1902	0·89	9·7	2	—	159	—	—
1903	0·90	10·1	2	—	161	—	—
1904	0·89	10·7	2	—	189	—	—
1905	0·92	11·5	6	—	196	—	—
1906	1·0	13·0	6	—	229	—	—
1907	1·1	13·8	7	—	267	—	—
1908	1·1	14·8	3	—	276	—	—
1909	1·1	15·0	7	—	252	—	—
1910	1·2	15·7	9	—	258	—	—
1911	1·3	17·6	12	—	221	—	—
1912	1·4	19·6	15	—	223	—	—
1913	1·6	21·3	17	—	259	—	—
1914	1·5	22·3	19	—	365	—	1·5
1915	1·7	20·5	20	—	416	—	1·8
1916	2·0	22·9	371	—	419	14·0	2·2
1917	2·3	26·4	773	—	386	25·4	2·6
1918	2·5	28·0	813	—	340	25·8	3·1
1919	2·6	31·3	814	—	326	28·7	3·5
1920	2·4	29·2	811	—	290	38·2	3·8
1921	2·6	26·2	932	—	298	33·1	5·1
1922	2·7	27·7	909	—	285	31·8	5·6
1923	2·7	28·9	959	—	251	26·2	6·1
1924	2·8	30·1	1,100	—	252	20·1	7·8
1925	3·1	31·5	1,300	—	266	23·2	9·1
1926	3·3	31·4	1,506	0·2	248	22·3	10·6
1927	3·5	33·5	1,685	0·3	248	28·1	12·1
1928	3·6	33·9	1,906	0·3	270 / 261	27·4	13·7
1929	3·9	34·3	2,294	0·4	278	28·7	15·1
1930	3·9	31·4	2,289	0·5	282	43·4	15·8
1931	3·6	28·0	1,883	0·4	273	76·6	16·0
1932	3·8	28·1	2,398	0·9	226	51·3	17·4
1933	4·6	32·5	3,198	1·7	202	46·9	19·5
1934	4·9	35·9	3,844	2·8	256	47·1	21·8
1935	5·2	37·8	4,705	5·1	316	41·5	24·7
1936	5·9	41·8	5,223	12·2	352	41·1	27·1
1937	6·9	45·3	5,801	18·1	353	53·1	30·2
1938	7·1	48·7	6,472	24·4	353	50·6	32·4
1939	7·8	51·1	6,696	34·5	334	54·7	34·1
1940	8·2	56·3	6,856	46·0	301	56·7	34·6
1941	8·5	56·5	6,844	48·5	275	53·6	37·7
1942	8·2	53·5	7,044	37·2	236	54·1	36·1
1943	8·3	55·5	7,650	25·9	247	45·5	37·7

Table J.3 (Continued)   Industrial production, index and selected series, 1885–1987

	Industrial production	Coal	Crude steel	Cars & commercial vehicles	Crude petroleum	Natural gas	Electricity
	Index nos., 1980 = 100	mn tons	'000 tons	'000	'000 tons	mn m³	bn kwh
1944	8·5	52·9	6,729	21·8	229	44·3	36·1
1945	3·7	29·9	1,963	8·2	221	40·9	21·9
1946	1·7	20·4	557	14·9	192	35·9	30·3
1947	2·1	27·2	952	11·3	183	39·2	32·8
1948	2·7	33·7	1,715	20·4	159	51·0	37·8
1949	3·5	38·0	3,111	28·7	194	57·8	41·5
1950	4·2	38·5	4,839	31·6	293	68·8	46·3
1951	5·7	43·3	6,502	38·5	336	82·8	47·9
1952	6·1	43·3	6,988	39·0	306	91·1	52·0
1953	7·4	46·5	7,662	49·8	296	110·5	57·5
1954	8·0	42·7	7,750	70·1	300	141·0	60·0
1955	9·0	42·4	9,408	68·9	314	155·5	65·2
1956	11·1	46·6	11,106	111·1	310	176·8	73·6
1957	12·9	51·7	12,570	182·0	321	243·6	81·3
1958	12·8	49·7	12,118	188·3	367	367·9	85·4
1959	15·3	47·3	16,629	262·8	406	506·8	99·1
1960	18·9	51·1	22,138	481·6	526	731·4	115·5
1961	22·3	54·5	28,268	813·8	657	950·3	132·0
1962	24·2	54·4	27,546	990·7	760	1,209	140·4
1963	26·6	52·1	31,501	1,284	785	1,695	160·2
1964	31·1	50·9	39,799	1,704	657	1,859	179·6
1965	32·6	49·5	41,161	1,876	671	1,727	190·3
1966	36·8	51·3	47,784	2,287	782	1,777	215·3
1967	43·9	47·5	62,154	3,147	788	1,859	244·9
1968	51·5	46·6	66,893	4,086	744	2,016	273·3
1969	65·2	44·7	82,167	4,675	749	2,157	316·3
1970	66·6	39·7	93,322	5,290	770	2,359	359·5
1971	68·4	33·4	88,557	5,811	752	2,434	385·6
1972	73·4	28·1	96,901	6,294	716	2,475	428·5
1973	86·3	22·4	119,322	7,083	700	2,595	470·2
1974	81·1	20·3	117,131	6,552	672	2,572	459·0
1975	72·6	19·1	102,313	6,942	606	2,436	475·8
1976	80·6	18·4	107,399	7,842	580	2,493	511·8
1977	83·9	18·3	102,405	8,514	592	2,804	532·6
1978	89·3	19·0	102,105	9,269	542	2,641	564·0
1979	95·6	17·7	111,748	9,636	482	2,414	589·6
1980	100·0	18·0	111,384	11,044	432	2,423	577·5
1981	101·0	17·7	101,676	11,180	396	2,337	583·2
1982	101·4	17·6	99,540	10,739	396	2,239	581·1
1983	104·6	17·1	96,984	11,118	420	2,114	555·5
1984	114·3	16·6	105,588	11,110	396	2,236	580·4
1985	118·5	16·4	105,276	12,356	528	2,318	598·1
1986	118·2	16·0	98,268	12,269	624	2,031	557·1
1987	122·4	13·1	91,920	12,258	600	2,134	. . .

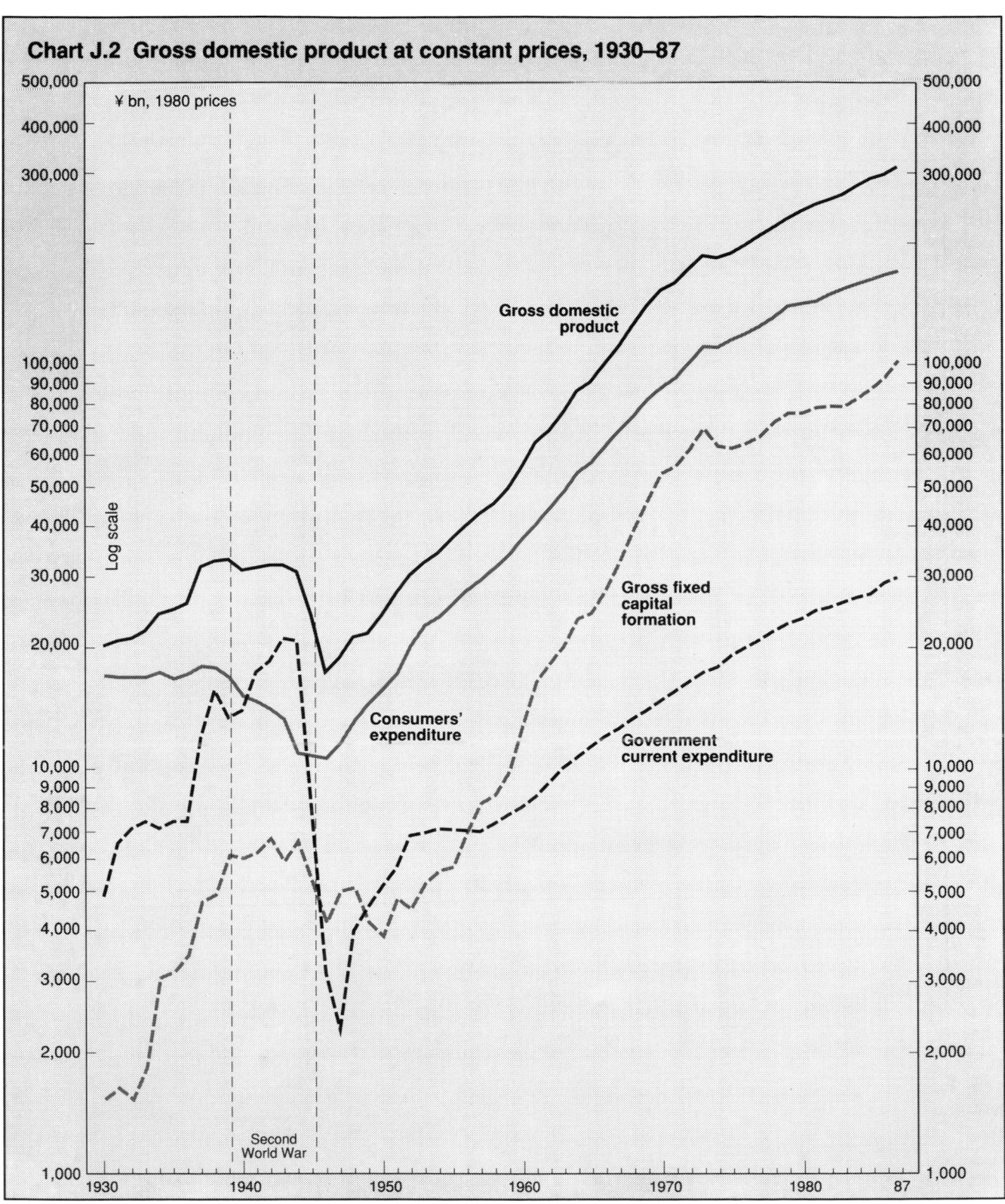

Chart J.2 Gross domestic product at constant prices, 1930–87

¥ bn, 1980 prices

Log scale

Gross domestic product

Gross fixed capital formation

Consumers' expenditure

Government current expenditure

Second World War

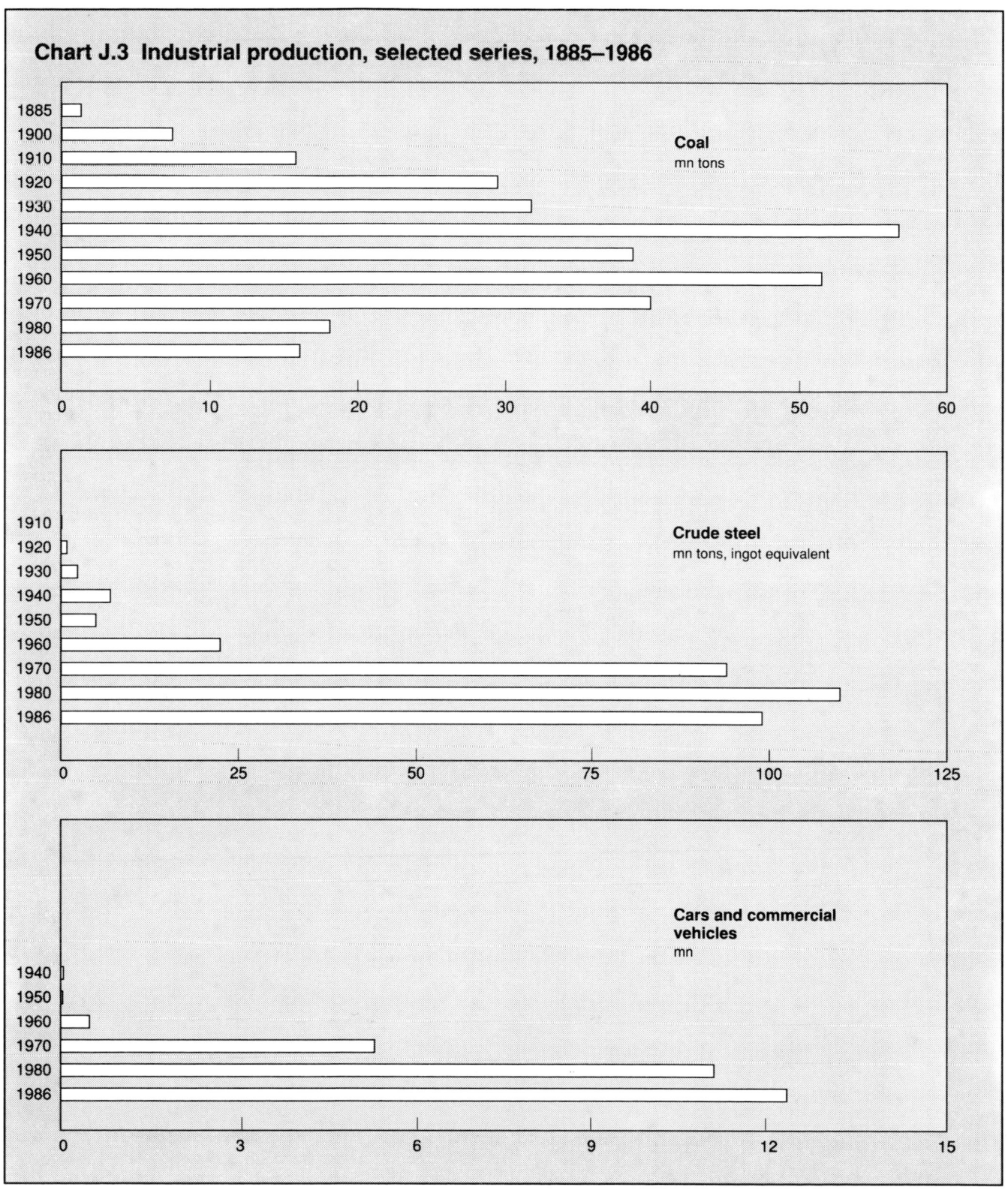

Chart J.3 Industrial production, selected series, 1885–1986

Coal
mn tons

1885	
1900	
1910	
1920	
1930	
1940	
1950	
1960	
1970	
1980	
1986	

0   10   20   30   40   50   60

Crude steel
mn tons, ingot equivalent

1910	
1920	
1930	
1940	
1950	
1960	
1970	
1980	
1986	

0   25   50   75   100   125

Cars and commercial vehicles
mn

1940	
1950	
1960	
1970	
1980	
1986	

0   3   6   9   12   15

Table J.4 Prices and income, 1900–87

	Consumer prices		Wholesale prices		Export prices	Import prices	Compensation of employees	National income
	All items	Food	All items	Producers' goods				
	Index nos., 1980 = 100						¥ bn	
1900	0·102	...	0·059	...	...	...	...	...
1901	0·100	...	0·057	...	...	...	...	...
1902	0·104	...	0·057	...	...	...	...	...
1903	0·110	...	0·061	...	...	...	...	...
1904	0·113	...	0·064	...	...	...	...	...
1905	0·116	...	0·069	...	...	...	...	...
1906	0·121	...	0·071	...	...	...	...	...
1907	0·130	...	0·076	...	...	...	...	...
1908	0·125	...	0·074	...	...	...	...	...
1909	0·123	...	0·070	...	...	...	...	...
1910	0·124	...	0·071	...	...	...	...	...
1911	0·133	...	0·074	...	...	...	...	...
1912	0·142	...	0·078	...	...	...	...	...
1913	0·146	...	0·078	...	...	...	...	...
1914	0·132	...	0·075	...	...	...	...	...
1915	0·124	...	0·076	...	...	...	...	...
1916	0·135	...	0·091	...	...	...	...	...
1917	0·161	...	0·115	...	...	...	...	...
1918	0·212	...	0·151	...	...	...	...	...
1919	0·281	...	0·185	...	...	...	2·6	12·5
1920	0·295	...	0·203	...	...	...	3·1	11·6
1921	0·277	...	0·157	...	...	...	3·7	12·4
1922	0·277	...	0·153	...	...	...	4·1	11·8
1923	0·059	...	0·156	...	...	...	4·4	11·4
1924	0·259	...	0·162	...	...	...	4·4	12·9
1925	0·255	...	0·158	...	...	...	4·3	13·6
1926	0·233	...	0·140	...	...	...	4·4	12·9
1927	0·221	...	0·133	...	...	...	4·6	13·1
1928	0·216	...	0·134	...	...	...	4·7	13·9
1929	0·213	...	0·130	...	...	...	4·5	13·0
1930	0·182	...	0·107	...	...	...	5·0	11·7
1931	0·159	...	0·090	...	...	...	4·5	10·5
1932	0·160	...	0·100	...	...	...	4·6	11·3
1933	0·171	...	0·115	...	...	...	4·8	12·4
1934	0·174	...	0·117	...	...	...	5·3	13·1
1935	0·178	...	0·120	...	...	...	5·5	14·4
1936	0·187	...	0·125	...	...	...	6·0	15·5
1937	0·204	...	0·152	...	...	...	6·8	18·6
1938	0·234	...	0·160	...	...	...	7·8	20·0
1939	0·262	...	0·177	...	...	...	9·6	25·4
1940	0·305	...	0·199	...	...	...	11·4	31·0
1941	0·308	...	0·213	...	...	...	13·8	35·8
1942	0·317	...	0·231	...	...	...	16·2	42·1
1943	0·336	...	0·247	...	...	...	20·8	48·4
1944	0·377	...	0·281	...	...	...	26·6	56·9
1945	0·554	...	0·424	...	...	...	...	...
1946	3·4	4·2	2·0	1·9	...	...	111	361
1947	7·3	8·5	5·8	4·9	...	...	315	968
1948	13·3	14·2	15·5	12·0	...	...	828	1,962
1949	17·5	17·8	25·3	18·3	...	...	1,144	2,737
1950	16·3	15·9	29·6	23·6	...	...	1,415	3,382
1951	19·0	18·4	41·4	36·3	...	...	1,819	4,525
1952	19·9	19·1	42·2	37·4	...	...	2,222	5,084
							2,330	5,567
1953	21·3	20·2	42·5	37·4	...	...	2,878	6,448
1954	22·6	21·8	42·2	35·9	...	...	3,189	7,231
1955	22·4	21·2	41·5	35·2	...	...	3,474	7,868
1956	22·5	20·9	43·3	38·4	...	...	3,956	8,670
1957	23·2	21·7	44·6	39·5	...	...	4,537	10,130
1958	23·1	21·5	41·7	35·9	...	...	4,953	10,544

258

Table J.4 (Continued)   Prices and income, 1900–87

	Consumer prices		Wholesale prices		Export prices	Import prices	Compensation of employees	National income
	All items	Food	All items	Producers' goods				
	Index nos., 1980 = 100						¥ bn	
1959	23·3	21·6	42·1	36·6	. . .	. . .	5,509	11,729
1960	24·2	22·4	42·6	36·6	67·7	29·3	6,453	14,180
1961	25·4	23·8	43·0	37·0	64·9	29·0	7,640	17,092
1962	27·2	25·7	42·3	36·3	64·9	29·4	9,120	19,135
1963	29·2	28·3	43·1	36·7	66·7	30·0	10,642	22,021
1964	30·4	29·4	43·2	36·7	69·6	31·0	12,449	25,409
1965	32·4	31·9	43·5	36·7	68·6	31·0	14,449	28,233
1966	34·1	33·1	44·5	37·8	66·4	29·7	16,780	32,799
1967	35·4	34·7	45·4	38·9	73·2	36·0	19,286	38,755
1968	37·3	37·0	45·7	38·5	98·0	60·4	22,477	46,652
1969	40·8	39·7	44·4	39·6	94·0	64·8	26,453	53,534
1970	42·3	42·7	48·4	41·1	93·4	68·2	31,895	63,550
1971	42·0	45·3	51·3	40·1	89·0	65·1	37,817	69,453
1972	42·3	47·3	53·3	40·5	83·1	53·7	44,026	80,026
1973	49·0	52·9	60·2	49·1	92·1	69·1	55,180	98,532
1974	65·2	67·8	73·7	67·3	100·0	100·0	70,010	116,192
1975	72·9	76·6	75·9	68·8	101·2	101·6	81,581	128,555
1976	79·7	83·6	79·7	73·4	105·1	109·6	92,020	145,809
1977	86·1	89·2	81·2	74·9	98·8	101·0	102,795	161,816
1978	89·4	92·3	79·1	71·7	99·4	97·6	111,079	178,770
1979	92·6	94·3	84·9	79·4	98·0	95·2	120,062	193,966
1980	100·0	100·0	100·0	100·0	100·0	100·0	130,398	209,143
1981	104·9	105·3	101·4	103·2	101·2	101·6	141,140	221,234
1982	107·8	107·2	103·2	110·4	105·2	109·6	149,059	232,543
1983	109·8	109·4	100·9	101·8	98·8	101·0	156,862	241,086
1984	112·2	112·5	100·6	99·2	99·5	97·6	165,311	256,459
1985	114·5	114·4	99·5	97·4	98·0	95·2	172,985	272,484
1986	115·2	114·6	90·4	64·8	83·2	61·1	181,660	283,751
1987	115·3	113·6	87·1	60·8	79·0	56·1	189,108	295,442

Table J.5   Population, 1885–1987

	Total population	Males	Females	Births	Age distribution		
					Under 15	15–64	65 & over
	mn			'000	mn		
1885	38·31	19·37	18·94	1,148	...	...	...
1886	38·54	19·48	19·06	1,127	...	...	...
1887	38·70	19·55	19·15	1,100	...	...	...
1888	39·03	19·72	19·31	1,214	...	...	...
1889	39·47	19·94	19·53	1,253	...	...	...
1890	39·90	20·15	19·75	1,190	...	...	...
1891	40·25	20·32	19·93	1,132	...	...	...
1892	40·51	20·44	20·07	1,263	...	...	...
1893	40·86	20·62	20·24	1,238	...	...	...
1894	41·14	20·75	20·39	1,274	...	...	...
1895	41·56	20·96	20·60	1,312	...	...	...
1896	41·99	21·16	20·83	1,351	...	...	...
1897	42·40	21·36	21·04	1,404	...	...	...
1898	42·89	21·59	21·30	1,458	...	...	...
1899	43·40	21·84	21·57	1,425	...	...	...
1900	43·85	22·05	21·80	1,470	...	...	...
1901	44·36	22·30	22·06	1,557	...	...	...
1902	44·96	22·61	22·36	1,570	...	...	...
1903	45·55	22·90	22·65	1,552	15·26	27·92	2·37
1904	46·14	23·20	22·94	1,500	...	...	...
1905	46·62	23·42	23·20	1,517	...	...	...
1906	47·04	23·60	23·44	1,461	...	...	...
1907	47·42	23·79	23·63	1,685	...	...	...
1908	47·97	24·04	23·92	1,734	16·40	29·02	2·54
1909	48·55	24·33	24·23	1,766	...	...	...
1910	49·18	24·65	24·53	1,782	...	...	...
1911	49·85	24·99	24·86	1,821	...	...	...
1912	50·58	25·37	25·21	1,817	...	...	...
1913	51·31	25·74	25·57	1,835	17·91	30·53	2·85
1914	52·04	26·11	25·93	1,883	...	...	...
1915	52·75	26·47	26·29	1,872	...	...	...
1916	53·50	26·84	26·66	1,873	...	...	...
1917	54·13	27·16	26·98	1,883	...	...	...
1918	54·74	27·45	27·29	1,856	19·21	32·41	3·12
1919	55·03	27·60	27·43	1,850	...	...	...
1920	55·96	28·04	27·92	2,105	20·42	32·60	2·94
1921	56·67	28·41	28·26	1,991	...	...	...
1922	57·39	28·80	28·59	1,969	...	...	...
1923	58·12	29·18	28·94	2,043	...	...	...
1924	58·88	29·57	29·31	1,999	...	...	...
1925	59·74	30·01	29·73	2,086	21·92	34·80	3·02
1926	60·74	30·52	30·22	2,104	...	...	...
1927	61·66	30·98	30·68	2,061	...	...	...
1928	62·60	31·45	31·15	2,136	...	...	...
1929	63·46	31·89	31·57	2,077	...	...	...
1930	64·45	32·39	32·06	2,085	23·58	37·81	3·06
1931	65·46	32·90	32·56	2,103	...	...	...
1932	66·43	33·36	33·07	2,183	...	...	...
1933	67·43	33·85	33·58	2,121	...	...	...
1934	68·31	34·29	34·02	2,044	...	...	...
1935	69·25	34·73	34·52	2,191	25·55	40·47	3·23
1936	70·11	35·10	35·01	2,102	...	...	...
1937	70·63	35·13	35·50	2,181	...	...	...
1938	71·01	35·13	35·88	1,928	...	...	...
1939	71·38	35·23	36·15	1,902	...	...	...
1940	71·93	35·39	36·54	2,116	26·37	42·11	3·45
1941	72·22	...	...	2,277	...	...	...
1942	72·88	...	...	2,234	...	...	...
1943	73·90	...	...	2,219	...	...	...
1944	74·43	...	...	2,274	...	...	...

Table J.5 (Continued)   Population, 1885–1987

	Total population	Males	Females	Births	Age distribution		
					Under 15	15–64	65 & over
	mn			'000	mn		
1945	72·15	...	...	1,902	26·48	41·97	3·70
1946	75·75	...	...	1,576	...	...	...
1947	78·10	38·13	39·97	2,679	27·57	46·79	3·74
1948	80·00	39·13	40·87	2,682	...	...	...
1949	81·77	40·06	41·71	2,697	...	...	...
1950	83·20	40·81	42·39	2,338	29·43	49·66	4·11
1951	84·54	41·49	43·05	2,138	...	...	...
1952	85·81	42·13	43·68	2,005	...	...	...
1953	86·98	42·72	44·26	1,868	...	...	...
1954	88·24	43·34	44·90	1,770	...	...	...
1955	89·28	43·86	45·42	1,731	29·80	54·73	4·75
1956	90·17	44·30	45·87	1,665	...	...	...
1957	90·93	44·67	46·26	1,567	...	...	...
1958	91·77	45·08	46·69	1,653	...	...	...
1959	92·64	45·50	47·14	1,626	...	...	...
1960	93·42	45·88	47·54	1,606	28·07	60·00	5·35
1961	94·29	46·30	47·99	1,589	...	...	...
1962	95·18	46·73	48·45	1,619	...	...	...
1963	96·17	47·21	48·96	1,660	...	...	...
1964	97·18	47·71	49·47	1,717	...	...	...
1965	98·28	48·24	50·04	1,824	25·17	66·93	6·18
1966	99·04	48·61	50·43	1,361	...	...	...
1967	100·20	49·18	51·02	1,936	...	...	...
1968	101·33	49·74	51·59	1,872	...	...	...
1969	102·54	50·33	52·21	1,890	...	...	...
1970	103·72	50·92	52·80	1,934	24·82	71·57	7·33
1971	105·15	51·61	53·54	2,001	...	...	...
1972	107·60	52·82	54·78	2,039	...	...	...
1973	109·10	53·61	55·49	2,092	...	...	...
1974	110·57	54·38	56·19	2,030	...	...	...
1975	111·94	55·09	56·85	1,901	27·22	75·85	8·87
1976	113·09	55·67	57·42	1,833	27·49	76·40	9·20
1977	114·15	56·20	57·95	1,755	27·65	76·95	9·55
1978	115·17	56·70	58·47	1,709	27·71	77·54	9·92
1979	116·13	57·18	58·95	1,643	27·66	78·16	10·31
1980	117·06	57·59	59·47	1,577	27·51	78·90	10·65
1981	117·88	58·00	59·88	1,529	27·60	79·27	11·01
1982	118·69	58·40	60·29	1,515	27·25	80·09	11·35
1983	119·48	58·79	60·69	1,509	26·91	80·90	11·67
1984	120·24	59·16	61·08	1,490	26·50	81·78	11·96
1985	121·05	59·50	61·55	1,432	26·03	82·51	12·47
1986	121·67	59·81	61·86	1,383	25·43	83·37	12·87
1987	122·26	...	...	...	24·75	84·19	13·32

Table J.6   Education, 1885–1986

| | Kindergarten | Elementary | Secondary | | Higher education | |
			Lower	Upper	Total	of which: Female
		No. of pupils '000			No. of students '000	
1885	...	3,097·4	23·2		11·8	...
1886	...	2,802·8	18·0		12·1	...
1887	...	2,713·6	19·3		14·1	...
1888	...	2,928·0	21·3		13·3	...
1889	...	3,032·1	22·6		14·5	...
1890	...	3,096·6	23·2		15·4	...
1891	...	3,154·0	24·5		17·0	...
1892	...	3,165·6	27·6		16·3	...
1893	...	3,337·8	31·3		14·7	...
1894	...	3,501·3	34·3		15·1	...
1895	...	3,670·6	46·1		16·1	...
1896	...	3,878·2	60·6		16·4	...
1897	...	3,995·1	78·4		18·9	...
1898	...	4,062·7	92·0		21·0	...
1899	...	4,303·1	105·2		22·7	...
1900	...	4,684·2	121·2		24·7	...
1901	...	4,981·4	144·1		28·6	...
1902	...	5,136·6	160·3		33·1	...
1903	...	5,085·1	171·6		33·6	...
1904	...	5,155·2	180·0		39·7	...
1905	...	5,349·6	191·5		41·9	...
1906	...	5,516·3	204·9		43·3	...
1907	...	5,715·4	217·7		45·7	...
1908	...	5,365·7	865·0		48·1	...
1909	...	5,972·0	749·3		48·8	...
1910	...	6,337·5	786·2		48·4	...
1911	...	6,454·9	848·6		50·4	...
1912	...	6,434·8	901·1		51·5	...
1913	...	6,469·2	941·3		55·6	...
1914	...	6,596·8	998·2		56·0	...
1915	...	6,743·8	1,058·1		56·7	...
1916	...	6,927·8	1,089·4		60·5	...
1917	...	7,153·5	1,114·5		64·0	...
1918	...	7,145·4	1,125·2		67·3	...
1919	...	7,580·4	1,221·5		68·4	...
1920	...	7,727·5	1,385·7		80·1	...
1921	...	7,867·2	1,540·5		91·4	...
1922	...	7,961·1	1,688·0		101·1	...
1923	...	8,017·4	1,826·0		110·1	...
1924	...	8,009·1	1,963·9		121·3	...
1925	...	7,893·6	2,069·1		134·0	...
1926	...	8,038·1	2,183·3		147·0	...
1927	...	8,196·7	2,284·9		154·7	...
1928	...	8,357·3	2,352·3		168·7	...
1929	...	8,540·5	2,375·7		177·3	...
1930	...	8,787·6	2,382·9		182·0	...
1931	...	9,072·8	2,349·7		181·9	...
1932	...	9,318·6	2,435·7		181·4	...
1933	...	9,484·8	2,611·6		182·0	...
1934	...	9,617·6	2,720·5		184·8	...
1935	144	9,797·6	2,821·4		187·0	...
1936	153	9,887·7	2,492·2		188·3	...
1937	162	10,054	3,072·3		190·2	...
1938	175	10,123	3,271·5		197·3	...
1939	176	10,253	3,492·1		215·8	...
1940	192	10,334	3,672·6		245·1	...
1941	211	10,381	3,856·8		244·6	...
1942	219	10,528	4,095·8		268·1	...
1943	235	10,631	4,426·7		360·7	...
1944	233	10,695	4,574·6		385·8	...

Table J.6 (Continued)   Education, 1885–1986

| | Kindergarten | Elementary | Secondary | | Higher education | |
| | | | Lower | Upper | Total | *of which:* Female |
	No. of pupils '000				No. of students '000	
1945	178	10,635	4,572·9		393·4	...
1946	144	10,257	4,510·3		431·9	...
1947	198	10,545	5,290·9		453·5	...
1948	199	10,782	4,793	1,204	12	2
1949	229	11,001	5,186	1,625	127	8
1950	225	11,191	5,333	1,935	225	19
1951	244	11,436	5,129	2,193	313	29
1952	371	11,163	5,076	2,343	400	42
1953	520	11,241	5,187	2,528	447	51
1954	612	11,767	5,664	2,545	492	59
1955	644	12,267	5,884	2,592	523	65
1956	651	12,632	5,962	2,702	547	69
1957	663	12,972	5,718	2,898	564	71
1958	674	13,508	5,210	3,057	578	74
1959	700	13,392	5,180	3,216	598	79
1960	742	12,591	5,900	3,239	626	86
1961	799	11,811	6,924	3,119	670	96
1962	856	11,057	7,328	3,282	727	109
1963	936	10,471	6,964	3,897	794	122
1964	1,061	10,031	6,476	4,634	853	134
1965	1,138	9,776	5,957	5,074	938	153
1966	1,222	9,584	5,556	4,997	1,044	177
1967	1,315	9,452	5,271	4,781	1,160	203
1968	1,420	9,383	5,043	4,522	1,270	228
1969	1,551	9,403	4,865	4,338	1,355	244
1970	1,675	9,493	4,717	4,232	1,407	253
1971	1,716	9,595	4,694	4,178	1,469	269
1972	1,842	9,696	4,688	4,155	1,529	287
1973	2,129	9,817	4,780	4,201	1,597	315
1974	2,233	10,089	4,736	4,271	1,659	343
1975	2,293	10,365	4,762	4,333	1,734	368
1976	2,371	10,610	4,834	4,386	1,792	388
1977	2,453	10,820	4,977	4,381	1,839	404
1978	2,498	11,147	5,048	4,415	1,862	410
1979	2,487	11,629	4,967	4,485	1,846	408
1980	2,407	11,827	5,094	4,622	1,835	405
1981	2,293	11,925	5,299	4,683	1,822	403
1982	2,228	11,902	5,624	4,601	1,818	405
1983	2,193	11,739	5,707	4,716	1,834	415
1984	2,133	11,464	5,829	4,892	1,843	425
1985	2,068	11,095	5,990	5,178	1,849	435
1986	2,019	10,665	6,106	5,259	1,880	453

Table J.7 Labour market: employment, 1885–1986

	Employed labour force	Agriculture, forestry & fishing	Mining	Manufacturing	Gas, electricity & water	Construction	Transport & communication	Distribution & services
				mn				
1885	21·16	16·76		1·55			2·85	
1886	21·46	16·86		1·64			2·96	
1887	21·76	16·96		1·74			3·06	
1888	22·04	17·05		1·83			3·16	
1889	22·31	17·12		1·92			3·27	
1890	22·58	17·20		2·01			3·37	
1891	22·83	17·24		2·11			3·48	
1892	23·09	17·30		2·19			3·59	
1893	23·32	17·34		2·29			3·69	
1894	23·55	17·37		2·38			3·81	
1895	23·77	17·39		2·47			3·92	
1896	23·98	17·39		2·56			4·03	
1897	24·20	17·39		2·65			4·15	
1898	24·38	17·38		2·74			4·26	
1899	24·57	17·36		2·83			4·38	
1900	24·77	17·33		2·93			4·51	
1901	24·96	17·29		3·04			4·63	
1902	25·12	17·24		3·13			4·75	
1903	25·30	17·19		3·23			4·88	
1904	25·44	17·11		3·32			5·01	
1905	25·60	17·04		3·37			5·19	
1906	25·73	16·94		3·42			5·37	
1907	25·86	16·85		3·56			5·46	
1908	25·97	16·74		3·69			5·54	
1909	26·09	16·63		3·75			5·71	
1910	26·17	16·49		3·89			5·79	
1911	26·26	16·35		3·98			5·92	
1912	26·35	16·21		4·08			6·06	
1913	26·42	16·06		4·17			6·19	
1914	26·47	15·88		4·25			6·34	
1915	26·53	15·72		4·32			6·49	
1916	26·56	15·52		4·44			6·59	
1917	26·59	15·33		4·55			6·71	
1918	26·62	15·13		4·63			6·86	
1919	26·62	14·91		4·68			7·03	
1920	27·26	14·85		4·59			7·82	
1921	27·50	14·84		4·64			8·02	
1922	27·73	14·82		4·71			8·20	
1923	27·97	14·81		4·75			8·41	
1924	28·21	14·80		4·82			8·59	
1925	28·44	14·79		4·87			8·79	
1926	28·68	14·77		4·91			8·99	
1927	28·91	14·76		4·95			9·20	
1928	29·15	14·75		4·99			9·41	
1929	29·38	14·73		4·87			9·78	
1930	29·62	14·72		5·07			9·83	
1931	28·99	14·80		4·74			9·45	
1932	29·18	14·83		4·92			9·42	
1933	29·78	14·79		5·26			9·72	
1934	30·79	14·78		5·85			10·16	
1935	31·40	14·77		6·22			10·41	
1936	30·86	14·57		6·20			10·09	
1937	31·16	14·53		6·47			10·17	
1938	31·47	14·49		6·74			10·25	
1939	31·78	14·45		7·08			10·25	
1940	32·48	14·40		7·66			10·42	
1941	32·58	14·28		8·11			10·19	
1942	32·60	14·17		8·59			9·84	
1947	34·66	17·65	...	6·69[a]	...	1·37	1·67	7·28

	Employed labour force	Agriculture, forestry & fishing	Mining	Manufacturing	Gas, electricity & water	Construction	Transport & communication	Distribution & services
				mn				
1948	34·93	17·09	0·61	6·33	...	1·36	1·64	7·88[a]
1949	36·12	18·58	0·45	6·65	...	1·25	1·78[a]	7·41
1950	36·48	18·53	0·47	6·04	...	1·35	1·59[a]	8·49
1951	36·74	17·18	0·54	6·25	...	1·44	1·85[a]	9·38
1952	37·56	17·19	0·62	6·31	...	1·52	1·93[a]	10·00
1953	39·36	16·69	0·60	7·19	0·16	1·63	(1·74)	11·35
1954	39·89	16·19	0·57	7·44	0·17	1·70	(1·69)	12·10
1955	41·19	16·54	0·49	7·56	0·18	1·81	(1·74)	12·84
1956	41·97	16·15	0·43	8·05	0·19	1·83	(1·85)	13·47
1957	42·81	14·67	0·50	8·53	0·22	2·17	1·89	14·83
1958	42·98	14·08	0·45	8·98	0·22	2·23	1·96	15·06
1959	43·35	13·48	0·48	8·96	0·23	2·43	2·07	15·70
1960	44·36	13·40	0·43	9·46	0·23	2·53	2·16	16·15
1961	44·98	13·03	0·38	10·11	0·23	2·74	2·25	16·24
1962	45·56	12·67	0·41	10·66	0·24	2·90	2·36	16·32
1963	45·95	11·94	0·33	11·08	0·25	2·90	2·43	17·02
1964	46·55	11·49	0·30	11·29	0·25	3·08	2·61	17·53
1965	47·30	11·13	0·29	11·50	0·26	3·28	2·68	18·16
1966	48·27	10·72	0·26	11·78	0·26	3·50	2·85	18·90
1967	49·20	10·36	0·26	12·52	0·27	3·59	2·89	19·29
1968	50·02	9·88	0·27	13·05	0·27	3·70	3·02	19·77
1969	50·40	9·46	0·24	13·45	0·27	3·71	3·11	20·11
1970	50·94	8·86	0·20	13·77	0·28	3·94	3·24	20·56
1971	51·21	8·15	0·19	13·83	0·29	4·14	3·33	21·22
1972	51·26	7·55	0·16	13·83	0·29	4·33	3·27	21·74
1973	52·59	7·05	0·13	14·43	0·34	4·67	3·37	22·48
1974	52·37	6·75	0·14	14·27	0·33	4·64	3·31	22·82
1975	52·23	6·61	0·16	13·46	0·32	4·79	3·32	23·48
1976	52·71	6·43	0·18	13·45	0·33	4·92	3·41	23·90
1977	53·42	6·34	0·19	13·40	0·31	4·99	3·41	24·67
1978	54·08	6·33	0·15	13·26	0·32	5·20	3·42	25·30
1979	54·79	6·13	0·12	13·33	0·33	5·36	3·49	25·94
1980	55·36	5·77	0·11	13·67	0·30	5·48	3·50	26·39
1981	55·81	5·57	0·10	13·85	0·31	5·44	3·44	26·98
1982	56·38	5·48	0·10	13·80	0·34	5·41	3·49	27·62
1983	57·33	5·31	0·10	14·06	0·36	5·41	3·50	28·43
1984	57·66	5·12	0·08	14·38	0·35	5·27	3·41	28·84
1985	58·07	5·09	0·09	14·53	0·33	5·30	3·43	29·07
1986	58·53	4·95	0·08	14·44	0·32	5·34	3·53	29·66

a   Including gas, electricity and water.

265

Table J.8 Labour market: other indicators, 1923–87

	Manufacturing				Industrial disputes		
	Average hrs worked per month	Average monthly earnings	Unemployment		Stoppages	Workers involved	Working days lost
			'000	%		'000	'000
		¥					
1923	283·0	46·26	. . .	. . .	. . .	. . .	. . .
1924	278·0	47·48	. . .	. . .	333	55	638
1925	278·6	47·14	. . .	. . .	293	40	361
1926	279·7	46·18	. . .	. . .	495	67	722
1927	276·0	52·64	. . .	. . .	383	47	1,177
1928	273·6	54·73	. . .	. . .	397	46	584
1929	272·8	55·52	. . .	. . .	576	77	572
1930	266·3	53·05	369	5·3	907	81	1,085
1931	264·0	49·37	423	6·1	998	65	980
1932	265·3	50·59	486	6·8	893	55	619
1933	271·7	50·55	409	5·6	410	49	385
1934	272·0	50·87	373	5·0	626	50	446
1935	272·8	50·49	356	4·6	590	38	301
1936	273·8	51·30	338	4·3	547	31	163
1937	275·6	53·03	295	3·7	628	124	338
1938	276·6	55·46	237	3·0	262	18	41
1939	276·3	54·69	. . .	. . .	358	73	35
1940	278·0	61·73	. . .	. . .	271	33	54
1941	280·0	69·12	. . .	. . .	159	11	. . .
1942	282·1	76·62	. . .	. . .	173	10	. . .
1943	282·9	88·56	. . .	. . .	292	11	. . .
1944	298·9	100·76	. . .	. . .	216	7	. . .
1945	204·9	88·47	. . .	. . .	95	36	. . .
1946	. . .	437·5	. . .	. . .	702	517	6,266
		¥ '000					
1947	183·4	1·8	370	. . .	464	219	5,036
1948	184·1	4·9	240	0·7	744	2,304	6,995
1949	182·8	8·4	380	1·0	554	1,122	4,321
1950	186·8 / 195·6	8·6 / 10·6	440	1·2	584	763	5,468
1951	192·8	11·7	390	1·1	576	1,163	6,015
1952	194·4	13·5	470	1·2	590	1,624	15,075
1953	196·7	15·3	450	1·1	611	1,341	4,279
1954	195·9	16·3	590	1·5	647	928	3,836
1955	198·0	16·7	680 / 760	1·6 / 1·8	659	1,033	3,467
1956	204·4	18·3	710	1·7	646	1,098	4,562
1957	202·9	19·3	590	1·4	827	1,557	5,634
1958	201·4	19·2	630	1·4	903	1,279	6,052
1959	204·7	20·8	650	1·5	887	1,216	6,020
1960	207·0	22·6	500	1·1	1,063	918	4,912
1961	203·4	24·8	440	0·9	1,401	1,680	6,150
1962	198·4	27·3	400	0·9	1,299	1,518	5,400
1963	196·9	30·2	400	0·9	1,079	1,183	2,770
1964	195·7	33·1	370	0·8	1,234	1,050	3,165
1965	191·8	36·1	390	0·8	1,542	1,682	5,669
1966	193·0	40·5	440	0·9	1,252	1,132	2,742
1967	193·9	45·6	630	1·3	1,214	733	1,830
1968	193·0	52·7	590	1·2	1,546	1,163	2,841
1969	190·0	61·8	570	1·1	1,783	1,412	3,634
1970	187·4	71·4	590	1·2	2,260	1,720	3,915
1971	184·3	81·0	640	1·4	2,527	1,896	6,029
1972	183·3	93·6	730	1·3	2,498	1,544	5,147
1973	182·0	116·3	680	1·3	3,326	2,236	4,604
1974	173·2	146·5	730	1·4	5,211	3,621	9,663
1975	167·8	163·7	1,000	1·9	3,391	2,732	8,016
1976	173·9	183·6	1,080	2·0	2,720	1,356	3,254
1977	174·5	200·8	1,100	2·0	1,712	692	1,519
1978	175·6	214·6	1,240	2·2	1,517	660	1,358

***Table* J.8 (Continued)**   **Labour market: other indicators, 1929–87**

	Manufacturing				Industrial disputes		
	Average hrs worked per month	Average monthly earnings	Unemployment		Stoppages	Workers involved	Working days lost
			'000	%		'000	'000
		¥					
1979	177·9	227·8	1,170	2·1	1,153	450	930
1980	178·2	244·6	1,140	2·0	1,133	563	1,001
1981	177·4	259·7	1,260	2·2	955	247	554
1982	177·0	269·6	1,360	2·4	944	216	538
1983	178·0	279·1	1,560	2·6	893	224	507
1984	180·5	292·3	1,610	2·7	596	155	354
1985	179·7	299·5	1,560	2·6	627	123	264
1986	178·2	305·4	1,670	2·8	620	118	253
1987	. . .	. . .	1,730	2·8	474	101	256

Table J.9　Public finance, 1885–1986

	Revenue					Expenditure				
	Taxes on personal income	Taxes on companies	Taxes on capital	Customs & excise duties	Total receipts	Defence	Education	Social services	Debt interest	Total expenditure
					¥ mn					
1885	...	...	...	2·1	62·2	15·5	...	...	14·1	61·1
1886	...	...	...	3·0	85·3	20·5	...	... ✓	24·1	83·2
1887	0·5	...	...	4·1	88·2	22·2	...	...	21·4	79·5
1888	1·1	...	...	4·6	93·0	22·5	...	...	20·7	81·5
1889	1·1	...	...	4·7	96·7	23·4	...	...	18·4	79·7
1890	1·1	...	...	4·4	106·5	25·7	...	...	20·3	82·1
1891	1·1	...	...	4·5	103·2	23·7	...	...	18·5	83·6
1892	1·1	...	...	5·0	101·5	23·8	...	...	18·5	76·7
1893	1·2	...	...	5·1	113·8	22·8	...	...	19·5	84·6
1894	1·4	...	...	5·8	98·2	20·7	...	...	19·7	78·1
1895	1·5	...	...	6·8	118·4	23·5	...	...	24·2	85·3
1896	1·8	...	...	6·7	187·0	73·2	...	...	30·5	168·9
1897	2·1	...	...	8·0	226·4	110·5	...	...	29·5	223·7
1898	2·4	...	...	9·1	220·1	112·4	...	...	28·4	219·8
1899	4·8	1·5	...	15·9	254·3	114·2	...	...	34·3	254·2
1900	6·4	2·2	...	17·0	295·9	133·1	...	...	34·8	292·8
1901	6·8	2·2	...	14·2	274·4	102·4	...	...	37·7	266·9
1902	7·5	2·3	...	19·6	297·3	85·8	...	...	42·8	289·2
1903	8·2	2·4	...	24·3	260·2	83·0	...	...	36·5	249·6
1904	14·4	3·8	...	31·6	327·5	(32·7)	...	...	31·6	277·1
1905	23·3	7·9	0·6	48·1	535·3	(34·5)	...	...	49·1	420·7
1906	26·3	9·4	1·4	58·1	530·4	129·7	...	...	151·2	464·3
1907	27·3	8·3	1·8	66·2	857·1	198·3	...	...	174·4	602·4
1908	32·1	8·9	2·4	59·8	794·9	213·4	...	...	176·8	636·4
1909	32·8	8·3	2·8	49·7	677·5	177·2	...	...	153·2	532·9
1910	31·7	7·5	3·1	57·8	672·9	185·2	...	...	154·3	569·2
1911	34·8	9·7	4·1	65·8	657·2	205·5	...	...	147·2	585·4
1912	38·9	11·5	3·6	82·0	687·4	199·6	...	...	141·7	593·6
1913	35·6	13·1	3·4	94·7	722·0	191·9	...	...	142·6	573·6
1914	37·2	13·2	3·3	67·6	734·6	171·0	...	...	142·9	648·4
1915	37·6	14·7	3·4	54·9	708·6	182·2	...	...	120·0	583·3
1916	51·3	26·7	4·1	63·3	813·3	211·4	...	...	115·8	591·0
1917	94·6	59·4	4·6	75·0	1,085	285·9	...	...	136·0	735·0
1918	122·8	62·0	4·6	105·3	1,479	368·0	...	...	136·6	1,017
1919	193·1	110·3	5·3	127·3	1,809	536·7	...	...	111·2	1,172
1920	190·3	127·9	7·0	109·8	2,001	649·8	...	...	94·9	1,360
1921	200·9	95·9	9·3	155·9	2,066	730·6	...	...	112·0	1,490
1922	229·1	91·7	11·8	180·9	2,087	604·8	...	...	115·2	1,430
1923	163·8	50·5	11·2	154·1	2,045	499·1	...	...	163·2	1,521
1924	210·0	66·2	14·2	199·8	2,127	455·2	...	...	187·9	1,625
1925	235·0	88·6	17·1	187·9	2,071	443·8	...	...	221·5	1,525
1926	209·6	64·9	18·4	233·0	2,056	434·2	...	...	233·2	1,579
1927	215·1	72·4	21·1	219·9	2,063	491·6	...	...	282·1	1,766
1928	206·7	65·8	29·2	234·1	2,006	517·2	...	...	285·7	1,815
1929	199·5	55·1	29·7	218·3	1,826	494·9	...	...	280·3	1,736
1930	200·6	63·6	32·9	183·3	1,597	442·6	...	...	272·5	1,558
1931	144·5	33·5	30·2	191·7	1,531	454·6	...	...	213·8	1,477
1932	136·1	37·3	30·2	178·1	2,045	686·4	...	...	241·5	1,950
1933	159·7	51·7	25·6	186·5	2,332	872·6	...	...	334·8	2,255
1934	196·4	71·9	27·2	219·3	2,247	941·9	...	...	361·3	2,163
1935	227·3	93·7	30·3	236·1	2,259	1,032·9	...	...	371·9	2,207
1936	276·6	125·8	31·8	278·5	2,372	1,078·2	...	...	363·4	2,282
1937	478·5	209·2	35·9	293·7	2,915	1,236·8	...	...	399·5	2,709
1938	732·8	314·3	45·5	322·7	3,595	1,167	...	...	502·4	3,288
1939	888·8	376·4	58·4	305·9	4,970	1,629	...	...	675·2	4,494
1940	1,488·7	182·9	56·6	297·5	6,445	2,226	...	...	903·0	5,860
1941	1,401·4	534·9	64·6	213·4	8,602	3,013	...	...	1,198·6	8,134
1942	2,236·2	775·9	86·1	203·1	9,192	(79)	...	...	1,597·1	8,277
1943	2,604·1	993·6	117·6	189·7	14,010	(2)	...	...	2,181·8	12,552
1944	4,040·6	1,326·5	145·6	85·6	21,040	(2)	...	...	3,106·8	19,872

	Revenue					Expenditure				
	Taxes on personal income	Taxes on companies	Taxes on capital	Customs & excise duties	Total receipts	Defence	Education	Social services	Debt interest	Total expenditure
					¥ mn					
1945	3,820·4	1,180·8	176·6	18·1	23,488	—	...	...	4,209·4	21,496
					¥ bn					
1946	18·1	1·3	0·18	0·02	118·9	—	...	...	5·5	115·2
1947	84·9	7·3	0·36	0·12	214·5	—	7·0	9·9	7·4	205·8
1948	191·5	28·1	0·46	0·62	508·0	—	20·7	18·8	9·6	462·0
1949	278·9	61·3	2·3	4·6	758·6	—	35·5	32·9	12·7	699·4
1950	220·1	83·8	2·7	9·7	716·8	13·2	16·2	48·6	58·4	633·3
1951	225·7	183·9	2·9	28·6	895·5	21·4	31·7	64·4	20·1	749·8
1952	269·9	186·0	2·8	57·5	1,079	104·1	37·2	93·4	30·9	873·9
1953	292·3	198·9	3·4	87·0	1,219	157·3	106·0	122·9	44·9	1,017
1954	285·6	200·3	4·3	101·5	1,185	154·7	118·6	136·9	40·3	1,041
1955	278·7	192·1	5·6	100·0	1,126	136·0	124·9	140·0	44·2	1,018
1956	304·9	259·8	7·1	132·8	1,233	134·5	132·7	136·8	38·1	1,069
1957	251·8	364·1	8·2	151·7	1,400	153·0	153·8	147·7	35·2	1,188
1958	259·3	308·3	8·4	164·3	1,454	151·5	163·1	162·7	66·6	1,332
1959	278·0	390·6	9·9	196·8	1,597	157·1	176·8	196·1	54·2	1,495
1960	390·6	573·4	12·3	240·9	1,961	163·5	220·0	231·1	26·5	1,743
1961	495·8	714·3	16·1	307·6	2,516	182·7	256·2	302·4	39·8	2,064
1962	579·5	780·4	22·1	343·5	2,948	217·3	305·6	369·3	67·3	2,557
1963	690·7	862·9	29·3	408·9	3,231	245·2	369·8	453·9	114·6	3,044
1964	837·4	975·4	32·6	484·3	3,447	281·3	408·8	517·0	45	3,311
1965	970·4	927·1	41·0	544·5	3,773	306	496	546	13	3,723
1966	1,084	1,032	38·0	577·5	4,552	346	564	640	42	4,459
1967	1,290	1,308	51·2	629·2	5,299	383	641	733	105	5,113
1968	1,613	1,592	60·8	687·2	6,060	433	727	851	193	5,937
1969	2,006	2,009	103·1	804·9	7,109	497	821	971	275	6,918
1970	2,428	2,567	134·2	924·4	8,459	591	965	1,152	287	8,188
1971	2,889	2,557	207·4	940·7	9,971	694	1,100	1,496	321	9,561
1972	3,726	2,992	260·4	1,003·6	12,794	813	1,310	1,880	454	11,932
1973	5,332	4,518	375·4	1,172·8	16,762	961	1,587	2,483	685	14,778
1974	5,350	5,816	437·7	1,151·0	20,379	1,225	2,308	3,126	847	19,100
1975	5,482	4,128	197·3	1,240·3	21,473	1,386	2,707	4,136	1,102	20,861
1976	6,213	4,792	216·6	1,552·4	25,076	1,518	2,996	4,878	1,843	24,468
1977	6,578	5,566	249·0	1,708·5	29,434	1,698	3,404	5,688	2,315	29,060
1978	7,753	7,913	286·9	1,892·1	34,907	1,863	3,881	6,735	3,232	34,096
1979	9,272	7,386	330·5	2,225·1	39,668	2,059	4,294	7,488	4,376	38,790
1980	10,800	8,923	439·9	2,237·4	44,041	2,250	4,606	8,170	5,492	43,405
1981	11,980	8,823	542·7	2,305·8	47,443	2,441	4,822	8,824	6,654	46,921
1982	12,846	9,135	633·0	2,322·2	48,001	2,572	4,830	9,186	6,907	47,245
1983	13,643	9,825	715	2,306·6	51,653	2,762	4,852	9,317	8,168	50,635
1984	14,064	11,340	777	2,381·0	52,183	2,951	4,921	9,777	9,233	51,481
1985	15,435	12,021	1,061	3,116·0	53,993	3,179	4,883	9,902	10,181	53,005
1986	16,827	13,091	1,351	3,184·1	53,825	3,312	4,852	10,127	10,664	53,640

Table J.10   Value of exports and imports by country, 1885–1987

	Total exports	Exports to:				Total imports	Imports from:			
		France	Germany	UK	USA		France	Germany	UK	USA
					¥ mn					
1885	37	7	—	3	16	29	1	2	13	3
1886	49	10	1	4	20	32	1	2	13	3
1887	52	10	1	4	22	44	2	4	19	3
1888	66	14	2	9	24	66	4	5	29	6
1889	70	14	2	8	25	66	3	5	26	6
1890	57	8	1	6	20	82	4	7	27	7
1891	80	15	2	6	30	63	3	5	20	7
1892	91	18	1	4	39	71	4	6	21	6
1893	90	20	1	5	28	88	3	7	28	6
1894	113	20	2	6	43	118	4	8	42	11
1895	136	22	3	8	54	129	5	12	45	9
1896	118	19	3	9	32	172	8	17	59	16
1897	167	26	2	9	52	221	5	18	65	27
1898	170	21	3	8	47	282	7	26	63	40
1899	223	29	4	11	64	224	6	18	45	38
1900	213	19	4	11	53	292	8	29	72	63
1901	261	27	5	12	72	263	4	28	51	43
1902	268	27	5	17	80	279	5	26	50	49
1903	301	34	5	17	83	327	5	27	49	46
1904	329	36	4	18	101	382	3	29	75	58
1905	335	27	4	13	94	502	5	43	115	104
1906	439	40	8	23	126	437	5	43	101	70
1907	452	43	11	22	131	512	7	48	116	81
1908	399	34	8	26	122	461	5	46	108	78
1909	437	42	8	27	132	431	6	40	86	54
1910	502	45	11	26	144	521	5	44	95	55
1911	523	44	12	24	143	581	6	57	111	81
1912	618	44	14	30	169	684	5	61	116	127
1913	717	60	13	33	185	795	6	68	123	122
1914	671	31	10	33	197	671	4	45	92	97
1915	793	42	—	69	204	636	4	6	58	103
1916	1,234	64	—	103	340	879	5	4	82	204
1917	1,752	98	—	203	479	1,201	4	3	93	360
1918	2,159	142	—	143	530	1,902	4	3	66	626
1919	2,379	67	—	112	828	2,501	9	—	128	766
1920	2,200	72	1	98	565	2,681	15	12	235	873
1921	1,503	35	2	33	496	1,940	12	48	184	574
1922	1,880	79	4	54	732	2,216	19	111	232	596
1923	1,686	26	3	40	606	2,393	22	120	237	512
1924	2,105	86	9	61	745	2,971	33	145	313	671
1925	2,670	59	12	60	1,006	3,105	33	124	227	665
1926	2,414	42	8	60	861	2,918	25	145	170	680
1927	2,383	54	11	65	834	2,712	27	131	153	674
1928	2,400	63	13	59	826	2,745	24	134	165	626
1929	2,604	45	13	63	914	2,765	26	157	153	654
1930	1,871	27	11	62	506	2,005	17	106	93	433
1931	1,480	16	8	53	425	1,686	12	73	63	342
1932	1,802	22	9	61	445	1,936	21	72	79	510
1933	2,351	39	12	89	492	2,464	22	96	83	621
1934	2,789	38	20	109	399	2,970	18	110	70	769
1935	3,276	43	27	120	536	3,272	20	121	82	810
1936	3,585	43	35	147	594	3,641	20	116	73	847
1937	4,188	47	43	168	639	4,765	28	177	106	1,270
1938	3,939	37	33	135	425	3,794	14	171	63	915
1939	5,163	26	25	132	642	4,165	14	141	24	1,002
1940	5,418	24	75	57	569	4,653	12	83	11	1,241
1941	4,384	—	35	4	278	4,088	1	70	5	572
1942	3,506	—	39	—	—	2,924	—	40	2	14
1943	3,055	—	15	—	—	2,939	—	121	—	5

270

Table **J.10 (Continued)** **Value of exports and imports by country, 1885–1987**

	Total exports	Exports to:				Total imports	Imports from:			
		France	Germany	UK	USA		France	Germany	UK	USA
					¥ bn					
1946	2·26	—	—	0·028	1·5	4·07	—	0·050	—	3·5
1947	10·15	0·004	0·021	0·624	1·8	20·27	—	0·159	—	17·6
1948	52·02	0·821	0·159	3·2	16·9	60·29	—	0·183	0·185	37·6
1949	169·8	1·8	0·315	12·6	30·7	284·5	1·2	2·3	1·5	176·8
1950	298·0	3·8	3·7	9·4	64·5	348·2	1·4	3·0	2·4	150·6
1951	488·8	7·0	7·8	19·4	66·6	737·2	8·0	6·1	12·0	250·1
1952	458·2	10·1	5·8	26·3	84·4	730·4	3·1	8·1	13·2	276·6
1953	458·9	4·2	5·7	11·9	84·2	867·5	9·6	13·6	17·6	273·5
1954	586·5	4·2	6·5	18·4	101·7	863·8	7·4	15·9	13·4	305·5
1955	723·8	4·2	9·1	21·9	164·2	889·7	5·5	16·6	13·7	278·6
1956	900·2	5·1	13·1	22·7	198·1	1,162·7	7·8	20·2	24·0	384·2
1957	1,028·9	6·5	21·4	26·5	217·6	1,542·1	10·4	51·6	35·5	584·3
1958	1,035·6	3·2	15·8	37·9	248·6	1,091·9	7·5	32·5	21·4	380·2
1959	1,244·3	4·3	17·0	37·2	376·8	1,295·8	9·0	37·3	37·3	401·6
1960	1,459·6	5·6	23·9	43·4	396·6	1,616·8	11·6	44·3	35·7	559·3
1961	1,524·8	6·3	30·0	41·3	384·1	2,091·8	14·1	69·5	49·4	754·5
1962	1,769·8	8·3	37·5	69·2	504·1	2,029·1	16·7	76·6	52·5	651·2
1963	1,962·8	11·3	41·6	56·1	542·5	2,425·1	18·2	79·1	53·7	747·8
1964	2,402·3	14·9	53·6	71·2	663·0	2,857·5	25·4	89·8	66·7	841·0
1965	3,042·6	17·6	77·4	73·8	892·5	2,940·8	22·5	80·2	58·5	851·9
1966	3,519·5	25·3	88·8	81·2	1,069·0	3,428·2	23·1	85·3	77·2	956·8
1967	3,759·0	27·9	77·4	106·5	1,084·3	4,198·7	31·4	131·0	92·6	1,156·3
1968	4,669·8	33·9	103·5	131·3	1,471·1	4,675·4	45·8	144·2	92·6	1,269·9
1969	5,756·4	43·2	141·4	125·4	1,784·8	5,408·5	53·8	160·3	118·9	1,472·4
1970	6,954·4	45·8	198·1	172·8	2,138·3	6,797·2	67·1	222·1	142·3	2,001·4
1971	8,392·8	66·7	229·3	200·0	2,621·9	6,910·0	69·6	212·9	146·2	1,748·0
1972	8,806·1	87·3	286·5	301·6	2,725·1	7,229·0	92·6	209·8	154·3	1,802·3
1973	10,031	98·1	344·7	368·6	2,568·2	10,404	145·9	303·2	206·2	2,518·4
1974	16,208	214·7	436·7	446·3	3,734·7	18,076	172·4	422·8	255·1	3,694·3
1975	16,545	207·5	492·3	436·7	3,312·1	17,170	148·5	337·6	240·4	3,441·5
1976	19,935	286·1	664·2	415·2	4,653·8	19,229	159·6	364·5	250·3	3,505·2
1977	21,648	269·9	747·5	524·4	5,292·2	19,132	151·0	403·8	258·0	3,357·4
1978	20,556	232·0	764·2	490·6	5,259·0	16,728	157·8	421·4	290·2	3,108·7
1979	22,532	305·3	933·0	674·5	5,772·8	24,245	235·0	563·6	366·1	4,456·9
1980	29,382	456·8	1,300·6	857·9	7,118·1	31,995	293·8	570·1	440·0	5,558·1
1981	33,469	485·9	1,308·9	1,054·1	8,518·7	31,464	256·9	532·5	594·1	5,552·2
1982	34,433	575·2	1,241·0	1,189·5	9,015·2	32,656	300·0	583·2	457·9	5,990·5
1983	34,909	477·0	1,396·4	1,184·1	10,178·6	30,015	309·5	573·3	461·3	5,885·3
1984	40,325	458	1,570	1,107	14,221	32,321	293	635	536	6,364
1985	41,956	496	1,646	1,132	15,583	31,085	317	700	432	6,213
1986	35,290	532	1,766	1,123	13,564	21,551	312	725	593	4,918
1987	33,315	584	1,871	1,221	12,148	21,737	416	893	443	4,582

Sources

(For sources used in specific tables, see Notes.)

1   Bank of Japan, *100 Year Statistics of the Japanese Economy*, Tokyo, 1966.
2   Bank of Japan, Explanatory notes and Supplement to **1**.
3   International Labour Office, *Technical Guide*, Geneva, Vol. II, 1972, 1976, 1980.
4   *Japan Statistical Year Book*, Statistics Bureau, Prime Minister's Office, Tokyo.
5   League of Nations, *Year Book of Labour Statistics*.
6   Maddison, Angus, *Phases of Capitalist Development*, Oxford University Press, 1982.
7   Mitchell, B.R., *International Historical Statistics: Africa and Asia*, New York University Press, 1982.
8   Organisation for Economic Cooperation and Development (OECD), *Labour Force Statistics*, annual and monthly, Paris.
9   OECD, *National Accounts, 1950–1979*, Vol. 1, Paris, 1981.
10 OECD, *National Accounts, 1960–1987*, Vol. 1, Paris, 1989.
11 *Statistical Year Book of the League of Nations*, Geneva.
12 Supplements to the United Nations *Statistical Year Book* and *Monthly Bulletin of Statistics*, New York, 1967, 1972 and 1977.
13 United Nations, *Monthly Bulletin of Statistics*, New York.
14 United Nations, *Statistical Year Book*, New York.
15 *Year Book of Labour Statistics*, ILO, Geneva.

Notes

Table J.1 Gross domestic product at current prices

Sources: **1, 9, 10**

From 1952, OECD data have been used. Data are classified according to the present system of national accounts from 1960 and on the former systems for 1952–59. For further details see **9**. Figures for exports and imports of goods and services and gross domestic product in 1987 have been estimated by the OECD Secretariat.

For 1930–50, data are taken from **1**. Figures refer to fiscal years beginning April 1 of year shown for 1946–50.

Table J.2 Gross domestic product at constant prices

Sources: **1, 9, 10**

OECD data have been used from 1952. See notes to Table J.1 for details of the national accounts system used. Figures for exports and imports of goods and services and gross domestic product in 1987 have been estimated by the OECD Secretariat.

For 1930–51 the figures are based on estimates published in **1**. Further details on the compilation of these estimates can be found in **2**. For 1946–50, the figures refer to fiscal years (beginning April 1) and not calendar years. Figures for 1930–51 have been roughly adjusted to 1980 prices. Each category of expenditure has been re-referenced independently and this means that the total for gross domestic product may not equal the sum of components.

Table J.3 Industrial production

Sources: **1, 4, 7, 13, 14**

Industrial production: the index includes mining, manufacturing, and electricity and gas. For 1885–1926, the series published in **1** (based on 1921–25 = 100) has been used. For the period 1927–30, figures given in **7** have been linked at 1930 to estimates made by Kasushi Ohkawa published in **1**.

For further details of method and coverage see **2**.

Coal: from 1975, the figures are for coal and lignite.

Cars and commercial vehicles: includes chassis for buses and trucks.

Crude petroleum: includes Formosa up to 1928 (first line).

Electricity: public supply only up to 1965. Includes electricity generated by industrial establishments (primarily for their own use) from 1966. Figures are for fiscal years (April 1) until 1982.

Natural gas: published figures are now given in terajoules. From 1977 the published figures have been converted to cubic metres using the conversion factors given in **13**.

Table J.4　Prices and income

Sources: **1, 4, 6, 9, 10**

Consumer prices: base weighted indices measuring changes in prices of goods and services consumed by city (non-farm) households. For 1900–45, the 'All items' index is the retail price index for Tokyo compiled by the Bank of Japan. This index has been linked to the consumer price index at 1946.

For the years 1885–1921, an index given in **6** has been linked on to the retail price index compiled by the Bank of Japan. The index in **6** is based on an earlier series compiled by the Bank of Japan. For further details see **6**.

Wholesale prices: up to 1955, referred to as the 'Tokyo wholesale price index'. It was considerably revised in 1952 and in 1955 the word 'Tokyo' was dropped, although the price data are still obtained mainly from Tokyo. The current series is linked to an earlier series compiled by the Bank of Japan.

The 'Producers' goods' index covers those commodities which are consumed in production. The current index includes raw materials, semi-finished goods, fuel and energy and building materials, but coverage has varied. From December 1982, substantial changes have been made in the presentation of data for the component categories of the wholesale price index. For details see **4**, 1984.

For further details of coverage and weights used see **2**.

Compensation of employees: OECD data have been used from 1952. The series includes wages and salaries in cash and in kind paid to employees together with contributions on behalf of employees to social security schemes and private pension funds. Figures for 1960–64 and for 1986 have been estimated by the OECD Secretariat.

For 1930–52 (first line), Japan Economic Planning Agency estimates published in **1** have been used; for 1919–29, estimates made by Yuzo Yamada published in **1** were used.

The figures for 1946–50 are for fiscal years (starting on April 1).

National income: OECD data have been used from 1952. National income is gross national product (gross domestic product plus net factor incomes from the rest of the world) minus consumption of fixed capital.

Figures for 1960–64 and for 1986 have been estimated by the OECD Secretariat.

For 1919–52, estimates made by Yuzo Yamada and the Japan Economic Planning Agency (see above) have been used. The figures for 1946–50 are for fiscal years.

For further details of these two series see **2**, **9** and **10**.

Table J.5　Population

Sources: **1, 4**

Current figures are for the *de facto* population at October 1 each year. For 1885–1919 the figures are at January 1 each year and cover the population of Hokkaido, Honshu, Shikoku, Kyushu and Okinawa. The total population figure for 1920 on this basis in 55·47 mn. The 1945 figures are from a Population Survey taken on November 1.

For 1945–71 Okinawa is excluded. For other territorial changes in the post-war period see **4**.

Age distribution: for the period up to 1921, the estimates of population by age are based on estimates published in **2**. These early estimates are not for the permanently domiciled population and have not been adjusted to the 1920 census results. The figures in the table have been calculated by obtaining the percentage in each age group in the early estimates, and applying these percentages to the total population figure shown in the table to get a rough estimate of the numbers in the different age groups consistent with the total population figure. For further details see **2**.

Table J.6　Education

Sources: **1, 4**

Compulsory education starts at age six years and is of nine years' duration. The current system was established after the Second World War although changes were introduced in 1961 when the present system came into force; primary, lower secondary and upper secondary pupils being distinguished. Figures which roughly correspond to this format are given from 1948 although they are not strictly comparable before 1961.

Kindergarten: includes pre-school and day nurseries.

Elementary: pupils spend six years in elementary schools as part of their compulsory schooling. For 1885–1947, the figures in this column refer to 'primary' education, that is, pupils enrolled in ordinary primary school courses, higher primary schools and special training schools.

Lower secondary: pupils complete their compulsory education with three years in what are now called lower secondary schools. For 1885–47, the figures refer to pupils enrolled in middle schools including higher primary schools, middle schools (pre-war system), girls' high schools, and upper secondary schools (pre-war).

Upper secondary: pupils in upper secondary schools usually complete a further three years before going on to university, junior college or technical college. Includes general education and vocational training.

Data are as at May 1 each year; for 1890–1951, as at March 1 each year; and for 1885–89, as at end-calendar year.

Higher education: includes students at universities and junior colleges. For 1885–1947 figures include universities, college preparatory courses, special collegiate courses (pre-war) and junior colleges.

Table J.7 Labour market: employment

Sources: **1, 5, 8**

From 1953, OECD data have been used. Figures are annual averages of those in employment and currently cover employees, self-employed, unpaid family workers working for at least one-third of normal working time and the armed forces (national self-defence forces). The temporarily stopped and the unemployed are not included.

From 1967, coverage of the survey on which the figures are based was changed. Figures were adjusted to the new definitions by the Japanese Bureau of Statistics back to 1957. Figures for 1957 on the previous basis are:

Employed labour force	43·03 mn
Agriculture	15.80 mn
Manufacturing	8·53 mn

For 1953–68, employment in gas, electricity and water industries has been estimated by the OECD Secretariat.

'Distribution and services' includes wholesale and retail trades, restaurants and hotels, finance, insurance, real estate and business services, commercial social and personal services and the national self-defence forces.

Okinawa is included in the figures from 1973.

For 1947–52, the data are taken from **5**. A new industrial classification was introduced in 1950 and earlier figures are therefore not strictly comparable. For the period 1885–1942, the figures are for the gainfully employed population based on estimates made by Kazushi Ohkawa published in **1**. The figures for this period in the third column include mining, manufacturing (excluding public and government owned companies) and gas and electricity industries. The figures in the fourth column include civil engineering and construction, transport and communication, commerce and the government sector.

Table J.8 Labour market: other indicators

Sources: **1, 4, 5, 7, 15**

Manufacturing: average hours worked and earnings per month: average hours worked include overtime. Average earnings include overtime and bonus payments as well as marriage allowances paid by employers. Data are based on surveys of establishments with 30 or more employees including administrative, technical, clerical and production workers. The sample design was revised in 1982.

The industrial classification was changed in 1950 and the figures are not strictly comparable before and after that date. The second figure given for 1950 is the average for October–December and this is consistent with the years that follow; the first figure is the average for January–September on the previous classification. From 1965, the tobacco industry is excluded from the figures.

There were revisions in the industry coverage in 1926, 1930, 1939 and 1946.

For 1926–38, public utilities, civil engineering and construction industries are included in the figures. Figures for hours worked for 1923–38 refer to normal working hours and not average hours worked.

For further details see **2**.

Unemployment: figures are annual averages. In 1955 there was a change in the coverage of the official statistics. For further details see **3**. The percentage figure is the number of unemployed expressed as a percentage of the civilian labour force.

Table J.9 Public finance

Sources: **1, 4, 7**

Total receipts: figures refer to central government revenue from all sources, including monopolies, for the fiscal years ending March 31 of year shown. Figures for 1885 are for nine months.

Taxes on companies: includes excess profits tax for 1918–28 and a company surtax for 1940–48.

Taxes on capital: includes inheritance and gift taxes.

Excise duties: duties on sugar, gasoline and, from 1985, tobacco.

Total expenditure: central government expenditure only. Figures used are those of the General Account for the fiscal year ending March 31 of the year shown.

Defence: figures for 1885–1944 are for total expenses in the ministries of the army and navy. They do not include the Extraordinary Military Special Account. After 1949, the figures refer to National Defence, that is, Japan's contribution to the support of US forces and the expenses of the Japanese Defence Agency.

Education: national government's share of expenditure on compulsory education and promotion of science and technology.

Social services: includes public assistance, social welfare, social insurance, public health services and measures for the unemployed.

Table J.10 Value of exports and imports by country

Sources: **1, 4, 7**

From 1952, the figures for Germany are for the Federal Republic of Germany. For 1885–1945, Japan includes South Sakhalin and Taiwan, and for 1910–45, Korea. Southern Ireland is included in the UK up to 1923.

SWEDEN

CONTENTS

Table S.1   Gross domestic product at current prices, 1885–1987

	Consumers' expenditure	Government current expenditure	Gross fixed capital formation	Value of physical change in stocks	Exports of goods & services	Imports of goods & services	**Gross domestic product at market prices**
				Skr mn			
1885	1,220	88	135	−10	271	−333	**1,370**
1886	1,129	90	144	−37	250	−290	**1,285**
1887	1,094	89	103	−14	267	−287	**1,252**
1888	1,142	92	125	6	304	−319	**1,350**
1889	1,237	93	146	25	324	−368	**1,457**
1890	1,295	95	149	23	321	−371	**1,512**
1891	1,367	97	122	42	338	−362	**1,604**
1892	1,368	97	126	1	328	−346	**1,574**
1893	1,330	100	113	−12	344	−320	**1,555**
1894	1,341	102	132	42	344	−340	**1,621**
1895	1,386	105	173	−86	357	−340	**1,595**
1896	1,437	106	179	26	392	−356	**1,784**
1897	1,538	112	226	1	415	−400	**1,892**
1898	1,717	114	249	−39	400	−445	**1,996**
1899	1,877	120	288	−79	419	−502	**2,123**
1900	1,954	128	300	−2	459	−525	**2,314**
1901	1,897	131	262	24	411	−461	**2,264**
1902	1,931	136	257	−45	435	−503	**2,211**
1903	2,026	141	316	34	486	−529	**2,474**
1904	2,093	151	332	16	464	−572	**2,484**
1905	2,144	157	329	−10	502	−574	**2,548**
1906	2,390	166	386	46	561	−640	**2,909**
1907	2,559	174	411	20	585	−673	**3,076**
1908	2,623	188	357	21	539	−599	**3,129**
1909	2,690	205	324	29	531	−614	**3,165**
1910	2,810	210	366	−13	659	−667	**3,365**
1911	2,790	219	401	3	736	−691	**3,458**
1912	3,002	230	418	−92	827	−783	**3,602**
1913	3,224	238	509	108	895	−846	**4,128**
1914	3,155	248	524	49	860	−725	**4,111**
1915	3,690	280	518	79	1,491	−1,173	**4,885**
1916	4,443	312	666	175	1,851	−1,221	**6,226**
1917	5,193	352	878	48	1,559	−878	**7,152**
1918	7,114	581	1,133	163	1,714	−1,363	**9,342**
1919	9,317	735	1,437	145	1,936	−2,533	**11,037**
1920	10,695	900	1,672	84	2,615	−3,314	**12,652**
1921	7,656	836	1,177	−101	1,230	−1,261	**9,537**
1922	6,038	754	896	−537	1,278	−1,115	**7,314**
1923	6,162	699	1,036	16	1,288	−1,296	**7,905**
1924	6,394	693	1,068	10	1,410	−1,425	**8,150**
1925	6,821	715	1,152	85	1,514	−1,446	**8,841**
1926	6,988	708	1,144	−37	1,588	−1,490	**8,901**
1927	7,104	697	1,167	12	1,810	−1,584	**9,206**
1928	7,289	729	1,296	−54	1,743	−1,714	**9,289**
1929	7,570	751	1,403	8	1,999	−1,786	**9,945**
1930	7,621	769	1,596	−88	1,752	−1,675	**9,975**
1931	6,850	798	1,320	−69	1,279	−1,430	**8,748**
1932	6,477	795	1,074	89	1,079	−1,154	**8,360**
1933	6,356	764	1,014	6	1,205	−1,095	**8,250**
1934	6,843	794	1,272	74	1,434	−1,306	**9,111**
1935	7,324	830	1,608	33	1,432	−1,475	**9,752**
1936	7,866	874	1,780	39	1,661	−1,641	**10,579**
1937	8,527	942	2,017	35	2,184	−2,123	**11,572**
1938	8,871	1,051	2,321	28	2,043	−2,081	**12,233**
1939	9,633	1,370	2,646	−4	2,150	−2,498	**13,297**
1940	10,579	1,897	2,503	113	1,710	−2,004	**14,798**
1941	11,527	2,286	2,597	57	1,717	−1,675	**16,509**
1942	12,147	2,468	3,277	8	1,677	−1,780	**17,797**
1943	13,165	2,616	3,753	11	1,551	−1,815	**19,281**

	Consumers' expenditure	Government current expenditure	Gross fixed capital formation	Value of physical change in stocks	Exports of goods & services	Imports of goods & services	**Gross domestic product at market prices**
				Skr mn			
1944	14,133	2,659	3,964	−69	1,203	−1,677	**20,213**
1945	14,708	2,590	3,662	30	2,055	−1,085	**21,960**
1946	17,313	2,382	4,841	18	3,160	−3,386	**24,328**
1947	19,464	2,635	5,768	−30	3,816	−5,220	**26,433**
1948	20,725	3,068	5,698	122	4,596	−4,945	**29,264**
1949	21,183	3,286	5,909	101	4,826	−4,333	**30,972**
1950	23,214	3,515	6,687	135	6,291	−6,102	**33,740**
				Skr bn			
1950	22·16	4·03	5·85	−0·18	7·10	−6·89	**32·07**
1951	24·70	5·07	7·28	1·61	11·22	−10·27	**39·59**
1952	27·34	6·16	8·47	0·99	10·20	−10·00	**43·16**
1953	28·53	6·77	9·29	−0·52	9·54	−9·18	**44·44**
1954	30·16	7·09	10·01	0·17	10·45	−10·60	**47·28**
1955	32·08	7·70	10·31	1·15	11·40	−11·82	**50·83**
1956	34·66	8·51	11·18	1·10	13·00	−13·18	**55·24**
1957	36·53	9·47	11·90	1·17	14·40	−14·50	**58·96**
1958	39·06	10·06	13·14	0·34	13·85	−14·19	**62·27**
1959	41·01	10·73	14·47	—	14·40	−14·37	**66·25**
1960	43·01	11·42	16·36	1·90	16·54	−17·00	**72·13**
1961	46·32	12·43	18·25	1·24	17·47	−17·09	**78·47**
1962	49·76	14·21	20·25	0·81	18·57	−18·28	**85·10**
1963	53·51	15·87	22·35	0·19	20·14	−19·91	**92·11**
1964	57·64	17·60	25·25	1·99	22·85	−22·58	**102·72**
1965	63·37	20·00	27·92	2·76	24·62	−25·59	**113·03**
1966	68·83	23·14	30·49	1·38	26·24	−27·09	**122·95**
1967	74·21	25·96	33·15	0·25	28·07	−28·14	**133·46**
1968	78·62	29·01	33·87	0·44	30·43	−30·70	**141·62**
1969	84·88	31·82	35·72	2·00	35·01	−35·59	**153·80**
1970	92·24	36·92	38·77	5·27	41·51	−42·48	**172·23**
1971	99·37	41·83	40·88	1·98	45·32	−43·17	**186·21**
1972	109·37	46·26	45·23	−0·18	49·28	−46·21	**203·76**
1973	120·68	51·38	49·61	−1·19	62·13	−55·87	**226·74**
1974	137·62	59·39	55·00	6·07	82·49	−84·45	**256·13**
1975	156·91	71·53	62·92	10·01	84·68	−85·26	**300·78**
1976	181·46	84·54	72·02	7·87	94·07	−99·77	**340·20**
1977	198·93	101·61	78·05	−2·40	101·33	−107·51	**370·02**
1978	220·48	115·07	80·10	−7·42	116·40	−112·17	**412·45**
1979	243·75	130·66	91·56	0·96	140·57	−145·20	**462·31**
1980	271·83	151·37	105·99	5·91	156·52	−166·52	**525·10**
1981	301·02	167·41	109·89	−5·59	172·53	−172·23	**573·04**
1982	336·65	182·71	118·24	−6·09	201·33	−205·16	**627·68**
1983	365·82	200·56	132·17	−9·59	249·53	−233·12	**705·37**
1984	402·00	218·04	146·58	−7·43	284·66	−254·27	**789·58**
1985	442·43	235·88	164·28	−1·35	303·51	−283·85	**860·88**
1986	484·79	253·70	170·77	−9·62	309·19	−277·05	**931·78**
1987	530·88	268·62	190·88	−6·14	326·12	−305·13	**1,005·23**

Table S.2 Gross domestic product at constant prices, 1885–1987

	Consumers' expenditure	Government current expenditure	Gross fixed capital formation	Value of physical change in stocks	Exports of goods & services	Imports of goods & services	**Gross domestic product at market prices**
				Skr bn, 1980 prices			
1885	21·96	3·93	2·75		4·37	−5·88	**25·26**
1886	21·56	4·12	3·09		4·18	−5·35	**24·89**
1887	21·30	4·09	2·29		4·66	−5·61	**25·24**
1888	21·12	4·22	2·86		5·02	−5·79	**25·59**
1889	22·11	4·26	3·03		4·87	−6·61	**27·18**
1890	22·76	4·36	3·04		5·04	−6·38	**27·52**
1891	23·58	4·45	2·55		5·34	−6·05	**28·54**
1892	24·08	4·45	2·69		5·20	−6·16	**28·26**
1893	24·47	4·52	2·51		5·64	−5·82	**29·07**
1894	25·51	4·69	2·88		5·62	−6·61	**31·80**
1895	25·88	4·82	3·79		5·92	−6·46	**30·91**
1896	26·57	4·78	3·67		6·34	−6·56	**34·99**
1897	26·88	5·21	4·31		6·13	−7·09	**35·75**
1898	28·65	5·25	4·60		5·71	−7·57	**35·91**
1899	30·92	5·81	4·89		5·77	−8·09	**36·87**
1900	30·51	6·10	4·85		6·00	−8·26	**38·83**
1901	30·77	6·27	4·60		5·65	−7·35	**39·72**
1902	31·03	6·34	4·60		6·24	−8·11	**38·39**
1903	32·63	5·68	5·48		6·93	−8·64	**42·49**
1904	33·21	6·01	5·81		6·65	−9·05	**43·17**
1905	33·66	6·17	5·53		7·26	−9·17	**43·68**
1906	36·44	7·36	6·26		7·72	−9·97	**48·88**
1907	37·72	5·91	6·20		7·81	−10·05	**48·94**
1908	38·15	6·27	5·83		7·51	−8·88	**49·31**
1909	38·50	6·83	5·16		7·03	−8·90	**50·38**
1910	40·43	7·06	5·64		8·66	−9·71	**53·55**
1911	40·24	7·29	6·12		9·77	−9·84	**55·70**
1912	40·80	7·66	6·28		10·70	−10·75	**54·46**
1913	44·13	7·85	7·40		11·11	−12·02	**62·39**
1914	40·97	8·18	7·11		9·93	−9·00	**60·88**
1915	40·83	9·24	5·99		15·31	−12·68	**63·18**
1916	43·53	9·37	5·70		14·92	−11·02	**71·31**
1917	41·46	9·27	5·30		8·45	−6·05	**65·10**
1918	41·49	10·43	5·84		7·24	−6·62	**60·84**
1919	47·14	11·19	6·54		7·39	−11·19	**62·23**
1920	51·96	11·42	6·99		8·42	−13·52	**70·83**
1921	48·60	9·60	7·25		6·57	−8·78	**62·41**
1922	50·85	12·57	7·18		9·02	−9·71	**59·13**
1923	52·56	13·16	7·34		8·85	−11·13	**64·04**
1924	54·20	14·06	8·11		10·64	−12·00	**68·89**
1925	55·27	14·32	9·21		11·78	−13·13	**75·50**
1926	59·10	14·68	9·35		12·70	−13·85	**78·67**
1927	60·81	14·95	9·93		15·14	−14·66	**82·33**
1928	61·95	15·94	11·33		14·59	−16·61	**82·57**
1929	66·95	16·43	12·26		17·34	−18·08	**89·48**
1930	73·27	17·62	14·17		16·01	−18·72	**92·52**
1931	69·75	18·41	12·19		13·05	−17·71	**83·69**
1932	66·94	18·61	9·47		10·92	−14·35	**81·53**
1933	66·60	18·02	9·77		12·29	−13·75	**82·57**
1934	69·46	18·97	11·93		14·35	−15·82	**90·61**
1935	73·28	19·40	15·02		14·63	−17·40	**95·10**
1936	77·44	20·16	16·40		16·73	−18·62	**101·92**
1937	78·57	20·59	14·54		17·56	−20·03	**108·71**
1938	83·23	21·81	18·10		17·74	−21·61	**112·73**
1939	88·23	26·72	21·38		19·56	−25·21	**118·93**
1940	83·51	34·18	17·83		13·22	−16·06	**117·73**
1941	79·28	38·31	17·58		12·20	−18·86	**115·54**
1942	78·43	39·16	20·38		11·17	−11·87	**115·93**

	Consumers' expenditure	Government current expenditure	Gross fixed capital formation	Value of physical change in stocks	Exports of goods & services	Imports of goods & services	**Gross domestic product at market prices**
				Skr bn, 1980 prices			
1943	82·60	41·51	22·62		10·43	−11·87	**123·66**
1944	88·67	37·98	23·90		7·77	−10·85	**130·56**
1945	92·49	36·99	20·52		12·04	−6·85	**142·32**
1946	108·60	32·47	28·33		19·35	−22·29	**157·14**
1947	116·90	30·91	32·27		22·28	−32·34	**166·46**
1948	119·24	36·03	31·21		24·61	−29·34	**175·53**
1949	118·79	38·57	31·71		25·06	−25·21	**182·88**
1950	125·99	41·27	35·48	−0·64	30·65	−33·69	**196·90**
1951	124·62	43·56	36·33	4·59	32·70	−38·65	**202·81**
1952	129·21	45·93	37·49	2·37	30·16	−36·40	**206·30**
1953	132·59	49·96	42·07	−1·55	31·32	−36·38	**212·97**
1954	138·04	52·32	46·65	0·54	34·65	−42·43	**225·69**
1955	142·32	53·22	46·30	3·31	36·47	−46·49	**232·48**
1956	146·39	55·89	47·64	2·96	39·90	−49·86	**240·20**
1957	148·63	57·52	48·84	3·02	43·48	−53·29	**245·89**
1958	152·27	59·98	53·65	0·93	43·50	−54·71	**251·69**
1959	157·80	63·01	59·01	—	46·15	−56·61	**264·81**
1960	160·28	63·60	61·15	5·12	51·83	−65·79	**274·90**
1961	168·80	65·78	66·05	3·31	54·53	−65·93	**290·52**
1962	174·39	69·93	70·24	2·07	58·94	−69·97	**302·90**
1963	182·10	76·56	74·99	0·37	63·24	−74·64	**319·03**
1964	189·40	78·84	80·66	5·69	70·86	−81·88	**340·80**
1965	197·45	82·61	83·92	8·37	74·81	−91·11	**353·82**
1966	201·27	87·18	87·74	4·06	78·44	−94·98	**361·22**
1967	205·87	91·24	92·43	1·17	82·77	−97·32	**373·37**
1968	214·34	97·43	93·03	0·85	89·07	−105·38	**386·96**
1969	223·85	102·54	97·03	3·72	99·28	−118·97	**406·34**
1970	231·66	110·82	100·18	13·40	107·87	−131·30	**432·65**
1971	231·87	113·24	99·61	5·94	113·02	−126·94	**436·73**
1972	239·82	116·01	103·76	−0·52	119·64	−131·98	**446·73**
1973	246·01	118·99	106·52	−1·96	136·03	−141·13	**464·46**
1974	254·32	122·65	103·29	10·97	143·25	−155·16	**479·31**
1975	261·43	128·38	106·48	15·07	129·95	−149·78	**491·55**
1976	272·30	132·91	108·46	10·78	135·56	−163·27	**496·75**
1977	269·47	136·87	105·27	−3·19	137·54	−157·14	**488·82**
1978	267·56	141·39	98·07	−9·36	148·27	−148·54	**497·38**
1979	274·03	148·08	102·44	0·36	157·36	−165·80	**516·48**
1980	271·83	151·37	105·99	5·90	156·52	−166·52	**525·10**
1981	270·43	154·44	100·32	−5·31	158·28	−154·65	**523·51**
1982	274·14	155·64	99·23	−5·18	165·26	−161·36	**527·73**
1983	269·27	156·88	100·79	−7·37	182·90	−161·94	**540·53**
1984	273·21	160·51	105·92	−3·68	195·23	−169·30	**561·88**
1985	281·27	163·92	112·30	−0·14	199·46	−182·91	**573·90**
1986	294·67	165·81	111·67	−5·07	206·06	−192·99	**580·15**
1987	305·87	167·95	118·60	−4·22	211·26	−205·23	**594·22**

Table S.3   Industrial production, index and selected series, 1885–1987

	Industrial production	Coal	Crude steel	Cars & commercial vehicles	Iron ore	Electricity
	Index nos., 1980 = 100	'000 tons	'000 tons	'000	'000 tons	mn kwh
1885	3·3	174	77	—	873	—
1886	3·1	170	78	—	872	—
1887	3·3	169	111	—	903	—
1888	3·5	169	114	—	960	—
1889	3·6	187	136	—	986	—
1890	3·9	188	168	—	941	—
1891	4·2	198	172	—	987	—
1892	4·4	199	160	—	1,294	—
1893	4·7	200	167	—	1,484	—
1894	5·1	196	168	—	1,927	—
1895	5·0	224	197	—	1,904	—
1896	5·6	226	257	—	2,039	—
1897	5·7	224	274	—	2,087	—
1898	6·1	236	264	—	2,303	—
1899	6·4	239	272	—	2,435	—
1900	6·6	252	300	—	2,610	—
1901	6·8	271	269	—	2,795	0·1
1902	7·1	305	286	—	2,897	0·1
1903	7·5	320	318	—	3,678	0·1
1904	7·8	321	333	—	4,085	0·2
1905	7·9	322	368	—	4,366	0·2
1906	8·7	297	398	—	4,503	0·2
1907	9·0	305	420	—	4,480	0·3
1908	8·8	305	438	—	4,713	0·4
1909	8·1	247	313	—	3,886	0·6
1910	9·5	303	472	—	5,549	0·8
1911	9·7	312	471	—	6,151	0·8
1912	10·1	360	515	—	6,699	1·2
1913	9·8	364	591	—	7,476	1·5
1914	9·3	367	507	—	6,589	...
1915	10·2	412	600	—	6,883	...
1916	10·6	415	614	—	6,987	...
1917	8·9	443	581	—	6,217	...
1918	7·4	404	545	—	6,624	...
1919	8·3	430	491	—	4,981	2·43
1920	9·3	440	437	—	4,519	2·61
1921	7·2	377	212	—	6,464	2·22
1922	8·5	379	311	—	6,201	2·68
1923	9·3	420	271	—	5,588	2·99
1924	10·6	438	501	—	6,500	3·52
1925	10·8	264	475	0·3	8,169	3·67
1926	11·9	384	495	0·3	8,466	4·01
1927	12·3	398	499	0·8	9,661	4·39
1928	13·4	359	576	1·2	4,669	4·41
1929	14·0	395	694	1·8	11,468	4·97
1930	14·4	398	611	2·3	11,236	5·12
1931	13·6	343	539	2·3	7,071	5·09
1932	12·5	333	528	2·9	3,299	4·90
1933	12·7	349	630	2·7	2,699	5·34
1934	15·5	415	862	3·2	5,253	6·03
1935	17·2	424	896	3·4	7,933	6·90
1936	18·9	456	977	4·5	11,250	7·43
1937	21·2	460	1,105	6·6	14,953	7·98
1938	21·4	431	972	7·0	13,928	8·16
1939	23·4	444	1,151	7·6	13,787	9·05
1940	21·2	498	1,145	(1·8)	11,295	8·62
1941	20·8	557	1,156	(0·1)	10,528	9·12
1942	21·9	582	1,228	(0·1)	9,727	9·80
1943	22·9	558	1,214	(0·2)	10,820	11·04
1944	24·4	570	1,197	(0·3)	7,253	12·43

Table S.3 (Continued)   Industrial production, index and selected series, 1885–1987

	Industrial production	Coal	Crude steel	Cars & commercial vehicles	Iron ore	Electricity
	Index nos., 1980 = 100	'000 tons	'000 tons	'000	'000 tons	mn kwh
1945	24·0	615	1,203	(0·5)	3,930	13·54
1946	29·1	488	1,203	8	6,867	14·20
1947	29·7	416	1,191	12	8,894	13·46
1948	31·8	374	1,257	12	13,286	14·08
1949	32·9	317	1,370	11	13,729	16·04
1950	34·1	309	1,437	17	13,611	18·18
1951	35·9	279	1,504	23	15,383	19·35
1952	34·7	347	1,666	22	16,949	20·55
1953	35·3	285	1,759	30	16,983	22·44
1954	36·5	267	1,840	44	15,325	23·96
1955	38·9	282	2,127	51	17,355	24·72
1956	40·1	294	2,399	57	18,947	26·63
1957	41·9	304	2,483	71	19,924	28·97
1958	42·5	319	2,407	91	18,312	30·35
1959	44·9	272	2,821	113	18,351	32·23
1960	49·7	251	3,189	129	21,690	34·72
1961	53·2	200	3,530	130	23,593	38·32
1962	56·2	148	3,573	148	22,526	40·62
1963	59·8	99	3,837	168	23,637	40·66
1964	65·8	84	4,447	185	26,619	45·40
1965	70·6	59	4,689	207	29,354	49·11
1966	73·0	40	4,727	199	27,987	50·66
1967	74·8	11	4,737	214	28,337	53·84
1968	78·4	20	5,043	243	32,419	56·25
1969	83·7	22	5,346	273	33,185	58·08
1970	89·1	12	5,462	305	31,509	60·64
1971	90·3	12	5,235	323	34,367	66·55
1972	92·7	10	5,225	355	33,979	71·68
1973	99·3	12	5,625	383	34,727	78·08
1974	105·3	11	5,941	374	36,153	75·13
1975	102·9	1	5,585	388	30,867	80·57
1976	102	12	5,149	393	29,862	86·42
1977	96	2	3,940	306	24,839	90·02
1978	94	16	4,302	331	21,063	92·90
1979	100	—	4,414	367	26,189	95·20
1980	100	—	4,236	328	26,922	96·70
1981	98	—	3,768	353	23,147	103·30
1982	97	—	3,900	370	14,744	100·05
1983	101	—	4,212	420	13,792	109·39
1984	107	—	4,704	373	17,806	123·84
1985	110	—	4,812	461	20,525	137·14
1986	110	—	4,704	466	20,529	138·65
1987	114	—	4,596	. . .	. . .	147·17

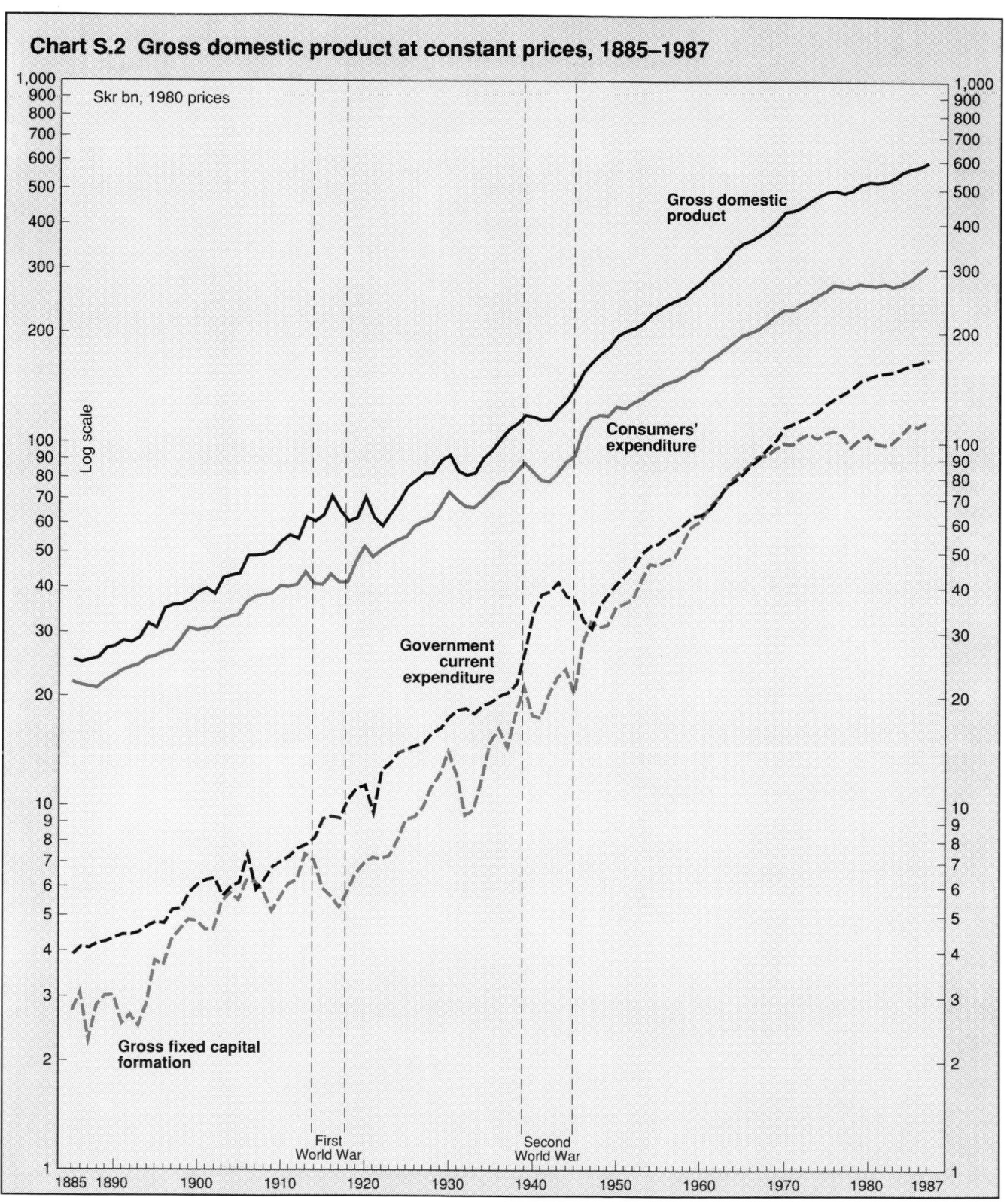

Chart S.2 Gross domestic product at constant prices, 1885–1987

Skr bn, 1980 prices

Log scale

Gross domestic product

Consumers' expenditure

Government current expenditure

Gross fixed capital formation

First World War

Second World War

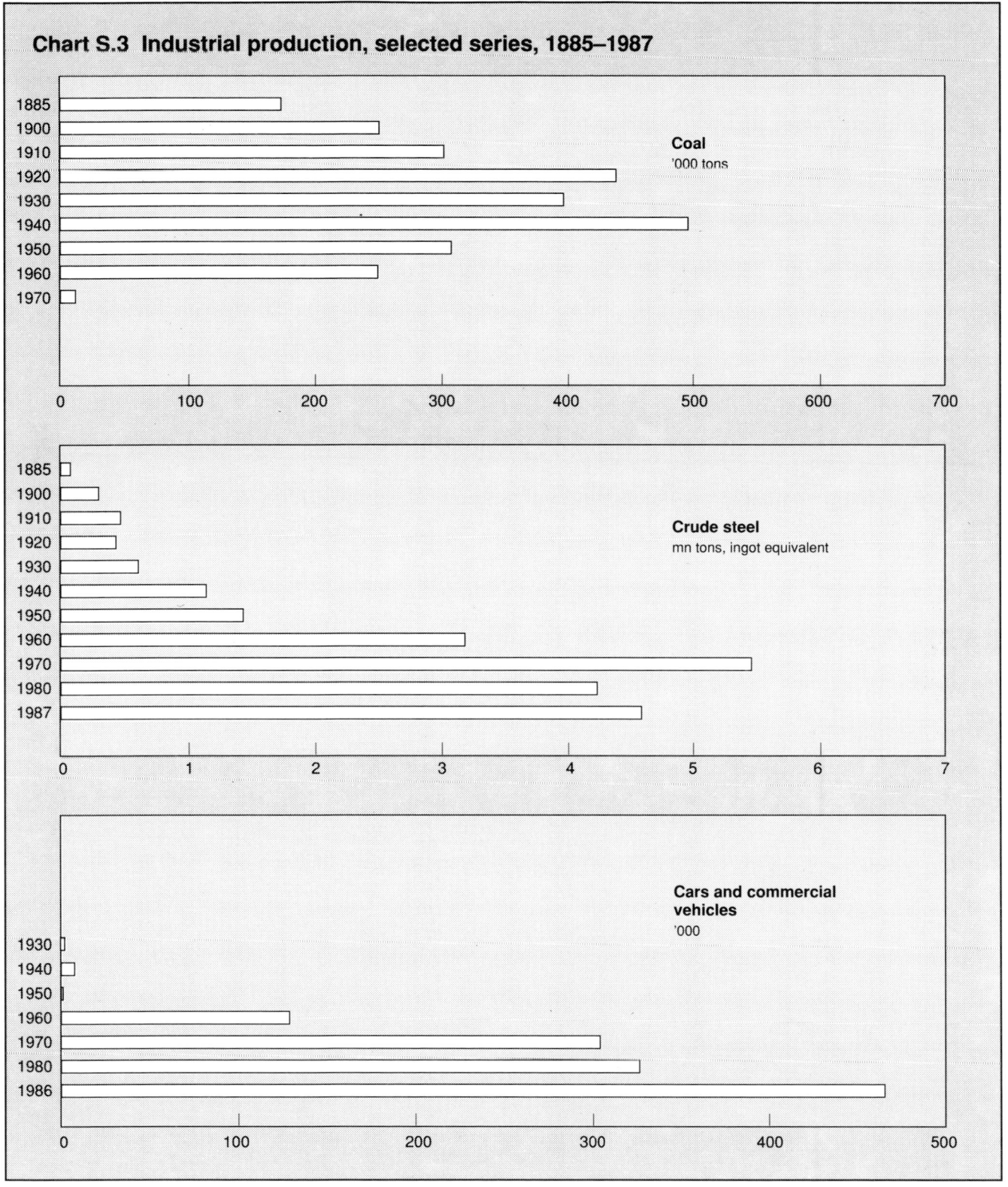

Chart S.3 Industrial production, selected series, 1885–1987

Coal
'000 tons

Crude steel
mn tons, ingot equivalent

Cars and commercial vehicles
'000

Table S.4   Prices and income, 1914–87

	Consumer prices		Wholesale prices	Import prices	Export prices	Compensation of employees	National income
	All items	Food	All items				
	Index nos., 1980 = 100					Skr bn	
1914	6·4	6·1	. . .	. . .	. . .	. . .	. . .
1915	. . .	. . .	. . .	. . .	. . .	. . .	. . .
1916	9·1	9·3	. . .	. . .	. . .	. . .	. . .
1917	10·9	11·0	. . .	. . .	. . .	. . .	. . .
1918	14·9	16·0	. . .	. . .	. . .	. . .	. . .
1919	17·2	19·4	. . .	. . .	. . .	. . .	. . .
1920	17·3	17·9	27·4	. . .	. . .	. . .	. . .
1921	14·8	14·6	16·9	. . .	. . .	. . .	. . .
1922	12·0	11·1	13·2	. . .	. . .	. . .	. . .
1923	11·2	10·0	12·4	. . .	. . .	. . .	. . .
1924	11·2	9·9	12·4	. . .	. . .	. . .	. . .
1925	11·4	10·3	12·3	. . .	. . .	. . .	. . .
1926	11·0	9·7	11·4	. . .	. . .	. . .	. . .
1927	10·9	9·3	11·1	. . .	. . .	. . .	. . .
1928	10·9	9·4	11·3	. . .	. . .	. . .	. . .
1929	10·8	9·1	10·7	. . .	. . .	. . .	. . .
1930	10·5	8·5	9·3	. . .	. . .	. . .	. . .
1931	(10·1)	7·9	8·5	. . .	. . .	. . .	. . .
1932	(10·0)	7·6	8·4	. . .	. . .	. . .	. . .
1933	9·7	7·4	8·2	. . .	. . .	. . .	. . .
1934	9·8	7·5	8·7	. . .	. . .	. . .	. . .
1935	10·0	7·8	9·2	. . .	. . .	. . .	. . .
1936	10·1	8·2	9·4	. . .	. . .	. . .	. . .
1937	10·3	8·5	10·5	. . .	. . .	. . .	. . .
1938	10·5	8·8	10·2	9	9	. . .	. . .
1939	10·7	9·0	10·6	. . .	. . .	. . .	. . .
1940	12·2	8·6	13·5	. . .	. . .	. . .	. . .
1941	14·1	11·7	15·8	. . .	. . .	. . .	. . .
1942	15·4	12·6	17·4	. . .	. . .	. . .	. . .
1943	15·8	12·6	18·1	. . .	. . .	7·98	. . .
1944	15·8	12·5	18·1	. . .	. . .	8·52	. . .
1945	15·7	12·4	17·9	. . .	. . .	9·21	. . .
1946	16·0	12·5	17·1	. . .	. . .	10·66	21·45
1947	16·1	13·1	18·3	18	20	12·16	23·17
1948	17·2	14·1	19·7	19	22	13·53	25·87
1949	17·5	14·3	19·9	19	21	13·94	27·21
1950	17·7	14·5	20·9	22	22	14·58	29·23
						15·93	29·19
1951	20·5	16·9	26·6	28	35	19·20	35·88
1952	22·1	19·0	28·2	30	34	22·53	38·77
1953	22·4	19·4	26·7	27	30	23·54	39·96
1954	22·6	19·4	26·5	27	29	24·87	42·75
1955	23·3	20·4	27·5	27	30	27·37	45·83
1956	24·3	21·8	28·9	28	30	29·42	49·80
1957	25·4	22·3	29·3	29	31	31·70	53·04
1958	26·6	23·1	28·7	27	30	33·19	56·04
1959	26·8	23·4	28·7	27	30	34·66	59·74
1960	27·8	24·8	29·5	27	30	38·61	64·86
1961	28·5	25·5	30·1	27	31	42·72	70·52
1962	29·8	27·7	30·7	27	30	47·85	76·38
1963	30·6	29·1	31·7	28	30	52·87	82·63
1964	31·7	30·2	33·1	29	31	58·77	92·47
1965	33·3	32·2	34·5	29	33	65·10	101·56
1966	35·4	34·3	35·5	30	33	72·39	110·28
1967	36·9	35·5	35·5	30	33	78·36	119·73
1968	37·6	35·7	35·9	30	33	84·45	127·24
1969	38·7	37·0	37·3	31	34	92·02	139·00
1970	41·3	40·1	39·8	33	37	103·02	155·82
1971	44·5	43·8	40·9	35	39	112·67	168·42
1972	47·1	47·8	42·6	35	41	123·31	184·34

Table S.4 (Continued)   Prices and income, 1914–87

	Consumer prices		Wholesale prices	Import prices	Export prices	Compensation of employees	National income
	All items	Food	All items				
	Index nos., 1980 = 100					Skr bn	
1973	50·3	50·6	47·8	40	45	132·66	205·30
1974	55·3	53·8	58·8	55	57	153·43	230·40
1975	60·8	60·1	63·8	57	66	183·74	271·05
1976	66·9	67·8	69·2	61	70	217·97	305·50
1977	74·6	77·7	74·9	69	74	245·10	328·81
1978	82·1	85·1	79·6	75	79	272·91	365·11
1979	87·9	89·6	88·2	87	89	299·95	409·32
1980	100·0	100·0	100·0	100	100	337·08	461·65
1981	112·1	115·0	110·0	111	109	368·36	497·12
1982	121·7	129·2	123·3	126	122	389·53	539·13
1983	132·6	144·2	136·9	142	136	421·60	603·86
1984	143·2	161·0	148·7	150	147	461·43	677·56
1985	153·8	172·9	157·0	154	153	502·38	738·90
1986	160·3	185·3	160·2	139	154	549·41	807·31
1987	167·0	191·1	165·2	142	160	595·66	872·51

Table S.5   Population, 1885–1986

	Total population	Males	Females	Births	Age distribution Under 15	Age distribution 15–64	Age distribution 65 & over
	mn			'000	mn		
1885	4·68	2·27	2·41	137	. . .	. . .	. . .
1886	4·72	2·29	2·43	140	. . .	. . .	. . .
1887	4·74	2·30	2·44	140	. . .	. . .	. . .
1888	4·75	2·30	2·45	136	. . .	. . .	. . .
1889	4·77	2·31	2·46	132	. . .	. . .	. . .
1890	4·79	2·32	2·47	134	1·59	2·82	0·37
1891	4·80	2·33	2·48	136	. . .	. . .	. . .
1892	4·81	2·33	2·48	130	. . .	. . .	. . .
1893	4·82	2·34	2·49	132	. . .	. . .	. . .
1894	4·87	2·36	2·51	131	. . .	. . .	. . .
1895	4·92	2·39	2·53	135	. . .	. . .	. . .
1896	4·96	2·41	2·55	134	. . .	. . .	. . .
1897	5·01	2·44	2·57	133	. . .	. . .	. . .
1898	5·06	2·47	2·60	137	. . .	. . .	. . .
1899	5·10	2·49	2·61	134	. . .	. . .	. . .
1900	5·14	2·51	2·63	138	1·67	3·04	0·43
1901	5·18	2·53	2·65	139	. . .	. . .	. . .
1902	5·20	2·54	2·66	137	. . .	. . .	. . .
1903	5·22	2·55	2·68	134	. . .	. . .	. . .
1904	5·26	2·57	2·69	135	. . .	. . .	. . .
1905	5·30	2·59	2·71	135	. . .	. . .	. . .
1906	5·34	2·61	2·73	137	. . .	. . .	. . .
1907	5·38	2·63	2·75	137	. . .	. . .	. . .
1908	5·43	2·66	2·77	139	. . .	. . .	. . .
1909	5·48	2·68	2·80	140	. . .	. . .	. . .
1910	5·52	2·70	2·82	136	1·75	3·30	0·47
1911	5·56	2·72	2·84	133	. . .	. . .	. . .
1912	5·60	2·74	2·86	133	. . .	. . .	. . .
1913	5·64	2·76	2·88	130	. . .	. . .	. . .
1914	5·68	2·78	2·90	129	. . .	. . .	. . .
1915	5·71	2·79	2·92	123	. . .	. . .	. . .
1916	5·76	2·82	2·94	122	. . .	. . .	. . .
1917	5·80	2·84	2·96	121	. . .	. . .	. . .
1918	5·81	2·85	2·96	118	. . .	. . .	. . .
1919	5·85	2·87	2·98	115	. . .	. . .	. . .
1920	5·90	2·90	3·01	139	1·73	3·68	0·50
1921	5·95	2·93	3·03	128	. . .	. . .	. . .
1922	5·99	2·94	3·04	117	. . .	. . .	. . .
1923	6·01	2·95	3·06	113	. . .	. . .	. . .
1924	6·04	2·96	3·07	109	. . .	. . .	. . .
1925	6·05	2·97	3·08	106	. . .	. . .	. . .
1926	6·07	2·98	3·09	102	. . .	. . .	. . .
1927	6·09	2·99	3·10	98	. . .	. . .	. . .
1928	6·11	3·00	3·11	98	. . .	. . .	. . .
1929	6·12	3·01	3·11	93	. . .	. . .	. . .
1930	6·14	3·02	3·12	94	1·53	4·05	0·57
1931	6·16	3·04	3·12	91	. . .	. . .	. . .
1932	6·19	3·05	3·14	90	. . .	. . .	. . .
1933	6·21	3·07	3·14	85	. . .	. . .	. . .
1934	6·23	3·08	3·15	85	. . .	. . .	. . .
1935	6·25	3·09	3·16	86	. . .	. . .	. . .
1936	6·27	3·10	3·17	89	. . .	. . .	. . .
1937	6·28	3·11	3·17	90	. . .	. . .	. . .
1938	6·31	3·13	3·18	94	. . .	. . .	. . .
1939	6·34	3·14	3·20	97	. . .	. . .	. . .
1940	6·37	3·16	3·21	96	1·30	4·47	0·60
1941	6·41	3·18	3·23	100	. . .	. . .	. . .
1942	6·46	3·21	3·25	114	. . .	. . .	. . .
1943	6·52	3·24	3·28	125	. . .	. . .	. . .
1944	6·60	3·28	3·32	135	. . .	. . .	. . .

Table S.5 (Continued)   Population, 1885–1986

	Total population	Males	Females	Births	Age distribution		
					Under 15	15–64	65 & over
	mn			'000	mn		
1945	6·67	3·32	3·35	135	...	..	...
1946	6·76	3·37	3·40	133	...	...	...
1947	6·84	3·41	3·44	129	...	...	...
1948	6·93	3·45	3·48	127	...	...	...
1949	6·99	3·48	3·51	121	...	...	...
1950	7·04	3·51	3·53	115	1·65	4·67	0·72
1951	7·10	3·54	3·56	110	1·67	4·70	0·73
1952	7·15	3·56	3·59	110	1·70	4·70	0·75
1953	7·19	3·58	3·61	110	1·71	4·71	0·77
1954	7·24	3·61	3·63	105	1·72	4·73	0·79
1955	7·29	3·63	3·66	107	1·73	4·76	0·80
1956	7·34	3·66	3·68	108	1·74	4·78	0·82
1957	7·39	3·69	3·70	107	1·74	4·82	0·83
1958	7·43	3·71	3·72	106	1·72	4·86	0·85
1959	7·47	3·72	3·74	105	1·69	4·91	0·87
1960	7·50	3·74	3·76	102	1·66	4·95	0·89
1961	7·54	3·76	3·78	105	1·67	4·98	0·89
1962	7·58	3·78	3·80	107	1·65	5·02	0·91
1963	7·63	3·81	3·82	113	1·61	5·07	0·95
1964	7·70	3·84	3·85	123	1·61	5·12	0·97
1965	7·77	3·88	3·89	123	1·63	5·15	0·99
1966	7·81	3·90	3·91	123	1·64	5·17	1·01
1967	7·87	3·93	3·94	121	1·65	5·19	1·03
1968	7·97	3·95	3·96	113	1·66	5·20	1·05
1969	8·04	3·98	3·99	108	1·66	5·23	1·07
1970	8·10	4·02	4·03	110	1·68	5·27	1·10
1971	8·12	4·04	4·06	114	1·68	5·29	1·13
1972	8·14	4·05	4·07	112	1·69	5·28	1·15
1973	8·16	4·05	4·08	110	1·69	5·27	1·18
1974	8·19	4·06	4·10	110	1·69	5·26	1·21
1975	8·22	4·07	4·12	104	1·69	5·26	1·24
1976	8·25	4·09	4·13	98	1·70	5·26	1·26
1977	8·27	4·10	4·15	96	1·69	5·27	1·29
1978	8·29	4·11	4·17	93	1·68	5·29	1·31
1979	8·31	4·11	4·18	96	1·65	5·31	1·33
1980	8·32	4·12	4·19	97	1·63	5·33	1·35
1981	8·32	4·12	4·20	94	1·60	5·35	1·37
1982	8·33	4·12	4·21	93	1·57	5·37	1·39
1983	8·33	4·12	4·21	92	1·54	5·38	1·40
1984	8·34	4·12	4·22	94	1·53	5·39	1·42
1985	8·35	4·12	4·23	98	1·52	5·39	1·44
1986	8·37	4·13	4·24	102	1·51	5·40	1·47

Table S.6　Education, 1885–1986

	Elementary	Secondary	Post-secondary	Higher education Total	of which: Females
		No. of pupils, '000		No. of students '000	
1885	611	...	...	...	...
1886	619	...	...	...	...
1887	628	...	...	...	...
1888	630	...	...	...	...
1889	636	14		...	...
1890	638	14		...	...
1891	641	14		...	...
1892	644	15		...	...
1893	648	15		...	...
1894	662	15		...	...
1895	670	15		...	...
1896	678	15		...	...
1897	689	16		...	...
1898	690	16		...	...
1899	690	17		...	...
1900	696	17		...	...
1901	717	18		...	...
1902	719	18		...	...
1903	723	19		...	...
1904	728	20		...	...
1905	729	21		...	...
1906	734	22		...	...
1907	740	22		...	...
1908	748	23		...	...
1909	753	23		...	...
1910	759	24		...	...
1911	764	24		...	...
1912	771	25		...	...
1913	777	26		...	...
1914	783	26		...	...
1915	701	27		...	...
1916	704	27		...	...
1917	706	28		9·0	...
1918	708	29		8·9	...
1919	707	30		9·2	...
1920	517	32		9·1	...
1921	534	34		8·8	...
1922	545	35		9·1	...
1923	548	36		9·0	...
1924	547	36		9·4	...
1925	548	36		9·1	...
1926	544	35		9·5	...
1927	545	34		9·7	...
1928	558	34		10·2	...
1929	574	35		10·1	...
1930	580	38		10·1	...
1931	584	42		10·6	...
1932	586	46		11·1	...
1933	589	50		11·3	...
1934	575	53		11·4	...
1935	557	55		11·7	...
1936	544	56		12·5	...
1937	532	57		12·5 / 11·7	...
1938	525	59		12·1	...
1939	520	61		12·1	...
1940	517	61		11·4	...
1941	510	62		8·4	2·3
1942	505	63		8·4	2·4
1943	502	64		8·5	2·4
1944	501	66		13·2	2·9

	Elementary	Secondary	Post-secondary	Higher education	
				Total	*of which:* Females
		No. of pupils, '000		No. of students '000	
1945	507		69	13·9	3·0
1946	513	72	20	13·9	2·9
1947	531	77	21	14·1	3·0
1948	545	84	21	14·6	3·0
1949	582	92	25	15·8	3·5
1950	607	100	26	16·9	4·0
1951	646	107	28	17·8	4·4
1952	682	113	29	18·6	4·8
1953	726	119	29	19·9	5·3
1954	756	114	30	21·0	5·9
1955	792	120	31	22·6	6·5
1956	815	130	31	25·8	7·9
1957	829	136	33	27·2	8·6
1958	835	140	34	30·6	9·7
1959	837	143	36	33·4	10·8
1960	843	142	66	37·0	12·5
1961	841	132	75	40·7	13·9
1962	837	121	82	45·0	15·8
1963	856	102	87	49·3	17·1
1964	867	163	82	60·2	22·1
1965	878	153	96	66·4	24·8
1966	891	154	97	79·9	29·4
1967	907	156	100	89·5	33·7
1968	911	154	58	100·3	38·2
1969	936	154	...	113·6	43·7
1970	954	148	...	120·1	45·8
1971	977		232	115·9	43·1
1972	989		235	113·6	42·6
1973	1,001		230	110·0	41·4
1974	1,016		221	108·5	42·2
1975	1,027		220	110·0	43·7
1976	1,033		221	113·8	46·6
1977	1,038		227	148·4	77·2
1978	1,043		237	156·8	83·1
1979	1,043		250	154·5	83·5
1980	1,032		269	158·4	86·3
1981	1,019		285	158·4	87·4
1982	999		303	162·5	90·5
1983	976		315	164·7	92·2
1984	959		311	164·6	92·4
1985	945		301	162·9	91·6
1986	934		292	161·4	90·4

Table S.7 Labour market: employment, 1885–1986

	Employed labour force	Agriculture, forestry & fishing	Mining & quarrying	Manufacturing	Construction	Gas, electricity & water	Transport & communication	Distribution & services
				'000				
1885	1,432	1,078	...	241	...	...	42	...
1886	1,428	1,076	...	237	...	...	42	...
1887	1,432	1,073	...	242	...	...	43	...
1888	1,443	1,070	...	255	...	...	43	...
1889	1,452	1,068	...	264	...	...	45	...
1890	1,461	1,066	...	275	...	...	46	...
1891	1,480	1,064	...	293	...	...	47	...
1892	1,480	1,062	...	292	...	...	49	...
1893	1,484	1,060	...	295	...	...	49	...
1894	1,499	1,059	...	310	...	...	49	...
1895	1,508	1,058	...	320	...	...	50	...
1896	1,539	1,057	...	351	...	...	52	...
1897	1,561	1,056	...	371	...	...	55	...
1898	1,585	1,055	...	396	...	...	56	...
1899	1,603	1,053	...	410	...	...	61	...
1900	1,618	1,051	...	421	...	...	65	...
1901	1,617	1,044	...	424	...	...	68	...
1902	1,622	1,036	...	431	...	...	68	...
1903	1,628	1,027	...	443	...	...	69	...
1904	1,635	1,019	...	455	...	...	73	...
1905	1,641	1,011	...	462	...	...	77	...
1906	1,645	1,002	...	479	...	...	80	...
1907	1,648	994	...	487	...	...	85	...
1908	1,641	990	...	480	...	...	86	...
1909	1,640	987	...	476	...	...	87	...
1910	1,653 / 1,931	979	...	495	...	...	90	367
1911	1,945	976	...	502	...	...	88	379
1912	1,959	973	...	514	...	...	90	381
1913	1,997	969	...	538	...	...	94	395
1914	1,999	967	...	545	...	...	96	391
1915	2,036	965	...	559	...	...	101	412
1916	2,072	962	...	589	...	...	104	416
1917	2,077	961	...	597	...	...	108	411
1918	2,104	961	...	583	...	...	113	448
1919	2,141	959	...	597	...	...	119	467
1920	2,191	956	...	628	...	...	121	485
1921	2,046	947	...	534	...	...	112	452
1922	2,070	937	...	530	...	...	117	486
1923	2,129	931	...	564	...	...	119	515
1924	2,133	924	...	589	...	...	121	498
1925	2,144	918	...	608	...	...	126	492
1926	2,201	915	...	626	...	...	130	529
1927	2,231	914	...	634	...	...	135	548
1928	2,282	911	...	666	...	...	136	568
1929	2,335	910	...	686	...	...	146	593
1930	2,376 / 2,616	907	...	694	240	...	151	624
1931	2,553	887	...	667	224	...	151	625
1932	2,483	872	...	638	202	...	148	624
1933	2,452	862	...	629	185	...	145	631
1934	2,546	872	...	684	203	...	143	643
1935	2,626	873	...	722	228	...	147	655
1936	2,695	869	...	754	248	...	155	668
1937	2,729	859	...	799	231	...	162	678
1938	2,781	856	...	813	247	...	166	699
1939	2,873	846	...	840	266	...	172	748
1940	2,737	828	...	834	175	...	168	732
1941	2,719	795	...	838	163	...	160	762
1942	2,792	762	...	880	193	...	167	789
1943	2,836	729	...	908	202	...	170	826

Table S.7 (Continued)   Labour market: employment, 1885–1986

	Employed labour force	Agriculture, forestry & fishing	Mining & quarrying	Manufacturing	Construction	Gas, electricity & water	Transport & communication	Distribution & services
				'000				
1944	2,843	724	. . .	924	203	. . .	179	812
1945	2,886	718	. . .	967	219	. . .	186	797
1946	2,931	689	. . .	985	241	. . .	201	816
1947	2,983	673	. . .	999	264	. . .	215	832
1948	2,981	659	. . .	1,013	240	. . .	221	849
1949	2·979	648	. . .	1,014	238	. . .	224	855
1950	2,977	626	17	1,020	242	19	226	863
				776				
1951	. . .	. . .	18	794	. . .	20	. . .	. . .
1952	. . .	. . .	19	781	. . .	20	. . .	. . .
1953	. . .	. . .	19	766	. . .	20	. . .	. . .
1954	. . .	. . .	19	798	. . .	20	. . .	. . .
1955	. . .	. . .	19	824	. . .	21	. . .	. . .
1956	. . .	. . .	20	830	. . .	22	. . .	. . .
1957	. . .	. . .	21	828	. . .	22	. . .	. . .
1958	. . .	. . .	20	822	. . .	23	. . .	. . .
1959	. . .	. . .	. . .	. . .	. . .	. . .	. . .	. . .
1960	. . .	. . .	. . .	. . .	. . .	. . .	. . .	. . .
1961	3,645	524	(20)	(1,168)	313	39	258	(1,205)
1962	3,690	485	(20)	(1,188)	288	36	261	(1,267)
1963	3,748	496	20	1,156	319	34	271	(1,306)
1964	3,719	470	25	1,163	323	32	276	(1,302)
1965	3,698	418	22	1,200	328	34	263	1,434
1966	3,733	373	19	1,165	336	36	279	1,525
1967	3,695	366	16	1,135	341	34	267	1,536
1968	3,737	340	22	1,139	339	37	280	1,580
1969	3,782	322	22	1,137	343	31	291	1,636
1970	3,854	314	21	1,064	371	24	266	1,794
1971	3,860	300	18	1,054	352	27	268	1,841
1972	3,863	287	19	1,046	331	26	268	1,886
1973	3,879	276	18	1,066	316	27	269	1,905
1974	3,962	264	20	1,120	294	31	271	1,962
1975	4,062	261	21	1,138	290	32	272	2,048
1976	4,088	254	21	1,100	294	33	275	2,109
1977	4,099	248	18	1,060	297	32	279	2,163
1978	4,115	251	15	1,023	290	32	277	2,229
1979	4,180	242	15	1,026	284	34	290	2,287
1980	4,232	237	15	1,026	286	37	295	2,336
1981	4,225	237	14	984	288	37	293	2,373
1982	4,220	236	14	946	277	40	300	2,405
1983	4,224	229	15	941	267	40	295	2,437
1984	4,196	195	15	947	258	39	292	2,449
1985	4,243	189	15	964	257	40	298	2,479
1986	4,269	179	14	976	257	40	302	2,497

Table S.8   Labour market: other indicators, 1903–87

	Manufacturing				Industrial disputes		
	Average hrs worked	Average hourly earnings	Unemployment		Stoppages	Workers involved	Working days lost
		Skr	'000	%		'000	'000
1903	...	...	...	...	142	25	642
1904	...	...	...	...	215	12	386
1905	...	...	...	...	189	33	2,390
1906	...	...	...	...	290	19	479
1907	...	...	...	...	312	24	514
1908	...	...	...	...	302	40	1,842
1909	...	...	...	...	138	302	11,800
1910	...	...	...	...	76	4	39
1911	...	...	...	...	98	21	570
1912	...	...	...	...	116	10	292
1913	...	3·81	...	...	119	10	303
1914	...	3·88	...	...	115	14	620
1915	...	4·12	...	...	80	5	83
1916	...	4·58	...	...	227	21	475
1917	...	5·65	...	...	475	47	1,109
1918	...	8·16	...	...	708	61	1,436
1919	...	10·30	...	...	440	81	2,296
1920	...	11·79	(14)	(9·6)	486	139	8,943
1921	...	11·97	(44)	(30·5)	347	50	2,663
1922	...	8·65	(29)	(21·1)	392	76	2,675
1923	...	8·19	(17)	(11·9)	206	103	6,907
1924	...	8·23	(24)	(11·5)	261	24	1,205
1925	...	8·43	(32)	(13·8)	239	146	1,560
1926	...	8·54	(36)	(14·4)	206	53	1,711
1927	...	8·50	(38)	(14·0)	189	10	400
1928	...	8·59	(35)	(12·5)	201	72	4,835
1929	...	9·05 / 1·25	33	11·2	180	13	667
1930	...	1·29	42	11·8	261	21	1,021
1931	...	1·29	65	16·7	193	41	2,627
1932	...	1·27	91	22·2	182	50	3,095
1933	46·0	1·22	97	23·4	140	32	3,434
1934	47·0	1·22	85	18·0	103	14	760
1935	47·4	1·24	81	15·1	98	17	788
1936	47·6	1·26	72	12·6	60	4	438
1937	47·2	1·29	67	10·8	67	31	861
1938	46·3	1·37	67	10·9	85	29	1,284
1939	45·6	1·42	64	9·2	45	2	159
1940	46·6	1·53	85	11·8	38	4	78
1941	47·0	1·64	85	11·3	34	2	94
1942	47·2	1·79	57	7·5	139	1	53
1943	47·3	1·86	44	5·7	167	7	94
1944	47·2	1·90	39	4·9	214	7	228
1945	47·4	1·90	36	4·5	163	133	11,321
1946	46·8	2·05	28	3·2	137	1	27
1947	...	2·34	24	2·8	81	57	125
1948	...	2·53	26	2·8	47	6	151
1949	...	2·62	26	2·7	31	1	21
1950	...	2·73	22	2·2	23	2	41
1951	...	3·30	18	1·8	28	15	531
1952	...	3·92	22	2·3	32	2	79
1953	50·3	4·11	27	2·8	20	26	582
1954	...	4·29	26	2·6	45	8	24
1955	50·3	4·64	25	2·5	18	4	159
1956	49·7	5·04	19	1·7	12	2	4
1957	49·7	5·34	24	1·9	20	2	53
1958	48·8	5·67	32	2·5	10	0·1	15
1959	48·3	5·93	27	2·0	17	1	24
1960	47·7	6·32	19	1·4	31	1	18
1961	47·1	6·82	17	1·2	12	0·1	2

	Manufacturing				Industrial disputes		
	Average hrs worked	Average hourly earnings	Unemployment		Stoppages	Workers involved	Working days lost
		Skr	'000	%		'000	'000
1962	47·1	7·29	19	1·3	10	4	5
1963	46·6	7·91	20	1·4	24	3	25
1964	46·3	8·78	17	1·1	14	2	34
1965	46·0	8·78	44	1·2	8	0·2	4
1966	46·0	9·60	59	1·6	26	29	352
1967	45·1	10·44	80	2·1	7	0·1	0·4
1968	44·3	11·17	85	2·2	7	0·4	1
1969	43·4	12·15	73	1·9	41	9	112
1970	43·1	13·52	59	1·5	134	27	156
1971	42·3	14·91	101	2·5	60	63	839
1972	40·9	16·76	107	2·7	44	7	11
1973	40·0	18·19	98	2·5	48	4	12
1974	39·1	20·30	80	2·0	85	17	58
1975	38·4	23·79	67	1·6	86	24	366
1976	38·0	27·01	66	1·6	73	9	25
1977	37·9	29·51	75	1·8	35	13	87
1978	37·7	33·03	94	2·2	99	8	37
1979	37·6	36·01	88	2·1	207	32	29
1980	37·6	39·63	86	2·0	212	747	4,478
1981	37·4	43·18	108	2·5	68	99	209
1982	37·6	45·67	137	3·1	46	5	2
1983	37·7	48·45	151	3·5	92	14	37
1984	38·1	53·98	136	3·1	206	24	31
1985	38·3	58·58	124	2·8	160	124	504
1986	38·3	62·65	117	2·7	75	66	683
1987	38·4	67·04	84	1·9	72	11	15

Table S.9 Public finance, 1885–1987

	Revenue				Expenditure				
	Taxes on income & property	Customs & excise (excluding auto taxes)	Automobile taxes	Total receipts	Defence	Education	Social services	Debt interest[a]	Total expenditure[b]
				Skr mn					
1885	11	49	. . .	88	. . .	. . .	. . .	. . .	85
1886	9	53	. . .	84	. . .	. . .	. . .	. . .	87
1887	9	45	. . .	75	. . .	. . .	. . .	. . .	91
1888	9	59	. . .	91	. . .	. . .	. . .	. . .	90
1889	9	63	. . .	97	. . .	. . .	. . .	. . .	93
1890	10	66	. . .	101	. . .	. . .	. . .	. . .	98
1891	10	60	. . .	94	. . .	. . .	. . .	. . .	102
1892	10	61	. . .	95	. . .	. . .	. . .	. . .	101
1893	11	62	. . .	98	. . .	. . .	. . .	. . .	105
1894	14	66	. . .	110	. . .	. . .	. . .	. . .	101
1895	14	70	. . .	116	. . .	. . .	. . .	. . .	103
1896	10	76	. . .	121	. . .	. . .	. . .	. . .	106
1897	9	81	. . .	137	. . .	. . .	. . .	. . .	118
1898	9	87	. . .	144	. . .	. . .	. . .	. . .	125
1899	9	98	. . .	155	. . .	. . .	. . .	. . .	135
1900	9	101	. . .	152	. . .	. . .	. . .	. . .	151
1901	6	94	. . .	140	. . .	. . .	. . .	. . .	153
1902	12	95	. . .	147	. . .	. . .	. . .	. . .	167
1903	27	98	. . .	171	82	30	20	. . .	188
1904	21	106	. . .	176	. . .	. . .	. . .	. . .	188
1905	22	109	. . .	185	. . .	. . .	. . .	. . .	189
1906	24	103	. . .	187	. . .	. . .	. . .	. . .	196
1907	27	116	. . .	204	. . .	. . .	. . .	. . .	209
1908	25	121	. . .	200	. . .	. . .	. . .	. . .	216
1909	28	110	. . .	189	. . .	. . .	. . .	. . .	232
1910	31	123	. . .	221	. . .	. . .	. . .	. . .	236
1911	36	127	. . .	236	. . .	. . .	. . .	. . .	249
1912	37	132	. . .	249	. . .	. . .	. . .	. . .	254
1913	41	135	. . .	264	. . .	. . .	. . .	. . .	259
1914	45	126	. . .	261	. . .	. . .	. . .	. . .	271
1915	44	128	. . .	365	. . .	. . .	. . .	. . .	413
1916	65	140	. . .	413	. . .	. . .	. . .	. . .	434
1917	114	97	. . .	636	. . .	. . .	. . .	. . .	650
1918	259	92	. . .	766	. . .	. . .	. . .	. . .	1,718
1919	277	208	. . .	891	. . .	. . .	. . .	. . .	849
1920	307	288	. . .	892	. . .	. . .	. . .	. . .	945
1921	298	275	. . .	767	. . .	. . .	. . .	. . .	1,116
1922	188	283	. . .	672	. . .	. . .	. . .	. . .	938
1923	(9)	(147)	. . .	(277)	. . .	. . .	. . .	. . .	(389)
1924	143	304	9	672	. . .	. . .	. . .	. . .	775
1925	145	311	19	653	. . .	. . .	. . .	. . .	714
1926	152	294	22	653	. . .	. . .	. . .	. . .	758
1927	151	316	25	673	. . .	. . .	. . .	. . .	810
1928	150	316	32	707	. . .	. . .	. . .	. . .	740
1929	149	320	40	733	. . .	. . .	. . .	. . .	792
1930	151	335	44	779	. . .	. . .	. . .	. . .	811
1931	166	321	51	783	. . .	. . .	. . .	. . .	819
1932	163	322	59	736	. . .	. . .	. . .	. . .	894
1933	148	330	73	741	. . .	. . .	. . .	. . .	1,067
1934	140	344	79	783	. . .	. . .	. . .	. . .	973
1935	156	383	88	903	. . .	. . .	. . .	. . .	1,108
1936	183	416	97	995 / 831	123	154	205	. . .	1,118
1937	233	443	107	949	154	160	222	. . .	1,199
1938	264	488	117	1,069	172	196	270	. . .	1,119
1939	366	537	130	1,244	234	231	233	. . .	1,372
1940	513	664	127	1,570	1,289	236	252	. . .	1,578
1941	750	768	30	1,730	2,010	255	400	. . .	2,880
1942	851	919	30	1,942	1,847	275	476	. . .	3,878

	Revenue				Expenditure				
	Taxes on income & property	Customs & excise (excluding auto taxes)	Automobile taxes	Total receipts	Defence	Education	Social services	Debt interest[a]	Total expenditure[b]
					Skr mn				
1943	993	1,140	31	2,330	2,065	288	536	. . .	4,085
1944	1,178	1,287	34	2,687	2,007	305	557	. . .	4,503
1945	1,330	1,323	32	2,875	1,772	309	719	. . .	4,618
1946	1,408	1,472	83	3,173	823	329	566	. . .	5,232
1947	1,178	1,643	203	3,237	729	384	558	. . .	4,537
1948	2,056	1,579	263	4,179	756	482	960	. . .	4,108
1949	2,077	1,714	436	4,626	855	537	1,400	. . .	4,844
1950	2,035	1,639	444	4,474	954	535	1,451	. . .	5,675
1951	2,754	1,815	472	5,426	1,191	571	1,517	335	5,834
1952	4,124	2,125	411	7,507	1,476	704	1,673	362	6,447
1953	4,100	2,218	520	7,808	1,787	873	1,878	319	7,831
1954	4,492	2,332	602	8,535	1,882	947	2,186	365	9,485
1955	4,600	2,512	819	8,907	2,056	1,006	2,416	377	10,077
1956	5,212	2,821	1,043	10,072	2,163	1,107	2,549	466	10,721
1957	5,600	2,977	1,018	10,691	2,281	1,268	3,200	492	11,963
1958	6,210	3,560	1,062	12,019	2,512	1,444	3,473	612	13,024
1959	6,401	3,938	1,086	12,605	2,600	1,574	3,821	640	14,630
1960	6,468	4,630	1,182	13,657	2,733	1,815	4,087	759	15,184
1961	7,669	5,912	1,265	16,641	2,738	1,929	4,479	896	16,373
1962	8,277	6,552	1,227	18,007	3,088	2,210	4,670	909	17,394
1963	8,647	7,546	1,587	19,869	3,446	2,509	5,560	798	18,754
1964	8,545	8,377	1,820	20,927	3,706	2,892	5,676	817	21,483
					Skr bn				
1964					4·25	4·38	4·56	0·82	17·63
1965	10·63	8·98	1·96	24·26	4·53	5·05	5·31	0·89	19·94
1966	11·93	10·85	2·22	28·02	5·04	5·79	6·37	0·94	23·22
1967	12·67	12·10	2·38	30·44	4·88	6·66	7·20	0·98	25·65
1968	12·89	13·17	2·56	32·10	5·32	7·12	8·48	1·14	28·98
1969	14·08	13·91	2·76	34·84	5·54	7·68	9·65	1·36	31·77
1970	17·05	14·16	3·04	38·89	5·70	9·00	11·83	1·76	36·57
1971	18·44	16·91	3·22	44·38	6·26	9·91	14·11	2·09	41·53
1972	19·77	20·01	3·33	50·30	6·36	10·91	16·18	2·01	45·95
1973	18·27	21·76	3·45	52·65	7·37	11·75	18·24	2·23	52·00
1974	20·96	23·31	3·62	59·13	8·06	13·10	21·57	2·69	60·06
1975	28·09	25·53	3·69	70·02	9·79	15·49	26·37	3·81	72·24
1976	40·63	30·9	3·89	91·37	10·63	17·89	32·27	4·23	85·51
1977	45·02	35·1	4·57	101·98	11·58	21·40	40·56	5·51	102·80
1978	46·15	40·7	4·89	109·29	12·51	23·78	47·48	7·02	116·29
1979	51·76	43·9	6·45	116·26	13·81	27·37	53·54	8·98	132·11
1980	57·62	44·1	7·03	128·56	16·03	31·21	63·04	14·58	153·16
1981	34·06	56·0	8·54	155·29	17·90	34·22	69·75	23·01	169·76
1982	36·25	61·0	9·19	167·13	19·09	37·76	77·71	26·47	185·46
1983	39·53	69·9	10·65	191·28	19·45	40·93	87·53	43·73	203·68
1984	48·90	76·8	10·78	221·17	20·74	43·30	96·55	48·20	221·58
1985	67·79	91·0	13·26	222·12	22·46	46·51	105·14	60·39	239·65
1986	60·41	95·9	17·78	233·09	. . .	. . .	. . .	66·51	. . .
1987	77·28	107·6	17·25	274·05	. . .	. . .	. . .	63·81	. . .

a Fiscal years, 1964–87.
b Excluding debt interest, 1964–85.

Table S.10 Value of exports and imports by country, 1885–1987

	Total exports	Exports to: Europe	of which: UK	of which: Germany	USA	Total imports	Imports from: Europe	of which: UK	of which: Germany	USA
					Skr mn					
1885	246	...	122	19	0·8	337	...	85	101	8·6
1886	228	...	111	21	2·6	296	...	77	92	8·7
1887	247	...	110	24	2·8	291	...	74	89	6·6
1888	282	...	130	27	1·1	323	...	94	94	4·2
1889	302	...	142	36	1·4	372	...	111	116	5·9
1890	304	...	137	37	0·9	376	...	109	118	8·2
1891	323	...	146	38	0·7	368	...	99	120	13
1892	328	...	150	48	2·4	359	...	95	116	13
1893	328	...	151	44	0·7	332	...	86	113	11
1894	298	...	124	39	—	345	...	98	120	12
1895	311	...	131	43	0·1	343	...	98	116	11
1896	340	...	144	44	0·7	357	...	99	118	9
1897	358	...	150	46	0·2	399	...	121	135	7
1898	345	...	149	50	0·1	446	...	139	158	10
1899	358	...	157	55	—	503	...	155	184	10
1900	391	...	169	65	—	526	...	177	188	9
1901	353	...	150	60	—	460	...	132	169	11
1902	392	...	150	63	—	502	...	130	197	10
1903	441	...	162	71	—	530	...	139	206	13
1904	415	...	149	72	—	572	...	149	222	9
1905	450	419	159	85	10	574	511	140	220	41
1906	504	465	171	97	12	638	551	159	231	60
1907	525	482	182	109	14	674	581	177	238	61
1908	482	444	169	103	10	597	509	152	210	60
1909	473	423	156	97	16	614	533	157	213	48
1910	593	518	191	124	23	669	579	164	230	53
1911	663	582	196	134	24	690	592	161	240	55
1912	760	666	223	171	32	783	675	189	274	60
1913	817	718	238	179	34	846	719	207	290	77
1914	772	690	258	175	41	727	604	184	239	78
1915	1,316	1,244	330	486	34	1,142	698	214	251	322
1916	1,556	1,422	320	438	75	1,139	823	164	420	214
1917	1,350	1,262	216	352	50	759	639	65	288	96
1918	1,350	1,276	253	293	19	1,233	1,075	149	448	83
1919	1,576	1,399	512	131	62	2,534	1,585	669	269	646
1920	2,278	1,918	825	185	129	3,314	2,178	915	500	779
1921	1,097	887	327	119	97	1,259	904	218	325	243
1922	1,154	897	285	103	133	1,114	874	268	314	167
1923	1,142	892	359	90	128	1,294	973	284	342	214
1924	1,261	977	363	133	153	1,424	1,058	308	353	227
1925	1,360	1,077	367	206	143	1,446	1,084	291	378	219
1926	1,419	1,091	386	189	173	1,490	1,147	221	460	199
1927	1,617	1,273	448	271	175	1,584	1,237	264	485	201
1928	1,575	1,231	393	198	166	1,708	1,292	275	531	252
1929	1,812	1,410	450	275	198	1,783	1,377	309	548	261
1930	1,550	1,233	395	225	161	1,662	1,310	263	533	229
1931	1,122	880	300	114	133	1,428	1,139	201	472	178
1932	947	734	242	90	100	1,155	920	194	339	125
1933	1,079	814	285	115	131	1,096	877	197	320	113
1934	1,302	1,018	328	186	129	1,305	1,049	255	350	154
1935	1,297	981	322	187	156	1,476	1,185	285	358	189
1936	1,514	1,171	374	241	188	1,633	1,301	314	399	223
		1,147	355	240	187		1,130	222	357	211
1937	2,000	1,506	452	314	220	2,123	1,431	284	437	294
1938	1,843	1,445	430	335	165	2,082	1,363	253	454	337
1939	1,889	1,477	418	369	179	2,499	1,701	327	620	414
1940	1,328	1,162	112	491	54	2,004	1,455	115	769	276
1941	1,345	1,250	21	558	13	1,674	1,416	19	870	128
1942	1,319	1,196	28	530	25	1,780	1,404	7	808	73
1943	1,172	1,098	2	538	0·6	1,814	1,507	14	894	48
1944	853	750	6	345	2	1,677	1,324	9	798	44

	Total exports	Exports to:				Total imports	Imports from:			
		Europe	*of which:*		USA		Europe	*of which:*		USA
			UK	Germany				UK	Germany	
					Skr mn					
1945	1,758	1,271	278	. . .	233	1,084	605	57	88	176
1946	2,547	1,819	390	19	185	3,386	1,750	340	38	801
1947	3,240	2,174	491	21	349	5,220	2,533	444	110	1,640
1948	3,979	2,845	671	147	292	4,945	3,149	860	103	692
1949	4,250	3,173	728	316	247	4,333	2,890	747	282	416
1950	5,707	4,174	812	708	356	6,102	4,072	1,215	649	524
					Skr bn					
1951	9·23	6·66	1·75	0·93	0·48	9·18	6·12	1·49	1·22	0·86
1952	8·13	6·19	1·35	0·96	0·47	8·95	6·09	1·28	1·59	0·86
1953	7·66	5·72	1·45	0·88	0·52	8·16	5·73	1·34	1·49	0·66
1954	8·20	6·31	1·52	1·01	0·38	9·19	6·69	1·46	1·87	0·73
1955	8·93	7·01	1·75	1·18	0·44	10·34	7·36	1·41	2·26	1·01
1956	10·07	7·70	1·79	1·38	0·52	11·43	8·08	1·58	2·52	1·17
1957	11·06	8·48	1·98	1·57	0·53	12·57	8·73	1·74	2·77	1·61
1958	10·80	8·08	1·76	1·54	0·63	12·25	8·83	1·72	2·86	1·30
1959	11·42	8·56	1·71	1·72	0·91	12·49	9·05	1·72	2·84	1·32
1960	13·27	10·23	2·12	2·02	0·85	15·01	10·69	1·95	3·21	1·89
1961	14·20	11·39	2·12	2·23	0·71	15·15	11·22	2·14	3·36	1·72
1962	15·13	12·06	2·00	2·31	0·85	16·15	12·27	2·32	3·56	1·64
1963	16·57	13·26	2·24	2·34	0·92	17·55	13·25	2·62	3·77	1·77
1964	19·01	15·42	2·65	2·73	1·04	19·95	14·98	3·01	4·29	2·00
1965	20·54	16·65	2·72	2·97	1·24	22·64	17·16	3·33	4·88	2·15
1966	22·07	17·55	2·80	2·84	1·52	23·70	18·06	3·65	4·77	2·22
1967	23·42	18·36	3·12	2·58	1·71	24·32	18·62	3·57	4·69	2·25
1968	25·55	20·04	3·78	2·96	1·97	26·52	20·08	3·60	4·96	2·45
1969	29·46	23·23	3·84	3·46	1·85	30·57	23·80	4·22	5·81	2·62
1970	35·15	28·19	4·40	4·14	2·10	36·25	28·25	5·00	6·86	3·16
1971	39·22	30·49	5·17	4·30	2·49	36·19	28·27	5·10	6·85	2·88
1972	41·75	32·76	6·14	4·48	2·94	38·62	30·69	5·02	7·27	2·76
1973	53·15	42·33	7·86	5·39	3·22	46·34	37·17	5·73	9·15	3·06
1974	70·51	55·40	9·33	6·94	3·74	69·95	54·89	7·78	13·16	4·59
1975	72·01	55·10	7·85	7·20	3·76	74·87	58·14	8·18	14·35	4·89
1976	80·20	62·27	9·03	7·92	3·68	83·23	62·70	8·76	15·68	5·60
1977	85·68	65·88	9·35	8·66	4·60	90·25	66·92	9·65	16·88	6·44
1978	98·21	73·31	10·64	10·78	6·20	92·72	68·95	10·33	17·11	6·78
1979	118·15	89·33	13·63	13·33	7·02	122·95	92·20	14·90	21·25	9·01
1980	131·00	100·00	13·04	16·10	7·02	141·64	101·39	16·73	23·78	10·33
1981	144·88	105·52	14·46	16·37	8·88	146·04	104·39	17·48	23·68	11·81
1982	168·13	122·86	16·87	17·61	11·96	173·93	129·20	21·33	30·08	14·68
1983	210·52	152·93	22·86	23·92	18·55	200·37	155·27	27·75	34·32	16·70
1984	242·49	171·31	24·81	28·13	27·50	217·88	170·22	29·74	38·41	17·67
1985	260·48	185·80	25·77	29·90	30·23	244·65	189·30	33·16	43·86	20·51
1986	265·10	195·77	27·67	30·66	29·87	232·61	180·76	24·20	47·73	18·24
1987	281·43	210·01	28·67	33·35	30·07	257·41	201·47	23·52	56·18	17·78

Sources

(For sources used in specific tables, see Notes.)

1 *Historisk Statistik for Sverige*, Central Bureau of Statistics, Stockholm, 1960.
2 Johansson, Osten, *The Gross Domestic Product of Sweden and its Composition, 1861–1955*, Stockholm Economic Studies, New Series VIII, Stockholm, 1967.
3 Krantz, O. and Nilsson, Carl-Axel, *Swedish National Product, 1861–1970, New Aspects on Methods and Measurement*, Liber Läromedel, Lund, 1975.
4 League of Nations, *International Statistical Year Book, 1926*, Geneva, 1927.
5 Mitchell, B.R., *European Historical Statistics, 1750–1975*, 2nd rev. edn., Macmillan, London, 1980.
6 Organisation for Economic Cooperation and Development (OECD), *Labour Force Statistics*, annual, Paris.
7 OECD, *National Accounts, 1950–1979*, Vol. 1, Paris, 1981.
8 OECD, *National Accounts, 1960–1987*, Vol. 1, Paris, 1989.
9 *Statistisk Årsbok*, annual, Central Bureau of Statistics, Stockholm.
10 United Nations, *Monthly Bulletin of Statistics*, New York.
11 United Nations, *Statistical Year Book*, New York.
12 *Year Book of Education Statistics*, National Central Bureau of Statistics, Stockholm.
13 *Year Book of Labour Statistics*, International Labour Office, Geneva.

Notes

Table S.1 Gross domestic product at current prices

Sources: **2, 7, 8**

OECD data have been used from 1950. Figures are on the present system of national accounts from 1950.

For the period 1885–1949, estimates published in **2** have been used. Krantz and Nilsson also published estimates of the Swedish national product in 1975 (see **3**) but their estimates were not quite so detailed as those published in **2**. For the most part, the two sets of estimates agreed in the early years although there were some differences.

Table S.2 Gross domestic product at constant prices

Sources: **2, 7, 8**

OECD data have been used from 1950. Figures are on the present system of national accounts. Consumers' expenditure and government current expenditure for 1986 and 1987 estimated by OECD Secretariat.

For the period 1885–1949, estimates published in **2** at constant (1913) prices have been roughly converted to 1980 prices by linking the two series at 1950. Each category of expenditure has been re-referenced separately for this period; this means that the totals for gross domestic product may not equal the sum of the components. See also note in Table S.1 about estimates by Krantz and Nilsson.

Table S.3 Industrial production

Sources: **1, 5, 9, 10**

Industrial production: excludes public utilities. Figures given in **5** have been linked to provide a continuous series from 1885.

Coal: no further data available on coal output from 1979.

Cars and commercial vehicles: figures refer to deliveries of cars from 1980. Figures for 1940–45 are for passenger cars only.

Table S.4 Prices and income

Sources: **1, 7, 8, 9**

Consumer prices: The 'All items' index includes taxes and social benefits. Current index based on 1988 expenditure patterns.

Wholesale price index: from 1968 this is the producer price index for mining, quarrying and manufacturing. Before this date it is a general price index for home produced goods.

Export and import prices: unit value index numbers.

Compensation of employees: OECD data have been used from 1950. Figures include all payments by resident producers of wages and salaries to their employees, in kind and in cash, and of contributions, paid or imputed, to social security and pension schemes on behalf of their employees.

For the period 1943–50 (first line), estimates in **1** have been used.

National income: OECD data have been used from 1950. National income is gross national product (gross domestic product plus net factor income from the rest of the world) minus consumption of fixed capital (depreciation).

Table S.5   Population

Sources: **1, 5, 6,**

Total population: OECD data have been used from 1950. Estimates are for mid-year.

For 1885–1949, estimates are for population at December 31 each year.

Age distribution: figures are for census years up to 1950.

Births: figures are for live births.

Table S.6   Education

Sources: **1, 4, 5, 9, 12**

Compulsory schooling starts at the age of 7; the minimum school leaving age is now 16 years (previously 14 and 15).

Elementary: pupils at comprehensive schools in the age range 7–15 years. Before the change to the comprehensive or integrated system, these figures refer to pupils at *grundskolan* and *folkskolan*.

For the years 1885–1951, figures are for pupils at what were called primary schools. Dates of returns vary but currently figures are for September 15 each year.

Secondary and post-secondary: figures currently refer to pupils in integrated upper secondary schools in September each year.

For 1946–70, post-secondary pupils are those at schools other than gymnasium, including vocational training of all kinds, and people's colleges. Because of the complexity of the data, these figures are incomplete.

For 1889–1945, figures refer to pupils at gymnasium.

Higher education: from 1967 the figures are for registered students at universities; earlier data were for the number of students enrolled. The basis of counting was changed in 1961. Figures include students at universities and colleges although the coverage has varied over the period. Undergraduate education underwent some changes in 1977 which widened the concept of higher education and amended the regulations concerning qualifications and selection; see **12**, 1980.

In 1937, the method of counting was changed at the University of Uppsala, two figures given for this year.

Table S.7   Labour market: employment

Sources: **2, 6**

OECD data have been used from 1950 in so far as data were available. Currently, the total labour force excludes conscript servicemen but includes certain military personnel. Figures are annual averages of the monthly labour force surveys.

For the years 1950–64 armed forces were included in the total labour force and the figures are averages of labour force surveys taken in February, May, August and November (no survey in February 1961). OECD (OEEC) figures are incomplete for 1950–61.

For 1885–1950, estimates are taken from **2**. Total labour force excludes building and construction for the years 1885–1930 (first line) and commerce, hotels and restaurants, banking, insurance and domestic service from 1885 to 1910 (first line).

Table S.8   Labour market: other indicators

Sources: **1, 4, 11, 13**

Average hours worked: average hours actually worked per week in manufacturing. Up to 1946, figures include the mining industry and relate to November each year.

Average earnings: average hourly earnings in manufacturing, adults only, in the second quarter each year including holidays, sick pay and payments in kind.

For the period 1929–49 the figures are for males only. For 1929–44 they include mining, construction, commerce and transport. For 1913–29 (first line) the figures refer to average earnings per day in manufacturing, mining, construction, commerce and transport.

Unemployment: OECD data have been used from 1950. Data are taken from **4** and **11** before 1950. Agricultural workers are excluded up to 1939.

For 1920–28 the figures refer to trade unionists only, and are the average of end-June and end-December figures for these years. The percentage figure is currently the ratio of the unemployed to the total labour force.

Table S.9   Public finance

Sources: **1, 5, 9**

Total receipts: central government only; revenue from all sources. Calendar years up to 1922; fiscal years ending June 30 of year shown from 1924. The figure for 1923 is for the first half-year. From 1936 (second line) some items excluded from receipts.

Taxes on income and property: includes taxes on individuals and taxes on companies. From 1981, taxes on income, profits and capital gains; taxes on property from 1981 were as follows.

Year ending June 30	Skr mn
1981	2,358
1982	2,741
1983	3,284
1984	4,172

Total expenditure: includes current and capital expenditure up to 1963. Calendar years up to 1922; fiscal years ending June 30 of year shown for 1924–63. The figure for 1923 is for the first half year.

From 1964, the figures are for all levels of government; calendar years; current expenditure only. Debt interest is not included in the total expenditure for these years.

Up to 1964, central government expenditure only.

Social services: includes expenditure on health and welfare which in turn includes pensions, unemployment benefit, child care and care of the elderly and handicapped.

Social security expenditure (a relatively small item) is not included from 1964.

Table S.10 Values of exports and imports by country

Sources: **1, 5, 9**

From 1936 (second line), exports are classified according to country of consumption and imports according to country of origin. Before this date, they are classified according to the country from which goods were bought or sold.

1898–1901 Statistics for exports to Norway are incomplete in this period.

1894 A revaluation of exports in this year revealed over-valuation in earlier years.

From 1948 figures for Germany are for the Federal Republic of Germany.

Part IV

Analytical tables and charts

Growth triangles; nine countries, 1950–87

Notes

The tables and charts in this section bring together some of the data from the tables in Parts II and III so that an idea of comparative movements in different countries can be obtained. The tables should be used in conjunction with the country tables, as the data are subject to the qualifications pointed out in the notes to the tables.

Some additional comparative data not derived from the tables in Parts II and III are also given.

TABLES AND CHARTS

CONTENTS

Table IV.1 Rates of growth of total output,[a] nine countries, 1885–1987

	UK	USA	Australia	Canada	France	Germany	Italy	Japan	Sweden
					Annual averages, %				
1885–1900	2·04	4·08[b]	1·64	2·80[e]	1·74	3·23	1·11	3·10	2·87
1900–13	1·67	3·91	3·73	5·21	1·70	2·93	2·54	2·47	3·65
1920–29	1·73	3·69[c]	2·04	3·65	4·77	4·09[f]	2·34	3·36	2·60
1929–38	1·86	0·10[d]	1·53	−0·23	−0·5	2·65	1·67	4·59	2·57
1950–60	2·70	3·25	3·85	4·51	4·46	7·67	5·39[g]	8·45	3·34
1960–73	3·12	3·84	5·16	5·30	5·31	4·28	5·16	9·20	4·03
1973–87	1·64	2·41	2·76	3·44	2·12	1·82	2·42	3·67	1·76
1885–1938	1·37	2·93[b]	1·97	2·76[e]	1·27	2·27	1·81	3·37	2·82
1950–87	2·45	3·14	3·90	4·36	3·86	4·34	4·15[g]	6·89	3·00

a Measured from the expenditure side.   b 1889–1900; 1889–1939.   c 1920–28.   d 1929–39.   e 1890–1900; 1890–1938.
f 1925–29.   g 1951–60; 1951–87.
Sources Table 2 for each country. For the UK the average estimate has been used from 1950. For France and Japan, where the components of gross domestic product are not available before 1930 or 1938, the source used is Angus Maddison, *Phases of Capitalist Development*, Oxford University Press, 1982.

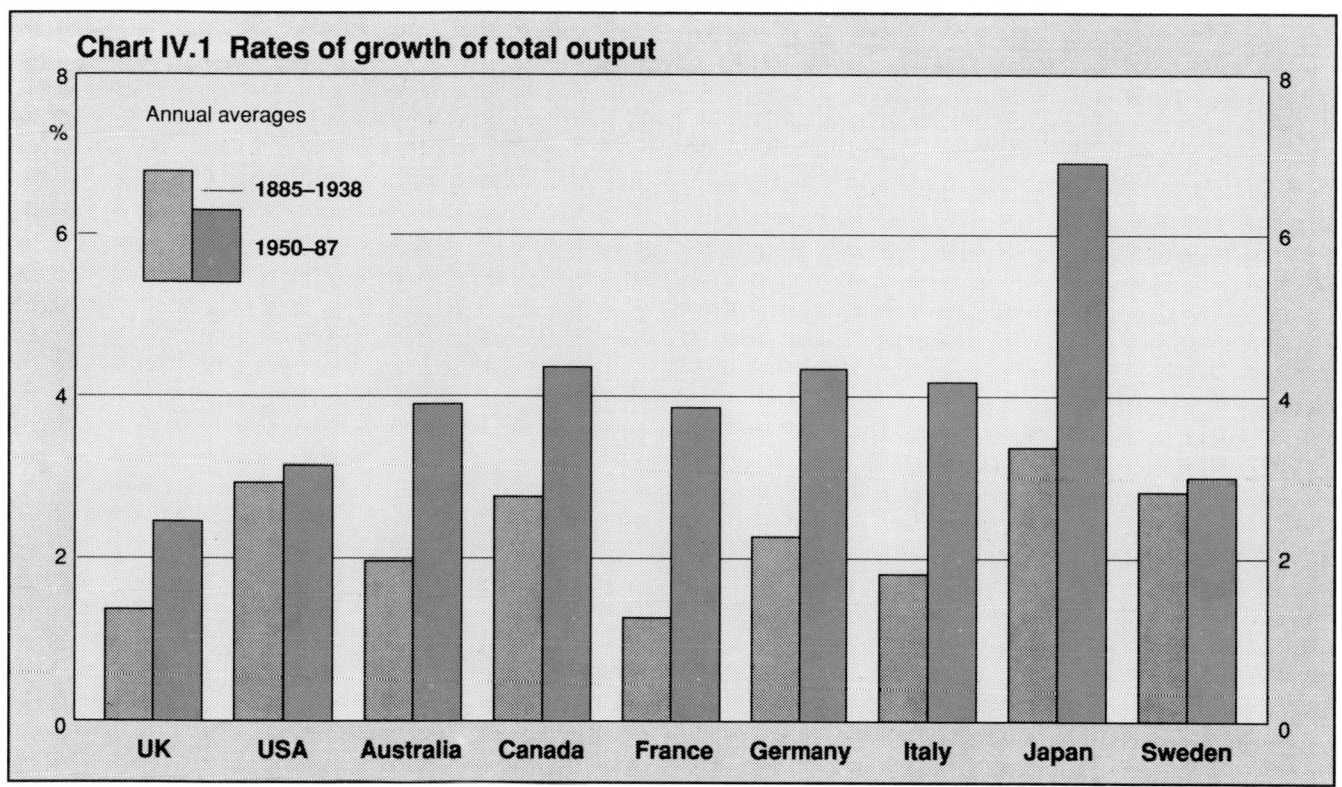

Chart IV.1 Rates of growth of total output

Annual averages
— 1885–1938
  1950–87

See Notes to Table IV.1 above.

Table IV.2　Rates of growth of total productivity,[a] nine countries, 1885–1986

	UK	USA	Australia	Canada	France	Germany	Italy	Japan	Sweden
	Annual averages, %								
1885–1900	0·60	2·24[c]	−0·83[d]	1·71[d]	2·02[d]	2·42[d]	1·20[d]	1·90[g]	2·05
1900–13	0·81	1·68	1·02	2·71	1·83	1·42	2·37	...	2·03
1920–29	1·98	2·76	0·70	1·48[e]	...	...	...	...	1·89
1929–38	0·79	1·31	−0·19	−0·85	2·83	2·34	2·97	3·42	0·63
1950–60	2·05	2·68	2·30	2·70	4·83[f]	5·25	4·33[g]	6·50	1·70
1960–70	2·39	2·68	2·58	2·19	4·59	4·33	5·95	8·60	3·81
1970–80	1·31	1·17	1·61	1·45	3·09	2·81	2·53	3·70	1·00
1980–86	2·66[b]	1·53[b]	1·43	1·45	1·87	1·81	1·54	2·64	1·53
1885–1938	0·72	1·94[c]	0·76[d]	1·48[d]	2·23[d]	1·80[d]	2·09[d]	2·68[g]	1·57
1950–86	2·07[b]	2·05[b]	2·04	2·00	3·66[f]	3·74	3·75[f]	5·66	2·00

a　Output per person employed in the whole economy in all countries except the USA where output per man hour is used. Output in the USA measurement refers to the business sector from 1950 and to the 'gross private domestic product' before then.
b　1980–87; 1950–87.　c　1889–1900; 1889–1938.　d　1890–1900; 1890–1938.　e　1921–29.　f　1954–60; 1954–86.
g　1890–1913; 1890–1938.
Sources Tables UK.12 and US.12; Tables 2 and 7 for other countries. Where figures not given in tables, data for pre-war period derived from Maddison, *op. cit.* Long-run growth rate (1890–1938) for Australia, Canada, France, Germany, Italy and Japan also derived from Maddison.

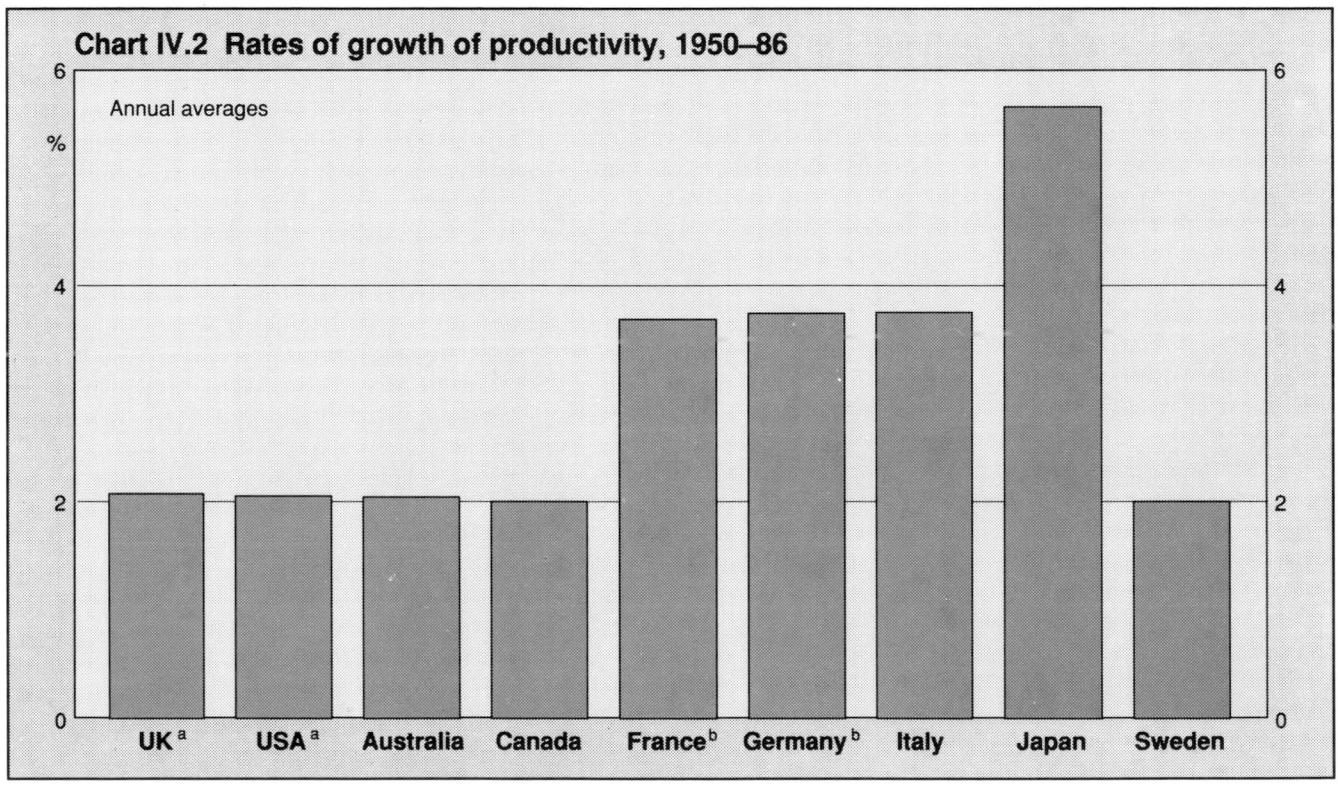

Chart IV.2　Rates of growth of productivity, 1950–86

a　1950–87.　b　1954–86.

Table IV.3   Gross domestic product per head, nine countries, selected periods, 1885–1986

	UK	USA	Australia	Canada	France	Germany	Italy	Japan	Sweden
	£ (1985)	$(1982)	A$ (1980)	C$ (1980)	Fr (1980)	DM (1980)	L'000 (1980)	¥ '000 (1980)	Skr (1980)
1885	1,694	2,681[a]	3,361	2,061[b]	8,798[c]	3,648	1,199	146	5,397
1900	2,009	3,410	2,939	2,457	10,694[c]	4,937	1,305[e]	203	7,565
1913	2,230	4,437	3,730	3,137	12,455[c]	6,044	1,532[e]	238	11,062
1920	2,077	4,678	3,448	3,190	11,011[c]	6,089[d]	1,647[e]	289	12,005
1938	2,603	5,474	3,694	3,330	14,746[c]	8,280	1,947[e]	464	17,865
1950	2,994	7,904	4,944	5,527	18,059	7,076	2,017	291	27,969
1970	4,765	11,781	8,117	9,244	39,963	18,678	5,438	1,471	53,414
1986	6,425	15,303	10,330	14,284	55,689	26,249	7,721	2,449	69,313

a   1889.   b   1890.   c   1886, 1901, 1911, 1921, 1936.   d   1925.   e   1901, 1911, 1921,1936.
Sources Tables UK.2 and UK.9; US.2 and US.9; Tables 2 and 5 for other countries. France and Japan from 1885–1920 derived from Maddison, *op. cit.*

Table IV.4 Gross domestic product per head, nine countries, at current prices and current purchasing power parities, 1970–86

	UK	USA	Australia	Canada	France	Germany	Italy	Japan	Sweden
					US$				
1970	3,273	4,922	3,465	3,969	3,215	3,413	3,045	2,811	3,855
1971	3,514	5,275	3,786	4,356	3,528	3,651	3,231	3,048	4,062
1972	3,743	5,735	4,043	4,762	3,871	3,953	3,461	3,375	4,330
1973	4,286	6,347	4,479	5,406	4,314	4,391	3,922	3,829	4,791
1974	4,631	6,810	4,894	6,067	4,826	4,797	4,427	4,070	5,378
1975	5,053	7,334	5,462	6,737	5,287	5,204	4,660	4,531	6,035
1976	5,570	8,094	5,934	7,497	5,883	5,855	5,216	4,986	6,454
1977	6,009	8,933	6,320	8,191	6,440	6,445	5,668	5,548	6,753
1978	6,676	9,969	6,881	9,092	7,107	7,120	6,198	6,197	7,348
1979	7,413	10,952	7,748	10,184	7,955	8,069	7,058	7,038	8,289
1980	7,905	11,804	8,486	11,131	8,773	8,891	7,982	7,954	9,173
1981	8,422	13,077	9,296	12,306	9,526	9,594	8,700	8,852	9,855
1982	9,061	13,424	9,717	12,516	10,331	10,144	9,252	9,615	10,560
1983	9,678	14,282	9,978	13,205	10,694	10,669	9,568	10,172	11,167
1984	10,224	15,705	10,979	14,427	11,203	11,418	10,247	11,012	12,031
1985	10,913	16,548	11,765	15,366	11,701	12,114	10,833	11,798	12,655
1986	11,498	17,324	12,084	16,105	12,218	12,741	11,406	12,339	13,111

Source OECD National Accounts, 1988.

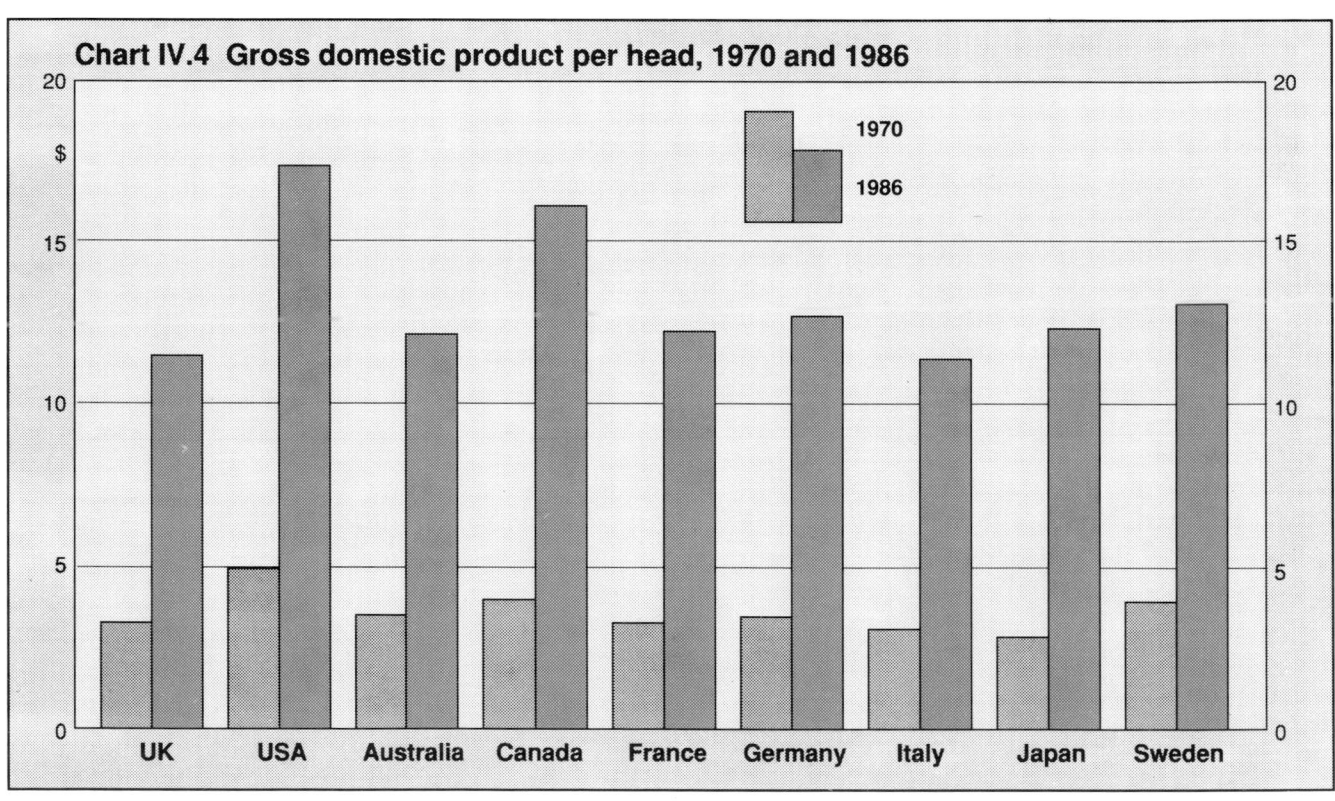

Chart IV.4 Gross domestic product per head, 1970 and 1986

Table IV.5 Output per head, selected commodities, nine countries, selected periods, 1885–1986

	UK	USA	Australia	Canada	France	Germany	Italy	Japan	Sweden
Coal (tons)									
1885	4·50	1·05[b]	1·17	0·59[c]	0·53[d]	1·58	—	0·03	0·04
1900	5·56	2·53	1·72	0·98	0·84[e]	2·67	0·01[e]	0·17	0·05
1913	6·40	4·47	2·62	1·67	1·00[f]	4·14	0·02[f]	0·42	0·06
1920	5·33	4·84	2·46	1·80	0·75[g]	4·37[i]	0·03[g]	0·52	0·07
1938	4·86	2·74	2·26	1·17	1·12[h]	5·56	0·04[h]	0·69	0·07
1950	4·35	3·08	2·97	1·27	1·26	3·93	0·04	0·46	0·04
1970	2·60	2·67	5·85	0·71	0·75	3·70	0·03	0·38	—
1986	1·84	3·28	10·61	1·19	0·27	3·30	0·03	0·13	—
Crude steel (tons)									
1885	0·05	0·03[b]	—	—	0·02[d]	0·03	—	—	0.02
1900	0·12	0·13	—	0·005	0·04[e]	0·12	—	—	0·06
1913	0·17	0·32	—	0·11	0·10[f]	0·26	0·02[f]	—	0·10
1920	0·21	0·39	0·05	0·13	0·08[g]	0·20[i]	0·02[g]	0·01	0·07
1938	0·22	0·37	0·17	0·11	0·16[h]	0·33	0·05[h]	0·09	0·15
1950	0·33	0·58	0·16	0·22	0·21	0·25	0·05	0·06	0·20
1970	0·50	0·58	0·55	0·53	0·47	0·74	0·33	0·90	0·67
1986	0·26	0·30	0·43	0·55	0·32	0·61	0·40	0·81	0·56
Cars and commercial vehicles[a]									
1913	0·75	4·8	—		1·0[f]	0·27	—	—	—
1920	—	17·9	—	10·5	1·4[g]	0·79[i]	—	—	—
1938	9·4	22·1	12·0	13·3	5·0[h]	4·9	1·2[h]	—	1·1
1950	15·5	43·8	7·1	27·4	8·5	6·3	2·8	—	2·4
1970	37·7	31·9	38·2	54·4	54·0	63·1	35·0	51·0	37·7
1986	21·1	32·2	21·3	72·1	57·7	72·9	32·2	100·8	55·7

a   Car production per '000 of population.   b   1889.   c   1890.   d   1886.   e   1901.   f   1911.   g   1921.   h   1936.   i   1925.
Sources Tables UK.4 and UK.9 and US.4 and US.9; Tables 3 and 5 for other countries.

Table IV.6 Expenditure per head, selected items, UK and USA, selected periods, 1885–1986

	Food		Clothing & footwear		Cars & motorcycles		Other consumer durables	
	UK	USA	UK	USA	UK	USA	UK	USA
	£ (1985)	$ (1982)	£ (1985)	$ (1982)	£ (1985)	$ (1982)	£ (1985)	$ (1982)
1885	...	650·8[a]	...	169·3	—	—	...	139.3[c]
1900	325·4	813·4[a]	92·8	206·3	—	...	43·7[b]	176·1[c]
1910	314·1	937·2[a]	87·8	244·6	1·7	...	41·7[b]	205·6[c]
1920	333·1	1,002·8[a]	97·9	235·7	5·7	...	33·4	227·2[c]
1930	411·4	923·6	97·4	267·3	11·3	110·5	52·3	259·1
1938	424·9	1,072·4	103·0	253·5	17·4	92·5	65·3	234·2
1950	498·8	1,290·9	106·5	290·9	8·0	271·2	57·2	529·9
1960	505·9	1,414·0	131·6	291·6	49·4	272·3	126·4	542·3
1970	519·4	1,630·9	161·1	351·1	91·4	358·4	170·4	792·3
1980	529·7	1,742·7	211·3	506·6	135·3	458·1	273·7	1,085·2
1986	547·0	1,868·1	280·1	653·7	189·8	731·7	387·9	1,596·9

a   Perishables – see notes to Table US.7.
b   Including other non-durable items – see notes to Table UK.7.
c   Including cars, etc.
Sources Tables UK.7, UK.9, US.7, US.9.

***Table* IV.7** Distribution of employment, UK, USA and Japan, selected periods, 1900–86

	% employment in:								
	Agriculture			Manufacturing			Distribution and services[e]		
	UK[a]	USA[b]	Japan	UK[a]	USA[b]	Japan[c]	UK[a]	USA[b]	Japan[d]
1900	13	41	70	33	20	12	36	17	18
1910	12	33	63	33	23	15	36	19	22
1920	9	27	55	35	27	17	32	20	29
1930	8	23	50	32	21	17	39	23	33
1950	3	11	44	37	26	17	31	28	23
1960	3	8	51	35	26	21	35	33	36
1970	2	4	30	34	25	27	40	38	40
1980	1	3	17	27	20	25	48	44	48
1986	1	3	8	21	17	25	53	48	51

a   Figures are for 1901 and 1911 and after 1930 refer to employees only; this affects the percentage particularly in agriculture and distribution and services.
b   US figures for agriculture include the self-employed, working proprietors, etc; other figures are for employees.
c   Before 1950, figures include mining and quarrying and public utilities.
d   Before 1950, construction and transport and communication included.
e   Distribution and services excludes transport and communication but includes (for the UK) public administration.
Sources Tables UK.11, US.11, J.7.

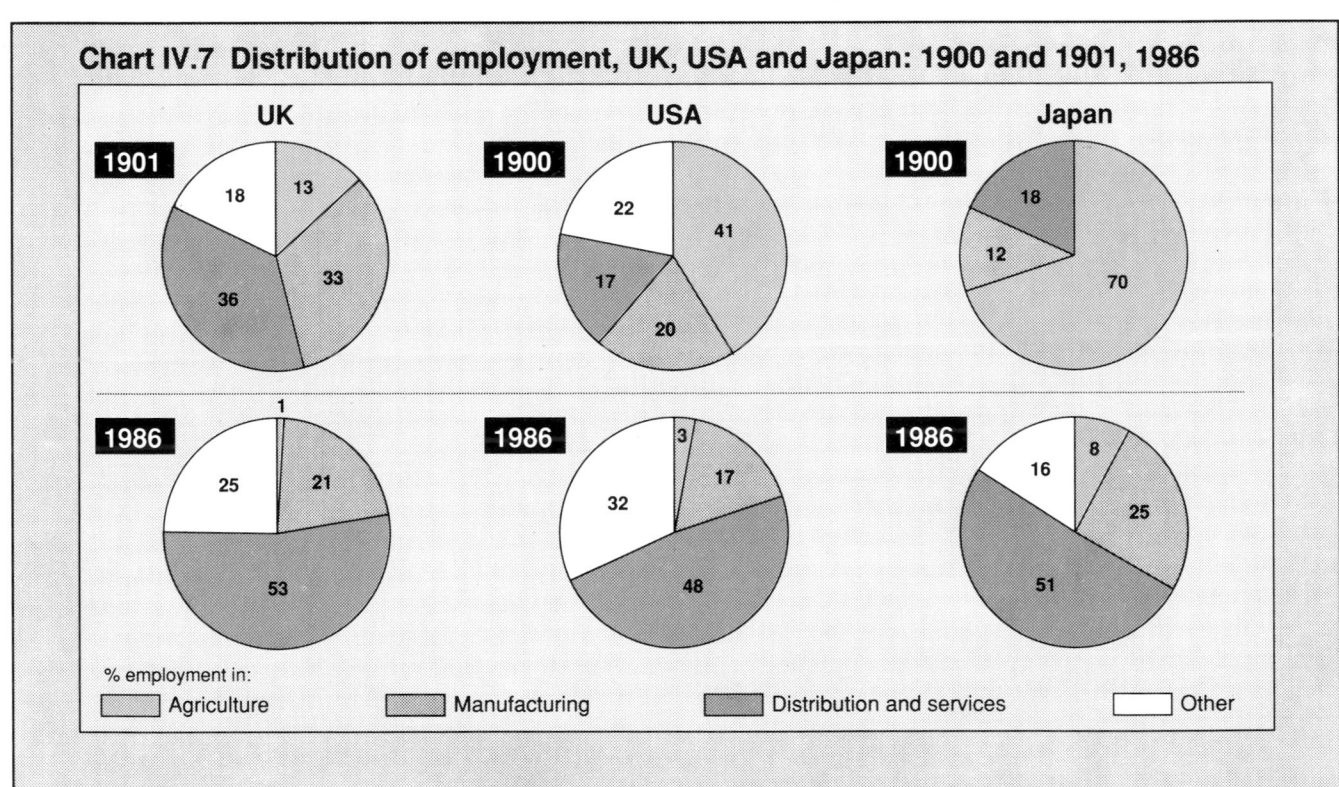

Chart IV.7 Distribution of employment, UK, USA and Japan: 1900 and 1901, 1986

See Notes to Table IV.7 above.

308

***Table* IV.8** Distribution of employment, France, Germany and Italy, selected periods, 1950–1986

	% employment in:								
	Agriculture			Manufacturing[b]			Distribution and services		
	France[a]	Germany	Italy[a]	France[a]	Germany	Italy[a]	France[a]	Germany	Italy[a]
1950	28	25	43	27	43	30	30	32	26
1960	22	16	33	28	39	37	33	32	30
1970	14	9	20	27	39	39	41	36	40
1980	9	6	14	26	34	38	49	44	48
1986	7	5	11	23	32	33	55	48	56

a   First figure is for 1954.
b   Includes mining and quarrying, construction and public utilities in Italy for all periods and in Germany for 1950. The figure shown against 1960 for Germany is for 1961 and refers to manufacturing only.
c   Includes transport and communication for Italy for all periods and for Germany for 1950.
Sources Tables F.7, G.7, It.7.

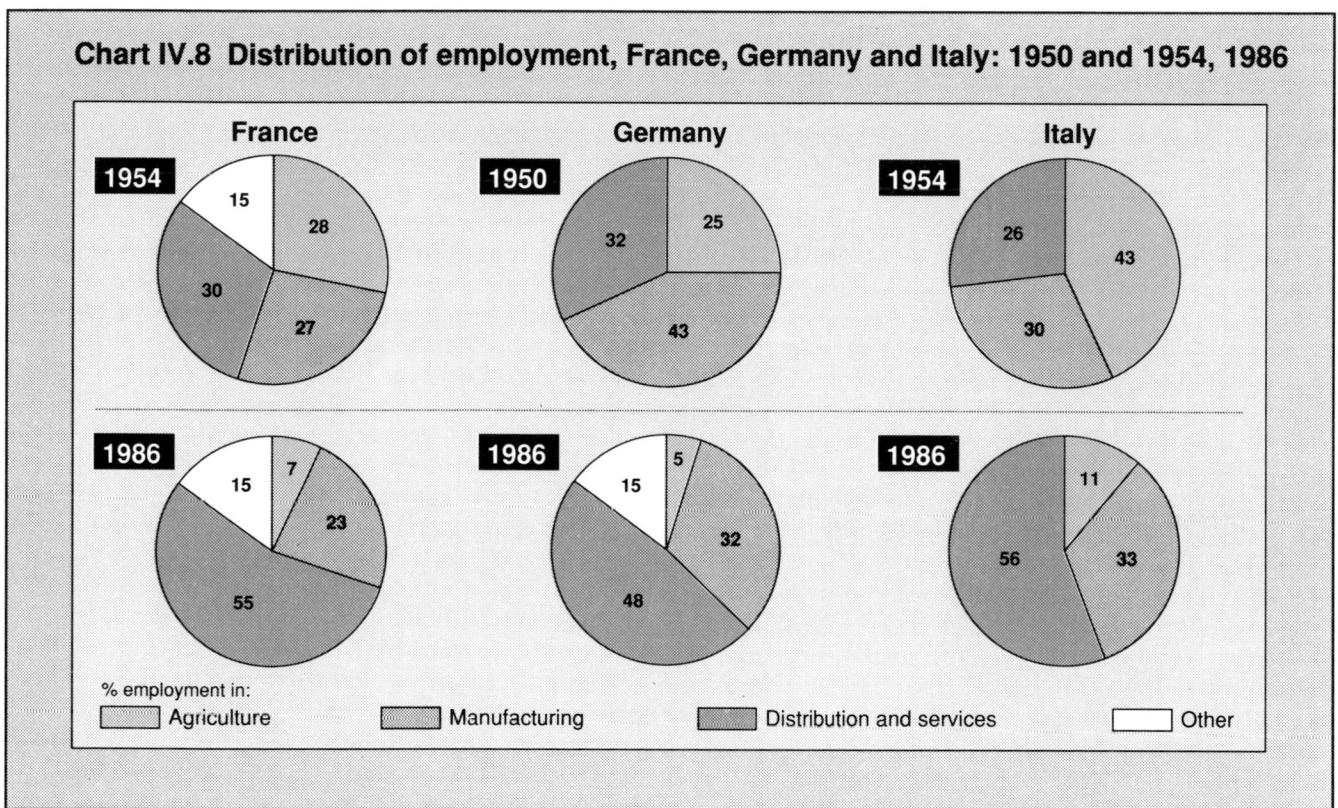

Chart IV.8 Distribution of employment, France, Germany and Italy: 1950 and 1954, 1986

See Notes to Table IV.8 above.

Table IV.9 Distribution of employment, Australia, Canada and Sweden, selected periods, 1885–1986

	% employment in:								
	Agriculture			Manufacturing			Distribution and services		
	Australia	Canada	Sweden	Australia	Canada	Sweden	Australia	Canada	Sweden
1885	. . .	. . .	75	. . .	. . .	17	. . .	. . .	. . .
1900	. . .	. . .	65	. . .	. . .	26	. . .	. . .	. . .
1910	25	. . .	51	21	. . .	26	32	. . .	19
1920	24	37[a]	44	22	18[a]	29	34	. . .	22
1930	26	34	38	18	19	29	38	. . .	26
1950	14	23	21	29	26	26	36	34	29
1960	11	13	14[b]	28	25	32[b]	40	45	33[b]
1970	8	8	8	26[c]	22	28	48	54	47
1980	6	5	6	20	20	24	55	59	55
1986	6	5	4	16	17	23	59	63	58

a   1921.
b   1961.
c   Including public utilities.
Sources Tables A.7, C.7, S.7.

Chart IV.9 Distribution of employment, Australia, Canada and Sweden: 1950 and 1986

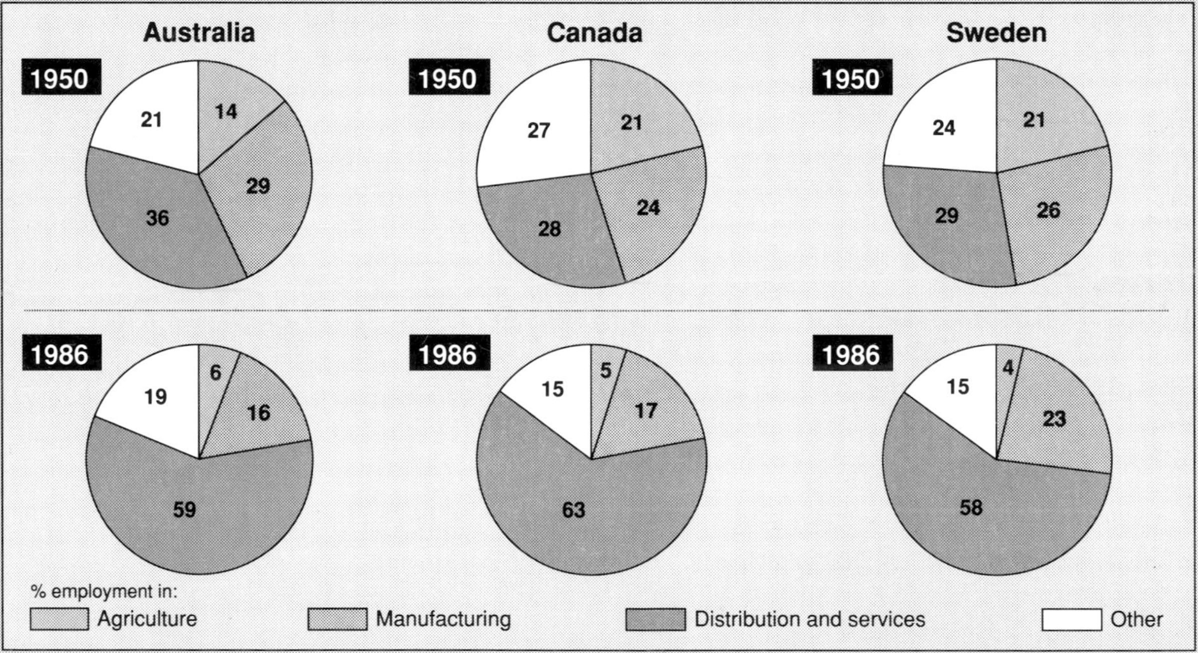

% employment in:
Agriculture   Manufacturing   Distribution and services   Other

See Notes to Table IV.9 above.

Table IV.10 Population trends, nine countries, selected periods, 1885–1986

	UK	USA	Australia	Canada	France	Germany	Italy	Japan	Sweden
Total population growth (1950 = 100)						*1938 = 100*			
1885	71·2	37·2	32·9	33·1	91·1[a]	68·1	60·9[f]	46·0	66·5
1900	81·4	50·0	46 1	38·7	92·0[b]	80·9	69·4[b]	52·7	73·0
1920	86·5	69·9	65·5	62·4	92·7[c]	90·0[e]	81·2[c]	67·3	83·8
1938	93·9	85·2	84·4	81·3	98·4[d]	100·0	91·8[d]	85·3	89 6
						1950 = 100			
1950	100·0	100·0	100·0	100·0	100·0	100·0	100·0	100·0	100·0
1970	110·0	134·7	152·9	155·4	121·3	126·8	112·8	124·7	115·1
1980	111·4	149·5	179·7	175·3	128·8	128·7	120·0	140·7	118·2
1986	112·2	159·7	195·2	186·7	132·4	127·6	121·0	146·2	118·9

% population in different age groups

Under 15 years

	UK	USA	Australia	Canada	France	Germany	Italy	Japan	Sweden
1885	34·8[g]	35·2[h]	. . .	25·3[g]	27·0[a]	33·0[h]	32·2[f]	. . .	33·2[h]
1900	32·5	34·3	35·2[b]	34·5[b]	25·7[b]	32·8	34·4[b]	33·5[i]	32·5
1920	28·2	31·7	31·8[c]	34·3[c]	22·4[c]	23·7[i]	31·1[c]	36·5	29·3
1938	21·9	25·6	27·5[p]	28·7	24·4[d]	21·6[j]	30·7[d]	36·9[m]	20·4[n]
1950	22·4	26·8	26·6	29·7	22·7	21·8	26·7	35·4	23·4
1970	24·1	28·2	28·9	30·3	24·8	23·2	22·9	23·9	20·7
1980	21·0	22·6	25·2	23·0	22·4	18·2	20·4	23·5	19·6
1986	19·0	21·6	23·1	21·2	20·9	15·1[k]	16·8	20·9	18·0

15–64 years

	UK	USA	Australia	Canada	France	Germany	Italy	Japan	Sweden
1885	60·2[g]	59·9[h]	. . .	70·2[g]	65·0[a]	61·9[h]	62·7[f]	. . .	58·9[h]
1900	62·8	61·5	60·3[b]	60·5[b]	65·8[b]	62·3	59·6[b]	61·3[i]	59·1
1920	65·8	63·6	63·6[c]	60·9[c]	68·4[c]	70·5[i]	61·7[c]	58·3	62·4
1938	69·4	67·8	66·1[p]	64·9	65·5[d]	70·6[j]	61·9[d]	58·4[m]	70·2[n]
1950	67·0	64·7	65·3	62·7	65·9	68·9	66·0	59·7	66·3
1970	62·9	61·9	62·8	61·7	62·3	63·6	66·5	69·0	65·1
1980	64·1	66·1	65·1	67·5	63·7	66·3	66·7	67·4	64·1
1986	65·7	66·3	66·5	68·1	65·9	70·0[k]	69·7	68·5	64·5

65 years and over

	UK	USA	Australia	Canada	France	Germany	Italy	Japan	Sweden
1885	5·0[g]	3·8[h]	. . .	4·6[g]	8·0[a]	5·1[h]	5·1[f]	. . .	7·7[h]
1900	4·8	4·1	4·5[b]	5·0[b]	8·4[b]	4·9	6·1[b]	5·2[i]	8·4
1920	6·0	4·6	4·6[c]	4·8[c]	9·2[c]	5·8[i]	7·2[c]	5·2	8·5
1938	8·6	6·5	6·5[p]	6·4	10·0[d]	7·8[j]	7·5[d]	4·7[m]	9·4[n]
1950	10·7	8·1	8·1	7·6	11·4	9·3	8·1	4·9	10·2
1970	13·0	9·8	8·3	8·0	12·9	13·2	10·5	7·1	13·6
1980	14·9	11·3	9·6	9·5	13·9	15·5	12·8	9·1	16·2
1986	15·3	12·1	10·4	10·7	13·2	14·8[k]	13·5	10·6	17·6

a 1886. b 1901. c 1921. d 1936. e 1925. f 1881. g 1891. h 1890. i 1925. j 1939. k 1985. l 1903.
m 1935. n 1940. p 1933.

Notes Germany refers to the German Reich before 1950 and then to the Federal Republic of Germany. UK includes Southern Ireland before 1920.
  Age distribution: figures for Germany are for those under 14 years and 14–64 years for 1900–55; figures for Italy are for those under 14 years and 14–64 years from 1959.

Sources Tables UK.9 and US.9; Table 5 for other countries.

311

Chart IV.10 Age distribution, selected periods

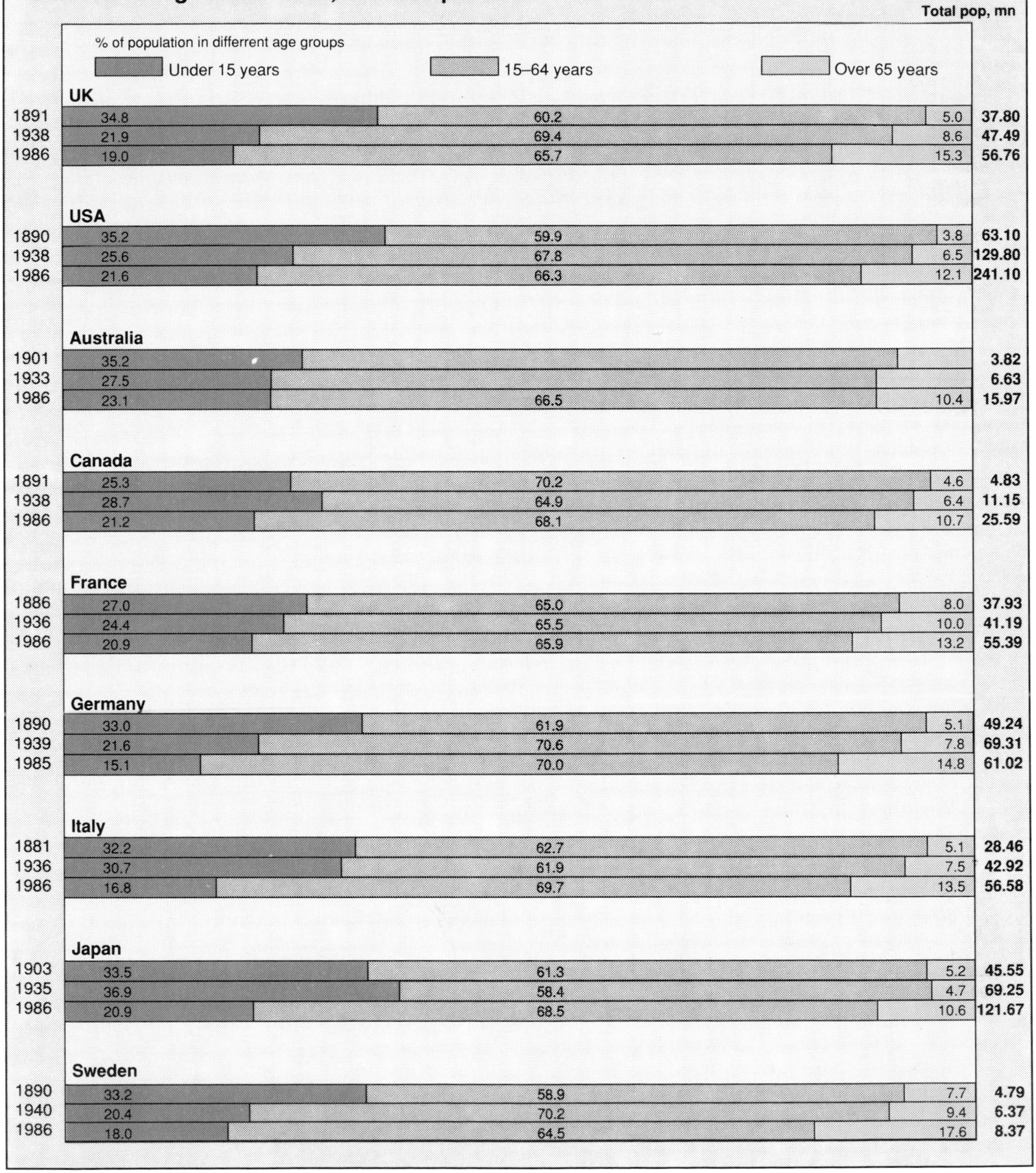

Total pop, mn

% of population in different age groups

| ■ Under 15 years | ▨ 15–64 years | □ Over 65 years |

UK

	Under 15	15–64	Over 65	Total pop, mn
1891	34.8	60.2	5.0	**37.80**
1938	21.9	69.4	8.6	**47.49**
1986	19.0	65.7	15.3	**56.76**

USA

	Under 15	15–64	Over 65	Total pop, mn
1890	35.2	59.9	3.8	**63.10**
1938	25.6	67.8	6.5	**129.80**
1986	21.6	66.3	12.1	**241.10**

Australia

	Under 15	15–64	Over 65	Total pop, mn
1901	35.2			**3.82**
1933	27.5			**6.63**
1986	23.1	66.5	10.4	**15.97**

Canada

	Under 15	15–64	Over 65	Total pop, mn
1891	25.3	70.2	4.6	**4.83**
1938	28.7	64.9	6.4	**11.15**
1986	21.2	68.1	10.7	**25.59**

France

	Under 15	15–64	Over 65	Total pop, mn
1886	27.0	65.0	8.0	**37.93**
1936	24.4	65.5	10.0	**41.19**
1986	20.9	65.9	13.2	**55.39**

Germany

	Under 15	15–64	Over 65	Total pop, mn
1890	33.0	61.9	5.1	**49.24**
1939	21.6	70.6	7.8	**69.31**
1985	15.1	70.0	14.8	**61.02**

Italy

	Under 15	15–64	Over 65	Total pop, mn
1881	32.2	62.7	5.1	**28.46**
1936	30.7	61.9	7.5	**42.92**
1986	16.8	69.7	13.5	**56.58**

Japan

	Under 15	15–64	Over 65	Total pop, mn
1903	33.5	61.3	5.2	**45.55**
1935	36.9	58.4	4.7	**69.25**
1986	20.9	68.5	10.6	**121.67**

Sweden

	Under 15	15–64	Over 65	Total pop, mn
1890	33.2	58.9	7.7	**4.79**
1940	20.4	70.2	9.4	**6.37**
1986	18.0	64.5	17.6	**8.37**

See Notes to Table IV.10.

Table IV.11   Rates of growth of consumer prices, nine countries, 1885–1987

	UK	USA	Australia	Canada	France	Germany	Italy	Japan	Sweden
	Annual averages, %								
1885–1900	0·00	−0·51	−1·75[a]	−0·6[a]	0·00	0·64	0·00	3·44	0·5
1900–13	0·75	1·33	2·44	2·80	0·62	2·03	1·40	2·03	1·0
1920–29	−4·51	−1·73	−1·35	−2·37	5·49	3·25[b]	2·95	−3·96	−5·24
1929–38	−0·64	−2·24	−1·43	−1·84	1·48	−2·28	−0·38	1·01	−0·31
1950–60	3·97	2·07	5·58	2·23	5·72	1·87	2·90	3·95	4·51
1960–73	4·97	3·13	3·48	3·25	4·11	3·21	4·61	5·43	4·56
1973–80	14·79	8·83	11·22	9·35	10·54	4·52	15·71	10·19	9·82
1980–87	6·02	4·59	8·09	6·51	7·35	2·72	10·67	2·03	7·33
1885–1938	1·05	0·84	0·92[a]	1·16[a]	3·76	1·16	3·32	2·52	1·38
1950–87	6·76	4·20	6·38	4·71	6·38	3·01	7·39	5·29	6·07

a   1890–1900; 1890–1938.
b   1924–29.
Sources Tables UK.8 and US.8; Table 4 for other countries. For Canada, Japan and Sweden, before 1920, some data derived from Maddison, _op. cit._

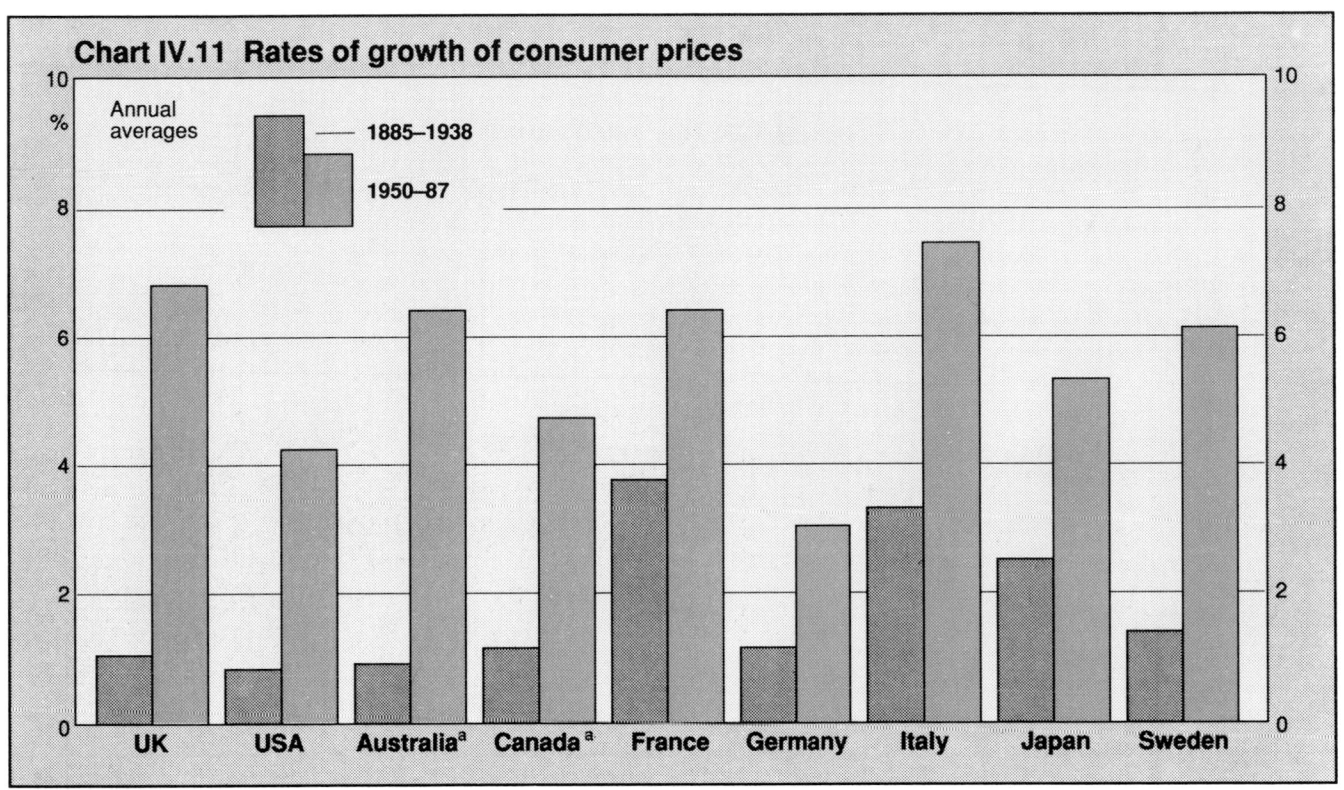

Chart IV.11 Rates of growth of consumer prices

a 1890–1938.

313

***Table* IV.12** **Rates of growth of earnings in manufacturing, nine countries, 1900–1986**

	UK	USA	Australia	Canada	France	Germany	Italy	Japan	Sweden
				Annual averages, %					
1900–13	1·03	...	3·72	1·04[b]	...	...	...	...	...
1920–29	...	−0·55	1·98	0·26	...	...	...	...	...
1929–38	0·00[a]	−1·28	−0·72	0·77	5·33	−2·27	0·61	1·21[c]	1·02
1950–60	6·59	4·32	6·55	5·26	9·43	7·20	4·84	7·57	8·39
1960–73	7·96	4·76	8·75	5·70	9·21	8·64	10·98	12·60	8·13
1973–86	11·49	6·67	11·20	8·32	12·08	5·68	19·81	7·43	9·51
1950–86	8·86	5·32	8·9[d]	6·52	10·31	7·15	12·03	9·34	8·70

a 1924–37.
b 1890–1910.
c 1923–38.
d 1950–85.
Sources Tables UK.12 and US.12; Table 8 for other countries.

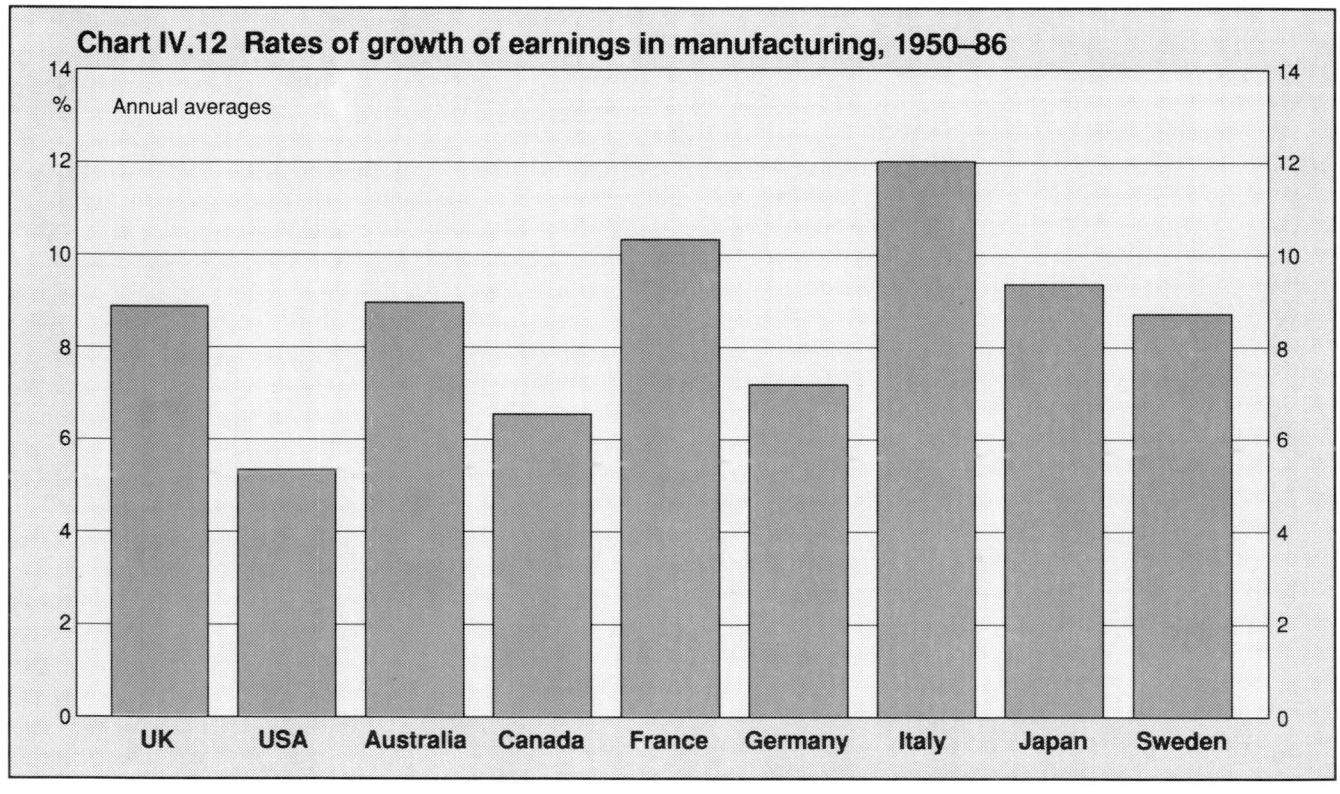

Chart IV.12 Rates of growth of earnings in manufacturing, 1950–86

Table IV.13 Contribution of selected taxes to total revenue, nine countries, selected periods, 1885–1986

	UK	USA	Australia	Canada	France	Germany	Italy	Japan	Sweden
	Annual averages, %								
Taxes on income									
1885	16·9	—	...	—	13·2	...	22·6	0·6[b]	12·5
1900	19·2	—	10·2	1·0	12·7	...	25·7	2·9	5·9
1920	43·1	21·9[a]	36·8	12·2	5·9	...	10·4	15·9	34·4
1938	42·7	15·9	43·8	14·0	14·8	43·4	29·4	29·1	24·7
1950	33·5	52·0	48·2	37·7	17·5	33·2	31·7	42·4	45·5
1970	33·8	43·7	56·2	38·4	28·3	43·7	39·2	59·0	43·8
1980	31·8	44·3	53·7	38·7	33·2	51·5	47·9	44·8	44·8
1986	32·6	39·9	53·6	39·1	32·3	50·1	46·0	55·6	25·9
Customs and excise duties									
1885	50·0	90·6	...	74·1	29·2	...	14·4	3·4	55·7
1900	46·4	91·2	83·7[c]	72·8	28·4	...	12·1	5·7	66·4
1920	23·4	18·3	40·8	55·4	16·9	21·0	3·4	5·5	32·2
1938	41·2	13·2	53·9	18·4[d]	25·5	26·3	5·0	9·0	45·7
1950	31·5	12·5	24·7	16·9	9·5	22·7	0·4	1·4	36·6
1970	24·2	5·9	18·8	5·9	12·6	18·1	2·1	10·9	36·4
1980	24·6	4·0	19·9	4·5	10·5	13·2	0·03	5·1	34·3
1986	27·5	3·3	17·5	4·4	11·2	12·7	—	5·9	41·1

a 1922.   b 1887.   c 1901.   d 1937.

Notes For Sweden, taxes on income include property taxes up to 1980. For other countries, taxes on income include taxes on companies except for Italy.
Sources Tables UK.18 and US.18; Table 9 for other countries.

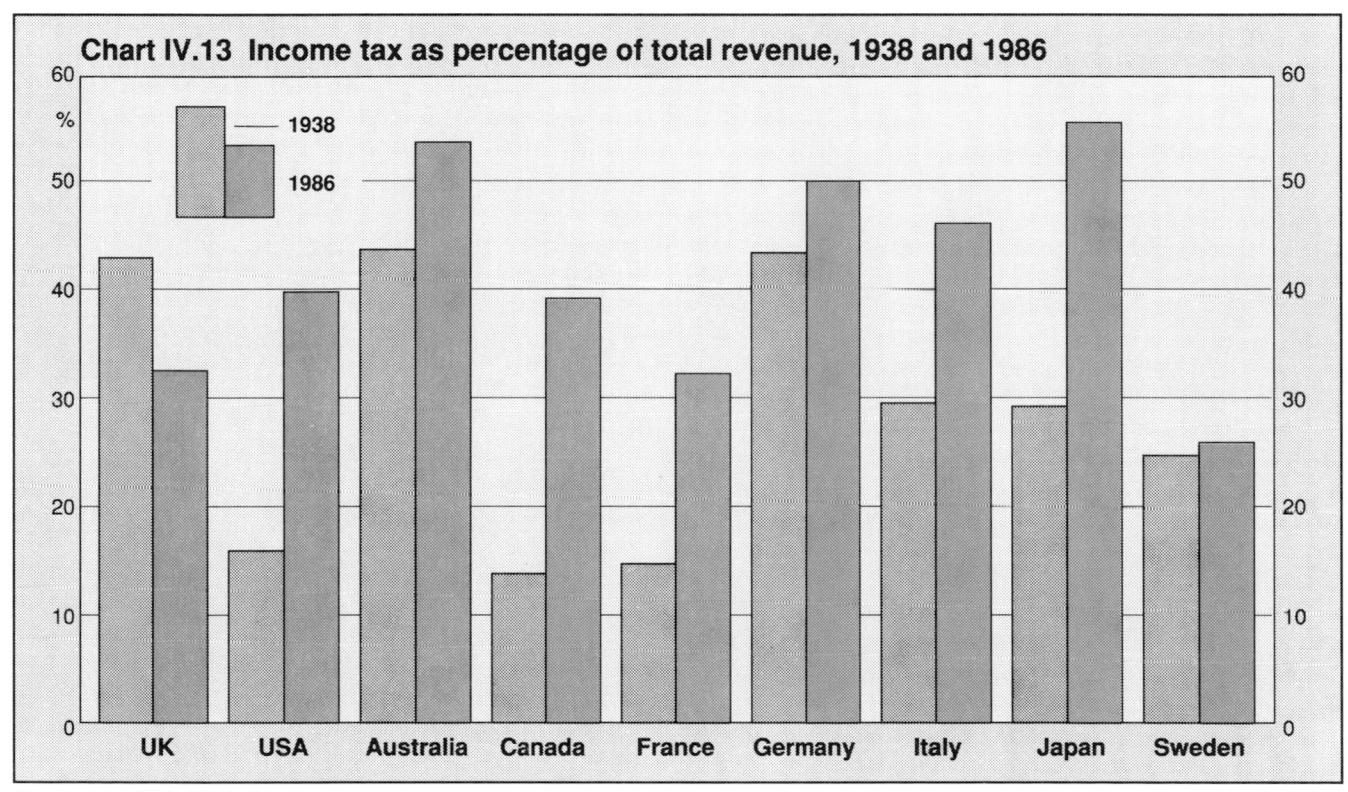

Chart IV.13 Income tax as percentage of total revenue, 1938 and 1986

See Notes to Table IV.13 above.

***Table* IV.14** Distribution of public expenditure, nine countries, selected periods, 1885–1986

	UK	USA	Australia	Canada	France	Germany	Italy	Japan	Sweden
	% share of total expenditure								
Defence									
1885	26·7[a]	...	...	...	17·3	...	21·9	25·4	...
1900	48·0	9·6[b]	...	...	18·0	...	21·5	45·5	45·6[f]
1925	12·5	9·2[c]	...	...	12·0	4·0	28·6	29·1	...
1938	29·8	5·8	...	2·9[d]	16·2[d]	42·7	20·2	35·5	15·4
1950	19·1	17·2	27·3	14·7	17·7	16·7	21·3	2·1	16·8
1970	11·8	24·1	27·6	5·5	16·8	10·1	...	7·2	15·6
1980	11·0	16·0	12·3	3·7	17·4	5·5	4·1	5·2	10·5
1986	11·3	18·6	13·8	4·0[e]	16·1	5·5	3·8	6·2	9·4[h]
Education									
1885	20·9[a]	...	...	...	4·8	...	...	...	...
1900	18·0[a]	15·7[b]	...	...	5·5	...	...	...	15·9[f]
1920	6·1	18·4[c]	...	...	3·0	13·6[g]	2·5	...	...
1938	8·8	15·0	...	10·2[d]	6·3[d]	...	5·0	...	17·5
1950	8·2	13·7	16·0	10·7	6·6	7·5	8·6	2·6	9·4
1970	12·1	17·7	23·1	19·1	20·5	12·6	...	11·8	24·6
1980	12·2	16·6	26·1	13·7	24·4	9·8	11·4	10·6	20·4
1986	12·6	15·2	23·1	12·0	22·7	8·9	8·6	9·1	19·4[h]
Social services									
1885	[a]	...	...	...	...	...	...	...	...
1900	[a]	6·0[b]	...	...	...	...	...	...	10·6[f]
1920	16·4	5·2[c]	...	...	...	33·6[g]	0·6	...	...
1938	23·8	10·8	...	20·6[d]	...	...	0·9	...	24·1
1950	26·9	8·1	14·0	21·0	22·3	27·0	5·4	7·7	25·6
1970	30·3	30·5	14·8	31·9	14·6	20·6	...	14·1	32·3
1980	35·6	39·5	19·8	34·1	19·9	45·7	25·7	18·8	41·2
1986	43·5	36·3	20·6	36·8	18·4	47·0	25·5	18·9	43·9[h]
Total public expenditure as % of GDP									
1885	8·9[a]	...	...	...	...	...	13·2	...	6·2
1900	14·5	2·8	...	...	...	...	12·5	...	6·5
1920	27·2	7·2	...	...	...	...	27·2	...	7·5
1938	28·5	19·7	...	21·7[d]	18·4	37·9	23·2	12·3	9·1
1950	34·5	21·3	5·9	22·0	23·2	28·6	22·5	16·0	17·7
1970	40·5	31·3	10·4	35·5	22·7	29·1	19·7	11·2	21·2
1980	45·1	32·6	15·5	43·0	19·5	50·1	36·6	18·1	29·2
1986	44·5	35·1	17·6	47·2	20·2	47·0	45·1	16·2	27·8

a 1890; education includes social services in 1890 and 1900.
b 1902.
c 1922.
d 1937.
e 1983.
f 1903.
g 1925.
h 1985.
Sources Tables UK.18 and US.18; Table 9 for other countries.

***Table* IV.15 Commodity composition, external trade, UK, selected periods, 1885–1987**

	% share of total imports of:				% share of total exports[a] of:			
	Food, drink & tobacco	Basic materials	Fuels	Finished manufactures	Non-manufactures	Fuels	Manufactures	Machinery & transport equipment
1885	43·1	40·7		15·9	31·0		69·0	...
1900	42·1	31·7	1·3	24·3[b]	18·6	11·0	69·8	0·8
1920	39·3	37·0	3·7	5·3	18·4	8·0	72·7	4·6
1938	46·5	26·1	5·2	7·1	18·2	8·8	70·7	22·0
1950	39·1	35·2	7·6	4·0	13·1	3·5	80·5	35·9
1970	22·3	15·8	10·4	23·1	9·8	2·6	84·5	41·4
1980	12·5	8·4	14·0	36·3	10·1	13·6	74·0	34·6
1987	10·8	6·1	6·5	48·7	9·8	10·9	76·4	36·1

a   These rows do not add to 100% because miscellaneous items (eg parcel post) have been included in the total.
b   Includes semi-manufactures.
Sources Tables UK.13 and UK.14.

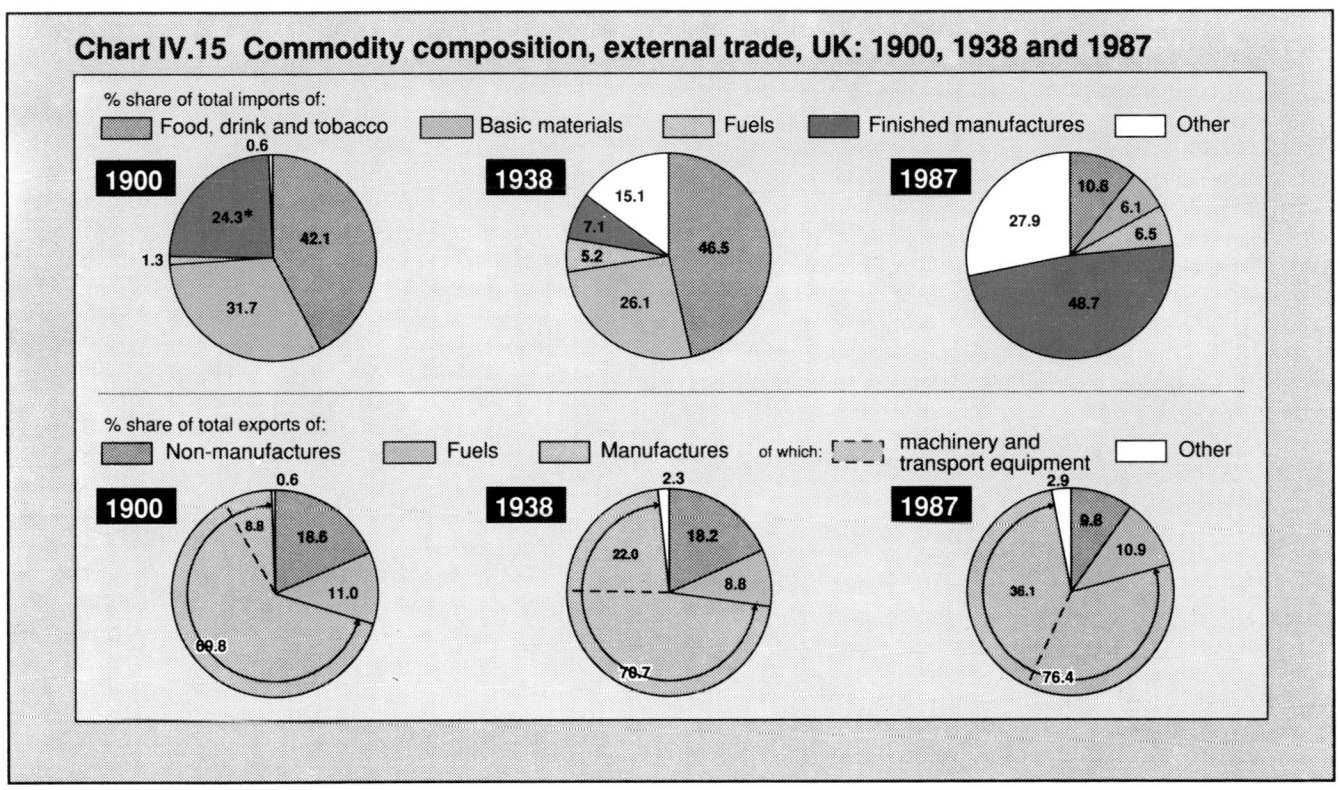

Chart IV.15 Commodity composition, external trade, UK: 1900, 1938 and 1987

% share of total imports of:
Food, drink and tobacco   Basic materials   Fuels   Finished manufactures   Other

1900 — 0·6, 24·3*, 1·3, 31·7, 42·1
1938 — 15·1, 7·1, 5·2, 26·1, 46·5
1987 — 27·9, 10·8, 6·1, 6·5, 48·7

% share of total exports of:
Non-manufactures   Fuels   Manufactures   of which: machinery and transport equipment   Other

1900 — 0·6, 8·8, 18·6, 11·0, 69·8
1938 — 2·3, 22·0, 18·2, 8·8, 70·7
1987 — 2·9, 9·8, 10·9, 36·1, 76·4

* Includes semi-manufactures.

Table IV.16 Commodity composition, external trade, USA, selected periods, 1885–1987

	% share of total imports of:				% share of total exports of:			
	Food, feeds & beverages	Industrial materials & supplies	Petroleum & products	Consumer[a] goods (incl. autos)	Food, feeds & beverages	Industrial materials & supplies	Fuels & lubricants	Consumer goods[a] (incl. autos)
1885	33·9	34·3	—	31·7	43·8	39·1	7·7	15·0
1900	27·2	48·9	—	23·9	39·2	35·4	7·5	23·8
1920	34·4	49·0	0·6	16·6	24·7	34·5	11·6	38·9
1938	28·9	58·7	2·0	9·6	14·0	50·4	14·4	15·5
1950	29·5	61·3	6·6	6·3	14·4	42·4	7·6	15·5
1970	14·9	36·9	7·1	32·0	13·3	31·0	3·6	15·1
1980	7·3	51·6	32·0	25·2	15·9	30·1	3·6	15·1
1987	6·0	26·5	10·4	42·1	9·7	26·1	3·0	17·4

a   Including capital goods, 1885, 1900 and 1920.
Sources Tables US.13 and US.14.

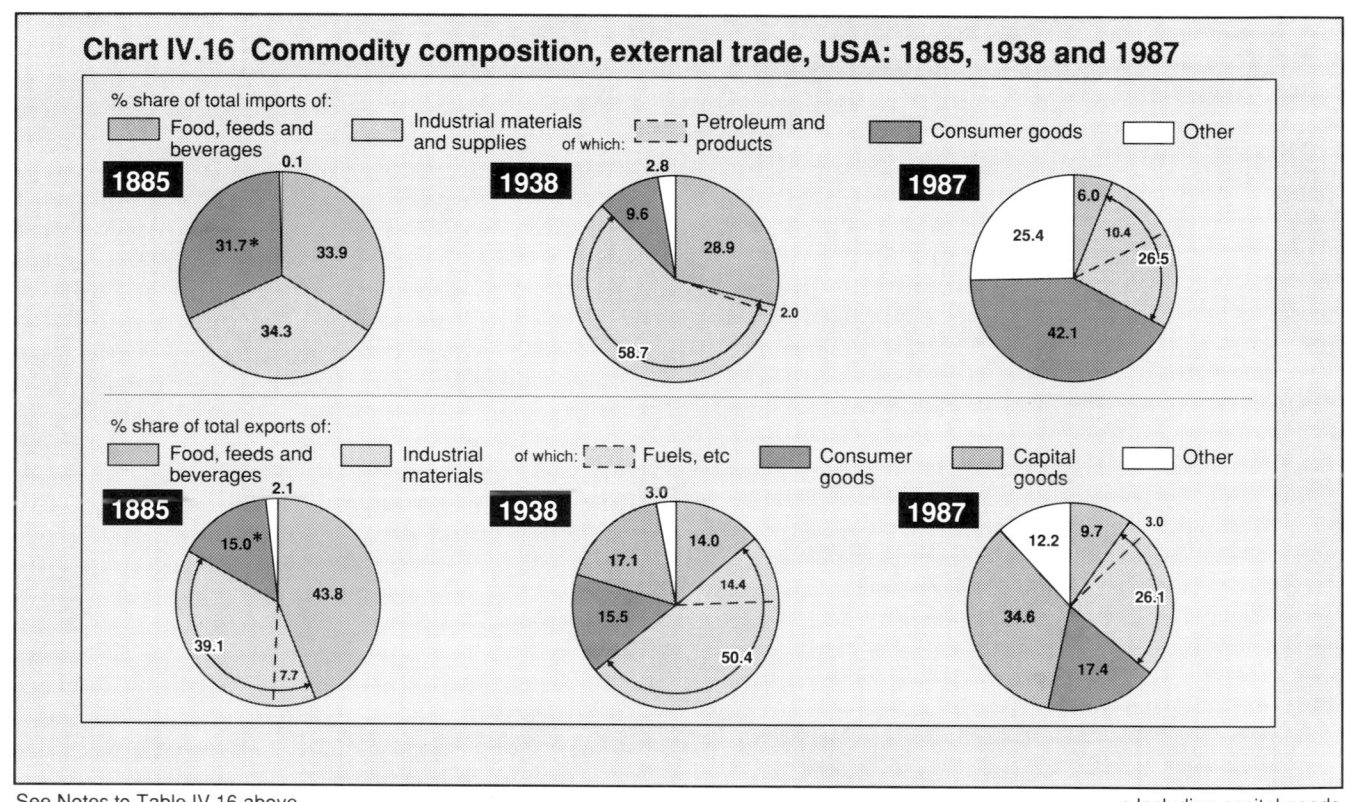

Chart IV.16 Commodity composition, external trade, USA: 1885, 1938 and 1987

See Notes to Table IV.16 above.

∗ Including capital goods.

***Table* IV.17   Exports of manufactures, shares of eight countries, 1970–87**

	UK[a]	USA	Canada	France	Germany	Italy	Japan	Sweden	Total value 11 industrial countries
	%								£ mn
1970	10·6	18·6	6·2	8·8	19·9	7·2	11·7	3·4	154·3
1971	10·8	17·1	6·0	8·9	20·1	7·3	13·0	3·3	173·9
1972	9·9	16·2	5·7	9·3	20·3	7·6	13·2	3·3	204·7
1973	9·1	16·1	5·1	9·6	22·1	6·8	12·7	3·4	271·9
1974	8·5	17·1	4·5	9·2	21·7	6·8	14·3	3·3	364·8
1975	9·1	17·7	4·3	10·2	20·3	7·5	13·6	3·5	391·7
1976	8·5	17·3	4·7	9·8	20·6	7·1	14·7	3·4	439·9
1977	9·0	15·8	4·6	9·9	20·8	7·6	15·5	3·1	501·6
1978	8·9	15·3	4·5	9·8	20·8	7·8	15·7	3·0	603·0
1979	9·1	16·0	4·2	10·5	20·9	8·4	13·7	3·1	721·8
1980	9·7	17·0	4·0	10·0	19·9	7·9	14·9	2·9	837·5
1981	8·5	18·6	4·6	9·2	18·4	7·7	17·9	2·8	818·6
1982	8·4	17·6	4·9	9·0	19·7	7·9	17·3	2·8	774·2
1983	7·9	16·9	5·5	8·9	19·0	8·1	18·5	2·8	769·7
1984	7·6	17·2	6·3	8·5	18·1	7·7	20·1	2·8	820·5
1985	7·9	16·7	6·3	8·5	18·7	7·8	19·7	2·9	864·1
1986	7·6	14·0	5·4	8·8	20·7	8·2	19·4	3·0	1,048·3
1987	8·1	13·7	4·9	9·0	21·5	8·4	18·1	3·0	1,231·1

a   UK share of exports of manufactures for 1899–1969 are shown in Part I, Table I.11.
Notes Eleven industrial countries comprise USA, Canada, France, Germany, Italy, Netherlands, Belgium/Luxembourg, UK, Sweden, Switzerland, Japan.
Source *Overseas Trade Statistics Annual Supplement*, 1988.

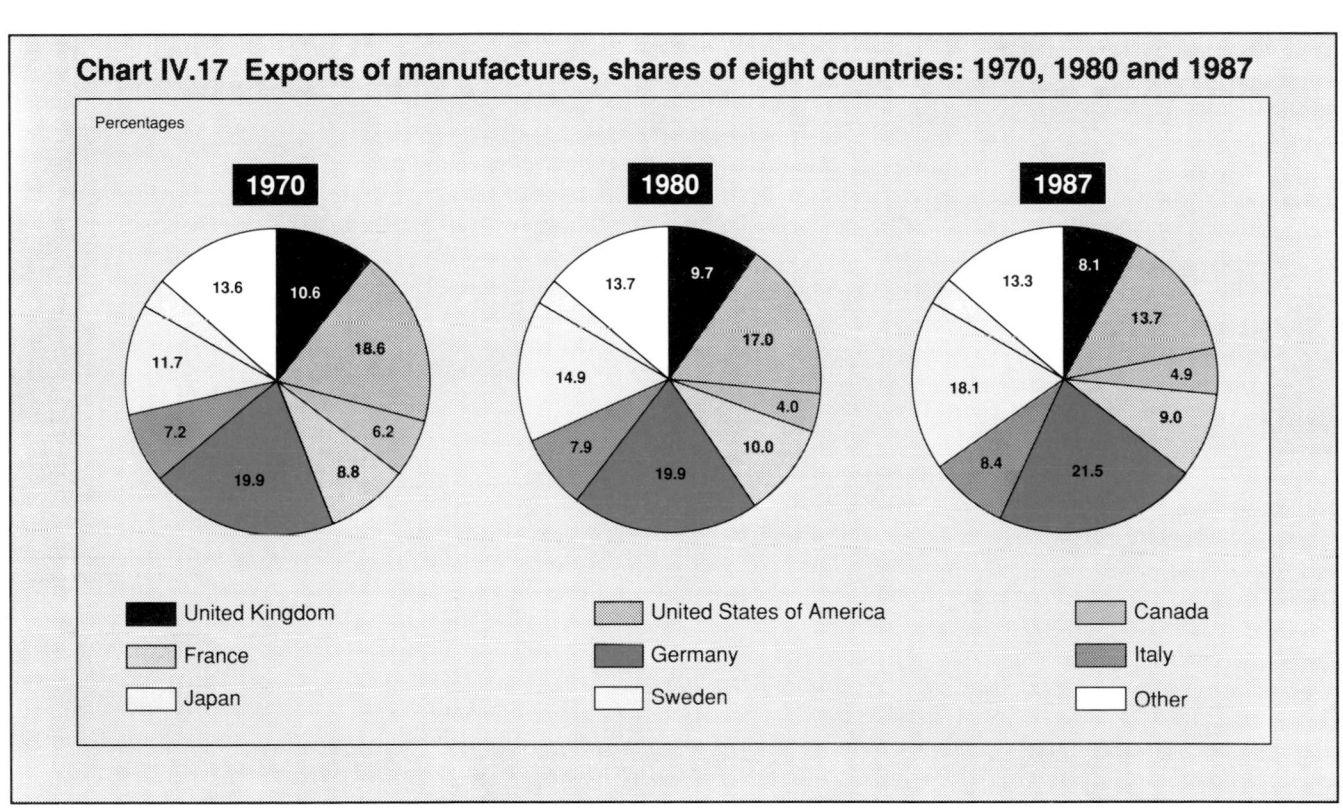

Chart IV.17 Exports of manufactures, shares of eight countries: 1970, 1980 and 1987

Percentages

1970

1980

1987

■ United Kingdom   United States of America   Canada
France   Germany   Italy
Japan   Sweden   Other

Table IV.18   External trade by area, UK, selected periods, 1885–1987

	% imports from:			% exports to:		
	European Community	North America	Japan	European Community	North America	Japan
1885	32·6	26·1	0·1	35·8	14·0	0·8
1900	34·0	31·2	0·4	33·3	13·6	2·8
1910	27·7	22·0	0·6	29·0	16·0	1·9
1920	14·8	17·6	1·6	31·2	11·6	1·8
1930	31·3	13·4	0·8	33·6	10·8	1·2
1938	19·7	21·7	1·0	26·1	10·0	0·4
1950	21·0	15·1	0·3	21·2	11·4	0·1
1960	22·3	20·4	0·9	22·4	15·7	0·8
1970	29·2	20·6	1·5	32·5	15·2	1·8
1980	44·2	15·1	3·5	45·8	11·3	1·3
1987	52·7	11·5	5·8	49·4	16·3	1·9

Source Table UK.15.

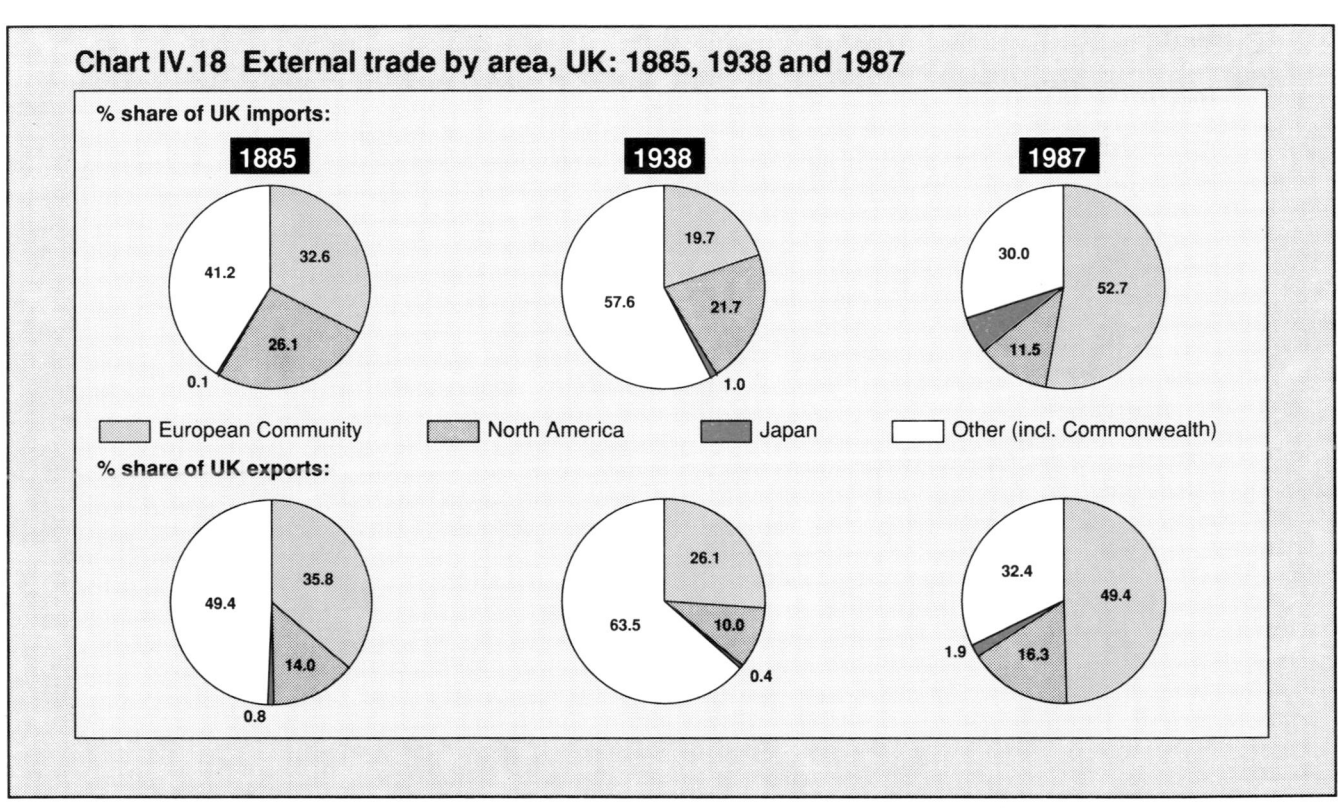

Chart IV.18 External trade by area, UK: 1885, 1938 and 1987

% share of UK imports:

1885 — 41.2, 32.6, 26.1, 0.1
1938 — 57.6, 19.7, 21.7, 1.0
1987 — 30.0, 52.7, 11.5

European Community   North America   Japan   Other (incl. Commonwealth)

% share of UK exports:

1885 — 49.4, 35.8, 14.0, 0.8
1938 — 63.5, 26.1, 10.0, 0.4
1987 — 32.4, 49.4, 16.3, 1.9

320

Table IV.19 External trade by area, USA, selected periods, 1885–1987

	% imports from:			% exports to:		
	UK	Germany[a]	Japan	UK	Germany[a]	Japan
1885	23·7	10·9	2·1	53·6	8·4	0·4
1900	18·8	11·4	3·9	38·3	13·4	2·0
1910	17·4	10·9	4·2	29·0	14·3	1·3
1920	9·7	1·7	7·9	22·2	3·8	4·6
1930	6·9	5·8	9·1	17·6	7·2	4·3
1940	5·9	—	6·0	25·1	—	5·6
1950	3·7	1·2	2·0	5·3	4·3	4·1
1960	6·6	6·0	7·6	7·2	6·2	7·0
1970	5·4	7·7	14·6	5·9	6·3	10·8
1980	4·0	4·8	12·5	5·7	5·0	9·4
1987	4·2	6·6	20·5	5·5	4·6	11·1

a Federal Republic of Germany from 1950.
Source Table US.15.

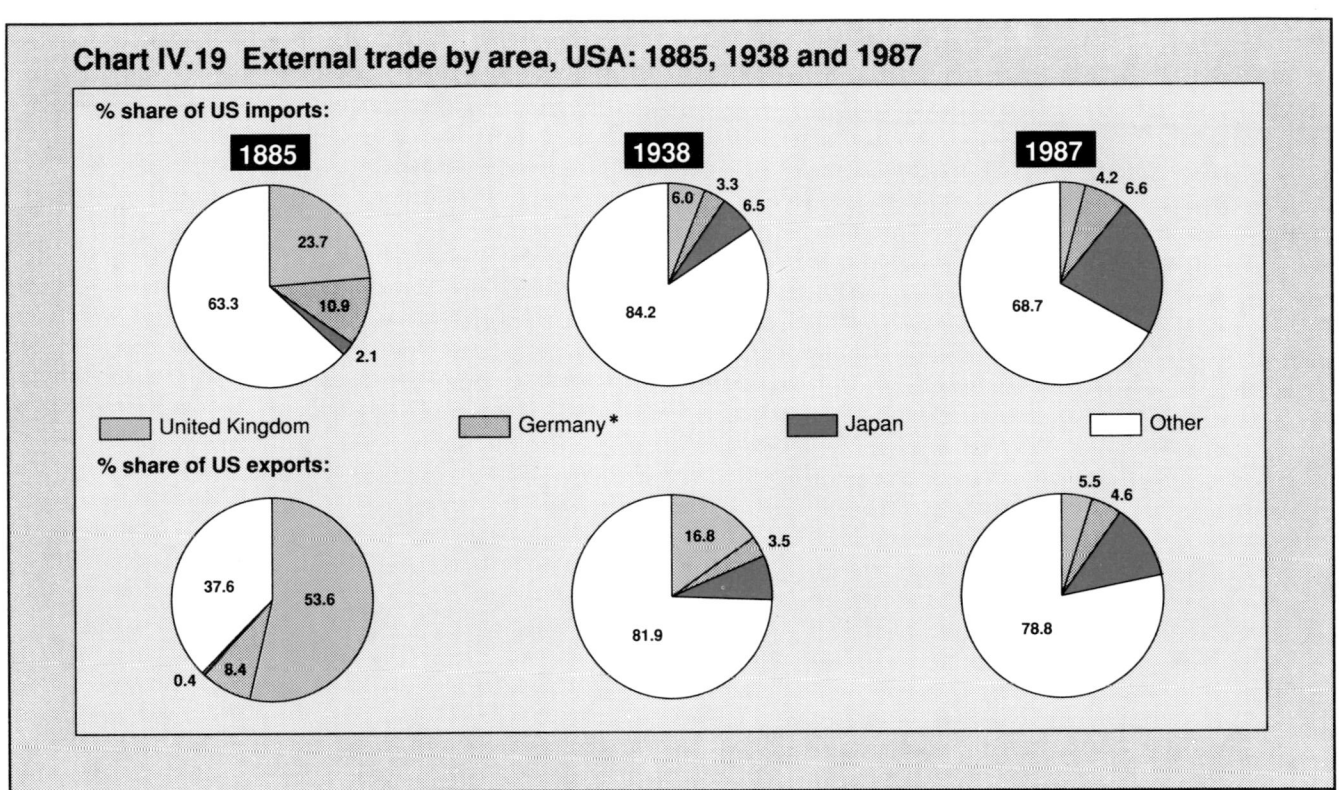

Chart IV.19 External trade by area, USA: 1885, 1938 and 1987

% share of US imports:

1885 — 63.3, 23.7, 10.9, 2.1
1938 — 84.2, 6.0, 3.3, 6.5
1987 — 68.7, 4.2, 6.6

United Kingdom   Germany*   Japan   Other

% share of US exports:

1885 — 37.6, 53.6, 0.4, 8.4
1938 — 81.9, 16.8, 3.5
1987 — 78.8, 5.5, 4.6

* Federal Republic of Germany.

Table IV.20 UK share of trade with France, Germany, Italy and Japan, selected periods, 1885–1987

	% total exports to UK from:				% total imports from UK in:			
	France	Germany	Italy	Japan	France	Germany	Italy	Japan
1885	26·9	15·9	7·5	8·1	13·1	15·5	21·5	44·8
1900	29·9	18·6	11·2	5·3	14·5	12·5	21·2	24·5
1910	20·5	14·7	10·1	5·1	13·0	8·6	14·8	18·2
1920	15·8	9·2	11·9	4·4	20·7	16·6	17·2	8·8
1930	16·1	10·1	9·8	3·3	10·1	6·2	9·7	4·6
1938	11·6	7·0	5·6	3·4	7·0	5·7	6·5	1·7
1950	9·2	4·3	11·4	3·1	3·7	4·3	5·5	0·7
1960	5·0	4·5	6·9	3·0	3·6	4·6	5·1	2·2
1970	3·9	3·6	3·8	2·5	4·6	3·9	3·8	2·1
1980	7·0	6·5	6·1	2·9	5·4	6·7	4·4	1·4
1987	8·8	8·8	7·4	3·7	7·1	7·2	5·3	2·0

Sources Table 10 for France, Germany, Italy and Japan.

GROWTH TRIANGLES

CONTENTS

UK **Rates of change of gross domestic product at constant factor cost (average estimate), 1950–87**

Initial year	1951	1952	1953	1954	1955	1956	1957	1958	Terminal year 1959	1960	1961	1962	1963	1964	1965	1966	1967	1968
1950	2·7	1·5	2·3	2·7	2·9	2·7	2·5	2·2	2·4	2·7	2·7	2·6	2·7	2·9	2·9	2·8	2·8	2·9
1951		0·3	2·1	2·7	3·0	2·6	2·5	2·1	2·3	2·7	2·7	2·6	2·7	2·9	2·9	2·8	2·8	2·9
1952			3·8	4·0	3·9	3·2	2·9	2·4	2·6	3·0	2·9	2·8	2·9	3·1	3·1	3·0	3·0	3·0
1953				4·1	3·9	3·0	2·7	2·1	2·4	2·9	2·8	2·7	2·8	3·1	3·0	2·9	2·9	3·0
1954					3·8	2·5	2·2	1·6	2·1	2·7	2·7	2·5	2·7	3·0	2·9	2·9	2·8	2·9
1955						1·2	1·4	0·9	1·7	2·5	2·5	2·3	2·5	2·9	2·9	2·8	2·7	2·8
1956							1·7	0·7	1·8	2·8	2·7	2·5	2·7	3·1	3·0	2·9	2·9	3·0
1957								−0·3	1·9	3·1	3·0	2·6	2·9	3·3	3·2	3·1	3·0	3·1
1958									4·1	4·9	4·1	3·4	3·5	3·9	3·7	3·5	3·3	3·4
1959										5·7	4·1	3·2	3·4	3·8	3·7	3·4	3·2	3·4
1960											2·5	1·9	2·6	3·4	3·3	3·0	2·9	3·1
1961												1·3	2·7	3·6	3·4	3·1	3·0	3·1
1962													4·1	4·8	4·2	3·6	3·3	3·5
1963														5·6	4·2	3·4	3·1	3·3
1964															2·8	2·3	2·3	2·8
1965																1·8	2·0	2·8
1966																	2·1	3·2
1967																		4·3
1968																		
1969																		
1970																		
1971																		
1972																		
1973																		
1974																		
1975																		
1976																		
1977																		
1978																		
1979																		
1980																		
1981																		
1982																		
1983																		
1984																		
1985																		
1986																		

1969	1970	1971	1972	1973	1974	1975	1976	1977	Terminal year 1978	1979	1980	1981	1982	1983	1984	1985	1986	1987	Initial year
2·8	2·8	2·7	2·7	2·9	2·8	2·6	2·6	2·6	2·6	2·6	2·5	2·3	2·3	2·4	2·3	2·4	2·4	2·4	**1950**
2·8	2·8	2·7	2·7	3·0	2·8	2·6	2·6	2·6	2·6	2·6	2·5	2·3	2·3	2·4	2·3	2·4	2·4	2·4	**1951**
3·0	2·9	2·9	2·9	3·1	2·9	2·7	2·7	2·7	2·7	2·7	2·5	2·4	2·4	2·4	2·4	2·4	2·5	2·5	**1952**
2·9	2·9	2·8	2·8	3·0	2·8	2·7	2·7	2·7	2·7	2·7	2·5	2·4	2·3	2·4	2·4	2·4	2·4	2·5	**1953**
2·9	2·8	2·7	2·7	3·0	2·8	2·6	2·6	2·6	2·6	2·6	2·4	2·3	2·3	2·3	2·3	2·3	2·4	2·4	**1954**
2·8	2·8	2·7	2·7	2·9	2·7	2·5	2·5	2·5	2·6	2·6	2·4	2·2	2·2	2·3	2·2	2·3	2·3	2·4	**1955**
2·9	2·9	2·8	2·8	3·0	2·8	2·6	2·6	2·6	2·6	2·6	2·4	2·3	2·3	2·3	2·3	2·3	2·4	2·4	**1956**
3·0	3·0	2·9	2·8	3·1	2·8	2·6	2·6	2·6	2·7	2·7	2·4	2·3	2·3	2·3	2·3	2·4	2·4	2·4	**1957**
3·3	3·2	3·1	3·1	3·4	3·0	2·8	2·8	2·8	2·8	2·8	2·6	2·4	2·4	2·4	2·4	2·5	2·5	2·5	**1958**
3·3	3·2	3·0	3·0	3·3	3·0	2·7	2·7	2·7	2·7	2·7	2·5	2·3	2·3	2·4	2·3	2·4	2·4	2·5	**1959**
3·0	2·9	2·8	2·8	3·1	2·8	2·5	2·6	2·6	2·6	2·6	2·3	2·2	2·2	2·2	2·2	2·3	2·3	2·4	**1960**
3·1	2·9	2·8	2·8	3·2	2·8	2·5	2·6	2·6	2·6	2·6	2·3	2·2	2·1	2·2	2·2	2·2	2·3	2·3	**1961**
3·3	3·1	3·0	2·9	3·3	2·9	2·6	2·6	2·6	2·7	2·7	2·4	2·2	2·2	2·3	2·2	2·3	2·3	2·4	**1962**
3·2	3·0	2·8	2·8	3·3	2·8	2·5	2·5	2·5	2·6	2·6	2·3	2·1	2·1	2·2	2·1	2·2	2·2	2·3	**1963**
2·7	2·6	2·4	2·5	3·0	2·6	2·2	2·3	2·3	2·4	2·4	2·1	1·9	1·9	2·0	2·0	2·1	2·1	2·2	**1964**
2·7	2·5	2·4	2·4	3·0	2·5	2·2	2·2	2·3	2·3	2·3	2·0	1·8	1·8	1·9	1·9	2·0	2·1	2·2	**1965**
2·9	2·7	2·5	2·5	3·2	2·6	2·2	2·3	2·3	2·4	2·4	2·0	1·8	1·8	1·9	1·9	2·0	2·1	2·2	**1966**
3·4	2·9	2·6	2·6	3·4	2·7	2·2	2·3	2·3	2·4	2·4	2·0	1·8	1·8	1·9	1·9	2·0	2·1	2·2	**1967**
2·4	2·2	2·0	2·2	3·2	2·4	1·9	2·0	2·1	2·2	2·2	1·9	1·6	1·6	1·8	1·8	1·9	1·9	2·1	**1968**
	2·0	1·8	2·1	3·4	2·4	1·9	2·0	2·1	2·2	2·2	1·8	1·6	1·6	1·7	1·7	1·8	1·9	2·0	**1969**
		1·5	2·1	3·9	2·5	1·8	2·0	2·1	2·2	2·2	1·8	1·5	1·5	1·7	1·7	1·8	1·9	2·0	**1970**
			2·7	5·1	2·8	1·9	2·1	2·1	2·3	2·3	1·8	1·5	1·5	1·7	1·7	1·9	1·9	2·1	**1971**
				7·4	2·9	1·7	1·9	2·0	2·2	2·3	1·7	1·4	1·4	1·6	1·6	1·8	1·9	2·0	**1972**
					−1·6	−1·2	0·1	0·7	1·2	1·4	0·9	0·6	0·8	1·0	1·1	1·3	1·4	1·6	**1973**
						−0·8	0·9	1·5	1·8	2·0	1·3	1·0	1·1	1·3	1·4	1·6	1·7	1·9	**1974**
							2·7	2·6	2·7	2·7	1·7	1·2	1·3	1·6	1·6	1·8	1·9	2·1	**1975**
								2·5	2·8	2·7	1·5	1·0	1·1	1·5	1·5	1·7	1·9	2·1	**1976**
									3·0	2·8	1·1	0·6	0·8	1·3	1·3	1·6	1·8	2·0	**1977**
										2·7	0·2	−0·2	0·3	0·9	1·1	1·4	1·6	1·9	**1978**
											−2·3	−1·7	−0·5	0·5	0·7	1·2	1·5	1·8	**1979**
												−1·1	0·3	1·4	1·5	1·9	2·1	2·4	**1980**
													1·8	2·7	2·4	2·7	2·8	3·0	**1981**
														3·6	2·6	3·0	3·0	3·2	**1982**
															1·6	2·7	2·8	3·1	**1983**
																3·7	3·4	3·6	**1984**
																	3·0	3·5	**1985**
																		4·1	**1986**

USA Rates of change of gross national product at constant market prices, 1950–87

Initial year	1951	1952	1953	1954	1955	1956	1957	1958	Terminal year 1959	1960	1961	1962	1963	1964	1965	1966	1967	1968
1950	9·8	6·8	5·9	4·1	4·3	3·9	3·6	3·1	3·4	3·2	3·2	3·4	3·4	3·5	3·7	3·8	3·7	3·8
1951		3·8	3·9	2·1	3·0	2·8	2·6	2·1	2·6	2·5	2·5	2·8	2·9	3·0	3·2	3·4	3·4	3·4
1952			3·9	1·3	2·7	2·5	2·3	1·8	2·4	2·3	2·4	2·7	2·8	3·0	3·2	3·4	3·3	3·4
1953				−1·3	2·0	2·0	1·9	1·4	2·1	2·1	2·2	2·5	2·7	2·9	3·1	3·3	3·3	3·3
1954					5·4	3·7	3·0	2·1	2·8	2·7	2·7	3·0	3·1	3·3	3·5	3·7	3·6	3·7
1955						2·0	1·8	1·0	2·1	2·2	2·2	2·6	2·8	3·1	3·3	3·5	3·5	3·5
1956							1·7	0·4	2·2	2·2	2·3	2·8	2·9	3·2	3·5	3·7	3·6	3·7
1957								−0·8	2·5	2·4	2·4	3·0	3·1	3·4	3·7	3·9	3·8	3·8
1958									5·7	3·9	3·5	3·9	3·9	4·1	4·4	4·5	4·3	4·3
1959										2·2	2·4	3·3	3·5	3·8	4·1	4·3	4·2	4·1
1960											2·5	3·9	3·9	4·2	4·5	4·7	4·4	4·4
1961												5·2	4·6	4·8	5·0	5·1	4·8	4·7
1962													4·0	4·6	5·0	5·1	4·7	4·6
1963														5·2	5·4	5·5	4·8	4·7
1964															5·6	5·6	4·7	4·5
1965																5·6	4·2	4·2
1966																	2·8	3·4
1967																		4·1
1968																		
1969																		
1970																		
1971																		
1972																		
1973																		
1974																		
1975																		
1976																		
1977																		
1978																		
1979																		
1980																		
1981																		
1982																		
1983																		
1984																		
1985																		
1986																		

1969	1970	1971	1972	1973	1974	1975	1976	1977	1978	1979	1980	1981	1982	1983	1984	1985	1986	1987	Initial year
3·7	3·5	3·5	3·5	3·6	3·4	3·2	3·3	3·3	3·4	3·4	3·2	3·2	3·0	3·0	3·1	3·1	3·1	3·1	1950
3·3	3·1	3·1	3·2	3·3	3·1	2·9	3·0	3·1	3·2	3·1	3·0	3·0	2·8	2·8	2·9	2·9	2·9	3·0	1951
3·3	3·1	3·1	3·2	3·3	3·1	2·9	3·0	3·1	3·1	3·1	3·0	3·0	2·8	2·8	2·9	2·9	2·9	2·9	1952
3·3	3·1	3·0	3·1	3·2	3·1	2·9	2·9	3·0	3·1	3·1	3·0	2·9	2·7	2·8	2·9	2·9	2·9	2·9	1953
3·6	3·3	3·3	3·4	3·5	3·3	3 1	3·1	3·2	3·3	3·3	3·1	3·1	2·9	2·9	3·0	3·0	3·0	3·0	1954
3·5	3·2	3·2	3·3	3·4	3·2	2·9	3·0	3·1	3·2	3·2	3·0	3·0	2·8	2·8	2·9	2·9	2·9	3·0	1955
3·6	3·3	3·3	3·4	3·5	3·2	3·0	3·1	3·2	3·2	3·2	3·1	3·0	2·8	2·8	3·0	3·0	3·0	3·0	1956
3·7	3·4	3·4	3·5	3·6	3·3	3·1	3·2	3·2	3·3	3·3	3·1	3·1	2·9	2·9	3·0	3·0	3·0	3·0	1957
4·1	3·8	3·7	3·8	3·9	3·6	3·3	3·4	3·4	3·5	3·5	3·3	3·2	3·0	3·0	3·2	3·2	3·2	3·2	1958
4·0	3·6	3·5	3·6	3·7	3·4	3·1	3·2	3·3	3·4	3·4	3·2	3·1	2·9	2·9	3·1	3·1	3·1	3·1	1959
4·2	3·7	3·6	3·7	3·8	3·5	3·2	3·3	3·4	3·5	3·4	3·2	3·2	2·9	2·9	3·1	3·1	3·1	3·1	1960
4·4	3·9	3·7	3·9	4·0	3·6	3·3	3·4	3·4	3·5	3·5	3·3	3·2	2·9	3·0	3·1	3·1	3·1	3·1	1961
4·3	3·7	3·6	3·7	3·8	3·5	3·1	3·2	3·3	3·4	3·4	3·2	3·1	2·8	2·9	3·0	3·0	3·0	3·0	1962
4·3	3·6	3·5	3·7	3·8	3·4	3·0	3·2	3·3	3·4	3·3	3·1	3·1	2·8	2·8	3·0	3·0	3·0	3·0	1963
4·1	3·4	3·3	3·5	3·7	3·2	2·8	3·0	3·1	3·3	3·2	3·0	2·9	2·6	2·7	2·9	2·9	2·9	2·9	1964
3·7	2·9	2·9	3·2	3·4	3·0	2·6	2·8	2·9	3·1	3·0	2·8	2·8	2·4	2·5	2·7	2·8	2·8	2·8	1965
3·1	2·2	2·4	2·8	3·1	2·6	2·2	2·5	2·7	2·9	2·8	2·6	2·6	2·3	2·3	2·6	2·6	2·6	2·6	1966
3·2	2·1	2·2	2·8	3·2	2·6	2·1	2·4	2·6	2·9	2·8	2·6	2·6	2·2	2·3	2·5	2·6	2·6	2·6	1967
2·4	1·1	1·6	2·4	3·0	2·4	1·9	2·2	2·5	2·8	2·7	2·5	2·4	2·1	2·2	2·5	2·5	2·5	2·6	1968
	−0·3	1·3	2·5	3·1	2·4	1·8	2·2	2·5	2·8	2·8	2·5	2·4	2·1	2·2	2·5	2·5	2·5	2·6	1969
		2·8	3·8	4·2	3·0	2·2	2·6	2·9	3·2	3·1	2·8	2·7	2·3	2·3	2·6	2·7	2·7	2·7	1970
			4·9	5·0	3·1	2·0	2·6	2·9	3·2	3·1	2·8	2·7	2·2	2·3	2·6	2·7	2·7	2·7	1971
				5·1	2·3	1·1	2·0	2·5	3·0	2·9	2·5	2·4	1·9	2·1	2·5	2·5	2·5	2·6	1972
					−0·5	−0·9	1·0	1·9	2·5	2·5	2·1	2·1	1·6	1·8	2·2	2·3	2·3	2·4	1973
						−1·3	1·8	2·7	3·3	3·1	2·6	2·5	1·9	2·0	2·5	2·6	2·6	2·6	1974
							4·8	4·7	4·8	4·2	3·4	3·1	2·3	2·5	2·9	2·9	2·9	3·0	1975
								4·6	4·9	4·1	3·0	2·8	1·9	2·1	2·7	2·7	2·8	2·8	1976
									5·2	3·8	2·5	2·3	1·4	1·7	2·4	2·5	2·5	2·6	1977
										2·4	1·1	1·4	0·4	1·0	1·9	2·1	2·2	2·3	1978
											−0·2	0·9	−0·3	0·7	1·8	2·1	2·2	2·3	1979
												1·9	−0·3	0·9	2·4	2·5	2·6	2·7	1980
													−2·6	0·5	2·5	2·7	2·7	2·8	1981
														3·5	5·0	4·5	4·0	3·9	1982
															6·6	4·9	4·2	4·0	1983
																3·3	3·1	3·1	1984
																	2·8	3·1	1985
																		3·3	1986

327

AUSTRALIA Rates of change of gross domestic product at constant market prices, 1950–87

Initial year	1951	1952	1953	1954	1955	1956	1957	1958	Terminal year 1959	1960	1961	1962	1963	1964	1965	1966	1967	1968
1950	2·0	0·9	2·7	3·5	3·7	3·4	3·2	3·7	3·9	3·8	3·6	3·9	4·1	4·3	4·1	4·3	4·2	4·5
1951		−0·2	3·0	4·0	4·2	3·7	3·5	4·0	4·1	4·1	3·8	4·0	4·3	4·5	4·3	4·4	4·4	4·7
1952			6·2	6·0	5·6	4·7	4·2	4·7	4·8	4·6	4·2	4·4	4·7	4·8	4·6	4·8	4·7	5·0
1953				5·9	5·4	4·2	3·7	4·4	4·5	4·4	4·0	4·2	4·5	4·7	4·5	4·7	4·6	4·9
1954					4·9	3·4	3·0	4·0	4·3	4·1	3·7	4·0	4·4	4·6	4·4	4·6	4·5	4·8
1955						1·9	2·0	3·7	4·1	4·0	3·5	3·9	4·3	4·6	4·3	4·5	4·5	4·8
1956							2·2	4·6	4·8	4·5	3·8	4·3	4·6	4·9	4·6	4·8	4·7	5·0
1957								7·1	6·2	5·2	4·2	4·7	5·0	5·3	4·9	5·1	4·9	5·3
1958									5·3	4·3	3·3	4·1	4·6	5·0	4·6	4·8	4·7	5·1
1959										3·4	2·3	3·7	4·5	4·9	4·5	4·8	4·6	5·1
1960											1·2	3·9	4·8	5·3	4·7	5·0	4·8	5·3
1961												6·6	6·7	6·7	5·6	5·8	5·4	5·9
1962													6·8	6·8	5·3	5·6	5·2	5·8
1963														6·8	4·5	5·2	4·8	5·6
1964															2·2	4·3	4·1	5·3
1965																6·5	5·1	6·4
1966																	3·7	6·3
1967																		9·0
1968																		
1969																		
1970																		
1971																		
1972																		
1973																		
1974																		
1975																		
1976																		
1977																		
1978																		
1979																		
1980																		
1981																		
1982																		
1983																		
1984																		
1985																		
1986																		

1969	1970	1971	1972	1973	1974	1975	1976	1977	1978	1979	1980	1981	1982	1983	1984	1985	1986	1987	Initial year
4·6	4·6	4·6	4·6	4·6	4·5	4·4	4·3	4·2	4·2	4·1	4·1	4·0	3·9	3·9	3·9	3·9	3·9	3·9	**1950**
4·7	4·7	4·8	4·7	4·7	4·6	4·5	4·4	4·3	4·3	4·2	4·2	4·1	3·9	4·0	4·0	4·0	4·0	3·9	**1951**
5·0	5·0	5·0	5·0	4·9	4·8	4·7	4·6	4·5	4·5	4·4	4·3	4·3	4·1	4·1	4·1	4·1	4·1	4·1	**1952**
4·9	4·9	5·0	4·9	4·9	4·7	4·6	4·5	4·4	4·4	4·3	4·3	4·2	4·0	4·0	4·0	4·1	4·0	4·0	**1953**
4·8	4·9	4·9	4·9	4·8	4·7	4·6	4·5	4·3	4·3	4·2	4·2	4·1	3·9	4·0	4·0	4·0	4·0	3·9	**1954**
4·8	4·9	4·9	4·9	4·8	4·7	4·6	4·5	4·3	4·3	4·2	4·2	4·1	3·9	3·9	4·0	4·0	3·9	3·9	**1955**
5·1	5·1	5·1	5·0	5·0	4·8	4·7	4·6	4·4	4·4	4·3	4·3	4·2	4·0	4·0	4·0	4·0	4·0	4·0	**1956**
5·3	5·3	5·3	5·2	5·2	5·0	4·8	4·7	4·5	4·5	4·4	4·4	4·3	4·0	4·1	4·1	4·1	4·1	4·0	**1957**
5·2	5·2	5·2	5·1	5·0	4·8	4·7	4·6	4·4	4·4	4·3	4·2	4·1	3·9	3·9	4·0	4·0	4·0	3·9	**1958**
5·1	5·2	5·2	5·1	5·0	4·8	4·7	4·6	4·4	4·4	4·2	4·2	4·1	3·9	3·9	3·9	4·0	3·9	3·9	**1959**
5·3	5·4	5·4	5·2	5·2	4·9	4·8	4·6	4·4	4·4	4·3	4·2	4·1	3·9	3·9	4·0	4·0	3·9	3·9	**1960**
5·9	5·8	5·8	5·6	5·5	5·2	5·0	4·9	4·6	4·6	4·5	4·4	4·3	4·0	4·0	4·1	4·1	4·0	4·0	**1961**
5·8	5·7	5·7	5·5	5·4	5·1	4·9	4·7	4·5	4·5	4·3	4·3	4·1	3·9	3·9	4·0	4·0	3·9	3·9	**1962**
5·6	5·6	5·5	5·4	5·2	4·9	4·7	4·6	4·3	4·3	4·2	4·1	4·0	3·7	3·8	3·8	3·9	3·8	3·8	**1963**
5·3	5·4	5·4	5·2	5·1	4·8	4·6	4·4	4·1	4·2	4·0	4·0	3·8	3·6	3·6	3·7	3·7	3·7	3·7	**1964**
6·1	6·0	5·9	5·6	5·4	5·0	4·8	4·6	4·3	4·3	4·1	4·1	3·9	3·6	3·7	3·8	3·8	3·7	3·7	**1965**
6·0	5·9	5·8	5·5	5·3	4·9	4·6	4·4	4·1	4·1	4·0	3·9	3·8	3·5	3·5	3·6	3·7	3·6	3·6	**1966**
7·2	6·6	6·3	5·8	5·6	5·0	4·7	4·5	4·1	4·2	4·0	3·9	3·8	3·4	3·5	3·6	3·7	3·6	3·6	**1967**
5·4	5·5	5·4	5·1	4·9	4·4	4·1	3·9	3·6	3·7	3·5	3·5	3·4	3·0	3·2	3·3	3·3	3·3	3·3	**1968**
	5·5	5·4	4·9	4·7	4·2	3·9	3·7	3·4	3·5	3·3	3·3	3·2	2·9	3·0	3·1	3·2	3·2	3·2	**1969**
		5·3	4·7	4·5	3·8	3·6	3·4	3·1	3·3	3·1	3·1	3·0	2·6	2·8	3·0	3·1	3·0	3·1	**1970**
			4·0	4·0	3·3	3·2	3·0	2·7	3·0	2·8	2·9	2·8	2·4	2·6	2·8	2·9	2·9	2·9	**1971**
				4·1	3·0	2·9	2·8	2·4	2·8	2·7	2·7	2·6	2·2	2·5	2·7	2·8	2·8	2·8	**1972**
					1·9	2·3	2·3	2·0	2·5	2·4	2·5	2·4	2·0	2·3	2·5	2·7	2·7	2·8	**1973**
						2·6	2·6	2·0	2·7	2·5	2·6	2·5	2·1	2·4	2·6	2·8	2·8	2·8	**1974**
							2·5	1·7	2·7	2·5	2·6	2·5	2·0	2·3	2·6	2·8	2·8	2·8	**1975**
								1·0	2·8	2·5	2·7	2·5	1·9	2·3	2·6	2·8	3·0	2·9	**1976**
									4·7	3·3	3·3	2·9	2·1	2·5	2·9	3·1	3·0	3·1	**1977**
										1·9	2·6	2·3	1·4	2·1	2·5	2·8	2·8	2·9	**1978**
											3·2	2·5	1·3	2·1	2·7	3·0	2·9	3·0	**1979**
												1·8	0·3	1·8	2·5	2·9	2·9	3·0	**1980**
													−1·2	1·8	2·8	3·2	3·1	3·2	**1981**
														4·8	4·8	4·7	4·2	4·1	**1982**
															4·8	4·7	4·0	3·9	**1983**
																4·5	3·6	3·6	**1984**
																	2·7	3·1	**1985**
																		3·5	**1986**

329

CANADA Rates of change of gross domestic product at constant market prices, 1950–87

Initial year	1951	1952	1953	1954	1955	1956	1957	1958	Terminal year 1959	1960	1961	1962	1963	1964	1965	1966	1967	1968
1950	4·4	6·4	5·9	4·1	5·1	5·6	5·2	4·8	4·7	4·5	4·4	4·6	4·6	4·8	4·9	5·0	4·9	4·9
1951		8·3	6·6	4·0	5·3	5·9	5·3	4·9	4·7	4·5	4·4	4·6	4·6	4·8	4·9	5·0	4·9	4·9
1952			4·8	1·9	4·3	5·3	4·7	4·3	4·2	4·0	3·9	4·2	4·3	4·5	4·6	4·8	4·7	4·7
1953				−1·1	4·0	5·4	4·7	4·2	4·1	3·9	3·8	4·2	4·3	4·5	4·6	4·8	4·6	4·7
1954					9·1	8·7	6·6	5·5	5·2	4·8	4·5	4·8	4·9	5·0	5·1	5·3	5·1	5·1
1955						8·2	5·4	4·3	4·2	3·9	3·8	4·2	4·3	4·6	4·7	4·9	4·7	4·8
1956							2·5	2·3	2·8	2·8	2·9	3·5	3·8	4·1	4·4	4·6	4·4	4·5
1957								2·1	3·0	2·9	3·0	3·8	4·0	4·3	4·6	4·8	4·6	4·7
1958									3·9	3·3	3·3	4·2	4·3	4·7	4·9	5·2	4·9	4·9
1959										2·8	2·9	4·3	4·5	4·9	5·1	5·3	5·0	5·0
1960											3·1	5·0	5·0	5·4	5·6	5·8	5·3	5·3
1961												6·9	6·0	6·1	6·2	6·3	5·7	5·6
1962													5·1	5·8	6·0	6·1	5·5	5·4
1963														6·5	6·5	6·5	5·6	5·5
1964															6·4	6·5	5·3	5·3
1965																6·6	4·7	4·9
1966																	2·9	4·0
1967																		5·1
1968																		
1969																		
1970																		
1971																		
1972																		
1973																		
1974																		
1975																		
1976																		
1977																		
1978																		
1979																		
1980																		
1981																		
1982																		
1983																		
1984																		
1985																		
1986																		

								Terminal year											Initial year
1969	1970	1971	1972	1973	1974	1975	1976	1977	1978	1979	1980	1981	1982	1983	1984	1985	1986	1987	
4·9	4·8	4·8	4·8	5·0	4·9	4·8	4·9	4·8	4·8	4·8	4·7	4·6	4·4	4·4	4·4	4·4	4·4	4·4	**1950**
4·9	4·8	4·8	4·9	5·0	5·0	4·9	4·9	4·8	4·8	4·8	4·7	4·6	4·4	4·4	4·4	4·4	4·4	4·4	**1951**
4·7	4·6	4·7	4·7	4·8	4·8	4·7	4·8	4·7	4·7	4·7	4·6	4·5	4·3	4·2	4·3	4·3	4·3	4·2	**1952**
4·7	4·6	4·6	4·7	4·8	4·8	4·7	4·8	4·7	4·7	4·7	4·5	4·5	4·2	4·2	4·3	4·3	4·2	4·2	**1953**
5·1	4·9	5·0	5·0	5·1	5·1	5·0	5·0	5·0	4·9	4·9	4·8	4·7	4·4	4·4	4·4	4·4	4·4	4·4	**1954**
4·8	4·7	4·7	4·8	4·9	4·9	4·8	4·8	4·8	4·8	4·7	4·6	4·5	4·3	4·2	4·3	4·3	4·3	4·2	**1955**
4·5	4·4	4·5	4·6	4·7	4·7	4·6	4·7	4·6	4·6	4·6	4·4	4·4	4·1	4·1	4·2	4·2	4·1	4·1	**1956**
4·7	4·6	4·6	4·7	4·9	4·8	4·7	4·8	4·7	4·7	4·7	4·5	4·5	4·2	4·1	4·2	4·2	4·2	4·2	**1957**
5·0	4·8	4·8	4·9	5·0	5·0	4·9	4·9	4·8	4·8	4·8	4·6	4·6	4·3	4·2	4·3	4·3	4·2	4·2	**1958**
5·1	4·8	4·9	4·9	5·1	5·1	4·9	5·0	4·9	4·9	4·8	4·7	4·6	4·3	4·2	4·3	4·3	4·3	4·2	**1959**
5·3	5·0	5·1	5·1	5·3	5·2	5·1	5·1	5·0	5·0	4·9	4·8	4·7	4·3	4·3	4·4	4·4	4·3	4·3	**1960**
5·6	5·3	5·3	5·3	5·5	5·4	5·2	5·2	5·1	5·1	5·0	4·8	4·8	4·4	4·3	4·4	4·4	4·4	4·3	**1961**
5·4	5·1	5·1	5·2	5·4	5·3	5·1	5·1	5·0	5·0	4·9	4·7	4·7	4·3	4·2	4·3	4·3	4·3	4·2	**1962**
5·5	5·1	5·1	5·2	5·4	5·3	5·1	5·1	5·0	5·0	4·9	4·7	4·6	4·2	4·2	4·3	4·3	4·2	4·2	**1963**
5·3	4·8	4·9	5·0	5·3	5·2	4·9	5·0	4·9	4·9	4·8	4·6	4·5	4·1	4·1	4·2	4·2	4·1	4·1	**1964**
5·0	4·5	4·7	4·8	5·1	5·0	4·8	4·9	4·8	4·8	4·7	4·5	4·4	4·0	3·9	4·0	4·1	4·0	4·0	**1965**
4·4	4·0	4·3	4·5	4·9	4·8	4·6	4·7	4·6	4·6	4·5	4·3	4·3	3·8	3·8	3·9	3·9	3·9	3·9	**1966**
5·2	4·3	4·6	4·8	5·3	5·1	4·8	4·9	4·8	4·8	4·7	4·4	4·4	3·9	3·8	4·0	4·0	3·9	3·9	**1967**
5·3	3·9	4·5	4·7	5·3	5·1	4·7	4·9	4·7	4·7	4·6	4·4	4·3	3·8	3·7	3·9	3·9	3·9	3·9	**1968**
	2·6	4·1	4·6	5·3	5·1	4·7	4·8	4·7	4·7	4·6	4·3	4·2	3·7	3·6	3·8	3·8	3·8	3·8	**1969**
		5·6	5·6	6·2	5·7	5·1	5·2	5·0	4·9	4·8	4·5	4·4	3·8	3·7	3·9	3·9	3·9	3·9	**1970**
			5·5	6·5	5·7	5·0	5·2	4·9	4·8	4·7	4·3	4·3	3·6	3·5	3·7	3·8	3·8	3·8	**1971**
				7·4	5·9	4·8	5·1	4·8	4·7	4·6	4·2	4·1	3·4	3·4	3·6	3·7	3·6	3·6	**1972**
					4·3	3·4	4·3	4·1	4·2	4·1	3·7	3·7	2·9	3·0	3·3	3·4	3·3	3·4	**1973**
						2·6	4·3	4·0	4·1	4·1	3·6	3·6	2·8	2·8	3·1	3·3	3·3	3·3	**1974**
							6·0	4·7	4·7	4·4	3·8	3·8	2·8	2·8	3·2	3·3	3·3	3·4	**1975**
								3·5	4·0	3·9	3·3	3·4	2·3	2·4	2·9	3·0	3·0	3·1	**1976**
									4·5	4·1	3·3	3·3	2·0	2·2	2·8	3·0	3·0	3·1	**1977**
										3·8	2·6	3·0	1·4	1·8	2·5	2·8	2·8	2·9	**1978**
											1·5	2·5	0·6	1·2	2·2	2·6	2·7	2·8	**1979**
												3·6	0·2	1·2	2·4	2·8	2·9	3·0	**1980**
													−3·3	−0·1	2·0	2·6	2·7	2·9	**1981**
														3·1	4·7	4·6	4·2	4·2	**1982**
															6·2	5·3	4·6	4·4	**1983**
																4·5	3·8	3·8	**1984**
																	3·1	3·5	**1985**
																		3·9	**1986**

331

FRANCE Rates of change of gross domestic product at constant market prices, 1950–87

Initial year	1951	1952	1953	1954	1955	1956	1957	1958	Terminal year 1959	1960	1961	1962	1963	1964	1965	1966	1967	1968
1950	5·6	4·5	3·8	3·9	4·0	4·3	4·5	4·3	4·2	4·5	4·5	4·7	4·7	4·9	4·8	4·9	4·8	4·8
1951		3·3	2·9	3·3	3·6	4·0	4·3	4·1	4·0	4·3	4·4	4·6	4·7	4·8	4·8	4·8	4·8	4·8
1952			2·5	3·3	3·7	4·2	4·5	4·3	4·1	4·5	4·6	4·7	4·8	4·9	4·9	4·9	4·9	4·8
1953				4·1	4·3	4·8	5·1	4·6	4·4	4·7	4·8	5·0	5·0	5·1	5·1	5·1	5·1	5·0
1954					4·6	5·2	5·4	4·8	4·4	4·8	4·9	5·1	5·1	5·2	5·2	5·2	5·1	5·1
1955						5·8	5·8	4·8	4·4	4·9	5·0	5·2	5·2	5·3	5·3	5·2	5·2	5·1
1956							5·8	4·3	3·9	4·7	4·8	5·1	5·1	5·3	5·2	5·2	5·1	5·0
1957								2·9	3·0	4·3	4·6	4·9	5·0	5·2	5·1	5·1	5·1	5·0
1958									3·1	5·0	5·1	5·5	5·4	5·6	5·4	5·4	5·3	5·2
1959										6·9	6·1	6·2	6·0	6·1	5·8	5·7	5·6	5·4
1960											5·4	5·9	5·7	5·8	5·6	5·5	5·4	5·2
1961												6·5	5·8	6·0	5·7	5·5	5·4	5·2
1962													5·2	5·8	5·4	5·3	5·2	5·0
1963														6·3	5·5	5·4	5·2	5·0
1964															4·7	4·9	4·8	4·6
1965																5·1	4·8	4·6
1966																	4·6	4·4
1967																		4·2
1968																		
1969																		
1970																		
1971																		
1972																		
1973																		
1974																		
1975																		
1976																		
1977																		
1978																		
1979																		
1980																		
1981																		
1982																		
1983																		
1984																		
1985																		
1986																		

1969	1970	1971	1972	1973	1974	1975	1976	1977	1978	1979	1980	1981	1982	1983	1984	1985	1986	1987	Initial year
4·9	4·9	4·9	4·9	4·9	4·8	4·6	4·6	4·6	4·5	4·5	4·4	4·3	4·2	4·1	4·0	4·0	3·9	3·9	**1950**
4·9	4·9	4·9	4·9	4·9	4·8	4·6	4·6	4·5	4·5	4·4	4·3	4·2	4·2	4·1	4·0	3·9	3·9	3·8	**1951**
5·0	5·0	5·0	4·9	5·0	4·9	4·6	4·6	4·6	4·5	4·5	4·4	4·3	4·2	4·1	4·0	3·9	3·9	3·8	**1952**
5·1	5·1	5·1	5·1	5·1	5·0	4·7	4·7	4·7	4·6	4·5	4·4	4·3	4·3	4·1	4·0	4·0	3·9	3·9	**1953**
5·2	5·2	5·2	5·1	5·1	5·0	4·8	4·7	4·7	4·6	4·6	4·5	4·3	4·3	4·1	4·0	4·0	3·9	3·9	**1954**
5·2	5·2	5·2	5·2	5·2	5·1	4·8	4·8	4·7	4·6	4·6	4·4	4·3	4·3	4·1	4·0	4·0	3·9	3·8	**1955**
5·2	5·2	5·2	5·1	5·1	5·0	4·7	4·7	4·6	4·6	4·5	4·4	4·3	4·2	4·1	4·0	3·9	3·8	3·8	**1956**
5·1	5·2	5·1	5·1	5·1	5·0	4·7	4·6	4·6	4·5	4·5	4·3	4·2	4·1	4·0	3·9	3·8	3·8	3·7	**1957**
5·3	5·4	5·3	5·2	5·2	5·1	4·8	4·7	4·7	4·6	4·5	4·4	4·3	4·2	4·0	3·9	3·9	3·8	3·7	**1958**
5·6	5·6	5·5	5·4	5·4	5·2	4·9	4·8	4·8	4·7	4·6	4·5	4·3	4·2	4·1	4·0	3·9	3·8	3·8	**1959**
5·4	5·4	5·3	5·3	5·3	5·1	4·8	4·7	4·6	4·5	4·5	4·3	4·2	4·1	4·0	3·8	3·8	3·7	3·6	**1960**
5·4	5·4	5·3	5·3	5·3	5·1	4·7	4·7	4·6	4·5	4·4	4·3	4·1	4·0	3·9	3·8	3·7	3·6	3·6	**1961**
5·3	5·3	5·2	5·1	5·2	5·0	4·6	4·5	4·5	4·4	4·4	4·2	4·0	3·9	3·8	3·7	3·6	3·5	3·5	**1962**
5·3	5·3	5·2	5·1	5·1	5·0	4·5	4·5	4·4	4·3	4·3	4·1	3·9	3·9	3·7	3·6	3·5	3·4	3·4	**1963**
5·1	5·1	5·1	5·0	5·0	4·8	4·4	4·3	4·2	4·2	4·1	4·0	3·8	3·7	3·6	3·5	3·4	3·3	3·3	**1964**
5·1	5·2	5·1	5·0	5·1	4·8	4·3	4·3	4·2	4·1	4·1	3·9	3·7	3·7	3·5	3·4	3·3	3·2	3·2	**1965**
5·2	5·3	5·2	5·0	5·1	4·8	4·2	4·2	4·1	4·1	4·0	3·8	3·7	3·6	3·4	3·3	3·2	3·1	3·1	**1966**
5·5	5·5	5·3	5·1	5·1	4·8	4·2	4·2	4·1	4·0	3·9	3·8	3·6	3·5	3·3	3·2	3·1	3·1	3·0	**1967**
6·8	6·2	5·7	5·3	5·3	4·9	4·2	4·2	4·1	4·0	3·9	3·7	3·5	3·5	3·3	3·2	3·1	3·0	3·0	**1968**
	5·6	5·1	4·9	5·0	4·6	3·8	3·8	3·7	3·7	3·6	3·5	3·3	3·2	3·0	2·9	2·8	2·8	2·8	**1969**
		4·7	4·5	4·8	4·3	3·4	3·5	3·5	3·5	3·4	3·3	3·1	3·0	2·8	2·7	2·7	2·6	2·6	**1970**
			4·3	4·8	4·2	3·1	3·3	3·3	3·3	3·3	3·1	2·9	2·9	2·7	2·6	2·5	2·5	2·5	**1971**
				5·3	4·2	2·7	3·1	3·1	3·1	3·1	2·9	2·7	2·7	2·5	2·4	2·4	2·3	2·3	**1972**
					3·1	1·4	2·3	2·5	2·7	2·8	2·6	2·4	2·4	2·3	2·2	2·1	2·1	2·1	**1973**
						−0·3	1·9	2·3	2·6	2·7	2·5	2·3	2·4	2·2	2·1	2·0	2·0	2·1	**1974**
							4·2	3·7	3·5	3·5	3·1	2·8	2·7	2·5	2·3	2·3	2·3	2·2	**1975**
								3·2	3·2	3·2	2·8	2·5	2·5	2·2	2·1	2·1	2·1	2·1	**1976**
									3·3	3·2	2·7	2·3	2·4	2·1	2·0	1·9	1·9	2·0	**1977**
										3·2	2·4	2·0	2·1	1·8	1·7	1·7	1·8	1·8	**1978**
											1·6	1·4	1·8	1·5	1·5	1·5	1·6	1·6	**1979**
												1·2	1·8	1·5	1·4	1·5	1·6	1·6	**1980**
													2·5	1·6	1·5	1·5	1·6	1·7	**1981**
														0·7	1·0	1·2	1·4	1·6	**1982**
															1·3	1·5	1·7	1·8	**1983**
																1·6	1·9	2·0	**1984**
																	2·1	2·1	**1985**
																		2·2	**1986**

Terminal year

GERMANY Rates of change of gross domestic product at constant market prices, 1950–87

Initial year	1951	1952	1953	1954	1955	1956	1957	1958	1959	1960	1961	1962	1963	1964	1965	1966	1967	1968
1950	10·0	9·2	8·8	8·4	9·0	8·7	8·2	7·6	7·6	7·7	7·4	7·2	6·8	6·8	6·7	6·5	6·1	6·0
1951		8·4	8·2	7·9	8·8	8·4	7·9	7·3	7·3	7·4	7·1	6·9	6·5	6·5	6·5	6·2	5·8	5·8
1952			8·0	7·7	8·9	8·4	7·8	7·1	7·1	7·3	7·0	6·7	6·4	6·4	6·3	6·1	5·6	5·6
1953				7·4	9·4	8·6	7·8	6·9	7·0	7·2	6·9	6·6	6·2	6·2	6·2	5·9	5·5	5·5
1954					11·4	9·1	7·9	6·8	6·9	7·2	6·8	6·5	6·1	6·1	6·1	5·8	5·3	5·3
1955						6·9	6·2	5·3	5·8	6·3	6·0	5·8	5·4	5·5	5·5	5·3	4·8	4·9
1956							5·5	4·5	5·4	6·2	5·8	5·6	5·2	5·4	5·4	5·1	4·6	4·7
1957								3·5	5·3	6·4	5·9	5·7	5·2	5·4	5·4	5·1	4·6	4·6
1958									7·2	7·8	6·7	6·2	5·5	5·7	5·6	5·3	4·7	4·8
1959										8·5	6·5	5·9	5·1	5·4	5·4	5·0	4·4	4·5
1960											4·5	4·6	4·0	4·6	4·7	4·4	3·8	4·0
1961												4·6	3·7	4·6	4·8	4·4	3·7	3·9
1962													2·7	4·6	4·8	4·4	3·5	3·8
1963														6·5	5·9	4·9	3·6	4·0
1964															5·3	4·1	2·7	3·4
1965																2·9	1·4	2·7
1966																	−0·1	2·6
1967																		5·4
1968																		
1969																		
1970																		
1971																		
1972																		
1973																		
1974																		
1975																		
1976																		
1977																		
1978																		
1979																		
1980																		
1981																		
1982																		
1983																		
1984																		
1985																		
1986																		

| | | | | | | | Terminal year | | | | | | | | | | | | Initial year |
1969	1970	1971	1972	1973	1974	1975	1976	1977	1978	1979	1980	1981	1982	1983	1984	1985	1986	1987	
6·1	6·0	5·9	5·8	5·8	5·5	5·2	5·2	5·2	5·1	5·0	4·9	4·8	4·6	4·5	4·4	4·4	4·3	4·3	**1950**
5·9	5·8	5·7	5·6	5·6	5·3	5·0	5·1	5·0	4·9	4·9	4·7	4·6	4·4	4·3	4·3	4·2	4·2	4·1	**1951**
5·7	5·7	5·5	5·5	5·4	5·2	4·9	4·9	4·8	4·8	4·7	4·6	4·5	4·3	4·3	4·2	4·1	4·0	4·0	**1952**
5·6	5·6	5·4	5·3	5·3	5·1	4·8	4·8	4·7	4·6	4·6	4·5	4·3	4·2	4·1	4·0	4·0	3·9	3·9	**1953**
5·5	5·4	5·3	5·2	5·2	4·9	4·6	4·7	4·6	4·5	4·5	4·4	4·2	4·0	4·0	3·9	3·9	3·8	3·7	**1954**
5·0	5·0	4·9	4·9	4·8	4·6	4·3	4·3	4·3	4·2	4·2	4·1	3·9	3·8	3·7	3·7	3·6	3·6	3·5	**1955**
4·9	4·9	4·8	4·7	4·7	4·5	4·2	4·2	4·1	4·1	4·1	4·0	3·8	3·6	3·6	3·5	3·5	3·4	3·4	**1956**
4·9	4·9	4·7	4·7	4·7	4·4	4·1	4·1	4·1	4·0	4·0	3·9	3·8	3·6	3·6	3·5	3·5	3·4	3·3	**1957**
5·0	5·0	4·8	4·8	4·8	4·5	4·1	4·2	4·1	4·1	4·1	3·9	3·8	3·6	3·6	3·5	3·5	3·4	3·3	**1958**
4·8	4·8	4·6	4·6	4·6	4·3	3·9	4·0	3·9	3·9	3·9	3·8	3·6	3·4	3·3	3·3	3·3	3·2	3·2	**1959**
4·3	4·4	4·3	4·3	4·3	4·0	3·6	3·7	3·7	3·6	3·7	3·5	3·4	3·2	3·1	3·1	3·1	3·0	3·0	**1960**
4·3	4·4	4·2	4·2	4·3	4·0	3·6	3·7	3·6	3·6	3·6	3·5	3·3	3·1	3·1	3·0	3·0	3·0	2·9	**1961**
4·3	4·4	4·2	4·2	4·2	3·9	3·5	3·6	3·6	3·6	3·5	3·5	3·4	3·3	3·1	3·0	3·0	2·9	2·9	**1962**
4·5	4·6	4·4	4·4	4·4	4·0	3·5	3·7	3·6	3·6	3·6	3·5	3·3	3·1	3·0	3·0	2·9	2·9	2·9	**1963**
4·1	4·3	4·1	4·1	4·1	3·8	3·3	3·4	3·4	3·4	3·4	3·3	3·1	2·9	2·8	2·8	2·8	2·7	2·7	**1964**
3·8	4·1	3·9	3·9	4·0	3·6	3·1	3·3	3·2	3·2	3·3	3·1	3·0	2·7	2·7	2·7	2·6	2·6	2·6	**1965**
4·2	4·4	4·1	4·1	4·2	3·7	3·1	3·3	3·3	3·2	3·3	3·2	3·0	2·7	2·7	2·7	2·6	2·6	2·6	**1966**
6·3	5·9	5·1	4·9	4·9	4·2	3·5	3·7	3·6	3·5	3·6	3·4	3·2	2·9	2·8	2·8	2·8	2·8	2·7	**1967**
7·2	6·1	5·0	4·8	4·8	4·0	3·2	3·5	3·4	3·3	3·4	3·2	3·0	2·7	2·7	2·7	2·6	2·6	2·6	**1968**
	5·0	3·9	4·0	4·1	3·4	2·5	2·9	2·9	2·9	3·0	2·9	2·7	2·4	2·3	2·4	2·3	2·3	2·3	**1969**
		2·9	3·5	3·9	3·0	2·0	2·6	2·6	2·7	2·8	2·7	2·4	2·2	2·1	2·2	2·2	2·2	2·2	**1970**
			4·1	4·4	3·0	1·8	2·5	2·6	2·6	2·8	2·6	2·4	2·1	2·1	2·1	2·1	2·1	2·1	**1971**
				4·6	2·4	1·1	2·1	2·3	2·4	2·6	2·5	2·2	1·9	1·9	2·0	2·0	2·0	2·0	**1972**
					0·3	−0·7	1·3	1·7	1·9	2·3	2·2	1·9	1·6	1·6	1·7	1·7	1·8	1·8	**1973**
						−1·6	1·8	2·2	2·4	2·7	2·5	2·1	1·8	1·8	1·9	1·9	1·9	1·9	**1974**
							5·3	4·1	3·7	3·8	3·3	2·8	2·3	2·2	2·2	2·2	2·2	2·2	**1975**
								2·9	2·9	3·3	2·8	2·3	1·8	1·7	1·9	1·9	1·9	1·9	**1976**
									2·8	3·4	2·7	2·1	1·6	1·5	1·7	1·8	1·8	1·8	**1977**
										4·1	2·7	1·9	1·2	1·3	1·5	1·6	1·7	1·7	**1978**
											1·4	0·8	0·3	0·6	1·0	1·2	1·3	1·4	**1979**
												0·2	−0·2	0·3	0·9	1·2	1·3	1·4	**1980**
													−0·7	0·4	1·2	1·4	1·6	1·6	**1981**
														1·5	2·1	2·1	2·1	2·1	**1982**
															2·8	2·4	2·3	2·2	**1983**
																2·0	2·1	2·1	**1984**
																	2·3	2·1	**1985**
																		1·9	**1986**

ITALY   Rates of change of gross domestic product at constant market prices, 1951–87

Initial year	1952	1953	1954	1955	1956	1957	1958	1959	Terminal year 1960	1961	1962	1963	1964	1965	1966	1967	1968	1969
1951	4·3	5·8	5·1	5·4	5·2	5·2	5·2	5·3	5·4	5·6	5·7	5·7	5·4	5·3	5·3	5·4	5·5	5·5
1952		7·2	5·4	5·8	5·5	5·4	5·3	5·4	5·5	5·8	5·8	5·8	5·5	5·3	5·4	5·5	5·5	5·6
1953			3·6	5·0	4·9	4·9	4·9	5·1	5·3	5·6	5·7	5·6	5·4	5·2	5·2	5·4	5·4	5·5
1954				6·5	5·5	5·4	5·2	5·5	5·6	5·9	5·9	5·9	5·6	5·3	5·4	5·5	5·6	5·6
1955					4·6	4·9	4·8	5·2	5·4	5·8	5·8	5·8	5·4	5·2	5·3	5·4	5·5	5·5
1956						5·2	4·9	5·4	5·6	6·0	6·0	6·0	5·6	5·3	5·4	5·5	5·6	5·6
1957							4·7	5·5	5·7	6·3	6·2	6·1	5·6	5·3	5·4	5·5	5·6	5·6
1958								6·3	6·2	6·8	6·6	6·4	5·8	5·4	5·5	5·6	5·7	5·7
1959									6·1	7·0	6·7	6·4	5·7	5·2	5·3	5·5	5·6	5·6
1960										7·9	7·0	6·5	5·5	5·1	5·2	5·4	5·6	5·6
1961											6·0	5·7	4·7	4·4	4·7	5·0	5·2	5·3
1962												5·5	4·1	3·8	4·3	4·8	5·1	5·2
1963													2·8	3·0	3·9	4·7	5·0	5·2
1964														3·2	4·5	5·3	5·6	5·6
1965															5·8	6·4	6·4	6·3
1966																6·9	6·6	6·4
1967																	6·3	6·1
1968																		5·9
1969																		
1970																		
1971																		
1972																		
1973																		
1974																		
1975																		
1976																		
1977																		
1978																		
1979																		
1980																		
1981																		
1982																		
1983																		
1984																		
1985																		
1986																		

1970	1971	1972	1973	1974	1975	1976	1977	Terminal year 1978	1979	1980	1981	1982	1983	1984	1985	1986	1987	Initial year
5·5	5·3	5·2	5·3	5·2	4·8	4·9	4·8	4·7	4·7	4·7	4·5	4·4	4·3	4·3	4·2	4·2	4·1	**1951**
5·5	5·3	5·2	5·3	5·2	4·9	4·9	4·8	4·7	4·7	4·7	4·5	4·4	4·3	4·3	4·2	4·2	4·1	**1952**
5·4	5·2	5·1	5·2	5·1	4·7	4·8	4·7	4·6	4·6	4·6	4·4	4·3	4·2	4·2	4·1	4·1	4·0	**1953**
5·6	5·3	5·2	5·3	5·2	4·8	4·8	4·7	4·6	4·6	4·6	4·5	4·3	4·2	4·2	4·1	4·1	4·1	**1954**
5·5	5·3	5·1	5·2	5·2	4·7	4·8	4·6	4·5	4·6	4·5	4·4	4·2	4·1	4·1	4·1	4·0	4·0	**1955**
5·6	5·3	5·2	5·3	5·2	4·7	4·8	4·6	4·5	4·6	4·5	4·4	4·2	4·1	4·1	4·0	4·0	4·0	**1956**
5·6	5·3	5·2	5·3	5·2	4·7	4·8	4·6	4·5	4·5	4·5	4·4	4·2	4·1	4·0	4·0	4·0	3·9	**1957**
5·7	5·4	5·2	5·3	5·2	4·7	4·8	4·6	4·5	4·5	4·5	4·3	4·2	4·0	4·0	4·0	3·9	3·9	**1958**
5·6	5·3	5·1	5·2	5·2	4·6	4·7	4·5	4·4	4·4	4·4	4·3	4·1	4·0	3·9	3·9	3·8	3·8	**1959**
5·6	5·2	5·0	5·2	5·1	4·5	4·6	4·4	4·3	4·3	4·3	4·2	4·0	3·9	3·8	3·8	3·8	3·7	**1960**
5·3	4·9	4·8	4·9	4·9	4·3	4·4	4·2	4·1	4·1	4·1	4·0	3·8	3·7	3·7	3·6	3·6	3·6	**1961**
5·2	4·8	4·6	4·8	4·8	4·1	4·2	4·1	4·0	4·0	4·0	3·9	3·7	3·6	3·5	3·5	3·5	3·5	**1962**
5·2	4·7	4·5	4·8	4·7	4·0	4·1	4·0	3·9	3·9	3·9	3·8	3·6	3·5	3·5	3·4	3·4	3·4	**1963**
5·6	5·0	4·8	5·0	4·9	4·1	4·3	4·1	4·0	4·0	4·0	3·8	3·6	3·5	3·5	3·5	3·4	3·4	**1964**
6·0	5·3	5·0	5·2	5·1	4·2	4·3	4·1	4·0	4·1	4·1	3·9	3·7	3·5	3·5	3·5	3·4	3·4	**1965**
6·1	5·2	4·9	5·1	5·0	4·0	4·2	4·0	3·9	3·9	3·9	3·8	3·5	3·4	3·4	3·3	3·3	3·3	**1966**
5·8	4·8	4·4	4·8	4·7	3·7	3·9	3·7	3·6	3·7	3·7	3·5	3·3	3·2	3·2	3·1	3·1	3·1	**1967**
5·5	4·2	4·0	4·5	4·5	3·3	3·6	3·4	3·3	3·5	3·5	3·3	3·1	3·0	3·0	3·0	3·0	3·0	**1968**
5·2	3·4	3·3	4·2	4·2	2·9	3·3	3·1	3·0	3·2	3·3	3·1	2·9	2·7	2·8	2·8	2·8	2·8	**1969**
	1·6	2·4	3·9	3·9	2·4	2·9	2·8	2·8	3·0	3·1	2·9	2·7	2·6	2·6	2·6	2·6	2·7	**1970**
		3·2	5·0	4·7	2·6	3·2	3·0	2·9	3·2	3·2	3·0	2·8	2·6	2·7	2·7	2·7	2·7	**1971**
			6·8	5·4	2·4	3·2	2·9	2·9	3·2	3·3	3·0	2·7	2·6	2·6	2·6	2·7	2·7	**1972**
				4·1	0·2	2·0	2·0	2·1	2·6	2·7	2·5	2·3	2·2	2·3	2·3	2·3	2·4	**1973**
					−3·7	1·0	1·3	1·6	2·3	2·5	2·3	2·1	2·0	2·1	2·1	2·2	2·3	**1974**
						5·7	3·8	3·4	3·8	3·8	3·3	2·9	2·7	2·7	2·7	2·7	2·8	**1975**
							1·9	2·3	3·1	3·3	2·9	2·4	2·2	2·3	2·4	2·4	2·5	**1976**
								2·7	3·7	3·8	3·1	2·5	2·3	2·4	2·5	2·5	2·6	**1977**
								4·8	4·3	3·3	2·5	2·2	2·4	2·4	2·5	2·5		**1978**
									3·8	2·5	1·7	1·6	1·9	2·0	2·2	2·3		**1979**
										1·1	0·7	0·8	1·4	1·7	1·9	2·0		**1980**
											0·2	0·6	1·5	1·8	2·0	2·2		**1981**
												1·0	2·1	2·3	2·5	2·6		**1982**
													3·1	3·0	2·9	3·0		**1983**
														2·8	2·8	2·9		**1984**
															2·8	3·0		**1985**
																3·1		**1986**

337

JAPAN Rates of change of gross domestic product at constant market prices, 1950–87

Initial year									Terminal year									
	1951	1952	1953	1954	1955	1956	1957	1958	1959	1960	1961	1962	1963	1964	1965	1966	1967	1968
1950	12·3	11·3	9·9	8·8	8·7	8·5	8·3	7·9	8·0	8·5	8·7	8·7	8·7	8·8	8·6	8·7	8·8	9·0
1951		10·4	8·8	7·7	7·8	7·7	7·6	7·3	7·5	8·0	8·4	8·4	8·4	8·6	8·4	8·5	8·6	8·8
1952			7·1	6·3	6·9	7·0	7·0	6·8	7·1	7·7	8·1	8·2	8·2	8·4	8·2	8·3	8·5	8·7
1953				5·5	6·9	7·0	7·0	6·7	7·1	7·8	8·3	8·3	8·3	8·5	8·3	8·4	8·6	8·8
1954					8·2	7·7	7·5	7·1	7·4	8·2	8·7	8·6	8·6	8·8	8·5	8·7	8·8	9·1
1955						7·3	7·2	6·7	7·2	8·2	8·7	8·7	8·6	8·9	8·6	8·7	8·9	9·1
1956							7·0	6·4	7·1	8·4	9·0	8·9	8·8	9·1	8·7	8·9	9·0	9·3
1957								5·7	7·2	8·9	9·5	9·3	9·1	9·4	8·9	9·1	9·2	9·5
1958									8·7	10·5	10·8	10·2	9·8	10·0	9·4	9·5	9·6	9·9
1959										12·3	11·8	10·7	10·1	10·3	9·5	9·6	9·7	10·0
1960											11·4	10·0	9·3	9·8	8·9	9·1	9·3	9·7
1961												8·5	8·3	9·2	8·3	8·7	9·0	9·4
1962													8·1	8·3	8·7	8·3	9·1	9·6
1963														11·0	8·4	8·9	9·3	9·9
1964															5·7	7·9	8·8	9·6
1965																10·1	10·3	10·9
1966																	10·5	11·3
1967																		12·1
1968																		
1969																		
1970																		
1971																		
1972																		
1973																		
1974																		
1975																		
1976																		
1977																		
1978																		
1979																		
1980																		
1981																		
1982																		
1983																		
1984																		
1985																		
1986																		

									Terminal year										Initial year
1969	1970	1971	1972	1973	1974	1975	1976	1977	1978	1979	1980	1981	1982	1983	1984	1985	1986	1987	
9·1	9·2	9·0	8·9	8·9	8·4	8·2	8·1	8·0	7·9	7·8	7·6	7·5	7·4	7·2	7·2	7·1	7·0	6·9	**1950**
9·0	9·0	8·8	8·8	8·7	8·3	8·0	7·9	7·8	7·7	7·6	7·5	7·4	7·2	7·1	7·0	6·9	6·8	6·7	**1951**
8·9	9·0	8·7	8·7	8·6	8·2	7·9	7·8	7·7	7·6	7·5	7·4	7·3	7·1	7·0	6·9	6·8	6·7	6·6	**1952**
9·0	9·1	8·8	8·8	8·7	8·2	8·0	7·8	7·7	7·6	7·5	7·4	7·3	7·1	7·0	6·9	6·8	6·7	6·6	**1953**
9·2	9·3	9·0	8·9	8·9	8·4	8·1	7·9	7·8	7·7	7·6	7·5	7·3	7·2	7·0	7·0	6·9	6·7	6·7	**1954**
9·3	9·4	9·0	9·0	8·9	8·4	8·1	7·9	7·8	7·7	7·6	7·4	7·3	7·1	7·0	6·9	6·8	6·7	6·6	**1955**
9·5	9·5	9·2	9·1	9·0	8·4	8·1	8·0	7·8	7·7	7·6	7·4	7·3	7·1	7·0	6·9	6·8	6·7	6·6	**1956**
9·7	9·7	9·3	9·2	9·1	8·5	8·2	8·0	7·9	7·7	7·6	7·5	7·3	7·1	7·0	6·9	6·8	6·7	6·6	**1957**
10·0	10·0	9·6	9·5	9·4	8·7	8·3	8·1	8·0	7·8	7·7	7·5	7·4	7·2	7·0	6·9	6·9	6·7	6·6	**1958**
10·2	10·2	9·7	9·5	9·4	8·7	8·3	8·1	7·9	7·8	7·6	7·5	7·3	7·1	7·0	6·9	6·8	6·6	6·5	**1959**
9·9	9·9	9·4	9·3	9·2	8·4	8·0	7·8	7·7	7·5	7·4	7·2	7·1	6·9	6·7	6·6	6·6	6·4	6·3	**1960**
9·7	9·8	9·2	9·1	9·0	8·2	7·8	7·6	7·4	7·3	7·2	7·0	6·9	6·7	6·5	6·4	6·4	6·2	6·1	**1961**
9·9	9·9	9·3	9·2	9·0	8·2	7·7	7·5	7·4	7·2	7·1	6·9	6·8	6·6	6·4	6·3	6·3	6·1	6·0	**1962**
10·2	10·2	9·4	9·3	9·1	8·2	7·7	7·5	7·3	7·2	7·0	6·9	6·7	6·5	6·3	6·3	6·2	6·0	5·9	**1963**
10·0	10·1	9·2	9·1	8·9	7·9	7·4	7·2	7·0	6·9	6·8	6·6	6·4	6·2	6·1	6·0	5·9	5·8	5·7	**1964**
11·1	10·9	9·8	9·6	9·3	8·1	7·6	7·3	7·1	7·0	6·8	6·7	6·5	6·3	6·1	6·0	6·0	5·8	5·7	**1965**
11·5	11·1	9·8	9·5	9·2	7·9	7·3	7·0	6·9	6·7	6·6	6·4	6·2	6·0	5·9	5·8	5·7	5·6	5·5	**1966**
11·9	11·3	9·6	9·3	9·0	7·5	6·9	6·7	6·5	6·4	6·3	6·1	5·9	5·7	5·6	5·5	5·5	5·3	5·3	**1967**
11·8	11·0	8·7	8·5	8·4	6·8	6·2	6·0	5·9	5·8	5·7	5·6	5·5	5·3	5·1	5·1	5·1	4·9	4·9	**1968**
	10·2	7·2	7·5	7·5	5·8	5·2	5·1	5·1	5·1	5·1	5·1	4·9	4·8	4·7	4·7	4·7	4·5	4·5	**1969**
		4·2	6·1	6·6	4·7	4·2	4·3	4·4	4·5	4·6	4·5	4·5	4·3	4·2	4·3	4·3	4·2	4·2	**1970**
			8·0	7·8	4·8	4·2	4·3	4·5	4·5	4·6	4·6	4·5	4·3	4·2	4·3	4·3	4·2	4·2	**1971**
				7·6	3·2	3·0	3·4	3·7	4·0	4·1	4·1	4·1	4·0	3·9	4·0	4·0	3·9	3·9	**1972**
					−1·2	0·7	2·0	2·8	3·2	3·5	3·7	3·7	3·6	3·5	3·6	3·7	3·6	3·7	**1973**
						2·6	3·6	4·1	4·3	4·5	4·5	4·4	4·2	4·1	4·1	4·2	4·0	4·0	**1974**
							4·7	4·9	4·9	5·0	4·8	4·7	4·4	4·2	4·3	4·3	4·2	4·2	**1975**
								5·2	5·1	5·1	4·9	4·7	4·4	4·2	4·3	4·3	4·1	4·1	**1976**
									5·0	5·0	4·8	4·5	4·2	4·0	4·1	4·2	4·0	4·0	**1977**
										5·1	4·7	4·4	4·0	3·8	4·0	4·1	3·9	3·9	**1978**
											4·3	4·1	3·6	3·5	3·8	3·9	3·7	3·8	**1979**
												3·8	3·3	3·2	3·6	3·8	3·6	3·7	**1980**
													2·8	3·0	3·6	3·9	3·6	3·7	**1981**
														3·1	4·0	4·2	3·7	3·8	**1982**
															4·9	4·7	4·0	4·0	**1983**
																4·6	3·5	3·7	**1984**
																	2·4	3·3	**1985**
																		4·2	**1986**

SWEDEN Rates of change of gross domestic product at constant market prices, 1950–87

Initial year	1951	1952	1953	1954	1955	1956	1957	1958	Terminal year 1959	1960	1961	1962	1963	1964	1965	1966	1967	1968
1950	3·0	2·3	2·6	3·4	3·3	3·3	3·2	3·1	3·3	3·3	3·5	3·6	3·7	3·9	3·9	3·8	3·8	3·8
1951		1·7	2·4	3·6	3·4	3·4	3·2	3·1	3·3	3·4	3·6	3·6	3·8	4·0	4·0	3·8	3·8	3·8
1952			3·2	4·5	4·0	3·8	3·5	3·3	3·6	3·6	3·8	3·8	4·0	4·2	4·1	4·0	4·0	3·9
1953				5·8	4·4	4·0	3·6	3·3	3·6	3·6	3·9	3·9	4·0	4·3	4·2	4·1	4·0	4·0
1954					3·0	3·1	2·9	2·7	3·2	3·3	3·6	3·7	3·8	4·1	4·1	3·9	3·9	3·9
1955						3·3	2·8	2·6	3·3	3·4	3·7	3·8	4·0	4·2	4·2	4·0	3·9	3·9
1956							2·3	2·3	3·3	3·4	3·8	3·9	4·1	4·4	4·3	4·1	4·0	4·0
1957								2·3	3·7	3·7	4·2	4·2	4·3	4·7	4·5	4·3	4·2	4·1
1958									5·1	4·4	4·8	4·6	4·7	5·1	4·9	4·5	4·4	4·3
1959										3·7	4·6	4·5	4·7	5·0	4·8	4·4	4·3	4·2
1960											5·5	4·8	5·0	5·4	5·0	4·6	4·4	4·3
1961												4·2	4·7	5·3	4·9	4·4	4·2	4·1
1962													5·2	5·9	5·2	4·4	4·2	4·1
1963														6·6	5·2	4·1	3·9	3·9
1964															3·7	2·9	3·0	3·2
1965																2·1	2·7	3·0
1966																	3·3	3·4
1967																		3·6
1968																		
1969																		
1970																		
1971																		
1972																		
1973																		
1974																		
1975																		
1976																		
1977																		
1978																		
1979																		
1980																		
1981																		
1982																		
1983																		
1984																		
1986																		
1987																		

1969	1970	1971	1972	1973	1974	1975	1976	Terminal year 1977	1978	1979	1980	1981	1982	1983	1984	1985	1986	1987	Initial year
3·8	3·9	3·8	3·7	3·7	3·7	3·7	3·6	3·4	3·3	3·3	3·3	3·2	3·1	3·1	3·1	3·1	3·0	3·0	1950
3·9	4·0	3·8	3·8	3·8	3·7	3·7	3·6	3·4	3·3	3·3	3·3	3·2	3·1	3·1	3·1	3·1	3·0	3·0	1951
4·0	4·1	3·9	3·9	3·9	3·8	3·8	3·7	3·5	3·4	3·4	3·3	3·2	3·1	3·1	3·1	3·1	3·0	3·0	1952
4·0	4·2	4·0	3·9	3·9	3·9	3·8	3·7	3·5	3·4	3·4	3·3	3·2	3·1	3·1	3·1	3·1	3·0	3·0	1953
3·9	4·1	3·9	3·8	3·8	3·8	3·7	3·6	3·4	3·3	3·3	3·2	3·1	3·0	3·0	3·0	3·0	3·0	2·9	1954
4·0	4·1	3·9	3·8	3·8	3·8	3·7	3·6	3·4	3·3	3·3	3·3	3·1	3·0	3·0	3·0	3·0	2·9	2·9	1955
4·0	4·2	4·0	3·9	3·9	3·8	3·8	3·6	3·4	3·3	3·3	3·3	3·1	3·0	3·0	3·0	3·0	2·9	2·9	1956
4·2	4·3	4·1	4·0	4·0	3·9	3·8	3·7	3·4	3·4	3·4	3·3	3·1	3·1	3·0	3·1	3·0	3·0	2·9	1957
4·4	4·5	4·2	4·1	4·1	4·0	3·9	3·8	3·5	3·4	3·4	3·3	3·2	3·1	3·1	3·1	3·1	3·0	3·0	1958
4·3	4·5	4·2	4·0	4·0	4·0	3·9	3·7	3·4	3·3	3·3	3·3	3·1	3·0	3·0	3·0	3·0	2·9	2·9	1959
4·3	4·5	4·2	4·0	4·0	4·0	3·9	3·7	3·4	3·3	3·3	3·2	3·1	3·0	2·9	3·0	2·9	2·9	2·9	1960
4·2	4·4	4·1	3·9	3·9	3·9	3·8	3·6	3·3	3·2	3·2	3·1	2·9	2·8	2·8	2·9	2·8	2·8	2·8	1961
4·2	4·5	4·1	3·9	3·9	3·8	3·7	3·5	3·2	3·1	3·1	3·1	2·9	2·8	2·8	2·8	2·8	2·7	2·7	1962
4·0	4·4	3·9	3·7	3·8	3·7	3·6	3·4	3·0	3·0	3·0	2·9	2·8	2·6	2·6	2·7	2·7	2·6	2·6	1963
3·5	4·0	3·5	3·4	3·4	3·4	3·3	3·1	2·8	2·7	2·8	2·7	2·5	2·4	2·4	2·5	2·5	2·4	2·4	1964
3·5	4·0	3·5	3·3	3·4	3·4	3·3	3·1	2·7	2·6	2·7	2·6	2·4	2·4	2·4	2·4	2·4	2·4	2·4	1965
3·9	4·5	3·8	3·5	3·6	3·5	3·4	3·2	2·8	2·7	2·8	2·7	2·5	2·4	2·4	2·5	2·4	2·4	2·4	1966
4·2	4·9	3·9	3·6	3·6	3·6	3·4	3·2	2·7	2·6	2·7	2·6	2·4	2·3	2·3	2·4	2·4	2·3	2·3	1967
4·9	5·6	4·0	3·6	3·7	3·6	3·4	3·1	2·6	2·5	2·6	2·5	2·3	2·2	2·2	2·3	2·3	2·2	2·3	1968
	6·3	3·6	3·2	3·3	3·3	3·2	2·9	2·3	2·2	2·4	2·3	2·1	2·0	2·0	2·2	2·2	2·1	2·1	1969
		0·9	1·6	2·4	2·6	2·6	2·3	1·7	1·7	2·0	1·9	1·7	1·7	1·7	1·9	1·9	1·8	1·9	1970
			2·3	3·1	3·1	3·0	2·6	1·9	1·9	2·1	2·0	1·8	1·7	1·8	1·9	2·0	1·9	1·9	1971
				3·9	3·5	3·2	2·7	1·8	1·8	2·1	2·0	1·8	1·7	1·7	1·9	1·9	1·9	1·9	1972
					3·1	2·8	2·2	1·3	1·4	1·8	1·8	1·5	1·4	1·5	1·6	1·8	1·7	1·8	1973
						2·5	1·8	0·7	0·9	1·5	1·5	1·3	1·2	1·3	1·6	1·6	1·6	1·7	1974
							1·1	−0·3	0·4	1·2	1·3	1·0	1·0	1·2	1·5	1·5	1·5	1·6	1975
								−1·6	0·1	1·3	1·4	1·0	1·0	1·2	1·5	1·6	1·6	1·6	1976
									1·7	2·8	2·4	1·7	1·5	1·7	2·0	2·0	1·9	2·0	1977
										3·8	2·7	1·7	1·5	1·7	2·0	2·0	1·9	2·0	1978
											1·7	0·7	0·7	1·1	1·7	1·8	1·7	1·8	1979
												−0·3	0·2	1·0	1·7	1·8	1·7	1·8	1980
													0·8	1·6	2·4	2·3	2·1	2·1	1981
														2·4	3·1	2·8	2·4	2·4	1982
															3·9	3·0	2·4	2·4	1983
																2·1	1·6	1·9	1984
																	1·1	1·7	1985
																		2·4	1986

INDEX TO TABLES

343